Exploring Police Integrity

Sanja Kutnjak Ivković • M. R. Haberfeld

Editors

Exploring Police Integrity

Novel Approaches to Police Integrity
Theory and Methodology

 Springer

Editors
Sanja Kutnjak Ivković
School of Criminal Justice
Michigan State University
East Lansing, MI, USA

M. R. Haberfeld
John Jay College of Criminal Justice
City University of New York
New York, NY, USA

ISBN 978-3-030-29064-1   ISBN 978-3-030-29065-8   (eBook)
https://doi.org/10.1007/978-3-030-29065-8

This Springer imprint is published by the registered company Springer Nature Switzerland AG
The registered company address is: Gewerbestrasse 11, 6330 Cham, Switzerland

Dedicated to Carl B. Klockars—with regrets that he is unable to share the joy of this book with us.

Sanja Kutnjak Ivković
M.R. Haberfeld

Dedicated to my loving family—thank you for your unconditional love, understanding, and patience.

Sanja Kutnjak Ivković

Dedicated to my two driving forces, my daughters Nellie and Mia, and to the new light in my life, my granddaughter Amelia.

M.R. Haberfeld

Preface

Police integrity is a pervasive issue of interest to scholars, police administrators, and general public. As numerous newspaper stories, criminal investigations, court cases, and independent commission investigations across the world demonstrate, police officers sometimes may not be able to resist these temptations. Although the reasons may vary, from a simple greed and the lack of skill to implicit bias and disrespect of human rights while achieving the greater good, the fact remains that police are not immune from such (mis) behaviors. Consequently, the study of the police has been largely the study of their shortcomings, failures, scandals, corruption, racism, and brutality. Whereas the policing literature has expanded in the last 30 years to new topics such as community policing, problem-oriented policing, evidence-based policing, terrorism, and the use of technology in policing, the ubiquitous problems associated with (lack of) integrity still haunt policing. Police integrity and police misconduct continue to be the topics of great concern not only in the USA but also across the world.

To avoid problems associated with attempts to measure the nature and extent of police misconduct directly, Klockars and Kutnjak Ivković have flipped the issue by instead focusing on the study of police integrity. A quarter of a century ago, Klockars and Kutnjak Ivković have proposed the theory of police integrity and developed accompanying methodology with which to measure police integrity empirically. Since the mid-1990s, Klockars, Kutnjak Ivković, and Haberfeld have studied police integrity across the world. They have defined what police integrity is and did so in an innovative way that distinguishes it from the traditional ways of defining corruption, brutality, and other forms of misconduct. The resulting paradigm offers both cross-sectional and time-series features because the resulting measurement tool—implemented by means of a survey—captures not only the contours of integrity within a particular police agency and across a multitude of agencies at a particular point in time but also the dynamics of the changes in the contours of integrity within police agencies over time. The confirmed ability of this instrument to capture the culture of integrity and, consequently, compare and benchmark police integrity across different police agencies has yielded the tool with which to assess the strength of police cultures both across multiple police agencies intra-nationally and, for the first time in the history of policing, across a multitude of countries, with a rich set of cross-national findings and implications.

Exploring Police Integrity provides a unique perspective in the world of police integrity research because it expands the police integrity theory and methodology and tests its reliability and validity. The book *explores* police integrity by providing a detailed analysis of the theoretical arguments and methodological approaches: every aspect of the police integrity theory is studied with a magnifying lens, methodology of police integrity is expanded, and the reliability and validity of the related methodology are tested.

The book is divided into four distinct parts, each consisting of chapters that address particular elements of the police integrity theory and methodology. The exploration of police integrity is not limited to a single country. Rather, based on surveys of police officers and citizens from countries as diverse as Armenia (Chap. 3), Australia (Chap. 11), Belgium (Chap. 16), Bosnia and Herzegovina (Chap. 8), Croatia (Chaps. 4, 9, and 15), Estonia (Chap. 6), Serbia (Chap. 9), Slovenia (Chap. 10), South Africa (Chap. 5), Uganda (Chap. 7), and USA (Chaps. 2, 10, and 13), the book provides a comparative, cross-cultural exploration of police integrity, understood as resistance to *various forms* of police misconduct from the four-dimensional theoretical perspective.

Part I: Studying Classical Police Integrity Theory and Methodology

The first part of the book presents classical police integrity studies, studies that have utilized the police integrity theory and the related methodology to measure the contours of police integrity among police officers (Chaps. 1, 2, and 3).

In Chap. 1, Kutnjak Ivković and Haberfeld set the stage for the book's conceptual framework by describing the classical police integrity theory and the related methodology. They also provide a systematic overview of the last 25 years of extant research on police integrity grounded in the police integrity theory and explore the ways the original theory and methodology have been used and expanded. The chapter compares and contrasts results from different studies, identifies common patterns across studies, and develops a classification based on their goals and procedures. It also systematizes the studies assessing the validity or reliability of the classical methodology developed to measure police integrity.

In Chap. 2, Kutnjak Ivković, Haberfeld, and Peacock focus on police culture and engage in an exploration of potential differences among the police officer, supervisor, and administrator culture(s) of police integrity. While the traditional approach in the study of police integrity relies on the line officer/supervisor dichotomy, this chapter differentiates across three levels of police hierarchy. The study, based on the 2013/2014 survey of US police officers, tests the argument that the hierarchical organizational structure of police agencies resulting in a division of labor among line officers, first-line supervisors, and chief executives results in somewhat overlapping yet distinct and nuanced police cultures. While line officers, first-line supervisors, and administrators evaluate the seriousness of misconduct at about the same level and expect similarly harsh discipline, their views about appropriate discipline and, particularly, their expressed willingness to report misconduct vary with their rank.

In Chap. 3, Khechumyan and Kutnjak Ivković explore the extent to which centralized systems, such as the Armenian police, are able to create identical levels of police integrity across all subunits of the same system. Unlike decentralized police systems, in which each police agency is required to create its own set of official rules (e.g., USA), subunits in centralized systems are all subject to the same set of official rules created by the headquarters. Based on a 2013 survey of the Armenian police officers from three police agencies, the chapter explores the contours of police agency across the three subunits. The results point toward a complex variation across subunits. On the one hand, evaluations of misconduct seriousness and knowledge of official rules are very similar across the three agencies, directionally consistent with the notion that centralized systems create uniform levels of police integrity. On the other hand, the results indicate large differences across subunits in their perceptions of appropriate discipline and the police officers' willingness to report misconduct, suggesting that smaller units within centralized systems create somewhat distinct cultures of police integrity.

Part II: Expanding the Police Integrity Theory

The second part of the book includes studies that have expanded the classical theory of police integrity either by extending it to a new environment (Chap. 6) or by connecting the police integrity theory with another theoretical concept (Chaps. 5, 6, 7, and 8).

In Chap. 4, Kutnjak Ivković, Haberfeld, Cajner Mraović, Prpić, Hamm, and Wolf connect police integrity and organizational justice. Prior research suggests that perceptions of organizational justice (i.e., how fairly police officers perceive that they have been treated by their police agencies) are related to many issues that are also potentially linked with police integrity, such as police officers' greater internalization of organizational goals, increased supervisor trust, greater rule compliance, and the reduced extent of misconduct. Based on the 2018 survey of police officers from the Croatian capital of Zagreb, the chapter extends the literature addressing relative and absolute judgments of police misconduct seriousness by considering the influence of perceptions of organizational justice—separated into distributive, procedural, and interactional justice—on the police officers' evaluations of misconduct seriousness. Multivariate models demonstrate that, even when controlled for demographic and organizational factors, police officers' evaluations of organizational justice are strong predictors of their evaluations of misconduct seriousness in most of the scenarios.

In Chap. 5, Sauerman, Kutnjak Ivković, and Meyer study the nature of the relation between police integrity and community policing, an issue unexplored by prior studies. The primary question addressed is whether, and to what extent, adherence to, and support for, the philosophy and principles of community policing affect organizational integrity of the South African

Police Service. Community policing, established as a basis of police transformation in South Africa, rests on public trust, which seems to be related to the public perceptions of police misconduct. Based on a 2010–2013 survey of the South African police officers, the results indicate that the experience in community policing and education about community policing are not related to the classical measures of police integrity. On the other hand, the police officers' personal desire to be included in community policing seems to be strongly related to the classical measures of police integrity. The authors posit that teaching the police officers to internalize community policing in South Africa may be a critical factor in enhancing the otherwise decreasing level of trust in the police.

In Chap. 6, Vallmüür extends the classical theory of police integrity by employing the perspective of green criminology to develop the theory of green police integrity. The importance of the environment is formally recognized globally, but the scale of environmental crime is vast and expanding. While the necessity of the police in tackling environmental crime is growing, the theory of police integrity and its methodology had studied neither the nature of green integrity in the police nor the characteristics of police agencies that have high levels of green integrity. The purpose of Chap. 6 is to expand the theory of police integrity with that of green police integrity and present a designated tool to study green integrity in the police. Grounded in several different areas of environmental crime, Vallmüür creates a new typology of police integrity scenarios. Based on the 2018 survey of Estonian police officers, the results show that, compared to the classical police integrity scenarios, police officers are less likely to label green police integrity scenarios as violations of official rules, evaluate them as serious, expect harsh discipline for such violations, and be willing to report them.

In Chap. 7, Wagner and Hout connect police integrity with the topics of police effectiveness and organizational environment. Based on the 2015 survey of the Ugandan police, the study focuses on ten aspects of police officers' perceptions of the institutional environment and police effectiveness. The results show that the perceptions of police effectiveness and organizational environment are strongly interrelated and that they impact police officers' views of police integrity. Put differently, the authors find that the perceived institutional environment and police effectiveness have additional explanatory power for policy integrity. In addition, Chap. 7 analyzes the impact of perceptions of the institutional environment and police effectiveness among Ugandan police officers to assess the reliability of police integrity methodology. When the authors combine dimensions of the perceived institutional environment and police effectiveness in two indices and analyze their relation with the measures of police integrity, they reported that these subjective perceptions of the institutional environment and police effectiveness feed into attitudes toward police integrity.

In Chap. 8, Datzer, Kutnjak Ivković, Mujanović, and Morgan go beyond classical police integrity research to explore the relation between police integrity (specifically the respondents' willingness to report as a measure of the third dimension of the theory) and police officers' education. While the rationale is clear—higher education can lead police officers to become more ethical and less supportive of the abuse of police authority—extant literature exploring the relation between police education and police performance, attitudes of high integrity, and police misconduct yields mixed results. Based on the 2017 survey of police officers from Bosnia and Herzegovina, Datzer and colleagues find no strong evidence supporting the argument that there is a relation between the *level* of education (e.g., high-school education, college education) and the adherence to the code of silence. The police educational system in Bosnia and Herzegovina provides opportunities to assess this relation further and explore the relation between the *type* of education (university-based vs. police-college-based) and the code of silence. While the results indicated no relation for supervisors, Datzer and colleagues documented a strong effect of the interaction between the type and level of line officers' police education on the code of silence.

Part III: Expanding the Police Integrity Methodology

The third section of the book incorporates studies that have expanded the classical methodology of measuring police integrity either by including new types of respondents (Chaps. 9, 10, and 11) or new demographic characteristics in the questionnaire (Chap. 12).

In Chap. 9, Kutnjak Ivković, Cajner Mraović, Božović, Prprović, and Nemec expanded the classical police integrity methodology, designed to measure the contours of police integrity among police officers, by surveying the public. This extension is based on the approach first promulgated by Klockars and colleagues (2002) as a way to adjust the classical police integrity methodology to fit a public opinion survey. In Chap. 9, Kutnjak Ivković and colleagues add to this approach a comparative perspective. Based on a 2016 survey of college students in Croatia and Serbia, the study compares public opinion about police misconduct and police integrity in Croatia and Serbia. Whereas the application of the police integrity measures yields some differences between the two countries in the students' own views of police integrity, particularly in their perceptions of seriousness, their estimates of how police officers from their countries would view police integrity are very similar and indicative that they do not perceive the police in their country to have a high level of police integrity.

In Chap. 10, Lim also studies public views of police integrity and further expands the topic by comparing public views of police integrity with the police views of police integrity. Lim notes that police officers are recruited from the communities they serve and, accordingly, their views on police integrity should be similar to the views expressed by community members. At the same time, as police officers climb the police administration hierarchy and assume new responsibilities, their views change as well. Based on the original US survey by Klockars and colleagues (1997) and Lim's surveys of Texas police officers and Midwestern students from the 2010s, the author finds that highly ranked police officers (e.g., chief, sheriff, constable) and middle-ranked police officers (e.g., sergeant, lieutenant) share similar evaluations of police misconduct seriousness. At the same time, their evaluations of misconduct seriousness are quite different from line officers' evaluations. Furthermore, although the students evaluate police misconduct as far less serious than any group of police officers does, regardless of rank, the bottom line is that students' evaluations of police misconduct seriousness are most similar with the line officers' estimates of misconduct seriousness.

In Chap. 11, Lobnikar, Meško, Hölzl, and Prislan expand the methodological boundaries by including students as respondents in their survey and comparing public views on police integrity with the police officer views. Lobnikar and colleagues focus on the measures of the first dimension of the theory of police integrity—evaluations of misconduct seriousness. The authors not only compare citizen and police officer own evaluations of misconduct seriousness but also compare citizen and police officer assessments of how most police officers would evaluate examples of police misconduct. Based on the 2010s surveys of Slovenian police officers and citizens, Lobnikar and colleagues show that, for almost all forms of police misconduct included in the questionnaire, citizens themselves evaluate such misconduct as less serious than police officers do. The differences are both statistically significant and large in magnitude. Similarly, when Lobnikar and colleagues compare police officer and citizen estimates of most police officers' evaluations of misconduct seriousness, they find large and statistically significant differences indicating that residents have a much more negative view of the police than the police officers themselves do.

In Chap. 12, Porter and Prenzler add to the extant literature by incorporating gender as a demographic characteristic into their version of the police integrity questionnaire and expand the classical police integrity methodology. Although both the overall number and proportion of women in policing have increased since the 1960s, policing remains a male-dominated profession, particularly at the supervisory and administrative levels of the police hierarchy. Chapter 12 builds upon extant research concerning gender differences in ethical attitudes and behavior. The authors study the relation between gender and several measures of police integrity (e.g., perceptions of seriousness, rule violations, willingness to report). Based on the 2013 survey of Australian police officers, the authors find relatively few gender differences in the police officers' own estimates of misconduct seriousness, recognition of police misconduct as rule-violating behavior, severity of appropriate discipline, and willingness to report. On the other hand, Porter and Prenzler report more prominent gender differences in the respondents' perceptions of social culture and organizational culture, with female police officers having less positive opinions about colleagues' evaluations of misconduct seriousness and their willingness to report. At the same time, female police officers expect less severe discipline than male police officers do and are more likely to evaluate such discipline as fair.

Part IV: Exploring Validity and Reliability of Police Integrity Methodology

The fourth and last section of the book consists of chapters that assess the validity of the police integrity methodology (Chaps. 13 and 14) and its reliability (Chaps. 15 and 16).

In Chap. 13, Maskály, Donner, and Chen explore the validity of the classical police integrity methodology. They apply a modern psychometric approach to assess the validity of the measures of the first dimension of the theory (i.e., estimates of misconduct seriousness, recognition of police misconduct as rule-violating behavior) and the third dimension of the theory (i.e., expressed willingness to report misconduct). Based on the original US data collected by Klockars and colleagues (1997, 2000, 2006), Maskály and colleagues rely on the item-response theory approach to assess the validity. To increase the understanding of the measurement of police integrity, the authors develop valid and reliable latent constructs of five dimensions while, at the same time, considering potential inter-relationships among the constructs. Their analyses show that, despite some challenges both in the design of a few scenarios (e.g., running an off-duty security system business) and some questions (e.g., appropriate discipline), classical police corruption methodology, developed by Klockars and colleagues (1997), is a valid way to measure police integrity.

In Chap. 14, Kutnjak Ivković, Cajner Mraović, and Sudar explore the reliability of the police integrity methodology by examining two applications of the survey in Croatia conducted over a 20-year time span. During this period, Croatia has experienced systematic and extensive transformation of its political, legal, and economic system, any and all of which could have affected public views of the police and of police misconduct. Two groups of college students were surveyed two decades apart, in 1996 and 2016. The results indicate that, in accordance with the transformation taking place in the society at large, students surveyed in 2016 express personal attitudes associated with the higher levels of police integrity (i.e., more likely to assess misconduct as violating official rules, select harsher discipline as appropriate, and state that they would be more likely to report misconduct). On the other hand, the two administrations of the survey do not capture dramatic changes in the way students evaluate the police. The authors argue that the absence of large differences in the views of the police is a consequence of the mixed messages that the Croatian society sends about police corruption (e.g., enactment of stricter laws, emphasis on the reform on the one hand, countered by persistent inability or unwillingness to discipline or punish top police administrators and politicians for corruption).

In the final chapter of this book, Chap. 15, Van Droogenbroeck, Spruyt, Kutnjak Ivković, and Haberfeld study the short-term and long-term effects of a one-day training called the *Holocaust, Police and Human Rights (HPM) Project* on police officers' views of police integrity. Based on three 2017 surveys of the Belgian police, this chapter analyzes whether police integrity can be taught or cultivated through police integrity training. The training teaches police officers about the causes and mechanisms of group violence, while reminding them that they have individual responsibility to act when they witness misconduct. In the process, as they compare the results on the pre-test, post-test, and follow-up surveys, the authors indirectly assess the reliability of police integrity methodology. The results show that the HPM training affects both the police officers' perceptions of misconduct seriousness and their willingness to report misconduct. The effect seems to be stronger on the police officers' evaluations of the ethnic prejudice scenario—the primary target of the HPM training—than on the classical police integrity scenarios describing the use of excessive force and a case of internal corruption. The effect is both immediate and sustainable for over a month after the training has been completed.

In Conclusion

The book you are holding in your hands, *Exploring Police Integrity*, is a joint effort of 32 scholars across the world. They have diligently collected the data, expanded the theory of police integrity and the related methodology, and provided answers to many challenging research questions. For the first time, validity of the police integrity methodology has been assessed. In their contributions, these scholars discuss their findings in the context of extant scholarly works and propose ideas for the next wave of police integrity research.

East Lansing, MI   Sanja Kutnjak Ivković
New York, NY   M. R. Haberfeld

Contents

About the Editors

Sanja Kutnjak Ivković is a Professor at the School of Criminal Justice, Michigan State University. She holds a Doctorate in Criminology (Ph.D., University of Delaware) and a Doctorate in Law (S.J.D., Harvard University). Dr. Kutnjak Ivković is currently serving as Chair of the *American Society of Criminology* International Division. Dr. Kutnjak Ivković has served as Vice Chair (2009–2011) and Chair (2011–2013) of the *Academy of Criminal Justice Sciences* International Section and is a Co-founder and Co-chair of the *Law and Society Association* Collaborative Research Network on Lay Participation. Dr. Kutnjak Ivković received the 2017 *Mueller Award for Distinguished Contributions to International Criminal Justice*, Academy of Criminal Justice Sciences International Section. Her research focuses on comparative and international criminology, criminal justice, and law. Dr. Kutnjak Ivković is the Author of *Reclaiming Justice: The International Tribunal for the Former Yugoslavia and Local Courts* (Oxford University Press, 2011; co-authored with John Hagan), *Enhancing Police Integrity* (Springer, 2006; co-authored with Carl Klockars and Maria R. Haberfeld), *The Fallen Blue Knights: Controlling Police Corruption* (Oxford University Press, 2005), and *Lay Participation in Criminal Trials* (Austin & Winfield, 1999). Dr. Kutnjak Ivković is also an Editor of *Measuring Police Integrity* (Springer, 2015; co-edited with Maria H. Haberfeld) and *Contours of Police Integrity* (Sage, 2004; co-edited with Carl Klockars and Maria R. Haberfeld). Her book *Reclaiming Justice: The International Tribunal for the Former Yugoslavia and Local Courts*, co-authored with John Hagan, won the 2014 Academy of Criminal Justice Sciences International Section Book Award. The *Contours of Police Integrity* book received the American Society of Criminology International Division Honorable Mention. Her work has appeared in leading academic and law journals such as the *Law and Society Review*; the *Journal of Criminal Law and Criminology*; *Criminology and Public Policy*; *Law and Policy*; the *Stanford Journal of International Law*; the *Cornell International Law Journal*; *Crime, Law, and Social Change*; the *European Journal of Criminology*; *Policing and Society*; *Policing: An International Journal of Police Strategies and Management*; and *Police Quarterly*.

M. R. Haberfeld is a Professor of Police Science at John Jay College of Criminal Justice in New York City. She holds a Ph.D. in Criminal Justice from the City University of New York. Dr. Haberfeld served in the Israel Defense Forces in a counter-terrorist unit and left the army at the rank of a Sergeant. Later she served in the Israel National Police and left the force at the rank of Lieutenant. Dr. Haberfeld is one of the co-creators of the Police Leadership Program for the NYPD sworn officers and its Academic Director since its creation in 2001. In addition, Dr. Haberfeld has created the Law Enforcement Leadership Institute for Police Chiefs in NY State and an online Law Enforcement Leadership Certificate. Dr. Haberfeld has trained police forces around the country and the world, including the Dominican Republic, the Czech Republic, Poland, India, China, Cyprus, Turkey, Mongolia, and Taiwan, and has conducted research in over 70 police departments in the USA and in 35 countries. Dr. Haberfeld also developed and trained some units of the US Armed Forces, including the US Marines. Her publications include *A New Understanding of Terrorism* (Co-editor, Springer, 2010), *Modern Piracy and Maritime Terrorism* (Co-editor, Kendall Hunt Publishing, 2012), *Terrorism Within Comparative International Context* (co-author, Springer, 2009), *Russian Organized Corruption Networks and Their International Trajectories* (co-author, Springer, 2011), *Critical Issues in Police Training* (Pearson, 2002, 2013, 2018), *Police Organization and Training: Innovations in Research and Practice* (Co-editor, Springer, 2011), *Police Leadership: Organizational and Managerial Decision Making Process* (Pearson, 2012), *Policing Muslim Communities* (co-author, 2012), *Match-Fixing in International Sports* (Co-editor, Springer, 2013), *Introduction to Policing: The Pillar of Democracy* (co-author, Carolina Academic Press, 2014, 2017), and *Measuring Police Integrity Across the World* (Co-editor, Springer, 2015). Dr. Haberfeld is also Series Editor of *Springer Briefs in Policing*, where she recently co-edited three briefs on community policing and technology (2018, 2019).

About the Authors

Vladimir Božović is an Advisor to the Minister of Interior, Serbia. He holds a Ph.D. in Security Studies from the University of Belgrade. Dr. Božović is a lawyer and an expert in the field of security studies. Dr. Božović was Inspector General of the Department of Public Security at the Ministry of Interior of Serbia from 2004 to 2007 and the State Secretary at the Ministry of Interior, in charge of internal control and international cooperation, between 2012 and 2014. In May 2015, he was appointed Advisor to the President of the Government of the Republic of Serbia in charge of regional cooperation and relation with church and religious communities.

Tiffany Chen is a Graduate Student at the University of Texas at Dallas, USA. After completing her Undergraduate Degree in Criminology, she has been pursuing a Master's Degree in Accounting at the Jindal School of Management at the University of Texas at Dallas. After completing her degree, Ms. Chen hopes to work in an environment in which she can blend her passion for criminology and accounting.

Darko Datzer is an Associate Professor at the Faculty of Criminal Justice, Criminology and Security Studies, University of Sarajevo, Bosnia and Herzegovina. He obtained a Ph.D. in Criminal Justice from the University of Sarajevo, elaborating on detection and gathering and the use of evidence in bribery cases. His present research covers a wide range of corruption issues, criminal confiscation, and property crime, primarily from criminal law and criminological perspectives. Dr. Datzer is the author of the monograph *Criminology of Corruption* (published by Faculty of Criminal Justice, Criminology and Security Studies Press, 2016), a co-author of *Overtly About Police and Corruption* (2006), and a Co-editor of several volumes on criminal confiscation.

Christopher M. Donner is an Assistant Professor in the Department of Criminal Justice and Criminology at Loyola University Chicago, USA. He received his Ph.D. in Criminology from the University of South Florida. His current research focuses on criminological theory testing among non-traditional forms of deviance, such as police misconduct, cybercrime, and sports doping. His recent research has been published in the *Journal of*

Criminal Justice, Deviant Behavior, Policing and Society, and *International Criminal Justice Review*.

Filip Van Droogenbroeck is a Research Professor at the Sociology Department at the Vrije Universiteit Brussel, Belgium. He holds a Bachelor's Degree in Social Work (BSc., Economische Hogeschool Sint-Aloysius) and Master and Doctorate degrees in Sociology (MSc., Ph.D., Vrije Universiteit Brussel). His main research interests include sociology of youth, educational policy, compassion and altruism research, and sociology of education. Dr. Van Droogenbroeck currently coordinates projects such as the "Teaching and Learning International Survey (TALIS 2018 Flanders)" and the "Holocaust, Police and Human Rights Project." Recently, Dr. Van Droogenbroeck received the 2018 European Varela Award, awarded by the Mind and Life Institute for the research project "Compassionate Attitude Training in a Challenging School Context: An Effectiveness Study Assessing the Impact on Well-Being, Prosocial Attitudes and Behavior, and Sociopsychological Attitudes Concerning Prejudice" for its intellectual rigor and societal value.

Joseph A. Hamm is an Assistant Professor, jointly appointed in Michigan State University's School of Criminal Justice and Environmental Science and Policy Program, USA. He holds a Ph.D. from the University of Nebraska-Lincoln in Law-Psychology (2014) and a Master of Legal Studies from the University of Nebraska College of Law (2013). His research addresses public trust in governance entities like the police, courts, and natural resource authorities. Dr. Hamm serves as an Associate Editor of the *Journal of Trust Research* and on the editorial board of *Psychology, Public Policy, and Law*. His work has been published in the *Journal of Experimental Criminology*; the *Journal of Public Administration, Research, and Theory*; and *Ecology and Society*.

Aljaž Hölzl holds a B.A. in Criminal Justice and Security from the Faculty of Criminal Justice and Security, University of Maribor, Slovenia.

Wil Hout is a Professor of Governance and International Political Economy at the International Institute of Social Studies, Erasmus University Rotterdam, the Netherlands. He received a Ph.D. in International Relations from Leiden University. His research focuses on international cooperation and on governance issues in developing countries. His work has been published in the *European Journal of International Relations, Development and Change*, the *Journal of Development Studies, Third World Quarterly, Critical Asian Studies, Development Policy Review*, the *Revue Internationale de Politique Comparée*, the *Journal of African Economies*, and *Acta Politica*. Dr. Hout is the author of *The Politics of Aid Selectivity* (Routledge, 2007), co-author of *Political Economy and the Aid Industry in Asia* (with Jane Hutchison, Caroline Hughes, and Richard Robison, Palgrave Macmillan, 2014), and Co-editor of *Regionalism Across the North-South Divide* (with Jean Grugel, Routledge, 1999). His most recent book, co-authored with M.A. Mohamed

Salih, is *A Political Economy of African Regionalisms: An Overview of Asymmetrical Development* (Edward Elgar, 2019).

Aleksandr Khechumyan is a Guest Researcher at the Max Planck Institute for Foreign and International Criminal Law, Germany. He holds a Diploma in Law (equivalent to an LL.B.) from the Police Academy of the Republic of Armenia (2000), an LL.M. Degree in International Human Rights Law from the University of Essex, UK (2010), and a Dr.jur. Degree from the Albert Ludwig University of Freiburg, Germany (2017). Dr. Khechumyan's research interests focus on implementation of human rights standards in criminal justice, aging, and human rights and police corruption. Dr. Khechumyan has published in journals such as *Policing: An International Journal of Police Strategies and Management*, the *European Journal on Criminal Policy and Research*, the *International Journal of Comparative and Applied Criminal Justice*, and the *European Human Rights Law Review*. His recent book, *Imprisonment of the Elderly and Death in Custody*, was published by Routledge in 2018.

Hyeyoung Lim is an Associate Professor at the Department of Criminal Justice, University of Alabama at Birmingham, USA. She holds a Doctorate in Criminal Justice (Ph.D., Sam Houston State University). Her primary research interests include police decision-making, police use of force, police organizational behaviors, and police-community relations. A recently developed line of her research focuses on cybersecurity and cyberpolicing.

Branko Lobnikar is an Associate Professor of Security Studies and Head of the Policing and Security Studies Department at the Faculty of Criminal Justice and Security, University of Maribor, Slovenia. He holds a Ph.D. in Human Resources Management from the University of Ljubljana. As former Police Officer and Police Supervisor, Dr. Lobnikar serves as an OSCE International Expert and was a Member of the management board of European Diploma in Policing, an international Leonardo da Vinci project of senior police managers training, a short-time Expert of the Council of Europe, and a short-time Expert of DCAF. His areas of expertise comprise policing, human resources management, and deviant behavior within organizations. Dr. Lobnikar has authored papers on various aspects of policing and police deviance management and co-edited *Handbook on Policing in Central and Eastern Europe* (Springer). Currently, Dr. Lobnikar is involved in the study of police integrity, (de)radicalization, and community policing. Dr. Lobnikar is a National Coordinator of an H2020 project— IMPRODOVA (*Improving Frontline Responses to High Impact Domestic Violence*).

Jon Maskály is an Assistant Professor in the criminology program at the School of Economic, Political and Policy Sciences at the University of Texas at Dallas, USA. He holds a Doctorate in Criminology (Ph.D., University of South Florida). His research focuses on police-community relationships, specifically the factors that enhance or erode the strength of these relationships. A recent line of research focuses on police integrity from a comparative perspective. Additionally, Dr. Maskály has expertise in quantitative methods, including psychometrics and latent variable modeling. Recent publications have appeared in *Crime & Delinquency*, *Deviant Behavior*, the *Journal of Criminal Justice*, *Policing and Society*, and *Social Science Research*.

Michael Meyer is Emeritus Professor of Criminal Justice at the University of North Dakota, USA. He received his Ph.D. in Sociology and M.P.A. from the University of Oklahoma as well as M.A. and B.S. degrees from the University of Hawaii, Manoa. In 2003–2004, he was a Fulbright Senior Researcher/Lecturer at Tshwane University of Technology, Pretoria, South Africa. He has been a recipient of two National Endowment for the Humanities Fellowships at Princeton University (Anthropology and Law) and the University of Pennsylvania (18th Century British Literature). His research interests focus on police and community, police legitimacy, police integrity, and policing in transitional societies, and he has published several articles with South African colleagues on cynicism and isolation among South African Police Service officers, integrity in the South African Police Service, as well as the integration of women into the South African Police Service.

Gorazd Meško is a Professor of Criminology at the Faculty of Criminal Justice and Security, University of Maribor, Slovenia, and past President of the European Society of Criminology. He holds a Ph.D. in Social Education from the University of Ljubljana. Dr. Meško has been a Visiting Scholar at the University of Cambridge (1995, 2001, 2009–2015) and at the University of Oxford (1996, 1999) and an Honorary Visiting Scholar at the University of Leicester (2004–2008). His recent books include *Handbook on Policing in Central and Eastern Europe* (Springer, 2013; co-edited with Chuck Fields, Andrej Sotlar, and Branko Lobnikar) and *Trust and Legitimacy in Criminal Justice: European Perspectives* (Springer, 2015; co-edited with Justice Tankebe). His research interests include the legitimacy of criminal justice, community policing, safety and security in local communities, and crime prevention. Dr. Meško is currently a Lead Researcher in projects on plural and rural policing in Slovenia.

Skyler Morgan is currently a Master's Student at the School of Criminal Justice at Michigan State University, USA. Upon completion of his master's degree, Mr. Morgan will be pursuing his Ph.D. in Criminology and Criminal Justice at Arizona State University. His research interests include corrections, gender and sexuality, and terrorism. His recent work has appeared in *Police Practice and Research: An International Journal*.

Irena Cajner Mraović is an Associate Professor at the Centre for Croatian Studies, University of Zagreb, Croatia, and a Representative at the City Assembly of the City of Zagreb. She graduated from the University of Zagreb and received a Ph.D. in Special Education Sciences. Dr. Cajner Mraović was the Dean of the Police College, an Advisor on Community Policing to the Minister of the Interior, and the Head of the Police Academy. Her research interests include policing, juvenile crime, and crime prevention. She has authored numerous scholarly papers, books, and manuals. Dr. Cajner Mraović has also mentored students who have received international awards for their work.

Eldan Mujanović is an Associate Professor at the Faculty of Criminal Justice, Criminology and Security Studies, University of Sarajevo, Bosnia and Herzegovina. He obtained a Ph.D. in Criminal Justice from the University of Sarajevo, addressing the issue of international police cooperation in the detection and proving of motor vehicle thefts. Currently, Dr. Mujanović is involved in research projects focusing on asset recovery, crimes against property, international police cooperation, and combating corruption. Dr. Mujanović is the Author of *International Police Cooperation* monograph (2015) and a Co-editor of several volumes on criminal confiscation.

Nikolina Nemec is a Senior Associate on the Development Project in Town Ludbreg in the Department of Tourism, Entrepreneurship, and Development Projects, Croatia. She has a Master's Degree in Sociology from the Centre for Croatian Studies at the University of Zagreb. Ms. Nemec has also completed a postgraduate specialist degree *Adapting to the European Union: The Project Management and the Use of EU Funds and Programmes* from the Faculty of Political Science at the University of Zagreb. Her work focuses on applying and implementing projects co-founded by the European Union. Ms. Nemec also studies urban security and migration, victimization, community-oriented policing, and police integrity.

Robert Peacock is an Assistant Professor in the Steven J. Green School of International and Public Affairs at Florida International University, USA. Peacock received an MBA in Finance from Ohio University and a B.A. in Public Policy from the University of Michigan prior to completing his Ph.D. in Criminal Justice from Michigan State University. Dr. Peacock's research interests are broadly focused on enforcement agency policies and practices in relation to police misconduct and corruption. His studies primarily seek to evaluate the effect that agency policies, notably officer selection and training, have on officer integrity and agency legitimacy.

Louse E. Porter is a Senior Lecturer in the School of Criminology and Criminal Justice at Griffith University, Australia, and Member of the Griffith Criminology Institute. She holds a Ph.D. in Psychology and M.Sc. in Investigative Psychology (University of Liverpool, UK). Her research applies social, psychological, and criminological perspectives to behavior in policing and offending contexts. Her current policing research focuses on police misconduct and police use of force. Dr. Porter is co-author of *Police Integrity Management in Australia* (CRC Press, 2012; co-authored with Tim Prenzler), and Dr. Porter co-edited a recent special issue of the *European Journal of Policing Studies* on changes in policing to improve service delivery (with Garth den Heyer).

Tim Prenzler is a Professor in the School of Criminology and Criminal Justice, Griffith University, Australia, and a Chief Investigator in the Australian Research Council Centre of Excellence in Policing and Security. He holds a Ph.D., M.A., and B.A. (Hons.). Dr. Prenzler has contributed to a number of textbooks and co-edited (with Hennessey Hayes) *An Introduction to Crime and Criminology* (Pearson, 2009). Dr. Prenzler is the Author of *Police Corruption: Preventing Misconduct and Maintaining Integrity* (CRC Press/Taylor & Francis, 2009) and *Ethics and Accountability in Criminal Justice* (Australian Academic Press, 2009) and co-author (with Rick Sarre) of *The Law of Private Security in Australia*, second edition (Thomson Lawbook Co., 2009). Apart from integrity research, his current work includes studies on police and security officer safety, security industry regulation, reducing welfare fraud, and improving the integration of women police.

Kaja Prislan is an Assistant Professor at the Faculty of Criminal Justice and Security, University of Maribor, Slovenia, working in the Department of Policing and Security Studies in collaboration with the Department of Information Security. She holds a Ph.D. in Security Sciences from the University of Maribor. Her research interests focus on information security and management in policing and security organizations. Dr. Prislan is currently a project member of different national and international projects related to policing and high-impact crimes. Her recent publications include *Measuring Information Security Performance with 10 by 10 Model for Holistic State Evaluation* (2016, PLOS One) and *The Code of Silence and Female Police Officers in Slovenia: Gender Differences in Willingness to Report Police Misconduct* (2016, *Policing: An International Journal of Police Strategies and Management*).

Marko Prpić is a High-School Teacher of Croatian Language and Literature and a Doctoral Student at the Faculty of Education and Rehabilitation Sciences, University of Zagreb, Croatia. He holds a Master's Degree in Croatology and a Master's Degree in Sociology from the University of Zagreb. His research focuses on formal and informal social control, prevention of deviance in school and police, police integrity, organizational justice, and procedural justice. His recent work includes articles on *Police Management for Community Policing: The Case of Croatia* (Interdisciplinary Management Research XIV, 2018; co-authored with Dražen Vitez and Marin Pucar) and *Depoliticisation as Key Component of Police Reforms in Post-Socialist Countries: The Case of Croatia* (international scientific conference Researching Security: Approaches, Concepts and Policies proceedings; University of St. Kliment Ohridski and Faculty of Security, 2018; co-authored with Irena Cajner Mraović and Vladimir Faber).

Barbara Prprović is a Project Associate of the Croatian Red Cross Society in Čakovec, Croatia. She holds a Master's Degree in Sociology. Her scientific research interests are comparative and international criminology, delinquency, and victimology. Her recent publications include a scientific paper called "Comparative Analysis of the Quality of Policing in Local Slovenian and Croatian Multicultural Communities" (2016; Lobnikar, B., Prprović, B., Nemec, N., Banutai, E., Prislan, K., Cajner Mraović, I.), published in the *Journal of Criminal Justice and Criminology*, Ljubljana, Slovenia.

Adri Sauerman is a Legal Counsel in the mineral resource and peripheral industries. A Fulbright alumnus (Florida State University), he has a professional background as Advocate (Barrister) to the High Court of South Africa with a history of interacting with both the country's justice department and police service. His research interests in the latter and his work with Dr. Kutnjak Ivković on international criminology, criminal justice, and law have during the past 15 years appeared in several national and international books, academic journals, and conferences.

Bram Spruyt is an Associate Professor of Sociology and Head of the Sociology Department at the Vrije Universiteit Brussel, Belgium. He holds a Doctorate in Sociology (Ph.D., Vrije Universiteit Brussel). Dr. Spruyt teaches sociology, cultural sociology, and researching culture. His main research interests include public opinion research, youth research, sociology of education, and cultural sociology. His recent work was published in, among others, *Political Psychology*, *Political Research Quarterly*, *Social Forces*, and *Social Science Research*. Bram Spruyt is Member of the Young Academy of Belgium.

Dorotea Sudar is a Recruitment Consultant at the Croatian Employment Service, Croatia. She holds an M.A. Degree in Philosophy and Sociology from the Centre for Croatian Studies, University of Zagreb. Her research focuses on criminology and public perception of criminology in a local (Croatian) society. Ms. Sudar won the Rector's Prize for her student paper "Social Context as a Dimension of the Police Integrity Theory." This paper is a product of cooperation between the School of Criminal Justice, Michigan State University, and the Centre for Croatian Studies, University of Zagreb.

Birgit Vallmüür is an Independent Researcher defending her Ph.D. in Government and Politics at Tallinn University, Estonia, in summer 2019. Previously, Ms. Vallmüür has served as an Advisor to both private- and public-sector organizations, was a Senior Civil Servant, and was employed in the academia. Ms. Vallmüür holds an M.A. in Public Management from Tallinn University. Her latest research is focused on green police integrity and she is passionate about green criminology. Ms. Vallmüür has published about police integrity in Estonia and has explored the gender neutrality of police integrity in Estonia.

Natascha Wagner is an Associate Professor of Development Economics at the Institute of Social Studies, Erasmus University Rotterdam, the Netherlands. She holds a Doctorate in International Economics from the Graduate Institute of International and Development Studies, Geneva (Switzerland). Her research interests lie in international economics, development, education, and health. Dr. Wagner has participated in various impact evaluation projects in

Africa and Asia, ranging from good governance to public health and rural infrastructure programs and applying experimental as well as quasi-experimental impact evaluation techniques. In her research, Dr. Wagner applies quantitative microeconomic methods to interdisciplinary questions such as gender and ethnicity bias in student evaluations of teaching, norms and policing, inclusiveness in community-driven development, and peer mentoring for health service uptake. Dr. Wagner has published articles in, among others, *Health Economics, Economics of Education Review, Journal of Development Studies*, and *World Development*.

Scott Wolfe is an Associate Professor in the School of Criminal Justice at Michigan State University, USA. He received his Ph.D. in Criminology and Criminal Justice from Arizona State University. Dr. Wolfe's research focuses on policing, organizational justice, legitimacy, and criminological theory. Currently, Dr. Wolfe is Co-principal investigator on a National Institute of Justice grant evaluating a police officer social interaction and de-escalation training program with a randomized controlled trial. Dr. Wolfe's recent research has appeared in the *Journal of Research in Crime and Delinquency, Justice Quarterly*, and *Law and Human Behavior*.

Part I

Studying Classical Police Integrity Theory and Methodology

Exploring Empirical Research on Police Integrity

Sanja Kutnjak Ivković and M. R. Haberfeld

Introduction

Almost 25 years ago, Klockars and Kutnjak Ivković (e.g., 2004) have proposed a theory of police integrity and developed the methodology to measure police integrity across police agencies. The first applications of the police integrity theory and methodology resulted in pioneering empirical research projects, conducted both in the United States (e.g., Klockars et al. 2000) and abroad (e.g., Kutnjak Ivković and Klockars 1998, 2000). A couple of years later, the methodology was updated to cover different forms of police misconduct (e.g., Klockars et al. 2006). According to the National Research Council of the National Academies (2004, p. 274), this research approach has been evaluated as showing "considerable promise" and the body of extant research has started to grow significantly.

Kutnjak Ivković (2015a, p. 17) pointed out in 2015 that, "[a] search of various electronic sources to date uncovered four books, 14 dissertations, 20 book chapters, 42 journal articles, and eight reports published utilizing this approach." Empirical research built upon this theoretical and methodological approach has expanded in several different directions. Its exploration of the contours of police integrity has covered more than 30 countries (e.g., Klockars et al. 2004a; Kutnjak Ivković 2015a; Kutnjak Ivković and Haberfeld 2015). Its research subjects were not only police officers, but also citizens (e.g., Bjerregaard and Lord 2004; Kuo 2018; Kutnjak Ivković et al. 2004; Meyer et al. 2013; Pagon et al. 2004). The methodology has been updated and expanded (e.g., Datzer et al. 2019; Gottschalk 2010; Kutnjak Ivković et al. 2019; Porter and Prenzler 2019), while the theory has been tested and extended (e.g., Donner et al. 2018a, 2018b; Hickman et al. 2016a; Kutnjak Ivković 2015a; Kutnjak Ivković et al. 2019; Vallmüür 2019). Finally, the validity and reliability of the methodology have been assessed (e.g., Davis et al. 2015; Hickman et al. 2016a; Maskály et al. 2019a, 2019b).

This chapter provides a systematic overview of the extant research on police integrity and explores the ways in which the original theory and methodology have been used and expanded. The analysis is based on an up-to-date review of the police integrity literature. The chapter compares and contrasts results from different studies, identifies common patterns across studies, and develops a classification based on the study's goals and procedures.

S. Kutnjak Ivković
School of Criminal Justice, Michigan State University, East Lansing, MI, USA
e-mail: kutnjak@msu.edu

M. R. Haberfeld (✉)
John Jay College of Criminal Justice, New York, NY, USA
e-mail: mhaberfeld@jjay.cuny.edu

Classical Theory of Police Integrity and Related Methodology

Theory of Police Integrity

Unlike the "rotten-apple" approach, individualistic in nature and grounded in the notion that police misconduct is a consequence of character failures of individual police officers (see, e.g., Knapp Commission 1972), the theory of police integrity (e.g., Klockars and Kutnjak Ivković 2004; Klockars et al. 2000, 2006) is organizational in nature. It focuses on "rotten orchards" or "rotten barrels" (see, e.g., Punch 2009), proposing how features of the police organization—what police agency does or does not do—influence the level of police integrity prevailing in the police agency. The theory's basic tenets are outlined in four dimensions.

The first dimension of the theory connects the existence of official rules prohibiting police misconduct and the level of police integrity in the police agency (e.g., Klockars and Kutnjak Ivković 2004; Klockars et al. 2000, 2006). The theory emphasizes the importance of the official rules delineating allowed and prohibited behavior, the way in which these rules are communicated to the police officers, and the extent to which police officers accept these official rules. Accordingly, a police agency of high integrity is an agency in which official rules prohibiting misconduct have been put in place and enforced, and in which they are taught, communicated to, and supported by, its police officers (e.g., Kutnjak Ivković 2015a).

The second dimension of the theory proposes that there is a positive relation between the level of police integrity in the police agency and the existence of, as well as reliance on, the methods of internal control (e.g., Klockars and Kutnjak Ivković 2004; Klockars et al. 2000, 2006). The theory takes into account that, to control police misconduct in their agencies, police agencies may rely on both reactive internal methods (e.g., internal investigation, discipline) and proactive internal methods (e.g., education in ethics, integrity testing; Kutnjak Ivković 2015a). Accordingly, a police agency of high integrity is an agency in which both proactive and reactive internal mechanisms of control have been used regularly and consistently (e.g., Klockars and Kutnjak Ivković 2004; Klockars et al. 2000, 2006).

The third dimension of the theory argues that the extent of police integrity and the strength of the code of silence are negatively related (e.g., Klockars and Kutnjak Ivković 2004; Klockars et al. 2000, 2006). The code of silence exists in every police agency because of the para-military organization of the police. The police agency's efforts in curtailing the code of silence are critical for the level of police integrity in the police agency. Accordingly, a police agency of high integrity is a police agency in which the code of silence is weak and does not protect serious forms of police misconduct (e.g., Kutnjak Ivković 2015a).

The fourth dimension of the theory links the level of police integrity in the police agency and the larger social, political, and economic environment in which police agencies operate (e.g., Klockars and Kutnjak Ivković 2004; Klockars et al. 2000, 2006). Through the establishment, teaching, and enforcement of the laws, the operation of external control systems, and the creation of culture intolerant of misconduct by governmental employees, the societies at large shape the level of police integrity in their police agencies. Accordingly, a police agency of high integrity is a police agency in which external negative societal influences have been controlled and positive societal influences embraced.

Measuring Police Integrity

The methodological approach developed by Klockars and Kutnjak Ivković (2004) rests on the premise that police integrity can be measured directly, without the resistance that any attempts at measuring police misconduct directly might face. The authors argue that police integrity can be assessed both quantitatively and qualitatively (see, e.g., Klockars et al. 2006). The focus on this chapter is on the questionnaires designed to measure police corruption quantitatively. The idea is to present the respondents with the hypothetical examples of police misconduct and ask them questions of fact and opinion, thereby tapping into different dimensions of police integrity.

The first questionnaire that Klockars and Kutnjak Ivković (2004) designed, called the police corruption questionnaire, contained 11 hypothetical scenarios. Because it was designed as the mirror opposite of police corruption, it mostly contained descriptions of various forms of police corruption, based on the Roebuck and Barker's typology (1974). In addition, Klockars and Kutnjak Ivković (2004) included one scenario describing the use of excessive force (Table 1). These scenarios contain short descriptions of police misconduct that should be applicable to the police on patrol in modern, developed societies (e.g., Klockars et al. 2000).

Because police integrity incorporates more than the opposite of for-gain police corruption, in the late 1990s, Klockars et al. (2000, 2004a, 2004b, 2006) have designed the second questionnaire, the police integrity questionnaire. That questionnaire contains a broader spectrum of different forms of police misconduct. Grounded in the same guiding principles, the 11 scenarios in the police integrity questionnaire include examples of police corruption, use of excessive force, planting of evidence, and falsification of official documents (Table 2). To allow a potential comparison of the data collected by the administration of the police corruption questionnaire and

Table 1 Police Corruption Questionnaire Scenarios

	Scenario description
Scenario 1	A police officer runs his own private business in which he sells and installs security devices, such as alarms, special locks, etc. He does this work during his off-duty hours
Scenario 2	A police officer routinely accepts free meals, cigarettes, and other items of small value from merchants on his beat. He does not solicit these gifts and is careful not to abuse the generosity of those who give gifts to him
Scenario 3	A police officer stops a motorist for speeding. The officer agrees to accept a personal gift for half of the amount of the fine in exchange for not issuing a citation
Scenario 4	A police officer is widely liked in the community, and on holidays local merchants and restaurant and bar owners show their appreciation for his attention by giving him gifts of food and liquor
Scenario 5	A police officer discovers a burglary of a jewelry shop. The display cases are smashed and it is obvious that many items have been taken. While searching the shop, he takes a watch, worth about two days' pay for that officer. He reports that the watch had been stolen during the burglary
Scenario 6	A police officer has a private arrangement with a local auto body shop to refer the owners of the cars damaged in the accidents to the shop. In exchange for each referral, he receives a payment of 5% of the repair bill from the shop owner
Scenario 7	A police officer, who happens to be a very good auto mechanic, is scheduled to work during the coming holidays. A supervisor offers to give him these days off, if he agrees to tune-up his supervisor's personal car. Evaluate the SUPERVISOR'S behavior
Scenario 8	At 2 A.M. a police officer, who is on duty, is driving his patrol car on a deserted road. He sees a vehicle that has been driven off the road and is stuck in a ditch. He approaches the vehicle and observes that the driver is not hurt but is obviously intoxicated. He also finds that the driver is a police officer. Instead of reporting this accident and offense he transports the driver to his home
Scenario 9	A police officer finds a bar on his beat which is still serving drinks a half hour past its legal closing time. Instead of reporting this violation, the police officer agrees to accept a couple of free drinks from the owner
Scenario 10	Two police officers on foot patrol surprise a man who is attempting to break into an automobile. The man flees. They chase him for about two blocks before apprehending him by tackling him and wrestling him to the ground. After he is under control both officers punch him a couple of times in the stomach as punishment for fleeing and resisting
Scenario 11	A police officer finds a wallet in a parking lot. It contains the amount of money equivalent to a full-day's pay for that officer. He reports the wallet as lost property, but keeps the money for himself

Table 2 Police Integrity Questionnaire Scenarios

	Scenario description
Scenario 1	A police officer is widely liked in the community. Local merchants and restaurant owners regularly show their appreciation for his attention by giving him gifts of food, cigarettes, and other items of small value
Scenario 2	A police officer is aware that there is a felony warrant for a long-time friend of his. Although he sees his friend frequently over a period of more than a week and warns his friend of its existence, he does not arrest him
Scenario 3	A police officer discovers a burglary of a hardware store. The display cases are smashed and many items have obviously been taken. While searching the store, he takes an expensive pocketknife and slips it into his pocket. He reports that the knife has been stolen during the burglary
Scenario 4	An officer who was severely beaten by a person resisting arrest, has just returned to duty. On patrol, the officer approaches a person standing in a dimly lit alley. Suddenly, the person throws a gym bag at the officer and begins to run away. The officer fatally shoots the person, striking him in the back. It was later determined that the person was unarmed
Scenario 5	A police officer is scheduled to work during coming holidays. The supervisor offers to give him these days off, if he agrees to run some personal errands for the supervisor. Evaluate the SUPERVISOR'S behavior
Scenario 6	In responding with her male partner to a fight in a bar, a young, female officer receives a black eye from one of the male combatants. The man is arrested, handcuffed, and, as he is led into the cells, the male member of the team punches him very hard in the kidney area saying, "hurts, doesn't it"
Scenario 7	A police officer stops a motorist for speeding. As the officer approaches the vehicle, the driver yells, "What the hell are you stopping me for?" The officer replies, "Because today is 'Arrest an Asshole Day'"
Scenario 8	At 2:00 a.m. a police officer, who is on duty, is driving his patrol car on a deserted road. He sees a vehicle that has been driven off the road and is stuck in a ditch. He approaches the vehicle and observes that the driver is not hurt but is obviously intoxicated. He also finds that the driver is a police officer. Instead of reporting this accident and offense, he transports the driver to his home
Scenario 9	A police officer has a private arrangement with a local auto body shop to refer the owners of cars damaged in accidents to the shop. In exchange for each referral, he receives a payment of 5% of the repair bill from the shop owner
Scenario 10	A police officer arrests two drug dealers involved in a street fight. One has a large quantity of heroin on his person. In order to charge them both with serious offenses, the officer falsely reports that the heroin was found on both men
Scenario 11	A police sergeant, without intervening, watches officers under his supervision repeatedly strike and kick a man arrested for child abuse. The man has previous child abuse arrests. Evaluate the SERGEANT'S behavior

the data collected by the administration of the police integrity questionnaire, the police integrity questionnaire contains five scenarios describing police corruption from the police corruption questionnaire (Scenarios 1, 3, 5, 8, and 9); the five scenarios were either completely unchanged or were slightly modified.

Upon reading the description of misconduct contained in each scenario, police officers participating in the study are asked to respond to seven identical questions. These questions

match the dimensions of the police integrity theory (Table 3). Three questions are intended to measure the first dimension of the theory—knowledge of and support for organizational rules—Klockars et al. (2000, 2004a, 2004b, 2006). One of them directly tests the respondents' knowledge of official rules ("Would this behavior be regarded as a violation of official policy in your agency?"). Two additional questions tap into the same dimension by looking at the respondents' perceptions of misconduct

Table 3 Questions and Answers

	Questions and answers
First dimension	1. How serious do YOU consider this behavior to be? Not at all serious　　　　Very serious 　　1　　2　　3　　4　　5 2. How serious do MOST POLICE OFFICERS IN YOUR AGENCY consider this behavior to be? Not at all serious　　　　Very serious 　　1　　2　　3　　4　　5 3. Would this behavior be regarded as a violation of official policy in your agency? Definitely not　　　　Definitely yes 　　1　　2　　3　　4　　5
Second dimension	4. If an officer in your agency engaged in this behavior and was discovered doing so, what, if any, discipline do YOU think *SHOULD* follow. 　1. NONE　　　　　　　　　　4. PERIOD OF SUSPENSION 　2. VERBAL REPRIMAND WITHOUT PAY 　3. WRITTEN REPRIMAND　　　　5. DEMOTION IN RANK 　　　　　　6. DISMISSAL 5. If an officer in your agency engaged in this behavior and was discovered doing so, what, if any, discipline do YOU think *WOULD* follow. 　1. NONE　　　　　　　　　　4. PERIOD OF SUSPENSION 　2. VERBAL REPRIMAND WITHOUT PAY 　3. WRITTEN REPRIMAND　　　　5. DEMOTION IN RANK 　　　　　　6. DISMISSAL
Third dimension	6. Do you think YOU would report a fellow police officer who engaged in this behavior? Definitely not　　　　Definitely yes 　　1　　2　　3　　4　　5 7. Do you think MOST POLICE OFFICERS IN YOUR AGENCY would report a fellow police officer who engaged in this behavior? Definitely not　　　　Definitely yes 　　1　　2　　3　　4　　5

seriousness ("How serious do you consider this behavior to be?") and their perceptions of other police officers' support ("How serious do most police officers in your agency consider this behavior to be?").

The questionnaire also incorporates two questions measuring the second dimension of the theory. The questionnaire does not contain any questions assessing the internal system of control in general. Rather, it features two questions asking about the discipline that the respondents expect their police agency to mete out for the behavior described ("If an officer in your agency engaged in this behavior and was discovered doing so, what, if any, discipline do you think would follow?") and the discipline the respondents think is appropriate for such behavior ("If an officer in your agency engaged in this behav-

ior and was discovered doing so, what, if any, discipline do you think should follow?"). A comparison of the respondents' answers to these two questions yields a measure of the respondents' perceptions of disciplinary fairness.

The third dimension of the theory—the code of silence and its control—is represented in the questionnaire with a question asking the respondents to express their willingness to report misconduct described in each scenario ("Do you think you would report a fellow police officer who engaged in this behavior?"). In addition, the questionnaire asks the respondents to estimate how likely the other police officers in their police agency would be to do the same ("Do you think most police officers in your agency would report a fellow police officer who engaged in this behavior?").

Finally, while the questionnaire contains a few questions about the size and nature of the police agency, it does not include any measures tapping into the fourth dimension of the theory (the influence of the society at large on police integrity).

Overview of Police Integrity Research

We have conducted an extensive search of various electronic resources to generate a list of existing publications that have utilized police integrity theory and the related methodology. Our search was limited to publications in English or publications in other languages that have an abstract in English. Our investigation yielded about 170 publications, including journal articles, book chapters, books, reports, and doctoral dissertations.

We have classified existing studies into "classic" police integrity studies, police integrity studies expanding theoretical arguments, police integrity studies expanding methodology, and police integrity studies assessing validity and reliability of the police integrity methodology. Whereas every study on our list utilizes the police integrity theory and the associated methodology and, hence, could be classified as a "classic" police integrity study, we strove to classify each study into only one category. To that end, if a study provided a basic overview of police integrity in a particular police agency or country and added a methodological or theoretical extension to the classical approach, we classified such studies based on the additional contribution they are making. If a study made a major contribution in rarely explored two categories (e.g., tested the validity and connected the theory of integrity with another theory), we included such a study into both categories.

Classic Police Integrity Research

"Classic" police integrity research studies satisfy three criteria. First, the authors have used at least several of the original scenarios from the police corruption questionnaire and/or the police integ-

rity questionnaire. Second, these studies have primarily focused on assessing the contours of police integrity and do not seek to expand the approach in either methodological and/or theoretical aspects. Third, they have to include police officers as respondents and not include any additional groups (e.g., students, citizens, police personnel). We made an exception and included a few additional studies in which the authors not only measured police integrity using the classical methodology (and hence should be classified here), but also expanded it by creating new scenarios (and hence should be classified under the methodological extensions category). Because we tried to provide an example of at least one publication assessing police integrity in every country in which police integrity methodology was used and these were the only studies from some of the countries (e.g., Belgium, Kenya, Malaysia, Uganda), we included them in this category as well. Ultimately, about 80 studies belong to this category of classic police integrity studies.

To date, the police integrity theory and methodology have been used to measure the extent of police integrity in more than 30 countries across the world (Table 4). The studies included countries from all but one continent (Table 4): Africa (Eritrea, Kenya, South Africa, Uganda), Asia (Armenia, China, Japan, Malaysia, Pakistan, Russia, South Korea, Thailand, Turkey), Australia and Oceania (Australia), Europe (Austria, Belgium, Bosnia and Herzegovina, Croatia, Czech Republic, Estonia, Finland, Hungary, Netherlands, Norway, Poland, Romania, Slovenia, Sweden, UK), and North America (Canada, USA). The overwhelming majority of the studies in this category are single-country studies (69 studies out of 82 studies or 84%), while only a small proportion included comparative studies (13 studies out of 82 studies or 16%; Tables 4 and 5). All of these studies clearly show how diverse the contours of police integrity are across the world.

The first questionnaire, the police corruption questionnaire, has been used more often than the second questionnaire (Tables 4 and 5). Although both versions of the questionnaire have been

Table 4 Classical Police Integrity Single-Country Studies

Authors	Year	Country/city	Survey	Sample	Topic
Kutnjak Ivković and Khechumyan	2013	Armenia (2 cities)	1st questionnaire	468 police officers	Exploring police integrity in Armenia
Khechumyan and Kutnjak Ivković	2015	Armenia (10 departments)	2nd questionnaire	959 police officers	Exploring police integrity in Armenia
Edelbacher and Kutnjak Ivković	2004	Austria (national)	1st questionnaire	1932 police officers	Measuring police integrity in Austria
Porter, Prenzler, and Hine	2015	Australia (several agencies)	2nd questionnaire	856 police officers	Measuring police integrity in Australia
Porter and Prenzler	2016	Australia (several agencies)	2nd questionnaire	856 police officers	Assessing the code of silence
Van Droogenbroeck et al.	2019	Belgium (national)	2nd questionnaire	207 police officers	Measuring the effects on ethics training on police integrity in Belgium
Kutnjak Ivković	2004b	Bosnia and Herzegovina (Sarajevo)	1st questionnaire	451 police officers	Comparing supervisor and line officer views of police integrity in Bosnia
Kutnjak Ivković and Shelley	2005	Bosnia and Herzegovina (Sarajevo)	1st questionnaire	451 police officers	Measuring police integrity in Bosnia and Herzegovina
Alain	2004	Canada (Quebec)	1st questionnaire	455 police officers	Measuring police integrity in Canada
Wu et al.	2018	China (national)	1st questionnaire	353 police officers	Measuring police integrity in China
Kutnjak Ivković and Klockars	2000	Croatia (national)	1st questionnaire	1649 police officers	Comparing the supervisor and line officer willingness to report
Kutnjak Ivković and Klockars	2004	Croatia (national)	1st questionnaire	1649 police officers	Measuring police integrity in Croatia
Kutnjak Ivković	2012	Croatia (national)	2nd questionnaire	966 police officers	Exploring the relation between police integrity and rank
Kutnjak Ivković	2015b	Croatia (national)	2nd questionnaire	966 police officers	Measuring police integrity in Croatia
Kutnjak Ivković, Morgan, Cajner Mraovic, and Borovec	2019e	Croatia (national)	2nd questionnaire	966 police officers	Studying the relation between the code of silence and police assignment
Kutnjak Ivković and Shelley	2007	Czech Republic (1 region)	1st questionnaire	600 police officers	Measuring police integrity in the Czech Republic
Desta	2013	Eritrea (national)	1st questionnaire (9 scenarios +1 added)	107 top police administrators	Measuring police integrity in Eritrea

(continued)

Table 4 (continued)

Authors	Year	Country/city	Survey	Sample	Topic
Vallmüür	2015	Estonia (national)	2nd questionnaire	112 police officers	Measuring police integrity in Estonia
Puonti, Vuorinen, and Kutnjak Ivković	2004	Finland (national)	1st questionnaire	378 police officers	Measuring police integrity in Finland
Kremer	2000	Hungary (national)	1st questionnaire	609 police officers	Comparing supervisor and line officer views about the code of silence
Kremer	2004	Hungary (national)	1st questionnaire	609 police officers	Measuring police integrity in Hungary
Johnson	2003	Japan (Tokyo)	1st questionnaire	182 police officers	Measuring police integrity in Japan
Johnson	2004	Japan (Tokyo)	1st questionnaire	182 police officers	Measuring police integrity in Japan
Mathenge	2014	Kenya (national)	1st questionnaire	150 police officers	Measuring police integrity in Kenya
Yunus, Bustaman, Khalid	2013	Malaysia (local)	Based on first questionnaire, developed new scenarios	100 local government employees	Measuring integrity in Malaysia
Bakri et al.	2017	Malaysia (capital)	New scenarios	189 police officers	Measuring integrity of in Malaysia
Punch, Huberts, and Lamboo	2004	The Netherlands (3 police agencies)	1st questionnaire	795 police officers	Measuring police integrity in the Netherlands
Gottschalk	2010	Norway	1st questionnaire	21 police managers	Measuring police integrity in Norway
Chattha and Kutnjak Ivković	2004	Pakistan (Lahore)	1st questionnaire	499 police officers	Measuring police integrity in Pakistan
Haberfeld	2004	Poland (national)	1st questionnaire	1477 police officers	Measuring police integrity in Poland
Cheloukhine et al.	2015	Russia (2 regions)	2nd questionnaire	106 police officers	Measuring police integrity in Russia
Pagon and Lobnikar	2000	Slovenia (national)	1st questionnaire	767 police officers	Comparing supervisor and line officer perceptions of the code of silence
Pagon and Lobnikar	2004	Slovenia (national)	1st questionnaire	767 police officers	Measuring police integrity in Slovenia
Kutnjak Ivković et al.	2000	Slovenia (national)	1st questionnaire	767 police officers	Measuring the code of silence
Lobnikar and Mesko	2015a	Slovenia (national)	2nd questionnaire	583 police officers	Measuring police integrity in Slovenia
Lobnikar and Mesko	2015b	Slovenia (national)	2nd questionnaire	550 police officers	Measuring police integrity in Slovenia
Kutnjak Ivković and Sauerman	2011	South Africa (national)	1st questionnaire	379 police supervisors	Studying the code of silence in South Africa

(continued)

Table 4 (continued)

Authors	Year	Country/city	Survey	Sample	Topic
Kutnjak Ivković and Sauerman	2012	South Africa (national)	1st questionnaire	379 police supervisors; 771 police officers	Comparing the code of silence with the 2005 and 2007 surveys
Kutnjak Ivković and Sauerman	2013	South Africa (national)	1st questionnaire	379 police supervisors	Exploring the code of silence among supervisors in South Africa
Kutnjak Ivković and Sauerman	2015	South Africa (national)	1st questionnaire	379 police supervisors	Measuring police integrity in South Africa
Matlala et al.	2016	South Africa (1 province)	1st questionnaire	390 police officers	Measuring police integrity in one South-African province
Newham	2002	South Africa (Johannesburg)	1st questionnaire	104 police officers	Measuring police integrity in South Africa
Newham	2004	South Africa (Johannesburg)	1st questionnaire	104 police officers	Measuring police integrity in South Africa
Reyneke-Cloete and Meyer	2016	South Africa (Gauteng)	1st questionnaire	160 police officers	Measuring police integrity in South Africa
Sauerman and Kutnjak Ivković	2008	South Africa (national)	1st questionnaire	379 police supervisors	Measuring police integrity in South Africa
Sauerman and Kutnjak Ivković	2015	South Africa (national)	2nd questionnaire	871 police officers	Measuring police integrity in South Africa
Kutnjak Ivković and Kang	2011	South Korea (2 police academies)	1st questionnaire	329 police officers	Measuring police integrity in South Korea
Kang and Kutnjak Ivković	2015	South Korea (national)	2nd questionnaire	335 police officers	Measuring police integrity in South Korea
Torstensson Levander and Ekenvall	2004	Sweden (national)	1st questionnaire	1590 police officers	Measuring police integrity in Sweden
Khruakham and Lee	2013	Thailand (national)	1st questionnaire	295 police officers	Measuring police integrity in Thailand
Phetthong and Kutnjak Ivković	2015	Thailand (national)	2nd questionnaire	274 police officers	Measuring police integrity in Thailand
Dayioglu	2007	Turkey (3 cities)	1st questionnaire (modified + new scenarios)	633 police officers	Focusing on attitudes toward the use of force among the Turkish police officers
Wagner and Hout	2019	Uganda	1st questionnaire (modified + new scenarios)	600 police officers	Studying the relation between police integrity and police effectiveness
Westmarland	2004	UK (southeast)	1st questionnaire	275 police officers	Measuring police integrity in the UK
Westmarland	2005	UK (southeast)	1st questionnaire	275 police officers	Focusing on the measures of seriousness and willingness to report in the UK

(continued)

Table 4 (continued)

Authors	Year	Country/city	Survey	Sample	Topic
Westmarland and Rowe	2018	UK (3 police agencies)	1st questionnaire	520 police officers	Comparing attitudes toward the code of silence by rank and police agency
Kargin	2009	USA (Philadelphia)	1st questionnaire (6 scenarios)	499 police officers	Examining influences on peer reporting intentions
Klockars and Kutnjak Ivković	2004	USA (national; 30 agencies)	1st questionnaire	3235 police officers	Measuring police integrity across the U.S.A
Klockars, Kutnjak Ivković, and Haberfeld	2004b	USA (national; 30 agencies)	1st questionnaire	3235 police officers	Measuring police integrity in the USA
Klockars, Kutnjak Ivković, and Haberfeld	2006	USA (national; 30 agencies)	1st questionnaire	3235 police officers	Measuring police integrity across the U.S.A
Klockars, Kutnjak Ivković, Harver, and Haberfeld	1997	USA (national; 30 agencies)	1st questionnaire	3235 police officers	Measuring police integrity across the U.S.A
Klockars, Kutnjak Ivković, Harver, and Haberfeld	2000	USA (national; 30 agencies)	1st questionnaire	3235 police officers	Measuring police integrity across the U.S.A
Kutnjak Ivković, Haberfeld, and Peacock	2013	USA (4 police agencies)	2nd questionnaire	1500 police agencies	Measuring police integrity across four U.S. police agencies
Kutnjak Ivković, Haberfeld, and Peacock	2015	USA (national, 11 agencies)	2nd questionnaire	664 police officers	Measuring police integrity across the U.S.A
Kutnjak Ivković, Haberfeld, and Peacock	2019d	USA (11 police agencies)	2nd questionnaire	664 police officers	Exploring cultures of police integrity by police officer rank (line officers, supervisors, administrators)
Lee, Lim, Moore, and Kim	2013	USA (national; 30 agencies)	1st questionnaire	3235 police officers	Linking organizational structure with the line officers' attitudes toward police corruption
Lim and Sloan	2016	USA (Texas)	1st questionnaire; 2nd questionnaire	553 police officers	Connecting police officers' willingness to report with their views about misconduct seriousness and rank
Micucci and Gomme	2005	USA (national; 30 agencies)	1st questionnaire	3235 police officers	Comparing support for the use of excessive force by the length of service and supervisory position

Table 5 Classical Police Integrity Multi-Country Studies

Authors	Year	Country/city	Survey	Sample	Topic
Andreescu et al.	2012a, 2012b	Romania (national)/ USA (national)	1st questionnaire	75 police officers 140 police officers	Measuring police integrity in Romania and the United States
Ekenvall	2003	Croatia Sweden USA	1st questionnaire	3235 police officers; 1579 police officers; 1649 police officers	Analyzing potential differences in police integrity across Croatia, Sweden, and the United States
Haberfeld et al.	2000	Croatia (national) Poland (national) Slovenia (national) USA (national)	1st questionnaire	1649 police officers; 767 police officers; 1477 police officers; 3235 police officers	Comparing perceptions of disciplinary environments in Croatia, Poland, Slovenia, and the United States
Huberts, Lamboo, and Punch	2003	The Netherlands/USA	1st questionnaire	795 police officers 3235 police officers	Measuring police integrity in the Netherlands/USA
Johnson	2003	Japan (Tokyo); USA (national)	1st and 2nd questionnaires	182 police officers 3235 police officers	Comparing of Japanese and U.S. views on police integrity
Klockars, Kutnjak Ivković, and Haberfeld	2004a, 2004b	14 countries (Austria, Canada, Croatia, Finland, Hungary, Japan, Netherlands, Pakistan, Poland, Slovenia, South Africa, Sweden, UK, USA)	1st questionnaire	14 samples	Analyzing police integrity in a comparative perspective
Khruakham and Lee	2013	Thailand; USA (national); Sweden (national); Finland (national); the Netherlands (3 police agencies)	1st questionnaire	295 police officers (cadets)	Measuring police integrity in Thailand and comparing with police integrity in the USA, The Netherlands, Sweden, and Finland
Kutnjak Ivković	2005	Croatia (national); Finland (national); USA (national)	1st questionnaire	1649 police officers; 378 police officers; 3235 police officers	Exploring cross-cultural differences in perceptions of misconduct seriousness
Kutnjak Ivković and Haberfeld	2015	10 countries (Armenia, Australia, Croatia, Estonia, Russia, Slovenia, South Africa, South Korea, Thailand, USA)	2nd questionnaire	10 samples	Analyzing police integrity in a comparative perspective

(continued)

Table 5 (continued)

Authors	Year	Country/city	Survey	Sample	Topic
Kutnjak Ivković, Haberfeld, Kang, Peacock, Sauerman	2016a	Croatia (national); South Africa (national); South Korea (national); USA (national)	2nd questionnaire	966 police officers; 871 police officers; 335 police officers; 604 police officers	Comparing perceived disciplinary environments
Kutnjak Ivković and Shelley	2008b	Bosnia and Herzegovina (Sarajevo); Czech Republic (1 region)	1st questionnaire	451 police officers; 600 police officers	Comparing the contours of police integrity in Bosnia and the Czech Republic
Pagon, Kutnjak Ivković, and Lobnikar	2000	Slovenia (national); Croatia (national); USA (national)	1st questionnaire	696 police officers; 215 college students; 1649 police officers; 3235 police officers	Comparing Slovenian, Croatian, and the US views
Vito, Wolfe, Higgins, and Walsh	2011	USA (Southern Police Institute); USA (national)	1st questionnaire	307 police managers	Comparing U.S. middle-manager views with the U.S., Croatian, and Finnish police supervisor views

available for close to two decades and the police integrity questionnaire covers more forms of police misconduct, the police corruption questionnaire, somewhat older and featured in a prominent NIJ publication available online free of charge (Klockars et al. 2000), seems to have been utilized more frequently. In addition, scholars have used both versions of the questionnaire in a few countries (e.g., Armenia, Croatia, Slovenia, South Africa, South Korea, Thailand, USA). Because the two versions of the questionnaire share five common scenarios (see, e.g., Klockars et al. 2006; Kutnjak Ivković 2015a), administrations of both versions of the questionnaire over time provide opportunities for a direct comparison of the results.

In terms of the content of the classic police integrity studies, most of the studies are providing an overall assessment of police integrity in a specific territorial unit, typically by analyzing the results of the measures of three organizational dimensions of police integrity (Tables 4 and 5). A smaller number of studies focused only on one dimension of the theory, such as the first dimension measured through evaluations of

misconduct seriousness (e.g., Kutnjak Ivković 2004a, 2004b), the second dimension measured through perceptions of expected and appropriate discipline (e.g., Haberfeld et al. 2000; Kutnjak Ivković et al. 2016b), or the third dimension measured through the respondents' perceived willingness to report (e.g., Kremer 2000; Kutnjak Ivković et al. 2018; Kutnjak Ivković and Sauerman 2013; Kutnjak Ivković and Shelley 2008a; Pagon and Lobnikar 2000). In addition, several studies also incorporated measures of two dimensions into the analysis (e.g., Kutnjak Ivković and Klockars 1998; Kutnjak Ivković et al. 2016b; Kutnjak Ivković and Sauerman 2012; Kutnjak Ivković and Shelley 2010; Porter and Prenzler 2016; Westmarland 2005).

To minimize the chances of a potential identification of the respondents and thereby enticing police officers to answer the questions honestly, both the police corruption questionnaire and the police integrity questionnaire contain a very limited number of demographic questions (see, e.g., Klockars and Kutnjak Ivković 2004; Klockars et al. 2000, 2006; Kutnjak Ivković 2015a): the respondents' length of service, rank, supervisory position, and assignment. Some of the studies from the classical police integrity studies have explored the relation between the levels of police integrity and these demographic variables (e.g., Kremer 2000; Kutnjak Ivković et al. 2004, Kutnjak Ivković 2012; Kutnjak Ivković and Klockars 2000; Kutnjak Ivković and Shelley 2008a; Kutnjak Ivković et al. 2018, 2019; Lee et al. 2013; Lim and Sloan 2016; Micucci and Gomme 2005; Pagon and Lobnikar 2000; Vito et al. 2011; Westmarland and Rowe 2018).

Police Integrity Research Expanding the Theoretical Arguments

The studies we classify in this category have either expanded the theory of police integrity or have used the police integrity theory and connected it with elements of other theories or theoretical concepts. We classified about 40 studies into this category (Table 6).

While both questionnaires contain measures of the first three dimensions of the police integ-

Table 6 Studies Expanding Theoretical Arguments

Authors	Year	Country/city	Survey	Sample	Topic
Bucak	2012	Turkey	1st questionnaire	617 police officers	Exploring the impact of police cynicism on police integrity
Chappell and Piquero	2004	USA (Philadelphia)	1st questionnaire (5 scenarios)	483 police officers	Applying social learning theory to predict citizen complaints
Charles	2008	USA (1 police agency)	1st questionnaire	152 police officers	Testing the effect of modern racism, self-esteem, and universality-diversity orientation of police officers on police integrity
Donner et al.	2016	USA (several agencies)	1st questionnaire	101 police officers	Examining the relation between social control theory and police integrity among police supervisors
Donner et al.	2018a	USA (several agencies)	1st questionnaire	1072 police officers	Studying the relation between self-control and willingness to report
Donner et al.	2018b	USA (several agencies)	1st questionnaire	1072 police officers	Exploring the relation between effective parenting, self-control, and adherence to the code of silence
Gamarra	2011	USA (5 police agencies)	1st questionnaire	233 police officers	Studying the effect of police training techniques, policing model, and police accountability measures on police integrity
Greene, Piquero, Hickman, and Lawton	2004	USA (Philadelphia)	1st questionnaire (6 scenarios)	499 police officers	Analyzing district-level influence on views of police integrity
Bakri et al.	2017	Malaysia	1st questionnaire	189 police officers	Studying whether police integrity moderates the relation between fraud risk elements and asset misappropriation
Hickman	2005	USA (Philadelphia)	1st questionnaire (6 scenarios)	499 police officers	Exploring district-level influence and cynicism on police integrity

(continued)

Table 6 (continued)

Authors	Year	Country/city	Survey	Sample	Topic
Hickman et al.	2016b	USA (Philadelphia)	1st questionnaire (6 scenarios)	499 police officers	Testing the relation between attitudes toward ethical behavior and willingness to report
Hickman et al.	2016a	USA (Philadelphia)	1st questionnaire (6 scenarios)	499 police officers	Linking police cynicism and district-level predictors with willingness to report.
Kargin	2009	USA (Philadelphia)	1st questionnaire (6 scenarios)	499 police officers	Examining the effect of cynicism and attitudes toward professional conduct at the individual level and peer associations and reinforcement as organizational factors on reporting intentions
Khechumyan and Kutnjak Ivković	2019	Armenia (2 rural and 1 urban police agency)	2nd questionnaire	959 police officers	Studying differences in police integrity between urban and rural police agencies
Kutnjak Ivković	2015a	None	1st questionnaire 2nd questionnaire	None	Expanding the theory of police integrity
Kutnjak Ivković, Haberfeld, and Peacock	2018	USA (national, 11 agencies)	2nd questionnaire	664 police officers	Connecting willingness to report with justice theories
Kutnjak Ivković and Khechumyan	2014	Armenia (2 cities)	1st questionnaire	468 police officers	Comparing police integrity in rural and urban settings in Armenia
Kutnjak Ivković and Klockars	1998	Croatia (national)	1st questionnaire	1649 police officers	Exploring the influence of justice theory and deterrence theory on the code of silence
Kutnjak Ivković and Klockars	2002	Croatia	1st questionnaire	504 college students; 379 police high school students; 223 police college students	Exploring potential differences in the perceptions of police integrity among college students, police high school students, and police college students
Kutnjak Ivković, Haberfeld, and Peacock	2016	USA (11 police agencies)	2nd questionnaire	604 police officers	Connecting justice theories and the code of silence
Kutnjak Ivković and Shelley	2010	Czech Republic (1 region)	1st questionnaire	600 police officers	Exploring the relation between the code of silence and disciplinary fairness; comparing supervisor and line officer views about the code
Kutnjak Ivković and Sauerman	2016	South Africa (national)	2nd questionnaire	871 police officers	Comparing police integrity across three police agency types
Kutnjak Ivković et al.	2016b	Croatia (national)	2nd questionnaire	1315 police officers	Linking police integrity and community policing

(continued)

Table 6 (continued)

Authors	Year	Country/city	Survey	Sample	Topic
Kutnjak Ivković et al.	2016c	Croatia (national)	2nd questionnaire	945 police officers	Testing the influence of the society at large on police integrity in a centralized police system
Kutnjak Ivković et al.	2019c	Croatia (capital)	2nd questionnaire (revised)	495 police officers	Connecting police integrity and organizational justice
Long, Cross, Shelley, and Kutnjak Ivković	2013	USA (national; 30 agencies)	1st questionnaire	3235 police officers	Exploring the relation between normative order, legitimacy, fairness, and willingness to report
Marche	2009	USA (national; 30 agencies)	1st questionnaire	3235 police officers	Analyzing the data by supervisory status, length of service, and agency size
Pagon, Kutnjak Ivković, and Lobnikar	2000	Slovenia (national); Croatia (national); USA (national)	1st questionnaire	696 police officers; 215 college students; 1649 police officers; 3235 police officers	Comparing police and public views of police corruption; comparing Slovenian, Croatian, and the US views
Pogarsky and Piquero	2004	USA (mid-sized southwestern police department)	1st questionnaire (1 modified scenario)	210 police officers	Exploring the influence of deterrence considerations on the intention to commit misconduct
Porter and Alpert	2017	Australia	2nd questionnaire	577 police officers	Studying the link between hostility, experience with violence, cynicism, and attitudes supportive on crime fighting on willingness to report
Raines	2010	USA (national; 30 agencies)	1st questionnaire	3235 police officers	Analyzing whether police officer tendency to report is influenced by individual, peer, or agency characteristics
Sauerman et al.	2019	South Africa (national)	2nd questionnaire	871 police officers	Exploring the relation between police integrity and community policing
Schafer and Martinelli	2008	USA (one police agency)	1st questionnaire	478 police officers	Studying the link between perceptions of ethics training, disciplinary system, reform initiatives with police integrity
Smith	2009	USA (Kentucky)	1st questionnaire	50 police officers	Linking attitudes on police integrity with emotional intelligence
Tasdoven and Kaya	2014	Turkey	1st questionnaire	335 police officers	Testing the influence of ethical leadership on willingness to report
Vallmüür	2019	Estonia	1st questionnaire (revised)	149 police officers	Developing and testing the theory of green police integrity

(continued)

Table 6 (continued)

Authors	Year	Country/city	Survey	Sample	Topic
Wagner and Hout	2019	Uganda (10 districts)	1st questionnaire	600 police officers	Exploring the link between perceptions of institutional environment and police effectiveness on police integrity
Wolfe and Piquero	2011	USA (Philadelphia)	1st questionnaire	483 police officers	Examining the role of organizational justice in predicting police misconduct
Zschoche	2011	USA (national, 8 police agencies)	1st questionnaire	1083 police officers	Measuring the effect of anomie, decoupling, and moral disengagement on police susceptibility to police corruption

rity theory, which are organizational in nature and apply to the specific police agency where the respondents are surveyed, the questionnaire does not include any measures of the fourth dimension of the theory, which is societal in nature. In the original writings about the influence of the social, economic, and political environment on the extent of police integrity, Klockars and colleagues (2000, 2004a, 2004b, 2006; Klockars and Kutnjak Ivković 2004) proposed that the characteristics of the larger environment influence the level of police integrity in a police agency. The authors continue by giving examples of a range of jurisdictions in the United States with different histories of public misconduct and conclude that, "public expectations about police integrity exert vastly different pressures on police agencies in different jurisdictions" (Klockars and Kutnjak Ivković 2004, p. 1.5).

Kutnjak Ivković (2015, p. 10) expanded the argument by proposing that, "[s]ocieties shape the level of misconduct of their public servants by establishing and nurturing a culture intolerant of misconduct, promulgating governing rules for ethical behavior of its employees, and by teaching and enforcing these rules (or, conversely, failing do to so)." Kutnjak Ivković (2015) brought the argument into a comparative arena, where she connected the country's ranking on the Transparency International Corruption Perceptions Index that measures the level of tolerance of public corruption society-wide with the country's results on the police integrity survey. In

their comparative paper, Kutnjak Ivković and Haberfeld (2015, p. 365) explore the results of classical police integrity studies from 10 countries and provide further evidence that, "[l]egal, social, political, and historical conditions shape police agencies and the behavior of the police officers they employ."

We found a few studies that sought to assess the fourth dimension (Table 6). Hickman and colleagues (2016a, 2016b) studied the relation between the respondents' willingness to report and district-level measures (e.g., violent crime rate, socio-economic status, residential stability, and population heterogeneity) and individual-level measures. Kutnjak Ivković et al. (2016a) assessed the influence of the society at large (e.g., type of police administration, community perceptions of safety, and community perceptions of police powers) on the police officers' integrity levels in a Croatian centralized police system. In a study of Armenian police, Khechumyan and Kutnjak Ivković (2019) compared the views about police integrity across rural and urban environments. Although the authors did not include measures of community characteristics into the model, Khechumyan and Kutnjak Ivković (2019) were able to compare the results across two types of communities and concluded that urban police agencies tended to have stronger codes of silence than suburban/rural police agencies did.

The original works by Klockars et al. (2000, 2004a, 2004b, 2006) developed the core theoretical arguments. Kutnjak Ivković et al. (2015)

expanded the description of each of the four dimensions. In the discussion of the first dimension of the theory, Kutnjak Ivković et al. (2015) specified the nature of the legal rules that regulate police misconduct and explained how their application may be different depending on the level of centralization of the police system (i.e., centralized vs. decentralized police systems). While discussing the second dimension of the theory, Kutnjak Ivković et al. (2015) elaborated on the various mechanisms of misconduct control and their effectiveness, as well as illustrated their diversity on several comparative examples. While discussing the third dimension of the theory, Kutnjak Ivković et al. (2015) linked the extent of the code of silence with the overall level of police integrity. Finally, while discussing the fourth dimension of the theory, Kutnjak Ivković et al. (2015) expanded theoretical arguments by elaborating on the relation between the levels of police integrity in the police agency and the levels of public integrity in the society at large. The arguments from Kutnjak Ivković et al. (2015) rest upon the results of comparative police integrity studies.

Vallmüür's study (2019) is one of the very few studies we found that has expanded the theory of police integrity across all four dimensions by applying it to a new area: green police integrity. It is based on the idea of green criminology and green or environmental crime (e.g., acts and omissions that potentially harm the environment, humans, and other species even if these are not recognized by criminal, civil, or administrative law). As Vallmüür (2019) argues, green theory of police integrity mirrors the theory of police integrity, but it also takes a more critical perspective because it involves forms of police misconduct that harm the environment and are not necessarily seen as such in national legislation. The theory of green police integrity also focuses on specialized techniques for controlling environmental police misconduct. Vallmüür (2019) argues that, because such forms of police misconduct are difficult to regulate, preventive measures may be more effective than reactive measures. The theory further proposes that the code of silence could be particularly strong in the cases of green police misconduct. Finally, the

expanded theory also recognizes the importance of the larger environment, particularly the views about environmental crimes, for the extent of green police integrity.

The original work by Klockars et al. (2000, 2004a, 2004b, 2006) tested the organizational effect on the level of police integrity and reported a substantial extent of variation of agency-level police integrity across the 30 police agencies in the U.S. sample. Marche (2009, p. 463) subsequently used the same dataset to develop "an economic model of police corruption" and concluded that, in five out of eleven scenarios, the size of the police agency was related with the respondents' evaluations of misconduct seriousness. Raines (2010, p. 207) reanalyzed the same dataset and concluded that, "the size of agency does not appear to impact greatly officer attitudes and behavior regarding misconduct." Similarly, Sauerman et al. (2019) report that the type of police agency (e.g., nationalized police, metropolitan, traffic) in South Africa is not related to several measures of police integrity, with the exception of expected discipline.

Close to one-half of the studies in this category expanded the theoretical framework by testing the effect of one or more theoretical concepts on police integrity (Table 6). A number of these theoretical concepts originated in the policing literature, such as police cynicism (e.g., Bucak 2012; Hickman et al. 2016a, 2016b; Kargin 2009; Porter and Alpert 2017), community policing (e.g., Kutnjak Ivković et al. 2016a; Sauerman et al. 2019), police effectiveness (e.g., Wagner and Hout 2019), police training (e.g., Gamarra 2011; Schafer and Martinelli 2008; Van Droogenbroeck et al. 2019), and ethics/ethical police leadership (e.g., Hickman et al. 2016a, 2016b; Kargin 2009; Schafer and Martinelli 2008; Tasdoven and Kaya 2014). Other concepts originate from psychological studies, sociological studies, or economic studies (e.g., Charles 2008; Hanim et al. 2017).

Finally, more than one-third of the studies in this group tried to connect the police integrity theory with other existing theories (Table 6). Justice theories were the most popular (e.g., Kutnjak Ivković and Klockars 1998; Kutnjak Ivković and Shelley 2010; Kutnjak Ivković et al.

2016, 2018, 2019; Long et al. 2013; Wolfe and Piquero 2011), followed by social control theory (e.g., Donner et al. 2016, 2018a, 2018b), social learning theory (e.g., Chappell and Piquero 2004), deterrence theory (e.g., Kutnjak Ivković and Klockars 1998), and anomie theory (e.g., Zschoche 2011). All these studies not only introduce elements of other theories, but also include variables that measure these concepts. Their major contribution is in the area of theoretical development because they typically use already existing measures of these theoretical concepts. Most of these studies (e.g., Donner et al. 2016, 2018a, 2018b; Long et al. 2013) utilize these additional theories to explain police officers' (un) willingness to report.

Police Integrity Research Expanding the Methodology

Although some of the studies that have expanded theoretical arguments also introduced methodological expansions (e.g., measures of organizational justice, measures of social control, measures of green police integrity), this category of studies incorporates studies that have primarily focused on expanding the police integrity methodology. We classified 42 studies into this category (Table 7).

Because both the police corruption questionnaire and the police integrity questionnaire (see, e.g., Klockars and Kutnjak Ivković 2004; Klockars et al. 2000, 2006; Kutnjak Ivković et al. 2015) purposely feature only a very limited number of demographic characteristics (e.g., length of service, rank, supervisory position, assignment), scholars engaging in police integrity research have included additional demographic characteristics into their modified versions of the police corruption questionnaire or the police integrity questionnaire. Slightly more than one-quarter of the studies in this category (11 out of 42 studies or 26.2%; Table 7) added demographic characteristics such as gender, education (e.g., Datzer et al. 2019; Kucukuysal 2008), age (e.g., Kucukuysal 2008), and race (e.g., Charles 2008). Gender is by far the most frequently added demographic char-

acteristic, with 10 out of 11 studies either merely including the respondents' gender in the questionnaire or focusing the paper exclusively on gender differences (e.g., Andreescu et al. 2012a, 2012b; Bjerregaard and Lord 2004; Charles 2008; Kucukuysal 2008; Lobnikar et al. 2016; McDevitt et al. 2011; Pagon et al. 2004; Porter and Prenzler 2019; Vallmüür 2016; Wagner et al. 2017).

The second type of methodological extensions included modifying the existing scenarios or designing completely new scenarios. About one-third (15 out of 42 studies or 35.7%; Table 7) of the studies in the category of methodological extensions introduced some type of modification to the scenarios. In some cases, these modifications were carried out because the focus of the study was not on police integrity in general, but on a specific type of misconduct (e.g., use of excessive force: Dayioglu 2007; court cases: Gottschalk 2009a, 2009b; motor-vehicle accidents: Servino 2013; counterproductive behavior: Yunus et al. 2013; fraud: Hanim et al. 2017), theoretical arguments (e.g., organizational justice: Kutnjak Ivković et al. 2019; Vallmüür 2019), or local conditions (e.g., Wagner et al. 2017).

The third type of methodological extensions focused on expanding the choice of types of respondents. These studies account for about one-half studies in this category (21 out of 42 or 50.0%; Table 7).[1] While Klockars et al. (2000) originally designed the questionnaires to measure the level of *police* integrity, relied on the *organizational* theory of police integrity, and included *police officers* as respondents, very soon they expanded the study to include college students and modified the questionnaire to fit the new category of respondents (e.g., Klockars and Kutnjak Ivković 1999; Klockars et al. 2002).

---

[1]The percentages in this category exceed 100% because some of the studies included information that would result in a classification into more than one category (e.g., a modified questionnaire and new demographic characteristic). There are 42 unique studies, but we counted such studies as both studies on demographic characteristics and studies on new scenarios. There are 11 studies on demographic characteristic, 21 studies on public opinions, and 15 studies on new scenarios, yielding a count of 47 studies.

Table 7 Studies Expanding Methodology

Authors	Year	Country/city	Survey	Sample	Topic
Andreescu, Kelling, Voinic, and Tonea	2012b	Romania (Romanian Police Academy)	1st questionnaire (10 scenarios)	293 police officers	Comparing male and female police officers' attitudes about police integrity
Bjerregaard and Lord	2004	USA (Southeastern public university)	1st questionnaire (10 scenarios)	443 students	Comparing criminal-justice majors' and other majors' views about police misconduct; gender comparisons
Cetinkaya	2010	Turkey (national)	1st questionnaire (2 scenarios +1 added)	596 police cadets	Exploring the relation between seriousness and willingness to report and socio-economic and cultural characteristics of Turkish cadets
Charles	2008	USA (1 metropolitan police agency)	1st questionnaire (6 scenarios added)	142 police officers	Exploring police integrity and police officer race and gender
Datzer et al.	2019	Bosnia and Herzegovina (national)	2nd questionnaire	1006 police officers	Studying the relation between education and willingness to report
Dayioglu	2007	Turkey (3 cities)	1st questionnaire (modified + new scenarios)	633 police officers	Focusing on attitudes toward the use of force among the Turkish police officers
Desta	2013	Eritrea (national)	1st questionnaire (9 scenarios +1 added)	107 top police administrators	Measuring police integrity in Eritrea
Gottschalk	2009a, 2009b	Norway	1st questionnaire	21 police managers	Comparing scenarios with actual court cases in Norway
Hanim et al.	2017	Malaysia	1st questionnaire (modifications)	189 police officers	Studying whether police integrity moderates the relation between fraud risk elements and asset misappropriation
Jenks, Johnson, and Matthews	2014	USA (national; 30 agencies)	1st questionnaire	3235 police officers	Creating police integrity indices
Kucukuysal	2008	Turkey (3 cities)	1st questionnaire (9 scenarios)	507 police officers	Examining the relation between police integrity and police organizational culture and individual police officer characteristics (gender, age, education)
Kuo	2018	Taiwan	1st questionnaire (modified, new scenarios)	297 police officers; 268 gaming workers	Comparing police officer and gaming worker perceptions of police integrity

(continued)

Table 7 (continued)

Authors	Year	Country/city	Survey	Sample	Topic
Klockars and Kutnjak Ivković	1999	Croatia, USA	1st questionnaire	1649 police officers; 504 college students; 3235 police officers; 375 college students	Exploring similarities and differences in the assessments of misconduct seriousness between police officer and colleges student views across the two countries
Klockars et al.	2002	USA	1st questionnaire	3235 police officers; 375 college students	Contrasting the environments of integrity between police officers and college students
Kutnjak Ivković	2004a	Croatia (national; university); USA (national; university)	1st questionnaire	1649 police officers; 504 students; 3235 police officers; 375 students	Studying views of police misconduct seriousness and comparing them between police offices and citizens across two countries
Kutnjak Ivković and Klockars	2002	Croatia	1st questionnaire	504 college students; 379 police high school students; 223 police college students	Comparing views about police integrity across different categories of citizens
Kutnjak Ivković et al.	2002a, 2002b	Croatia Slovenia	1st questionnaire	1649 police officers; 504 college students; 696 police officers; 215 college students	Comparing police and citizen evaluations of police misconduct seriousness across two countries
Kutnjak Ivković et al.	2002a, 2002b	Croatia	1st questionnaire; 2nd questionnaire	854 college students	Exploring public views about police integrity and their estimates about police views of police integrity
Kutnjak Ivković et al.	2004	Croatia	1st questionnaire	1649 police officers; 534 college students; 511 college students; 379 police high school students; 223 police college students	Comparing evaluations of police misconduct seriousness among police officers, college students, police high school students, and police college students
Kutnjak Ivković et al.	2019c	Croatia (capital)	2nd questionnaire (new scenarios)	495 police officers	Connecting police integrity and organizational justice
Kutnjak Ivković et al.	2019b	Croatia (capital)	1st questionnaire; 2nd questionnaire	504 students; 382 students	Comparing citizen views of the police and police integrity over time

(continued)

Table 7 (continued)

Authors	Year	Country/city	Survey	Sample	Topic
Kutnjak Ivković et al.	2019a	Croatia Serbia	2nd questionnaire	381 students; 404 students	Comparing citizen views about police integrity in Croatia and Serbia
Lim	2019	USA	1st questionnaire	police officers; students	Comparing police officers and citizen views about police misconduct
Lobnikar et al.	2016	Slovenia (national)	2nd questionnaire	408 police officers	Studying the effect of gender on willingness to report misconduct
Lobnikar et al.	2019	Slovenia	2nd questionnaire	550 police officers 338 citizens	Comparing police officer and citizen views on police integrity
McDevitt et al.	2011	USA (7 police agencies)	1st questionnaire (3 scenarios)	unknown	Focusing on differences by the size of community served; gender differences
Meyer, Steyn, and Gopal	2013	South Africa (Gauteng)	1st questionnaire (modified for students)	160 police officers; 186 students	Comparing police officer and student views about police integrity
Pagon, Kutnjak Ivković, and Lobnikar	2000	Slovenia	1st questionnaire (modified for students)	767 police officer; 254 college students	Contrasting police officer and college student views on police integrity
Pagon, Lobnikar, and Anzelj	2004	Slovenia	2nd questionnaire	95 police officers and 247 students	Comparing gender differences between police officers and students
Pogarsky and Piquero	2004	USA (mid-sized southwestern police department)	1st questionnaire (1 modified scenario)	210 police officers	Exploring the influence of deterrence considerations on the intention to commit misconduct
Porter and Prenzler	2019	Australia (national)	2nd questionnaire	856 police officers	Exploring gender differences in perceptions of police integrity in Australia
Rothwell and Baldwin	2006	USA (Georgia)	1st questionnaire (modified for civilian employees)	198 police officers; 184 civilian employees	Focusing on reporting differences between police officers and civilian employees
Rothwell and Baldwin	2007a	USA (Georgia)	1st questionnaire (modified for civilian employees)	198 police officers; 184 civilian employees	Comparing police officers' and civilian employees' willingness to report
Rothwell and Baldwin	2007b	USA (Georgia)	1st questionnaire	198 police officers	Examining differences in willingness to report between citizen employees and police officers
Servino	2013	USA (153 police agencies)	1st questionnaire (new scenarios)	153 police chiefs/ administrators	Focusing on police officer injuries in motor-vehicle incidents
Vallmüür	2016	Estonia (national)	2nd questionnaire	109 police officers	Exploring gender-neutrality in police integrity

(continued)

Table 7 (continued)

Authors	Year	Country/city	Survey	Sample	Topic
Vallmüür	2019	Estonia	1st questionnaire (new scenarios)	149 police officers	Developing new scenarios for green police integrity
Wagner et al.	2017	Uganda	1st questionnaire (modified + new scenarios)	600 police officers	Studying the relation gender and police integrity
White	2008	USA (Florida Gulf Coast University; national; 30 agencies)	1st questionnaire (4 scenarios with gratuities)	265 students	Comparing police officer and student attitudes about police integrity with the emphasis on gratuities
Wright	2010	UK (northern)	1 questionnaire (some + some new added)	723 police officers and police staff	Comparing police officer and staff views about police integrity
Yun	2003	South Korea (Chungnam Province)	1 questionnaire (4 scenarios +4 added)	321 police officers	Studying the influence of the length of service, supervisory position, and type of community on views of police integrity
Yunus, Bustaman, Khalid	2013	Malaysia (local)	1st questionnaire (new scenarios)	100 local government employees	Measuring integrity of local governmental employees in Malaysia

This provided Klockars and Kutnjak Ivković (1999); Klockars and colleagues (2002) with an opportunity to explore similarities and differences in the assessments of police integrity between police officers and colleges students, even in a comparative perspective (Klockars and Kutnjak Ivković 1999). Studies in this category primarily focused on comparing police officer and citizen views (16 out of 21 studies or 76.2%), with the remaining studies explored the differences across college majors (e.g., Bjerregaard and Lord 2004) or countries (e.g., Kutnjak Ivković et al. 2019).

Police Integrity Research Assessing Reliability and Validity

Finally, the remaining studies have tested the validity and/or reliability of the police integrity methodology. We classified 11 studies into this category. About one-half explore the reliability, and the rest explore the validity of the approach.

A subset of the studies explored reliability of the police integrity approach. (i.e., consistency or repeatability of results using the same instrument; Table 8). In case of police integrity, there are two instruments—the police corruption questionnaire and the police integrity questionnaire—designed on the same principles. Comparative studies not included in this category (e.g., Klockars et al. 2004a, 2004b; Kutnjak Ivković and Haberfeld 2015) provide evidence of reliability. In particular, although absolute evaluations of seriousness vary across countries, relative evaluations of seriousness (i.e., how scenarios tend to be evaluated compared to other scenarios in the questionnaire) tend to be quite similar across the countries (e.g., Kutnjak Ivković et al. 2015). Stealing from a crime scene, accepting a bribe from a motorist stopped for speeding, and abusing deadly force are the forms of police misconduct typically evaluated as the most serious in the questionnaire, most likely to be evaluated as rule-violating behaviors, typically associated with the harshest discipline, and least likely to be protected by the code of silence. On the other hand, accepting gratuities, verbal abuse, and internal corruption were typically evaluated as the least serious forms of misconduct, least likely to be

Table 8 Studies Assessing Reliability and Validity

Authors	Year	Country/city	Survey	Sample	Topic
Alain et al.	2018	One country in North America; one country in Continental Europe	1st questionnaire	455 police officers; 1520 police officers	Exploring the Psychometric Qualities of the police integrity methodology
Davis et al.	2015	USA (9 police agencies)	1st questionnaire	police officers	Reliability of the police integrity methodology
Hickman et al.	2016a	USA (Philadelphia)	1st questionnaire (6 scenarios)	499 police officers	Providing reliability assessments of the initial study by Klockars and colleagues
Jenks, Johnson, and Matthews	2014	USA (national; 30 agencies)	1st questionnaire	3235 police officers	Creating police integrity indices
Klockars, Kutnjak Ivković, and Haberfeld	2006	USA (national; 30 agencies; Charleston; Charlotte-Mecklenburg; St. Petersburg)	1st questionnaire; 2nd questionnaire	3235 police officers; 1544 police officers	Assessing the changes in police officer views on police integrity in three police agencies
Kutnjak Ivković	2009	Croatia	2nd questionnaire	927 police officers	Comparing police officer perceptions over time
Kutnjak Ivković et al.	2019	Croatia	1st questionnaire; 2nd questionnaire	504 college students; 382 college students	Comparing citizen perceptions over time
Maskalay et al.	2019b	Many countries	1st questionnaire; 2nd questionnaire	Many respondents	Assessing the validity of the police integrity scale in a comparative context
Maskalay et al.	2019a	USA (national)	1st questionnaire	3232 police officers	Improving the measurement of police integrity
Van Droogenbroeck et al.	2019	Belgium	2nd questionnaire (new scenario)	207 police officers	Measuring the effects of police training over time
Wagner and Hout	2019	Uganda	1st questionnaire	600 police officers	Testing the external validity of the scenarios

evaluated as rule-violating behavior, typically associated with the most lenient discipline, and most likely to be protected by the code of silence. In addition, empirical studies consistently demonstrate that the measures of police integrity (e.g., seriousness, discipline, willingness to report) are closely related.

Another approach used in the studies is to re-test the same population after a certain period of time has passed (i.e., test-retest reliability). In the first such study, Klockars et al. (2006) compared the results of the application of the police corruption questionnaire in three U.S. police agencies with the results of the application of the police integrity questionnaire in the same police agencies within two years. While there was either no change or only some minimal change in the police officers' opinions in Charleston and

Charlotte-Mecklenburg, thus suggesting a substantial degree of reliability, there was a visible change in the police officers' views in St. Petersburg, but in only one scenario (Klockars et al. 2006, p. 142). This change in the police officers' views about the acceptance of gratuities was a consequence of the new policy and its application in the police agency. In other words, the results showed a high degree of reliability of the police integrity methodology.

A few other studies compared either police officer (e.g., Kutnjak Ivković 2009) or citizen views (e.g., Kutnjak Ivković et al. 2019) over time and provided further evidence of reliability. In some studies, the opinions changed relatively little over time, while in others (e.g., Klockars et al. 2006), as a result of outside influences (e.g., ethics training in human rights: Van Droogenbroeck et al. 2019; Kutnjak Ivković 2009; change in policy and its implementation: Klockars et al. 2006), the views have changed over time in accordance with the change in these external factors.

A handful of studies also explored the validity—the degree of overlap between what is supposed to be measured and what is actually being measured—of the police integrity approach (Table 8). Maskály and colleagues (2019a; b) investigate the criterion validity that explores "the relationship between test scores and some known external criterion variable that adequately indicates the quantity being measured" (Huizinga and Elliott 1986, p. 308). To that end, Maskály et al. (et al. 2019a, 2019b) compare the results of the prior police integrity studies from different countries with the external country-level measures of integrity and corruption (e.g., Transparency International Corruption Perceptions Index, the International Crime Victimization Survey, the World Value Survey, and the World Governance Indicators). Maskály and colleagues (et al. 2019a, 2019b) conclude that there is relatively robust evidence of criterion validity of the measures, although the strength of this relationship varies across criteria.

Some of the studies focused on the psychometric properties of the police integrity methodology (e.g., Alain et al. 2018; Jenks et al. 2014;

Maskály et al. 2019a, 2019b; Wolfe and Piquero 2011), particularly the unidimensionality of the constructs. Jenks and colleagues (2014) concluded that, based on the original U.S. sample of 30 police agencies, the scenarios in the police corruption questionnaire did not coalesce into a single latent factor of police corruption, but into two factors. In the Philadelphia study, Wolfe and Piquero (2011) run the principal component analysis to conclude that scenarios loaded into two categories as well, namely less serious and more serious forms of corruption. On an example of the data coming from a North-American country and a European country, Alain et al. (2018, p. 1) use the item-response theory and found the police corruption questionnaire and methodology to be "very robust." Alain and colleagues elaborate (2018, p. 11): "while it is likely that police culture in regions B and A differ significantly (if only, for instance, because one is in North America and the other in Continental Europe), the survey tool and the type of response analysis proposed here seem to be capable of comparing the respondents' levels of integrity regardless of national professional police cultures." Finally, Maskály and colleagues (2019b) use latent trait models to reassess the validity of the measures from the original U.S. sample. In the end, they conclude (Maskály et al. 2019b): "Our analyses confirm that the Klockars et al. (1997) methodology is a valid way to measure police integrity; however, we find there are several dimensions of police integrity that, while related, are distinct from one another."

Conclusion

A quarter of a century has passed since the first groundwork has been outlined and the theory of police integrity and the related methodology developed (Klockars and Kutnjak Ivković 2004). Since the mid-1990s, more than 170 studies have relied on this theory and methodology. Classical police integrity studies have explored the contours of police integrity in more than 30 countries. In addition, scholars have proposed theoretical and methodological extensions of the original work. Finally, a handful of studies have tested the validity and the reliability of the methodology; their results provided a consistent and favorable evaluation of the methodology.

Despite the breadth and depth of the extant research on police integrity, as evinced by the analyses in this chapter, a number of open research questions remain. The theory of police integrity, as proposed by Klockars and Kutnjak Ivković (2004) and extended by Kutnjak Ivković et al. (2015), is relatively sparse with the explanations of how dimensions of the theory are internally connected and, furthermore, how measures of each dimension are related, and whether all dimensions are equally important for police integrity. A few studies (e.g., Maskály et al. 2019b) testing the psychometric properties of the methodology report that some of the measures, such as perceptions of seriousness, are not as closely related to one another as other measures are.

While the influence of the society at large on the level of police integrity in a police agency is listed as a separate dimension of the police integrity theory, the existing police integrity work (e.g., Klockars and Kutnjak Ivković 2004; Klockars et al. 2000, 2004a, 2004b, 2006) provided neither detailed explanations about the role of this fourth dimension nor any measures for it. Although some comparative studies (e.g., Kutnjak Ivković and Haberfeld 2015) seemed to have preliminary evidence supportive of the relevance and importance of the fourth dimension, other studies found very limited evidence once organizational dimensions are entered into the model (e.g., Kutnjak Ivković et al. 2016a). In future research, scholars should expand the theoretical discussion about the fourth dimension and its connection to the other dimensions, seeking to explore how the importance of the societal dimension compares with the importance of the organizational dimensions of the theory, as well as to identify the key societal characteristics that adequately capture the influence of the society at large on police integrity.

With further refinement of the police integrity theory and the introduction of the measures of the fourth dimension, future research likely needs to incorporate multivariate models to account for the individual-, agency-, and societal-level variables. Although a few existing studies have already started to incorporate individual, agency/unit, and/or societal variables into their analyses (e.g., McDevitt et al. 2011; Kutnjak Ivković et al. 2016a), not necessarily at different levels, this process has just begun.

In the end, although the police integrity theory and the related methodology are already over twenty years old, the field is ripe for further studies of police integrity, be they classical police integrity studies, studies extending the theory and/or methodology of police integrity, or studies testing its reliability and validity. As a tool proven to be resilient, reliable, and relatively inexpensive to administer, police integrity methodology should be of wide interest to scholars and practitioners alike. When police scholars and practitioners think about "measuring what matters," police integrity should be high on their list.

References

Alain, M. (2004). An exploratory study of Quebec's Police Officers' attitudes toward ethical dilemmas. In C. B. Klockars, S. Kutnjak Ivković, & M. R. Haberfeld (Eds.), *The contours of police integrity* (pp. 40–56). Thousand Oaks, CA: Sage.

Alain, M., Rousseau, M., & Carrer, F. (2018). Measuring police integrity: Futile exercise or worthwhile effort in personnel management? Revisiting survey data from two previous studies in order to assess the psychometric qualities of the Klockars questionnaire. *Journal of Police and Criminal Psychology*, Forthcoming.

Andreescu, V., Keeling, D., Vito, G. T., & Voinic, M. C. (2012a). Romanian and American Police Officers' perceptions of professional integrity and ethical behavior. *Revista Romậna de Sociologie, 23*(3–4), 185–207.

Andreescu, V., Keeling, D. G., Voinic, M. C., & Tonea, B. N. (2012b). Future Romanian law enforcement: Gender differences in perceptions of police misconduct. *Journal of Social Research and Policy, 3*(1), July 2012. Retrieved from http://www.academia.edu/3114941/Future_Romanian_Law_Enforcement_Gender_Differences_in_Perceptions_of_Police_Misconduct.

Bakri, H. H. M., Mohamed, N., & Said, J. (2017). Mitigating asset misappropriation through integrity and fraud risk elements. *Journal of Financial Crime, 24*(2), 242–255.

Bjerregaard, B., & Lord, V. B. (2004). An examination of the ethical and value orientation of criminal justice students. *Police Quarterly, 7*(2), 262–284.

Bucak, S. (2012). *An examination of police cynicism in Turkey and its impacts on officers' perception of corruption.* (Order No. 3558466, University of Illinois at Chicago). *ProQuest Dissertations and Theses,* 214. Retrieved from http://ezproxy.msu.edu/login?url=http://search.proquest.com/docview/1343688917?accountid=12598. (1343688917).

Cetinkaya, N. (2010). *Perceptions of police corruption among Turkish police cadets.* ProQuest Dissertations and Theses, 123-n/a. Retrieved from http://ezproxy.msu.edu/login?url=http://search.proquest.com/docview/744399134?accountid=12598. (744399134).

Chappell, A. T., & Piquero, A. R. (2004). Applying social learning theory to police misconduct. *Deviant Behavior, 25,* 89–108.

Charles, S. (2008). Professional integrity, modern racism, self-esteem, and universality-diversity orientation of police officers in a large urban police agency. *DigitalResearch@Fordham.*

Chattha, Z. N., & Kutnjak Ivković, S. (2004). Police misconduct: The Pakistani paradigm. In C. B. Klockars, S. Kutnjak Ivković, & M. R. Haberfeld (Eds.), *The contours of police integrity* (pp. 175–194). Thousand Oaks, CA: Sage Publications.

Cheloukhine, S., Kutnjak Ivković, S., Haq, Q., & Haberfeld, M. R. (2015). Police integrity in Russia. In S. Kutnjak Ivković & M. Haberfeld (Eds.), *Police integrity across the world.* New York: Springer.

Datzer, D., Kutnjak Ivković, S., Mujanovic, E., & Morgan, S. (2019). A complex relation between the code of silence and education. In S. Kutnjak Ivković & M. Haberfeld (Eds.), *Exploring police integrity.* New York: Springer.

Davis, R. C., Ortiz, C. W., Euler, S., & Kuykendall, L. (2015). Revisiting "Measuring What Matters:" Developing a suite of standardized performance measures for policing. *Police Quarterly, 18*(4), 469–495.

Dayioglu, M. (2007). *Police officers' attitudes toward use of force in the Turkish national police.* ProQuest Dissertations and Theses, 193 p. Retrieved from http://ezproxy.msu.edu/login?url=http://search.proquest.com/docview/304891501?accountid=12598. (304891501).

Desta, Y. (2013). Applying a US police integrity measurement tool to the Eritrean context: Perceptions of top-level Eritrean police officers regarding police misconduct. *Journal of Organizational Transformation & Social Change, 10*(3), 238–261.

Donner, C., Maskaly, J., & Fridell, L. (2016). Social bonds and police misconduct: An examination of social control theory and its relationship to workplace deviance among police supervisors. *Policing: An International Journal of Police Strategies & Management, 39*(2), 416–431.

Donner, C. M., Maskaly, J., & Thompson, K. N. (2018a). Self-control and the police code of silence: Examining the unwillingness to report fellow officers' misbehavior among a multi-agency sample of police recruits. *Journal of Criminal Justice, 56,* 11–19.

Donner, C.M., Maskaly, J., Nicole Popovich, N., & K. N. Thompson (2018b). Exploring the relationship between effective parenting, self-control, and adherence to the police code of silence. *Deviant Behavior,* forthcoming.

Edelbacher, M., & Kutnjak Ivković, S. (2004). Ethics and the police: Studying police integrity in Austria. In C. B. Klockars, S. Kutnjak Ivković, & M. R. Haberfeld (Eds.), *The contours of police integrity* (pp. 19–39). Thousand Oaks, CA: Sage.

Ekenvall, B. (2003). Police attitudes toward fellow officers' misconduct: The Swedish case and a comparison with the USA and Croatia. *Journal of Scandinavian Studies in Criminology and Crime Prevention, 3*(2), 210–232.

Gamarra, A. O. (2011). *Call of duty: A question of police integrity.* ProQuest Dissertations and Theses, 261. Retrieved from http://ezproxy.msu.edu/login?url=http://search.proquest.com/docview/907104941?accountid=12598. (907104941).

Gottschalk, P. (2009a). Crime-based survey instrument for police integrity measurement. *Policing: An International Journal of Police Strategies & Management, 33*(1), 52–68.

Gottschalk, P. (2009b). *Knowledge management in police oversight: Law enforcement integrity and accountability.* Irvine, CA: Universal-Publishers..

Gottschalk, P. (2010). Police integrity surveys: A court-based survey approach. *International Journal of Management and Enterprise Development, 8*(3), 243–259.

Greene, J. R., Piquero, A. R., Hickman, M. J., & Lawton, B. A. (2004). *Police integrity and accountability in philadelphia: Predicting and assessing police misconduct.* National Institute of Justice. Retrieved from http://www.ncjrs.gov/pdffiles1/nij/grants/207823.pdf.

Haberfeld, M. R. (2004). The heritage of police misconduct: The case of the Polish police. In C. B. Klockars, S. Kutnjak Ivković, & M. R. Haberfeld (Eds.), *The contours of police integrity* (pp. 95–210). Thousand Oaks, CA: Sage.

Haberfeld, M. R., Klockars, C. B., Kutnjak Ivković, S., & Pagon, M. (2000). Police officer perceptions of the disciplinary consequences of police corruption in Croatia, Poland, Slovenia, and the United States. *Police Practice and Research: An International Journal, 1*(1), 41–72.

Hanim, H., Bakri, M., Mohamed, N., & Said J. (2017). Mitigating asset misappropriation through integrity and fraud risk elements: Evidence emerging economie. *Journal of Financial Crime, 24*(2), 242–255.

Hickman, M. J. (2005). *Self-reported and official police problem behavior: Identifying the roles of context, individual, and data.* ProQuest Dissertations and Theses, Retrieved from http://ezproxy.msu.edu/login?url=http://search.proquest.com/docview/305393854?accountid=12598. (305393854).

Hickman, M. J., Piquero, A. R., Powell, Z. A., & Greene, J. (2016a). Expanding the measurement of police integrity. *Policing: An International Journal of Police Strategies & Management, 39*(2), 246–267.

Hickman, M. J., Powell, Z. A., Piquero, A. R., & Greene, J. (2016b). Exploring the viability of an attitudes toward ethical behavior scale in understanding police integrity outcomes. *Policing: An International Journal of Police Strategies & Management, 39*(2), 319–337.

Huberts, L., Lamboo, T., & Punch, M. (2003). Police integrity in the Netherlands and the United States: Awareness and alertness. *Police Practice and Research, 4*(3), 217–232.

Huizinga, D., & Elliott, D. S. (1986). Reassessing the reliability and validity of self-report delinquent measures. *Journal of Quantitative Criminology, 2*, 293–327.

Jenks, D., Johnson, L. M., & Matthews, T. (2014). Examining police integrity: Categorizing corruption vignettes. In M. Guzman, A. M. Das, & D. Das (Eds.), *The evolution of policing*. Boca Raton, FL: CRC.

Johnson, D. T. (2003). Above the law? Police integrity in Japan. *Social Science Japan Journal, 6*(1), 19–37.

Johnson, D. T. (2004). Police integrity in Japan. In C. B. Klockars, S. Kutnjak Ivković, & M. R. Haberfeld (Eds.), *The contours of police integrity*. Thousand Oaks, CA: Sage.

Kang, W., & Kutnjak Ivković, S. (2015). Police integrity in South Korea. In S. Kutnjak Ivković & M. Haberfeld (Eds.), *Police integrity across the world*. New York: Springer.

Kargin, V. (2009). *An investigation of factors proposed to influence police officers' peer reporting intentions.* ProQuest Dissertations and Theses, Retrieved from http://ezproxy.msu.edu/login?url=http://search.proquest.com/docview/305066516?accountid=12598. (305066516).

Khechumyan, A., & Kutnjak Ivković, S. (2015). Police integrity in Armenia. In S. Kutnjak Ivković & M. Haberfeld (Eds.), *Police integrity across the world*. New York: Springer.

Khechumyan, A., & Kutnjak Ivković, S. (2019). Exploring differences in police integrity within a centralized police system. In S. Kutnjak Ivković & M. Haberfeld (Eds.), *Exploring police integrity*. New York: Springer.

Khruakham, S., & Lee, J. (2013). Cross-nation comparison of the intolerance to police misconduct: findings from a Thai police cadet survey. *International Journal of Police Science and Management, 15*(3), 237–245.

Klockars, C. B., & Kutnjak Ivković, S. (1999). The measurement of police delinquency. In W. Laufer & F. Adler (Eds.), *The criminology of criminal law. Advances in criminological theory* (Vol. 8, pp. 87–106). Transaction: New Brunswick, NJ.

Klockars, C. B., & Kutnjak Ivković, S. (2004). Measuring police integrity. In M. J. Hickman, A. R. Piquero, & J. R. Greene (Eds.), *Police integrity and ethics.* Belmont, CA: Wadsworth.

Klockars, C. B., Kutnjak Ivković, S., Harver, W. E., & Haberfeld, M. R. (1997). *The measurement of police integrity.* Final Report Submitted to the U.S. Department of Justice, Office of Justice Programs, National Institute of Justice.

Klockars, C. B., Kutnjak Ivković, S., Harver, W. E., & Haberfeld, M. R. (2000). *The measurement of police integrity.* Research in Brief. U.S. Department of Justice, Office of Justice Programs, National Institute of Justice. Washington, DC: Government Printing Office.

Klockars, C. B., Haberfeld, M. R., Kutnjak Ivković, S., & Uydess, A. (2002). A minimum requirement for police corruption. In R. A. Silverman, T. P. Thornberry, B. Cohen, & B. Krisberg (Eds.), *Crime and justice at the millennium: Essays by and in Honor of Marvin E. Wolfgang*. New York, NY: Springer.

Klockars, C. B., Kutnjak Ivković, S., & Haberfeld, M. R. (2004a). The contours of police integrity. In C. B. Klockars, S. Kutnjak Ivković, & M. R. Haberfeld (Eds.), *The contours of police integrity* (pp. 1–18). Thousand Oaks, CA: Sage.

Klockars, C. B., Kutnjak Ivković, S., & Haberfeld, M. R. (2004b). Police integrity in the United States of America. In C. B. Klockars, S. Kutnjak Ivković, & M. R. Haberfeld (Eds.), *The contours of police integrity* (pp. 265–282). Thousand Oaks, CA: Sage.

Klockars, C. B., Kutnjak Ivković, S., & Haberfeld, M. R. (2006). *Enhancing police integrity*. Dordrecht: Springer.

[Knapp Commission]. Commission to Investigate Allegations of Police Corruption and the City's Anti-Corruption Procedures. (1972). *Report on police corruption*. New York: G. Braziller.

Kremer, F. (2000). Comparing supervisor and line officer opinions about the code of silence: The case of Hungary. In M. Pagon (Ed.), *Policing in Central and Eastern Europe: Ethics, integrity, and human rights* (pp. 211–219). Ljubljana: College of Police and Security Studies.

Kremer, F. (2004). Police integrity in Hungary. In C. B. Klockars, S. Kutnjak Ivković, & M. R. Haberfeld (Eds.), *The contours of police integrity* (pp. 116–130). Thousand Oaks, CA: Sage.

Kucukuysal, B. (2008). *Determinants of Turkish Police Officers' perception of integrity: Impact of organizational culture* (Doctoral dissertation, University of Central Florida Orlando, Florida).

Kuo, S. Y. (2018). Police misconduct in Taiwan: Comparing perceptions of the police and electronic gaming service workers. *Crime, Law and Social Change, 69*, 657–679.

Kutnjak Ivković, S. (2004a). Evaluating the seriousness of police misconduct: A cross-cultural comparison of police officer and citizen views. *International Criminal Justice Review, 14*, 25–48.

Kutnjak Ivković, S. (2004b). Sharing the view: Line officer and supervisor evaluations of police corruption seriousness in Bosnia and Herzegovina. In G. Mesko, M. Pagon, & G. Dobovsek (Eds.), *Dilemmas of contemporary criminal justice* (pp. 312–322). Ljubljana: Faculty of Criminal Justice, University of Maribor.

Kutnjak Ivković, S. (2005). Police (Mis)Behavior: A cross-cultural study of corruption seriousness.

Policing: An International Journal of Police Strategies and Management, 28(3), 546–566.

Kutnjak Ivković, S. (2009). The Croatian police, police integrity, and transition toward democratic policing. *Policing: An International Journal of Police Strategies and Management, 32*(3), 459–488.

Kutnjak Ivković, S. (2012). Exploring the relation between police integrity and rank: A Croatian example. *International Criminal Justice Review, 22*(4), 372–396.

Kutnjak Ivković, S. (2015a). Studying police integrity. In S. Kutnjak Ivković & M. Haberfeld (Eds.), *Police integrity across the world*. New York: Springer.

Kutnjak Ivković, S. (2015b). Police integrity in Croatia. In S. Kutnjak Ivković & M. Haberfeld (Eds.), *Police integrity across the world*. New York: Springer.

Kutnjak Ivković, S., & Haberfeld, M. R. (2015). A comparative perspective on police integrity. In S. Kutnjak Ivković & M. Haberfeld (Eds.), *Police integrity across the world*. New York: Springer.

Kutnjak Ivković, S., & Kang, W. (2011). Police integrity in South Korea. *Policing: An International Journal of Police Strategies and Management, 35*(1), 76–103.

Kutnjak Ivković, S., & Khechumyan, A. (2013). The state of police integrity in Armenia: Findings from the police integrity survey. *Policing: An International Journal of Police Strategies and Management, 36*(1), 70–90.

Kutnjak Ivković, S., & Khechumyan, A. (2014). Measuring police integrity among urban and rural police in Armenia: From local results to global implications. *International Journal of Comparative and Applied Criminal Justice, 38*(1), 39–61.

Kutnjak Ivković, S., & Klockars, C. B. (1998). The code of silence and the Croatian police. In M. Pagon (Ed.), *Policing in Central and Eastern Europe: Organizational, managerial, and human resource aspects* (pp. 329–347). Ljubljana: College of Police and Security Studies.

Kutnjak Ivković, S., & Klockars, C. B. (2000). Comparing police supervisor and line officer opinions about the code of silence: The case of Croatia. In M. Pagon (Ed.), *Policing in Central and Eastern Europe: Ethics, integrity, and human rights* (pp. 183–195). Ljubljana: College of Police and Security Studies.

Kutnjak Ivković, S., & Klockars, C. B. (2002). Public views about police corruption: The case of Croatia. In M. Pagon (Ed.), *Policing in Central and Eastern Europe: Deviance, violence, and victimization* (pp. 283–296). Ljubljana: College of Police and Security Studies.

Kutnjak Ivković, S., & Klockars, C. B. (2004). Police integrity in Croatia. In C. B. Klockars, S. Kutnjak Ivković, & M. R. Haberfeld (Eds.), *The contours of police integrity* (pp. 56–74). Thousand Oaks, CA: Sage.

Kutnjak Ivković, S., & Sauerman, A. (2011). Measuring the code of silence among the South African Police: Findings from a SAPS Supervisor Survey. In C. Gould & G. Newham (Eds.), *Toward a coherent strategy for crime reduction in South Africa beyond 2010* (pp. 74–87). Institute for Security Studies: Pretoria.

Kutnjak Ivković, S., & Sauerman, A. (2012). The code of silence: Revisiting South African police integrity. *South African Crime Quarterly, 40*(June), 15–24.

Kutnjak Ivković, S., & Sauerman, A. (2013). Curtailing the code of silence among the South African Police. *Policing: An International Journal of Police Strategies and Management, 36*(1), 175–198.

Kutnjak Ivković, S., & Sauerman, A. (2015). Threading the thin blue line: Transition toward democratic policing and the integrity of the South African Police Service. *Policing and Society, 25*(1), 25–52.

Kutnjak Ivković, S., & Sauerman, A. (2016). Police integrity in South Africa: a tale of three police agency types. *Policing: An International Journal of Police Strategies & Management, 39*(2), 268–283.

Kutnjak Ivković, S., & Shelley, T. O. (2005). The Bosnian police and police integrity: A continuing story. *European Journal of Criminology, 2*(4), 428–454.

Kutnjak Ivković, S., & Shelley, T. O. (2007). Police integrity and the Czech police officers. *International Journal of Comparative and Applied Criminal Justice, 31*(1), 21–49.

Kutnjak Ivković, S., & Shelley, T. O. (2008a). The police code of silence and different paths toward democratic policing. *Policing and Society, 18*(4), 445–473.

Kutnjak Ivković, S., & Shelley, T. O. (2008b). The contours of police integrity across Eastern Europe: The case of Bosnia and Herzegovina and the Czech Republic. *International Criminal Justice Review, 18*(1), 59–82.

Kutnjak Ivković, S., & Shelley, T. O. (2010). The code of silence and disciplinary fairness: A comparison of Czech police supervisor and line officer views. *Policing: An International Journal of Police Strategies and Management, 33*(3), 548–574.

Kutnjak Ivković, S., Klockars, C. B., Lobnikar, B., & Pagon, M. (2000). Police integrity and the code of silence: A case of the Slovenian Police Force. In G. Mesko (Ed.), *Corruption in Central and Eastern Europe at the turn of millennium* (pp. 85–102). Ljubljana: College of Police and Security Studies.

Kutnjak Ivković, S., Klockars, C. B., Cajner-Mraovic, I., & Ivanusec, D. (2002a). Controlling police corruption: The Croatian perspective. *Police Practice and Research: An International Journal, 3*(1), 55–72.

Kutnjak Ivković, S., Pagon, M., Klockars, C. B., & Lobnikar, B. (2002b). A comparative view of public perceptions of police corruption. In M. Pagon (Ed.), *Policing in Central and Eastern Europe: Deviance, violence, and victimization* (pp. 297–310). Ljubljana: College of Police and Security Studies.

Kutnjak Ivković, S., Cajner-Mraovic, I., & Ivanusec, D. (2004). The measurement of seriousness of police corruption. In G. Mesko, M. Pagon, & G. Dobovsek (Eds.), *Dilemmas of contemporary criminal justice* (pp. 300–311). Ljubljana: Faculty of Criminal Justice, University of Maribor.

Kutnjak Ivković, S., Haberfeld, M., & Peacock, R. (2013). Rainless West: The integrity survey's role in agency accountability. *Police Quarterly, 16*(2), 148–176.

Kutnjak Ivković, S., Haberfeld, M., & Peacock, R. (2015). Police integrity in the United States. In S. Kutnjak Ivković & M. Haberfeld (Eds.), *Police integrity across the world*. New York: Springer.

Kutnjak Ivković, S., Haberfeld, M., Kang, W., Peacock, R., & Sauerman, A. (2016a). A multi-country comparative study of the perceived police disciplinary environments. *Policing: An International Journal of Police Strategies and Management, 39*(2), 338–353.

Kutnjak Ivković, S., Cajner Mraović, I., & Borovec, K. (2016b). Does community policing matter for police integrity? *Journal of Criminal Investigation and Criminology, 67*(4), 313–325.

Kutnjak Ivković, S., Cajner Mraović, I., & Borovec, K. (2016c). An empirical test of the influence of society at large on police integrity in a centralized police system. *Policing: An International Journal of Police Strategies & Management, 39*(2), 302–318.

Kutnjak Ivković, S., Haberfeld, M., & Peacock, R. (2018). Decoding the code of silence. *Criminal Justice Policy Review, 29*(2), 172–189.

Kutnjak Ivković, S., Cajner-Mraovic, I., Božović, V., Prprović, B., & Nemec, N. (2019a). Public views about police misconduct and police integrity in a comparative perspective. In S. Kutnjak Ivković & M. Haberfeld (Eds.), *Exploring police integrity*. New York: Springer.

Kutnjak Ivković, S., Cajner-Mraovic, I., & Sudar, D. (2019b). The speed of progress: Comparing citizen perceptions of police corruption in Croatia over time. In S. Kutnjak Ivković & M. Haberfeld (Eds.), *Exploring police integrity*. New York: Springer.

Kutnjak Ivković, S., Haberfeld, M., Cajner Mraović, I., Prpić, M., Hamm, J. A., & Wolfe, S. (2019c). Seriousness of police (mis)behavior and organizational justice. In S. Kutnjak Ivković & M. Haberfeld (Eds.), *Exploring police integrity*. New York: Springer.

Kutnjak Ivković, S., Haberfeld, M., & Peacock, R. (2019d). Overlapping shades of blue: Exploring police officer, supervisor, and administrator cultures of police integrity. In S. Kutnjak Ivković & M. Haberfeld (Eds.), *Exploring police integrity*. New York: Springer.

Kutnjak Ivković, S., Morgan, S. J., Cajner Mraović, I., & K. Borovec (2019e). Does the police code of silence vary with police assignment? An empirical exploration of the relation between the code and assignment. *Police Problems and Practices*, Forthcoming.

Lee, H., Lim, H., Moore, D. D., & Kim, J. (2013). How police organizational structure correlates with frontline officers' attitudes toward corruption: a multilevel model. *Police Practice and Research, 14*(5), 386–401.

Lim, H. (2019). Similar, different or somewhere in between? The police officer and citizen views on police misconduct. In S. Kutnjak Ivković & M. Haberfeld (Eds.), *Exploring police integrity*. New York: Springer.

Lim, H., & Sloan, J. J. (2016). Police officer integrity: A partial replication and extension. *Policing: An International Journal of Police Strategies & Management, 39*(2), 284–301.

Lobnikar, B., & Meško, G. (2015a). Perception of police corruption and the level of integrity among Slovenian police officers. *Police Practice and Research, 16*(4), 341–353.

Lobnikar, B., & Meško, G. (2015b). Police integrity in Slovenia. In S. Kutnjak Ivković & M. Haberfeld (Eds.), *Police integrity across the world*. New York: Springer.

Lobnikar, B., Prislan, K., Čuvan, B., & Meško, G. (2016). The code of silence and female police officers in Slovenia: Gender differences in willingness to report police misconduct. *Policing: An International Journal of Police Strategies & Management, 39*(2), 387–400.

Lobnikar, B., Meško, G., Hölzl, A., & Prislan, K. (2019). Slovene resident and police officer evaluations of the harm caused by different types of police deviance. In S. Kutnjak Ivković & M. Haberfeld (Eds.), *Exploring police integrity*. New York: Springer.

Long, M., Cross, J. E., Shelley, T. O., & Kutnjak Ivković, S. (2013). The normative order of reporting police misconduct: Examining the roles of offense seriousness, legitimacy, and fairness. *Social Psychology Quarterly, 76*(3), 242–267.

Marche, G. E. (2009). Integrity, culture, and scale: An empirical test of the big bad police agency. *Crime, Law and Social Change, 51*, 463–486.

Maskály, J., Kutnjak Ivković, S., Haberfeld, M. R., Donner, C. M., Chen, T., & Meyers, M. (2019a). Assessing the validity of police integrity scale in a comparative context. *Policing & Society*. Forthcoming.

Maskály, J., Donner, C. M., & Chen, T. (2019b). Improving the measurement of police integrity: An application of LTM to the Klockars et al. (1997) scales. In S. Kutnjak Ivković & M. Haberfeld (Eds.), *Exploring police integrity*. New York: Springer.

Mathenge, G. D. (2014). An empirical study to measuring corruption and integrity in Kenyan police agency: An ethical perspective. *Public Policy and Administration Research, 4*(2).

Matlala, R. L. G., Mistry, D., & Phala, A. (2016). Measuring the integrity of law enforcement officers in Gauteng Province. *The International Journal of Social Sciences and Humanities Invention, 3*(11), 2969–2980.

McDevitt, J., Posick, C., Zschoche, R., Rosenbaum, D. P., Buslik, M., & Fridell, L. (2011). *Police integrity, responsibility, and discipline*. National Institute of Justice. Retrieved from http://www.nationalpoliceresearch.org/storage/updated-papers/Police%20Integrity%20Responsibility%20and%20Discipline.pdf.

Meyer, M. E., Steyn, J., & Gopal, N. (2013). Exploring the public parameter of police integrity. *Policing: An International Journal of Police Strategies & Management, 36*(1), 140–156.

Micucci, A. J., & Gomme, I. M. (2005). American police and subcultural support for the use of excessive force. *Journal of Criminal Justice, 33*, 487–500.

National Research Council. (2004). *Fairness and effectiveness in policing: The evidence*. Committee to Review Research on Police Policy and Practices. Wesley

Skogan and Kathleen Frydl, editors. Committee on Law and Justice, Division of Behavioral and Social Sciences and Education. Washington, DC: The National Academies Press.

Newham, G. (2002). Promoting police integrity at station level: The case of the Hillbrow police station. *Urban Forum, 13*(3), 20–52.

Newham, G. (2004). Out of step: Integrity and the South Africa Police Service. In C. B. Klockars, S. Kutnjak Ivković, & M. R. Haberfeld (Eds.), *The contours of police integrity* (pp. 232–247). Thousand Oaks, CA: Sage.

Pagon, M., & Lobnikar, B. (2000). Comparing supervisor and line officer opinions about the code of silence: The Case of Slovenia. In M. Pagon (Ed.), *Policing in Central and Eastern Europe: Ethics, integrity, and human rights* (pp. 197–209). Ljubljana: College of Police and Security Studies.

Pagon, M., & Lobnikar, B. (2004). Police integrity in Slovenia. In C. B. Klockars, S. Kutnjak Ivković, & M. R. Haberfeld (Eds.), *The contours of police integrity* (pp. 212–231). Thousand Oaks, CA: Sage.

Pagon, M., Kutnjak Ivković, S., & Lobnikar, B. (2000). Police integrity and attitudes toward police corruption: A comparison between the police and the public. In M. Pagon (Ed.), *Policing in Central and Eastern Europe: Ethics, integrity, and human rights* (pp. 383–396). Ljubljana: College of Police and Security Studies.

Pagon, M., Lobnikar, B., & Anelj, D. (2004). Gender differences in leniency towards police misconduct. In G. Mesko, M. Pagon, & B. Dobovsek (Eds.), *Policing in Central and Eastern Europe—Dilemmas of contemporary criminal justice* (pp. 1–16). Ljubljana: Faculty of Criminal Justice, University of Maribor.

Phetthong, N., & Kutnjak Ivković, S. (2015). Police integrity in Thailand. In S. Kutnjak Ivković & M. Haberfeld (Eds.), *Police integrity across the world*. New York: Springer.

Pogarsky, G., & Piquero, A. R. (2004). Studying the reach of deterrence: Can deterrence theory help explain police misconduct? *Journal of Criminal Justice, 32*(4), 371–386.

Porter, L. E., & Alpert, G. P. (2017). Understanding police recruits' attitudes toward public interactions: An Australian example. *Police Quarterly, 20*(4), 449–480.

Porter, L. E., & Prenzler, T. (2016). The code of silence and ethical perceptions: Exploring police officer unwillingness to report misconduct. *Policing: An International Journal of Police Strategies & Management, 39*(2), 370–386.

Porter, L. E., & Prenzler, T. (2019). Exploring gender differences in the Australian context: Organizational and cultural dimensios of ethical attitudes. In Kutnjak Ivković, S. & M. Haberfeld (Eds.), *Exploring Police Integrity*. New York: Springer.

Porter, L. E., Prenzler, T., & Hine, K. (2015). Police integrity in Australia. In S. Kutnjak Ivković & M. Haberfeld (Eds.), *Police integrity across the world*. New York: Springer.

Pounti, A., Vuorinen, S., & Kutnjak Ivković, S. (2004). Sustaining police integrity in Finland. In C. B. Klockars, S. Kutnjak Ivković, & M. R. Haberfeld (Eds.), *The contours of police integrity* (pp. 95–115). Thousand Oaks, CA: Sage.

Punch, M. (2009). *Police corruption: Deviance, accountability and reform in policing*. Portland, OR: Willan.

Punch, M., Huberts, L. W. J. C., & Lamboo, M. E. D. (2004). Integrity, perceptions, and investigations in The Netherlands. In C. B. Klockars, S. Kutnjak Ivković, & M. R. Haberfeld (Eds.), *The contours of police integrity* (pp. 161–175). Thousand Oaks, CA: Sage.

Raines, J. (2010). *Ethics in policing: Misconduct and integrity*. Burlington, MA: Jones & Bartlett Learning.

Reyneke-Cloete, S., & Meyer, M. E. (2016). Viewing integrity in the South African Police Service among non-commissioned officers in Gauteng Province. *Acta Criminologica: Southern African Journal of Criminology, 29*(2), 87–106.

Roebuck, J. B., & Barker, T. (1974). A typology of police corruption. *Social Problems, 21*(3), 423–437.

Rothwell, G. R., & Baldwin, J. N. (2006). Ethical climates and contextual predictors of whistle-blowing. *Review of Public Personnel Administration, 26*(3), 216–244.

Rothwell, G. R., & Baldwin, J. N. (2007a). Whistle-blowing and the code of silence in police agencies policy and structural predictors. *Crime & Delinquency, 53*(4), 605–632.

Rothwell, G. R., & Baldwin, J. N. (2007b). Ethical climate theory, whistle-blowing, and the code of silence in police agencies in the state of Georgia. *Journal of Business Ethics, 70*(4), 341–361.

Sauerman, A., & Kutnjak Ivković, S. (2008). Measuring the integrity of the South African Police Service during Transitional Times. *Acta Criminologica, 2*, 21–39.

Sauerman, A., & Kutnjak Ivković, S. (2015). Police integrity in South Africa. In S. Kutnjak Ivković & M. Haberfeld (Eds.), *Police integrity across the world*. New York: Springer.

Sauerman, A., Kutnjak Ivković, S., & Meyer, M. (2019). Exploring the relation between support for community policing and police integrity in South Africa. In S. Kutnjak Ivković & M. Haberfeld (Eds.), *Exploring police integrity*. New York: Springer.

Schafer, J. A., & Martinelli, T. J. (2008). First-line supervisor's perceptions of police integrity. *Policing: An international journal of police strategies and management, 31*(2), 306–323.

Servino, C. (2013). *Driving forces: Factors affecting police officer injuries in motor vehicle incidents in the United States*. (Order No. 3590166, University of Nevada, Las Vegas). *ProQuest Dissertations and Theses,* 152. Retrieved from http://ezproxy.msu.edu/login?url=http://search.proquest.com/docview/14314 54710?accountid=12598. (1431454710).

Smith, M. V. (2009). *Police perceptions of integrity: The relationship between emotional intelligence and moral development among police officers. ProQuest Dissertations and Theses,* 167. Retrieved from http://ezproxy.msu.edu/login?url=http://search.pro-quest.com/docview/305165879?accountid=12598. (305165879).

Tasdoven, H., & Kaya, M. (2014). The impact of ethical leadership on police officers' code of silence and integrity: Results from the Turkish National Police. *International Journal of Public Administration, 37*, 529–541.

Torstensson Levander, M., & Ekenvall, B. (2004). Homogeneity in moral standards in Swedish police culture. In C. B. Klockars, S. Kutnjak Ivković, & M. R. Haberfeld (Eds.), *The contours of police integrity* (pp. 251–265). Thousand Oaks, CA: Sage.

Vallmüür, B. (2015). Police integrity in Estonia. In S. Kutnjak Ivković & M. Haberfeld (Eds.), *Police integrity across the world*. New York: Springer.

Vallmüür, B. (2016). Exploring gender-neutrality of police integrity in Estonia. *Policing: An International Journal, 39*(2), 401–415.

Vallmüür, B. (2019). The contours of an organizational theory of Green police integrity. In S. Kutnjak Ivković & M. Haberfeld (Eds.), *Exploring police integrity*. New York: Springer.

Van Droogenbroeck, F., Spruyt, B., Kutnjak Ivković, S., & Haberfeld, M. R. (2019). The effects of ethics training on police integrity. In S. Kutnjak Ivković & M. Haberfeld (Eds.), *Exploring police integrity*. New York: Springer.

Vito, G. F., Wolfe, S., Higgins, G. E., & Walsh, W. F. (2011). Police integrity: Rankings of scenarios on the Klockars scale by "Management Cops". *Criminal Justice Review, 36*, 152–164.

Wagner, N., & Hout, W. (2019). Police integrity and the perceived effectiveness of policing: Evidence form a survey among Ugandan police officers. In S. Kutnjak Ivković & M. Haberfeld (Eds.), *Exploring police integrity*. New York: Springer.

Wagner, N., Rieger, M., Bedi, A., & Hout, W. (2017). Gender and policing norms: Evidence form survey experiments among police officers in Uganda. *Journal of African Economies, 26*(4), 492–515.

Westmarland, L. (2004). Policing integrity: Britain's Thin Blue Line. In C. B. Klockars, S. Kutnjak Ivković, & M. R. Haberfeld (Eds.), *The contours of police integrity* (pp. 75–93). Thousand Oaks, CA: Sage.

Westmarland, L. (2005). Police ethics and integrity: Breaking the blue code of silence. *Policing and Society, 15*(2), 145–165.

Westmarland, L., & Rowe, M. (2018). Police ethics and integrity: Can a new code overturn the blue code? *Policing and Society, 28*(7), 854–870.

White, D. A. (2008). *Assessing the differences in opinion regarding gratuities in law enforcement. ProQuest Dissertations and Theses,* 139-n/a. Retrieved from http://ezproxy.msu.edu/login?url=http://search.pro-quest.com/docview/304836939?accountid=12598. (304836939).

Wolfe, S. E., & Piquero, A. R. (2011). Organizational justice and police misconduct. *Criminal Justice and Behavior, 38*(4), 332–353.

Wright, B. (2010). Civilianising the 'blue code'? An examination of attitudes to misconduct in the police extended family. *International Journal of Police Science and Management, 12*(3), 339–356.

Wu, G., Makin, D. A., Li, Y., Boateng, F. D., & Abess, G. (2018). Police integrity in China. *Policing: An International Journal, 41*(5), 563–577.

Yun, I. (2003). *A study of police officers' perceptions of police deviance: From an occupational socialization perspective. ProQuest Dissertations and Theses,* 89–89 p. Retrieved from http://ezproxy.msu.edu/login?url=http://search.proquest.com/docview/305329643?accountid=12598. (305329643).

Yunus, O. M., Bustaman, H., & Khalid, K. (2013). Conducive business environment: A measurement of local authority integrity. *The Journal of Interdisciplinary Networks*, 213–220.

Zschoche, R. (2011). *A multilevel model of police corruption: Anomie, decoupling, and moral disengagement* (Doctoral dissertation, University of South Florida).

Overlapping Shades of Blue: Exploring Police Officer, Supervisor, and Administrator Cultures of Police Integrity

Sanja Kutnjak Ivković, M. R. Haberfeld, and Robert Peacock

Introduction

Police integrity is defined as "the normative inclination among police to resist temptations to abuse the rights and privileges of their occupation" (Klockars et al. 2006, p. 1). This definition deliberately does not elaborate on who the police in this definition are. Thus, it allows for the possibility that the "police" could be individual police officers, groups of police officers, or entire police agencies (Klockars et al. 2006). Hence, police integrity can then be studied at the micro-level (i.e., individual police officer level), meso-level (i.e., level of subunits within each police agency), and macro-level (i.e., police agency level or country level). The majority of the extant research on police integrity focuses either on the individual police officer level (for an overview, see Kutnjak Ivković 2015) or the agency and/or country level (e.g., Klockars et al. 2000, 2004; Kutnjak Ivković and Haberfeld 2015; Kutnjak Ivković et al. 2016; Micucci and Gomme 2005). There is relatively limited research on the meso level (e.g., Hickman et al. 2016; Kutnjak Ivković et al. 2016; Lim and Sloan 2016; Raines 2010).

In addition to studying police integrity across different units within a police agency at the meso level (i.e., across different units of the police agency), police integrity could be studied at the meso level by looking at different levels of police hierarchy as well. A typical American police agency is "a complex bureaucracy, characterized by a hierarchical structure and an authoritarian management style" (Walker and Katz 2011, p. 105). At the lowest level of the hierarchical structure are line officers, such as patrol officers. The next level of the hierarchy includes first-line supervisors, such as Sergeants, Corporals, and Lieutenants. At the top of the hierarchy are police managers or police administrators, such as Captains, Majors, and Police Chiefs/Sheriffs. This organizational structure implies a clear division of labor between workers, first-line supervisors, and chief executives (Walker and Katz 2011, p. 105). Yet, empirical studies on police integrity typically focus only on the division between non-supervisors and supervisors (e.g., Bucak 2012; Kargin 2009; Kremer 2000; Kucukuysal 2008; Kutnjak Ivković 2004; Kutnjak Ivković and Klockars 2000; Kutnjak Ivković and Shelley 2008, 2010; Kutnjak Ivković

S. Kutnjak Ivković
School of Criminal Justice, Michigan State University, East Lansing, MI, USA
e-mail: kutnjak@msu.edu

M. R. Haberfeld (✉)
John Jay College of Criminal Justice, City University of New York, New York, NY, USA
e-mail: mhaberfeld@jjay.cuny.edu

R. Peacock
Steven J. Green School of International and Public Affairs, Florida International University, Miami, FL, USA
e-mail: rpeacock@fiu.edu

© Springer Nature Switzerland AG 2019
S. Kutnjak Ivković, M. R. Haberfeld (eds.), *Exploring Police Integrity*,
https://doi.org/10.1007/978-3-030-29065-8_2

et al. 2016, 2018; Lee et al. 2013; Lim and Sloan 2016; Long et al. 2013; Marche 2009; Micucci and Gomme 2005; Pagon and Lobnikar 2000; Porter and Prenzler 2016; Rothwell and Baldwin 2006, 2007a, b) that potentially hides any differences between first-line supervisors and the police administrators.

This chapter explores the contours of police integrity across the police agencies' hierarchical structure. Instead of relying on the traditional non-supervisor/supervisor dichotomy, we differentiate across three levels of the police hierarchy (line officers, first-line supervisors, and administrators). We study the potential differences among line officer, first-line supervisor, and management views on police integrity. We start by comparing their opinions about official rules and their violations (misconduct seriousness, rule-violating behavior) and continue by exploring their attitudes toward the internal system of control (views about appropriate and expected discipline, evaluations of discipline fairness). We also contrast the adherence to the code of silence (willingness to report) across police officers from three hierarchical levels. Thus, our study provides additional information about potential similarities and differences in the views and opinions across the police hierarchical structure and contributes toward more in-depth understanding of police culture(s).

Rank and Police Culture

The differences between rank and file should be understood within the context of some of the themes that represent the model of *culture,* from which the different subcultural themes evolve (Mayhall et al. 1995). Police culture is viewed as "accepted practices, rules, and principles of conduct that are situationally applied, and generalized rationales and beliefs" (Manning 1989, p. 360). Police culture has traditionally been described as characterized by a cynical perspective, *the us versus them* attitude, a suspicious worldview, an isolated social life, a strong code of silence, and sexism (e.g., Chan 1997, p. 43). The underlying assumption is that these practices, unofficial rules, and principles are widely shared by police officers, forming a monolithic and universal police culture.

The first cultural theme refers to culture as being *Organic* and *Super-organic,* which indicates that the way it evolves depends on people, but, at the same time, it also outlives them in terms of the actual life span and provides a continued impact on societies (Bidney 1944; Kroeber 1917). In the case of police subculture, it can be said that much is derived from the subcultural patterns that were developed by members of the organization long before the new cadre joins it. The new recruits inherit certain behavioral tendencies, including the ones related to ethical and/or unethical behavior, as part of their organizational socialization that occurs both during their academy training and their field training.

One way of teaching the norms of police subculture and transferring the *organic* and *supraorganic* cultural themes is through sharing "war stories" that in the police profession manifest in the way that officers perceive and respond to various situations and interact with members of the public (Haberfeld et al. 2018). According to Sklansky (2007), rather than being labeled as "black" or "white," the officers are labeled as "blue" to reflect their membership in the police subculture. Therefore, the color "blue" represents the membership in the police profession that transcends the membership in any other subcultural group (Sklansky 2007) and, at the same time, creates a unified theme for police officers across different police agencies.

Cultural themes are not just observed by members of the group and the outsiders, but they are also inferred by the police rookies. Sometimes, the interpretation of a given behavioral pattern or reaction to a situation surpasses the mere observation of the facts; new recruits observe the behaviors of their Field Training Officers (FTOs) to learn how to respond to situations. However, not all behaviors that the rookies will observe are lawful or within the legal discretion of the FTO. At this point, the recruits move from just observing the behavior of the more senior officers to inferring the meaning of such behaviors and translating what they observe into meaningful concepts for their own future actions or/and inactions.

The inference process will differ from one officer to another as they will be based on personal biases and experiences of each individual officer as well as the police cultural or subcultural theme. Police subculture will always reflect an adaptation process of the members of a given department to behavioral themes that are not just observed but also inferred, which may differ by rank and supervisory status (Haberfeld 2013).

To further complicate the way behaviors are exhibited and interpreted, additional subcultural themes of "ideal" and "manifest" (Bidney 1944) add yet another dimension to the possible differences between rank and file. An "ideal" action or reaction will exhibit itself in a way that people believe their behavior should be, while a "manifest" action or reaction, on the other hand, will exhibit itself in the way police officers really behave, which is not always synonymous with the "ideal" one. Behavior that might have been acceptable to a police officer while he or she was a line officer may not necessarily be acceptable to the same police officer once the police officer attains a supervisory status. Thus, compared to line officers, supervisors might strive to behave more often in accordance with the "ideal" role and the official rules they are expected to uphold and enforce.

Early research on police culture (e.g., Niederhoffer 1967; Skolnick 1994; Skolnick and Fyfe 1993; Westley 1970) implies that there is one police subculture, shared by police officers across the country, which is secretive, hostile to the public, closely-knit, and opposed to accountability. Loftus (2010) notes that the understanding of police culture and subculture relies heavily on ethnographies conducted several decades ago, where the researchers identified recurring themes within police dispositions and practices over time and space. His ethnographic research, conducted in one of the British police agencies, explored how much of the classic characteristics of police culture have survived over the years (Loftus 2010) and showed that the officers display remarkable continuity with older patterns.

More recent research has challenged the basic notions of a single police culture (e.g., Chan 1997; Haarr 1997; Herbert 1998; Paoline et al.

2000). As police organizations have started to recruit and hire police officers of different gender, race, ethnicity, and sexual orientation, the police culture should change as well and become less likely to be shared by all police officers (e.g., Chan 1997; Haarr 1997; Herbert 1998; Paoline et al. 2000). In fact, separate police cultures may develop across groups of officers, depending on their demographic characteristics. However, extant research does not appear to provide a very strong evidence of large differences based on gender (e.g., Poteyeva and Sun 2009) and/or race/ethnicity (e.g., Britz 1997; Ingram and Terrill 2014; Paoline et al. 2000).

Despite these changes in the police culture that have started to occur in the last two to three decades, potential differences between the line officer and supervisor police culture(s) seem to have predated these developments. The attitudes and values of the traditional police culture seemed to be more strongly adopted by line officers than supervisors (e.g., Crank 2014; Manning 1997; Paoline and Terrill 2014; Reuss-Ianni 1983). In their seminal work on cops and managers, Reuss-Ianni and Ianni (1983) found that the NYPD officers believed that the headquarters personnel have become allied with the politicians and that their behaviors differ from the line officers' behavior based on these alliances. In fact, Reuss-Ianni and Ianni (1983) described two separate subcultures that have developed as a result of somewhat different strains experienced by line officers and supervisors. According to Reuss-Ianni and Ianni (1983), the "street cop culture," which incorporates the values and attitudes of traditional police culture, is primarily shared by line officers, while the "management cop culture," which incorporates broader concerns about the police agency and the society at large, is primarily shared by supervisors (Reuss-Ianni and Ianni 1983). Other research has also indicated that the police culture is not as monolithic as was originally assumed. A U.S. study conducted by Silver et al. (2017) showed that the supervisory status and the adherence to the values of the traditional police culture were negatively related; supervisors were less likely than line officers to accept the values associated with the traditional police culture. While examining the British police officers, Waddington (1999) found significant differences in professional values between lower-ranking officers and their supervisors.

On the other hand, Paoline (2001, p. 151) found subcultural differences across clusters of line officers (e.g., traditionalists, law enforcers, old-pros, peacekeepers, and lay-lows), which further called into question the assumption about one monolithic culture of policing. Yet, his research indicated that the supervisory position is not a key variable affecting police officer views; "like patrol officers, street supervisors are interpreting and coping with the occupational and organizational environments in the same ways as their subordinates." Similarly, Terrill et al.'s (2003) research indicates that those officers who closely embody the values of the police culture are more coercive compared to the officers who differentially align with the culture, suggesting that the police use of force is a function of officers' varying attitudinal commitments to the traditional view of police culture and yet, again, not necessarily attributed to the differences between rank and file.

Rank and Police Integrity

The definition of police integrity is built into the theory of police integrity (see Klockars and Kutnjak Ivković 2004; Klockars et al. 2000, 2004, 2006). To allow the empirical testing of the theory of police integrity, Klockars and colleagues (see Klockars and Kutnjak Ivković 2004; Klockars et al. 2000, 2004, 2006) have developed a methodological approach as well. The police officer survey includes a series of vignettes describing examples of police misconduct, followed by a series of seven identical questions.

The theory of police integrity is built on four dimensions. The *first dimension* of the theory puts emphasis on the official rules (Klockars and Kutnjak Ivković 2004; Klockars et al. 2000, 2004, 2006). In particular, the theory argues that the way in which the official rules are made and communicated to/understood by the police officers is critical for the level of police integrity

(Klockars and Kutnjak Ivković 2004; Klockars et al. 2000, 2004, 2006; Kutnjak Ivković 2015). In the police integrity survey, there is a related question measuring the police officers' familiarity with official rules. In addition, there are also questions assessing how serious police officers evaluate examples of police misconduct. The *second dimension* of the theory proposes that police integrity is related to the quality and effectiveness of the internal system of control (Klockars and Kutnjak Ivković 2004; Klockars et al. 2000, 2004, 2006; Kutnjak Ivković 2015). One of the possible outcomes of the functioning internal systems of control is actual discipline that is meted out to police officers who have been found responsible of engaging in misconduct. There are two questions in the questionnaire related to this theoretical dimension: the first question inquiries about the discipline that the respondents view as the appropriate for such misconduct and the second question inquiries about the discipline that the respondents think that would really occur in their agency. The *third dimension* of the theory argues that the level of police integrity is negatively related to the strength of the code of silence (Klockars and Kutnjak Ivković 2004; Klockars et al. 2000, 2004, 2006; Kutnjak Ivković 2015). Two questions in the questionnaire tap into the police officers' code of silence. The *fourth dimension* links the level of police integrity and the legal, social, political, and economic conditions in the society at large (Klockars and Kutnjak Ivković 2004; Klockars et al. 2000, 2004, 2006; Kutnjak Ivković 2015). While the questionnaire does not have any questions exploring the characteristics of the society at large, information about these characteristics can be collected separately and used to analyze potential differences in the contours of police integrity across different environments (see, e.g., Klockars et al. 2004; Kutnjak Ivković and Haberfeld 2015; Kutnjak Ivković et al. 2016).

The police integrity theory and methodology (see Klockars and Kutnjak Ivković 2004; Klockars et al. 2000, 2004, 2006) have been used extensively to study police integrity across the world (for a summary see e.g., Klockars et al. 2004; Kutnjak Ivković and Haberfeld 2015). The bulk of the extant research has explored the contours of police integrity across police agencies and only a small subset of these studies has explored potential differences across police hierarchies. Typically, this was done by dichotomizing rank and comparing non-supervisor views with supervisor views (e.g., Kargin 2009; Kremer 2000; Kutnjak Ivković 2004; Kutnjak Ivković and Klockars 2000; Kutnjak Ivković and Shelley 2008, 2010; Kutnjak Ivković et al. 2016, 2018; Lee et al. 2013; Lim and Sloan 2016; Long et al. 2013; Marche 2009; Micucci and Gomme 2005; Pagon and Lobnikar 2000; Porter and Prenzler 2016; Rothwell and Baldwin 2006, 2007a, b) and only rarely by exploring police integrity across the three or more hierarchical levels[1] (e.g., Bucak 2012; Kucukuysal 2008; Raines 2010; Yun 2003).

Rank and Evaluations of Seriousness

About a dozen studies have examined the relation between rank and perceptions of misconduct seriousness (Bucak 2012; Kucukuysal 2008; Kutnjak Ivković 2004; Lee et al. 2013; Marche 2009; Micucci and Gomme 2005; Raines 2010; Yun 2003). The data were collected in a number of countries across the world, from Bosnia and Herzegovina (Kutnjak Ivković 2004), South Korea (Yun 2003), and Turkey (Bucak 2012; Kucukuysal 2008) to the United States (Marche 2009; Micucci and Gomme 2005; Raines 2010; Lee et al. 2013). Virtually all of these studies relied on the first questionnaire that mostly focused on police corruption (e.g., Klockars et al. 2000, 2004).

The results of these studies do not produce a uniform picture. On the one hand, in the study of line officers and supervisors in Bosnia and Herzegovina (Kutnjak Ivković 2004), a bivariate comparisons yielded very few differences between supervisors and non-supervisors in their evaluations of seriousness; out of 11 scenarios, line officer and supervisor evaluations of seriousness were statistically different in only 2 scenar-

ios. In both of these scenarios, describing the use of excessive force and off-duty business, supervisors evaluated these scenarios as more serious (Kutnjak Ivković 2004). Similarly, Yun (2003) found that supervisors and non-supervisors exhibited statistically significant differences in their evaluations of misconduct seriousness in only 1 scenario (describing an improper search) out of 8 scenarios. Furthermore, the hierarchical linear modeling (HLM) analysis of the U.S. data revealed that rank was not a significant predictor of the respondents' evaluations of seriousness (Lee et al. 2013). While Kucukuysal (2008) demonstrated significant differences across ranks in 5 out of 9 scenarios in the bivariate analysis of the Turkish data, the rank effects disappeared in the multivariate analyses of evaluations of seriousness.

On the other hand, Raines (2010) found that the supervisory position mattered in the U.S. data. When scenarios were grouped into four categories of police misconduct (conflict of interest, exploiting authority, abuse of authority, and malfeasance), statistically significant differences between supervisors and non-supervisors were reported in all four types of scenarios. In all of them, supervisors evaluated scenarios as more serious (Raines 2010). Rank remained an important variable predicting the respondents' estimates of seriousness in multivariate models as well (Raines 2010). When reanalyzing the same data set, Marche (2009) found that the supervisory status was directly related to the perceptions of seriousness in 10 out of 11 scenarios. Although using a somewhat different methodology, Micucci and Gomme (2005) also found that supervisors were also more likely to evaluate one of these scenarios—the use of excessive force—as more serious than non-supervisors.

Four of these studies also relied on a more detailed classification of rank (Bucak 2012; Kucukuysal 2008; Raines 2010; Yun 2003). Raines (2010) combined rank and assignment to classify respondents into officers, detectives, first-line managers, mid-level managers, and senior managers. There were no large differences in their seriousness evaluations of malfeasance, but officers in the study provided the least serious

---

[1] We do not count police assignments as different hierarchical levels.

evaluations of the three other types of miscon-duct and the mid-level and senior managers pro-vided the most serious evaluations (Raines 2010). Studies from other countries seemed to suggest that the differences may not be as strong as Raines (2010) reported. In the factor analysis of Turkish data that merged seriousness estimates of 9 scenarios, Kucukuysal (2008) reported that rank (measured as police officers, sergeants, and higher officers) was insignificant. Although Bucak (2012) found that line officers evaluated the three scenarios as less serious in bivariate analyses than either group of managers, rank was not a significant predictor of seriousness in the multivariate models of Turkish data. Similarly, Yun (2003) noticed some differences across the ranks (e.g., Captains and Lieutenants provided the highest aggregate evaluations of seriousness across 8 scenarios) in his analysis of South Korean data, but the differences were neither sta-tistically significant nor large.

Rank and Discipline Severity and Fairness

The least frequently examined theoretical dimen-sion—discipline—also had the smallest number of studies exploring the relation of rank and the perceptions of discipline severity (e.g., Kutnjak Ivković et al. 2016; Kutnjak Ivković and Shelley 2010; Micucci and Gomme 2005; Raines 2010). The results of these few studies are mixed as well: a few studies found no differences between supervisors and non-supervisors in their percep-tions of discipline, while other studies reported that supervisor and non-supervisor views about expected and appropriate discipline were quite different.

On the one hand, Kutnjak Ivković and Shelley (2010) analyzed the influence of rank on the Czech respondents' perceptions of both expected and appropriate discipline. They reported that the Czech supervisors and non-supervisors had very similar views about both expected and appropri-ate discipline. In particular, the supervisory level

was not significantly related with the views about the appropriate discipline in any of the scenarios (Kutnjak Ivković and Shelley 2010), while the supervisory level and the views about the expected discipline were statistically signifi-cantly related in only 1 out of 10 scenarios (Kutnjak Ivković and Shelley 2010). Similarly, the subsequent U.S. study (Kutnjak Ivković et al. 2016) revealed that the supervisor and non-supervisor estimates of discipline their agency would mete out were almost identical; statistically-significant differences were reported in only 1 out of 11 scenarios (Kutnjak Ivković et al. 2016). The supervisor and non-supervisor views seemed to diverge more when the analysis focused on the views about appropriate disci-pline. Although there were no statistically signifi-cant differences in the respondents' views of appropriate discipline by rank in the majority of the scenarios (6 out of 11), in a strong minority of the scenarios (5 out of 11), supervisors advocated more severe discipline than non-supervisors. Both of these studies also found that the supervi-sor and non-supervisor estimates of discipline fairness were not statistically significantly differ-ent in the majority of the scenarios (Kutnjak Ivković and Shelley 2010; Kutnjak Ivković et al. 2016). In other words, supervisors and non-supervisors seem to express similar views of dis-cipline fairness.

On the other hand, two other studies (Micucci and Gomme 2005; Raines 2010), both analyzing the same national U.S. data set (Klockars et al. 2000), reported larger differences in the supervi-sor and non-supervisor views of appropriate and expected discipline. Specifically, Micucci and Gomme (2005) examined only the use of force scenario and found that, compared to non-supervisors, supervisors both expected and sup-ported more severe discipline. Raines (2010) took into account all 11 scenarios and grouped them into 4 types of police misconduct. Raines (2010) found statistically significant differences between supervisors and non-supervisors in their views about both appropriate and expected discipline.

Rank and Expressed Willingness to Report

The relation between rank and the code of silence has also been a topic of even more studies than perceptions of seriousness and discipline. Studies from Australia (Porter and Prenzler 2016), Bosnia and Herzegovina (Kutnjak Ivković and Shelley 2008), Croatia (Kutnjak Ivković and Klockars 2000), Czech Republic (Kutnjak Ivković and Shelley 2008, 2010), Hungary (Kremer 2000), and the USA (Kargin 2009; Kutnjak Ivković et al. 2016, 2018; Long et al. 2013; Micucci and Gomme 2005; Raines 2010; Rothwell and Baldwin 2006, 2007a, b) explored the potential differences in the line officer and supervisor code(s) of silence. While most of the studies used the original or modified version of the police corruption questionnaire (Kargin 2009; Kremer 2000; Kutnjak Ivković and Klockars 2000; Kutnjak Ivković and Shelley 2008, 2010; Micucci and Gomme 2005; Raines 2010; Rothwell and Baldwin 2006, 2007a, b), several other studies relied on the police integrity questionnaire (e.g., Kutnjak Ivković et al. 2016, 2018; Porter and Prenzler 2016). A common feature across the studies is that they dichotomized rank (i.e., supervisors, non-supervisors) in their analyses.

As was the case for perceptions of seriousness and discipline, estimates of the respondents' willingness to report—a measure of the code of silence—did not produce a uniform picture either. On the one hand, several studies from Eastern Europe (Croatia, Hungary, and Slovenia) in the early 2000s (Kremer 2000; Kutnjak Ivković and Klockars 2000; Pagon and Lobnikar 2000) reported that supervisors seemed to be much more likely to say that they would report than the line officers were. The differences between the line officers' and supervisors' codes of silence were strong and systematic (e.g., line officers were less likely to say that they would report in 11 out of 11 scenarios; Kremer 2000; Kutnjak Ivković and Klockars 2000; Pagon and Lobnikar 2000). A couple of years later, Kutnjak Ivković and Shelley (2008, 2010) compared the respondents' expressed willingness to report in two other East-European countries (Bosnia and

Herzegovina and the Czech Republic) and found no statistically significant differences in all scenarios in Bosnia and Herzegovina (10 out of 10) and in the majority of scenarios in the Czech Republic (7 out of 10). However, when the supervisor and line officer codes differed in the Czech Republic, the supervisor code seems to be narrower, just like the previous studies from Eastern Europe have demonstrated (Kutnjak Ivković and Shelley 2008). Kutnjak Ivković and Shelley (2010, p. 571) concluded that, "[t]he existence of a more homogeneous code of silence among the line officers and supervisors in BiH [than in the Czech Republic] is potentially a consequence of a stronger camaraderie among the police developed during the war."

Empirical studies from the United States mostly found that the rank has an effect on the respondents' willingness to report. In the studies based on the U.S. dataset created by Klockars et al. (2000, 2006), scholars have reported that rank does matter, both as a result of bi-variate and multi-variate analyses (e.g., Long et al. 2013; Micucci and Gomme 2005; Raines 2010). Regardless of whether the authors focused on the use of excessive force (e.g., Micucci and Gomme 2005), original corruption scenarios (e.g., Long et al. 2013), or reclassified corruption scenarios (e.g., Raines 2010), supervisors in the study were more likely to say that they would report than line officers. A new U.S. sample (Kutnjak Ivković et al. 2016, 2018) tested the relation on a more heterogeneous set of police misconduct types. Nevertheless, the results were quite similar: in the majority of the scenarios, line officers were more likely to say that they would adhere to the code of silence than supervisors (Kutnjak Ivković et al. 2016, 2018). Similarly, in a series of papers exploring the rank differences among civilian employees and police officers, Rothwell and Baldwin (2006, 2007a, b) consistently found that the supervisory status is one of the most significant predictors of the employees' expressed willingness to report.

In the reanalysis of the police integrity data from Philadelphia, Kargin (2009) classified scenarios into three categories based on their evaluations of seriousness. While Kargin (2009)

initially found that the supervisory status and expressed willingness to report were related in bi-variate analyses, his multivariate models revealed that the supervisory status was no longer a significant predictor of the respondents' expressed willingness to report. Similarly, Porter and Prenzler (2016) analyzed Australian data and found that the supervisory effect disappears in multi-variate models.

Methodology

Questionnaire

The police integrity questionnaire (Klockars et al. 1997, 2006) was used to survey U.S. police officers. This questionnaire was designed to measure police integrity (Klockars et al. 2006), viewed as the resistance to temptations of various sources. Consequently, the questionnaire contains scenarios describing different forms of police misconduct (e.g., Klockars et al. 2006). Out of 11 scenarios included in the questionnaire, 5 describe examples of police corruption, ranging in their severity from the acceptance of free meals and gifts to the theft of money from a crime scene. There are also 4 scenarios that provide examples of the use of excessive force, ranging in their severity from verbal abuse to the abuse of deadly force (see, e.g., Klockars et al. 2006; Kutnjak Ivković 2015). Finally, there are two scenarios that contain examples of other forms of police misconduct, such as falsification of the official report and failure to execute a search warrant (e.g., Kutnjak Ivković 2015). The scenarios describe the behavior that a police officer on the beat might experience and, hence, are "realistic in modern, industrial societies" (Kutnjak Ivković 2015, p. 12).

The scenarios are followed by a series of seven identical questions. One group of questions targeted the first dimension of the theory. The first question asked the respondents to assess the seriousness of the behavior ("How serious do you consider this behavior to be?"). The answers ranged on a 5-item scale from 1 = "not at all serious" to 5 = "very serious." A parallel question

focused on the others' evaluations of seriousness ("How serious do most police officers in your agency consider this behavior to be?"). The questions also asked the respondents to assess whether the behavior described in the scenario is a violation of official policy ("Would this behavior be regarded as a violation of official policy in your agency?"). The answers were offered on a 5-item scale, ranging from 1 ("definitely not") to 5 ("definitely yes").

The second dimension of the theory was measured through questions about discipline. The first question focused on the discipline that would be appropriate ("If an officer in your agency engaged in this behavior and was discovered doing so, what, if any, discipline do you think should follow?"), while the second question explored discipline that would actually be meted out by the police agency ("If an officer in your agency engaged in this behavior and was discovered doing so, what, if any, discipline do you think would follow?"). The answers range on a 6-item scale from "no discipline" to "dismissal." The issue of discipline fairness can be assessed by comparing the answers to the first question about the appropriate discipline and the second question about the expected discipline. If the outcome is zero, this would imply that the respondents perceive the discipline they think that their police agency would met our as fair. If the outcome is larger than zero (i.e., a positive number), this would imply that the respondents perceive the discipline they think that their police agency would met out as too lenient. If the outcome is smaller than zero (i.e., a negative number), this would imply that the respondents perceived the discipline they think that their police agency would met out as too harsh.

The third dimension of the theory was measured through two questions as well. The first question asked the respondents to express their own willingness to report misconduct ("Do you think you would report a fellow police officer who engaged in this behavior?").

The parallel question focused on the estimates of others' willingness to report ("Do you think most police officers in your agency would report a fellow police officer who engaged in this behavior?"). Both questions used a 5-item scale, ranging from 1 ("definitely not") to 5 ("definitely yes").

The practice with the police integrity surveys has been to keep the number of demographic questions to the minimum. The rationale is that this would minimize the potential identification of the respondents and entice them to participate in the study (see, e.g., Kutnjak Ivković et al. 2015). We followed this practice and asked the respondents a very small number of demographic questions: rank, supervisory position, assignment, and type of agency in which they work. Also, the questionnaire contains two questions asking about their fellow officers' willingness to be truthful ("Do you think that most police officers would give their honest opinions in filling out this questionnaire?") and, lastly, their own willingness to respond truthfully ("Did you?").

The Sample

With about 18,000 independent police agencies in the United States (BJS 2011), it is not realistic to survey them all. Similarly, because of their heterogeneity (e.g., federal, state, rural, municipal, transit, park, university), it is not feasible to generate a representative sample of these agencies. Thus, the 11 police agencies from the Midwest and East Coast of the United States surveyed in this study constitute such a convenience sample. Our sample includes a heterogeneous group of local police agencies, ranging in their size (e.g., small, large) and jurisdiction (e.g., municipal, rural). A Bureau of Justice Statistics (2011) survey of local police agencies suggests that the 11 agencies taking part in the study generally reflect the range of law enforcement officers working in large, medium, and small cities in the U.S.A. (for details see Kutnjak Ivković et al. 2015).

The data were collected through an online survey. The police administrators in each police agency emailed sworn police officers in their agencies inviting them to participate in the survey. The email also contained our cover letter describing the study, informing the respondents

that their participation is voluntary and that they can withdraw from the study at any point, and enlisting potential risks and benefits from participation in the study (Kutnjak Ivković et al. 2015). The email provided the link and password for Survey Monkey. A follow-up email was sent a couple of weeks later reminding the respondents to participate if they chose to do so (Kutnjak Ivković et al. 2015). The sample response rate for the 11 police agencies was 37.4%,[2] consistent with what the literature suggests for one-time web surveys (e.g., Shih and Fan 2008).

The overall number of respondents who filled out the survey is 664. About 8% of the respondents did not answer the questions about their rank, so we omitted their answers from the further analyses and included the responses by 612 respondents. Based on their ranks, we classified the respondents into three groups: line officers, supervisors, and administrators (Table 1). The distribution of respondents across these three groups corresponds well to a structure of a hierarchical organization that has a wide bottom level (line officers are 72.9% of the sample), a somewhat narrower middle level (immediate supervisors are 21.7% of the sample), and a narrow top level (administrators are 5.4% of the sample; Table 1).

In terms of their experience, there is a logical difference across the three groups of respondents; while only about one-third of line officers have been police officers for over 15 years, this was the case for three-quarters of immediate supervisors and almost all administrators (Table 1). Both line officers and immediate supervisors mostly worked in patrol, while most administrators wrote that they worked in the administration (Table 1). Furthermore, the majority of line officers and immediate supervisors are spread across large and medium-sized police agencies, the

---

[2]Web-based surveys traditionally have lower response rates than the surveys which are mailed, emailed, faxed, or phoned (e.g., Manfreda et al. 2008). In their comparison of survey modes, Shih and Fan (2008) found that the average web-based survey had a response rate of 34%.

Table 1 Respondents' Demographic Characteristics

Rank	Line officers Recruit, corporal, officer, detective, deputy	Supervisors Sergeant, lieutenant	Administrators Captain, major, colonel, chief/sheriff	Chi-square (Phi)
Number of respondents	446	133	33	
Percent of sample	72.9%	21.7%	5.4%	
Supervisory position				
Yes	0.9%	100%	100%	588.2*** (.984)
Length of service				
Up to 5 years	16.2%	0.8%	3.1%	121.3***
6 to 15 years	51.9%	21.8%	3.1%	(.446)
Over 15 years	31.9%	77.4%	93.8%	
Type of assignment				
Patrol	52.0%	54.9%	18.2%	153.4***
Investigative	18.1%	7.5%	6.1%	(.502)
Special operations	12.4%	10.5%	6.1%	
Administrative	3.6%	19.5%	66.7%	
Other	13.8%	7.5%	3.0%	
Type of police agency				
Very large or large	46.3%	43.7%	60.7%	14.0 (.151)
Medium	40.7%	42.9%	21.2%	
Small or very small	13.0%	13.5%	18.2%	
Others telling the truth				
Yes	81.3%	87.2%	84.8%	2.6 (.066)
Respondents themselves telling the truth				
Yes	98.2%	99.2%	98.3%	1.1 (.043)

majority of administrators are employed in large police agencies (Table 1).

The last two questions in the questionnaire asked respondents whether they and their fellow police officers responded honestly while filling out the questionnaire. The overwhelming majority of the respondents across all three groups (81% for line officers, 87% for immediate supervisors, and 85% for administrators) thought that their fellow officers would provide truthful answers. When directly asked whether the respondents themselves answered honestly, almost all respondents—regardless of the place in the organizational hierarchy—answered positively (Table 1). Only answers by the respondents who stated that they answered honestly will be used in the analyses and the answers by the respondents who stated that they have lied or did not answer this question will be omitted from the analyses.

Results

Rank and the First Dimension (Seriousness and Rule Violations)

The questions tapping into the first dimension of the theory focused on the respondents' estimates of misconduct seriousness and recognition of behavior as rule-violating. We will compare the police officers' views across the three groups of respondents (line officers, supervisors, administrators).

The respondents were first asked to assess how *serious* they view the behavior in each questionnaire (Table 2). According to the three groups of respondents, the behavior described in 11 scenarios seems to vary greatly in its seriousness, from the behavior evaluated as the least serious, such as the acceptance of free meals and gifts from merchants (Scenario 1), to the behavior evaluated as the most serious, such as the theft of a knife from a crime scene (Scenario 3). A comparison of the rank-order on scenarios based on their mean values across the three groups of respondents clearly showed that the relative rankings of these scenarios across groups of respondents were strongly related (Spearman's rho for line and supervisors is .991, p < .001; Spearman's rho for line and administrators is .991, p < .001; Spearman's rho for supervisors and administrators is .982, p < .001). Put differently, the relative seriousness of each scenario—its standing compared to the standing of other scenarios in the questionnaire—was quite uniform across the three groups of respondents.

We also compared at the absolute evaluations of seriousness across the three groups of respondents (Table 2). In about one-half of the scenarios (6 scenarios or 54% of the scenarios), there were no statistically significant differences across the three groups of respondents, suggesting that their evaluations of seriousness were very similar. On the other hand, in a large minority of the scenarios (5 scenarios or 45% of the scenarios)—almost of all them on the least serious side of the seriousness scale—the respondents' own estimates of seriousness were statistically different. The post-hoc analyses provided further evidence about the pairs of groups of respondents (e.g., line officers v. supervisors or 1 v. 2 in the tables) that were statistically different. In all such pairs, the higher rank was associated with the higher evaluations of seriousness (Table 2). A further exploration of the issue revealed that, out of 7 pairs with statistically significant differences, 5 pairs or 71% involved a comparison of line officer and administrator mean values; in each and every of these scenarios, administrators tended to evaluate the behavior as more serious than line officers.

We will now compare the respondents' predictions of other police officers' estimates of seriousness (Table 3). The results show that the respondents assumed that other police officers would be able to differentiate across the scenarios and view the acceptance of free meals and

Table 2 Respondents' Own Views about Misconduct Seriousness

	Line officers		Supervisors		Administrators		
	Mean	Rank	Mean	Rank	Mean	Rank	F-test
Scenario 1: Free Meals/Gifts from Merchants	3.13	1	3.27	1	3.34	1	.883
Scenario 2: Failure to Arrest Friend with Warrant	4.31	5	4.51	4	4.56	5	2.900
Scenario 3: Theft of Knife from Crime Scene	4.98	11	5.00	11	4.94	11	1.327
Scenario 4: Unjustifiable Use of Deadly Force	4.84	9	4.87	9	4.88	8	.150
Scenario 5: Supervisor Offers Holiday for Errands	4.13	4	4.57	5	4.53	4	12.173*** (1 v. 2; 1 v. 3)
Scenario 6: Officer Strikes Prisoner Who Hurt Partner	4.32	6	4.64	6	4.78	6	7.881*** (1 v. 3)
Scenario 7: Verbal Abuse "Arrest an Asshole Day"	3.27	2	3.70	2	3.91	2	9.075*** (1 v. 3)
Scenario 8: Cover-Up of Police DUI & Accident	3.66	3	3.73	3	4.23	3	2.893[a] (1 v. 3; 2 v. 3)
Scenario 9: Auto-Body Shop 5% Kickback	4.59	8	4.78	8	4.88	8	4.520* (no sig. pairs)
Scenario 10: False Report on Drug Dealer	4.91	10	4.96	10	4.91	10	.830
Scenario 11: Sgt. Fails to Halt Beating	4.49	7	4.77	7	4.88	8	8.308*** (1 v. 3)

* p < .05; ** p < .01; *** p < .001; [a] p < .10

gifts from merchants (Scenario 1) as the least serious and a theft of a knife from a crime scene (Scenario 3) as the most serious (Table 3). When we compared the scenarios for each group of respondents based on the rank-order of the scenarios, the analyses revealed that the relative rankings of other police officers' views of seriousness and the category of respondents were strongly related (Spearman's rho for line and supervisors is .964, p < .001; Spearman's rho for line and administrators is .966, p < .001; Spearman's rho for supervisors and administrators is .979, p < .001). In other words, the relative ranking of each scenario based on the others' estimated evaluations of seriousness seemed to be very similar across the three groups of respondents.

The analyses of the absolute estimates of others' evaluations of seriousness across the three groups of respondents (Table 3) provided additional evidence of the similarity with which line officers, supervisors, and administrators perceived that other officers would evaluate the seriousness of these scenarios. In fact, in the overwhelming majority of the scenarios (8 out of 11 or 73%), the mean values across the three groups were so similar that they resulted in no statistically significant differences (Table 3). Out of the three scenarios with differences (Scenario 5: Supervisor Offers Holidays for Errands; Scenario 6: Officer Strikes Prisoner Who Hurt Partner; Scenario 11: Sgt. Fails to Halt Beating), two of them involve the only two scenarios in the questionnaire describing misconduct committed by a supervisor. In one of these scenarios (Scenario 5: Supervisor Offers Holidays for Errands), we found statistically significant pairs indicating that, compared to both supervisors and administrators, line officers perceived that other officers would evaluate this behavior as less serious.

Our next step in the analysis was to ascertain how closely the respondents' own views correspond with how they perceive that most police officers in their agencies would respond. Because of the self-serving bias (e.g., Larwood and Whittaker 1977; Svenson 1981; Weinstein 1980), we expected that the respondents' own estimates

Table 3 Respondents' Estimates of Others' Views about Misconduct Seriousness

	Line officers		Supervisors		Administrators		
	Mean	Rank	Mean	Rank	Mean	Rank	F-test
Scenario 1: Free Meals/Gifts from Merchants	2.77	1	2.73	1	2.72	1	.073
Scenario 2: Failure to Arrest Friend with Warrant	4.14	6	4.25	4	4.31	4.5	.963
Scenario 3: Theft of Knife from Crime Scene	4.89	11	4.93	11	4.88	11	.723
Scenario 4: Unjustifiable Use of Deadly Force	4.81	10	4.87	10	4.84	9.5	.716
Scenario 5: Supervisor Offers Holiday for Errands	3.84	4	4.29	5	4.38	6	11.562*** (1 v. 2; 1 v. 3)
Scenario 6: Officer Strikes Prisoner Who Hurt Partner	4.11	5	4.39	6	4.31	4.5	3.933* (no sig. pairs)
Scenario 7: Verbal Abuse "Arrest an Asshole Day"	3.13	2	3.34	2	3.50	2	2.461
Scenario 8: Cover-Up of Police DUI & Accident	3.46	3	3.42	3	3.65	3	.388
Scenario 9: Auto-Body Shop 5% Kickback	4.38	8	4.49	7	4.69	7.5	2.245
Scenario 10: False Report on Drug Dealer	4.80	9	4.82	9	4.84	9.5	.135
Scenario 11: Sgt. Fails to Halt Beating	4.35	7	4.53	8	4.69	7.5	3.664* (no sig. pairs)

* p < .05; ** p < .01; *** p < .001; [a] p < .10

of seriousness would be higher than the estimates they attributed to other police officers in their agencies. Indeed, our results confirm the existence of self-serving bias among line officers (11 out of 11 scenarios with statistically significant differences), supervisors (10 out of 11 scenarios with statistically significant differences), and administrators (7 out of 11 scenarios with statistically significant differences; Table 4) as their own estimates of seriousness were higher than the estimates they provided for other officers.

A more interesting comparison for our purposes explores the size of the differences between own and others' estimates among the three groups of respondents. Because line officers typically constitute the majority of employees in a police agency and the administrators the smallest group of employees in hierarchical police agencies, we anticipated that the differences between own views and others' views ("most police officers in your police agency") would be the smallest among line officers and largest among administrators. Our results confirmed this idea; the mean of differences for line officers were the smallest (0.175), while the mean of differences for supervisors (0.249) and for administrators (0.275) were somewhat larger. Furthermore, if we use the rule of thumb that differences of .50 or larger are substantively important, there was no scenario in which we found such differences for line officers, 1 for supervisors, and 2 for administrators (Table 4).

Another measure we used to assess the respondents' level of police integrity focused on the respondents' familiarity with legal rules. While the respondents' familiarity with official rules seemed to vary across the scenarios, there was less heterogeneity in their views across the scenarios than there was in their perceptions of misconduct seriousness. Across all three groups of respondents, the mean values were close to the violation side of the scale (i.e., the behavior is viewed as "definitely a violation" of official rules); in fact, there was no scenario in which the mean value was below 4 on a 5-point scale (Table 5), suggesting that all scenarios have been recognized as rule-violating across all groups of respondents. In the scenarios involving the behaviors evaluated as the most serious (e.g., Scenario 3: Theft of Knife from Crime Scene; Scenario 6: Officer Strikes Prisoner Who Hurt Partner; Scenario 9: Auto-Body Shop 5% Kickback; Scenario 10: False Report on Drug Dealer; Scenario 11: Sgt. Fails to Halt Beating), virtually all line officers, supervisors, and administrators in our sample recognized and labeled such behaviors as rule-violating. The acceptance of free meals and gifts from merchant (Scenario 1) was least likely to be recognized as rule violating by the respondents from all three groups.

There were very few differences in the line officer, supervisor, and administrator labeling of behavior as rule violating (Table 5). In fact, in 8 out of 11 scenarios or 73% there were no statistically significant differences in the respondents' evaluations across the three groups of respondents. In only 3 scenarios or 27% (Scenario 3: Theft of Knife from Crime Scene; Scenario 5: Supervisor Offers Holiday for Errands; Scenario 7: Verbal Abuse "Arrest an Asshole Day") there were statistically significant differences, suggesting that the rank and evaluation of behavior as rule violating were positively related: in all 3 scenarios with statistically significant differences, administrators were more likely than line officers to recognize and label this behavior as rule violating.

Our analysis of the relative order in which the behavior described in the scenarios has been evaluated as rule violating again suggested that the line officers, supervisors, and administrators have about the same likelihood of recognizing behavior as rule violating. Specifically, the rank-order on scenarios based on their mean values across the three groups of respondents showed a great deal of similarity (Spearman's rho for line and supervisors is .931, p < .001; Spearman's rho for line and administrators is .954, p < .001; Spearman's rho for supervisors and administrators is .968, p < .001). Put differently, the relatively likelihood that each scenario will be evaluated as rule violating—its standing compared to the standing of other scenarios in the questionnaire—was uniform across the three groups of respondents.

Table 4 Comparing Respondents' Own Estimates and Estimates of Others' Evaluations of Seriousness

	Line officers			
	Own mean	Others' mean	Difference	T-test
Scenario 1: Free Meals/Gifts from Merchants	3.13	2.77	+.36	9.212***
Scenario 2: Failure to Arrest Friend with Warrant	4.31	4.14	+.17	6.534***
Scenario 3: Theft of Knife from Crime Scene	4.98	4.89	+.09	5.715***
Scenario 4: Unjustifiable Use of Deadly Force	4.84	4.81	+.03	2.948**
Scenario 5: Supervisor Offers Holiday for Errands	4.13	3.84	+.29	8.843***
Scenario 6: Officer Strikes Prisoner Who Hurt Partner	4.32	4.11	+.21	7.345***
Scenario 7: Verbal Abuse "Arrest an Asshole Day"	3.27	3.13	+.14	5.044***
Scenario 8: Cover-Up of Police DUI & Accident	3.66	3.46	+.20	5.441***
Scenario 9: Auto-Body Shop 5% Kickback	4.59	4.38	+.21	7.705***
Scenario 10: False Report on Drug Dealer	4.91	4.80	+.09	5.297***
Scenario 11: Sgt. Fails to Halt Beating	4.49	4.35	+.14	5.599***
	Supervisors			
	Own mean	Others' mean	Difference	T-test
Scenario 1: Free Meals/Gifts from Merchants	3.27	2.73	+.54	7.505***
Scenario 2: Failure to Arrest Friend with Warrant	4.51	4.25	+.26	5.880***
Scenario 3: Theft of Knife from Crime Scene	5.00	4.93	+.07	2.782**
Scenario 4: Unjustifiable Use of Deadly Force	4.87	4.87	.00	.00
Scenario 5: Supervisor Offers Holiday for Errands	4.57	4.29	+.28	4.990***
Scenario 6: Officer Strikes Prisoner Who Hurt Partner	4.64	4.39	+.25	4.595***
Scenario 7: Verbal Abuse "Arrest an Asshole Day"	3.70	3.34	+.36	6.025***
Scenario 8: Cover-Up of Police DUI & Accident	3.73	3.42	+.31	4.890***
Scenario 9: Auto-Body Shop 5% Kickback	4.78	4.49	+.29	4.929***
Scenario 10: False Report on Drug Dealer	4.96	4.82	+.14	4.013***
Scenario 11: Sgt. Fails to Halt Beating	4.77	4.53	+.24	4.299***
	Administrators			
	Own mean	Others' mean	Difference	T-test
Scenario 1: Free Meals/Gifts from Merchants	3.34	2.72	+.62	4.706***
Scenario 2: Failure to Arrest Friend with Warrant	4.56	4.31	+.25	2.784**
Scenario 3: Theft of Knife from Crime Scene	4.94	4.88	+.06	1.438
Scenario 4: Unjustifiable Use of Deadly Force	4.88	4.84	+.04	1.000
Scenario 5: Supervisor Offers Holiday for Errands	4.53	4.38	+.15	1.973
Scenario 6: Officer Strikes Prisoner Who Hurt Partner	4.78	4.31	+.46	3.695**
Scenario 7: Verbal Abuse "Arrest an Asshole Day"	3.91	3.50	+.41	3.738**
Scenario 8: Cover-Up of Police DUI & Accident	4.23	3.65	+.58	3.815**
Scenario 9: Auto-Body Shop 5% Kickback	4.88	4.69	+.19	2.675*
Scenario 10: False Report on Drug Dealer	4.91	4.84	+.07	1.000
Scenario 11: Sgt. Fails to Halt Beating	4.88	4.69	+.19	2.675*

* $p < .05$; ** $p < .01$; *** $p < .001$; [a] $p < .10$

Table 5 Respondents' Own Views about Rule Violations

	Line officers		Supervisors		Administrators		
	Mean	Rank	Mean	Rank	Mean	Rank	F-test
Scenario 1: Free Meals/Gifts from Merchants	4.13	1	4.15	1	4.09	1	.030
Scenario 2: Failure to Arrest Friend with Warrant	4.55	5	4.57	3	4.66	3	.212
Scenario 3: Theft of Knife from Crime Scene	4.99	11	5.00	10.5	4.94	11	3.449* (1 v. 3; 2 v. 3)
Scenario 4: Unjustifiable Use of Deadly Force	4.69	6	4.66	4.5	4.81	6	.539
Scenario 5: Supervisor Offers Holiday for Errands	4.32	2.5	4.66	4.5	4.75	4	8.282*** (1 v. 3)
Scenario 6: Officer Strikes Prisoner Who Hurt Partner	4.85	9	4.93	9	4.91	9.5	1.641
Scenario 7: Verbal Abuse "Arrest an Asshole Day"	4.42	4	4.76	6	4.78	5	9.341*** (1 v. 2; 1 v. 3)
Scenario 8: Cover-Up of Police DUI & Accident	4.32	2.5	4.42	2	4.48	2	.839
Scenario 9: Auto-Body Shop 5% Kickback	4.77	7	4.89	7	4.90	8	2.810
Scenario 10: False Report on Drug Dealer	4.94	10	5.00	10.5	4.91	9.5	2.123
Scenario 11: Sgt. Fails to Halt Beating	4.81	8	4.92	8	4.87	7	2.311

$*\ p < .05; **\ p < .01; ***\ p < .001; {}^a\ p < .10$

Rank and the Second Dimension (Internal Discipline)

The second dimension of the theory targeted the operation of the police agency's internal system of control. We include two measures related to internal discipline. Our first measure included the question seeking respondents' views about what they thought should be appropriate discipline for the behavior described in each scenario (Table 6). The respondents could have selected one disciplinary option, ranging from "no discipline" to "dismissal," which they would deem appropriate for such behavior. The respondents' views about the appropriate discipline differed across their ranks in about one-half of scenarios (6 out of 11 or 55%). These scenarios are typically in the midrange based on their seriousness and include different forms of misconduct, from the use of excessive force to corruption. In all of these scenarios, the higher rank was associated with the views that harsher discipline should be more appropriate. Specifically, there were 9 statistically significant pairs (Table 6) and, in all of

these pairs, a higher-ranked category of respondents (e.g., supervisors, administrators) advocated for a more severe form of discipline than a lower-ranked category of respondents, such as line officers (Table 6).

When we explored the scenarios based on the relative harshness of discipline that the respondents thought should be appropriate—that is, the relative order of scenarios compared to the other scenarios in the questionnaire—the results again revealed a great deal of similarity across the three groups of respondents (Spearman's rho for line and supervisors is .989, p < .001; Spearman's rho for line and administrators is .973, p < .001; Spearman's rho for supervisors and administrators is .989, p < .001). In other words, the relative severity of appropriate discipline for each scenario was quite uniform across the three groups of respondents.

The second measure of the police agency's disciplinary environment focused on the respondents' estimates of the expected discipline (i.e., discipline they expect their police agency to mete out for the behavior described in the questionnaire).

Table 6 Respondents' Own Views about Appropriate Discipline

	Line officers		Supervisors		Administrators		
	Mean	Rank	Mean	Rank	Mean	Rank	F-test
Scenario 1: Free Meals/Gifts from Merchants	2.16	1	2.25	1	2.31	1	.950
Scenario 2: Failure to Arrest Friend with Warrant	3.28	5	3.38	4	3.74	4	2.145
Scenario 3: Theft of Knife from Crime Scene	5.45	11	5.58	11	5.74	11	2.088
Scenario 4: Unjustifiable Use of Deadly Force	5.31	10	5.36	9.5	5.53	9	.324
Scenario 5: Supervisor Offers Holiday for Errands	3.27	4	3.67	5	4.14	5	10.177*** (1 v. 3; 2 v. 3)
Scenario 6: Officer Strikes Prisoner Who Hurt Partner	3.70	6	4.00	6	4.17	6	4.250* (no sig. pairs)
Scenario 7: Verbal Abuse "Arrest an Asshole Day"	2.46	2	2.79	2	2.97	2	11.934*** (1 v. 2; 1 v. 3)
Scenario 8: Cover-Up of Police DUI & Accident	2.98	3	3.17	3	3.37	3	1.721
Scenario 9: Auto-Body Shop 5% Kickback	4.12	7	4.48	7	5.25	8	11.301*** (1 v. 3; 2 v. 3)
Scenario 10: False Report on Drug Dealer	5.15	9	5.36	9.5	5.69	10	4.505* (1 v. 3)
Scenario 11: Sgt. Fails to Halt Beating	4.32	8	4.61	8	5.21	7	7.193** (1 v. 3; 2 v. 3)

* $p < .05$; ** $p < .01$; *** $p < .001$; [a] $p < .10$

The results show that the three groups of respondents were in agreement about the expected discipline in about one-half of the scenarios (6 out of 11 scenarios or 55%; Table 7). Put differently, in a minority of the scenarios, but close to one-half of the scenarios (5 out of 11 scenarios or 45%), there were statistically significant differences in their views about the expected discipline. In each and every one of these five scenarios, involving corruption, planting of evidence, and falsifying official records, line officers expected less severe discipline than administrators (Table 7). At the same time, line officers' views about expected discipline were statistically different from the first-line supervisors' views of expected discipline in only one scenario (Scenario 5: Supervisor Offers Holiday for Errands). Such a finding also implied that supervisor and administrator disciplinary expectations are not identical; in three scenarios, first-line supervisors expected less severe discipline than administrators (Table 7).

Our next set of analyses focused on the differences across the three groups in the relative harshness of the expected discipline. To that end, we have compared the rankings of scenarios for each group and discovered a substantial degree of similarity in their relative assessments of harshness of expected discipline (Spearman's rho for line and supervisors is .964, $p < .001$; Spearman's rho for line and administrators is .927, $p < .001$; Spearman's rho for supervisors and administrators is .973, $p < .001$). In other words, the relative severity of expected discipline for each scenario was quite uniform across the three groups of respondents.

Finally, we explore perceptions of disciplinary fairness by comparing the respondents' views about the disciplinary option they deemed to be appropriate with the disciplinary option they expected to be meted out by their police agencies (Table 8). As described earlier, this comparison can result in a zero value (expected discipline evaluated as "fair"), a negative number (expected

Table 7 Respondents' Estimates of Expected Discipline

	Line officers		Supervisors		Administrators		
	Mean	Rank	Mean	Rank	Mean	Rank	F-test
Scenario 1: Free Meals/Gifts from Merchants	2.36	1	2.44	1	2.25	1	.803
Scenario 2: Failure to Arrest Friend with Warrant	3.25	4	3.25	3	3.77	4	2.862[a] (1 v. 3; 2 v. 3)
Scenario 3: Theft of Knife from Crime Scene	5.33	10	5.35	11	5.63	11	1.167
Scenario 4: Unjustifiable Use of Deadly Force	5.44	11	5.29	10	5.53	9	.736
Scenario 5: Supervisor Offers Holiday for Errands	2.87	3	3.43	5	3.90	5	14.643*** (1 v. 2; 1 v. 3)
Scenario 6: Officer Strikes Prisoner Who Hurt Partner	3.91	6	3.97	6	4.18	6	.767
Scenario 7: Verbal Abuse "Arrest an Asshole Day"	2.76	2	2.85	2	3.06	2	2.181
Scenario 8: Cover-Up of Police DUI & Accident	3.41	5	3.38	4	3.33	3	.059
Scenario 9: Auto-Body Shop 5% Kickback	4.20	7	4.38	7	5.06	8	6.238** (1 v. 3; 2 v. 3)
Scenario 10: False Report on Drug Dealer	5.09	9	5.18	9	5.61	10	2.852[a] (1 v. 3; 2 v. 3)
Scenario 11: Sgt. Fails to Halt Beating	4.40	8	4.55	8	4.97	7	3.234* (1 v. 3)

$* p < .05;\ ** p < .01;\ *** p < .001;\ ^a p < .10$

discipline evaluated as "too harsh"), and a positive number (expected discipline evaluated as "too lenient").

Although the specific percentage of the respondents who evaluated expected discipline as fair differed across scenarios within each group of respondents, the results across the groups indicate that the majority of the respondents in each group evaluated the expected discipline as fair (Table 8). However, several indicators show that line officers seemed to be least likely to evaluate expected discipline as fair, while administrators were most likely to evaluate it as fair (Tables 8 and 9). First, discipline was evaluated to be unfair by at least one-quarter of line officers in 6 out of 11 scenarios and at least one-quarter of supervisors and administrators in only 1 scenario each

(Scenario 1: Free Meals/Gifts from Merchants; Table 8). Second, the number of scenarios in which at least 85% of the respondents in each group evaluated discipline as fair (Table 9) was much larger for administrators (7 out of 11 scenarios or 64%) than either line officers (1 out of 11 scenarios or 9%) or supervisors (2 out of 11 scenarios or 18%; Tables 8 and 9). Third, in the majority of the scenarios (8 out of 11), 80% or fewer of line officers evaluated expected discipline as fair (Table 9). On the other hand, in the majority of the scenarios (8 out of 11), between 75 and 85% of supervisors evaluated expected discipline as fair (Table 9). Finally, in the majority of the scenarios (7 out of 11), at least 85% of the administrators evaluated discipline as fair (Table 9).

Table 8 Respondents' Estimates of Discipline Fairness

	Line officers			Supervisors		
	Fair	Too harsh	Too lenient	Fair	Too harsh	Too lenient
Scenario 1: Free Meals/Gifts from Merchants	62.6%	26.7%	10.8%	65.9%	17.5%	16.7%
Scenario 2: Failure to Arrest Friend with Warrant	73.6%	13.4%	13.1%	78.6%	4.3%	17.1%
Scenario 3: Theft of Knife from Crime Scene	83.2%	5.8%	10.9%	82.9%	4.1%	13.0%
Scenario 4: Unjustifiable Use of Deadly Force	89.6%	7.2%	3.2%	93.9%	2.6%	3.5%
Scenario 5: Supervisor Offers Holiday for Errands	67.6%	6.1%	26.3%	82.4%	2.8%	14.8%
Scenario 6: Officer Strikes Prisoner Who Hurt Partner	75.9%	18.7%	5.3%	82.8%	7.8%	9.5%
Scenario 7: Verbal Abuse "Arrest an Asshole Day"	71.5%	25.9%	2.6%	89.4%	8.9%	1.6%
Scenario 8: Cover-Up of Police DUI & Accident	64.0%	31.2%	4.8%	77.8%	18.5%	3.7%
Scenario 9: Auto-Body Shop 5% Kickback	78.4%	12.4%	9.2%	82.9%	8.1%	9.0%
Scenario 10: False Report on Drug Dealer	85.0%	6.7%	8.3%	83.9%	3.4%	12.7%
Scenario 11: Sgt. Fails to Halt Beating	71.8%	16.4%	11.8%	81.2%	9.9%	8.9%

	Administrators			
	Fair	Too harsh	Too lenient	Chi-square (Phi)
Scenario 1: Free Meals/Gifts from Merchants	68.8%	12.5%	18.8%	9.275[a] (.128)
Scenario 2: Failure to Arrest Friend with Warrant	93.5%	3.2%	3.2%	13.923** (.160)
Scenario 3: Theft of Knife from Crime Scene	93.5%	0.0%	6.5%	3.648 (.082)
Scenario 4: Unjustifiable Use of Deadly Force	100.0%	0.0%	0.0%	6.751 (.114)
Scenario 5: Supervisor Offers Holiday for Errands	85.7%	0.0%	14.3%	12.460* (.155)
Scenario 6: Officer Strikes Prisoner Who Hurt Partner	89.3%	7.1%	3.6%	11.935* (.152)
Scenario 7: Verbal Abuse "Arrest an Asshole Day"	77.4%	16.1%	6.5%	19.133** (.188)
Scenario 8: Cover-Up of Police DUI & Accident	76.7%	13.3%	10.0%	11.927* (.152)
Scenario 9: Auto-Body Shop 5% Kickback	90.3%	0.0%	9.7%	5.656 (.105)
Scenario 10: False Report on Drug Dealer	96.8%	0.0%	3.2%	7.260 (.118)
Scenario 11: Sgt. Fails to Halt Beating	82.8%	0.0%	17.2%	9.263[a] (.142)

* $p < .05$; ** $p < .01$; *** $p < .001$; [a] $p < .10$

Table 9 Number of Scenarios by Percent of Respondents Evaluating Discipline as Fair

	Line officers	Supervisors	Administrators
60–75%	6 (S1, S2, S5, S7, S8, S11)	1 (S1)	1 (S1)
75.1–80%	2 (S6, S9)	2 (S2, S8)	2 (S7, S8)
80.1–85%	2 (S3, S10)	6 (S3, S5, S6, S9, S10, S11)	1 (S11)
85.1–90%	1 (S4)	1 (S7)	2 (S5, S6)
90.1–95%	0	1 (S4)	3 (S2, S3, S9)
95.1–100%	0	0	2 (S4, S10)
Total number of scenarios	11	11	11

Rank and the Third Dimension (The Code of Silence)

The third dimension of the theory focused on the control of the code of silence. The respondents' expressed willingness to report misconduct was our first measure of the respondents' own views on police integrity (Table 10). The respondents' expressed willingness to report varied greatly across the scenarios for each group. The respondents across all three groups seemed to be least likely to say that they would report a police officer who accepts free meals and gifts from merchants (Scenario 1) and most likely to be willing to report a colleague who stole a knife from a crime scene (Scenario 3) or abused deadly force (Scenario 4).

Despite these initial similarities, there was a great deal of difference in the respondents' expressed willingness to report. In 10 out of 11 scenarios or 91% there were statistically significant differences across the three groups of respondents. Upon further examination of the post-hoc significant pairs (Table 10), we counted 20 significant pairs (e.g., 1 v. 2; 1 v. 3). In all of them, the higher-ranked police officers expressed greater willingness to report misconduct than lower-ranked police officers, such as line officers. Most of the pairs with differences included line officers and one of the groups of supervisors (18 out of 20 pairs), while there were very few statistically significant differences between supervisors and administrators (2 out of 20 pairs). In other words, in almost all scenarios, line officers were less likely to say that they would report misconduct than were either the supervisors and/or administrators. The differences between the mean values tended to be

Table 10 Respondents' Own Willingness to Report

	Line officers		Supervisors		Administrators		
	Mean	Rank	Mean	Rank	Mean	Rank	F-test
Scenario 1: Free Meals/Gifts from Merchants	2.23	1	2.74	1	3.31	1	14.882*** (1 v. 2; 1 v. 3; 2 v. 3)
Scenario 2: Failure to Arrest Friend with Warrant	3.40	4	4.23	4	4.44	4	25.196*** (1 v. 2; 1 v. 3)
Scenario 3: Theft of Knife from Crime Scene	4.61	10	4.91	11	4.88	10	9.268*** (1 v. 2; 1 v. 3)
Scenario 4: Unjustifiable Use of Deadly Force	4.77	11	4.90	10	4.91	11	2.906
Scenario 5: Supervisor Offers Holiday for Errands	3.43	5	4.31	5	4.69	5	31.198*** (1 v. 2; 1 v. 3)
Scenario 6: Officer Strikes Prisoner Who Hurt Partner	3.56	6	4.36	6	4.72	6	25.344*** (1 v. 2; 1 v. 3)
Scenario 7: Verbal Abuse "Arrest an Asshole Day"	2.51	2	3.64	3	4.19	3	48.497*** (1 v. 2; 1 v. 3; 2 v. 3)
Scenario 8: Cover-Up of Police DUI & Accident	2.93	3	3.44	2	3.68	2	8.009*** (1 v. 3)
Scenario 9: Auto-Body Shop 5% Kickback	3.97	8	4.61	8	4.75	7	19.318*** (1 v. 2; 1 v. 3)
Scenario 10: False Report on Drug Dealer	4.52	9	4.81	9	4.86	9	9.414*** (1 v. 3)
Scenario 11: Sgt. Fails to halt beating	3.94	7	4.55	7	4.84	8	18.309*** (1 v. 2; 1 v. 3)

$* p < .05; ** p < .01; *** p < .001; {}^{a} p < .10$

quite large and even in some scenarios exceed 1 on a 5-point scale (Scenario 1: Free Meals/Gifts from Merchants; Scenario 2: Failure to Arrest Friend with Warrant; Scenario 5: Supervisor Offers Holiday for Errands; Scenario 6: Officer Strikes Prisoner Who Hurt Partner; Scenario 7: Verbal Abuse "Arrest an Asshole Day").

At the same time, there was a great degree of similarity in the relative order of each scenario based on the respondents' willingness to report. Specifically, the rank-order of the scenarios based on the mean values of their own willingness to report for each category of respondents suggested that the relative rankings of these scenarios across groups of respondents were strongly related (Spearman's rho for line and supervisors is .982, p < .001; Spearman's rho for line and administrators is .982, p < .001; Spearman's rho for supervisors and administrators is .982, p < .001). Put differently, the relative expressed willingness to report misconduct described in each scenario— its standing compared to the standing of other scenarios in the questionnaire—was uniform across the three groups of respondents.

The respondents' views about others' willingness to report tended to be less heterogeneous than their own expressed willingness to report. In about one-half of the scenarios (6 scenarios or 55%) we detected statistically significant differences across the three groups of respondents in their estimates of others' willingness to report. However, in only four of these scenarios—evaluated to be on the less serious side—the post-hoc test revealed statistically significant pairs (Table 11). None of these pairs included statistically significant differences between supervisor and administrator estimates of others' willingness to report; rather, the line officers were typically less likely to say that others would report than the supervisors and/or administrators were (Table 11).

We also studied the degree of similarity across the three groups of respondents in their relative assessments of others' willingness to report (Table 11). The rank-order of scenarios based on their relative order (i.e., how the mean value for each scenario compares to the mean values for the remaining ten scenarios) revealed a great degree

Table 11 Respondents' Estimates of Others' Willingness to Report

	Line officers		Supervisors		Administrators		
	Mean	Rank	Mean	Rank	Mean	Rank	F-test
Scenario 1: Free Meals/Gifts from Merchants	2.11	1	2.31	1	2.34	1	1.889
Scenario 2: Failure to Arrest Friend with Warrant	3.19	4	3.65	4	3.94	5	10.106*** (1 v. 3)
Scenario 3: Theft of Knife from Crime Scene	4.30	10	4.50	10	4.56	10	3.585* (no sig. pairs)
Scenario 4: Unjustifiable Use of Deadly Force	4.67	11	4.81	11	4.84	11	2.394
Scenario 5: Supervisor Offers Holiday for Errands	3.24	5	3.94	6	4.13	6	19.244*** (1 v. 2; 1 v. 3)
Scenario 6: Officer Strikes Prisoner Who Hurt Partner	3.38	6	3.67	5	3.91	4	4.153* (1 v. 3)
Scenario 7: Verbal Abuse "Arrest an Asshole Day"	2.43	2	2.88	2	3.09	3	8.800*** (1 v. 3)
Scenario 8: Cover-Up of Police DUI & Accident	2.86	3	2.90	3	2.94	2	.074
Scenario 9: Auto-Body Shop 5% Kickback	3.74	7	4.05	8	4.19	7.5	5.032* (no sig. pairs)
Scenario 10: False Report on Drug Dealer	4.27	9	4.27	9	4.41	9	.285
Scenario 11: Sgt. Fails to Halt Beating	3.78	8	4.02	7	4.19	7.5	3.104

$* p < .05$; $** p < .01$; $*** p < .001$; [a] $p < .10$

of agreement across the three groups of respondents (Spearman's rho for line and supervisors is .982, p < .001; Spearman's rho for line and administrators is .961, p < .001; Spearman's rho for supervisors and administrators is .980, p < .001). In other words, the three groups of respondents were in agreement about the other officers' relative willingness to report misconduct.

Finally, we explored the size of the differences between own and others' estimates of willingness to report for each group. In line with self-serving bias, there were statistically significant differences between the respondents' own expressed willingness to report and estimated others' willingness to report for all three groups of respondents (11 out of 11 scenarios for line officers and supervisors and 10 out of 11 scenar-

ios for administrators; Table 12). More importantly, the size of the differences between own estimates and others' estimates was not the same across the three groups. Compared to supervisors and administrators, the line offices' own expressed willingness to report was most similar to the estimated others' willingness to report. In particular, the mean of differences between own and others' estimates was the smallest (0.173) for line officers and much larger for both first-line supervisors (0.500) and administrators (0.612). Finally, if we use the rule of thumb evaluating differences of means of .50 or larger as substantively important, there was no scenario in which we found such differences for line officers, while we found 7 such scenarios for supervisors and 8 for administrators (Table 12).

Table 12 Comparing Respondents' Own Estimates and Estimates of Others' Willingness to Report

	Line officers			
	Own mean	Others' mean	Difference	T-test
Scenario 1: Free Meals/Gifts from Merchants	2.23	2.11	.12	3.37**
Scenario 2: Failure to Arrest Friend with Warrant	3.40	3.19	.21	5.22***
Scenario 3: Theft of Knife from Crime Scene	4.61	4.30	.31	10.20***
Scenario 4: Unjustifiable Use of Deadly Force	4.77	4.67	.10	4.41***
Scenario 5: Supervisor Offers Holiday for Errands	3.43	3.24	.19	5.17***
Scenario 6: Officer Strikes Prisoner Who Hurt Partner	3.56	3.38	.18	5.26***
Scenario 7: Verbal Abuse "Arrest an Asshole Day"	2.51	2.43	.08	2.30*
Scenario 8: Cover-Up of Police DUI & Accident	2.93	2.86	.07	2.11*
Scenario 9: Auto-Body Shop 5% Kickback	3.97	3.74	.23	6.84***
Scenario 10: False Report on Drug Dealer	4.52	4.27	.25	8.04***
Scenario 11: Sgt. Fails to Halt Beating	3.94	3.78	.16	5.26***
	Supervisors			
	Own mean	Others' mean	Difference	T-test
Scenario 1: Free Meals/Gifts from Merchants	2.74	2.31	.43	5.97***
Scenario 2: Failure to Arrest Friend with Warrant	4.23	3.65	.58	7.72***
Scenario 3: Theft of Knife from Crime Scene	4.91	4.50	.41	6.63***
Scenario 4: Unjustifiable Use of Deadly Force	4.90	4.81	.09	3.16**
Scenario 5: Supervisor Offers Holiday for Errands	4.31	3.94	.37	5.17***
Scenario 6: Officer Strikes Prisoner Who Hurt Partner	4.36	3.67	.69	8.73***
Scenario 7: Verbal Abuse "Arrest an Asshole Day"	3.64	2.88	.76	9.09***
Scenario 8: Cover-Up of Police DUI & Accident	3.44	2.90	.54	6.90***
Scenario 9: Auto-Body Shop 5% Kickback	4.61	4.05	.56	8.05***
Scenario 10: False Report on Drug Dealer	4.81	4.27	.54	8.00***
Scenario 11: Sgt. Fails to Halt Beating	4.55	4.02	.53	7.38***

(continued)

Table 12 (continued)

	Administrators			
	Own mean	Others' mean	Difference	T-test
Scenario 1: Free Meals/Gifts from Merchants	3.31	2.34	.97	5.31***
Scenario 2: Failure to Arrest Friend with Warrant	4.44	3.94	.50	4.55***
Scenario 3: Theft of Knife from Crime Scene	4.88	4.56	.32	3.30**
Scenario 4: Unjustifiable Use of Deadly Force	4.91	4.84	.07	1.00
Scenario 5: Supervisor Offers Holiday for Errands	4.69	4.13	.56	4.19***
Scenario 6: Officer Strikes Prisoner Who Hurt Partner	4.72	3.91	.81	4.76***
Scenario 7: Verbal Abuse "Arrest an Asshole Day"	4.19	3.09	1.10	5.40***
Scenario 8: Cover-Up of Police DUI & Accident	3.68	2.94	.74	4.00***
Scenario 9: Auto-Body Shop 5% Kickback	4.75	4.19	.56	3.36**
Scenario 10: False Report on Drug Dealer	4.86	4.41	.45	3.74**
Scenario 11: Sgt. Fails to Halt Beating	4.84	4.19	.65	3.96***

* $p < .05$; ** $p < .01$; *** $p < .001$; [a] $p < .10$

Conclusion

This chapter has explored the contours of police integrity across the police agencies' hierarchical structure. Instead of using the traditional supervisor/non-supervisor way of dichotomizing rank, we have not only included the comparison of the supervisor and non-supervisor views on police integrity, but have also compared the first-line supervisor views with the police administrator views. Our results indicate that non-supervisors, first-line supervisors, and administrators had similar views about the measures of the first dimension of the police integrity theory. Although there were a few scenarios with statistically significant differences across the three groups, the big picture is that, in the majority of the scenarios, there were no statistical differences across the non-supervisor, first-line supervisor, and administrator evaluation of misconduct seriousness and evaluation of behavior as rule violating. To that end, our findings provide additional support to the studies reporting no differences in the evaluations of seriousness by supervisory status (e.g., Bucak 2012; Lee et al. 2013).

At the same time, because we did find a few statistically significant differences as well, there was some evidence supporting the argument that the respondents' own evaluations of seriousness

may not be as uniform and homogeneous as some of the earlier studies indicated. Specifically, we found statistically significant differences in the respondents' own evaluations of seriousness in 5 out of 11 scenarios or nearly one-half of the scenarios. Thus, our results also provide some support to the previous studies reporting differences in the evaluations of seriousness by non-supervisors and supervisors (e.g., Kutnjak Ivković 2004; Marche 2009; Micucci and Gomme 2005; Raines 2010).

The exploration of the second dimension of the theory of police integrity produced an even greater degree of heterogeneity of views across the three groups of respondents. To begin with, compared to supervisors, non-supervisors thought that less severe discipline would be appropriate in the majority of the scenarios (6 out of 11). There results fit well with the results of the earlier U.S. studies (e.g., Micucci and Gomme 2005; Raines 2010). Yet, we found no statistically significant differences in the expected discipline in the majority of the scenarios, which fits well with the no-difference results reported in extant literature (e.g., Kutnjak Ivković and Shelley 2010; Kutnjak Ivković et al. 2016). Before we draw the final conclusion, we need to keep in mind that this no-difference result applies to the majority of the scenarios and that we also documented that, in almost one-half of the scenarios (but definitely less than 50%), there were significant differences among the three groups of respondents in their views of expected discipline. Put differently, non-supervisors, first-line supervisors, and administrators differed in some scenarios in what they expect the actual discipline would be. There were also some differences in the fairness evaluations as well; compared to non-supervisors, supervisors, particularly administrators, were much more likely to evaluate expected discipline as fair.

Finally, the exploration of the measures of the third dimension—the code of silence—resulted in the greatest degree of heterogeneity among non-supervisors, first-line supervisors, and administrators. While all police integrity measures ask about the respondents' options, questions about willingness to report carry with them an extra element—a predicted action or the lack thereof. Non-supervisors were not only more likely to say that they would adhere to the code of silence themselves than first-line supervisors and/or administrators, but they were also more likely to say that most police officers would do the same. Our results are in full agreement with the findings of earlier East-European studies (e.g., Kremer 2000; Kutnjak Ivković and Klockars 2000; Pagon and Lobnikar 2000) and other U.S. studies (Rothwell and Baldwin 2006, 2007a, b; Kutnjak Ivković et al. 2016, 2018; Long et al. 2013; Micucci and Gomme 2005; Raines 2010) reporting that rank matters for the adherence to the code of silence.

Regardless of which measure of police integrity we used, we noticed a common feature across almost all scenarios with statistically significant differences. Simply put, if there are differences, at least one group of supervisors, if not both, expressed attitudes associated with higher integrity than non-supervisors. Such a finding comes as no surprise, having in mind earlier studies that systematically reported that, if there are differences in views and opinions between supervisors and non-supervisors, supervisors were more likely to evaluate misconduct as serious, expect harsher discipline, and are would be more willing to say that they would report misconduct than non-supervisors (e.g., Kremer 2000; Kutnjak

Ivković 2004; Kutnjak Ivković and Klockars 2000; Kutnjak Ivković et al. 2016, 2018; Long et al. 2013; Marche 2009; Micucci and Gomme 2005; Pagon and Lobnikar 2000; Raines 2010).

Furthermore, our results provide a very strong evidence of the need to differentiate among supervisors. Put differently, not all levels of supervisors in the hierarchical organization share the same view. To begin with, while the differences between the first-line supervisors and administrators were not statistically significant often (there were 9 such instances in the measurement of seriousness, discipline, and willingness to report), they demonstrate that these two groups of supervisors do not have identical views. In virtually all of these instances, as expected, administrators exhibited attitudes associated with higher levels of integrity than the first-line supervisors. Furthermore, we counted 47 instances in which the non-supervisor views on all seven measures (own and others' seriousness, rule-violations, appropriate and expected discipline, and own and others' willingness to report) were different from the first-line supervisor and/or administrator views. However, when views of the non-supervisors differed from the view of any group of supervisors, in about two-thirds of these instances (33 out of 47), the non-supervisors' views were systematically different from the administrators' views, and in only about one-third of these instances (14 out of 47), non-supervisor views were different from the first-line supervisor views. Put differently, the first-line supervisors were more likely to share their views with non-supervisors than administrators. This issue is most obvious when evaluations of discipline fairness are explored; the percentage of non-supervisors who evaluated expected discipline as fair was 80% and the smallest percentage among all three groups, followed by about 85% of first-line supervisors and 90% of administrators who evaluated discipline as fair. Such results indicate that, compared to administrators' views, the first-line supervisors' views were more similar to non-supervisor views. These findings are by no means surprising, having in mind the fact that, by their role in the police hierarchy (e.g., Walker and Katz 2011), the first-line supervisors were much closer in the police hierarchy to non-supervisors than police administrators are.

In the end, our study demonstrates that police officers, regardless of the rank, differentiate across different measures of police integrity. It also shows that rank matters. While the non-supervisor, first-line supervisor, and administrator views are more similar in their views about misconduct seriousness and recognition of behavior as rule violating (the first dimension of the theory), their views tend to diverge more about the views about appropriate and expected discipline (the second dimension of the theory) and, particularly, in their expressed willingness to report (the third dimension of the theory). Our study has empirically shown the existence of three distinct but partly overlapping police cultures of integrity: the non-supervisor culture, the first-line supervisor culture, and the administrator culture. The results of our analyses clearly demonstrate the need to include a more complex differentiation of the respondents' rank and supervisory status into future studies.

References

Bidney, D. (1944). On the concept of culture and some cultural fallacies. *American Anthropologist, 46*(1), 30–44.

Britz, M. T. (1997). The police subculture and occupational socialization: Exploring individual and demographic characteristics. *American Journal of Criminal Justice, 21*(2), 127–146.

Bucak, S. (2012). *An examination of police cynicism in turkey and its impacts on officers' perception of corruption.* (Order No. 3558466, University of Illinois at Chicago). *ProQuest Dissertations and Theses,* 214. Retrieved from http://ezproxy.msu.edu/login?url=http://search.proquest.com/docview/13436 88917?accountid=12598. (1343688917).

Bureau of Justice Statistics (2011). Census of State and Local Law Enforcement Agencies, 2008. Washington, DC: US Department of Justice. Retrieved from: http://www.bjs.gov/content/pub/pdf/csllea08.pdf.

Chan, J. B. L. (1997). *Changing police culture: Policing in a multicultural society.* Cambridge: Cambridge University Press.

Crank, J. (2014). *Understanding police culture* (2nd ed.). London: Routledge.

Haarr, R. H. (1997). Patterns of integration in a police patrol bureau: Race and gender barriers to integrate. *Justice Quarterly, 14*(1), 53–85.

Haberfeld, M. R. (2013). *Critical issues in police training* (3rd ed.). Upper Saddle River, NJ: Pearson Custom.

Haberfeld, M. R., Lieberman, C. A., & Horning, A. (2018). *Introduction to policing: The pillar of democracy* (2nd ed.). Durham, NC: Carolina Academic.

Herbert, S. (1998). Police subculture reconsidered. *Criminology, 36*(2), 343–369.

Hickman, M. J, Piquero, A. R., Powell, Z. A., & Greene, J. (2016). Expanding the measurement of police integrity. *Policing: An International Journal of Police Strategies & Management, 39*(2), 246–267.

Ingram, J. R., & Terrill, W. (2014). Relational demography and officer occupational attitudes: The influence of workgroup context. *Journal of Criminal Justice, 42,* 309–320.

Kargin, V. (2009). *An investigation of factors proposed to influence police officers' peer reporting intentions.* *ProQuest Dissertations and Theses.* Retrieved from http://ezproxy.msu.edu/login?url=http://search.proquest.com/docview/305066516?accountid=12598. (305066516).

Klockars, C. B., Kutnjak Ivković, S., Harver, W. E., & Haberfeld M. R. (1997). The Measurement of Police Integrity. Final Report Submitted to the U.S. Department of Justice, Office of Justice Programs, National Institute of Justice.

Klockars, C. B., Kutnjak Ivković, S., Harver, W. E., & Haberfeld, M. R. (2000). *The Measurement of Police Integrity.* Research in brief. U.S. Department of Justice, Office of Justice Programs, National Institute of Justice. Washington, DC: Government Printing Office.

Klockars, C. B., Kutnjak Ivković S. (2004). Measuring Police Integrity. In Piquero, A. R., Greene, J.R., & M. J. Hickman (Eds.). Police Integrity and Ethics. Wadsworth Publishing. (pp. 1.3–1.20).

Klockars, C. B., Kutnjak Ivković, S., & Haberfeld, M. R. (Eds.). (2004). *The contours of police integrity.* Newbury Park, CA: Sage.

Klockars, C. B., Kutnjak Ivković, S., & Haberfeld, M. R. (2006). *Enhancing police integrity.* Dordrecht: Springer.

Kremer, F. (2000). Comparing supervisor and line officer opinions about the code of silence: The case of Hungary. In M. Pagon (Ed.), *Policing in Central and Eastern Europe: Ethics, integrity, and human rights* (pp. 211–219). Ljubljana: College of Police and Security Studies.

Kroeber, A. L. (1917). The superorganic. *American Anthropologist, 19*(2), 163–213.

Kucukuysal, B. (2008). *Determinants of Turkish police officers' perception of integrity: Impact of organizational culture* (Doctoral dissertation, University of Central Florida Orlando, Florida).

Kutnjak Ivković, S. (2004). Sharing the view: Line officer and supervisor evaluations of police corruption seriousness in Bosnia and Herzegovina. In G. Mesko, M. Pagon, & G. Dobovsek (Eds.), *Dilemmas of contemporary criminal justice* (pp. 312–322). Ljubljana: Faculty of Criminal Justice, University of Maribor.

Kutnjak Ivković, S. (2015). Studying police integrity. In S. Kutnjak Ivković & M. Haberfeld (Eds.), *Police integrity across the world*. New York: Springer.

Kutnjak Ivković, S., & Haberfeld, M. R. (Eds.). (2015). *Police integrity across the world*. New York: Springer.

Kutnjak Ivković, S., & Klockars, C. B. (2000). Comparing police supervisor and line officer opinions about the code of silence: The case of Croatia. In M. Pagon (Ed.), *Policing in central and Eastern Europe: Ethics, integrity, and human rights* (pp. 183–195). Ljubljana: College of Police and Security Studies.

Kutnjak Ivković, S., & Shelley, T. O. (2010). The code of silence and disciplinary fairness: A comparison of Czech police supervisor and line officer views. *Policing: An International Journal of Police Strategies and Management, 33*(3), 548–574.

Kutnjak Ivković, S., & Shelley, T. O. (2008). The police code of silence and different paths toward democratic policing. *Policing and Society, 18*(4), 445–473.

Kutnjak Ivković, S., Haberfeld, M., & Peacock, R. (2016). Does discipline fairness matter for the police code of silence? Answers from the U.S. supervisors and line officers. *Policing: An International Journal of Police Strategies and Management, 39*(2), 354–369.

Kutnjak Ivković, S., Haberfeld, M., & Peacock, R. (2018). Decoding the code of silence. *Criminal Justice Policy Review, 29*(2), 172–189.

Larwood, L., & Whittaker, W. (1977). Managerial myopia: Self-serving bias in organizational planning. *Journal of Applied Psychology, 62*, 194–198.

Lee, H., Lim, H., Moore, D. D., & Kim, J. (2013). How police organizational structure correlates with frontline officers' attitudes toward corruption: A multilevel model. *Police Practice and Research, 14*(5), 386–401.

Lim, H., & Sloan, J. J. (2016). Police officer integrity: A partial replication and extension. *Policing: An International Journal of Police Strategies and Management, 39*(2), 284–301.

Loftus, B. (2010). Police occupational culture: Classic themes, altered times. *Policing and Society, 20*(1), 1–20.

Long, M., Cross, J. E., Shelley, T. O., & Kutnjak Ivković, S. (2013). The normative order of reporting police misconduct: Examining the roles of offense seriousness, legitimacy, and fairness. *Social Psychology Quarterly, 76*(3), 242–267.

Manning, P. (1989). Occupational culture. In W. G. Bailey (Ed.), *The encyclopedia of police science*. New York: Garland.

Manning, P. K. (1997). Police work: The social organization of police work. Prospect Heights, IL: Waveland. Press, Inc.

Manfreda, K. L, Bosnjak, M., Berzelak, J., Haas, I., & Vehovar V. (2008). Web Surveys versus other Survey Modes: A Meta-Analysis Comparing Response Rates. *International Journal of Market Research, 50*(1), 79–104.

Marche, G. E. (2009). Integrity, culture, and scale: An empirical test of the big bad police agency. *Crime, Law and Social Change, 51*, 463–486.

Mayhall, P., Barker, T., & Hunter, R. D. (1995). *Police-community relations and the administration* (3rd ed.). Englewood Cliff, NJ: Prentice Hall.

Micucci, A. J., & Gomme, I. M. (2005). American police and subcultural support for the use of excessive force. *Journal of Criminal Justice 33*: 487–500.

Niederhoffer, A. (1967). *Behind the shield*. Garden City, NY: Anchor Books.

Pagon, M., & Lobnikar, B. (2000). Comparing supervisor and line officer opinions about the code of silence: The case of Slovenia. In M. Pagon (Ed.), *Policing in Central and Eastern Europe: Ethics, integrity, and human rights* (pp. 197–209). Ljubljana: College of Police and Security Studies.

Paoline, E. A. (2001). *Rethinking police culture: Officers' occupational attitudes*. New York: LFB Scholarly.

Paoline, E. A., & Terrill, W. (2014). *Police culture: Adapting to the strains of the job*. Durham, NC: Carolina Academic.

Paoline, E. A., Myers, S. M., & Worden, R. E. (2000). Police culture, individualism, and community policing: Evidence from two police departments. *Justice Quarterly, 17*(3), 575–605.

Porter, L. E., & Prenzler, T. (2016). The code of silence and ethical perceptions: Exploring police officer unwillingness to report misconduct. *Policing: An International Journal of Police Strategies and Management, 39*(2), 370–386.

Poteyeva, M., & Sun, I. Y. (2009). Gender differences in police officers' attitudes: Assessing current empirical evidence. *Journal of Criminal Justice, 37*, 512–522.

Raines, J. (2010). *Ethics in policing: Misconduct and integrity*. Burlington, MA: Jones & Bartlett Learning.

Reuss-Ianni, E., & Ianni, F. A. (1983). *Street cops and management cops: The two cultures of policing*. New York, NY: Transaction Publishers.

Reuss-Ianni, E. (1983). Two cultures of policing. New Brunswick, NJ:Transaction Books.

Rothwell, G. R., & Baldwin, J. N. (2006). Ethical climates and contextual predictors of whistle-blowing. *Review of Public Personnel Administration, 26*(3), 216–244.

Rothwell, G. R., & Baldwin, J. N. (2007a). Whistle-blowing and the code of silence in police agencies policy and structural predictors. *Crime & Delinquency, 53*(4), 605–632.

Rothwell, G. R., & Baldwin, J. N. (2007b). Ethical climate theory, whistle-blowing, and the code of silence in police agencies in the state of Georgia. *Journal of Business Ethics, 70*(4), 341–361.

Shih, T. H., Fan X. (2008). Comparing Response Rates from Web and Mail Surveys: A Meta-Analysis. *Field Methods, 20*(3), 249–271.

Silver, J. R., Roche, S. P., Bilach, T. J., & Bontrager Ryon, S. (2017). Traditional police culture, use of force, and procedural justice: Investigating individual, organizational, and contextual factors. *Justice Quarterly, 34*(7), 1272–1309.

Sklansky, D. A. (2007). Seeing blue: Police reform, occupational culture, and cognitive burn-in. In M. O'Neill

& M. Marks (Eds.), *Police occupational culture: New debates and directions*. Amsterdam: Elsevier Science.

Skolnick, J. (1994). *Justice without trial*. New York: Macmillan.

Skolnick, J., & Fyfe, J. (1993). *Above the law: Police and the excessive use of force*. New York: The Free Press.

Svenson, O. (1981). Are we all less risky and more skillful than our fellow drivers? *Acta Psychologica, 94*, 143–148.

Terrill, W., Paoline, E. A., III, & Manning, P. K. (2003). Police culture and coercion. *Criminology, 41*(4), 1003–1034.

Waddington, P. A. (1999). Police (canteen) sub-culture. An appreciation. *British Journal of Criminology, 39*(2), 287–309.

Walker, S., & Katz, C. M. (2011). *The police in America: An introduction*. New York: McGraw Hill.

Weinstein, N. D. (1980). Unrealistic optimism about future life events. *Journal of Personality and Social Psychology, 39*, 806–820.

Westley, W. A. (1970). *Violence and the police*. Cambridge, MA: MIT Press.

Yun, I. (2003). *A study of police officers' perceptions of police deviance: From an occupational socialization perspective. ProQuest Dissertations and Theses*, 89 p. Retrieved from http://ezproxy.msu.edu/login?url=http://search.proquest.com/docview/305329643?accountid=12598. (305329643).

Exploring Differences in Police Integrity Within a Centralized Police System

Aleksandr Khechumyan and Sanja Kutnjak Ivković

Introduction

Police integrity is defined as "the normative inclination among police to resist temptations to abuse the rights and privileges of their occupation" (Klockars et al. 2006, p. 1). Systematic empirical exploration of police integrity was sparked by the development of the theory of police integrity and its accompanying methodology (Klockars and Kutnjak Ivković 2004; Klockars et al. 1997). Scholars studied police integrity both in general (for an overview, see Kutnjak Ivković 2015) and with a focus on specific topics such as perceptions of seriousness (e.g., Klockars et al. 2004; Klockars and Kutnjak Ivković 1999; Kutnjak Ivković et al. 2004, 2005; Kutnjak Ivković et al. 2016a; Yun 2003), the code of silence (e.g., Hickman et al. 2016; Kremer 2000; Kutnjak Ivković et al. 2016c, 2017; Kutnjak Ivković and Shelley 2010; Kutnjak Ivković and Sauerman 2012; Lim and Sloan 2016; Pagon and Lobnikar 2000;

A. Khechumyan (✉)
Max Planck Institute for Foreign and International Criminal Law, Freiburg im Breisgau, Germany

S. Kutnjak Ivković
Michigan State University School of Criminal Justice, East Lansing, MI, USA
e-mail: kutnjak@msu.edu

Rothwell and Baldwin 2007), or discipline and disciplinary fairness (e.g., Kutnjak Ivković and Klockars 1998; Kutnjak Ivković et al. 2016b; Kutnjak Ivković and Shelley 2010).

Most of the extant research focused on the exploration of police integrity in a single country (see Kutnjak Ivković 2015). Among such studies, very few have explored potential differences *within* the country. In decentralized systems, in which multiple police agencies create and enforce their own official rules, extant research detected varying levels of police integrity across the surveyed agencies (e.g., Klockars et al. 1997, 2006, 2013). On the other hand, studies have just begun to investigate potential cross-agency differences in the way rules have been understood and applied in centralized police systems, in which the official rules and their enforcement *should* be applied consistently across all subunits (e.g., Kutnjak Ivković and Khechumyan 2014; Kutnjak Ivković et al. 2016a; Yun 2003).

This chapter explores potential differences in the contours of police integrity across a centralized police system. It moves beyond focusing on a single concept (e.g., seriousness, the code of silence) and engages in a multi-concept exploration of police integrity. Its main line of inquiry is the degree to which centralized systems, such as the Armenian police, were able to create uniform levels of police integrity across the parts of large system.

© Springer Nature Switzerland AG 2019
S. Kutnjak Ivković, M. R. Haberfeld (eds.), *Exploring Police Integrity*,
https://doi.org/10.1007/978-3-030-29065-8_3

Theory of Police Integrity and Centralized Police Systems

The theory of police integrity (see e.g., Klockars and Kutnjak Ivković 2004; Klockars et al. 1997) seeks to explain the factors critical for the development and maintenance of high integrity of the police. The key tenants of the theory (see, e.g., Klockars and Kutnjak Ivković 2004; Klockars et al. 1997, 2006; Kutnjak Ivković 2015) are explained through the four dimensions.

The first dimension focuses on the organizational rules and the way they are made and communicated to the police officers (see, e.g., Klockars and Kutnjak Ivković 2004; Klockars et al. 1997, 2006; Kutnjak Ivković 2015). The theory states that police officers in agencies of high integrity should know and support the official rules. These official rules could include constitutional norms, various laws (both procedural and substantive), as well as internal agency rules (Kutnjak Ivković 2015, p. 5).

In decentralized police systems—systems with multiple agencies and multiple centers of control —the basic legal documents, such as the constitution or criminal code, may apply equally to every agency, but each agency is also authorized to make its own set of internal administrative rules (Kutnjak Ivković 2015, p. 5). To complicate matters further, countries may have more than one layer of government, thus creating additional rules applicable to only certain subsets of police agencies. Thus, official rules could be quite different across police agencies within a decentralized system.

Indeed, empirical studies tapping into the police officers' knowledge of official rules and perceived seriousness of police misconduct show a substantial degree of heterogeneity across police agencies within the heavily decentralized U.S. system (e.g., Chappell and Piquero 2004; Greene et al. 2004; Hickman 2005; Klockars et al. 2000, 2006; Marche 2009; McDevitt et al. 2011; Schafer and Martinelli 2008; Vito et al. 2011). The first indications of this diversity were found in the 30-agency study (Klockars et al. 2000, 2004), in which the authors were able to rank police agencies based on the police officers'

perceptions of misconduct seriousness. Whereas differences across some agencies (e.g., Agency 2 and Agency 23) were quite large (Klockars et al. 2000), there were also substantial similarities in perceptions of seriousness for some scenarios and some agencies.

Decentralized police systems are not only housed within federations, but also within their constituent states, in which the same constitutional norms and laws should apply to all agencies. In such systems, local governments create second-level legal documents such as ordinances. With a few exceptions, a comparison of integrity levels across three types of police agencies within the same country (South Africa), yielded no statistical differences in the respondents' knowledge of official rules across agency types (Kutnjak Ivković and Sauerman 2016). Similarly, Kutnjak Ivković and Sauerman (2016) mostly found there was an absence of extensive differences in the respondents' perceptions of seriousness.

In countries with centralized police systems, not only are the constitutional norms and laws applicable to all police agencies, but the internal agency rules, created at the headquarters, are applicable to all police agencies in the system. In such centralized police systems, individual police agencies have little or no control over the content of official rules. In reality, as centralized police systems could be quite large, both in terms of the number of sworn officers and the size of the territory they are covering, the ways the police officers understand the rules and police administrators apply them in different parts of the country could be quite divergent.

To date, very few studies of police integrity explored variations within centralized systems. Yun (2003) compared the perceptions of seriousness between an urban police agency and a rural police agency in South Korea. In the overwhelming majority of the scenarios, Yun (2003) found no statistically significant differences in the perceptions of seriousness between the respondents from these two agencies. Similarly, in the 2008–2009 Armenian study, Kutnjak Ivković and Khechumyan (2014) found very few differences in the respondents' familiarity with official rules and their perceptions of misconduct seriousness across two police agencies serving different types of communities. In other words, the authors found more similarities than differences across these two police agencies. In a recent study, Kutnjak Ivković et al. (2016a) also found mostly similarities in the perceptions of seriousness. The few differences were largely driven by the finding that officers working in smaller rural areas perceived misconduct as more serious than officers in larger urban agencies did (Kutnjak Ivković et al. 2016a).

The second dimension focuses on the various techniques police agencies use to detect and investigate police misconduct and determine discipline (see, e.g., Klockars and Kutnjak Ivković 2004; Klockars et al. 1997, 2006; Kutnjak Ivković 2015). The theory proposes that the police agency of high integrity relies on various mechanisms of detection and control and systematically disciplines police officers who engage in misconduct (Kutnjak Ivković 2015).

Just like the official agency rules differ across agencies in the countries with decentralized police systems, so could the investigations of misconduct and applications of discipline. There could be substantial variation across police agencies both in terms of the available disciplinary options and in terms of consistency of their application, thereby creating divergent disciplinary environments both in terms of harshness and consistency of discipline application.

Klockars and Kutnjak Ivković (2004) designed the "common" disciplinary scale for their U.S. survey. The empirical application of the questionnaire on 30 U.S. police agencies uncovered substantial differences in the expected discipline police agencies would mete out. A comparison of the two agencies on the opposite ends of integrity continuum suggested that these agencies have created quite divergent disciplinary environments, particularly with respect to the most serious forms of corruption (Klockars et al. 2000). The qualitative work performed in three of the surveyed police agencies, perceived and shown to be of high integrity, further revealed that disciplinary environments differ not only across police agencies from the opposite sides of the police integrity scale, but also across agencies on the

same, high end of the police integrity scale (Klockars et al. 2006).

Subsequent U.S. studies in other agencies further contributed toward the understanding that disciplinary environments could be quite different (Chappell and Piquero 2004; Greene et al. 2004; Hickman 2005; Kutnjak Ivković et al. 2013). A study of potential differences across agency types in South Africa (Kutnjak Ivković and Sauerman 2016) indicates that, of all the measures of police integrity, perceptions of disciplinary environments exhibited the most variation across agency types. In other words, while knowledge of official rules, evaluations of discipline seriousness, as well as willingness to report misconduct are quite similar across agency types, different agency types seem to create different disciplinary environments.

The potential for creating different disciplinary environments has been noted in the studies of centralized police systems as well. In the 2008–2009 Armenian study—the only study of centralized systems exploring the issue of discipline— Kutnjak Ivković and Khechumyan (2014) reported almost no differences in the respondents' perceptions of misconduct seriousness, their knowledge of official rules, and the code of silence. Yet, the authors (Kutnjak Ivković and Khechumyan 2014) noted that, "we did find the largest and most systematic differences in the perceptions of disciplinary environments (i.e., police officers' estimates of discipline their agency would mete out). In particular, police officers employed in the capital consistently reported that they expected a harsher discipline than the police officers employed in a regional police department did."

The third dimension of the theory focuses on the code of silence and the police efforts to curtail it (see, e.g., Klockars and Kutnjak Ivković 2004; Klockars et al. 1997, 2006; Kutnjak Ivković 2015). The theory proposes that the code of silence would neither be very strong nor would protect serious forms of misconduct in the police agencies of high integrity (Kutnjak Ivković 2015).

The initial U.S. study of police integrity (Klockars et al. 2000) explored potential agency differences in the extent of the code of silence and found substantial differences across two agencies on the opposite ends of integrity scale (Klockars et al. 2000, p. 8):

> In both agencies, few officers said that they or their police colleagues would report any of the least serious types of corrupt behavior ... Officers from Agency 2 reported that they and their colleagues would report the behavior described in the seven other cases. In Agency 23, however, there was no case that the majority of officers indicated they would report. In sum, while The Code is under control in Agency 2, it remains a powerful influence in Agency 23, providing an environment in which corrupt behavior can flourish.

Several studies performed comparisons of the code of silence within decentralized systems. Lim and Sloan (2016) explored the code of silence among police supervisors in Texas. They found that a "deviant climate" in the police agency is a stronger predictor of police officers' unwillingness to report than either individual-level characteristics or community-level characteristics. Similarly, Hickman and colleagues (2016) found that officer-level differences were irrelevant for the code of silence when compared with the district-level differences in respondents' willingness to report misconduct.

Empirical studies of the agency comparisons within centralized systems are rare. In the 2008–2009 study of Armenian police, Kutnjak Ivković and Khechumyan (2014) found statistically significant differences in the code of silence between the two agencies, one located in an urban setting and the other located in a rural setting, in about one-half of the scenarios. Without exception, the code of silence in the larger, urban police agency seems to have been much stronger than the code in the smaller, rural police agency. These differences were not only limited to the behaviors evaluated as the least serious, but were also present for some of the behaviors evaluated as the most serious (Kutnjak Ivković and Khechumyan 2014).

The fourth dimension of the theory emphasizes the importance of social, economic, and political conditions prevailing in society for the level of police integrity in a police agency (see, e.g., Klockars and Kutnjak Ivković 2004; Klockars et al. 1997, 2006; Kutnjak Ivković 2015). The theory proposes that society creates a culture intolerant of misconduct and reduces the extent of misconduct among its public service employees by developing, teaching, and enforcing the rules prohibiting misconduct (Kutnjak Ivković 2015).

Comparative studies of police integrity (e.g., Klockars et al. 2004; Kutnjak Ivković and Haberfeld 2015) demonstrate that various measures of police integrity exhibit substantial variation across countries. In fact, there seems to be a strong and positive relation between the country's score on the police integrity questionnaire and the country's ranking on the Transparency International Corruption Perceptions Index (Kutnjak Ivković 2015). However, no study to date has explored empirically how closely connected police integrity is with various country-related factors.

Studies of police integrity in decentralized countries indicate that police agencies in such systems create different levels of integrity (e.g., Klockars et al. 2000, 2006). However, exploration of the relation between policy integrity and societal factors remains a rare pursuit. In their book "Enhancing Police Integrity," Klockars et al. (2006) examine the political and social effects on the level of police integrity in St. Petersburg, Florida, Charleston, South Carolina, and Charlotte-Mecklenburg, North Carolina. These influences ranged from the enactment of the Sunshine Laws in Florida, to the existence of a citizen review board in Charlotte-Mecklenburg, and the influence of the tourist industry in Charleston.

Existing studies on police integrity in centralized countries (Kutnjak Ivković and Khechumyan 2014; Yun 2003) sought to detect any potential differences across police agencies, but they have rarely focused on the effects of social, political, or economic conditions on police integrity from different parts of the country. Kutnjak Ivković et al. (2016a) designed a project to explore the role that community characteristics play on the contours of police integrity across police administrations from different parts of the country. They used the community characteristics and the police classification based on local conditions to compare evaluations of misconduct seriousness across different police administrations within the centralized Croatian police system (Kutnjak Ivković et al. 2016a). The results showed that, upon controlling for organizational characteristics, community characteristics were independent predictors of the respondents' assessments of misconduct seriousness in only a few scenarios (Kutnjak Ivković et al. 2016a).

Armenia and Police Integrity

Upon adopting the Declaration of Independence from the former USSR in 1990, Armenia has initiated a transition toward becoming a Western-style democracy (The Supreme Council of the ASSR 1990). The independence from the USSR came with the change in the power structure as well. The communist party, which dominated and controlled the country for decades, lost its grip on power in 1990. Eventually, many experienced police officers, particularly in supervisory positions, who were members of the communist party were replaced by the new police officers who were strong supports of the newly established government. The replacements were often more experienced in guerilla fighting than in policing. At the time, the Ministry of Internal Affairs and the Militiya, headed by Vano Siradeghyan, had virtually unlimited powers and lacked accountability (Avagyan and Hiscock 2005).

Bayley (2006) argued that the process of democratization of a country also includes democratization of its police. Although the process of transition from authoritarianism to democracy in Armenia has been ongoing since the early 1990s, the police had not experienced any major democratization processes until the end of the 20th century. As a result of the new Law on Police (2001) and the Law on Police Service (2002), in 2003 the police were established as a new and independent governmental agency (Police of the Republic of Armenia 2013) concerned with providing protection of life and property, as well as assisting individuals and organizations in protecting their rights and legitimate interests.

The Armenian police are a centralized and hierarchical organization. The head of the organization is the Police Chief (The Law on Police 2001, Article 9; The Law on Police Service 2002, Article 13). The police have 21 subunits (Police of the Republic of Armenia 2014). The organization of the police follows the territorial organization of the country: each of the ten regions has a special provincial police agency. In addition, Yerevan, the capital city, constitutes a separate administrative entity with a separate police agency. These provincial departments are further subdivided into 52 local police stations (Police of the Republic of Armenia 2014), where majority of everyday regular police work is performed.

Organizational Rules

According to the Law on Police Service (2002), the rights and duties of the police are regulated at the nationwide level by several key pieces of legislation. Some of them are fundamental legal documents, such as the Armenian Constitution, while others are nationwide laws regulating the police work exclusively, such as the Law on Police Service and the Law on Police (2001), or regulating the operation of the criminal justice system in general, such as Code of Criminal Procedures (1998) and the Criminal Code (2003). All of these laws should apply to every police agency and every police officer in the country.

The laws create the legal basis for the development of a democratic police agency. In addition to defining the police, the Law on Police (2001) establishes police responsibilities. In fact, it explicitly prohibits the use of torture, inhumane or degrading treatment, or other forms of violence by the police (2001, Article 5). Similarly, the Criminal Code (2003) contains a special section defining crimes committed in the official capacity. Furthermore, the Code of Criminal Procedures (1998) imposes additional boundaries on police work as it regulates the police role, responsibilities, and functions during criminal investigation (Articles 27, 57), thus developing basic rules for the protection of constitutional rights and liberties of defendants during criminal investigation.

By 2003, the majority of the key legal statutes regulating police work have been enacted. In 2008–2009—5 years after the enactment of the laws—Kutnjak Ivković and Khechumyan (2013, 2014) explored police officers' familiarity with legal rules. A sample of police officers was asked to review ten examples of police corruption and one example of the use of excessive force and assess whether they constitute violations of official rules. A strong majority of surveyed police officers had no problems recognizing all these behaviors as examples of rule violations (Kutnjak Ivković and Khechumyan 2013). At the same time, the respondents had an easier time recognizing very serious forms of police corruption, such as the acceptance of a bribe and an opportunistic theft, than less serious forms of police corruption, such as the corruption of authority and internal corruption.

In 2013—10 years after the enactment of the official rules—Khechumyan and Kutnjak Ivković (2015) performed another sweep of the survey. They reported that police officers in their nationwide sample had no problems recognizing as rule-violating most of the forms of police misconduct, including police corruption, use of excessive force, falsifying official documents, and planting evidence. Among the behaviors least likely to be recognized as rule-violating was corruption of authority, internal corruption, and failing to stop a beating (Khechumyan and Kutnjak Ivković 2015, p. 52).

Detection and Investigation of Police Misconduct

The official rules established in the 2000s have set the ground rules by both defining what police misconduct is and outlining the procedure of determining police officers' responsibility. To begin, the Police Law (2001, Article 43) sets the legal basis for police officers to be found liable if they intentionally abuse their office or if they fail to fulfill their responsibilities. Similarly, the Police Disciplinary Code (2005, Article 5.1) requires that police officers fulfill their responsibilities prescribed by the laws and other legal

directives. In addition, the Police Disciplinary Code (2005, Article 10) contains rules of ethics, such as respect for human rights and prohibition of financial political support. Finally, the Law on Police Service (2002, Article 42) explicitly prohibits police misconduct, such as the acceptance of kickback and being under the influence of alcohol while on duty.

Legal rules also differentiate between internal disciplinary procedures and criminal investigation (Police Disciplinary Code 2005, Article 8). An internal procedure could be initiated based on the information coming from the citizens and organizations, as well as supervisors and media (Police Disciplinary Code 2005, Article 18). It can be performed by a special unit or by the police officer's chain of command (Police Disciplinary Code 2005). If the case involves a potentially serious violation of official rules, the evidence is reviewed by the Police Disciplinary Committee, composed of police officers and citizens (Police Disciplinary Code 2005, Article 43.1). Once the supervisors or the Police Disciplinary Committee determine that a police officer had violated the rules, a disciplinary recommendation is made to the Chief of Police, who reaches the final decision about discipline (Police Disciplinary Code 2005, Article 8). Discipline can range from reprimand to dismissal.

For a long time, despite the legal norms guaranteeing public access to information about public services, the number of police officers disciplined each year has not been publicly available (see Transparency International 2003). In 2010, OSCE published that, in the period between 2006 and 2009, there were fewer than 300 complaints per year (OSCE 2010), and that the numbers *decreased* over time. Eventually, 167 officers were fired and 625 officers received some other discipline (OSCE 2010). In the 2010s, the police started to provide information about the outcomes of police disciplinary procedures performed by the Internal Security Department (the investigations performed by the chain of command are not included in the online publications). In general, the numbers posted by the police suggest a much higher rate of investigations and discipline. In 2012, administrative investigations were conducted in 571 cases, resulting in disciplinary actions concerning 175 officers (Internal Security Department 2013), out of which about one-quarter were dismissed. At the same time, the most frequently applied disciplinary sanction was the most lenient discipline: reprimand (Internal Security Department 2014).

In the 2008–2009 police integrity survey, Kutnjak Ivković and Khechumyan (2013) found that, out of 11 scenarios primarily describing police corruption, the respondents expected to be dismissed in only two scenarios. As for the remaining scenarios, the respondents expected either no discipline at all or only the least severe discipline legally possible (i.e., reprimand). The 2013 police integrity survey (Khechumyan and Kutnjak Ivković 2015) revealed very similar results. Although the questionnaire included a greater variety of forms of police misconduct, the respondents expected dismissal in only three out of 11 scenarios (Khechumyan and Kutnjak Ivković 2015, p. 57). In accordance with the results of the first survey, the respondents expected either no discipline at all or only very mild discipline for the behaviors described in the majority of scenarios (Khechumyan and Kutnjak Ivković 2015).

The Code of Silence

Although it is broadly accepted that the code of silence exists in every police agency (see, e.g., Klockars et al. 2006), the extent of the code of silence among the police in Armenia has been unknown to date. An essential ingredient in striving to ascertain the extent of the code of silence is the enactment of legal rules that can be interpreted to imply that participating in the code is against the law (e.g., Khechumyan and Kutnjak Ivković 2015). In particular, the Police Disciplinary Code (2005) shares the responsibility of maintaining discipline between supervisors and line officers. If a police officer fails to assist supervisors in the maintenance of discipline, the officer could be investigated and eventually disciplined (Police Disciplinary Code 2005, Article 10). Participating in the code of silence could be

viewed as a failure to assist the supervisor in the maintenance of a disciplinary environment.

The first empirical study measuring the contours of the code, conducted in 2008–2009 (Kutnjak Ivković and Khechumyan 2013), detected the presence of a sturdy code of silence. It seems that the code would cover almost all behaviors described in the police corruption questionnaire (Kutnjak Ivković and Khechumyan 2013). The only behavior that was not as protected by the code was opportunistic theft (Kutnjak Ivković and Khechumyan 2013). The results of the second empirical study measuring the contours of the code, conducted in 2013 (Khechumyan and Kutnjak Ivković 2015), are similar. Although the code does not appear to be as sturdy as it had been reported in the first study, in almost one-half of the scenarios, the majority of the respondents indicated that they would not report the described misconduct (Khechumyan and Kutnjak Ivković 2015, p. 59).

Influence of Social and Political Environment

Although Armenia's government is seeking to implement reforms and democratize the country, NGOs and other international observers have consistently raised questions about the success of these reform efforts and the quality of democracy achieved as a result (e.g., U.S. Department of State 2012). Since independence, Armenia's transition toward democracy has been far from smooth, riddled with a war, economic collapse, banning of political parties, assassination of country's leadership, and disputed parliamentary and presidential elections (Freedom House 1998–2013). The Freedom House (2013) consistently evaluates Armenia as "partly free," thus indicating that the country is not able to guarantee full protection of civil and political rights (Freedom House 1998–2013).

The police are perceived as serving the government and oppressing the opponents of the regime (e.g., Transparency International 2003, p. 40). The NGOs and European institutions claim that the human rights violations are occurring on a regular basis (e.g., Freedom House 2013; Council of Europe 2004, 2007, 2011, 2012). Freedom House (2013) reported that the police are viewed as using excessive force not only to carry out arrests, but also to extract confessions. Similarly, the Council of Europe (2004, 2007, 2011, 2012) cites the European Committee for Prevention of Torture and Inhuman or Degrading Treatment's reports that document large-scale use of excessive force on detainees in police custody. Such findings correlate strongly with the reports by the Armenian Ombudsman (2012).

Corruption and the lack of determination to address it in a systematic way are perceived as serious challenges (e.g., Freedom House 2010; UN Human Rights Committee 2012). Bribery and other forms of corruption seem to be widespread among different elements of the criminal justice system, including the judiciary (Ombudsman 2013) and the police (Council of Europe 2011). The European Committee for Prevention of Torture and Inhuman or Degrading Treatment (Council of Europe 2011) reports that police officers request payments for detainees in their custody to obtain special privileges or in exchange for the detainees' release. The UN Human Rights Committee (2012, para. 22) noted its concern "at the lack of convincing results in the fight against high-level corruption and the resulting lack of public trust in the administration of justice."

Public views and views of the experts about the corruption are aligned with these NGO reports. Armenia's ranking on the Transparency International Corruption Perceptions Index, based on both public and expert views on corruption, has remained relatively low. Between 2003 and 2012, Armenia received a score of about 2.5–3 on a 10-point scale, suggesting widespread corruption in the country (Transparency International 2011, 2012). Once Transparency International changed the ranking system, Armenia's score remained very similar (36 out of 100), still suggesting extensive corruption (Transparency International 2014b). The Global Corruption Barometer revealed in 2014 that 66% of the participants in its Armenian survey thought that the police are corrupt or extremely corrupt (Transparency International 2014a). Furthermore, about one-quarter of the respondents reported paying a bribe to the police (Transparency International 2014b). In the end, the majority of the respondents also evaluated the governmental actions against corruption as ineffective (Transparency International 2011).

Methodology

Questionnaire

To measure the levels of police integrity, we used the police integrity questionnaire developed by Klockars et al. (2006). A cover letter preceeds the questionnaire, instructing the respondents to assume that the officer described in the questionnaire had been a police officer for 5 years, had a satisfactory employment record, and had not been disciplined in the past. The questionnaire is completed anonymously: the respondents are asked not to write their name or other identifying information on the questionnaire and, to prevent potential identification of the respondents, the number of questions regarding demographic information is kept at the absolute minimum.

The first police integrity questionnaire (Klockars and Kutnjak Ivković 2004; Klockars et al. 2004) almost exclusively focused on police corruption. The second police integrity questionnaire (Klockars et al. 2006)—used in this study—includes several different forms of police misconduct. These forms range from police corruption and use of excessive force to planting of evidence and falsifying official records.

Although the police integrity questionnaire works well in cross-cultural applications (Kutnjak Ivković and Haberfeld 2015), descriptions of police misconduct included in the questionnaire have to be adjusted to fit the local conditions. While most of the scenarios worked well in Armenia, Scenario 7 (Verbal Abuse "Arrest Asshole Day"), scenario describing a traffic stop during which a police officer verbally abuses the driver, created problems. At the outset, regular police are not in charge of regulating traffic and controlling safety on the roads. Rather, these responsibilities are entrusted to specialized police agencies—the traffic police. Because our sampling strategy included regular police only, we had to adjust this scenario to make it applicable to regular police. In searching for a close substitute, we exploited the fact that regular police may be assigned to patrol demonstrations and rallies, during which shouting, verbal exchanges, and clashes with protesters are quite possible. Hence, we reworded Scenario 7 so that it focuses on the verbal abuse of young activists, instead of the verbal abuse of a motorist.

After the respondents read the description of each hypothetical scenario, they are asked to answer the same seven questions. These questions explore the respondents' perceptions of misconduct seriousness, their knowledge of the official rules, their views about the appropriate and expected discipline, and their support for the code of silence. With the exception of discipline questions, all other questions rely on a five-point Likert scale. The two questions about discipline need to be adjusted to the legal rules in each country. To maintain consistency across countries to the highest degree possible, although intermediate disciplinary options may vary from country to country, disciplinary scales in each country start with "no discipline" and end with "dismissal." According to the Law on Police Service (2002), a police officer engaging in police misconduct anywhere in Armenia can be disciplined with a range of disciplinary options, from "reprimand," "severe reprimand," "salary reduction," "incompatibility with the occupied position," "demotion to one step lower position," "demotion to one step lower rank," to "dismissal." We merely added "no discipline" at the beginning and created the 8-item Likert scale for the questions about the appropriate and expected discipline.

Upon answering questions concerning 11 hypothetical scenarios, the respondents completed only a very limited number of demographic questions. Because our goal was to execute an anonymous survey, the questionnaire feature only a few demographic questions. These questions inquired about the length of the respondents' police experience, rank, assignment, and supervisory position. While the questions about the

length and supervisory position are left in their original form, consistent across all countries, we adjusted the questions about rank and assignment to fit the Armenian framework. We also included a question about respondents' gender.

The Sample

The Armenian police are a centralized police agency, composed of 21 specialized departments, Yerevan City Department, and ten provincial departments (Police of the Republic of Armenia 2014). The nature of the police integrity survey is such that it contains descriptions of the behaviors typical for uniformed police officers patrolling the beat. Because we wanted the respondents to evaluate the behaviors they could plausibly encounter in the course of carrying out their everyday duties, the sampling frame was limited to regular police; we purposely excluded specialized police agencies and administrative bodies that do not have direct supervisory control over officers patrolling the beats.

The ten provincial departments and the Yerevan City Department are in charge and control the operation of smaller administrative units underneath them, such as local police stations (2001, Article 9). To capture views of police officers from different parts of the country, our sampling frame included all provincial departments and the Yerevan city Department.[1] In a manner characteristic of the overall level of governmental transparency, the overall number of police officers in Armenia is classified information, as is the information concerning the numbers of police officers employed in provincial departments and the Yerevan City Department.

During the summer of 2013, the police administration granted us access to police officers patrolling the beat in 9 out of 10 provincial departments and in the Yerevan City Department. About 1,000 police officers agreed to participate in the study and 969 have returned filled out questionnaires (response rate 97%). Our overall

---

[1] For technical reasons, one of the ten provincial departments could not be included in the study.

Table 1 Basic Socio-Economic Indicators by Region (Early 2016)

Region	Agency 8	Agency 9	Agency 10
Geographic location in the country	Northwest	North	West
Proportion of the country's territory	9%	12%	0.7%
Population (absolute numbers)	243,200	225,000	1,073,700
Population (proportion in the country's residents)	8.1%	7.5%	35.8%
Percent of urban population in the region	58.4%	52.1%	n/a
Crime rate per 100,000 residents	4.1	5.1	7.8
Leading branches of economy	Agriculture; industry	Agriculture; industry	Service; retail trade; construction business; industry
Unemployment rate per 100,000 residents	0.830	0.798	1.183
The rate of families with poverty benefit per 100,000 residents	62.3	89.7	15.9
The rate of retired persons per 100,000 residents	168.2	200.4	157.3

Source: The Demographic Handbook of Armenia (2016)

sample of police officers is composed of police officers from all ten surveyed police agencies (Khechumyan and Kutnjak Ivković 2015). Because we strive to attain sufficient statistical power to assess potential differences in police integrity across police agencies within the same system, we focused on the responses we received from three police agencies (Agency 8, Agency 9, and Agency 10) with the largest numbers of respondents, discarding the remaining agencies because they each featured substantially smaller numbers of respondents.

The three regions in which the three agencies are located are somewhat heterogeneous in their characteristics (Table 1). Regions housing Agency 8 and Agency 9 each cover about 10% of Armenia's territory (Table 1), while the region housing Agency 10 covers only 1%. On the other hand, the region housing Agency 10 accounts for about one-third of the population, while the regions housing Agency 8 and Agency 9 each account for about 10% of the population (Table 1). Among the three regions, the region housing Agency 10 has the highest crime rate, highest unemployment rate, and the lowest rate of families in poverty (Table 1).

The overwhelming majority of the respondents from the three agencies are line officers (Table 2). There are no significant differences across the agencies in the percent of respondents performing supervisory roles (Table 2). On the other hand, the respondents from Agency 8 and Agency 9 tended to be somewhat more experienced than the respondents from Agency 10 were (Table 2); only about one-quarter of the respondents from Agency 8 and Agency 9 had 5 years of experience or fewer, while over one-third of the respondents from Agency 10 had 5 years of experience or fewer (Table 2). The percentage of respondents assigned to special operations and administrative jobs is rather similar across the three agencies in our sample; compared to the respondents from Agency 8 and Agency 9, respondents from Agency 10 tended to be somewhat more likely to be assigned to the position of neighborhood inspector and less likely to be assigned to patrol (Table 2). Finally, there are no statistically significant differences across the agencies in the proportion of female respondents (Table 2).

The last question in the questionnaire asked the respondents to state whether they have provided honest answers while filling out the questionnaire. Out of 576 respondents from all three agencies, 94.3% answered affirmatively. There are no statistically significant differences across the three agencies in the percent of respondents who stated that they answered truthfully (Table 2). In subsequent analyses, we excluded the responses from the respondents who stated that they had lied or had not responded to this question.

Table 2 Sample Characteristics by Agency

	Agency 8 (N = 99)	Agency 9 (N = 97)	Agency 10 (N = 426)	Chi-Square	Phi
Supervisory position				2.54	.066
No	86.6%	84.0%	89.6%		
Yes	13.4%	16.0%	10.4%		
Length of service				25.65**	.208**
Up to 5 years	23.5%	24.7%	38.9%		
6–10 years	18.4%	14.0%	19.2%		
11–15 years	23.5%	26.9%	15.7%		
16–20 years	13.3%	18.3%	16.2%		
Over 20 years	21.4%	16.1%	10.0%		
Type of assignment				27.73**	.216**
Patrol	18.6%	18.8%	6.5%		
Neighborhood Inspector	33.0%	42.7%	51.0%		
Special operations	39.2%	33.3%	33.1%		
Administrative	5.2%	2.1%	3.7%		
Other	4.1%	3.1%	5.7%		
Gender				5.74	.101
Male	91.6%	96.7%	88.7%		
Female	8.4%	3.3%	11.3%		
Reported telling truth				3.43	.077
No	3.2%	7.6%	5.9%		
Yes	96.8%	92.4%	94.1%		

$* p < .05; ** p < .01; *** p < .001$

Results

Knowledge of Organizational Rules and Assessment of Misconduct Seriousness

All 11 scenarios in the questionnaire describe violations of official rules. In addition, 6 out of 11 scenarios (Scenario 2: Fails to Arrest Friend with Warrant; Scenario 3: Theft of Knife from Crime Scene; Scenario 4: Unjustified Use of Deadly Force; Scenario 6: Officer Strikes a Prisoner who Hurt Partner; Scenario 9: Falls Report of Drug on Drug Dealer; Scenario 11: Sgt. Fails to Halt Beating) violate criminal law as well. To study the respondents' familiarity with the official rules, we asked the respondents to assess each of the scenarios and evaluate whether the behaviors they describe violate official rules using a 5-point Likert scale, ranging from 1 = "definitely not a violation" to 5 = "definitely a violation."

Respondents from all three agencies evaluated all scenarios as rule violations. Specifically, the mean values for every scenario are around or above 4 on a 5-point scale in which 5 is considered to be "definitely a violation" (Table 3). The overall picture emerging from the results is very clear: the respondents' level of familiarity with official rules was very similar across the three police agencies. There were statistically significant differences across the agencies in only one scenario (Table 3; Scenario 10: False Report on Drug Dealer). The subsequent Tukey post-hoc analysis revealed that the respondents from Agency 8 were more likely to evaluate falsifying the report as rule violation than the respondents from either Agency 9 or Agency 10 were.

There were also very pronounced similarities across the three agencies. For example, the respondents from all three agencies evaluated the same scenario as the least likely to be a violation of official rules (Scenario 8: Cover-Up of Police DUI Accident). Similarly, the respondents from

Table 3 Respondents' Assessment of Rule Violations by Police Agency

	Agency 8		Agency 9		Agency 10		
	Mean	Rank	Mean	Rank	Mean	Rank	F-test
Scenario 1—Free Meals, Gifts from Merchants	4.43	4	4.31	4	4.30	2	.41
Scenario 2—Fail to Arrest Friend with Warrant	4.64	9	4.52	8	4.51	7	.65
Scenario 3—Theft of Knife from Crime Scene	4.90	11	4.85	11	4.85	11	.32
Scenario 4—Unjustifiable Use of Deadly Force	4.48	6	4.23	2.5	4.36	4	1.10
Scenario 5—Supervisor: Holiday Off for Errands	4.52	7.5	4.59	9	4.63	10	.51
Scenario 6—Officer Strikes Prisoner Who Hurt Partner	4.38	3	4.23	2.5	4.43	5	1.12
Scenario 7—Verbal Abuse of Young Activists	4.44	5	4.44	6	4.55	8	.88
Scenario 8—Cover-Up of Police DUI Accident	3.92	1	4.04	1	3.78	1	1.22
Scenario 9—Auto-Body Shop 5% Kickback	4.52	7.5	4.48	7	4.44	6	.18
Scenario 10—False Report on Drug on Dealer	4.89	10	4.64	10	4.62	9	3.38*(1 v. 2; 1 v. 3 at $p < .10$)
Scenario 11—Sgt. Fails to Halt Beating	4.27	2	4.41	5	4.32	3	.310

$* p < .05$; $** p < .01$; $*** p < .001$
Spearman's rho: Agency 8 and Agency 9: .881***; Agency 8 and Agency 10: .838**; Agency 9 and Agency 10: .888***

all three agencies evaluated the same scenario (Scenario 8: Cover-Up of Police DUI Accident) as the most likely to be a violation of official rules (Table 3).

To assess relative measures of seriousness—the extent of perceived seriousness of each scenario in relation to the other scenarios in the questionnaire—we rank-ordered each agency's respondents' mean responses to all of the scenarios ("Rank" in Table 3) and correlated those rankings for each agency with the rankings from the other two agencies. Correlation coefficients—all above .800—show a very strong and positive correlation between the pairs of rankings (Table 3; Spearman's rho = .881 for Agency 8 and Agency 9; Spearman's rho = .838 for Agency 8 and Agency 10; Spearman's rho = .888 for Agency 9 and Agency 10).

A question in the questionnaire, accompanying each scenario, inquired about the respondents' own assessments of misconduct seriousness. While answering the question, the respondents could have selected an answer from a 5-point Likert scale, ranging from 1 = "not serious at all" to 5 = "very serious."

The respondents from the three agencies showed very clearly that there is a substantial degree of difference across the perceived seriousness of the scenarios. They evaluated the 11 scenarios to vary from the scenarios perceived as the least serious, such as Scenario 8 (Cover-Up of Police DUI) and Scenario 11 (Sgt. Fails to Halt Beating), to the scenarios perceived as the most serious, such as Scenario 3 (Theft of Knife from Crime Scene) and Scenario 10 (False Report on Drug on Dealer; Table 4).

There was a substantial degree of similarity in the respondents' evaluations of seriousness across the three agencies. In particular, in 9 out of 11 scenarios, there were no statistically significant differences across the three agencies in the respondents' evaluations of seriousness (Table 4). In other words, the respondents from the three police agencies provided very similar evaluations of seriousness in the overwhelming majority of scenarios in the questionnaire, indicating that the contours of police integrity seem to be very similar across the three agencies.

There were only two scenarios with statistically significant differences in the perceptions of seri-

Table 4 Respondents' Evaluation of Scenario Seriousness by Police Agency

	Agency 8		Agency 9		Agency 10		
	Mean	Rank	Mean	Rank	Mean	Rank	F-test
Scenario 1—Free Meals, Gifts from Merchants	4.01	4	4.01	4	4.14	4	.54
Scenario 2—Fail to Arrest Friend with Warrant	4.66	9	4.35	6	4.27	6	4.28* (1 v. 3)
Scenario 3—Theft of Knife from Crime Scene	4.90	11	4.88	11	4.81	11	1.10
Scenario 4—Unjustifiable Use of Deadly Force	4.36	6	4.00	2.5	4.08	3	2.02
Scenario 5—Supervisor: Holiday Off for Errands	4.51	8	4.42	8.5	4.57	9	.82
Scenario 6—Officer Strikes Prisoner Who Hurt Partner	4.07	5	4.06	5	4.20	5	.65
Scenario 7—Verbal Abuse of Young Activists	3.93	2	4.39	7	4.40	8	6.62** (1 v. 2; 1 v. 3)
Scenario 8—Cover-Up of Police DUI Accident	3.46	1	3.67	1	3.34	1	1.63
Scenario 9—Auto-Body Shop 5% Kickback	4.42	7	4.42	8.5	4.34	7	.27
Scenario 10—False Report on Drug on Dealer	4.81	10	4.54	10	4.60	10	2.23
Scenario 11—Sgt. Fails to Halt Beating	3.96	3	4.00	2.5	4.04	2	.13

$* p < .05$; $** p < .01$; $*** p < .001$

Spearman's rho: Agency 8 and Agency 9: .776**; Agency 8 and Agency 10: .745**; Agency 9 and Agency 10: .982***

ousness (Table 4). In the first scenario (Scenario 2: Fail to Arrest Friend with Warrant), respondents from Agency 8 evaluated failing to execute an arrest warrant on a friend to be more serious than respondents from Agency 10 (Table 4). On the other end, respondents from Agency 8 evaluated the scenarios describing a verbal assault of young activists (Scenario 7: Verbal Abuse of Young Activists) as less serious than respondents from either Agency 9 or Agency 10 (Table 4).

We also ranked the scenarios for each agency, starting from the scenarios with the lowest mean (i.e., perceived to be the least serious) to the scenarios with the largest mean (i.e., perceived to be the most serious; "Rank" in Table 4). This measure gives us a relative assessment of seriousness (i.e., how serious scenarios are compared to each other). We used bivariate correlation to assess the similarity of evaluations of seriousness across the three agencies. Spearman's correlation coefficients indicate a very strong correlation of the agency rankings (Spearman's rho for bivariate correlations across the agencies is above .740 and is statistically significant; Table 4), suggesting that there is a common understanding of relative misconduct seriousness across the three agencies. In addition, the respondents' assessments of seriousness for all three agencies were

very strongly positively related to their own perceptions that the described behavior is a violation of official rules (Spearman's rho = .934*** for Agency 8; Spearman's rho = .908*** for Agency 9; Spearman's rho = .955*** for Agency 10).

Views About Appropriate Discipline and Disciplinary Environment

We wanted to explore the respondents' perceptions of appropriate discipline for the misconduct featured in the scenarios, as well as their perceptions of actual discipline meted out by their police agencies. The question about appropriate discipline focused on the discipline that *should* follow and the question about the expected discipline focused on the discipline that *would* follow. As discussed earlier, answers to both questions were determined by the Armenian legal rules. Specifically, the 8-point Likert scale started with "no discipline" and ended with "dismissal." Other disciplinary options, placed between the ends of the scale, included "reprimand," "severe reprimand," "salary reduction," "incompatibility with the occupied position," "demotion to one step lower position," and "demotion to one step lower rank." Because some disciplinary options were selected very infrequently, we recoded the answers to create four categories for the chi-square analysis: none, reprimand ("reprimand" and "severe reprimand"), more serious discipline other than dismissal ("salary reduction," "incompatibility with the occupied position," "demotion to one step lower position," and "demotion to one step lower rank"), and dismissal.

Unlike the questions about rule violations and seriousness, we found substantial differences across the three agencies in the respondents' views of appropriate discipline (Table 5). In 6 out of 11 scenarios, the differences among the agencies were statistically significant (Table 5). In a nutshell, in a number of scenarios with differences (4 out of 6 scenarios), respondents from Agency 10 thought that somewhat more severe discipline is appropriate than the respondents from Agency 8 did (Table 5). Similarly, in a couple of scenarios with statistically significant differences (2 out of 6), the respondents from Agency 9 thought that somewhat more severe discipline is appropriate than the respondents from Agency 8 did.

Scenario 3 (Theft of Knife from Crime Scene) is the only scenario in which the differences were particularly visible on the more severe side of the scale—dismissal. The respondents from all three agencies evaluated this scenario as the most serious (Table 4). In particular, while only about 44% of the respondents in Agency 8 and Agency 9 thought that a police officer who steals from a crime scene should be dismissed, the majority of respondents (55%; Table 5) from Agency 10 thought the same.

Another scenario describing serious corruption (Scenario 9: Auto-Body Shop 5% Kickback) also suggests that the respondents from Agency 10 thought that more severe discipline was appropriate than the respondents from both Agency 8 and Agency 9 did. Specifically, the respondents from Agency 8 and Agency 9 were more likely to state that reprimand is the preferred discipline (62.9% and 63.5%, respectively; Table 5) than the respondents from Agency 10 were (46.9%).

In the last of the three scenarios with corruption (Scenario 5: Supervisor: Holiday Off for Errands), the differences were spread across disciplinary categories. The respondents from Agency 9 (24.7%; Table 5) were more likely to say that the supervisor who engages in internal corruption should not be disciplined at all than the respondents from Agency 8 were (8.0%; Table 5). Furthermore, the respondents from Agency 9 seemed to be more supportive of no discipline or less severe discipline than the respondents from Agency 10 were. Specifically, the respondents from Agency 9 (61.2%; Table 5) were more likely to advocate for "reprimand" than the respondents from Agency 10 were (49.4%; Table 5).

Among the scenarios with statistically significant differences, there were three scenarios describing the use of excessive force. In two of these scenarios (Scenario 4: Unjustifiable Use of Deadly Force; Scenario 7: Verbal Abuse of Young Activists), the respondents from Agency 8 thought that less severe discipline should be appropriate than the respondents from Agency 10. In particular, the percentage of respondents from Agency 8 who thought that a police officer who verbally abused activists should not be disciplined (35.5%; Table 5) was higher than the percentage of respondents from Agency 10 who thought the same (21.2%; Table 5). Similarly, the percentage of the respondents from Agency 8 (48.3%; Table 5) who expected "reprimand" for an unjustifiable use of deadly force was higher than the percentage of respondents from Agency 10 who thought the same (32.7%; Table 5).

The last scenario describing the use of excessive force with statistically significant differences is Scenario 11 (Sgt. Fails to Halt Beating). While the percentage of the respondents who thought that the Sergeant should not be disciplined for this behavior was very similar across the three agencies (26.1% for Agency 8, 27.4% for Agency 9, and 27.2% for Agency 10; Table 5), the respondents from Agency 9 (59.5%; Table 5) were much more likely to state that "reprimand" was the appropriate discipline than were the respondents from Agency 8 (39.8%; Table 5) and, to a certain extent, the respondents from Agency 10 (46.4%; Table 5).

To obtain a relative measure of discipline severity—how severe discipline should be appropriate for one scenario compared to the other

Table 5 Respondents' Views of Appropriate Discipline by Police Agency

	Agency 8				Agency 9				Agency 10				Chi-Square	Phi	Agency 8 Rank	Agency 9 Rank	Agency 10 Rank
	None	Reprimand	Some	Dismissal	None	Reprimand	Some	Dismissal	None	Reprimand	Some	Dismissal					
Scenario 1—Free Meals, Gifts from Merchants	24.7%	60.7%	9.0%	5.6%	27.3%	60.2%	4.8%	7.2%	26.5%	54.4%	5.4%	13.7%	8.16	.125	3	6	6
Scenario 2—Fail to Arrest Friend with Warrant	3.4%	64.4%	13.8%	18.4%	12.9%	62.4%	10.6%	14.1%	13.0%	60.3%	11.8%	14.9%	7.01	.115	7	8	7
Scenario 3—Theft of Knife from Crime Scene	2.2%	28.1%	25.8%	43.8%	1.2%	39.3%	15.5%	44.0%	2.0%	30.2%	12.6%	55.3%	13.60*	.160*	11	11	11
Scenario 4—Unjustifiable Use of Deadly Force	6.9%	48.3%	14.9%	29.9%	20.7%	40.2%	9.8%	29.3%	14.0%	32.7%	19.2%	34.1%	15.33*	.173*	10	10	10
Scenario 5—Supervisor: Holiday Off for Errands	8.0%	58.6%	27.6%	5.7%	24.7%	61.2%	9.4%	4.7%	15.9%	49.4%	26.5%	8.1%	20.23**	.196**	4.5	4	3
Scenario 6—Officer Strikes Prisoner Who Hurt Partner	25.0%	62.5%	6.8%	5.7%	29.8%	60.7%	4.8%	4.8%	21.0%	58.6%	10.3%	10.1%	8.72	.129	4.5	5	5
Scenario 7—Verbal Abuse of Young Activists	35.5%	56.7%	4.4%	3.3%	29.4%	67.1%	1.2%	2.4%	21.1%	66.3%	9.3%	3.4%	15.64*	.172*	2	2	2
Scenario 8—Cover-Up of Police DUI Accident	31.1%	63.3%	5.6%	0.0%	43.5%	54.1%	1.2%	1.2%	40.0%	56.7%	2.2%	1.1%	7.59	.119	1	1	1
Scenario 9—Auto-Body Shop 5% Kickback	7.9%	62.9%	6.7%	22.5%	21.2%	63.5%	7.1%	8.2%	18.2%	46.9%	13.4%	21.5%	22.56**	.206**	9	7	8
Scenario 10—False Report on Drug on Dealer	4.4%	56.0%	20.9%	18.7%	10.6%	49.4%	14.1%	25.9%	7.9%	46.6%	19.1%	26.4%	6.53	.111	8	9	9
Scenario 11—Sgt. Fails to Halt Beating	26.1%	39.8%	27.3%	6.8%	27.4%	59.5%	9.5%	3.6%	27.2%	46.4%	16.9%	9.5%	14.84*	.169*	6	3	4

*p < .05; **p < .01; ***p < .001

Spearman's rho: Agency 8 and Agency 9: .888***; Agency 8 and Agency 10: .920***; Agency 9 and Agency 10: .982***

scenarios in the questionnaire—we rank-ordered scenarios based on the percentage of the respondents who thought that the police officer should be dismissed for the behavior described in each scenario (Table 5). The relative order of appropriate discipline severity is very similar across the police agencies (Spearman's rho is above .800 for all three comparisons; Table 5).

A comparison of the respondents' views about the expected discipline across the three agencies revealed statistically significant differences in five out of 11 scenarios (of which four featured statistically significant differences in the domain of appropriate discipline as well). There were two scenarios describing police corruption (Scenario 5: Supervisor: Holiday Off for Errands; Scenario 9: Auto-Body Shop 5% Kickback). In the first of these scenarios, describing a case of internal corruption (Scenario 5: Supervisor: Holiday Off for Errands), the respondents from Agency 9 and Agency 10 were more likely to say that they would expect "no discipline" than the respondents from Agency 8 were. In the same scenario, the respondents from Agency 8 were also more likely to say that they would expect "reprimand" than the respondents from Agency 10 were (Table 6). In the second scenario featuring corruption (Scenario 9: Auto-Body Shop 5% Kickback), the respondents from Agency 8 and Agency 10 were more likely to expect dismissal than the respondents from Agency 9 were (47.2%; Table 6). At the same time, the respondents from Agency 10 were much less likely to expect "reprimand" than the respondents from either Agency 8 (64.0%) or Agency 9 were (60%; Table 6).

Statistically significant differences were found in three scenarios dealing with the use of excessive force. In particular, in Scenario 7 (Verbal Abuse of Young Activists), the respondents from Agency 9 were more likely to expect no discipline at all (28.0%; Table 6) than either the respondents from Agency 8 (11.8%; Table 6) or Agency 10 were (15.3%). At the same time, they were less likely to expect to be reprimanded for such behavior as well (Table 6). Similarly, the respondents from Agency 9 were more likely to expect no discipline at all when officer strikes a prisoner who hurt partner (Scenario 6; 25.9%;

Table 6) than the respondents from either Agency 8 (11.6%) or Agency 10 were (15.2%). At the same time, the respondents from Agency 10 were more likely to expect more severe discipline (26.7% for "some" and "dismissal" in Table 6) than the respondents from either Agency 8 (11.7%) or Agency 9 were (9.4%). Finally, in Scenario 11 (Sgt. Fails to Halt Beating), the respondents from Agency 10 (43.9%) were also less likely to say that they would expect a reprimand (and somewhat more likely to say that they would expected dismissal) that either the respondents from Agency 8 (58.6; Table 6) or Agency 9 were (61.0%).

We have also rank-ordered scenarios based on the percentage of respondents who have selected "dismissal" as the expected discipline for each scenario. While dismissal is not a frequently expected discipline (only for Scenario 3 about one-half of all respondents in all three agencies expect dismissal), the percentage of respondents who selected it varies across scenarios (Table 6). The relative order of expected discipline severity, that is, how severe discipline is for one scenario compared to the other scenarios in the questionnaire, is very similar across the three police agencies (Spearman's rho is at .900 or above for all three comparisons; Table 6).

The Code of Silence

To assess the degree to which the contours of the code of silence differed across the agencies, we asked the respondents to tell us whether they would report the behavior described in each scenario. The respondents could have selected one answer on a 5-point Likert scale, ranging from 1 = "definitely would not report" to 5 = "definitely would report."

The results show that the code of silence does seem to differ across police agencies within the same system and is far from being uniform across various parts of the same police system. In particular, out of 11 scenarios in the questionnaire, we found statistically significant differences across the police agencies in six (Table 7). These scenarios are heterogeneous as they involve one

Table 6 Respondents' Views of Expected Discipline by Police Agency

	Agency 8				Agency 9			
	None	Reprimand	Some	Dismissal	None	Reprimand	Some	Dismissal
Scenario 1—Free Meals, Gifts from Merchants	11.6%	72.1%	7.0%	9.3%	20.7%	62.2%	3.7%	13.4%
Scenario 2—Fail to Arrest Friend with Warrant	1.2%	54.9%	22.0%	22.0%	10.7%	63.1%	11.9%	14.3%
Scenario 3—Theft of Knife from Crime Scene	2.3%	29.1%	12.8%	55.8%	1.2%	40.0%	12.9%	45.9%
Scenario 4—Unjustifiable Use of Deadly Force	5.7%	35.6%	19.5%	39.1%	15.3%	38.8%	9.4%	36.5%
Scenario 5—Supervisor: Holiday Off for Errands	9.6%	61.4%	22.9%	6.0%	24.4%	59.8%	12.2%	3.7%
Scenario 6—Officer Strikes Prisoner Who Hurt Partner	11.6%	76.7%	4.7%	7.0%	25.9%	64.7%	3.5%	5.9%
Scenario 7—Verbal Abuse of Young Activists	11.8%	81.2%	4.7%	2.4%	28.0%	67.1%	3.7%	1.2%
Scenario 8—Cover-Up of Police DUI Accident	23.9%	71.6%	4.5%	0.0%	36.9%	56.0%	2.4%	4.8%
Scenario 9—Auto-Body Shop 5% Kickback	7.0%	64.0%	4.7%	24.4%	20.0%	60.0%	9.4%	10.6%
Scenario 10—False Report on Drug on Dealer	4.5%	48.3%	21.3%	25.8%	10.6%	50.6%	12.9%	25.9%
Scenario 11—Sgt. Fails to Halt Beating	11.5%	58.6%	18.4%	11.5%	22.0%	61.0%	12.2%	4.9%

	Agency 10				Chi-Square	Phi	Agency 8 Rank	Agency 9 Rank	Agency 10 Rank
	None	Reprimand	Some	Dismissal					
Scenario 1—Free Meals, Gifts from Merchants	22.6%	56.8%	5.4%	15.2%	9.33	.136	5	7	4
Scenario 2—Fail to Arrest Friend with Warrant	9.9%	59.3%	12.7%	18.1%	12.49	.155	7	8	7
Scenario 3—Theft of Knife from Crime Scene	2.5%	28.9%	11.8%	56.7%	4.98	.097	11	11	11
Scenario 4—Unjustifiable Use of Deadly Force	10.2%	33.5%	14.0%	42.3%	8.16	.126	10	10	10
Scenario 5—Supervisor: Holiday Off for Errands	20.4%	48.7%	22.1%	8.8%	14.39*	.167*	3	2	3
Scenario 6—Officer Strikes Prisoner Who Hurt Partner	15.2%	58.1%	10.0%	16.7%	24.15***	.217***	4	5	6
Scenario 7—Verbal Abuse of Young Activists	15.3%	68.9%	10.2%	5.6%	18.55***	.189***	2	1	2
Scenario 8—Cover-Up of Police DUI Accident	29.6%	64.9%	2.3%	3.2%	9.12	.132	1	3	1
Scenario 9—Auto-Body Shop 5% Kickback	14.4%	47.2%	14.1%	24.3%	22.04**	.205**	8	6	8
Scenario 10—False Report on Drug on Dealer	8.5%	45.0%	16.1%	30.3%	5.41	.101	9	9	9
Scenario 11—Sgt. Fails to Halt Beating	20.1%	43.9%	19.5%	16.4%	17.91**	.185***	6	4	5

*$p < .05$; **$p < .01$; ***$p < .001$

Table 7 Respondents' Expressed Willingness to Report by Police Agency

	Agency 8		Agency 9		Agency 10		
	Mean	Rank	Mean	Rank	Mean	Rank	F-test
Scenario 1—Free Meals, Gifts from Merchants	3.19	5	3.30	6	2.83	2	3.68* (2 v. 3 at p < .10)
Scenario 2—Fail to Arrest Friend with Warrant	3.68	7	3.41	7	3.19	8	3.54* (1 v. 3 at p < .10)
Scenario 3—Theft of Knife from Crime Scene	4.33	10	4.05	11	3.69	10	7.04** (1 v. 3)
Scenario 4—Unjustifiable Use of Deadly Force	4.37	11	3.88	9	3.79	11	5.41** (1 v. 2; 1 v. 3)
Scenario 5—Supervisor: Holiday Off for Errands	3.73	8	3.19	5	3.17	7	4.31* (1 v. 2; 1 v. 3)
Scenario 6—Officer Strikes Prisoner Who Hurt Partner	2.99	2.5	2.69	3	2.92	3	.80
Scenario 7—Verbal Abuse of Young Activists	2.99	2.5	2.67	2	3.00	5	1.36
Scenario 8—Cover-Up of Police DUI Accident	2.88	1	2.55	1	2.73	1	.88
Scenario 9—Auto-Body Shop 5% Kickback	3.20	6	3.47	8	3.10	6	1.67
Scenario 10—False Report on Drug on Dealer	4.02	9	3.79	10	3.56	9	3.44* (1 v. 3 at p < .10)
Scenario 11—Sgt. Fails to Halt Beating	3.10	4	2.87	4	2.97	4	.40

$* p < .05; ** p < .01; *** p < .001$
Spearman's rho: Agency 8 and Agency 9: .907***; Agency 8 and Agency 10: .920***; Agency 9 and Agency 10: .818**

scenario describing the use of excessive force (Scenario 4: Unjustifiable Use of Deadly Force), three scenarios describing police corruption (Scenario 1: Free Meals, Gifts from Merchants; Scenario 3: Theft of Knife from Crime Scene; Scenario 5: Supervisor: Holiday Off for Errands), and two scenarios describing other forms of police misconduct (Scenario 2: Fail to Arrest Friend with Warrant; Scenario 10: False Report on Drug on Dealer).

Despite the diversity of these scenarios (some are evaluated as very serious, others as very mild; Table 4), there appears a common pattern. In five out of six scenarios (83%), the mean for Agency 8 is higher than the mean for Agency 10, indicating that the code of silence is narrower in Agency 8 than in Agency 10. In addition, in one scenario the mean is significantly higher in Agency 9 than in Agency 10. Finally, there were two out of six scenarios in which there were statistically significant differences between the means from Agency 8 and Agency 9; in these two scenarios, the code

of silence seems to be narrower in Agency 8 than in Agency 9 (Table 7).

We ranked the scenarios from those with the lowest mean value (suggesting the strongest protection from the code) to the scenarios with the highest mean value (suggesting the weakest protection from the code). This measure gives us a relative assessment of the respondents' (un)willingness to report. In other words, the measure of relative willingness to report assesses the extent to which the code of silence would compare specific behavior described in one scenario with the extent to which the code would cover the behaviors in the other scenarios featured in the questionnaire. Spearman's correlation coefficients indicate very pronounced similarities of the agency rankings (Spearman's rho coefficients for bivariate correlations across the three pairs of agencies are all above .800 and are statistically significant; Table 7), suggesting the existence of common views about which behaviors would be more likely to be protected by the code of silence.

Conclusion

This chapter has tested the assumption that the contours of police integrity are the same across all elements of a police system, particularly police stations from the same centralized police system. A simple answer to the question we raised at the beginning is negative: the results of our empirical study clearly show that, despite the apparent and expected uniformity of a centralized system, the contours of police integrity vary across centralized police systems as well. A more complex answer is based on our desire to engage in an encompassing exploration of police integrity. Indeed, our empirical results show that the patterns of variation of the contours of police integrity across subunits are complex.

The theory of police integrity (Klockars and Kutnjak Ivković 2004; Klockars et al. 1997, 2006) emphasizes the way organizational rules are made and understood by police officers as one of its critical dimensions. We tested the police officers' knowledge of official rules and found that the level of the respondents' familiarity with legal rules is very similar across three subunits of the Armenian police system. Finding statistically significant differences in only one scenario (Scenario 10: False Report on Drug Dealer) led to the conclusion that the contours of police integrity are quite similar with respect to the respondents' understanding of official rules. Put differently, regardless of the location, police offices' familiarity with the legal rules is about the same. This is good news for the Armenian police.

Our results are strongly aligned with the results of prior empirical studies exploring knowledge of official rules in centralized systems (Kutnjak Ivković and Khechumyan 2014). Centralization of official rules—in this instance, national-level creation of official rules applicable to all subunits—seems to result in more uniformity in police officers' understanding of those rules than has been achieved in decentralized systems, in which each police agency has the capacity to create its own official rules. Indeed, empirical studies exploring consistency of knowledge of official rules in decentralized systems have shown that the knowledge of official rules could vary from agency to agency in a decentralized system (e.g., Chappell and Piquero 2004; Greene et al. 2004; Hickman 2005; Klockars et al. 2000; Kutnjak Ivković et al. 2013; Marche 2009; McDevitt et al. 2011; Schafer and Martinelli 2008; Vito et al. 2011).

We also used another measure related to the perceived organizational rules: respondents' evaluations of misconduct seriousness. Our results further indicated that the respondents' views across the three agencies are very similar too; we uncovered statistically significant differences in their perceptions of seriousness in only 20% of the scenarios. Extant research in centralized systems yielded similar results (e.g., Kutnjak Ivković et al. 2016a; Kutnjak Ivković and Khechumyan 2014; Yun 2003). Yun (2003) reported very few differences in the respondents' perceptions of seriousness in two South Korean cities. Kutnjak Ivković and Khechumyan (2014) found statistically significant differences in about 40% of the scenarios dealing with police corruption across two Armenian police agencies, but noted that these differences in seriousness evaluations were substantively important in a much smaller percent of scenarios, only about 20% (Kutnjak Ivković and Khechumyan 2014). That our scenarios with statistically significant differences in perceptions of seriousness do not form a uniform picture (e.g., one agency consistently evaluating scenarios as more serious than the other two agencies) is consistent with the results reported in Kutnjak Ivković and Khechumyan (2014), indicating the absence of a clear pattern in uniformly ranking the seriousness with which agencies perceive scenarios featured in the questionnaire. Moreover, although Kutnjak Ivković et al. (2016a) also found mostly similarities in the perceptions of seriousness, their findings suggested that the respondents from smaller rural agencies were more likely to evaluate misconduct as more serious than their counterparts from larger urban agencies did (Kutnjak Ivković et al. 2016a).

The theory of police integrity (Klockars and Kutnjak Ivković 2004; Klockars et al. 1997, 2006) elaborated on the quality and consistency of the application of control mechanisms. To that end, we measured both the respondents' views of what the appropriate discipline is for misconduct and what discipline they anticipate their agency would mete out. The presence of statistically significant differences in about one-half of the scenarios suggests a much greater degree of variation for measures of discipline, both appropriate and expected, than for the measures related to awareness of official rules.

Our results show that agency-level disciplinary environments are far from identical, thus accentuating the fact that contours of integrity could vary with respect to discipline. Although these results may signal to the police administrators that there is a need to develop a more consistent disciplinary system, these findings are not unexpected. Indeed, other empirical research, both in centralized and decentralized systems, suggests that disciplinary environments could be quite heterogeneous. Kutnjak Ivković and Khechumyan (2014) found strong support for such heterogeneity in their empirical study; they not only found substantial differences across the two agencies within the same centralized system, but also recorded that the differences in perceptions of disciplinary environments were the largest among all police integrity measures. Our study suggested that rural police agencies expected more severe discipline, while Kutnjak Ivković and Khechumyan (2014) reported a harsher disciplinary environment in the urban police agency. Similarly, while studying differences in police integrity among different agency types in South Africa, Kutnjak Ivković and Sauerman (2016) documented the greatest degree of heterogeneity of police integrity in the perceived disciplinary environments. Other studies of decentralized systems show further evidence of how different these disciplinary environments could be across agencies (e.g., Chappell and Piquero 2004; Greene et al. 2004; Hickman 2005; Klockars et al. 2000, 2006; Kutnjak Ivković et al. 2013).

The third dimension of the theory explains the importance of the strength of the code of silence, resulting from the police efforts to curtail it (see, e.g., Klockars and Kutnjak Ivković 2004; Klockars et al. 1997, 2006; Kutnjak Ivković 2015). One of the questions in the questionnaire sought to measure the extent of the code. The results of our study show that in over one-half of the scenarios there were statistically significant differences in the extent of the code of silence across the three agencies. A police agency, be it a small municipal agency or a large state agency, should be eager to control the code of silence. Although it is not realistic to expect that the code would be entirely homogeneous across different types of units (e.g., patrol v. vice) or different hierarchical levels (e.g., line officers v. supervisors), learning that the code of silence is measurably heterogeneous across geographically distinct parts of the same agency may be an indication that the code should be more efficiently controlled in the areas in which the code is stronger.

Our results are quite similar to the results reported in Kutnjak Ivković and Khechumyan (2014). In particular, both studies found differences in about one-half of the scenarios in the respondents' evaluations of willingness to report. Furthermore, both studies consistently reported that, if there were differences in the contours of the code, urban police agencies tended to have stronger codes of silence than suburban/rural police agencies did. However, our study contained samples from two rural police agencies; we found further differences, though not as pronounced, between the two rural police agencies as well. Our study provides further support for the general idea that the code of silence could vary dramatically across police agencies, regardless of whether these police agencies are part of the same centralized or decentralized system (e.g., Klockars et al. 2000, 2006; Kutnjak Ivković 2015; Lim and Sloan 2016).

In the end, our study provides very clear evidence that police integrity is a complex phenomenon. It shows that, even within centralized systems, the assumption that the level of police integrity is the same across all the elements of the system does not hold. While some elements of police integrity may be fairly homogeneous, such as knowledge of official rules or perceptions of misconduct seriousness, other elements, such as the perceptions of the disciplinary environment or the code of silence, could be quite heterogeneous.

Therefore, even in centralized systems, police agencies can create specific disciplinary environments and develop unique police cultures.

Future research can provide more in-depth explorations of the degree to which these disciplinary environments and police cultures differ. Also, it would be informative to study how these similar and partly overlapping, yet distinct environments get to be created. How is it possible that the seriousness evaluations are so similar across the centralized system while the willingness to report is not? Where does the differentiation start? Quite possibly, the socialization at the level of individual police stations may carry more weight in the shaping of police officers' views and attitudes. These and similar questions could be addressed in the next sweep of research concerning the very fundamentals of police integrity.

References

Avagyan, G., & Hiscock, D. (2005). *Security sector reform in Armenia*. Retrieved December 23, 2013, from www.saferworld.org.uk/downloads/pubdocs/Armenia_English.pdf

Bayley, D. (2006). *Changing the guard: Developing democratic policing abroad*. New York: Oxford University Press.

Chappell, A. T., & Piquero, A. R. (2004). Applying social learning theory to police misconduct. *Deviant Behavior, 25*, 89–108.

Code of Criminal Procedure of the Republic of Armenia. (1998). Retrieved February 25, 2014, from http://www.arlis.am/

Council of Europe. (2004). *Report to the Armenian Government on the visit to Armenia from 20 to 22 April 2004*. Retrieved December 12, 2013, from www.cpt.coe.int/documents/arm/2006-38-inf-eng.htm

Council of Europe. (2007). *Report to the Armenian Government on the visit to Armenia from 2 to 12 April 2006*. Retrieved January 12, 2014, from www1.umn.edu/humanrts/research/armenia/Report%20to%20the%20Armenian%20Government%202007.pdf

Council of Europe. (2011). *Report to the Armenian Government on the visit to Armenia from 20 to 21 May, 2010*. Retrieved January 12, 2014, from www.cpt.coe.int/documents/arm/2011-24-inf-eng.pdf

Council of Europe. (2012). *Report to the Armenian Government on the visit to Armenia from 5 to 7 December, 2011*. Retrieved January 13, 2014, from http://www.cpt.coe.int/documents/arm/2012-23-inf-eng.pdf

Criminal Code of the Republic of Armenia. (2003). Retrieved February 25, 2014, from http://www.arlis.am/

Freedom House. (2010). *Country reports: Armenia*. Retrieved January 12, 2014, from http://www.freedomhouse.org/template.cfm?page=22&year=2010&country=7772

Freedom House. (2013). *Country reports: Armenia*. Retrieved June 24, 2018, from https://freedomhouse.org/report/freedom-world/2013/armenia

Greene, J. R., Piquero, A. R., Hickman, M. J., & Lawton, B. A. (2004). *Police integrity and accountability in Philadelphia: Predicting and assessing police misconduct*. National Institute of Justice. Retrieved from http://www.ncjrs.gov/pdffiles1/nij/grants/207823.pdf

Hickman, M. J. (2005). *Self-reported and official police problem behavior: Identifying the roles of context, individual, and data. ProQuest Dissertations and Theses*. Retrieved from http://ezproxy.msu.edu/login?url=http://search.proquest.com/docview/305393854?accountid=12598

Hickman, M. J., Piquero, A. R., Powell, Z. A., & Greene, J. (2016). Expanding the measurement of police integrity. *Policing: An International Journal of Police Strategies & Management, 39*(2), 246–267.

Internal Security Department of RA Police. (2013). Retrieved January 11, 2014, from http://www.police.am/structure

Internal Security Department of RA Police. (2014). Retrieved January 11, 2014, from http://www.police.am/news/view/2014

Khechumyan, A., & Kutnjak Ivković, S. (2015). Police integrity in Armenia. In S. Kutnjak Ivković & M. Haberfeld (Eds.), *Police integrity across the world*. New York: Springer.

Klockars, C. B., & Kutnjak Ivković, S. (1999). The measurement of police delinquency. In W. Laufer & F. Adler (Eds.), *The criminology of criminal Law. Advances in criminological theory* (Vol. 8, pp. 87–106). New Brunswick, NJ: Transaction.

Klockars, C. B., & Kutnjak Ivković, S. (2004). Measuring police integrity. In M. J. Hickman, A. R. Piquero, & J. R. Greene (Eds.), *Police integrity and ethics*. Belmont, CA: Wadsworth.

Klockars, C. B., Kutnjak Ivković, S., Harver, W. E., & Haberfeld, M. R. (1997). *The measurement of police integrity*. Final report submitted to the U.S. Department of Justice, Office of Justice Programs, National Institute of Justice.

Klockars, C. B., Kutnjak Ivković, S., Harver, W. E., & Haberfeld, M. R. (2000). *The measurement of police integrity*. Research in brief. U.S. Department of Justice, Office of Justice Programs, National Institute of Justice. Washington, DC: Government Printing Office.

Klockars, C. B., Kutnjak Ivković, S., & Haberfeld, M. R. (Eds.). (2004). *The contours of police integrity*. Newbury Park, CA: Sage.

Klockars, C. B., Kutnjak Ivković, S., & Haberfeld, M. R. (2006). *Enhancing police integrity*. New York: Springer.

Kremer, F. (2000). Comparing supervisor and line officer opinions about the code of silence: The case of Hungary. In M. Pagon (Ed.), *Policing in Central and*

Eastern Europe: Ethics, integrity, and human rights (pp. 211–219). Ljubljana, Slovenia: College of Police and Security Studies.

Kutnjak Ivković, S. (2004). Sharing the view: Line officer and supervisor evaluations of police corruption seriousness in Bosnia and Herzegovina. In G. Mesko, M. Pagon, & G. Dobovsek (Eds.), *Dilemmas of contemporary criminal justice* (pp. 312–322). Ljubljana, Slovenia: Faculty of Criminal Justice, University of Maribor.

Kutnjak Ivković, S. (2005). Police (Mis)behavior: A cross-cultural study of corruption seriousness. *Policing: An International Journal of Police Strategies and Management, 28*(3), 546–566.

Kutnjak Ivković, S. (2015). Studying police integrity. In S. Kutnjak Ivković & M. Haberfeld (Eds.), *Police integrity across the world.* New York: Springer.

Kutnjak Ivković, S., & Haberfeld, M. R. (Eds.). (2015). *Police integrity across the world.* New York: Springer.

Kutnjak Ivković, S., & Khechumyan, A. (2013). The state of police integrity in Armenia: Findings from the police integrity survey. *Policing: An International Journal of Police Strategies and Management, 36*(1), 70–90.

Kutnjak Ivković, S., & Khechumyan, A. (2014). Measuring police integrity among urban and rural police in Armenia: From local results to global implications. *International Journal of Comparative and Applied Criminal Justice, 38*(1), 39–61.

Kutnjak Ivković, S., & Klockars, C. B. (1998). The code of silence and the Croatian police. In M. Pagon (Ed.), *Policing in Central and Eastern Europe: Organizational, managerial, and human resource aspects* (pp. 329–347). Ljubljana, Slovenia: College of Police and Security Studies.

Kutnjak Ivković, S., & Sauerman, A. (2012). The code of silence: Revisiting south African police integrity. *South African Crime Quarterly, 40*(June), 15–24.

Kutnjak Ivković, S., & Sauerman, A. (2016). Police integrity in South Africa: A tale of three police agency types. *Policing: An International Journal of Police Strategies and Management, 39*(2), 268–283.

Kutnjak Ivković, S., & Shelley, T. O. (2010). The code of silence and disciplinary fairness: A comparison of Czech police supervisor and line officer views. *Policing: An International Journal of Police Strategies and Management, 33*(3), 548–574.

Kutnjak Ivković, S., Cajner-Mraović, I., & Ivanusec, D. (2004). The measurement of seriousness of police corruption. In G. Mesko, M. Pagon, & G. Dobovsek (Eds.), *Dilemmas of contemporary criminal justice* (pp. 300–311). Ljubljana, Slovenia: Faculty of Criminal Justice, University of Maribor.

Kutnjak Ivković, S., Haberfeld, M., & Peacock, R. (2013). Rainless west: The integrity survey's role in agency accountability. *Police Quarterly, 16*(2), 148–176.

Kutnjak Ivković, S., Cajner Mraović, I., & Borovec, K. (2016a). An empirical test of the influence of society at large on police integrity in a centralized police system. *Policing: An International Journal of Police Strategies and Management, 39*(2), 302–318.

Kutnjak Ivković, S., Haberfeld, M., Kang, W., Peacock, R., & Sauerman, A. (2016b). A multi-country comparative study of the perceived police disciplinary environments. *Policing: An International Journal of Police Strategies and Management, 39*(2), 338–353.

Kutnjak Ivković, S., Haberfeld, M., & Peacock, R. (2016c). Does discipline fairness matter for the police code of silence? Answers from the U.S. supervisors and line officers. *Policing: An International Journal of Police Strategies and Management, 39*(2), 354–369.

Kutnjak Ivković, S., Haberfeld, M., & Peacock, R. (2017). Decoding the code of silence. *Criminal Justice Policy Review, Forthcoming.*

Law on Police Disciplinary Code. (2005). Retrieved February 7, 2014, from http://www.arlis.am/

Law on Police Service. (2002). Retrieved February 7, 2014, from http://www.arlis.am/

Lim, H., & Sloan, J. J. (2016). Police officer integrity: A partial replication and extension. *Policing: An International Journal of Police Strategies and Management, 39*(2), 284–301.

Marche, G. E. (2009). Integrity, culture, and scale: An empirical test of the big bad police agency. *Crime, Law and Social Change, 51*, 463–486.

McDevitt, J., Posick, C., Zschoche, R., Rosenbaum, D. P., Buslik, M., Fridell, L. (2011). *Police integrity, responsibility, and discipline.* National Institute of Justice. Retrieved from http://www.nationalpoliceresearch.org/storage/updated-papers/Police%20Integrity%20Responsibility%20and%20Discipline.pdf

Ombudsman of the Republic of Armenia. (2012). *Annual report.* Retrieved February 7, 2014, from http://www.ombuds.am/

Ombudsman of the Republic of Armenia. (2013). *Ad hoc report on Fair Trial Rights.* Retrieved February 7, 2014, from http://www.ombuds.am/

OSCE. (2010). *Police accountability in the Republic of Armenia.* Retrieved February 7, 2014, from http://194.8.63.155/yerevan/68198

Pagon, M., & Lobnikar, B. (2000). Comparing supervisor and line officer opinions about the code of silence: The case of Slovenia. In M. Pagon (Ed.), *Policing in Central and Eastern Europe: Ethics, integrity, and human rights* (pp. 197–209). Ljubljana, Slovenia: College of Police and Security Studies.

Police Law. (2001). Retrieved February 7, 2014, from http://www.arlis.am/

Police of the Republic of Armenia. (2013). Retrieved February 7, 2014, from http://www.police.am/about-the-police/

Police of the Republic of Armenia. (2014). Retrieved February 7, 2014, from http://www.police.am/en/structure/subdivisions

Rothwell, G. R., & Baldwin, J. N. (2007). Whistleblowing and the code of silence in police agencies policy and structural predictors. *Crime & Delinquency, 53*(4), 605–632.

Schafer, J. A., & Martinelli, T. J. (2008). First-line supervisor's perceptions of police integrity. *Policing: An International Journal of Police Strategies and Management, 31*(2), 306–323.

Statistical Committee of the Republic of Armenia. (2016). *2016 Demographic Handbook of Armenia*. Retrieved from http://www.armstat.am/en/?nid=82&id=1847

Transparency International. (2003). *National Integrity Systems Transparency International Country Reports: Armenia 2003*. Retrieved February 7, 2014, from http://www.transparency.org/policy_research/nis/nis_reports_by_country

Transparency International. (2011). *Global Corruption Barometer 2010 report*. Retrieved February 7, 2014, from http://www.transparency.org/policy_research/surveys_indices/gcb/2010/results

Transparency International. (2012) *Corruption perception index*. Retrieved February 7, 2014, from http://www.transparency.org/research/cpi/cpi_2011

Transparency International. (2014a). *Global corruption barometer 2013*. Retrieved February 5, 2014, from http://www.transparency.org/gcb2013/country?country=armenia&q=1#question1

Transparency International. (2014b). *Corruption perception index*. Retrieved February 7, 2014, from http://transparency.am/en/cpi

The Supreme Council of the Armenian Soviet Socialist Republic (1990). Armenian Declaration of Independence, Retrieved May 7, 2017, from https://www.gov.am/en/independence/

United Nations Human Rights Committee (2012). Concluding Observations adopted by the Human Rights Committee at its 105th session CCPR/C/ARM/CO2(2012)para.22. Retrieved February 1, 2014 from www2.ohchr.org/english/bodies/hrc/.../CCPR.C.ARM.CO.2-3_AV.doc

Vito, G. F., Wolfe, S., Higgins, G. E., & Walsh, W. F. (2011). Police integrity: Rankings of scenarios on the Klockars scale by "management cops". *Criminal Justice Review, 36*, 152–164.

Yun, I. (2003). *A study of police officers' perceptions of police deviance: From an occupational socialization perspective. ProQuest Dissertations and Theses.* 89 p. Retrieved from http://ezproxy.msu.edu/login?url=http://search.proquest.com/docview/305329643?accountid=12598

Part II

Expanding the Police Integrity Theory

Seriousness of Police (Mis)Behavior and Organizational Justice

Sanja Kutnjak Ivković, M. R. Haberfeld,
Irena Cajner Mraović, Marko Prpić,
Joseph A. Hamm, and Scott Wolfe

Introduction

The seminal study *The Measurement of Delinquency* by Selling and Wolfgang (1964) initiated a wave of studies exploring seriousness of crime (e.g., Figlio 1975; Kwan et al. 2000; Pease 1988; Rossi et al. 1985; Velez-Dias and Megargee 1971; Wolfgang et al. 1985). Various groups of respondents, from citizens to police officers, have been asked to evaluate seriousness of hypothetical scenarios describing a range of crimes.

S. Kutnjak Ivković · S. Wolfe
School of Criminal Justice, Michigan State University, East Lansing, MI, USA
e-mail: kutnjak@msu.edu; kutnjak@msu.edu

M. R. Haberfeld
John Jay College of Criminal Justice, City University of New York, New York, NY, USA
e-mail: makih@sprynet.com

I. Cajner Mraović (✉)
Department of Croatian Studies, University of Zagreb, Zagreb, Croatia

City Assembly of the City of Zagreb, Zagreb, Croatia

M. Prpić
The Faculty of Education and Rehabilitation Sciences, University of Zagreb, Zagreb, Croatia

J. A. Hamm
School of Criminal Justice and Environmental Science and Policy Program, Michigan State University, East Lansing, MI, USA
e-mail: jhamm@msu.edu

Whereas absolute evaluations of crime seriousness varied with respondent demographic characteristics (e.g., offender status, Velez-Dias and Megargee 1971; Figlio 1975; gender, Rossi et al. 1985; race, Rossi et al. 1985; Wolfgang et al. 1985; victim status, Wolfgang et al. 1985), the extent of agreement among respondent groups regarding the relative order of crime seriousness was remarkably high. Selling and Wolfgang (1964, p. 268) concluded that, "[a] pervasive social agreement about what is serious and what is not appears to emerge." However, these common judgments tend to be related to a number of factors, such as severity of legal penalties, extent of harm, offenders' level of culpability, and offenders' status (e.g., Hansel 1987; Kwan et al. 2000; Wolfgang et al. 1985).

Studies concerning crime severity typically do not include examples of police misconduct. Rather, studies exploring severity—or seriousness—of police misconduct are under the purview of policing research (e.g., Australian Criminal Justice Commission 1999; Huon et al. 1995; Knowles 1996; Martin 1994). Klockars et al. (2000, 2004, 2006) developed a comprehensive approach toward studying police misconduct by including perceptions of seriousness as an integral part of the study of police integrity. Subsequent studies have typically explored perceptions of misconduct seriousness as part of a larger study on police integrity (e.g., Alain 2004; Chattha and Kutnjak Ivković 2004; Cheloukhine

© Springer Nature Switzerland AG 2019
S. Kutnjak Ivković, M. R. Haberfeld (eds.), *Exploring Police Integrity*,
https://doi.org/10.1007/978-3-030-29065-8_4

et al. 2015; Edelbacher and Kutnjak Ivković 2004; Haberfeld 2004; Johnson 2004; Kang and Kutnjak Ivković 2015; Khechumyan and Kutnjak Ivković 2015; Kutnjak Ivković et al. 2015; Kutnjak Ivković and Klockars 2004; Kremer 2004; Lobnikar and Meško 2015; Newham 2004; Pagon and Lobnikar 2004; Phetthong and Kutnjak Ivković 2015; Porter et al. 2015; Pounti et al. 2004; Punch et al. 2004; Sauerman and Kutnjak Ivković 2015; Torstensson Levander and Ekenvall 2004; Westmarland 2004; Vallmuur 2015). In addition to recording similarity or differences in evaluations of seriousness across different forms of police misconduct, a number of studies explored factors that influence police officers' evaluations of misconduct seriousness, such as demographic factors, recognition of behavior as rule-violating, and harshness of expected discipline (e.g., Cheloukhine et al. 2015; Desta 2013; Hickman et al. 2016; Huberts et al. 2003; Johnson 2003; Kutnjak Ivković 2009, 2015a; Kutnjak Ivković et al. 2015; Kutnjak Ivković and Kang 2011; Kutnjak Ivković and Klockars 2004; Kutnjak Ivković and Sauerman 2015; Lobnikar and Meško 2015; Phetthong and Kutnjak Ivković 2015; Porter et al. 2015; Vallmuur 2015; Wu et al. 2018).

With a few exceptions (e.g., Wolfe and Piquero 2011), perceptions of organizational justice (i.e., how fairly police officers perceive that they have been treated by their police agencies) have not been included as a factor in prior research on police misconduct seriousness and/or police integrity. Yet, extant research on organizational justice documented that perceptions of organizational justice are related to many issues potentially related to police integrity, such as police officers' greater internalization of organizational goals, increased supervisor trust, greater rule compliance, and the reduced extent of misconduct (Bradford et al. 2014; Bradford and Quinton 2014; Carr and Maxwell 2018; Haas et al. 2015; Myhill and Bradford 2013; Nix and Wolfe 2016; Trinker et al. 2016; Van Craen and Skogan 2017; Wolfe and Nix 2017). Thus, we hypothesize that perceptions of organizational justice are related to the police officers' evaluations of misconduct seriousness.

This chapter explores the relation between evaluations of misconduct seriousness and per-

ceptions of organizational justice. Grounded in the theory of police integrity and the related methodology (e.g., Klockars et al. 2000, 2004, 2006), our study incorporates a number of hypothetical scenarios, ranging from police corruption and the use of excessive force, to organizational and interpersonal deviance. Our analyses first explore bivariate relations between perceptions of seriousness and different elements of organizational justice (i.e., procedural justice, distributive justice, interactional justice). In subsequent logistic regression models that control for demographic factors (e.g., length of service, supervisory position) and organizational factors (e.g., knowledge of official rules, severity of expected discipline), we assess the influence of organizational justice on the respondents' evaluations of misbehavior seriousness.

Police Misconduct Seriousness and Police Integrity

Direct measurement of police misconduct with any degree of accuracy is notoriously difficult for a host of reasons, from police officers' unwillingness to report on their own and their fellow police officers' misconduct to police administrators' reluctance to allow any study of police misconduct in their police agencies (see, e.g., Klockars et al. 2000, 2006). Klockars and Kutnjak Ivković (2003) addressed this issue by developing the theory and the related methodology to measure police integrity—the exact opposite of police misconduct.

The theory of police integrity (Klockars et al. 2000, 2004, 2006) contains four dimensions. The first dimension focuses on the organizational rules and the way they are made by the administration and communicated to, and understood by, police officers (Klockars and Kutnjak Ivković 2003; Klockars et al. 2000, 2004, 2006). Klockars and colleagues (2000, 2004, 2006) define a police agency of high integrity as an agency in which the official rules concerning misconduct are made, taught to the police officers, enforced on a continuous basis, and whose police officers are familiar with the rules and support them (Kutnjak Ivković 2015b). The second dimension discusses internal methods of misconduct control utilized by the police agency (Klockars and Kutnjak Ivković 2003; Klockars et al. 2000, 2004, 2006). Based on this dimension, a police agency of high integrity is expected to deploy both proactive methods and reactive methods of control (Kutnjak Ivković 2015b). The third dimension explores the extent of the code of silence and the police agency's efforts in curtailing it (Klockars and Kutnjak Ivković 2003; Klockars et al. 2000, 2004, 2006). According to this dimension of the theory, a police agency of high integrity controls the code of silence. The fourth dimension of the theory proposes that the society at large influences the level of integrity in the police agency (Klockars and Kutnjak Ivković 2003; Klockars et al. 2000, 2004, 2006).

Klockars and colleagues also developed a methodological approach that enables scholars and police administrators to measure the level of police integrity in a police agency. This approach utilizes a police officer survey in which police officers are asked to evaluate hypothetical scenarios describing examples of police misconduct. The first version of the questionnaire—the police corruption questionnaire (e.g., Klockars et al. 2000, 2004)—contains mostly scenarios describing police corruption. The second version of the questionnaire—the police integrity questionnaire (e.g., Klockars et al. 2006)—includes different forms of police misconduct, ranging from police corruption and the use of excessive force to a failure to react and a falsification of official documents.

In both versions of the questionnaire, each scenario description is followed by seven identical questions exploring perceptions of misconduct seriousness, violations of official rules, expected and appropriate discipline, and the perceptions of the code of silence. Two of these questions tap into the first theoretical dimension that we explore in this chapter. They ask the respondents to recognize whether the described behaviors violate official rules and thus directly test their knowledge of official rules. In addition, a question also asks the respondents to assess the seriousness of the described behaviors and express their support for the official rules.

Absolute Evaluations of Police Misconduct Seriousness

Since the development of the theory and methodology in the mid-1990s, empirical studies of police integrity have been conducted in 30 countries across the world (for an overview, see Klockars et al. 2004; Kutnjak Ivković and Haberfeld 2015). Studies have used either the first police corruption questionnaire (e.g., Alain 2004; Chattha and Kutnjak Ivković 2004; Edelbacher and Kutnjak Ivković 2004; Haberfeld 2004; Johnson 2004; Kutnjak Ivković and Klockars 2004; Kremer 2004; Newham 2004; Pagon and Lobnikar 2004; Pounti et al. 2004; Punch et al. 2004; Torstensson Levander and Ekenvall 2004; Westmarland 2004) or the second police integrity questionnaire (e.g., Cheloukhine et al. 2015; Kang and Kutnjak Ivković 2015; Khechumyan and Kutnjak Ivković 2015; Kutnjak Ivković 2015a; Kutnjak Ivković et al. 2015; Lobnikar and Meško 2015; Phetthong and Kutnjak Ivković 2015; Porter et al. 2015; Sauerman and Kutnjak Ivković 2015; Vallmuur 2015). Regardless of the questionnaire used, these studies of police integrity followed the Klockars and colleagues' methodological approach (e.g., Klockars et al. 2000, 2004, 2006) and, accordingly, they also included measures of police misconduct seriousness.

Various empirical studies have documented that perceptions of misconduct seriousness vary across the scenarios provided in the questionnaire (e.g., Alain 2004; Chattha and Kutnjak Ivković 2004; Cheloukhine et al. 2015; Edelbacher and Kutnjak Ivković 2004; Haberfeld 2004; Johnson 2004; Kang and Kutnjak Ivković 2015; Khechumyan and Kutnjak Ivković 2015; Kutnjak Ivković et al. 2015; Kutnjak Ivković and Klockars 2004; Kremer 2004; Lobnikar and Meško 2015; Newham 2004; Pagon and Lobnikar 2004; Phetthong and Kutnjak Ivković 2015; Porter et al. 2015; Pounti et al. 2004; Punch et al. 2004; Sauerman and Kutnjak Ivković 2015; Torstensson Levander and Ekenvall 2004; Westmarland 2004; Vallmuur 2015).

Comparative studies (e.g., Huberts et al. 2003; Khruakham and Lee 2013; Klockars et al. 2004;

Kutnjak Ivković 2005; Ivković and Haberfeld 2015; Kutnjak Ivković and Shelley 2008) provide extensive evidence about the degree to which these absolute evaluations of seriousness vary across countries. Indeed, the magnitude of these absolute differences across various countries could be large (e.g., Klockars et al. 2004; Kutnjak Ivković and Haberfeld 2015). Large cross-country differences could be linked with the country's social, economic, and legal characteristics. In fact, the fourth dimension of the police integrity theory predicts (e.g., Klockars et al. 2000, 2006; Kutnjak Ivković 2015b) that social, political, and legal environment is related to the evaluations of seriousness. Indeed, results concerning specific scenarios lend support to that prediction. In one study, absolute evaluations of seriousness of the use of excessive force scenarios in South Korea tended to be much lower than in other established democracies participating in the study, while the absolute evaluations of seriousness for police corruption scenarios seemed quite similar (Kutnjak Ivković and Haberfeld 2015). Officers in South Korea, like officers in other established democracies, put a lot of emphasis of addressing police corruption, but they had much more relaxed views about the use of excessive force than police officers in other established democracies did (Kutnjak Ivković and Haberfeld 2015). Similarly, Kutnjak and Shelley (2008) found that the Czech respondents consistently evaluated the behaviors as more serious than the Bosnian respondents, a finding that supports the argument that the conditions in the society at large may explain such differences.

Extant research has also explored the connection between the two measures of the first theoretical dimension (i.e., official rules and the way they are taught and accepted by police officers): perceptions of seriousness and the recognition of behavior as rule-violating. As expected, these two measures are strongly related; the studies that have explored this relation (e.g., Kutnjak Ivković 2015a; Kutnjak Ivković et al. 2015; Kutnjak Ivković and Sauerman 2015; Lobnikar and Meško 2015; Phetthong and Kutnjak Ivković 2015; Wu et al. 2018) have consistently found that, when police officers were more likely to label behavior as rule-violating, they were also more likely to evaluate it as more serious.

Research has also analyzed the relation between perceptions of seriousness and measures of other dimensions of the theory of police integrity. The theory proposes that other organizational components, such as the effectiveness of the police agency's internal control system (second dimension) and the agency's effectiveness of addressing the code of silence (third dimension; Klockars and Kutnjak Ivković, 2003), should be related to the evaluations of police seriousness (first dimension). The second dimension of the theory, that is, the effectiveness of the internal control system, is measured in the questionnaire through the respondents' views of expected discipline. In conclusion of their comparative 14-country study, Klockars et al. (2004, p. 13) elaborate on this relation:

> It appears that in each country the seriousness of officers' misconduct is, in large part, determined by the absolute level of discipline the organization is expected to visit on an offending officer. In almost every case, when the police organization is expected to punish an offense very severely, officers regard that offense as serious. Conversely, when organizations do not punish misbehavior severely, as is the case in Hungary, Pakistan, and South Africa, officers seem to have little ability to distinguish among the levels of seriousness with regard to misconduct.

The same conclusion was drawn in a number of other countries, as diverse as Australia (Porter et al. 2015), China (Wu et al. 2018), Croatia (Kutnjak Ivković 2015a), Eritrea (Desta 2013), Japan (Johnson 2003), South Africa (Kutnjak Ivković and Sauerman 2015), and South Korea (Kutnjak Ivković and Kang 2011). Simply put, when police officers expect that their police agency will discipline more severely for specific misconduct, they are also more likely to evaluate this behavior as serious.

The third dimension of the theory—the police agency's efforts to curtail its code of silence—is measured through the respondents' views of their own willingness to report misconduct. Akin to the strong relation between perceptions of seriousness and expected discipline, there is a strong relation between perceptions of seriousness and the respondents' expressed willingness to report misconduct (e.g., Cheloukhine et al. 2015; Hickman et al. 2016; Huberts et al. 2003; Kutnjak Ivković 2009; Kutnjak Ivković et al. 2015; Kutnjak Ivković and Kang 2011; Kutnjak Ivković and Klockars 2004; Kutnjak Ivković and Sauerman 2013, 2015; Lobnikar and Meško 2015; Phetthong and Kutnjak Ivković 2015; Porter et al. 2015; Vallmuur 2015; Wu et al. 2018). While willingness to report and perceptions of seriousness are strongly related, it appears that perceptions of seriousness influence the respondents' willingness to report (rather than vice versa).

In addition to the organizational dimensions, prior research has uncovered that some of the respondents' demographic characteristics may play a role in their estimates of seriousness. Supervisory position was one such characteristic; studies show that the supervisory position is positively related with the evaluations of seriousness (e.g., Kutnjak Ivković 2004; Raines 2010). Length of service was explored in Micucci and Gomme (2005), uncovering a complex relation between the length of service and evaluations of seriousness for the use of excessive force scenario: U.S. rookie police officers (below 1 year of service) and highly experienced police officers (with over 20 years of service) evaluated police misconduct as much more serious than their other colleagues did. However, the study did not control for the supervisory status, so it is quite possible that the highly experienced police officers in their study were actually almost all supervisors.

Gender has been explored in a few prior studies. Pagon and colleagues (Pagon et al. 2004) reported that gender was not a significant predictor of the Slovenian police officers' and students' evaluations of seriousness in the majority of scenarios, but in a few scenarios in which gender played a role, women viewed police misconduct as more serious than men did. On the other hand, the results of a U.S. student study suggested that gender was a significant predictor (women evaluated misconduct as more serious; Bjerregaard and Lord 2004). In the same study, Bjerregaard and Lord (2004) found that the students' major and career interests were not significant predictors of their evaluations of misconduct seriousness.

Relative Evaluations of Police Misconduct Seriousness

In addition to exploring absolute evaluations of seriousness, studies have also explored relative evaluations of seriousness (i.e., how serious one behavior is compared to the other behaviors in the questionnaire). The results of comparative studies demonstrate that, despite sometimes even very large differences in absolute evaluations of seriousness, relative evaluations of seriousness tend to be very similar across countries (e.g., Huberts et al. 2003; Klockars et al. 2004; Kutnjak Ivković 2004, 2005; Ivković and Haberfeld 2015; Kutnjak Ivković and Shelley 2008). Put differently, it seems that there is a shared hierarchy of relative seriousness of police misconduct across continents. Regardless of the specific absolute assessments of misconduct seriousness in a country, stealing an item from a crime scene or accepting a bribe from a motorist would consistently be evaluated as more serious than accepting gratuities (e.g., Klockars et al. 2004).

Khruakham and Lee (2013) compared the relative rankings of seriousness across five countries (Finland, The Netherlands, Sweden, Thailand, USA) and found them to be very similar, while the absolute assessments of seriousness by Thai police officers tended to be quite different from the evaluations provided by police officers from the other four countries. Similarly, Klockars and colleagues (Klockars et al. 2004, p. 13) summarized the results of their comparative study utilizing the police corruption questionnaire across 14 countries: "despite substantial differences in absolute scores, the rank order in which police officers from most countries evaluated the seriousness of the misconduct in the scenarios is remarkably similar." At the same time, Klockars and colleagues (2004) noted that, when they found differences in the rankings across the countries in specific scenarios (e.g., abuse of alcohol, use of excessive force), the deviations from the uniformed way in which these behaviors have been ranked in other countries were probably driven by cultural differences.

About a decade later, Kutnjak Ivković and Haberfeld (2015) engaged in a 10-country comparative study based on the police integrity questionnaire. They found a strong connection between the rankings in 8 out of 10 countries included in the study. The two outliers are related to the influence of the society at large on the evaluations of seriousness. For example, while the rankings were particularly strongly related across the four East-European countries (Armenia, Croatia, Estonia, and Slovenia) in the study, that similarity did not extend to the rankings reported by the Russian sample. Also, the ranking from South Korea did not fit well with the rest; because of the relatively tolerant attitudes toward the use of excessive force, the associated scenarios tended to be ranked as less serious than they were in other countries and, hence, resulted in a comparatively different ranking of the scenarios (Kutnjak Ivković and Haberfeld 2015).

The similarity of relative orders of seriousness seems to transcend police ranks as well. In a study comparing supervisor and line officer views from Croatia, Finland, and the U.S.A., Kutnjak Ivković (2005) reported not only that the rankings across groups of supervisors and groups of line officers from the three countries were similar, but also that they were similar across all six groups of line officers and supervisors, regardless of the country (e.g., line officers from Croatia and supervisors from Finland). Vito and colleagues (2011) provided further evidence of similarity in relative views of seriousness between U.S. sergeants and middle managers, as well as among supervisors in Croatia, Finland, and the U.S.A.

Some studies (e.g., Kutnjak Ivković 2004, 2005; Meyer et al. 2013; Wright 2010) compared police officers' and citizens' relative evaluations of misconduct seriousness. Kutnjak Ivković (2004, 2005) found that the rankings of police misconduct seriousness are quite similar between police officers and citizens. Meyer and colleagues (2013) compared rankings of South African police officers and students and concluded that

there is a substantial degree of similarity in relative rankings between these two groups. In a comparative paper exploring the U.S. and Croatian police officer and college student views, Kutnjak Ivković (2004) found not only that the same type of respondents (e.g., police officers, students) from the two countries ranked these scenarios in similar ways, but also that the rankings were similar across different types of respondents. Wright (2010, p. 348) explored potential differences in the views between police officers and civilian staff employed in the police stations in northern England. He noted that, "with few exceptions, there was a general agreement amongst both police officers and police staff in relation to the rank order of the scenarios in terms of seriousness, discipline and willingness to report" Wright (2010, p. 348).

Extant research has also explored how evaluations of seriousness change over time. Although absolute evaluations of seriousness of police corruption had changed over a period of 5 years, the relative estimates of seriousness remained stable (Kutnjak Ivković 2014): the respondents surveyed at the beginning and at the end of the five-year period evaluated the same scenarios as the least serious and the most serious. The current chapter extends this literature addressing relative and absolute judgements of police misconduct seriousness by considering the influence of perceptions of organizational justice on the respondents' evaluations of misconduct seriousness.

Organizational Justice as a Predictor of Police Attitudes and Behavior

Several decades of organizational behavior and management research demonstrate that employees' attitudes and behaviors are driven to a large degree by their perceptions of supervisor fairness (e.g., Colquitt et al. 2001). Employees that believe their supervisors treat them fairly and with respect are more likely to engage in a wide range of organizational citizenship behaviors, adhere to organizational goals, have higher levels of productivity, engage in less deviance, be more committed to their organization, and have higher job satisfaction (Ambrose and Schminke 2009; Cohen-Charash and Spector 2001; McFarlin and Sweeney 1992). Although somewhat inconsistently conceptualized across studies, most organizational justice research recognizes four components (Colquitt 2001). Distributive justice focuses on employees' evaluations of how fairly outcomes are distributed within their organization (e.g., promotions, salary; Adams 1965). The second component—procedural justice—centers on how fair organizational procedures are during decision-making processes and whether employees are given a voice (Leventhal 1980; Lind and Tyler 1988; Thibaut and Walker 1975). The third component—interactional justice—focuses on the extent of respect and dignity that supervisors provide to their subordinates (Bies and Moag 1986). Some scholars divide interactional justice into two more components: interpersonal and informational justice (see Colquitt 2001). Interpersonal justice deals with the level of respect and dignity that supervisors afford their subordinates while informational justice deals with communication from supervisors, specifically, the extent to which supervisors are candid, timely, and thorough in their communications with subordinates (Bies and Moag 1986).

Police researchers have explored the role of organizational justice in understanding officers' attitudes and behaviors with increased frequency in recent years. From an attitudinal standpoint, officers who believe they have been treated with organizational justice tend to be less cynical about their job and more committed to their department's goals (Bradford and Quinton 2014; Bradford et al. 2014). Such officers also hold more favorable attitudes toward the public and are more likely to support the use of community-oriented policing and procedurally-fair treatment of citizens (Myhill and Bradford 2013; Trinker et al. 2016). More broadly, officers have greater job satisfaction if they believe their supervisors are fair (Donner et al. 2016; Rosenbaum and McCarty 2017). The experience of organizational justice appears to cultivate greater organizational identification, internalization of organizational goals, supervisor trust, citizen trust, and self-legitimacy which, in turn, are associated with beneficial work-related outcomes among line-level officers (Bradford et al. 2014; Bradford and Quinton 2014; Carr and Maxwell 2018; Haas et al. 2015; Nix and Wolfe 2016; Van Craen and Skogan 2017; Wolfe and Nix 2017). Simply put, organizational justice produces favorable outcomes among police employees.

Much less research has explored the relationship between police officers' evaluations of organizational justice and deviant behavior. Trinkner and colleagues (2016), for example, found that procedural justice from supervisors cultivated an organizational climate where officers were significantly less likely to support the use of excessive force. Wolfe and Piquero (2011) demonstrated that officers who evaluated their superiors as organizationally fair had fewer self-reported citizen complaints, internal affairs investigations, and disciplinary charges against them. Importantly, these results were observed after controlling for officers' code of silence and noble-cause corruption attitudes, and their deviant colleague associations. Their analysis also revealed that officers who felt they were treated with organizational justice were less likely to adhere to the code of silence or harbor beliefs in noble-cause corruption.

From the extant literature we know that employees, in general, and police officers specifically, are more likely to hold favorable attitudes and engage in beneficial behaviors when they believe they have been treated in an organizationally fair manner. We also know that police officers are more likely to engage in misconduct when they believe their supervisors are organizationally unjust. What we do not know, however, is whether officers' evaluations of organizational justice are tied to their attitudes concerning the seriousness of various forms of misconduct. This is an interesting question because it could be the partial attitudinal explanation between organizational justice and deviant behavior. Officers may engage in more misconduct when they feel unfairly treated by their supervisors because such treatment helps cultivate attitudes that specific forms of misconduct are not serious. We explore this question in the analyses below.

Current Study

The current study seeks to contribute to the literature on police integrity by seeking to connect perceptions of police misconduct seriousness to perceptions of organizational justice. As discussed above, organizational justice is often associated with correlates like positive perceptions of supervisors, rule structures, and commitment to the organization. Although the causal order of these relations is unclear, organizational support theory suggests that, as officers experience more just outcomes, processes, interactions, and information-sharing from the organization in general and its leadership in particular, they will feel more obligated to reciprocate the behavior, more strongly incorporate the agency into their self-concept, and increase belief that positive behavior will be rewarded (Rhones and Eisenberger 2002). This obligation, identification, and/or belief in rewards for positive behavior then provide potential mechanisms by which increases in organizational justice might translate to a greater willingness to eschew police misconduct. The current research takes a first step toward understanding this relation by testing the correlation between organizational justice and police integrity in sample of police officers in Croatia.

Methodology

Questionnaire

The questionnaire contained 12 hypothetical scenarios. Several scenarios are based on the police integrity questionnaire developed by Klockars and colleagues (2006). Specifically, four scenarios provided examples of police corruption and additional three scenarios provided examples of the use of excessive force. These scenarios ranged in their seriousness, from the least serious scenario, describing the acceptance of gratuities (Scenario 1) and the verbal abuse of a citizen (Scenario 5), to the most serious scenarios, describing theft from a crime scene (Scenario 2) and the abuse of deadly force (Scenario 3;

Kutnjak Ivković 2015a, b; Kutnjak Ivković and Haberfeld 2015). The questionnaire also contained additional six scenarios addressing organizational deviance and interpersonal deviance (see Kutnjak Ivković et al. 2019; Table 1). The scenarios shown in tables (Tables 2, 3, 4, 5, 6, 7, 8, and 9) are based on the type of behavior and, within each group, classified based on the hypothesized evaluations of seriousness.[1]

Dependent Variables

Each scenario is followed by several identical questions. The first question tapped into the respondents' evaluations of misconduct seriousness. Possible answers ranged from $1 =$ "not at all serious" to $5 =$ "very serious." Because the distribution of answers was not normal, we dichotomized the answers for the analyses. Answers "1," "2," and "3″ were merged into "less serious" and answers "4″ and "5″ into "more serious." Because the distribution in two scenarios (Scenario 2: Theft; Scenario 4: Internal Corruption) was even more skewed toward the end of the seriousness scale, we dichotomized the variable as follows: "1″ through "4″ were classified as "not serious" and answer "5″ is classified as "more serious."

Organizational Independent Variables

In accordance with the first theoretical dimension, the next question asked the respondents to assess whether the behavior violates official rules. Possible answers were "1" = "yes," "2" = "no," and "3" = "not sure." Because our analyses focused on comparing the results by the respondents who were able to recognize the behavior as rule-violating (1 = "yes") and the

---

[1] The evaluations of seriousness for police corruption and the use of excessive force are based on the earlier police integrity survey of the Croatian police (e.g., Kutnjak Ivković 2015a, b). The ranking of the organizational deviance and interpersonal deviance scenarios is based on the hypothesized seriousness based on the Bennett and Robinson's typology (2000).

Table 1 Scenario Classification and Description

Scenario type and seriousness level	Scenario description
Police corruption	
Least serious	Scenario 1: A police officer is frequently seen in a neighborhood. Local merchants and restaurant owners regularly show their appreciation for his attention by giving him gifts of food and liquor and other items of small value
Medium seriousness	Scenario 4: A police officer is scheduled to work during coming holidays. The supervisor offers to give him these days off, if he agrees to run some personal errands for the supervisor. Evaluate the SUPERVISOR'S behavior
Most serious	Scenario 2: A police officer discovers a burglary of an appliance store. The display cases are smashed and many items have obviously been taken. While searching the store, he takes an expensive watch and slips it into his pocket. He reports that the watch, worth about a week's pay, has been stolen during the burglary
Use of excessive force	
Least serious	Scenario 5: A police officer stops a motorist for speeding. As the officer approaches the vehicle, the driver yells, "what the hell are you stopping me for?" the officer replies, "because today is 'arrest an asshole day'"
Medium seriousness	Scenario 7: A police sergeant, without intervening, watches officers under his supervision repeatedly strike and kick a man arrested for child abuse. The man has previous child abuse arrests. Evaluate the SERGEANT'S behavior
Most serious	Scenario 3: An officer, who was severely beaten by a person resisting arrest, has just returned to duty. On patrol, the officer approaches a person standing in a dimly lit alley. Suddenly, the person throws a gym bag at the officer and begins to run away. The officer fatally shoots the person, striking him in the back. It was later determined that the person was unarmed
Organizational deviance	
Least serious	Scenario 8: An officer is passed over for a day off on new Year's eve despite a promise from the supervisor. As a result, the officer could incur a financial loss for a nonrefundable family vacation. The police officer decides to call in sick for the new year Eve's shift and takes the trip
Medium seriousness	Scenario 6: At 2 a.m. a police officer, who is on duty, is driving his patrol car on a deserted road. He sees a vehicle that has been driven off the road and is stuck in a ditch. He approaches the vehicle and observes that the driver is not hurt but is obviously intoxicated. He also finds that the driver is a police officer. Instead of reporting this accident and offense he transports the driver to his home
Most serious	Scenario 11: Several days in a row, a police officer stays overtime to finish the paperwork. While filling out the forms requesting his overtime pay, he reports working 1 h longer each day than he had actually worked
Interpersonal deviance	
Least serious	Scenario 12: An officer is scheduled to attend a leadership training offered only to select members of the agency. After a disagreement with a supervisor, the officer is no longer on the list of officers scheduled to attend the training. The officer starts spreading a rumor that the supervisor's daughter is dating a drug addict. Evaluate the behavior of the officer
Medium seriousness	Scenario 9: Before the shift begins, several police officers gather in the police station to chat. After a few minutes, a male officer starts to taunt the female officers about their suitability for the job and makes jokes about their "other skills." evaluate the behavior of the male officer
Most serious	Scenario 10: A traffic light is broken and a police officer is sent to direct traffic an hour prior to the end of his shift. He is assured by the supervisor that he is going to be relieved by officer Jones within 1 h. After 4 h, the light is fixed. The officer gets back to the station and upon spotting officer Jones yells: "Why the fuck didn't you show up to relieve me?"

Table 2 Respondents' Views about Misconduct Seriousness by Procedural Justice

	Lowest procedural justice		Middle procedural justice		Highest procedural justice		Difference between highest and lowest	Chi-square	Phi
	% Serious	Rank	% Serious	Rank	% Serious	Rank			
Scenario 1: Gratuities	40.9%	5	46.7%	5	62.1%	5	21.2%	13.492**	.178
Scenario 4: Internal corruption	85.1%	11	88.1%	11	90.0%	11	4.9%		
	62.7%		62.2%		69.9%		7.2%	2.70	.079
Scenario 2: Theft	94.0%	12	97.0%	12	96.9%	12	2.9%		
	92.5%		90.4%		95.2%		2.7%	3.22	.086
Scenario 5: Verbal abuse	47.0%	6	58.8%	6	69.2%	6	22.2%	12.11**	.167
Scenario 7: Sgt. Watches	53.7%	7	64.0%	7	72.1%	7	18.4%	8.60*	.140
Scenario 3: Deadly force	64.2%	8	84.4%	10	84.7%	9	20.5%	15.64***	.190
Scenario 8: New year	29.9%	2	31.6%	2	41.5%	1	11.6%	5.14[a]	.108
Scenario 6: Protection of DUI	23.9%	1	28.7%	1	47.4%	2	23.5%	19.53***	.211
Scenario 11: Overtime forms	66.7%	9	76.5%	8	85.4%	10	18.7%	12.53**	.170
Scenario 12: Rumor	65.7%	4	66.9%	3	79.8%	4	14.1%	9.96**	.151
Scenario 9: Rude gender	68.2%	10	81.6%	9	79.0%	8	10.8%	4.89+	.106
Scenario 10: Cursing	34.3%	3	39.3%	4	56.8%	3	22.5%	16.47***	.194

* $p < .05$; ** $p < .01$; *** $p < .001$; + $p < .10$

respondents who were not able to do so (3 = "not sure") or openly stated that he behavior does not violate the rules (2 = "no"), we recoded answers "2" and "3" together as "no or not sure."

To measure the second dimension of the theory, the respondents were asked to estimate what the expected discipline would be. Possible answers ranged on an 8-point scale, from "none" to "dismissal." The first two answers (1 = "none" and 2 = "public warning") denote either no discipline at all or the mildest form of discipline that does not include any written discipline that is kept in the police officers' permanent file. All of the other answers ("3″ to "8″) describe realistic disciplinary options that result in a permanent record in police officers' personnel files. Specifically, answers "3″ to "6″ denote fine that increases in severity, from 10% of the salary (answer "3″) to 30% of the salary (answer "6″). Answer "7″ refers to the "possibility of no advancement," while answer "8″ represents the most serious disciplinary option—the dismissal. Again, because the answers were not normally distributed across the 8 categories, we have dichotomized them into "no discipline" (answers "1″ and "2″) and "some discipline" (answers "3″ through "8″).

Organizational Justice Independent Variables

The questionnaire contained seven questions inquiring about procedural justice from the organizational justice study by Wolfe and Piquero (2011). The answers to these questions ranged

Table 3 Respondents' Views about Misconduct Seriousness by Distributive Justice

	Lowest distributive justice		Middle distributive justice		Highest distributive justice		Difference between highest and lowest	Chi-square	Phi
	% Serious	Rank	% Serious	Rank	% Serious	Rank			
Scenario 1: Gratuities	37.4%	3	58.3%	4	62.1%	4	24.7%	18.83***	.209
Scenario 4: Internal corruption	86.4%	11	88.5%	11	90.9%	11	4.5%		
	65.6%		66.7%		66.9%		1.3%	0.06	.011
Scenario 2: Theft	95.2%	12	96.8%	12	96.8%	12	1.6%		
	91.2%		93.6%		94.2%		3.0%	1.03	.049
Scenario 5: Verbal abuse	50.4%	5	62.4%	5	70.9%	5	20.5%	12.45**	.168
Scenario 7: Sgt. Watches	53.2%	6	67.9%	6	75.3%	6	22.1%	15.67***	.189
Scenario 3: Deadly force	71.2%	10	87.8%	10	82.5%	7	11.3%	12.80**	.172
Scenario 8: New year	28.6%	2	36.3%	1	42.4%	1	13.8%	5.80+	.115
Scenario 6: Protection of DUI	24.6%	1	38.2%	2	47.5%	2	22.9%	15.65***	.188
Scenario 11: Overtime forms	69.6%	8.5	84.1%	9	84.1%	9	14.5%	11.69**	.163
Scenario 12: Rumor	64.3%	7	72.6%	7	82.8%	8	18.5%	12.61**	.169
Scenario 9: Rude gender	69.6%	8.5	78.3%	8	85.4%	10	15.8%	10.18**	.152
Scenario 10: Cursing	38.1%	4	44.6%	3	59.9%	3	21.8%	14.54**	.182

* $p < .05$; ** $p < .01$; *** $p < .001$; + $p < .10$

from 1 = "strongly disagree" to 5 = "strongly agree." Based on the seven questions tapping into procedural justice, we created the *procedural justice scale*. It ranges from 7 to 35, with the mean of 27.90 (Cronbach's alpha is .914). Because the answers were not normally distributed, we created three categories to denote low levels of procedural justice (scores 7 to 21, indicating an average answer of 3 or lower on each of the seven questions), medium levels of procedural justice (scores 22 to 28, indicating an average answer of between 3 and 4 on each of the seven questions), and high levels of procedural justice (scores 29 to 35, indicating an average answer of above 4 on each of the seven questions).

The questionnaire also incorporated five questions inquiring about distributive justice from the organizational justice study by Wolfe and Piquero (2011). These questions (questions 14, 15, 25a, 25b, and 26 in our questionnaire) all had answers ranging from 1 = "strongly disagree" to 5 = "strongly agree." Based on the five questions tapping into interactional justice, we created the *distributive justice scale*. It ranges from 5 to 25, with the mean of 17.86 (Cronbach's alpha is .793). Because the answers were not normally distributed, we created three categories to denote low levels of distributive justice (scores 5 to 15, indicating an average answer of 3 or lower on each of the five questions), medium levels of distributive justice (scores 16 to 20, indicating an average answer of between 3 and 4 on each of the five questions), and high levels of procedural justice (scores 21 to 25, indicating an average answer of above 4 on each of the five questions).

Table 4 Respondents' Views about Misconduct Seriousness by Interactional Justice

	Lowest interactional justice		Middle interactional justice		Highest interactional justice		Difference between highest and lowest	Chi-square	Phi
	% Serious	Rank	% Serious	Rank	% Serious	Rank			
Scenario 1: Gratuities	37.3%	4	51.5%	4	59.2%	4	21.9	11.39**	.163
Scenario 4: Internal corruption	81.3%	11	90.2%	11	90.3%	11	9.0%		.107
	62.7%		57.8%		71.2%		8.5%	6.49*	.122
Scenario 2: Theft	92.0%	12	97.1%	12	97.3%	12	5.3%	4.76+	.105
	88.0%		93.1%		94.6%		6.6%	3.87	.094
Scenario 5: Verbal abuse	48.0%	5	56.9%	5	68.7%	5	20.7%	12.40**	.168
Scenario 7: Sgt. Watches	53.3%	6	68.0%	7	69.3%	6	16.0%	6.86*	.125
Scenario 3: Deadly force	70.7%	10	81.4%	10	84.8%	9	14.1%	7.74*	.134
Scenario 8: New year	28.0%	1.5	30.1%	2	40.8%	1	12.8%	6.29*	.120
Scenario 6: Protection of DUI	28.0%	1.5	25.2%	1	45.4%	2	17.4%	16.45***	.193
Scenario 11: Overtime forms	63.5%	7	78.6%	9	85.1%	10	21.6%	16.80***	.196
Scenario 12: Rumor	64.0%	8	67.0%	6	79.3%	7	15.3%	10.30**	.153
Scenario 9: Rude gender	68.9%	9	77.7%	8	81.2%	8	12.3%	5.17+	.109
Scenario 10: Cursing	36.0%	3	36.9%	3	55.2%	3	19.2%	14.78**	.183

$* p < .05; ** p < .01; *** p < .001; + p < .10$

Table 5 Average Difference between the Lowest and Highest Seriousness Evaluations by Organizational Justice

	Procedural justice	Distributive justice	Interactional justice
Traditional Police corruption	9.7%	10.3%	12.1%
Traditional Excessive force	20.4%	18.0%	16.9%
Organizational deviance	17.9%	17.1%	17.2%
Interpersonal deviance	15.8%	18.7%	15.6%

Furthermore, the questionnaire also included four questions inquiring about interactional justice from the organizational justice study by Wolfe and Piquero (2011). These questions (questions 13, 20, 21, and 27 in our questionnaire) all had answers ranging from 1 = "strongly disagree" to 5 = "strongly agree." Based on the four questions tapping into interactional justice, we created the *interactional justice scale*. It ranges from 4 to 20, with the mean of 16.26 (Cronbach's alpha is .889). Because the answers were not normally distributed, we created three categories to denote low levels of interactional justice (scores 4 to 12, indicating an average answer of 3 or lower on each of the four questions), medium levels of interactional justice (scores 13 to 16, indicating an

Table 6 Logistic Regression of Own Seriousness (Police Corruption)[a]

	Scenario 1 (Gratuities)			Scenario 4 (Internal Corruption)			Scenario 2 (Theft)		
	b	s.e.	Odds	b	s.e.	Odds	b	s.e.	Odds
Supervisory status[b]	.449	.315	1.567	.454	.329	1.575	.311	.620	1.365
Length of service[c]									
6–15 years	−.579	.502	.561	.446	.481	1.562	.538	.854	1.713
Over 15 years	−.046	.479	.955	.561	.463	1.753	.485	.813	1.624
Organizational justice[d]									
Middle	.655+	.348	1.926	.205	.336	1.228	.424	.590	1.529
High	1.147***	.324	3.148	.110	.310	1.116	.477	.532	1.612
Violation of rules[e]	1.917***	.243	6.801	1.622***	.248	5.065	2.979***	.585	19.665
Expected discipline[f]	.445+	.242	1.560	.240	.237	1.272	.211	.465	1.235
Constant	−1.714	.517		−1.207	.511		−1.015	.955	
Model Nagelkerke R^2	.332			.191			.184		

* $p < .05$; ** $p < .01$; *** $p < .001$; + $p < .10$
[a]Reference category = "not serious"
[b]Reference category = "non-supervisor"
[c]Reference category = "0 to 5 years"
[d]Reference category = "low organizational justice"
[e]Reference category = "not a violation"
[f]Reference category = "more lenient discipline"

Table 7 Logistic Regression of Own Seriousness (Excessive Force)[a]

	Scenario 5 (Verbal Abuse)			Scenario 7 (Sgt. Watches)			Scenario 3 (Deadly Force)		
	b	s.e.	Odds	b	s.e.	Odds	b	s.e.	Odds
Supervisory status[b]	.243	.302	1.275	.136	.327	1.146	−.061	.409	.941
Length of service[c]									
6–15 years	−1.068=	.559	.344	.218	.511	1.243	.452	.529	1.571
Over 15 years	−1.146*	.548	.318	.917+	.496	2.501	1.278*	.525	3.589
Organizational justice[d]									
Middle	.688*	.341	1.991	.392	.351	1.479	.528	.399	1.695
High	1.032**	.316	2.808	.576+	.324	1.779	.797*	.356	2.218
Violation of rules[e]	1.515***	.236	4.551	2.054***	.275	7.798	1.443***	.322	4.235
Expected discipline[f]	.910***	.242	2.483	.255	.349	1.291	.556+	.320	1.743
Constant	−.548	.553		−1.946	.544		−1.166	.560	
Model Nagelkerke R^2	.275			.299			.237		

* $p < .05$; ** $p < .01$; *** $p < .001$; + $p < .10$
[d]Reference category = "low organizational justice"
[e]Reference category = "not a violation"
[a]Reference category = "not serious"
[b]Reference category = "non-supervisor"
[c]Reference category = "0 to 5 years"
[d]Reference category = "more lenient discipline"

average answer of between 3 and 4 on each of the four questions), and high levels of interactional justice (scores 17 to 20, indicating an average answer of above 4 on each of the four questions).

Because of the high correlation among the three justice scales (Pearson's coefficient for procedural justice and distributive justice = .798, $p < .001$; Pearson's coefficient for procedural

Table 8 Logistic Regression of Own Seriousness (Organizational Deviance)[a]

	Scenario 8 (New Year)			Scenario 6 (Protection of DUI)			Scenario 11 (Overtime forms)		
	b	s.e.	Odds	b	s.e.	Odds	b	s.e.	Odds
Supervisory status[b]	.357	.295	1.428	.443	.284	1.557	.376	.383	1.457
Length of service[c]									
6–15 years	−.023	.558	.977	−1.163*	.487	.312	−.898	.827	.407
Over 15 years	.593	.534	1.809	−1.251**	.468	.286	−1.288	.807	.276
Organizational justice[d]									
Middle	−.112	.359	.894	.623	.382	1.865	.269	.384	1.309
High	.254	.324	1.290	1.089**	.357	2.970	.799*	.360	2.23
Violation of rules[e]	1.731***	.247	5.702	1.577***	.288	4.838	1.601***	.308	4.957
Expected discipline[f]	.262	.264	1.300	.306	.257	1.358	1.162***	.303	3.195
Constant	−1.981	.554		−1.524	.516		.246	.827	
Model Nagelkerke R^2	.252			.232			.304		

$* p < .05; ** p < .01; *** p < .001; ^+ p < .10$
[a]Reference category = "not serious"
[b]Reference category = "non-supervisor"
[c]Reference category = "0 to 5 years"
[d]Reference category = "low organizational justice"
[e]Reference category = "not a violation"
[f]Reference category = "more lenient discipline"

Table 9 Logistic Regression of Own Seriousness (Interpersonal Deviance)[a]

	Scenario 12 (Rumor)			Scenario 9 (Rude Gender)			Scenario 10 (Cursing)		
	b	s.e.	Odds	b	s.e.	Odds	b	s.e.	Odds
Supervisory status[b]	−.175	.323	.840	.291	.376	1.337	.207	.282	1.229
Length of service[c]									
6–15 years	−.826	.630	.438	−1.053	.652	.349	−.450	.490	.638
Over 15 years	−6.21	.621	.537	−.931	.635	.394	−.626	.473	.535
Organizational justice[d]									
Middle	.460	.345	1.584	.784*	.382	2.190	.404	.330	1.498
High	.784*	.320	2.190	.594+	.343	1.811	1.048**	.304	2.851
Violation of rules[e]	1.559***	.281	4.756	2.171***	.274	8.766	1.250***	.241	3.491
Expected discipline[f]	.746*	.301	2.108	.376	.290	1.456	.619	.294	1.858
Constant	.315	.620		.156	.637		−.847	.497	
Model Nagelkerke R^2	.246			.296			.206		

$* p < .05; ** p < .01; *** p < .001; ^+ p < .10$
[a]Reference category = "not serious"
[b]Reference category = "non-supervisor"
[c]Reference category = "0 to 5 years"
[d]Reference category = "low organizational justice"
[e]Reference category = "not a violation"
[f]Reference category = "more lenient discipline"

justice and interactional justice = .854, p < .001; Pearson's coefficient for distributive justice and interactional justice = .743, p < .001), we have created a new scale *organizational justice* by adding up the values on the three justice scales (Cronbach's alpha is .905). Because the answers were not normally distributed, we created three categories to denote low levels of organizational justice (scores 16 to 48, indicating an average answer of 3 or lower on each of 16 questions), medium levels of organizational justice (scores 49 to 64, indicating an average answer of between 3 and 4 on each of the 16 questions), and high levels of organizational justice (scores 65 to 80, indicating an average answer of above 4 on each of the 16 questions).

Demographic Independent Variables

Following the approach developed by Klockars and Kutnjak Ivković (2003), the questionnaire contains very few measures of demographic characteristics. First, the respondents were asked to state whether they were supervisors. Possible answers were "yes" or "no." Second, there was a question about the respondents' length of service. The seven possible answers ranged from "less than 1 year" to "over 20 years." For multivariate analyses, the answers were merged into "less than 5 years," "5–15 years" and "over 15 years."

Analytical Plan

We first conduct bivariate analyses that explore the relation between perceptions of seriousness and the respondents' views on each of the three components of organizational justice (i.e., procedural justice, distributive justice, interactional justice). We do so by looking separately across scenarios belonging to particular types of misbehavior, including police corruption, use of excessive force, organizational deviance, and interpersonal deviance.

The next step in the analyses incorporates multivariate models of perceptions of seriousness. While controlling for respondents' demographic characteristics and organizational variables, we study the independent effect of organizational justice on seriousness evaluations.

The Sample

The data were collected in the fall of 2018 among the police officers employed in four police stations in the Croatian capital of Zagreb.

The research team distributed the paper-and-pencil survey to over 500 police officers. The questionnaire included a cover letter describing the study, informing the respondents that their participation is voluntary and that they can withdraw from the study at any point, and listing potential risks and benefits from participation in the study. About 500 police officers (N = 495) returned completed questionnaires, resulting in the response rate of 90%.

The last question in the questionnaire asked the respondents whether they have answered honestly. About 10% of the respondents (47 out of 495) either did not answer this question at all or had explicitly stated that they lied while filling out the questionnaire. Their answers were excluded from further analyses.

The overwhelming majority of the respondents are line officers or non-supervisors (82%). The respondents are mostly experienced police officers: 6% have been police officers for up to 5 years, 29% have been police officers from 6 to 15 years, and 65% have been police officers for at least 15 years.

Results

Bivariate Analyses of Seriousness Evaluations by Organizational Justice

The respondents were asked to assess the seriousness of traditional police corruption and excessive force scenarios, as well as the new workplace deviance scenarios including organizational deviance and interpersonal deviance. Their answers were dichotomized into "less serious" and "more serious" evaluations. The goal of our analyses is to explore the bivariate relation between the respondents' evaluations of seriousness and their perceptions of different elements of organizational justice. We begin by assessing the bivariate relation between the respondents' evaluations of misconduct seriousness and their perceptions of procedural justice (Table 2), distributive justice (Table 3), and interactional justice (Table 4).

The results of the bivariate analysis between the respondents' evaluations of seriousness and their assessments of *procedural justice* (Table 2) indicate that, in two-thirds of the scenarios (8 out of 12), the respondents' estimates of seriousness vary with their assessments of procedural justice in statistically significant ways. Specifically, the respondents who attributed the highest level of procedural justice were more likely to respond that misconduct is serious than the respondents with the lowest levels of procedural justice were. In addition, differences were marginally significant for two scenarios (Scenario 8: New Year; Scenario 9: Rude Gender). The respondents' evaluations of seriousness and perceptions of procedural justice were not related in only two scenarios (Scenario 2: Theft; Scenario 4: Internal Corruption), also evaluated to be the most serious in the whole questionnaire (i.e., ranked as #11 and #12; Table 2).

The next set of analyses explores the bivariate relation between the respondents' evaluations of seriousness and their assessments of *distributive justice* (Table 3). As with procedural justice, in more than two-thirds of the scenarios (9 out of 12) the respondents' estimates of seriousness vary with their assessments of distributive justice in statistically significant ways; the respondents with the highest level of distributive justice were also more likely to say that misconduct was serious than the respondents with the lowest levels of distributive justice were. Once again, the respondents' evaluations of seriousness and perceptions of distributive justice were not related in the two most serious in the whole questionnaire (Scenario 2: Theft; Scenario 4: Internal Corruption).

Finally, we also analyzed the bivariate relation between the respondents' evaluations of seriousness and their assessments of *interactional justice* (Table 4). Similarly to the results for procedural justice and distributive justice, our findings indicate that in over two-thirds of the scenarios (10 out of 12), the respondents' estimates of seriousness vary with their assessments of interactional justice in statistically significant ways; the respondents with the highest level of interactional justice were also more likely to say that misconduct was serious than the respondents with the lowest levels of interactional justice were. In addition, differences were marginally

significant for one scenario (Scenario 9: Rude Gender). The respondents' evaluations of seriousness and perceptions of interactional justice were not related in only two scenarios (Scenario 2: Theft; Scenario 4: Internal Corruption), also evaluated to be the most serious in the whole questionnaire.

We have also compared the importance of each of the components of organizational justice for the perceptions of seriousness across types of behavior (Table 5). As the average difference between the lowest and highest procedural justice score indicates,[2] the average differences were the smallest for the police corruption scenarios, suggesting that, among all four types of behavior, organizational justice has the weakest influence on evaluations of police corruption scenarios (Table 5). In fact, comparisons among scenarios that did not result in a statistically significant difference (Tables 2, 3, and 4) always involve at least one scenario from the police corruption group. Scenario 2 (Theft) and Scenario 4 (Internal Corruption) have been evaluated as the most serious in the whole questionnaire and their evaluations of seriousness were typically least affected by the respondents' perceptions of organizational justice, be it procedural justice, distributive justice, or interactional justice.[3] On the other hand, the remaining scenario in the police corruption group (Scenario 1: Gratuities) typically resulted in large differences in seriousness evaluations (e.g., over 20%) between the respondents who evaluated organizational justice as low and the respondents who evaluated organizational justice as high.

On the other hand, perceptions of organizational justice were significantly related to the evaluations of seriousness for the remaining three

---

[2]The average difference score for each group of police misconduct (e.g., police corruption, use of excessive force) is calculated by adding the percent difference between highest and lowest justice for each of the three scenarios that belong to that group of police misconduct and dividing the number by three.

[3]In 5 out of 6 comparisons, the differences were not statistically significant. In particular, the differences were not statistically significant in both scenarios for procedural justice and distributive justice and were not statically significant for Scenario 2 for Scenario 2.

forms of behavior (i.e., excessive force, organizational deviance, interactional deviance). The effect of procedural justice seems to be the strongest on the seriousness evaluations for scenarios describing the use of excessive force (Table 5). Accordingly, police officers who perceived that their supervisors are treating them fairly, both in terms of procedures and outcomes, seemed to be more likely to evaluate the use of excessive force as serious misconduct.

Organizational justice matters for organizational deviance and interpersonal deviance as well (Table 5). Unlike scenarios describing the use of excessive force, in regard to which procedural justice seems to have a somewhat stronger effect than either distributive justice or interactional justice does, the effect of all three elements of organizational justice (i.e., procedural justice, distributive justice, interactional justice) tends to be rather similar on the respondents' evaluations of misconduct seriousness for organizational deviance and interpersonal deviance. By contrast, distributive justice seems to have a somewhat stronger effect on scenarios describing interpersonal misconduct than either procedural justice or interactional justice does (Table 5).

Another way to look at the same data (Table 5) is to assess for each element of organization justice how strongly it affects various forms of behavior. Procedural justice tends to be particularly relevant for the use of excessive force and organizational deviance, and, to a certain degree, for interpersonal deviance (Table 5). Procedural justice seems to be the least relevant for police corruption scenarios which tend to be evaluated as the most serious; while procedural justice is not a significant factor in the respondents' assessment of seriousness for two types of police corruption, the influence on the least serious form of corruption in the questionnaire—the acceptance of gratuities—is as strong (21.2% difference; Table 2) as it was for the use of excessive force scenarios (20.4%; Table 5).

With the exception of the police corruption scenarios, distributive justice has a strong influence on the seriousness evaluations for the use of excessive force, organizational deviance, and interpersonal deviance scenarios (Table 5). The relation between distributive justice and evalua-

tions of police corruption seriousness is very similar to the relation between procedural justice and seriousness evaluations: while justice is not significantly related to the seriousness evaluations in two corruption scenarios, it is a highly significant predictor of the seriousness evaluation of the least serious example of corruption in the questionnaire (Table 3). In fact, the influence of distributive justice seems to be stronger for the scenario describing the use of gratuities (Scenario 1; 24.7%) than for any other scenario in the questionnaire (Table 3).

Finally, the influence of interactional justice seems to be relatively uniform across the four forms of misbehavior, with the influence on police corruption evaluations of seriousness probably being the weakest (Table 5). The only difference is that, unlike procedural justice and distributive justice, interactional justice is significantly connected to evaluations of police corruption in two out of the three scenarios (Table 4).

Out last set of analyses moved from the absolute evaluations of seriousness to the relative evaluations of seriousness. For each type of organizational justice and each level of procedural justice, we have rank-ordered each scenario from "1" = the least serious to "12" = the most serious (Tables 2, 3 and 4) and then estimated the Spearman bivariate correlation for each type of organizational justice.

Unlike the absolute evaluations of seriousness, the relative order of seriousness is related to neither the respondents' perceptions of procedural justice, distributive justice, nor interactional justice. The internal order of the misbehaviors respondents seem to be evaluating as the most serious and the least serious does not seem to be affected by the respondents' levels of organizational justice. Specifically, there was a strong bivariate correlation in the seriousness rankings across the three levels of procedural justice (Spearman's rho for lowest level of procedural justice and the middle level of procedural justice is .972, $p < .001$; Spearman's rho for lowest level of procedural justice and the highest level of procedural justice is .972, $p < .001$; Spearman's rho for middle level of procedural justice and the highest level of procedural justice is .965, $p < .001$). Similarly, there was a strong bivariate correlation in the seriousness rankings between the three levels of distributive justice (Spearman's rho for lowest level of distributive justice and the middle level of distributive justice is .984, p < .001; Spearman's rho for lowest level of distributive justice and the highest level of distributive justice is .942, p < .001; Spearman's rho for middle level of distributive justice and the highest level of distributive justice is .951, p < .001). Lastly, there was a strong bivariate correlation in the seriousness rankings between the three levels of interactional justice (Spearman's rho for lowest level of procedural justice and the middle level of interactional justice is .963, p < .001; Spearman's rho for lowest level of interactional justice and the highest level of interactional justice is .956, p < .001; Spearman's rho for middle level of interactional justice and the highest level of interactional justice is .979, p < .001).

Multivariate Models of Seriousness

To assess the influence of organizational justice on the respondents' evaluations of misconduct seriousness while controlling for the influence of organizational variables and demographic variables, we have performed logistic regressions (Tables 6, 7, 8, and 9) in which the respondents' evaluation of behavior seriousness is the dependent variable. The respondents' length of service and supervisory position are demographic independent variables in the models, and the respondents' estimates of rule violations and expected discipline are organizational independent variables in the models. Finally, organizational justice is included as an independent variable as well.[4] As explained earlier, organizational justice

has three categories, lowest organizational justice, medium organizational justice, and highest organizational justice.[5]

Organizational justice was a significant predictor of the respondents' evaluations of seriousness in the majority of the scenarios (8 out of 12 scenarios or about two-thirds of the scenarios; Tables 6, 7, 8, and 9) and a marginally significant predictor in one more scenario (Scenario 7: Sgt. Watches). The pattern is the same across all scenarios in which organizational justice is a significant predictor: the respondents who expressed higher levels of organizational justice also had higher odds of evaluating misconduct as serious (Tables 6, 7, 8, and 9).

The effect of organizational justice is not uniform across all types of misbehavior. Specifically, organizational justice had the weakest effect on police corruption (in only 1 out of 3 scenarios organizational justice had a statistically significant effect; Table 6) and the strongest effect on interpersonal deviance (in all 3 out of 3 scenarios organizational justice had a statistically significant effect; Table 9). Organizational deviance scenarios seem to lie somewhere between police corruption and interpersonal deviance (in 2 out of 3 scenarios there is the statistically significant effect). The effect of organizational justice on the evaluations of seriousness for the use of excessive force scenarios (2 scenarios with statistically significant effects and 1 more scenario in which the effect was marginally significant; Table 7) is closer to the evaluations of seriousness for the interpersonal deviance scenarios (3 scenarios with statistically significant effects; Table 9).

Out of the two organizational variables (knowledge of official rules, estimates of expected discipline), recognizing that misbehavior is a vio-

---

[4]However, because of the high correlation between the three measures of organizational justice (Spearman's rho for the correlation between categorical measures of procedural justice and distributive justice is .683; Spearman's rho for the correlation between categorical measures of procedural justice and interactional justice is .768; Spearman's rho for the correlation between categorical measures of distributive justice and interactional justice is .620), we could not use all three measures in the same model; instead, we used the measure of organizational justice created by calculating the sum of all three measures.

[5]We have also run the logistic regression models with the organizational justice as a numerical variable, but the results are very similar. In particular, organizational justice measures as a numerical scale was significant in 6 out of 12 scenarios, whereas organizational justice as a categorical scale was significant in 8 out of 12 scenarios. The use of organizational justice as a categorical scale allows us to draw conclusions not only whether organizational justice matters, but also where it matters (e.g., by comparing the views of the respondents with the lowest levels of organizational justice and the respondents with the highest levels of organizational justice).

lation of official rules was the stronger predictor of the respondents' evaluations of seriousness. Specifically, in all 12 scenarios, the respondents who evaluated behavior as rule-violating had higher odds of stating that the behavior is more serious than the respondents who did not evaluate behavior as rule-violating (Tables 6, 7, 8, and 9). In fact, across all four types of behavior, recognizing that the behavior violates official rules was *the* strongest predictor of the respondents' evaluations of behavior as serious. On the other hand, the severity of expected discipline was a significant predictor in about one-quarter of the scenarios (3 out of 12) and a marginally significant predictor in 2 more scenarios. In all these scenarios, the respondents who expected harsher discipline had higher odds of saying that the behavior is serious than the respondents who expected more lenient discipline.

Demographic characteristics carried little weight in the respondents' assessment of behavior seriousness. In particular, supervisory position was not a significant predictor in any of the scenarios (Tables 6, 7, 8, and 9), while the length of service was a significant predictor in less than one-third of the scenarios (Tables 6, 7, 8, and 9).

Conclusion

In the tradition of the seriousness of crime studies (e.g., Figlio 1975; Kwan et al. 2000; Pease 1988; Rossi et al. 1985; Selling and Wolfgang 1964; Velez-Dias and Megargee 1971; Wolfgang et al. 1985), we explored perceptions of seriousness of various types of police misconduct, including police corruption, use of excessive force, organizational deviance, and interpersonal deviance. Traditional studies of crime seriousness typically do not contain examples of police misconduct. Our study expands along this dimension by relying on the police integrity theory and the related methodology (e.g., Klockars et al. 2000, 2004, 2006) to explore the police views of misconduct seriousness and the potential connection between seriousness evaluations and perceptions of organizational justice.

Despite numerous studies utilizing the police integrity approach to explore perceptions of mis-conduct seriousness (e.g., Alain 2004; Chattha and Kutnjak Ivković 2004; Cheloukhine et al. 2015; Edelbacher and Kutnjak Ivković 2004; Haberfeld 2004; Johnson 2004; Kang and Kutnjak Ivković 2015; Khechumyan and Kutnjak Ivković 2015; Kutnjak Ivković et al. 2015; Kutnjak Ivković and Klockars 2004; Kremer 2004; Lobnikar and Meško 2015; Newham 2004; Pagon and Lobnikar 2004; Phetthong and Kutnjak Ivković 2015; Porter et al. 2015; Pounti et al. 2004; Punch et al. 2004; Sauerman and Kutnjak Ivković 2015; Torstensson Levander and Ekenvall 2004; Westmarland 2004; Vallmuur 2015), no previous study of which we are aware has tested the relation between police integrity/perceptions of organizational justice and misconduct seriousness. Based on the results of previous organizational justice studies (Bradford et al. 2014; Bradford and Quinton 2014; Carr and Maxwell 2018; Haas et al. 2015; Myhill and Bradford 2013; Nix and Wolfe 2016; Trinker et al. 2016; Van Craen and Skogan 2017; Wolfe and Nix 2017), we hypothesized that the perceptions of organizational justice and evaluations of misconduct seriousness are positively related. We assumed that police officers more likely to evaluate positively their experience with the police agency in general and with police supervisors in particular would also be more likely to feel the pressure to behave in the same way and believe that their police agencies would reward such positive behavior (Rhones and Eisenberger 2002). Consequently, they would be more willing to adhere to the higher levels of police integrity and express attitudes associated with higher police integrity.

Indeed, the results of our bivariate analyses and multivariate logistic regression models clearly support the hypothesis that police officers' evaluations of misconduct seriousness and perceptions of organizational justice are related; in at least two-thirds of the scenarios, police officers who expressed higher levels of organizational justice were also more likely to evaluate police misconduct as serious. This result remains strong and consistent across different types of police misconduct, from less serious forms of police corruption and use of excessive force to organizational deviance and interpersonal deviance. Typical exceptions from this finding are scenarios evaluated to be the most serious in the whole questionnaire (e.g., theft, internal corruption); in such cases, because the overwhelming majority of the respondents (over 85%) evaluated these behavior to be very serious, there seems to be very little room left for any other concepts to shape their estimates of seriousness. In other words, these misbehaviors are already evaluated as so serious that they are so ingrained that any outside influences may have a hard time reaching these evaluations and potentially affecting them.

Our study has very direct policy implications. If a police agency is interested in enhancing police integrity, in addition to the traditional approaches of developing rules, teaching, and enforcing them; investigating misconduct and disciplining police officers who engage in it; and circumventing the code of silence (e.g., Klockars et al. 2000, 2004, 2006), police administrators should be interested in how just the police agency in general and police supervisors in specific are perceived by police officers. Simply put, the more fair police officers perceive the police agency, the more likely the police officers are to maintain the belief that is incompatible with police misconduct. Furthermore, we have found not only that organizational justice in general is related to evaluations of misconduct seriousness, but also that *each* component of organizational justice (i.e., distributive justice, procedural justice, interactional justice) is related to evaluations of misconduct seriousness. What matters is not only whether the procedures that supervisors are using are evaluated as fair, but the interpersonal treatment that officers receive and the degree to which the outcomes themselves are perceived as fair also count in their evaluations of misconduct seriousness.

Our findings also demonstrate that relative evaluations of seriousness (i.e., how serious is each scenario evaluated compared to the other scenarios in the questionnaire) are not related to the police officers' perceptions of organizational justice. Put differently, assessments of how fairly the police officer thinks that his organization in general and the supervisors in particular are treating the officer do not influence the police

officer's relative assessment of whether opportunistic theft, internal corruption, or abuse of deadly force is more serious than the acceptance of gratuities or a verbal abuse of a citizen. Such a result is by no means surprising because both studies of crime seriousness (e.g., Hansel 1987; Kwan et al. 2000; Selling and Wolfgang 1964; Wolfgang et al. 1985) and police misconduct seriousness (e.g., Huberts et al. 2003; Klockars et al. 2004; Kutnjak Ivković 2004, 2005; Kutnjak Ivković and Haberfeld 2015; Kutnjak Ivković and Shelley 2008) consistently show that these relative evaluations of seriousness seem to be very similar across different groups of respondents and even different countries.

The current research presented in this chapter takes a first step toward understanding the relation between organizational justice and police integrity in a sample of police officers from Croatia. Future research can explore whether the strong relation that we found for the evaluations of misconduct seriousness, which is only one of the measures of the police integrity theory (Klockars et al. 2000, 2004, 2006), persists for other measures of the same theory. Second, our results indicate that the influence of the three components of organizational justice (i.e., distributive justice, procedural justice, and interactional justice) is not identical across different types of police misconduct. Future research could provide an in-depth analysis of the factors that affect the interplay between different components of organizational justice and different forms of police misconduct. Third, one of the notable findings from our research is that the relation between organizational justice and evaluations of seriousness seems to disappear for the most serious scenarios. Empirical research can test whether there is indeed a line beyond which organizational justice no longer matters for the evaluation of seriousness and, if so, where the line is. Fourth, research could explore whether the results we reported for Croatia remain stable across other countries and the degree to which social, political, legal, and economic conditions in each society potentially shape this relation.

References

Adams, J. S. (1965). Inequity in Social Exchange. *Advances in Experimental Social Psychology, 2*, 267–299. New York: Academic Press.

Alain, M. (2004). An exploratory study of Quebec's police officers' attitudes toward ethical dilemmas. In C. B. Klockars, S. Kutnjak Ivković, & M. R. Haberfeld (Eds.), *The contours of police integrity* (pp. 40–56). Thousand Oaks, CA: Sage.

Ambrose, M., & Schminke, M. (2009). The Role of Overall Justice Judgments in Organizational Justice Research: A Test of Mediation. *The Journal of applied psychology, 49*, 491–500.

Bennett, R. J., & Robinson, S. L. (2000). Development of a measure of workplace deviance. *Journal of Applied Psychology, 85*(3), 349–360.

Bies, R. J., & Moag, J. F. (1986). Interactional Justice: Communication Criteria of Fairness. In R- J- Lewicki, B. H. Sheppard, & M. H. Bazerman (Eds.), *Research on Negotiations in Organizations* (pp. 43–55), Vol. 1, Greenwich: JAI Press.

Bjerregaard, B., & Lord, V. B. (2004). An examination of the ethical and value orientation of criminal justice students. *Police Quarterly, 7*(2), 262–284.

Bradford, B., & Quinton, P. (2014). Self-legitimacy, police culture and support for democratic policing in an English constabulary. *British Journal of Criminology, 54*(6), 1023–1046.

Bradford, B., Quinton, P., Myhill, A., & Porter, G. (2014). Why do 'the law' comply? Procedural justice, group identification and officer motivation in police organizations. *European Journal of Criminology, 11*(1), 110–131.

Carr, J., & Maxwell, S. R. (2018). Police officers' perceptions of organizational justice and their trust in the public. *Police Practice and Research, 19*(4), 365–379.

Chattha, Z. N., & Kutnjak Ivković, S. (2004). Police misconduct: The Pakistani paradigm. In C. B. Klockars, S. Kutnjak Ivković, & M. R. Haberfeld (Eds.), *The contours of police integrity* (pp. 175–194). Thousand Oaks, CA: Sage.

Cheloukhine, S., Kutnjak Ivković, S., Haq, Q., & Haberfeld, M. R. (2015). Police integrity in Russia. In S. Kutnjak Ivković & M. Haberfeld (Eds.), *Police integrity across the world*. New York: Springer.

Cohen-Charash, Y., & Spector, P. E. (2001). The role of justice in organizations: A meta-analysis. *Organizational Behavior and Human Decision Processes, 86*(2), 278–321.

Colquitt, J. A. (2001). On the dimensionality of organizational justice: A construct validation of a measure. *Journal of Applied Psychology, 86*(3), 386–400.

Colquitt, J. A., Conlon, D. E., Wesson, M. J., Porter, C. O., & Ng, K. Y. (2001). Justice at the millennium: A meta-analytic review of 25 years of organizational justice research. *Journal of Applied Psychology, 86*, 425–445.

Criminal Justice Commission. (1999). *Ethics Surves of first year constables: summary of findings 1995–1999*. Brisbane: Criminal Justice Commission.

Desta, Y. (2013). Applying a US police integrity measurement tool to the Eritrean context: Perceptions of top-level Eritrean police officers regarding police misconduct. *Journal of Organizational Transformation & Social Change, 10*(3), 238–261.

Donner, C., Maskaly, J., & Fridell, L. (2016). Social bonds and police misconduct: An examination of social control theory and its relationship to workplace deviance among police supervisors. *Policing: An International Journal of Police Strategies & Management, 39*(2), 416–431.

Edelbacher, M., & Kutnjak Ivković, S. (2004). Ethics and the police: Studying police integrity in Austria. In C. B. Klockars, S. Kutnjak Ivković, & M. R. Haberfeld (Eds.), *The contours of police integrity* (pp. 19–39). Thousand Oaks, CA: Sage.

Figlio, R. M. (1975). The seriousness of offenses: An evauation of offenders and nonoffenders. *Journal of Criminal Law, Criminology, and Police Science, 66*, 189–200.

Haas, N. E., Van Craen, M., & Skogan, W. G. (2015). Explaining officer compliance: The importance of procedural justice and trust inside a police organization. *Criminology and Criminal Justice, 15*, 442–463.

Haberfeld, M. R. (2004). The heritage of police misconduct: The case of the polish police. In C. B. Klockars, S. Kutnjak Ivković, & M. R. Haberfeld (Eds.), *The contours of police integrity* (pp. 95–210). Thousand Oaks, CA: Sage.

Hansel, M. (1987). Citizen crime stereotypes—Normative consensus revisited. *Criminology, 25*, 455–485.

Hickman, M. J., Powell, Z. A., Piquero, A. R., Powell, Z. A., & Greene, J. (2016). Exploring the viability of attitudes toward ethical behavior scale in understanding police integrity outcomes. *Policing: An International Journal of Police Strategies and Management, 39*(2), 319–337.

Huberts, L., Lamboo, T., & Punch, M. (2003). Police integrity in the Netherlands and the United States: Awareness and alertness. *Police Practice and Research, 4*(3), 217–232.

Huon, G. F., Hesketh, B. L., Frank, M. G., McConkey, K. M., & McGrath, G. M. (1995). *Perceptions of ethical dilemmas*. Payneham: National Police Research Unit.

Johnson, D. T. (2003). Above the law? Police integrity in Japan. *Social Science Japan Journal, 6*(1), 19–37.

Johnson, D. T. (2004). Police integrity in Japan. In C. B. Klockars, S. Kutnjak Ivković, & M. R. Haberfeld (Eds.), *The contours of police integrity*. Thousand Oaks, CA: Sage.

Kang, W., & Kutnjak Ivković, S. (2015). Police integrity in South Korea. In S. Kutnjak Ivković & M. Haberfeld (Eds.), *Police integrity across the world*. New York: Springer.

Khechumyan, A., & Kutnjak Ivković, S. (2015). Police integrity in Armenia. In S. Kutnjak Ivković & M. Haberfeld (Eds.), *Police integrity across the world*. New York: Springer.

Khruakham, S., & Lee, J. (2013). Cross-nation comparison of the intolerance to police misconduct: Findings from a Thai police cadet survey. *International Journal of Police Science and Management, 15*(3), 237–245.

Klockars, C. B. & Kutnjak Ivković, S. (2003). Measuring Police Integrity. In Piquero, A. R., Greene, J. R., & M. J. Hickman (Eds.). *Police Integrity and Ethics.* Wadsworth Publishing. pp. 1.3–1.20.

Klockars, C. B. & Kutnjak Ivković, S. (2004). Measuring Police Integrity. In Hickman, M. J., Piquero, A. R., & J. R. Greene (Eds)., *Police Integrity and Ethics.* Belmont, CA: Wadsworth Publishing.

Klockars, C. B., Kutnjak Ivković, S., Harver, W. E., & Haberfeld, M. R. (2000). *The measurement of police integrity.* Research in brief. U.S. Department of Justice, Office of Justice Programs, National Institute of Justice. Washington, DC: Government Printing Office.

Klockars, C. B., Kutnjak Ivković, S., & Haberfeld, M. R. (Eds.). (2004). *The contours of police integrity.* Newbury Park, CA: Sage Publication.

Klockars, C. B., Kutnjak Ivković, S., & Haberfeld, M. R. (2006). *Enhancing police integrity.* New York: Springer.

Knowles, J. J. (1996). *The Ohio police behavior study.* Columbus, OH: Office of Criminal Justice Services.

Kremer, F. (2004). Police integrity in Hungary. In C. B. Klockars, S. Kutnjak Ivković, & M. R. Haberfeld (Eds.), *The contours of police integrity* (pp. 116–130). Thousand Oaks, CA: Sage.

Kutnjak Ivković, S. (2004). Evaluating the seriousness of police misconduct: A cross-cultural comparison of police officer and citizen views. *International Criminal Justice Review, 14*, 25–48.

Kutnjak Ivković, S. (2005). Police (Mis)behavior: A cross-cultural study of corruption seriousness. *Policing: An International Journal of Police Strategies and Management, 28*(3), 546–566.

Kutnjak Ivković, S. (2009). The Croatian police, police integrity, and transition toward democratic policing. *Policing: An International Journal of Police Strategies and Management, 32*(3), 459–488.

Kutnjak Ivković, S. (2014). Police misconduct. In M. Reisig & R. Kane (Eds.), *Handbook on police and policing.* New York: Oxford University Press.

Kutnjak Ivković, S. (2015a). Police integrity in Croatia. In S. Kutnjak Ivković & M. Haberfeld (Eds.), *Police integrity across the world.* New York: Springer.

Kutnjak Ivković, S. (2015b). Studying police integrity. In S. Kutnjak Ivković & M. Haberfeld (Eds.), *Police integrity across the world.* New York: Springer.

Kutnjak Ivković, S., & Haberfeld, M. (2015). A comparative perspective on police integrity. In S. Kutnjak Ivković & M. Haberfeld (Eds.), *Police integrity across the world.* New York: Springer.

Kutnjak Ivković, S., & Kang, W. (2011). Police integrity in South Korea. *Policing: An International Journal of Police Strategies and Management, 35*(1), 76–103.

Kutnjak Ivković, S., & Klockars, C. B. (2004). Police integrity in Croatia. In C. B. Klockars, S. Kutnjak Ivković, & M. R. Haberfeld (Eds.), *The contours of*

police integrity (pp. 56–74). Thousand Oaks, CA: Sage.

Kutnjak Ivković, S., & Sauerman, A. (2013). Curtailing the code of silence among the south African police. *Policing: An International Journal of Police Strategies and Management, 36*(1), 175–198.

Kutnjak Ivković, S. & Sauerman, A. (2015). Threading the thin blue line: Transition toward democratic policing and the integrity of the South African police service. *Policing and Society, 25*(1), 25–52.

Kutnjak Ivković, S., & Shelley, T. C. (2008). The contours of police integrity across Eastern Europe: The case of Bosnia and Herzegovina and the Czech Republic. *International Criminal Justice Review, 18*(1), 59–82.

Kutnjak Ivković, S., Haberfeld, S. M., & Peacock, R. (2015). Police integrity in the United States. In K. Ivković & M. Haberfeld (Eds.), *Police integrity across the world.* New York: Springer.

Kutnjak Ivković, S., Haberfeld, M. R., Cajner Mraovic, I., Prpic, M., Hamm, J., & Wolfe S. (2019). Exploring the Relation between Organizational Justice and Police Integrity. The 56th Meeting of the Academy of Criminal Justice Sciences, Baltimore, March 2019.

Kwan, Y. K., Ip, W. D., & Kwan, P. (2000). A crime index with Thurstone's scaling of crime severity. *Journal of Criminal Justice, 28*, 237–244.

Leventhal, G. S. (1980). What should be done with equity theory? New approaches to the study of fairness in social relationships. In K. J. Gergen, M. S. Greenberg, & R. H. Willis (Eds.), *Social exchange: Advances in theory and research* (pp. 27–55). New York: Plenum. https://doi.org/10.1007/978-1-4613-3087-5_2

Lind, E. A., & Tyler, T. R. (1988). Critical issues in social justice. *The social psychology of procedural justice.* New York: Plenum Press.

Lobnikar, B., & Meško, G. (2015). Police integrity in Slovenia. In S. Kutnjak Ivković & M. Haberfeld (Eds.), *Police integrity across the world* (pp. 183–212). New York: Springer.

Martin, C. (1994). *Illinois municipal officers' perceptions of police ethics.* Chicago, IL: Illinois Criminal Justice Information Authority.

McFarlin, D. B., & Sweeney, P. D. (1992). Distributive and procedural justice as predictors of satisfaction with personal and organizational outcomes. *Academy of Management Journal, 35*(3), 626–637.

Meyer, M. E., Steyn, J., & Gopal, N. (2013). Exploring the public parameter of police integrity. *Policing: An International Journal of Police Strategies & Management, 36*(1), 140–156.

Micucci, A. J., & Gomme, I. M. (2005). American police and subcultural support for the use of excessive force. *Journal of Criminal Justice, 33*, 487–500.

Myhill, A., & Bradford, B. (2013). Overcoming cop culture? Organizational justice and police officers' attitudes toward the public. *Policing: An International Journal of Police Strategies and Management, 36*(2), 338–356.

Newham, G. (2004). Out of step: Integrity and the South Africa police service. In C. B. Klockars, S. Kutnjak Ivković, & M. R. Haberfeld (Eds.), *The contours of police integrity* (pp. 232–247). Thousand Oaks, CA: Sage.

Nix, J., & Wolfe, S. E. (2016). Sensitivity to the Ferguson effect: The role of managerial organizational justice. *Journal of Criminal Justice, 47*, 12–20.

Pagon, M., & Lobnikar, B. (2004). Police integrity in Slovenia. In C. B. Klockars, S. Kutnjak Ivković, & M. R. Haberfeld (Eds.), *The contours of police integrity* (pp. 212–231). Thousand Oaks, CA: Sage.

Pagon, M., Lobnikar, B., & Anelj, D. (2004). Gender differences in leniency towards police misconduct. In G. Meško, M. Pagon, & B. Dobovsek (Eds.), *Policing in Central and Eastern Europe–Dilemmas of Contemporary Criminal Justice* (pp. 1–16). Ljubljana, Slovenia: Faculty of Criminal Justice, University of Maribor.

Pease, K. (1988). *Judgments of crime seriousness: Findings from the 1984 British crime survey*. London: Home Office.

Phetthong, N., & Kutnjak Ivković, S. (2015). Police integrity in Thailand. In S. Kutnjak Ivković & M. Haberfeld (Eds.), *Police integrity across the world*. New York: Springer.

Porter, L. E., Prenzler, T., & Hine, K. (2015). Police integrity in Australia. In K. Ivković & M. Haberfeld (Eds.), *Police integrity across the world* (pp. 67–96). New York: Springer.

Pounti, A., Vuorinen, S., & Kutnjak Ivković, S. (2004). Sustaining police integrity in Finland. In C. B. Klockars, S. Kutnjak Ivković, & M. R. Haberfeld (Eds.), *The contours of police integrity* (pp. 95–115). Thousand Oaks, CA: Sage.

Punch, M., Huberts, L. W. J. C., & Lamboo, M. E. D. (2004). Integrity, perceptions, and investigations in the Netherlands. In C. B. Klockars, S. Kutnjak Ivković, & M. R. Haberfeld (Eds.), *The contours of police integrity* (pp. 161–175). Thousand Oaks, CA: Sage.

Raines, J. (2010). *Ethics in policing: Misconduct and integrity*. Burlington, MA: Jones & Bartlett Learning.

Rhones, L., & Eisenberger, R. (2002). Perceived organizational support: A review of the literature. *Journal of Applied Psychology, 87*(4), 698–714.

Rosenbaum, D., & McCarty, W. (2017). Organizational justice and officer "buy in" in American policing. *Policing: An International Journal, 40*(1), 71–85.

Rossi, P. H., Simpson, J. E., & Miller, J. L. (1985). Beyond crime seriousness: Fitting the punishment to crime. *Journal of Quantitative Criminology, 1*, 59–90.

Sauerman, A., & Kutnjak Ivković, S. (2015). Police integrity in South Africa. In S. Kutnjak Ivković & M. Haberfeld (Eds.), *Police integrity across the world*. New York: Springer.

Selling, T., & Wolfgang, M. E. (1964). *The measurement of delinquency*. New York: Wiley.

Thibaut, J., & Walker, L. (1975). *Procedural Justice: A Psychological Analysis*. Lawrence Erlbaum Associates, Hillsdale.

Torstensson Levander, M., & Ekenvall, B. (2004). Homogeneity in moral standards in Swedish police culture. In C. B. Klockars, S. Kutnjak Ivković, & M. R. Haberfeld (Eds.), *The contours of police integrity* (pp. 251–265). Thousand Oaks, CA: Sage.

Trinker, R., Tyler, T. R., & Goff, P. A. (2016). Justice from within: The relations between a procedurally just organizational climate and police organizational efficiency, endorsement of democratic policing, and officer well-being. *Psychology, Public Policy, and Law, 22*(2), 158–172.

Vallmuur, B. (2015). Police integrity in Estonia. In K. Ivković & M. Haberfeld (Eds.), *Police integrity across the world* (pp. 125–152). New York: Springer.

Van Craen, M., & Skogan, W. G. (2017). Achieving fairness in policing: The link between internal and external procedural justice. *Police Quarterly, 20*(1), 3–23.

Velez-Dias, A., & Megargee, E. I. (1971). An investigation of differences in value judgments between youthful offenders and nonoffenders in Puerto Rico. *Journal of Criminal Law, Criminology, and Political Science, 61*, 549–553.

Vito, G. F., Wolfe, S., Higgins, G. E., & Walsh, W. F. (2011). Police integrity: Rankings of scenarios on the Klockars scale by "Management Cops". *Criminal Justice Review, 36*, 152–164.

Westmarland, L. (2004). Policing integrity: Britain's thin blue line. In C. B. Klockars, S. Kutnjak Ivković, & M. R. Haberfeld (Eds.), *The contours of police integrity* (pp. 75–93). Thousand Oaks, CA: Sage Publications.

Wolfe, S., & Nix, J. (2017). Police officers' trust in their agency: Does self-legitimacy protect against supervisor procedural injustice? *Criminal Justice and Behavior, 44*(5), 717–732.

Wolfe, S., & Piquero, A. R. (2011). Organizational justice and police misconduct. *Criminal Justice and Behavior, 38*(4), 332–353.

Wolfgang, M. E., Figlio, R. M., Tracy, P. E., & Singer, S. I. (1985). *The national survey of crime severity*. Retrieved from https://www.bjs.gov/content/pub/pdf/nscs.pdf

Wright, B. (2010). Civilianising the 'blue code'? An examination of attitudes to misconduct in the police extended family. *International Journal of Police Science and Management, 12*(3), 339–356.

Wu, G., Makin, D. A., Yongtao, L., Boatend, F. D., & Abess, G. (2018). Police integrity in China. *Policing: An International Journal of Police Strategies and Management, 41*(5), 563–577.

Exploring the Relation Between Support for Community Policing and Police Integrity in South Africa

Adri Sauerman, Sanja Kutnjak Ivković, and Michael Meyer

Introduction

The origins of contemporary policing in South Africa, as influenced by the unique features of the country's modern (colonial) history, can be traced to the development of the London Metropolitan Police in 1828. Indeed, while under British rule, South Africa would experience the establishment of several policing bodies and the introduction of principles such as equality before the law (Legassick and Ross 2010, p. 315). Conversely, much of Britain's ideologies would amount to mere rhetoric as its self-interest permeated the South African society, at times creating ethnic and racial division to ensure authority over mineral-rich territories (Giliomee and Mbenga 2007, pp. 159–164). Sadly, under both foreign and nationalist rule, South Africa's policing bodies would never rise above paramilitary forces focusing primarily on the protection of specific interests and groups from a majority population.

More recent, post-apartheid developments, have been largely influenced by the philosophy and strategy of community policing as developed in the United States and modified in practice elsewhere. Although there is no universally-agreed upon definition of community policing (e.g., Cordner 2014), some common features of community policing include a shift toward a new philosophical view that places the emphasis on police-community partnerships working to enhance the safety of the community and address community needs (e.g., Cordner 2014). As numerous publications demonstrate (e.g., Lab and Das 2003; Nalla and Newman 2013; Wisler and Onwudiwe 2009), community policing has become a standard police practice across the world. Community policing is more than an idea of policing with consent (Shearing 2013). It may mean reverting to the pre-colonial forms of informal justice (e.g., Lanre and Olabisi 2013; Ratsimbazafy et al. 2013) or returning policing to the people as an effort to achieve greater democratization, justice, and crime control (e.g., Borovec and Kutnjak Ivković 2013; Crichlow 2013; Feltes 2013; Fenoff and Garcia 2013; Malone 2013; Minnaar 2013; Ungar 2013).

This chapter explores one dimension of these developments, the potential relationship between the level of police integrity and support for community policing in the context of the Republic of

A. Sauerman (✉)
Barrister, Cape Town, South Africa
e-mail: adri@sauerman.net

S. Kutnjak Ivković
School of Criminal Justice, Michigan State University, East Lansing, MI, USA
e-mail: kutnjak@msu.edu

M. Meyer
University of North Dakota, Grand Forks, ND, USA
e-mail: michael.meyer2@und.edu

© Springer Nature Switzerland AG 2019
S. Kutnjak Ivković, M. R. Haberfeld (eds.), *Exploring Police Integrity*,
https://doi.org/10.1007/978-3-030-29065-8_5

South Africa. The primary question to be addressed is whether, and to what extent, adherence to, and support for, the philosophy and principles of community policing affect organizational integrity of the South African Police Service (SAPS). In addressing this question, we first briefly explore the history of developments in the policing of South Africa and then discuss the development of the concept and philosophy of "community policing," especially in the U.S.A. We describe the origins and developments of community policing in South Africa and the realization of transforming the country's police through the adoption of community policing. Finally, we present the results of an empirical examination (the first to be conducted) of the relation between police integrity and support of community policing in the South African Police Service.

A Brief History of the European Influence on Policing in South Africa

The earliest South African policing office was established by the Netherlands East India Company (*Verenigde Oost-Indiesche Compagnie*, abbreviated as VOC; Elphick and Malherbe 1989, p. 10). An organization driven by profit for its members, the VOC considered the order and security of the trading Fort of Cape of Good Hope essential from its establishment in 1652 and, as such, worthy of protection by a rudimentary police force. As the Fort steadily expanded to constitute a town, a paramilitary policing organization, the Dutch Watch (Photius.com), was formed in 1655 to lend "a new sense of security" to the colony (Elphick and Malherbe 1989, p. 13).

With the decline of Dutch power in Europe, Britain took administrative control of the Cape in 1795 and in 1825 established the Cape Constabulary, later superseded by the Cape Town Police Force in 1840. With the advent of British rule, the burgher militia was eventually disbanded. Changes in the basic structure of policing in the Cape continued over the next several years, resulting in a distinction between urban and rural policing. This distinction was eliminated by the

transfer of the Cape Mounted Police to the new South African Army and the integration of the Cape Peninsula Urban Police into the new South African Police in 1913. The South African Police (SAP), the first national policing organization, was an amalgamation of four colonial police forces: the Cape Colony, the Natal Colony, the Orange River Colony, and the Transvaal Colony.

Policing developments throughout the remainder of what now constitutes the territory of the Republic of South Africa have been uneven and are tied to political transitions associated with the history of the country. European developments in policing in what is now the KwaZulu-Natal province can be traced back to its origins in 1854 as a city police agency and reconstituted as the Durban Borough Police the following year (Newham et al. 2002). Although known to the Portuguese as far back as 1497, European settlement in the region of present-day Durban did not begin until after 1824 when, founded by merchants from the Cape Colony, the port was effectively placed under British rule and law. By the mid-1830s, a group of emigrant Afrikaner families—the Voortrekkers—left the Cape Colony to "plant new societies in the interior of southern Africa" (Elphick and Giliomee 1989, p. 560). By 1839, this group would already attempt the establishment of the Afrikaner Republic of Natalia, an effort that was met with British resistance. In fact, the British reasserted domain over Natal in 1843, thus reinstituting British law and practice to include the policing systems in place in the Cape Colony. In 1935, the attainment of city status resulted in Durban being brought under the jurisdiction of the South African Police, relegating the Durban City Police to the functions of administering city by-laws and traffic control (Newham et al. 2002). The loss of the Republic of Natalia led the Voortrekkers, in their quest for freedom from British rule, to establish new republics like the Orange Free State and the South African Republic, also referred to as the Transvaal Republic, among other smaller states, in the interior of South Africa.

Although the Voortrekkers sought independence from British rule and, by definition, independence from the Cape's governance, the British governor of the Cape nevertheless extended British sovereignty in 1848 over the newly settled land north of the Orange River, predictably leading to direct conflicts between the British and the Voortrekkers. Through these skirmishes, the Voortrekkers or Boers, reestablished their governing bodies north of the Vaal River and in 1852 Britain recognized the Transvaal Republic as an independent country. This was followed by the independence of the Orange Free State from Britain in 1854.

Because of numerous factors, including the control of trade routes to India, the discovery of gold on the borders of the Cape Colony, the Orange Free State, and the Transvaal, and European colonial expansion, the strategic value of independent territories shifted for Britain. Seeking to establish control over the two dominant Boer republics and several Zulu kingdoms, a series of events was set in motion that would lead to both the Anglo-Zulu War in 1879 and the First Anglo-Boer War (Giliomee and Mbenga 2007, p. 164). Even though the latter conflict was short-lived–from December 1880 to March 1881–Britain encountered fierce resistance in battle, withdrew, and granted the Republics the right to self-rule. This nominal independence of the Republics remained intact until the discovery of a major gold body just outside of present-day Johannesburg. Efforts on the part of Britain to reassert domain over the Republics to profit from the gold finds were rebuffed by the citizens of the Republics, leading to the Second Anglo-Boer War at the beginning of 1899. Despite facing early setbacks, the British were able to offically annex the two Republics in 1900 although the conflict became more costly still as it continued well into 1902. Less than 10 years later, on May 31, 1910, the former Cape Colony, Natal Colony, and the two Boer Republics were combined to create the Union of South Africa, the predecessor of the present-day Republic of South Africa.

Following the First Anglo-Boer War, the South African Republic, or Transvaal Republic, established a policing system in 1881, the South African Republic Police (*Zuid-Afrikaansche Republiek Politie*, abbreviated as ZARP) to enforce the laws. Given the rural and frontier character of the Republic, the ZARP was constituted as a paramilitary organization, with both law enforcement and civil order functions; during the Anglo-Boer War, it even functioned as a military unit of the Republic. Following Britain's efforts to re-exert control over the Boer Republics and the resulting Anglo-Boer War, Britain established the South African Constabulary in 1900 for the policing of territories in the Transvaal and Orange Free State captured from the Republics. As constituted, the South African Constabulary was another a paramilitary force under British Army control that functioned less in a law enforcement role than to exercise British civil authority over the captured territory.

After the cessation of hostilities and the assertion of British authority and military administration over the Republics, the South African Constabulary assumed more functional policing duties. Over the next several years, the force would be depleted because of its growing costs to Britain, and the Constabulary was eventually dissolved in 1908. Although Britain maintained the South African Constabulary through 1908, the ZARP also continued to exist until it was absorbed into the new South African Police following the establishment of the Union of South Africa.

Within the new Union, policing was reorganized along lines used in the former Cape Colony, resulting in the creation of two police forces, the South African Mounted Rifles (SAMR) and the South African Police (SAP) (2019). This division of forces was functional because SAP duties were focused on the policing of cities and urban areas under the Police Act of 1912 (Act 14 of 1912) as the regular police force of the Union. The SAMR, an amalgamation of the Cape Mounted Police, the Cape Mounted Rifles, Natal Police, and the Transvaal Police, was a military constabulary that during peace time undertook policing duties in the rural and predominantly Black areas within the Union. The SAMR was disbanded in 1920 with its members transferred to the new South African Police (2019).

The creation of the Union led to many changes in the social, political, and economic landscape of South Africa which, in turn, had implications for the development of the policing system. Among these was the Natives Land Act of 1913. It set aside only 7% of the agricultural lands on reserves for the Black population, which by the 1950s expanded to cover only 13% of the land area of South Africa (Encyclopaedia Britannica 2019). These reserves would later form a key part of the apartheid system, becoming the "homelands" of the apartheid era (Bell 2013) in the period from 1959. The Bantu Homelands Citizenship Act of 1970 defined Blacks "living throughout South Africa as legal citizens of the homelands designated for their particular ethnic groups—thereby stripping them of their South African citizenship and their few remaining civil and political rights" (Encyclopaedia Britannica 2019). Under the apartheid system, the Bantustans, run by Black elites collaborating with the South African government, were allowed to perform some functions of self-government, particularly in the realms of education, health, and law enforcement (Encyclopaedia Britannica 2019). The result was that each homeland created its own "police."

Following the collapse of apartheid and the establishment of a democratic South Africa, a new policing body for the whole country would be created, the South African Police Service (SAPS). This Service would involve the amalgamation of 11 organizations, the police from each of the Homelands, and the South African Police (SAP). The history of policing in South Africa is a history of division and conflict, be it racial conflict, ethnic conflict, social conflict, and conflict between nation states. For the first time in its modern history, the police would represent all of the county's people and thus desperately needed a method of doing so. Eventually, community policing would lead the way.

Origins of Community Policing

In American cities crime rates started to raise in the 1960s and 1970s. As it turned out, traditional ways of controlling crime, developed during the reform era of American policing (Kelling and Moore 1988), did not yield satisfactory results.

In addition, empirical research on traditional policing suggested that the traditional approaches to policing were not as helpful as expected in reducing crime (e.g., Eck 1984; Greenwood et al. 1977; Kelling et al. 1974; Spelman and Brown 1984). The fear of crime rose rapidly as well and, as empirical research uncovered, it was related to the extent of disorder in communities (Skogan and Maxfield 1981; Trojanowicz 1982), which traditional policing during the reform period did not address. At the same time, the quality of police-community relations, particularly in racial/ethnic minority communities, resulted in biased policing and the crisis of legitimacy (Kelling and Moore 1988).

One of the critical issues for any police strategy is to have a clear definition of what it is (see, e.g., Maguire and Mastrofski 2000). Community policing has suffered in this domain. According to the National Research Council's critical assessment of policing (2004), the definition of community policing has varied across time and place. As Manning put it (1997), community policing is a "semantic sponge" that incorporates not only ideological, political, and philosophical elements, but also cultural and occupational ones. To address this problem, California Attorney General's Office identified 12 points that embedded the basic concepts included in COPPS or Community Oriented and Problem Solving Policing, ranging from a call to reassess responsibility for public safety, while redefining the relationships between the public and the police, to a call for development of new skills through training and education (Program Planning Guide 1992).

As Cordner argues in his review essay about community policing (2014), with the lack of definitional clarity, the actual origin of community policing also becomes unclear. Although late in the progression of the concept, one view is that Kelling and Moore's paper (1988), published by the National Institute of Justice and Harvard University, initiated community policing. In addition, the traces of community policing could be found in Wilson and Kelling's essay "Broken Windows," published in the Atlantic Monthly in 1982, in which Willson and Kelling argued that the police should turn their resources to the disorder in the communities affecting the quality of life in neighborhoods (1982). An alternative view is that community policing was invented by police chiefs such as Chief Lee Brown of Houston, Texas, who implemented it in 1983 (Pate et al. 1985), or Chief Ray Davis of Santa Ana, California, who implemented it in the late 1970s (Davis 1985). The trail potentially goes even farther in the history of policing, into the early 1970s, with the San Diego and community profile initiative (Boydstun and Sherry 1975), team policing in the late 1960s (Sherman et al. 1973), or the National Institute on Police and Community Relations held at Michigan State University in the 1950s (Carter and Radelet 2002). Finally, the origin of community policing may be traced all the way to the beginning of modern policing in the nineteenth century, with Sir Robert Peel arguing that, "The police are the public and the public are the police; the police being only members of the public who are paid to give full time attention to duties which are incumbent on every citizen in the interests of community welfare and existence" (Home Office 2012).

Common Features of Community Policing

In the context of this definitional confusion, Cordner (2005, 2014) tried to pull together common elements of various community policing approaches and projects and identified four common features he calls "dimensions of community policing."

The first dimension is the *philosophical dimension*. Community policing is perceived as the new philosophy of policing; it goes beyond a single strategy or method and involves a new way of thinking about the police. This philosophical dimension includes the underlying values of community policing such as citizen input, broad police service, and personalized service. As Kelling and Moore (1988) emphasized, the role of the police shifts in the community-policing era from its law-enforcement focus to a broader view that incorporates order maintenance and service

to the community (Cordner 2010). The philosophical dimension of community policing requires that citizens and communities have an input in police policies, priorities, and decisions (Cordner 2005, 2014). Because they are parts of the government, police agencies are expected to be responsive and accountable to the communities that fund them (Cordner 2014). Finally, the philosophical dimension requires that the police service should be personalized. In striving to achieve policing tailored to the needs of every community, police agencies should first consider specific needs of each community (Cordner 2005).

The second dimension is the *strategic dimension* (Cordner 2014). It serves to translate the broad philosophical concepts and ideas contained in the philosophical dimension (e.g., citizen involvement) into specific programs and practices (e.g., community meetings). In an effort to enhance police-community relationships and secure time and resources for community policing, police operations should be re-oriented (Cordner 2014). First, the work of the police should include less emphasis on isolating forms of policing (e.g., car patrol) and more on the face-to-face operations (e.g., bicycle patrol, door-to-door policing). Second, police agencies need to find more efficient ways of dealing with traditional police functions such as handling emergency calls or investigating crimes (Cordner 2014). Another aspect of the strategic dimension is its preventive emphasis (Cordner 2014). While traditional policing is mostly reactive, community policing puts more emphasis on proactive and preventative activities, leading to the idea that crime prevention is "a big part of *every* police officer's job" (Cordner 2014, p. 156). Reactive policing is not completely eliminated; rather, it is supplemented with preventive and proactive policing. Finally, the third aspect of the strategic dimension includes establishing a geographic focus (Cordner 2014) to foster a stronger relationship between the police and the community.

The third dimension is the *tactical dimension* (Cordner 2014). It represents the next stage in transforming general ides of community policing into concrete programs. There are three separate components of this dimension: positive interaction, partnerships, and problem solving. In traditional policing, most of the contacts between the citizens and the police are involuntary (arrests, traffic stops) and, therefore, represent negative contacts. Because community policing expands beyond the basic elements of traditional policing, the number of negative contacts should be balanced by the number of positive contacts (Cordner 2005). Furthermore, a goal of community policing is to establish active partnerships among the police, other agencies, and citizens (Cordner 2014) and to allow both the police to become more integrated into the local community and the citizens to assume an active role in crime control and prevention. The third aspect of the tactical dimension is the problem-solving part. Traditional policing is described as having a tunnel vision with case-to-case orientation (e.g., as calls for service come in, police officers address them). While policing in the community policing era still involves responding to the calls for service and handling individual incidents, police officers should also try to address the underlying causes and conditions (Goldstein 1990).

The fourth dimension of community policing is the *organizational dimension* (Cordner 2014). Changes in the organization of police agencies, essential for the successful implementation of community policing, are *not* viewed as basic elements of community policing (Cordner 2005); however, they are critical for its implementation. Changing the structure of the police agencies to fit with community policing has included greater decentralization (more power at the lower level of the organization), flattening of the organization (to ease the communication between the police and the community), civilianization of some of the police services (citizen participation, allocation of police officers to other aspects of policing), and team work (to ease the problem solving; Cordner 2005). Another aspect of the organizational dimension includes the management of the organization. Compared to traditional

policing, in which managers emphasize the adherence to the official rules and mete out discipline for their violations, managers in the community policing era are more focused on developing organizational values and organizational culture (Cordner 2005).

Community Policing in South Africa

Prior to the advent of democratic reform in 1994, the South African Police (SAP), as an instrument of the apartheid government, was responsible for applying discriminatory laws and regulations. In this regard, the role of the police approximated that of a typical colonial police force with minority whites regarding the police as the guardians of their interests and the majority, Blacks, experiencing the same police as an instrument of their oppression (Nel and Bezuidenhout 1995). The South African Police (SAP) functioned as a security force rather than as an agency for crime prevention or crime control. Following the introduction of broad-based inclusion of the South African polity in the political process, a new South African police was to be constituted having the delegated task of maintaining order in society (Van Heerden 1982), but *in partnership* with the general citizenry, thus fostering a police/community partnership. In this setting, the police were to assume the role of an active partner with an obligation to convert the passive role of the community into that of a fully-active partner. In turn, the community as a passive partner would have a duty to help and support the active partner in keeping order (Van Heerden 1982; Mayet 1976). The prospects for participation and the willingness of the public to assist the police would depend, to a large extent, on the community's attitude towards the police and the attitude of the police toward communities. Any rift arising in the partnership would be reflected in the relationship between the community and the police, and in the image one has of the other leading to mutual mistrust (Mayet 1976).

Establishing Community Policing in the Republic of South Africa

With the adoption of the National Peace Accord in 1991, the implementation of police accountability to local communities in South Africa gained momentum. The National Peace Accord provided, among others, that the police shall be guided by the principle that they are accountable to society in rendering their services and shall therefore conduct themselves so as to secure and retain the respect and approval of the public. The Accord, signed by all major political parties, created various structures for the management of the transition to a democratic society and, relevant to police and community relations, called for the establishment of Local Peace Committees (LPCs); it was expected that the SAP would "consult regularly with local peace committees and community leaders" (Camay and Gordon 2000).

With the promulgation of The Interim Constitution of the Republic of South Africa (Act 200 of 1993, Section 221), local peace committees were to be reconstituted as Community-Police Forums, conceptualized as a means to facilitate a partnership between the police and the community and to engage in joint problem identification and consultative problem solving (Department of Safety and Security 1997). The Forums were to be designed not only to permit communities to make their policing concerns known to the police, but also to provide a vehicle for holding the police accountable to them (Pelser et al. 2002). Van Vuuren (2000) noted that this local and democratic oversight of policing activity was to be exercised with regard to the distribution of resources, operational policy, and accountability to the community, but not control of operations.

The Act directed the first parliament to establish Community-Police Forums (CPFs) at every police station (Pelser et al. 2002), with the functions of the promotion of accountability of the services to local communities and co-operation of communities with the police, monitoring of the effectiveness and efficiency of the police, advising the police regarding local police priorities, and evaluation of the provision of visible police services (Interim Constitution, Section 221, 2 (a)) in which accountability means that the institution must give explanation for the manner in which it performs every specific function for which it has been made responsible (Cloete 1996). Following from the directive of the Interim Constitution, Parliament made provision for a formal partnership between the police and the community in fulfilling the needs of the community regarding policing (South African Police Service Act, Act 68 of 1995, chapter "Police Integrity and the Perceived Effectiveness of Policing: Evidence from a Survey Among Ugandan Police Officers"), wherein, "A provincial or area community police board or a community police forum or sub-forum shall perform the functions it deems necessary and appropriate to achieve the objects contemplated in section 18, which may include the functions contemplated in section 221(2) of the [Interim] Constitution" (Act 68, Section 21 (1)). Section 18 provides for the establishment and maintenance of a partnership between the community and the police; promotion of communication between the police and the community; promotion of co-operation between the police and the community in fulfilling the needs of the community regarding policing; and the improvement in the rendering of police services to the community at National, Provincial, Area and local levels; and the improvement of transparency in the police and accountability of the police to the community; and the promotion of a joint problem identification and problem solving by the police and the community.

The Interim Constitution had made specific mention of Community Police Forums, but directed that implementation of police/community partnerships be enacted into law, thus the provisions in the Police Service Act. Although the Constitution of the Republic of South Africa (Act 108 of 1996) contains no provisions on police/community partnerships, many viewed the establishment of Community Police Forums as constitutionally mandated due to the Interim Constitution. In the context of these reformative efforts, the Police Act established the South African Police

Service (SAPS), replacing the South African Police (SAP) of the previous regime and as referred to by the National Peace Accord.

In April 1997, "partnership policing" became the focus of the SAPS when the Department of Safety and Security published its formal policy on community policing, *Community Policing Policy Framework and Guidelines*, in which a major objective of community policing was described as the establishment of an active partnership between the police and the community through which police-community relations could jointly be analyzed and appropriate solutions designed and implemented. In this effort, the police were expected to strive consciously to create an atmosphere in which potential community partners were willing and able to co-operate with the police (Fouche 2003). The CPFs were to build trust and legitimacy, particularly in those areas in which the relationship between the police and the community had been characterized by mistrust and conflict (White Paper on Safety and Security 1998), by engaging in joint problem identification and consultative problem solving with communities (Department of Safety and Security 1997), and as consultative forums designed to permit communities to make their policing concerns known to the police and to provide a vehicle for holding the police accountable to them (Pelser et al. 2002).

The evolution of these functions as expressed in legislation and policy have been traced by Pelser et al. (2002). During the period between 1993 and 1995, the focus was put on the oversight of the police, characterized by explicit monitoring and evaluations of CPF functions (Pelser et al. 2002). Between 1995 and 1997, the key issue was building relationships between the police and the community, characterized by a focus on liaison and communication functions of CPFs. In 1997, the lens refocused on the establishment of problem-solving "partnerships," intended to help improve police services and assist in reducing crime. By 1998, the emphasis shifted to directing CPFs towards co-operation with local government, community mobilization against crime, and other social crime prevention functions. Finally, in 2001, the focus became one of integrating CPFs with the liaison structures of other departments as part of an overall drive to bring communities on board.

Realizing the Goal of Transforming the Police

Minnaar (2010) has noted that the drafters of the interim constitution were quite aware of the need to transform the SAP into a more democratic and human-rights form of policing. Community policing was to be the core of this transformation and CPFs were to be the primary means by which community policing objectives were to be realized. However, as a result of the different legislation and policies, confusion and disagreement between community members and the responsible police officials regarding the functions of Community Police Forums was likely.

Three interpretations can be given to the function of the CPFs based on evolving policy. One interpretation saw the Forums as bodies for police accountability (a community control model). To those who would wish to direct the police, the word accountability became a euphemism for control. For others, accountability meant being called to account for actions and policies, implying *ex post facto* explanation rather than subordination (Oliver 1987). A second interpretation can be summarized as a community-responsibility model directed by the SAPS. A subtle manifestation of this perspective could be heard in the everyday language meaning of "CPF member" when spoken by SAPS personnel. For many SAPS members, a CPF member is a civilian or citizen and, importantly, not a SAPS member. Although as a "forum" the CPF is meant to bring police and citizens together as a consultative body, the SAPS usage of CPF tended to refer to community members as constituting a CPF. That is, there is the SAPS and then there are the CPFs (Meyer and Chiliza 2004). A third interpretation reconstructed the identification of CPF to Community Policing Forums (a partnership/collaboration model).

Given that South Africa followed a British model of police-community consultation forums, one could expect that similar teething problems encountered by liaison committees in Britain might also affect police-community consultation forums in South Africa. Some of the most important problems that could be anticipated were a lack of consensus among the police and the communities as to the real purposes and focus of such forums, resistance emanating from the ranks of police to the whole idea of liaison, and the lack of power of liaison forums to challenge operational policies of the police (Nel and Bezuidenhout 1995, p. 29).

Although there was clear legislation demanding the establishment of CPFs, there were no corresponding clear guidelines leading to a shared understanding of the functions and processes of CPFs by either members of the SAPS or community members. Regulation 6 of the SAPS Interim Regulations for CPFs and Boards (2001) provided that a community police forum, sub-forum, or board, *has no command and control* over the police or any part or member thereof. The management of the police is the responsibility of police management. The Constitution of the RSA 1996 (Act 108 of 1996, Section 207) provides that the National Commissioner of the SAPS shall exercise control over and manage the police service in accordance with the National Policing Policy and is accountable to the National Minister for Safety and Security. Following from this structure, the National Commissioner delegates his powers to the various management levels of the SAPS in order to put policy into effect. Meyer and Chiliza (2004), in their study of perspectives on the functions and processes of the CPFs, observed that community and SAPS members differed significantly on the issue of community oversight (accountability) of the SAPS, a community control model, leading to disputes between citizen members and police members over the operational independence of the SAPS (Shaw 2002). SAPS members were very protective of their operational independence and organizational control, and although community members appeared to perceive limits on their authority and tended to reject interference with the operational independence of the SAPS, resistance to community policing and CPFs by SAPS

members was evident, an observation also noted by Mistry (1997). Brogden and Nijhar (2005) discuss the differing perspectives of police and community members of the CPFs.

In his review, "The changing face of 'community policing' in South Africa, Post-1994," Minnaar (2010) observed that many of the challenges faced in the implementation of community policing in South Africa could be traced back to the apartheid period. Because of an absence (neglect) of effective crime control by state police in the black townships, policing developed as informal, but institutionalized, 'self-policing.' As a consequence, "Many [South Africans] thought that this new community policing was where citizens would police themselves merely under the supervision of the formal police agencies" (Minnaar 2010, p. 190). By 2002, Pelser and colleagues concluded that, essentially, community policing and CPFs appeared to have been subtly downgraded both as a practical matter and as a guiding philosophy. In essence, Community Policing was being replaced by other forms of policing, visible and sector policing, although in the name of Community Policing (Minnaar 2010).

There is some evidence that the concept of sector policing may have been introduced into the SAPS as early as 1993 or 1994, imported from either the U.S.A. or Britain. There was at least a passing reference to sector policing in the 1996 National Crime Prevention Strategy (Dixon and Rauch 2004). Dixon and Rauch identify the period between 1998 and 2003 as the "gestation phase" of sector policing with 2003, when the Police Service published the "Final Draft of the South African Police Service National Instruction on Sector Policing."

In July of 2009, sector policing became an official instruction that is now a "directed and official instrument of policing in South Africa" (Bezuidenhout 2011). In January of 2016, the SAPS indicated it was now focusing on going back to basic policing in order to address deficiencies and challenges related to the tried and tested, fundamental principles of policing, which had been neglected for a long period of time (IOL 2016). Specific issues to be addressed included discipline, enhanced visibility, and the targeted, informed deployment of operational resources. In 2017, Major General Moeketsi Sempe, then Deputy Provincial Commissioner of Policing for the Free State, made a research presentation, "The implementation of Sector Policing in South Africa: Successes and Challenges," describing the status of sector policing at that time. He noted that Sector Policing as a concept was viewed as an implementation tool to support the philosophy of community and partnership policing. To achieve this goal, sector crime forums were created in order to increase police/community interaction and consultation.

Although Sempe identified a number of successes associated with the implementation of sector policing (e.g., geographic domination and stability, enhancement of community interaction and consultation, improved visibility and quick response, and promotion of community/police relations), a number of persistent challenges were also identified. First, there was an incongruence between the definition of the concept of sector policing and its practical implementation. Second, there was a detachment of sector policing from being a community-police driven initiative to being a police-oriented concept, thus resulting in it being costly and resource-intensive. Third, sector policing policy frameworks were developed without the participation of civil society, NGOs, and other interest groups. Fourth, there was a noted absence of well-researched monitoring and evaluation tools to measure the effect and success of the implementation process. Fifth, the implementation of sector policing occurred outside the scope of community policing strategy.

After more than 25 years of community-oriented policing informing the philosophy and practice of policing in South Africa, it appears that the police have not yet found effective means to address what today continue to be significant challenges. Crime rates remain high; community trust and, thus, support for the police, remain low among many South Africans; and stories of corruption continue to plague the SAPS. While significant success on some levels has occurred, the story on the aspirations for community policing has yet to be concluded.

The Relation Between Police Integrity and Community Policing

As part of their task of assisting police agencies through initiatives aiming at establishing or enhancing programs that improve community-police relationships and build trust, the U.S. COPS Office has paid particular attention to police integrity. Carl R. Peed, a Director of the COPS Office (Peed 2003, p. 1) explained the link between community policing and police integrity:

> One essential principle of community policing is public trust. If trust does not exist between the public and their law enforcement agency then community policing efforts will not work. Integrity must be the foundation of everything we do, and is the cornerstone of community policing.

Over time, the COPS Office has indeed supported the idea of police integrity and equality of treatment (Office of Community Oriented Policing Services 2003). The erosion of trust in the police in the 1990s prompted the COPS Office and the National Institute of Justice (NIJ) to hold a national symposium on police integrity (Office of Community Oriented Policing Services 2003, p. 1):

> The COPS Office sponsored the first National Symposium on Police Integrity and followed up with a series of regional technical assistance conferences. The goal was to facilitate a national dialogue on significant integrity issues. The COPS Office expanded its investment in integrity to include racial profiling and hosted a problem solving working group on police stops and searches. COPS also organized the U.S. Department of Justice's Conference on Police-Community Relationships and participated in follow-up working groups. These efforts culminated in a police-integrity focus that concentrated on the effective use of early warning systems, complaint investigations, use of force policies, and racial profiling.

In July of 1996, about 200 police administrators, politicians, lawyers, and scholars attended the first National Symposium on Police Integrity (Gaffigan and McDonald 1997). The attendees agreed that police integrity is a good thing and that it should be enhanced (Klockars et al. 2006). Following the 1996 COPS/NIJ sponsored symposium, the NIJ decided to award grants for scholarly research on police integrity; both COPS and NIJ were to "consider ways to initiate case studies of departments that have an excellent track record pertaining to police integrity" (Greenberg 1997).

The study titled "Enhancing Police Integrity" was among the first to be funded: the study fit well because it was a case-study of three police agencies of high integrity (Klockars et al. 2006). It was based on the groundwork established in an earlier NIJ-funded project by Klockars et al. (2000) that proposed a theory of police organizational integrity and developed methodology to study police integrity.

Klockars and colleagues (Klockars et al. 2006, p. 1) define police integrity as "the normative inclination among police to resist temptations to abuse the rights and privileges of their occupation." The theory of police integrity that they propose has four dimensions (Klockars et al. 2006). The first dimension of the theory focuses on the way police agency's organizational rules are established by the administration, how they are communicated to the police officers, and the way they are understood by the police officers (Klockars and Kutnjak Ivković 2004, p. 1.4). This second dimension of the theory explores the quality of various techniques used by the police agency to detect and investigate police misconduct (Klockars and Kutnjak Ivković 2004, p. 1.4). The third dimension of the theory explores the extent of the police code of silence and the police agency's efforts in curtailing it (Klockars and Kutnjak Ivković 2004, p. 1.4). Lastly, the fourth dimension of the theory argues that the characteristics of the society at large—social, economic, and political—help shape the level of integrity in the police agency (Klockars and Kutnjak Ivković 2004).

This theoretical approach was accompanied with the methodological approach that allows for the study of police integrity as an organizational concept in a systematic, empirical, and quantitative manner (Klockars et al. 2006). The police officer survey—the key part of the methodology used in the study—includes hypothetical scenarios describing different forms of police misconduct. Police officers participating in the study are asked to assess how serious they evaluate mis-conduct, whether the examples of behavior described in the questionnaire violate official rules, what they think that the appropriate and expected discipline should and would be, and whether they would report such behavior to the supervisors. This methodological approach was used to survey police officers from over two dozen countries (for an overview, see Klockars et al. 2004; Kutnjak Ivković and Haberfeld 2015).

Despite this widespread push toward police integrity as a topic of interest, the understanding of police integrity varied substantially across conference organizers, presenters, and authors (Klockars et al. 2006). The topics addressed in the other COPS/NIJ-funded projects ranged from the development of the use of force policy, strengthening the internal review, improving citizen complaint processes, and enhancing integrity training, to establishing a citizen review board, collecting traffic stop data, and developing early intervention systems (Office of Community Oriented Policing Services 2003, pp. 1–2). McDevitt and colleagues from the Institute on Race and Justice at the Northeastern University (2008) estimated that the COPS Office funded 59 police agencies through the Creating a Culture of Integrity (CCI) initiative.

Since 1997, the COPS Office has provided funds to scholars to "build on and strengthen the police integrity initiatives developed by COPS for purposes of creating community policing environments that foster trust and mutual respect between police and citizens" (Office of Community Oriented Policing Services 2003, p. 1). In other words, strengthening police integrity should have a direct effect on respect for and trust in the police, a part of community policing. Police integrity should be related to community policing; as Peed (2003, p. 1) argued, "Integrity must be the foundation of everything we do, and is the cornerstone of community policing." In one of the prominent publications on community policing, the Bureau of Justice Assistance viewed integrity as one of the key values central to community policing (1994, p. 25). Consequently, attitudes supportive of community policing and attitudes of high integrity should be positively related.

At the same time, the results of several studies suggest an alternative view of this relation: the idea that attitudes supportive of community policing may not be related to the attitudes of high integrity at all. To begin, the National Research Council (2004) summarized years of research on the COP-funded large Project on Policing Neighborhoods. The Council (2004, p. 32) emphasized that, "[p]olice officers' views toward community policing bear little relationship to their behavior, suggesting that imbuing officers with the philosophy of community policing will do little to advance its implementation." In other words, supporting community policing in theory may do little when it gets to its actual implementation. Furthermore, research suggested that the views about community policing may not be related to police performance, be it in getting citizens to comply with police commands (McCluskey et al. 1999) or in the level of force used in the contacts with citizens (Terrill and Mastrofski 2004).

Additional evidence could be found in the only study directly measuring the strength of the relation between community policing and police integrity; Kutnjak Ivković et al. (2016) found a very weak relation between the two concepts. Although they used only one (albeit highly correlated) measure of police integrity (perceptions of seriousness), Kutnjak Ivković et al. (2016) included variables measuring the respondents' strength of support for community policing *and* their actual experience in community policing. The experience in community policing was a statistically significant predictor of evaluations of misconduct seriousness in less than one-third of all scenarios (3 out of 11 scenarios), while support for community policing was relevant in still fewer scenarios (1 out of 11 scenarios; Kutnjak Ivković et al. 2016). In other words, attitudes supportive of police integrity and community policing seem at best to be only weakly related.

In this study, we explore whether South African police officers' support for community policing correlates with their views of police integrity. With the end of the apartheid regime in South Africa, community policing was envisioned as a way to democratize policing. Community policing in South Africa, inspired by the U.S. and Belgian models of community polic-

ing (Minnaar 2013), became a part of the Constitution. We provide an in-depth analysis of how South African police officers' views of community policing relate to various measures of police integrity, from the police officers' evaluations of seriousness and their expressed willingness to report misconduct, to their assessments of whether the behavior violates official rules.

Methodology

Questionnaire

We used a modified version of the police integrity questionnaire (Klockars et al. 2006). The original questionnaire contains descriptions of 11 hypothetical scenarios. These scenarios include five cases describing police corruption, four cases describing the use of excessive force, and two cases describing other forms of misconduct (Klockars et al. 2006). The behavior described in the scenarios provides descriptions of realistic behaviors that police officers may experience in their everyday work (e.g., Klockars et al. 2006; Kutnjak Ivković 2015).

After the respondents read the description of the behavior in each scenario, they were asked to respond to the same seven questions (see, e.g., Klockars et al. 2006; Kutnjak Ivković and Haberfeld 2015; Kutnjak Ivković and Sauerman 2016; Sauerman and Kutnjak Ivković 2015). In this chapter, we use three measures of police integrity, primarily focusing on the questions tapping into the respondents' own views.

The first measure of police integrity includes the respondents' evaluations of misconduct seriousness. The question is asking the respondents to assess how serious the behavior in the scenario is. Possible answers range on a 5-point Likert scale from 1 = "not at all serious" to 5 = "very serious." Because the distribution of this variable for every scenario is skewed toward the serious side of the scale (about one-half or more respondents selected "very serious"), we dichotomized it into "not serious" (values 1 through 4) and "very serious" (value 5).

The second measure of police integrity we use in the study taps into the respondents' knowledge of official rules. It is asking the respondents to assess whether the behavior described in the questionnaire violates official rules. Possible answers range on a 5-point Likert scale from 1 = "definitely not a violation" to 5 = "definitely a violation." Because the distribution of this variable for every scenario is skewed toward the rule-violating side of the scale, we dichotomized it into "probably not a violation" (values 1 through 4) and "definitely a violation" (value 5).

The third measure of police integrity focuses on the code of silence. The question inquires whether the respondents would be willing to report misconduct described in the questionnaire. Possible answers range from 1 = "definitely would not report" to 5 = "definitely would report." Because the distribution of this variable for each scenario is skewed toward the reporting side, we dichotomized it into "probably would not report" (vales 1 through 4) and "definitely would report" (value 5).

To assess the respondents' level of familiarity with community policing, we have expanded the original police integrity questionnaire. The first community-policing question asked whether the respondent was personally involved in community-policing projects ("Are you personally involved in any community-policing projects?"). The second question tapped into the respondents' experience in working as a community-policing officer ("Do you work or have you ever worked as a community-policing officer?"). The third question inquired whether the respondents completed a course on community policing ("Have you received any training on community policing?"). To answer these questions, the respondents could have selected one of the two possible answers ("yes" and "no"). The fourth question was about the strength of the respondents' desire for community policing ("What is your personal desire to be part of the implementation of community policing?"). Possible answers ranged on a 5-point Likert scale: 1 = "very strong desire," 2 = "strong desire," 3 = "neither strong nor weak," 4 = "weak desire," 5 = "very weak desire."

The back of the questionnaire also contained a limited number of demographic questions (e.g., length of policing experience, police rank, police assignment, race, and gender). The very last question in the whole questionnaire asked the respondents whether they have lied while filling out the questionnaire. Answers by the respondents who skipped this question or explicitly answered that they had lied were not included in the analyses.

The Sample

The data were collected between 2010 and 2013. We surveyed both commissioned and non-commissioned SAPS officers across all nine provinces, resulting in a sample of 757 sworn SAPS officers (response rate of 87.5%).

Although they were all employed by the SAPS, a nationwide agency, and the respondents came from all nine provinces, the police officers in our sample are somewhat more likely to have come from Western Cape, Gauteng, and Kwazulu-Natal than from other provinces (Table 1). Furthermore, respondents were generally stationed in larger police agencies (23.5% from very large agencies, 13.2% from large agencies, and 27.8% from medium-sized police agencies; Table 1). Most of the respondents were experienced police officers (54.8%) because they reported having more than 10 years of experience (Table 1). Also, the majority of the respondents were employed in non-supervisory positions (62.6%; Table 1). The predominant assignments were patrol (28.9%) and investigation (34.9%; Table 1). Community policing was not a frequent assignment; only 11.6% of the respondents claimed to be employed as community-policing officers (Table 1). Furthermore, the majority of the respondents were black (57.1%) and male (71.5%; Table 1).

With community policing being popularized, it comes as no surprise that virtually all respondents (96%) have heard about the term community policing. The majority (60%) stated that they have personally being involved in community-policing projects, while about one-half (51%) claimed that they currently work or have worked as community-policing officers. About one-half (47%) also stated that they have received training on community policing. Finally, the respondents

Table 1 Respondents' Demographic Characteristics

	Number of Sworn Officers	Percent of Sworn Officers
Police agency size		
Very large (over 500 sworn)	178	23.5%
Large (201–500 sworn)	100	13.2%
Medium (76–200)	210	27.8%
Small (25–75)	142	18.8%
Very small (fewer than 25)	126	16.7%
Province		
Western cape	144	19.0%
Eastern cape	87	11.5%
Northern cape	49	6.5%
Free state	80	10.6%
Kwazulu-Natal	94	12.4%
Gauteng	108	14.3%
Mpumalanga	53	7.0%
North west	75	9.9%
Limpopo	67	8.9%
Length of service		
Up to 5 years	133	17.6%
6–10 years	209	27.6%
11–15 years	65	8.6%
16–20 years	99	13.1%
Over 20 years	251	33.2%
Supervisory position		
No	472	62.6%
Yes	282	37.4%
Type of assignment		
Patrol	219	28.9%
Detective/ investigative	264	34.9%
Communications	44	5.8%
Traffic	30	4.0%
COP	88	11.6%
Administrative	45	5.9%
Other	67	8.9%
Race		
White	124	16.4%
Black	432	57.1%
Colored	201	26.6%
Gender		
Men	536	71.5%
Women	216	28.5%

were asked about their personal desire to be a part of the community-policing implementation. Most of the respondents also had either "very

Table 2 Spearman's Correlation Coefficients for the COP Variables

	Involved	Worked	Course
Involved	1.000		
Worked	.523***	1.000	
Course	.323***	.334***	1.000
Desire	.358***	.298***	.178***

strong" (38%) or "strong" (45%) desire to be part of the community-policing implementation.

Analytical Strategy

Our analytical goal is to explore the relation between police integrity and community policing. To that end, we have used several measures of police integrity (seriousness, rule violation, willingness to report) and several measures of community policing (worked as a community-policing officer, involved in community-policing projects, completed a training on community policing, personal desire to be included in the implementation of community policing). Dependent variables in our logistic regression models will be perceptions of misconduct seriousness, violation of official rules, and own willingness to report misconduct for each scenario.

Although we have expected that the four variables measuring community policing would be highly correlated and we would need to create a community-policing scale, the data revealed this was not the case (Table 2). Most of the variable comparisons indicate a weak relation between variables (Spearman's rho is around .300; Table 2). In only one pair (worked as a community-policing officer and personally involved in community policing), the correlation was moderate (Spearman's rho is .523, Table 2). Such weak to moderate correlations should not result in multicollinearity. At the same time, the relations between these variables are not suitable for the common scale either. We have also tried to create a scale with these variables, but, as expected, the scale had "poor"/"questionable" internal consistency (Cronbach's alpha = .645 for 4 items), and we opted for including all four variables into the logistic regression analyses.

The Results

Seriousness

We utilize the logistic regression models to assess the relation between the respondents' estimates of misconduct seriousness and community-policing variables (*personal involvement, worked as a community-policing officer, taken a course, desire for community policing*). The models also include demographic characteristics as control variables. The results are shown in Table 3.

The logistic regression models show that the strength of the respondents' desire for community policing is the most powerful predictor of their evaluations of seriousness among the community-policing variables (Table 3); in 10 out of 11 scenarios, the respondents who said that they had a "very strong" personal desire to be included in the implementation of community policing also had higher odds of evaluating misconduct as serious than the respondents who had a weak personal desire to be included in the implementation of community policing (Table 3). In addition, in 5 out of 11 scenarios, the respondents who said that they had a somewhat weaker, but still "strong" desire to be included in the implementation of community policing also had higher odds of evaluating misconduct as serious than those respondents who had a weak desire to be included in the implementation of community policing.

The second most powerful predictor among the community-policing variables is the variable measuring whether the respondents have received some training on community policing (Table 3). This variable is a significant predictor in 7 out of 11 scenarios (Table 3), but the direction varies. In particular, in 4 scenarios, this variable is positively related to the perceptions of seriousness (i.e., the respondents who said that they have received some education on community policing also had *higher* odds of evaluating misconduct as serious than the respondents who said that they did not receive any training on community policing; Table 3), and in 3 scenarios it is negatively related to the perceptions of seriousness (i.e., the respondents who said that they have received some education on community policing had

lower odds of evaluating misconduct as serious than the respondents who said that they did not receive any training on community policing; Table 3).

Finally, the remaining two community-policing variables—participation in the community-policing projects and experience as a community-policing officer—were not significant predictors of the respondents' evaluations of seriousness in the overwhelming majority of scenarios (9 out of 11; Table 3).

Violation of Official Rules

The next step in our analyses is testing the effects of community-policing variables (*personal involvement, worked as a community-policing officer, taken a course, desire for community policing*) on the violation measure of police integrity. The models also include demographic characteristics as control variables. The results are shown in Table 4.

The logistic regression models of the recognition that the behavior in each scenario is rule-violating (Table 4) lead us to the same conclusion as the models for the evaluations of seriousness (Table 3) did: out of the community-policing variables, the strength of the respondents' desire to take part in the implementation of community policing is the most powerful predictor. In 8 out of 11 scenarios (Table 4), the respondents who said that they had a "very strong" personal desire to be included in the implementation of community policing also had higher odds of labeling misconduct as rule-violating than the respondents who had a weak personal desire to be included in the implementation of community policing (Table 4). The difference between the respondents who expressed "strong" desire and "weak desire" were smaller, and in only 3 out of 11 scenarios, the respondents who said that they had a "strong" desire to be included in the implementation of community policing also had higher odds of labeling misconduct as rule-violating than the respondents who had a weak desire to be included in the implementation of community policing.

Table 3 Logistic Regression of Own Seriousness[a]

	Scenario 1 (Gifts)			Scenario 2 (Warrant)			Scenario 3 (Theft)			Scenario 4 (Deadly F.)		
	b	s.e.	Odds	b	s.e.	Odds	b	s.e.	Odds	b	s.e.	Odds
Personally involved[b]	.023	.203	1.023	−.098	.246	.907	.695**	.259	2.003	−.505*	.239	.603
Worked as COP[c]	.192	.187	1.211	.397	.235	1.487	.282	.256	1.326	.382	.223	1.466
Course[d]	.352*	.172	1.422	−.239	.206	.787	.504*	.241	1.655	.003	.199	1.003
Desire for COP[e]												
Very strong	.606*	.253	1.833	1.295***	.290	3.651	.278	.343	1.321	1.052***	.294	2.863
Strong	.563*	.238	1.756	.392	.244	1.480	−.505	.290	.603	.005	.248	1.005
Supervisor[f]	−.415*	.201	.660	−.080	.243	.923	−.307	.277	.736	−.506*	.232	.603
Length of service[g]												
6–10 years	.488*	.239	1.629	.616*	.273	1.852	1.122***	.322	3.070	.343	.269	1.409
11–20 years	.385	.255	1.470	.481	.284	1.617	.801*	.336	2.227	.504	.286	1.655
Over 20 years	1.007***	.264	2.739	.786**	.303	2.194	.356	.332	1.428	.785**	.300	2.192
Gender[h]	.060	.179	1.062	−.337	.208	.714	−.698**	.229	.498	.172	.211	1.188
Race[i]												
Black	.997***	.242	2.710	.594*	.248	1.810	.857**	.288	2.356	.200	.251	1.221
Colored	1.233***	.268	3.433	1.091***	.301	2.978	.204	.311	1.226	.276	.289	1.318
Constant	−.2095	.352	.123	−.352	.363	.703	.382	.408	1.465	.477	.366	1.611
Model Nagelkerke R[2]	.125			.143			.193			.099		

	Scenario 5 (Supervisor)			Scenario 6 (Hurts)			Scenario 7 (Verbal)			Scenario 8 (DUI)		
	B	s.e.	Odds	B	s.e.	Odds	B	s.e.	Odds	B	s.e.	Odds
Personally involved[b]	−.152	.221	.859	.195	.203	1.215	−.304	.210	.738	−.032	.200	.968
Worked as COP[c]	.525*	.203	1.690	−.120	.189	.887	.551**	.195	1.735	−.301	.187	.740
Course[d]	−.401*	.185	.669	.412*	.173	1.510	−.563**	.177	.570	.371*	.170	1.450
Desire for COP[e]												
Very strong	1.505***	.263	4.503	.305	.248	1.356	.914***	.263	2.494	1.066***	.250	2.903
Strong	.733**	.235	2.081	.075	.230	1.078	.861***	.245	2.365	.760**	.233	2.138
Supervisor[f]	−.442*	.209	.643	−.405*	.198	.667	−.389	.200	.678	−.375	.196	.687
Length of service[g]												
6–10 years	.551*	.257	1.736	.243	.240	1.275	.713**	.245	2.040	.163	.236	1.177
11–20 years	.224	.266	1.251	.375	.257	1.455	.030	.258	1.031	.338	.249	1.402
Over 20 years	.353	.275	1.424	.165	.259	1.179	.109	.261	1.115	.519*	.256	1.681
Gender[h]	.778***	.202	2.177	−.037	.178	.963	.458*	.179	1.581	.388*	.175	1.474

	B	s.e.	Odds	B	s.e.	Odds	B	s.e.	Odds
Race[i]									
Black	.460	.235	1.584	1.111***	.232	3.038	.221	.225	1.247
Colored	.298	.265	1.347	.892**	.257	2.440	-.144	.253	.866
Constant	-.936	.348	.392	-.945	.336	.389	-1.053	.334	.349
Model Nagelkerke R^2	.176			.099			.071		

	Scenario 9 (Kickback)			Scenario 10 (Report)			Scenario 11 (Watch)		
	B	s.e.	Odds	B	s.e.	Odds	B	s.e.	Odds
Personally involved[a]	.220	.216	1.246	.328	.221	1.389	.284	.227	1.328
Worked as COP[b]	-.351	.204	.704	.087	.208	1.091	-.124	.214	.884
Course[c]	-.453*	.182	.636	-.333	.187	.716	-.109	.192	.897
Desire for COP[d]									
Very strong	1.600***	.263	4.955	.892**	.263	2.441	1.569***	.270	4.803
Strong	.253	.229	1.288	.069	.234	1.071	.801**	.234	2.229
Supervisor[e]	.241	.211	1.273	-.272	.218	.762	-.488*	.225	.614
Length of service[f]									
6–10 years	.353	.245	1.423	.883***	.252	2.417	.811**	.260	2.250
11–20 years	.423	.259	1.527	.854**	.267	2.348	.748**	.274	2.112
Over 20 years	.600*	.269	1.822	.857**	.274	2.357	1.049***	.288	2.854
Gender[g]	.604**	.192	1.829	-.028	.193	.973	.542**	.209	1.720
Race[h]									
Black	-.160	.240	.852	.488*	.233	1.629	.489*	.245	1.630
Colored	-.367	.267	.693	.935**	.273	2.547	.022	.272	1.022
Constant	-.384	.344	.681	-.683	.341	.505	-.967	.354	.380
Model Nagelkerke R^2	.157			.133			.155		

$*\ p < .05;\ **\ p < .01;\ ***\ p < .001$

[a] Reference category = "no"
[b] Reference category = "no"
[c] Reference category = "no"
[d] Reference category = "weak support"
[e] Reference category = "no"
[f] Reference category = "5 or fewer years"
[g] Reference category = "male"
[h] Reference category = "white"
[i] Reference category = "probably would not report"

Table 4 Logistic Regression of Rule Violations[a]

	Scenario 1 (Gifts)			Scenario 2 (Warrant)			Scenario 3 (Theft)			Scenario 4 (Deadly F.)		
	b	s.e.	Odds	b	s.e.	Odds	b	s.e.	Odds	b	s.e.	Odds
Personally involved[b]	.642**	.208	1.901	.191	.242	1.210	−.293	.253	.746	−.539*	.219	.583
Worked as COP[c]	−.276	.196	.759	−.126	.231	.882	.714**	.245	2.042	.155	.199	1.168
Course[d]	.262	.177	1.300	−.234	.205	.792	.281	.225	1.324	.231	.181	1.260
Desire for COP[e]												
Very strong	.637*	.249	1.890	1.484***	.303	4.412	.565	.318	1.759	.365	.267	1.441
Strong	.337	.229	1.401	.049	.243	1.050	.014	.273	1.014	.000	.243	1.000
Supervisor[f]	−.339	.206	.712	−.376	.240	.687	.164	.260	1.178	−.332	.207	.717
Length of service[g]												
6–10 years	.704**	.243	2.022	1.174***	.273	3.236	.416	.307	1.516	−.172	.262	.842
11–20 years	.423	.255	1.527	.758**	.277	2.134	.168	.318	1.183	−.131	.273	.877
Over 20 years	.880**	.267	2.411	1.213***	.298	3.363	.026	.328	1.026	.055	.280	1.057
Gender[h]	.404*	.187	1.497	−.194	.207	.824	−.382	.223	.683	.184	.192	1.201
Race[i]												
Black	.556	.228	1.744	.407	.257	1.502	.861**	.272	2.366	.007	.238	1.008
Colored	1.000***	.262	2.718	.289	.292	1.335	.282	.295	1.326	.259	.273	1.296
Constant	−1.397	.340	.247	−.179	.362	.836	.457	.399	1.580	.951	.357	2.588
Model Nagelkerke R[2]	.122			.174			.097			.040		

	Scenario 5 (Supervisor)			Scenario 6 (Hurts)			Scenario 7 (Verbal)			Scenario 8 (DUI)		
	b	s.e.	Odds	b	s.e.	Odds	b	s.e.	Odds	b	s.e.	Odds
Personally involved[b]	.246	.222	1.279	.018	.206	1.018	−.230	.204	.795	−.011	.203	.989
Worked as COP[c]	.172	.205	1.188	.281	.192	1.325	.264	.190	1.302	−.209	.187	.811
Course[d]	−.569**	.191	.566	.342	.177	1.408	−.574**	.173	.563	.004	.170	1.004
Desire for COP[e]												
Very strong	2.004***	.272	7.419	.720**	.250	2.055	.907***	.257	2.478	.933***	.249	2.543
Strong	1.733***	.247	5.657	.261	.227	1.298	.677**	.238	1.968	.495*	.229	1.640
Supervisor[f]	.334	.217	1.397	−.280	.204	.756	−.147	.197	.863	−.063	.197	.939
Length of service[g]												
6–10 years	.168	.263	1.183	.481	.246	1.618	.907***	.244	2.476	−.126	.237	.881
11–20 years	−.169	.275	.844	.333	.259	1.395	.307	.257	1.359	.231	.251	1.260
Over 20 years	−.241	.281	.786	.278	.264	1.320	.196	.261	1.217	.195	.256	1.215
Gender[h]	.477*	.200	1.612	−.039	.182	.962	.255	.178	1.290	.713***	.179	2.039

(Table continued from previous page)

	b	s.e.	Odds	b	s.e.	Odds	b	s.e.	Odds	b	s.e.	Odds
Race[i]												
Black	−.154	.254	.857	.561*	.228	1.753	−.710**	.214	.492	−.506*	.231	.603
Colored	−.630*	.280	.532	.405	.256	1.499	−1.152***	.201	.316	−.785**	.258	.456
Constant	−.793	.364	.453	−.675	.334	.509	−.283	.182	.754	−.046	.333	.955
Model Nagelkerke R²	.194			.090			.110			.077		

	Scenario 9 (Kickback)			Scenario 10 (Report)			Scenario 11 (Watch)		
	b	s.e.	Odds	b	s.e.	Odds	b	s.e.	Odds
Personally involved[b]	.322	.216	1.380	.184	.214	1.202	−.076	.217	.927
Worked as COP[c]	−.106	.203	.900	.430*	.201	1.537	.163	.204	1.177
Course[d]	−.667***	.184	.513	−.257	.182	.773	.222	.185	1.249
Desire for COP[e]									
Very strong	1.019***	.260	2.771	.412	.257	1.510	.885**	.260	2.423
Strong	−.184	.232	.832	−.148	.234	.863	.339	.232	1.404
Supervisor[f]	.482*	.213	1.620	−.005	.211	.995	.272	.218	1.313
Length of service[g]									
6–10 years	.275	.245	1.316	.636*	.247	1.888	.591*	.246	1.806
11–20 years	.438	.262	1.550	.623*	.262	1.864	.782**	.266	2.186
Over 20 years	.419	.269	1.520	.514	.267	1.671	.589*	.270	1.801
Gender[h]	.806***	.196	2.239	−.047	.187	.954	.425*	.196	1.530
Race[i]									
Black	.175	.237	1.192	.714**	.228	2.043	.150	.242	1.162
Colored	.155	.264	1.168	1.266***	.268	3.547	.081	.270	1.085
Constant	−.407	.343	.665	−.771	.337	.463	−.588	.347	.555
Model Nagelkerke R²	.148			.118			.073		

$* p < .05; ** p < .01; *** p < .001$

[a] Reference category = "probably would not report"
[b] Reference category = "no"
[c] Reference category = "no"
[d] Reference category = "no"
[e] Reference category = "weak support"
[f] Reference category = "no"
[g] Reference category = "5 or fewer years"
[h] Reference category = "male"
[i] Reference category = "white"

Unlike the results for the respondents' estimates of seriousness, for which the training in community policing turned out to the second strongest predictor, the remaining three community policing variables (training, involvement in projects, worked as a community-policing officer) were not statistically significant predictors in the majority of the scenarios in the specifications in which we used rule violations as a measure of police integrity (Table 4). Whether they received some education about community policing was a statistically significant predictor of the assessment that the behavior violates official rules in only 3 out of 11 scenarios (Table 4) and, in these scenarios, contrary to the expectations, the relation is negative. Similarly, involvement in community-policing projects was a statistically significant predictor in only 2 scenarios and experience as a community-policing officer in only 1 scenario (Table 4).

Willingness to Report Misconduct

Finally, we tested the relation between the respondents' expressed willingness to report and community policing (measured as *personal involvement, worked as a community-policing officer, taken a course, desire for community policing*). The models also include demographic characteristics as control variables. The results are shown in Table 5.

Our final set of logistic regression models confirms our findings related to the other two measures of police integrity. Specifically, out of the four measures of community policing, the respondents' personal desire for community policing has the strongest effect of the respondents' willingness to report misconduct (Table 5). In 9 out of 11 scenarios (Table 5), the respondents who said that they had a "very strong" personal desire to be included in the implementation of community policing also had higher odds of saying that they would report misconduct than the respondents who said that they had a weak personal desire to be included in the implementation of community policing (Table 5). The differences between the respondents who expressed

"strong" desire and "weak desire" were smaller; they were statistically significant in only 4 out of 11 scenarios in which the respondents who said that they had a "strong" desire to be included in the implementation of community policing also had higher odds of saying that they would report misconduct than the respondents who had a weak desire to be included in the implementation of community policing.

Logistic regression analyses of the respondents' willingness to report yielded the second most powerful predictor among the community-policing variables as the variable measuring whether the respondents have worked as community-policing officers (Table 5). This variable is a significant predictor in 7 out of 11 scenarios (Table 5). In all of those scenarios, the respondents who said that they worked as community-policing officers also had higher odds of saying that they would report misconduct than the respondents who said that they did not work as community-policing officers; Table 5).

Finally, the remaining two community-policing variables—participation in the community-policing projects and training in community policing—were not significant predictors of the respondents' expressed willingness to report in the overwhelming majority of scenarios (10 out of 11; Table 5).

Conclusion

Democratic changes that occurred in the mid-1990s, put the South African Police *Service* in the position in which the police could be held accountable by the local communities as they render their services to these communities. One way in which the police should represent all people, regardless of their race or ethnicity, was through the community policing approach, expected to be at the core of the transformation into a democratic police agency (Minnaar 2010).

Indeed, our data demonstrate that the concept of community policing has been shared with the South African police officers; almost all the respondents in our sample have heard about the concept of community policing. At the same

Table 5 Logistic Regression of Own Reporting[a]

	Scenario 1 (Gifts)			Scenario 2 (Warrant)			Scenario 3 (Theft)			Scenario 4 (Deadly F.)		
	b	s.e.	Odds	b	s.e.	Odds	b	s.e.	Odds	b	s.e.	Odds
Personally involved[b]	−.082	.208	.921	−.102	.206	.903	.196	.213	1.216	.054	.214	1.056
Worked as COP[c]	.536**	.192	1.710	.725***	.192	2.064	1.006***	.204	2.734	.459*	.201	1.583
Course[d]	−.331	.178	.718	−.327	.175	.721	−.037	.186	.963	−.183	.182	.832
Desire for COP[e]												
Very strong	1.146***	.291	3.146	.630*	.250	1.878	.332	.263	1.394	.520*	.261	1.682
Strong	1.365***	.277	3.914	.430	.231	1.537	−.331	.238	.719	−.230	.235	.794
Supervisor[f]	−.529**	.203	.589	.082	.201	1.086	.355	.219	1.427	−.361	.209	.697
Length of service[g]												
6–10 years	.300	.251	1.350	.640**	.239	1.897	.734**	.248	2.083	.535*	.247	1.707
11–20 years	.704**	.264	2.022	.172	.251	1.188	1.020***	.272	2.774	.637*	.264	1.892
Over 20 years	.964***	.180	2.622	1.067***	.263	2.906	.440	.271	1.553	.398	.265	1.488
Gender[h]	.173	.180	1.189	−.060	.180	.942	−.144	.189	.865	−.440*	.183	.644
Race[i]												
Black	.440	.243	1.553	.596**	.229	1.815	.242	.240	1.274	−.292	.239	.747
Colored	.327	.269	1.386	.382	.255	1.465	.202	.268	1.223	.045	.273	1.046
Constant	−2.301	.382	.100	−1.364	.338	.256	−.691	.348	.501	.518	.343	1.678
Model Nagelkerke R²	.128			.125			.163			.092		

(continued)

Table 5 (continued)

	Scenario 5 (Supervisor)			Scenario 6 (Hurts)			Scenario 7 (Verbal)			Scenario 8 (DUI)		
	b	s.e.	Odds	b	s.e.	Odds	b	s.e.	Odds	b	s.e.	Odds
Personally involved[b]	−.045	.209	.956	.318	.205	1.374	.222	.233	1.249	.237	.206	1.267
Worked as COP[c]	.682***	.191	1.978	−.010	.188	.990	.032	.211	1.033	−.272	.190	.762
Course[d]	−.375*	.177	.688	−.020	.173	.981	.029	.194	1.029	−.115	.173	.892
Desire for COP[e]												
Very strong	1.404***	.263	4.073	1.418***	.276	4.128	2.387***	.361	10.885	.895***	.254	2.448
Strong	.462	.247	1.588	.924***	.263	2.518	1.365***	.349	3.915	.157	.240	1.170
Supervisor[f]	.329	.199	1.390	−.063	.197	.939	−.047	.218	.954	−.142	.198	.868
Length of service[g]												
6–10 years	−.068	.245	.934	−.056	.244	.946	−.739**	.279	.478	−.277	.245	.758
11–20 years	−.070	.257	.932	−.138	.257	.871	−.165	.279	.848	.163	.253	1.177
Over 20 years	−.152	.261	.859	.082	.259	1.085	−.225	.283	.799	.173	.258	1.188
Gender[h]	.500**	.179	1.649	.429*	.177	1.536	1.104***	.195	3.017	.458**	.176	1.581
Race[i]												
Black	−.174	.232	.840	−.322	.230	.725	−.647*	.253	.523	−.180	.227	.835
Colored	−.405	.261	.667	−.564*	.260	.569	−1.315***	.301	.268	−.541*	.260	.582
Constant	−1.090	.347	.336	−1.283	.355	.277	−1.971	.429	.139	−.651	.338	.522
Model Nagelkerke R²	.142			.094			.227			.076		

	Scenario 9 (Kickback)			Scenario 10 (Report)			Scenario 11 (Watch)		
	b	s.e.	Odds	b	s.e.	Odds	b	s.e.	Odds
Personally involved[b]	.284	.211	1.328	.786***	.205	2.194	.375	.201	1.455
Worked as COP[c]	−.018	.194	.982	.689***	.187	1.991	.520**	.185	1.683
Course[d]	.051	.177	1.052	−.136	.175	.873	.031	.172	1.032
Desire for COP[e]									
Very strong	1.243***	.255	3.467	.280	.251	1.323	.816**	.257	2.261
Strong	−.125	.240	.882	−.399	.236	.671	.573*	.242	1.774
Supervisor[f]	.253	.203	1.288	−.373	.202	.689	.128	.196	1.136
Length of service[g]									
6–10 years	.156	.247	1.168	.370	.245	1.448	.075	.244	1.078
11–20 years	.144	.260	1.155	.509	.261	1.663	.374	.256	1.453
Over 20 years	−.061	.266	.941	.384	.265	1.468	.372	.259	1.450
Gender[h]	.683***	.183	1.980	.327	.183	1.387	.258	.179	1.294
Race[i]									
Black	.323	.237	1.382	−.197	.233	.821	.133	.228	1.133
Colored	−.031	.267	.970	.391	.261	1.479	−.276	.257	.759
Constant	−1.362	.350	.256	−.895	.342	.409	−1.542	.347	.214
Model Nagelkerke R²	.168			.170			.120		

*$p < .05$; ** $p < .01$; *** $p < .001$

[a]Reference category = "probably would not report"
[b]Reference category = "no"
[c]Reference category = "no"
[d]Reference category = "no"
[e]Reference category = "weak support"
[f]Reference category = "no"
[g]Reference category = "5 or fewer years"
[h]Reference category = "male"
[i]Reference category = "white"

time, the majority of the respondents either have been involved in community-policing projects or worked as community-policing officers themselves. In addition, the majority also expressed either a strong or very strong desire to be a part of the community policing program. There is no doubt the SAPS officers have at least some general idea about community policing.

Our results indicate that learning about community policing, taking part in community policing-projects, or working as community-policing officers is not systematically related to any of the three measures of police integrity (evaluations of misconduct seriousness, recognition of behavior as rule violating, willingness to report). Although the relation been police integrity and community policing has not been comprehensively explored in previous studies, the only other study measuring this relation and yielding similar results is the Croatian study (Kutnjak Ivković et al. 2016). While the Croatian study relied on only one measure of police integrity (perceptions of seriousness), our study has incorporated more measures of integrity (evaluations of misconduct seriousness, recognition of behavior as rule violating, willingness to report), nevertheless resulting in a similar conclusion.

Unlike the Croatian study (Kutnjak Ivković et al. 2016) in which the authors did not find a strong connection between perceptions of misconduct seriousness and any measures of community policing, the results of our study suggest that the respondents' strong personal desire to be involved in community policing matters for all three measures of police integrity. Out of all measures of community policing (involvement in projects, working as a community-policing officer, taking a course on community policing, exhibiting desire for involvement in community-policing project), the respondents' personal *desire* to be involved in community policing is the only community-policing measure that exhibits a consistent and strong relation with police integrity. Our results clearly show that the respondents who expressed a very stronger desire to be involved in community policing were also more likely to evaluate police misconduct as serious, more likely to evaluate behavior as rule-violating,

and more likely to say that they would report misconduct.

Although previous research (Kutnjak Ivković et al. 2016) and the findings from our study have found little relation between police integrity and community policing, there is some evidence that those respondents who had a high level of commitment (desire to be involved) to community policing also had higher levels of identification with seeing the various scenarios as more serious. The obvious question is why there is an absence of a stronger relation between police integrity and community policing.

A potential source of the lack of association may revolve around the question of the definition of community policing. This lack of clarity about what community policing is has plagued community policing since its conception. In a study of SAPS officer perceptions from one large township in South Africa regarding whether police understand the philosophy of community policing, 87% of the respondents said the police do understand the philosophy (Brogden and Nijhar 2005). However, only 73% of the officers at the rank of Captain and 67% of those at the rank of Superintendent agreed. There was a clear difference of opinion between those who carry out community policing activities and those responsible for overseeing the execution of community policing functions. In addition, there were clear indications of a disjuncture regarding community policing not only across ranks, but also between the police and the community. When community members were asked whether the police understood their role in policing, only two-thirds of the respondents agreed. Furthermore, only about one in five respondents agreed that community policing made a difference in crime prevention. In these circumstances, it is difficult to conclude that there are shared expectations and meanings regarding community policing. Consequently, it is not surprising that few statistically significant relations could be observed between the measures of integrity and community policing variables, with the exception of the respondents who had stated a "very strong" desire to be included in the implementation of community policing.

Another potential explanation lies in the context of the values that underlie the goals of community policing, mainly the legitimacy of shared responsibility for crime reduction and crime prevention between the police and the policed. There would also seem to be a logical connection between the community and the police regarding some level of community oversight of the police. Meyer and Chiliza's study (2004) identified the issue of operational independence of the police and how this affects the relationship between the police and the community. The authors concluded that community and SAPS members had quite different views about the appropriate level of community control over the police, with police officers being very protective of their operational independence and organizational control, and quite resistant to community oversight (Meyer and Chiliza 2004).

Furthermore, the lack of the relation between police integrity and community policing could be linked with how community policing is described to the police officers and how it is implemented. Taking a course that a police officer is not interested in taking or working on a community-policing assignment that the police officer does not want to do may not necessarily increase their acceptance of, and support for, community policing. Rather, police officers would need to internalize the underlying values of community policing and accept them as a way to increase trust in and legitimacy of the police. This is really critical because studies indicate that trust in, and legitimacy of, the police are generated through fair, community-oriented, and inclusive policing (Trinkner et al. 2016). Teaching the police officers to internalize community policing in South Africa may be a critical factor in enhancing the otherwise decreasing level of trust in the police.

References

Bell, C. (2013). Apartheid's roots: The natives land act. *BBC History*. Retrieved from http://www.bbc.co.uk/history/0/22786616

Bezuidenhout, D. (2011). Sector policing in South Africa: Case closed....Or not? *Pakistan Journal of Criminology, 3*(2&3), 11–25. Retrieved from http://www.pjcriminology.com/wp-content/uploads/2019/01/2-22.pdf.

Borovec, K., & Kutnjak Ivković, S. (2013). Croatia. In M. Nalla & G. Newman (Eds.), *Community policing in indigenous communities*. Boca Raton, FL: CRC, Taylor & Francis Group.

Boydstun, J. E., & Sherry, M. E. (1975). *San Diego community profile: Final report*. Washingon, DC: Police Foundation.

Brogden, M., & Nijhar, P. (2005). *Community policing: National and international models and approaches*. Portland, OR: Willan.

Bureau of Justice Assistance. (1994). *Understanding community policing: A framework for action*. Washington, DC: U.S. Department of Justice. Retrieved April 30, 2019, from https://www.ncjrs.gov/pdffiles/commp.pdf

Camay, P., & Gordon A. J. (2000). *The national peace accord and its structures*. Retrieved from http://www.ids.ac.uk/ids/civsoc/final/southafrica/saf4.doc

Carter, D. L., & Radelet, L. A. (2002). *Police and the community* (7th ed.). Englewood Cliffs, NJ: Prentice Hall.

Cloete, J. J. N. (1996). *Accountable government and administration for the Republic of South Africa*. Pretoria: J.L. van Schaik.

Constitution of the Republic of South Africa (Act 108 of 1996). (1996). Pretoria: Government Printers.

Cordner, G. (2005). Community policing: Elements and effects. In R. G. Dunham & G. P. Alpert (Eds.), *Critical Issues in Policing: Contemporary Readings* (5th ed.). Long Grove, IL: Waveland.

Cordner, G. (2010). *Reducing fear of crime: Strategies for police*. Washington, DC: Office of Community Oriented Policing Services. Retrieved April 30, 2019, from https://ric-zai-inc.com/Publications/cops-p173-pub.pdf

Cordner, G. (2014). Community policing. In M. Reisig & R. Kane (Eds.), *Handbook on police and policing*. New York: Oxford University Press.

Crichlow, V. J. (2013). Trinidad and Tobago. In M. Nalla & G. Newman (Eds.), *Community policing in indigenous communities*. Boca Raton, FL: CRC, Taylor & Francis Group.

Davis, R. C. (1985). Organizing the community for improved policing. In W. A. Geller (Ed.), *Police leadership in America: Crisis and opportunity*. New York: Praeger.

Department of Safety & Security. (1997). *Community policing policy framework and guidelines*. Pretoria: Government Printers.

Dixon, B., & Rauch, J. (2004). *Sector policing: Origins and prospect*. Institute of security studies. Monograph no. 97. March. Pretoria: Institute for Security Studies.

Eck, J. (1984). *Solving crimes: The investigation of burglary and robbery*. Washington, DC: Police Executive Research Forum.

Elphick, R., & Giliomee, H. (1989). Chapter 11—The origins and entrenchment of European dominance at the Cape, 1652-c.1840. In R. Elphick & H. Giliomee (Eds.), *The shaping of South African Society, 1652–1840*. Middletown, CT: Wesleyan University Press.

Elphick, R., & Malherbe, V. C. (1989). Chapter 1—The Khoisan to 1828. In R. Elphick & H. Giliomee (Eds.), *The shaping of South African Society* (pp. 1652–1840). Middletown, CT: Wesleyan University Press.

Encyclopaedia Britannica. (2019). *Bantustan: Historical territory, South Africa.* Retrieved from https://www.britannica.com/topic/Bantustan#

Feltes, T. (2013). Germany. In M. Nalla & G. Newman (Eds.), *Community policing in indigenous communities.* Boca Raton, FL: CRC, Taylor & Francis Group.

Fenoff, R., & Garcia, K. (2013). Mexico. In M. Nalla & G. Newman (Eds.), *Community policing in indigenous communities.* Boca Raton, FL: CRC, Taylor & Francis Group.

Fouche, H. (2003). Partnership policing in the Wierda bridge policing area. Unpublished master's thesis, Tshwane University of Technology.

Gaffigan, S. J., & McDonald, P. P. (Eds.). (1997). *Police integrity: Public service with honor.* Washington, DC: U.S. Department of Justice. Retrieved April 30, 2019, from https://www.ncjrs.gov/pdffiles/163811.pdf

Giliomee, H., & Mbenga, B. (2007). *New history of South Africa.* Cape Town, Tafelberg.

Goldstein, H. (1990). *Problem-oriented policing.* New York: McGraw-Hill.

Greenberg, S. F. (1997). Executive summary. In S. J. Gaffigan, & P. P. McDonald (Eds.). *Police integrity: Public service with honor.* Washington, DC: U.S. Department of Justice. Retrieved April 30, 2019, from https://www.ncjrs.gov/pdffiles/163811.pdf

Greenwood, P. W., Chaiken, J. M., & Petersilia, J. (1977). *The criminal investigation process.* Lexington, MA: D. C. Heath.

Home Office. (2012). *Definition of policing by consent. U.K. Government.* Retrieved April 30, 2019, from https://www.gov.uk/government/publications/policing-by-consent/definition-of-policing-by-consent

Interim Constitution of the Republic of South Africa (Act 200 of 1993). (1993). Pretoria: Government Printers.

IOl.(2016).*SAPS goes back to basics to fight crime.* Retrieved April 16, 2019, from https://www.iol.co.za/news/saps-goes-back-to-basics-to-fight-crime-1975680

Kelling, G. L., & Moore, M. H. (1988). *The evolving strategy of policing. Perspectives on Policing No. 4.* Washington, DC: National Institute of Justice. Retrieved April 30, 2019, from https://pdfs.semanticscholar.org/a614/21a27a6c4fa0e25962ef30e95a22371c1b9c.pdf

Kelling, G. L., Pate, T., Dieckman, D., & Brown, C. E. (1974). *The Kansas City preventive patrol experiment.* Washington, DC: Police Foundation.

Klockars, C. B., & Kutnjak Ivković, S. (2004). Measuring police Integrity. In M. J. Hickman, A. R. Piquero, & J. R. Greene (Eds.), *Police integrity and ethics.* Belmont, CA: Wadsworth.

Klockars, C. B., Kutnjak Ivković, S., Harver, W. E., & Haberfeld, M. R. (2000). *The measurement of police integrity.* Research in brief. U.S. Department of Justice, Office of Justice Programs, National Institute of Justice. Washington, DC: Government Printing Office. Retrieved April 30, 2019, from https://www.ncjrs.gov/pdffiles1/nij/181465.pdf

Klockars, C. B., Kutnjak Ivković, S., & Haberfeld, M. R. (Eds.). (2004). *The contours of police integrity.* Thousand Oaks, CA: Sage.

Klockars, C. B., Kutnjak Ivković, S., & Haberfeld, M. R. (2006). *Enhancing police integrity.* Dordrecht: Springer.

Kutnjak Ivković, S. (2015). Studying police integrity. In S. Kutnjak Ivković & M. Haberfeld (Eds.), *Police integrity across the world.* New York: Springer.

Kutnjak Ivković, S., & Haberfeld, M. R. (Eds.). (2015). *Police integrity across the world.* New York: Springer.

Kutnjak Ivković, S., & Sauerman, A. (2016). Police integrity in South Africa: A tale of three police agency types. *Policing: An International Journal of Police Strategies & Management, 39*(2), 268–283.

Kutnjak Ivković, S., Cajner Mraović, I., & Borovec, K. (2016). Does community policing matter for police integrity? *Journal of Criminal Investigation and Criminology, 67*(4), 313–325.

Lab, S. P., & Das, D. K. (2003). *International perspectives on community policing and crime prevention.* Upper Saddle River, NJ: Prentice Hall.

Lanre, I. O., & Olabisi, A. J. (2013). Nigeria. In M. Nalla & G. Newman (Eds.), *Community policing in indigenous communities.* Boca Raton, FL: CRC, Taylor & Francis Group.

Legassick, M., & Ross, R. (2010). From Slave Economy to Settler Capitalism: The Cape Colony and its Extensions, 1800–1854. In C. Hamilton, B. K. Mbenga, & R. Ross (Eds.), *The Cambridge history of South Africa. Vol. 1: From early times to 1885.* Cambridge: Cambridge University Press.

Maguire, E., & Mastrofski, S. (2000). Patterns of community policing in the United States. *Police Quarterly, 13*(4), 347–366.

Malone, M. F. (2013). Chile. In M. Nalla & G. Newman (Eds.), *Community policing in indigenous communities.* Boca Raton, FL: CRC, Taylor & Francis Group.

Manning, P. (1997). *Police work: The social Organization of Policing* (2nd ed.). Prospect Heights, IL: Waveland.

Mayet, H. R. (1976). *The role and image of the South African police in society from the point of view of the coloured people in Johannesburg.* Unpublished MA dissertation, University of South Africa.

McCluskey, J. D., Mastrofski, S. D., & Parks, R. B. (1999). To acquiesce or rebel: Predicting citizen compliance with police requests. *Police Quarterly, 2,* 389–416.

McDevitt, J., Farrell, A., and R. Wolff (2008). *Creating a culture of integrity.* COPS Evaluation Brief #3. Retrieved April 30, 2019, from https://ric-zai-inc.com/Publications/cops-p148-pub.pdf

Meyer, M. E. & Chiliza, D. J. (2004). *A comparison of citizen and police perceptions of the functions and operation of community police forums in the Durban North Policing Area of South Africa.* Paper presented at the 2004 Annual Meeting of the Midwestern Criminal Justice Association, Chicago, IL, September 30–October 2, 2004.

Minnaar, A. (2010). The changing face of 'community policing' in South Africa, post-1994. *Acta Criminologica: Southern African Journal of Criminology, 2*, 189–210.

Minnaar, A. (2013). South Africa. In M. Nalla & G. Newman (Eds.), *Community policing in indigenous communities*. Boca Raton, FL: CRC, Taylor & Francis Group.

Mistry, D. (1997). A review of community policing. In M. Shaw, L. Cramerer, D. Mistry, S. Oppler, & L. Muntingh (Eds.), *Policing the transformation: Further issues in South Africa's crime debate. ISS monograph no. 12* (pp. 40–49). Pretoria: Institute for Security Studies.

Nalla, M. K., & Newman, G. R. (2013). *Community policing in indigenous communities*. Boca Raton, FL: CRC.

National Research Council. (2004). Fairness and effectiveness in policing: The evidence. Committee to review research on police policy and practices. In W. Skogan & K. Frydl (Eds.), *Committee on law and justice, division of behavioral and social sciences and education*. Washington, DC: The National Academies Press.

Nel, F., & Bezuidenhout, J. (1995). *Human rights for the police*. Kenwyna: Juta.

Newham, G., Masuku, T., & Gomomo, L. (2002). *Metropolitan police services in South Africa, 2002.* Research report written for the Centre for the Study of Violence and Reconciliation, November 2002. Retrieved from https://www.researchgate.net/publication/237562001_Metropolitan_Police_Services_in_South_Africa_2002.

Office of Community Oriented Policing Services. (2003). *COPS fact sheet: Police integrity*. Retrieved April 30, 2019, from https://cops.usdoj.gov/pdf/fact_sheets/e10032081.pdf

Oliver, L. (1987). *Police, government and accountability*. London: MacMillan.

Pate, A. M., Skogan, W., Wycoff, M. A., & Sherman, L. W. (1985). *Coordinated community policing: Executive summary*. Washington, DC: Police Foundation.

Peed, C. R. (2003). *COPS fact sheet: Police integrity*. Office of Community Oriented Policing Services. Retrieved April 30, 2019, from https://cops.usdoj.gov/pdf/fact_sheets/e10032081.pdf

Pelser, E, Schnetler, J. & Louw, W. (2002). *Not everybody's business: Community policing in the SAPS's priority areas. ISS Monograph No. 71.* Pretoria: Institute of Security Studies.

Program Planning Guide (Monograph). (1992, August). *California Attorney General's office. Community Oriented Policing and Problem Solving (COPPS) definition and principles*. Washington, DC: Department of Justice.

Ratsimbazafy, J., Gore, M. L., & Rakotoniaina, L. J. (2013). Madagascar. In M. Nalla & G. Newman (Eds.), *Community policing in indigenous communities*. Boca Raton, FL: CRC, Taylor & Francis Group.

Sauerman, A., & Kutnjak Ivković, S. (2015). Police integrity in South Africa. In S. Kutnjak Ivković & M. Haberfeld (Eds.), *Police integrity across the world*. New York: Springer.

Sempe, M. (2017). *The implementation of Sector Policing in South Africa: Successes and challenges.* Retrieved April 16, 2019, from https://www.saps.gov.za/resource_centre/publications/gen_sempe_saps_research_colloquiumsector_policing.pdf

Shaw, M. (2002). *Crime and policing in post-apartheid South Africa: Transforming under fire*. Bloomington, IN: Indiana University Press.

Shearing, C. (2013). Foreword. In M. Nalla & G. Newman (Eds.), *Community policing in indigenous communities*. Boca Raton, FL: CRC, Taylor & Francis Group.

Sherman, L. W., Milton, C. H., & Kelley, T. V. (1973). *Team policing: Seven case studies*. Washington, DC: Police Foundation.

Skogan, W. G., & Maxfield, M. G. (1981). *Coping with crime*. Beverly Hills, CA: Sage.

South African Corps of Military Police. (2019). *SA mounted rifles, 1911–1922*. Retrieved from http://home.mweb.co.za/re/redcap/new-samr.htm

South African Police Service Act (Act 68 of 1995). (1995). Pretoria: Government Printers.

Spelman, W., & Brown, D. K. (1984). *Calling the police: Citizen reporting of serious crime*. Washington, DC: U.S. Department of Justice.

Terrill, W., & Mastrofski, S. D. (2004). Working the street: Does community policing matter? In W. G. Skogan (Ed.), *Community policing: Can it work?* Belmont, CA: Wadsworth.

Trinkner, R., Tyler, T. R., & Goff, P. A. (2016). Justice from within: The relations between a procedurally just organizational climate and police organizational efficiency, endorsement of democratic policing, and officer well-being. *Psychology, Public Policy, and Law, 22*(2), 158–172.

Trojanowicz, R. (1982). *An evaluation of the neighborhood foot patrol program in Flint, Michigan*. East Lansing, MI: Michigan State University.

Ungar, M. (2013). Argentina. In M. Nalla & G. Newman (Eds.), *Community policing in indigenous communities*. Boca Raton, FL: CRC, Taylor & Francis Group.

Van Heerden, T. J. (1982). *Introduction to police science*. Pretoria: University of South Africa.

Van Vuuren, J. W. J. (2000). Metropolitan policing: A pipe-dream of a realistic option for local crime problems. Pretoria: University of South Africa..

White Paper on Safety and Security. (1998). Pretoria: Government Printers.

Wilson, J. Q., & Kelling, G. L. (1982). Police and neighborhood safety: Broken windows. *Atlantic Monthly*, 29–38.

Wisler, D., & Onwudiwe, I. D. (2009). *Community policing: International patterns and comparative perspectives*. Boca Raton, FL: CRC.

The Contours of an Organizational Theory of Green Police Integrity

Birgit Vallmüür

Expanding the Theory of Police Integrity

The importance of the environment is recognized globally as reflected in the internationally agreed sustainable development goals adopted by the UN in 2015, two of which explicitly categorize protecting the environment as a major priority (UN 2015). At the same time, environmental crime is vast and expanding, thus increasingly harming wildlife populations, entire ecosystems, livelihoods of people, revenues of governments, as well as peace and security (Nellemann et al. 2016). Not only have environmental crimes been estimated to be the third (May 2017) or fourth largest illicit economy in the world, but they have also been rising by 2 to 3 times the rate of the global economy during the last decade (Nellemann et al. 2016).

Although the environment has received growing attention in numerous scientific disciplines, criminology has started to address matters of environmental harm only recently (see e.g. Natali 2013). Some criminologists have employed a *'legal-procedural approach'* studying violations of environmental law, others have used a *'socio-legal approach'*, considering environmental harms that may or may not necessarily be statutorily proscribed (South et al. 2013, p. 35; White 2013, p. 88; see also Gibbs and Boratto 2017). While there is no universal agreement on the term for this sub-field studying environmental harm and crime, the most frequently chosen term is *'green criminology'* (South et al. 2013; see also Natali 2013).

This chapter follows the view of South et al. (2013, p. 28) considering green criminology a *'capacious and evolving perspective'*—'a loose framework or set of intellectual, empirical and political orientations toward problems (harms, offences and crimes related to the environment, different species and the planet)'. This allows the inclusion of research from mainstream and critical theoretical perspectives as well as from interdisciplinary works and expanding the research focus to acts that cause harm that may and may not be proscribed (South et al. 2013).

It is difficult to fit environmental harms into traditional criminological understanding, because conceptions of 'harm' and 'crime' often do not correspond and overlap (South et al. 2013). Furthermore, identifying what constitutes 'environmental crime' is complicated because many types of harm may constitute 'normal social practice' and be legal, while environmentally disastrous (White 2013, p. 88). Thus, this chapter uses the term 'environmental crime' loosely—without these acts having to fall under criminal law in the particular country.

B. Vallmüür (✉)
BV Consulting Ltd, Tallinn, Estonia
e-mail: bv@bvc.ee

© Springer Nature Switzerland AG 2019
S. Kutnjak Ivković, M. R. Haberfeld (eds.), *Exploring Police Integrity*,
https://doi.org/10.1007/978-3-030-29065-8_6

A substantial challenge that researchers come across when studying environmental crimes is the diversity of acts that are considered crimes against the environment. The all-encompassing nature of the phenomenon and internal variety complicate studying the extensiveness, pervasiveness, and cost of these acts to society as a whole and specific victims, not to mention making it hard to identify appropriate mechanisms for preventing and controlling environmental crimes (Yeager and Simpson 2009). Environmental crimes include a heterogeneous group of crimes, committed by either individuals or corporations. Because they are very diverse, ranging from common acts in households to corporate strategies, it is difficult to capture them into a common scheme. The situation is further complicated because not all of them are violations of criminal law. Although the police have an increasingly important role in tackling environmental crime (see e.g. White 2016; INTERPOL 2015; Blindell 2006; Tomkins 2005), the theory of police integrity and its methodology, while including an increasing variety of violations (see e.g., Kutnjak Ivković 2015), have not included any environmental crimes in its focus and research instrument.

This chapter approaches this complexity by including various types of environmental crimes into the methodology of studying green police integrity. To do that, this chapter constructs a novel set of scenarios to capture the environmental crimes as they apply to police officers. To cover a multitude of behaviors that constitute harm against the environment and that are the most relevant to policing globally, this approach develops a new set of police misconduct scenarios addressing the areas of environmental crime based on the INTERPOL classification: biodiversity (poaching and trafficking threatened species), natural resources (forestry crime, fisheries crime, and illegal mining), and environmental quality (air, soil and water; White 2016). The study pilots that methodology in Estonia and addresses the nature of green police integrity among the Estonian police. It contains examples of police misconduct within each of the key areas and analyzes the Estonian police officer views

about the misconduct seriousness, estimates of rule violations, assessments of appropriate and expected behavior, and estimates of the respondents' willingness to report misconduct.

A Brief Introduction to Estonia and Its Police

The Republic of Estonia, located in northeastern Europe, regained its independence from the Soviet Union in 1991, is a member of the European Union (EU) since 2004, belongs to the Schengen area since 2007, and to the euro area since 2011. Estonia is categorized as a 'high-income economy' by the World Bank (2018) and has been classified as having an 'advanced economy' by the International Monetary Fund (2017). However, its GDP per capita in purchasing power standard (PPS) was only 75% of the EU28 average in 2016 (Eurostat 2017).

With a population of 1.32 million (Statistics Estonia 2018) and the total area of 45,227 km², Estonia is one of the smallest countries in the EU (Eurostat 2018). While the society of Estonia is not culturally uniform, as nationalities other than Estonian make up about 30.3% of the population (25.1% are Russian) (Statistics Estonia 2017), Estonia has been historically a Protestant country. It has also been categorized as Protestant ex-Communist society (Norris and Inglehart 2011; see also Vallmüür 2015).

The police in Estonia—the Police and Border Guard Board (henceforth PBGB)—is a police agency with a long but disrupted history (see Vallmüür 2015) and with its more than five thousand employees one of the biggest state agencies in Estonia (Police and Border Guard Board 2018a). It was formed in 2010 by merging the Police Board, Central Criminal Police, Public Order Police, Border Guard Board, and Citizenship and Migration Board. It was further expanded in 2012 when the former police prefectures, border guard territories as well as regional offices of Citizenship and Migration Board, were transformed into four territorial prefectures that were incorporated into it (Police and Border Guard Board 2018a). The last major transformations within this reform were carried out in October 2014, when the PBGB started a transformation into service-based management and the responsibilities of its regional agencies were increased (National Audit Office of Estonia 2016). With these changes the high level distinction in the structure between the Public Order Police and the Central Criminal Police was abolished (National Audit Office of Estonia 2016).

As the police organization in Estonia is centralized, all police agencies in Estonia adhere to the same rules (see e.g. Vallmüür 2015). While the National Audit Office of Estonia concluded that the quality of the services they audited at the PBGB has remained the same or improved, they state that the agency is currently facing troubles and, according to their prognosis, will be struggling with a personnel shortage as if the current recruiting trends continue, the number of employees will decrease 30% by 2025 (National Audit Office of Estonia 2016). Surprisingly, the lengthy report does not mention the investigation of environmental crimes and related changes. Namely, the investigation of environmental crimes in Estonia was transferred in 2011 from the PBGB to the Environmental Inspectorate (Act amending the Code of Criminal Procedure and acts pertaining to this act 2011).

The Four Organizational Dimensions of the Green Police Integrity Theory

Organizational Rules Governing Green Misconduct

The first dimension of the theory of police integrity focuses on the manner the administration establishes the police agency's organizational rules, the way these are communicated to the police officers, and how these are understood by the latter (Klockars and Kutnjak Ivković 2004). The theory suggests that in high integrity police agencies formal rules forbidding misconduct have been put in place, taught and enforced, and the police officers in these agencies not only

know, but also support these rules (Kutnjak Ivković 2015). The theory of green police integrity further considers how rules addressing offenses against the environment are established, communicated and perceived.

Hence, addressing green police integrity requires consideration of laws and rules that regulate the conduct of police officers in relation to environmental protection. Virtually every nation has established a legal regime to protect the environment, yet these environmental law schemes may have numerous forms (Burns 2017). Some nations secure environmental protection within a constitution, others place it to the statutory level. While some nations have positive rights, that place the duty of environmental protection on the government, thus making a healthy environment a right citizens are entitled to; others have created negative rights, restricting polluting (Burns 2017). The Constitution of the Republic of Estonia (1992) lays out already in the fifth paragraph that 'The natural wealth and resources of Estonia are national riches which must be used economically' and later specifies that 'Everyone has a duty to preserve the human and natural environment and to compensate for harm that he or she has caused to the environment'. Thus, environmental protection in Estonia is constitutionally a matter of individual responsibility, not a duty of the government (Boyd 2012).

Environmental protection in Estonia is addressed in numerous specific laws and acts that directly relate to police work such as the Penal Code (2001), the Code of Misdemeanor Procedure (2002), the Code of Criminal Procedure (2003), and the Law Enforcement Act (2011). According to the Law Enforcement Act (2011, Article 5.3–4) a threat to the environment is a *'significant threat'* and 'a threat of the occurrence of a serious environmental damage' is a *'serious threat'*.

In 2011, the investigation of environmental crimes in Estonia was transferred from the Police and Border Guard Board to the Environmental Inspectorate (The Act amending the Code of Criminal Procedure and acts pertaining to this act 2011), giving the Environmental Inspectorate the investigative jurisdiction 'in the case of criminal offences relating to violation of the requirements for the protection and use of the environment and the natural resources.'

However, if a competent law enforcement agency (such as the Environmental Inspectorate) is unable (in a timely manner) to counter a significant or a serious immediate threat or eliminate a disturbance, it is the responsibility of the police to apply urgent measures (based on 'urgent competence') and also to notify the competent agency immediately (Law Enforcement Act 2011, Article 6.3). However, the police are required to apply urgent measures only if this does not excessively obstruct the performance of the functions of the police (Law Enforcement Act 2011, Article 6.3). Furthermore, situations in which the elimination of some disturbance or the ascertainment and countering of a particular threat is not within the competence of any other law enforcement agency, it is within the responsibility of the police (Law Enforcement Act 2011). Hence, the police are required to be aware of the responsibilities of other law enforcement agencies and also recognize the instances that do not fall into the competence of any of these and respond.

Laws protecting the environment and addressing environmental law enforcement can be supported by specialized organizational rules within police agencies and hence, specialized internal rules have likely been established or environmental misconduct may be covered by broader statements. For example, an Estonian police officer and an employee of the PBGB is obligated to follow laws and other legal acts and be an example to other citizens with his/her law-obeying behavior (Police and Border Guard Board 2018b). This stems from the core values of the PBGB, oath of office of police (Police and Border Guard Act 2009), and legal acts such as the Civil Service Act (2012), professional requirements of a police officer, and internal acts such as Rules of Procedure of the PBGB and the procedure of notifying about corruption related information and exceptional cases related to a staff member (Police and Border Guard Board 2018b).

However, the existence of rules does not ensure the rules are known to the police officers. The rules also need to be taught. Yet, the manner and extent of teaching formal rules may vary not only across countries, but also within countries, and temporally, as during steady recruitment periods more time tends to be allocated to training compared to episodes of rapid hiring (Kutnjak Ivković 2015). Therefore, the mere existence of rules concerning environmental violations does not suffice and the awareness of these among the police still needs to be ensured.

In Estonia cordons, whose responsibilities include guarding border water bodies, also monitor marine pollution. Thus, the Estonian Academy of Security Sciences teaches the essence of marine pollution, discovering marine pollution, and responding to marine pollution under the subject of guarding the marine border in the module focusing on guarding the border both in the higher education Police Service curriculum and in the vocational education Police Officer curriculum (The Estonian Academy of Security Sciences 2018). In the module of public order there is a subject 'General requirements for behavior in public place' (Law Enforcement Act 2011) that includes how to police, when there is a prohibition to 'dirty, break, destroy or relocate an item in public use or use it in a manner other than for the prescribed purpose, including put waste in a place other than prescribed therefor, contaminate a body of water or a fountain' (The Estonian Academy of Security Sciences 2018).

The cadets are also explained the Law Enforcement Act (2011) Article 6.3, which stipulates the urgent competence of the police if a competent law enforcement agency is unable to counter a significant or a serious immediate threat, and the meaning of serious threat according to the Law Enforcement Act (2011, Article 5.4) (The Estonian Academy of Security Sciences 2018). Curiously, it appears that a threat to the environment, which is considered *'significant threat'* according to the Law Enforcement Act (2011, Article 5.3), is excluded from the curriculum. This suggests that the cadets in Estonia are introduced to specific paragraphs of laws, not the wider subjects like environmental ethics that are related to these, and the focus is specifically on policing these behaviors.

According to the theory of police integrity solely enacting laws and renewing rules does not suffice to create high integrity police organizations, as the enforcement of these rules is another critical component (Kutnjak Ivković 2015). The extent to which the rules governing green misconduct are followed in practice in a police organization is difficult to inquire directly, as also suggested by the underlying logic of the theory of police integrity (see e.g., Klockars and Kutnjak Ivković 2004), insight into this can be provided by the green police integrity survey. However, formal techniques that have been established to control misconduct can be studied directly and the following section focuses on these.

Techniques of Controlling Green Misconduct in the Police

The second dimension of the theory of police integrity covers a range of methods police agencies use to prevent, investigate, and discipline misconduct (Klockars and Kutnjak Ivković 2004; Klockars et al. 2006). Police agencies globally vary greatly according to the extent to which they employ these methods (Klockars and Kutnjak Ivković 2004). In a high integrity police agency the occupational police culture supports disciplining the violation of standards (Klockars et al. 2006). These agencies tend to use multiple misconduct-controlling methods spanning from preventive and proactive such as education in ethics and proactive investigation to reactive measures such as investigations and disciplining violations (Kutnjak Ivković 2015), as well as following up on citizen complaints and carrying out audits and external reviews (Klockars et al. 2006).

As environmental violations are possibly more difficult to regulate because of the multifaceted nature of these matters, measures that support prevention, such as education on environmental ethics and on the extent of environmental crime globally, as well as on its value, consequences, and linkages with other forms of serious crime, may prove to be more effective than specialized regulations explicitly forbidding

such behavior. Also, by investigating and disciplining environmental harms carried out, enabled, or not acted on by the police, the agency can likely communicate efficiently that misconduct harming the environment is not supported by the organization even if investigating environmental crimes is not the primary responsibility of the agency in the particular country. Especially as teaching values directly can be riddled with difficulties (see, e.g., Gould 1997).

When it comes to the enforcement of laws and rules that govern the behavior of police officers regarding offenses against the environment in Estonia, it can be argued that the PBGB have taken a reactive approach. Namely, specialized preventive and proactive organizational measures are not evident in the PBGB. Furthermore, the PBGB neither possess information about the internal training of relevant rules at the PBGB nor about the training programs and education of matters related to environmental harm and protection that the police officers have received prior to joining the police force (Police and Border Guard Board 2018b).

Thus, as discussed above, the PBGB is of the stance that a police officer is obligated to follow laws and other legal acts 'himself/herself' and to be an example to other citizens with his/her law-obeying behavior (Police and Border Guard Board 2018b). At the same time, no related organizational trainings are provided and relevant education at the Estonian Academy of Security Sciences is strictly limited to particular paragraphs in legal acts.

At the same time, there are clear principles for investigating environmental offences within the PBGB or involving its staff. The Internal Control Bureau of the PBGB processes the offenses of its employees in the PBGB. However, if an official carries out an environmental offense, then it is processed based on the competence either by the Environmental Inspectorate or by the PBGB Internal Control Bureau, while in practice it usually is processed by the Environmental Inspectorate. The Internal Control Bureau processes cases where the Internal Control Bureau or some other police unit discovered an environmental offense of an official, or the information about such an offense was received directly by the police. If the Environmental Inspectorate discovers the offense, then it is processed by their organization. However, the Environmental Inspectorate and the PBGB Internal Control Bureau have a functioning cooperation and the Environmental Inspectorate inform the latter of cases when an incident involving a PBGB official or employee is being processed by them. Also in practice, the PBGB have investigated hints about environmental violations carried out by their staff that they have received internally or from partnering organizations as well as from citizens and have generally involved the Environmental Inspectorate with whom they 'have a good cooperation' (Police and Border Guard Board 2018b).

There are examples demonstrating that environmental crime investigations involving police officials as offenders have led to a discipline. Namely, in 2014 there was an incident in Estonia where a five-person team of the Police and Border Guard Board border guard ship 'Pikker' was suspected of using the ship and its rubber boat for illegal fishing on two consecutive dates. A joint search carried out on the ship by the employees of the Internal Control Bureau of the Police and Border Guard Board and the Environmental Inspectorate followed and discovered fishing nets (Anvelt 2014, March 27). At the time the Deputy Director General (of the Police and Border Guard Board) in the field of Border Guard publicly condemned the actions of these employees (Anvelt 2014, March 27). In that process, the internal control of the Police and Border Guard Board engaged in intensive cooperation with the Environmental Inspectorate and the Police and the Border Guard Board started a disciplinary procedure that, indeed, led to the dismissal of the whole team (Police and Border Guard Board 2018b).

While a public statement by the Deputy Director General condemning environmental crimes on duty and the consequences of it sends a public message about how isolated environmental crimes are treated, another case from Estonia illustrates the linkages environmental crimes may have with other forms of police misconduct. Considering the involvement of police

administrators in unofficial practices communicates that de facto breaking the rules is permitted (Kutnjak Ivković 2015), the following case is a particularly interesting example. Specifically, in 2009 there was a high profile case involving the PBGB when the Estonian Internal Security Service discovered in an investigation that the Prefect of the East Prefecture at the time, who had previously been a long time Prefect of the South Prefecture, and his close team involving other leading figures and officials of these Prefectures, engaged in a combination of acts ranging from embezzlement and unauthorized surveillance to damaging of wild fauna by illegal hunting and illegal fishing with electricity (see e.g. Rudi and Berendson 2009, May 19). While eight officials including the Prefect were found guilty of embezzlement, three Leading Police Inspectors, one Senior Police Inspector, and two Commissars, were found guilty of damaging of wild fauna by illegal hunting and fishing and the police Prefect in the facilitation of that (Kalmre 2009, June 17).[1] These examples have made it publicly evident in Estonia that environmental crimes by police officers are not tolerated.

While the general police integrity theory suggests that training, deterrence, supervision, personnel management, and other methods are required to keep honest cops honest (Kutnjak Ivković 2015), it may hold especially true for the police officers' views on green crimes. As environmental crime may lack an observable 'victim' that is relatable to the 'usual perpetrator-victim model that police tend to prioritise' (Wright 2011, p. 340), then in situations where the police officers become desensitized during their work or develop 'compassion fatigue' (see e.g., Figley 1999; Andersen and Papazoglou 2015), environmental crimes could become more easily overlooked. At the same time, investigation and

---

[1]The police officers hunted in the dark with artificial light and with weapons not intended for hunting and without any relevant licenses, chasing and hunting from motor vehicles killing at least five mallard ducks, twenty roe deer, two beavers, a fox, a tawny owl and a long-eared owl using various police vehicles in the process and engaged in illegal fishing with the electric fishing equipment given to them by the Prefect (Kalmre 2009, June 17).

discipline measures may suffice for the enforcement. Therefore, specialized measures may be beneficial for controlling police misconduct that relates to environmental matters, however the preferred specifics of these are yet to be established by future research.

Curtailing the Blue Code of Green Police Misconduct

The third dimension of the organizational theory of classic police integrity addresses the blue curtain or the code of silence—the informal prohibition against reporting the observed misconduct of fellow police officers (Klockars and Kutnjak Ivković 2004) and the police agency's endeavors of diminishing it (Klockars et al. 2006). In a high integrity police agency the occupational culture is intolerant of members that abuse the position of their occupation (Klockars et al. 2006) and does not protect serious forms of misconduct (Kutnjak Ivković 2015). What types of behavior are protected by the blue code and to whom the protection extends varies not only among but also within police agencies—especially in large ones where the occupational police culture of integrity may vary extensively among precincts, service areas, task forces, and work groups (Klockars et al. 2000, p. 2). More recently, it has been suggested that not only the seriousness, but the more specific nature of misconduct could influence the code of silence used for example by different gender groups (see Vallmüür 2016). This, in turn, gives reason to explore to what extent green police misconduct or subcategories of it fall under the protection of the blue code, and whether these differ so much that the code of silence protecting these would need to be tackled separately.

Environmental crimes tend to be seen as not serious in general at international, regional, and national level (see e.g., Elliott 2007; Eurojust 2014), and by policy makers and law enforcement elites and organizations (Elliott 2007; Hayman and Brack 2002; Lin 2005), as well as by the police (Wright 2011), and at times even by judges (Edwards 1996, p. 236). Therefore, it could be expected that the blue code in case of green police misconduct is especially strong and these acts would be protected even in high integrity police organizations in the classical sense.

While circumscribing the blue code is an obligation of police organizations, many police administrators have been line officers, and thus they at least appreciate, if not feel affection, for the collegial nature of the subculture of policing and thus are hesitant to weaken these bonds (Klockars et al. 2006). The hesitance of implementing measures that are specialized for crimes that traditionally have not been the responsibility of the police, such as environmental violations, may be even higher, thus it could be hypothesized that such specialized measures are rare.

Estonia is one of the countries with the weakest code of silence when it comes to classic police misconduct and one where, according to earlier research, police officers have an accurate perception of how the blue code could manifest in their agency (Kutnjak Ivković and Haberfeld 2015). This makes considering the mechanisms established to counter the blue code in that agency, and exploring whether forms of environmental misconduct are included in these, particularly interesting.

The police organization in Estonia has a specialized internal directive by the Director General of the Police and Border Guard Board to address reporting offenses that involve the members of the police organization (Police and Border Guard Board 2014). The objective of that procedure is to ensure that the improper behavior of the PBGB officials, employees, auxilliary police officers, and the cadets of the Police and Border Guard College is discovered as early as possible, preventive and counter measures are urgently employed, and the relevant information is passed on as expediently as possible to the Bureau of Internal Control (Police and Border Guard Board 2018b). Following and implementing the procedure is mandatory by the officials of the police organization, auxilliary police officers, employment contract employees of the police organization, and the cadets of the Police and Border Guard College of the Estonian Academy of Security Sciences who serve as interns in the police organization and to other interns (together referred to as staff) (Police and Border Guard Board 2018b).

The officials are obligated to inform the Bureau of Internal Control of all violations known to them (including these carried out by themselves or by other officials) and not following that requirement is an occupational violation and punishable in a disciplinary manner (Police and Border Guard Board 2018b). The directive does not state that the police officers must report instances where a law has been broken, but includes situations that may be deemed unsuitable from the point of view of the public and media and may stem from both action and inaction. Such a phrasing allows considering behaviors and omissions that can be condemned by the public—including potentially harmful acts towards the environment that might not be considered serious crimes.

The Bureau of Internal Control has received and investigated tips from partnering organizations, citizens, and employees of the PBGB about potential environmental offenses conducted by the PBGB officials (Police and Border Guard Board 2018b). Yet, how widespread the willingness to report these acts is and what kind of acts would be reported can be studied with the research tool provided in this chapter.

Influence of Social, Economic and Political Environment

The fourth dimension of the organizational police integrity theory suggests that the social, economic, and political environment of a police agency influences the integrity in that agency (Klockars and Kutnjak Ivković 2004). As societies tend to 'shape the level of misconduct of their public servants by establishing and nurturing a culture intolerant of misconduct, promulgating governing rules for ethical behavior of its employees, and by teaching and enforcing these rules (or, conversely, failing to do so)', police organizations are strongly influenced by the views held and controls established by their societies (Kutnjak Ivković 2015, p. 10).

In addition, social, economic and political characteristics that predict environmental concern, may play a role in how police officers in agencies in different countries respond to situations involving environmental crimes. Whilst providing an extensive overview, Milfont (2012, p. 181) demonstrates that 'affluence and value orientations are the main determinants of the development of and differences in environmental engagement across cultures.' Namely, there is strong evidence that at the country-level affluence and value orientations like self-expression/post-materialist values are linked to higher environmental engagement (Milfont 2012).

At the same time, it has been shown that economic and political factors can determine enforcement decisions of the criminal environmental law in the police—not only is the police influenced by the economic aspects, but belonging to the executive branch of the government, the police can be relatively dependent on the political process (Almer and Goeschl 2011). When faced with scarce resources, the police 'are forced to consider opportunity cost arguments when deciding how much effort to put into enforcement' and 'political factors influence this decision at the margin' (Almer and Goeschl 2011, p. 627). For example, public environmental preferences increase the enforcement of environmental crimes, while pro-industry parties tend to have a decreasing effect, yet the police tend to 'respond to a growth of environmental crime with increased effort' to deter (Almer and Goeschl 2011, p. 627). While it is beyond the scope of this chapter, it is possible that potential decreased enforcement of environmental law in the police at the institutional level, stemming from economic and political reasons, lowers also green police integrity among the police officers and therefore national political cycles could have an influence.

Measuring Green Police Integrity

The majority of police integrity research to date has been carried out using two versions of police integrity surveys (see e.g., Kutnjak Ivković

2015). The first survey was mostly focused on corruption. While the majority of the scenarios in the first questionnaire described forms of police corruption, i.e. abusing the position for gain, from accepting gratuities to kickbacks and theft, the questionnaire also included a scenario describing the use of excessive force, and notably one scenario—that of being employed off duty—which may not be a violation of official rules in some police agencies. In addition to multiple police corruption examples, the second version of the general police integrity questionnaire provides a selection of four scenarios covering the use of excessive force, falsification of an official report, and a failure to execute a search warrant (see e.g. Kutnjak Ivković 2015). The questionnaire included multiple examples of similar types of misconduct that represented varying levels of seriousness that can be compared easily to each other already in the phase of designing the instrument by considering the law in a particular country as well as the typology of police corruption by Roebuck and Barker (1974).

As the current chapter focuses on various types of environmental harm, the seriousness of which is difficult to measure and compare, no such clear-cut rankings are done in the design phase of the questionnaire. In other words, there was no prior typology of the seriousness of environmental crimes in general, and no pre-existing typology of green police integrity in the extant literature, so the author had to create a new typology of green police integrity. In the process, the author applied the basic principles used in the design of the police integrity questionnaire. First, the motives have to be unambiguous, the scenarios need to be easily expressed by two or three short sentences and these must be 'compelling' to the police officers who read them (Klockars et al. 2006, p. 137). At the same time, it is possible that the motives are unambiguous only to a reasonable extent. For example, the seriousness a police officer assigns to a situation of wildlife trafficking by a friend may stem from loyalty to friends, concern for law, concern for endangered species, or from a combination of these motives.

Second, the approach seeks to allow studying the nuances of green police integrity by including a variety of scenarios that represent different types of environmental harm that police officers may encounter or cause. Considering a variety of environmental crimes may be especially beneficial, as the perceived seriousness of the act has been shown to be one of the key determinants of police integrity (see e.g., Kutnjak Ivković and Haberfeld 2015; Klockars et al. 2004). Yet, selecting and arranging a multitude of environmental crimes based on their perceived seriousness is a complex task because of the difficulties of assessing the harmfulness of these acts.

Third, the objective is to enable comparing and combining the research of green police integrity with that of general police integrity. Therefore, the main principles of the research instrument are kept the same as these of general police integrity, and the methodology uses the framework and research instrument of general police integrity in terms of questions and answers to the scenarios provided.

Fourth, in the general police integrity survey, there was a deliberate objective to create scenarios that would include police officers in patrol and enable comparative research. Following the approach of the general police integrity questionnaire (see e.g., Kutnjak Ivković 2015), the hypothetical scenarios are selected to be appropriate to the functions of a line police officer on patrol.

Fifth, as a central component of this framework is environmental harm, it is crucial that the level of environmental harm is kept reasonably comparable to the one included in this research instrument.[2] However, while in the first questionnaire of police integrity the majority of scenarios depicted forms of police corruption and thereby acceptance of gain, a deliberate effort was made to include the value of the gain acquired by corrupt behavior into the description of the scenario (Kutnjak Ivković 2015). There, instead of providing absolute values that would have created a different perception of seriousness based on the salary difference of police officials internation-

---

[2]For example, if an endangered species has to be replaced with another one for geographical reasons then a species with an equal level of being endangered should be chosen.

ally, the values were expressed in relative terms (Kutnjak Ivković 2015, p. 12). Maintaining the relative value of scenarios that include examples of transnational environmental crime is challenging, as the value of shipments in the global logistical chain may differ. Also there is no global price list for endangered species for these to be replaced with identical ones. Therefore, the extent of harm in the questionnaire is measured in total amounts such as units, kilos, and cargo loads that directly measure the harm caused to the environment.

The green police integrity questionnaire solicits police officers' responses to hypothetical scenarios describing different examples of environmental harm potentially encountered or committed by law enforcement officers. To focus on environmental crime areas that most closely apply to police work globally, the research instrument includes the three key areas of the INTERPOL Environmental Crime Programme: biodiversity (poaching and trafficking threatened species), natural resources (forestry crime, fisheries crime, and illegal mining), and environmental quality (air, soil and water).

The first area of INTERPOL Environmental Crime Programme focuses on biodiversity. Illegal wildlife trade has increased drastically during this millennium, involving small-scale smuggling and advanced international supply chains (May 2017). The annual value of the illegal wildlife trade is estimated at 7–23 billion USD (Nellemann et al. 2016). Two main commodities the market value consists of are ivory and rhino horn (May 2017). Rhino horn, which is the most expensive animal product, costing up to 65,000 USD per kilo, is more expensive than gold and exceeds even the price of cocaine and heroine in some countries (Anderson and Jooste 2014). As the smuggling routes of rhino horn involve Africa, Middle East, Europe, Asia (Nellemann et al. 2016; Christy 2016), and North America (Nellemann et al. 2016) it is a relevant commodity to study globally. Thus, smuggling rhino horn is included in the research instrument (Scenario 9) as an example of wildlife trafficking involving a widely known global commodity.

While Europe is first and foremost a transit hub for illegal wildlife trafficking, there are also species sourced from Europe for trafficking, such as highly endangered European eel (see e.g., Smith, 2017, December 8; Stein et al. 2016). At least 110 million glass eels have been trafficked from Europe within the current season and for every eel that is legally consumed, 3 to 5 are trafficked (SEG 2018). Therefore, studying that commodity has high regional importance and hence smuggling glass eels is included in the research instrument (Scenario 5) as an example of wildlife trafficking involving a regionally important commodity.

The second area of INTERPOL Environmental Crime Programme focuses on natural resources. Forests provide a multitude of ecosystem services from carbon storage, regulating climate and water supplies to forming a habitat for a multitude of species (Foley et al. 2005). At the same time, forestry crimes are estimated to form the largest turnover of all environmental crimes at 51–152 billion USD per year (Nellemann et al. 2016). Law enforcement officials are crucial in preventing and detecting forest crimes. Hence, a scenario of police officers noticing a potentially suspicious timber truck is included into the questionnaire (Scenario 4).

Marine biodiversity contributes from climate regulation and nutrient cycling to food provision (Beaumont et al. 2007). Illegal and unreported marine fishing create up to 16–36 billion USD in illicit profits annually, which is 14–33% of the global marine capture value, yet it is a conservative estimate due to excluding unregulated fishing as well as any IUU fishing in inland areas (May 2017). Although commercial fishing is one of the main causes behind globally declining fish stocks, recreational fisheries have been starting to contribute to fisheries declines (Cooke and Cowx 2006; Font and Lloret 2014). The police have a role in countering fishing crimes in supporting functions (see e.g., Beke and Blomeyer 2014, p. 25) and as specialized units (see e.g., NZPA 2012, October, 1). Therefore, a scenario involving illegal recreational fishing is included in the questionnaire (Scenario 8).

Modern society relies on minerals, but as these are 'non-renewable' and finite, their sustainable use is highly important (Prior et al. 2012). However, illegal mining is estimated at

12–48 billion USD annually (Nellemann et al. 2016). The most extracted materials globally are sand and gravel (Schandl et al. 2016). However, the scarcity and overexploitation of sand is seen as an 'emerging issue' (see Sutherland et al. 2017) that is yet to be systematically studied (Torres et al. 2017, September, 7). While extracting sand from coasts and rivers in modest amounts can be damaging stemming from the sensitivity of these areas (Schandl et al. 2016), there is a multitude of examples of industrial scale illegal beach sand mining. It has also occurred in developed economies like the UK (The Scotsman 2010, February, 11). Furthermore, beach sand mining is very common and it has been practiced for millennia (Cooper and Pilkey 2014, December, 8). Thus a scenario involving removing sand from a beach is included in the questionnaire (Scenario 11).

The third area of INTERPOL Environmental Crime Programme focuses on environmental quality. Air pollution is a serious environmental concern (INTERPOL and UNEP 2016). However, as open waste burning is frequently excluded from inventories, emissions of air pollutants tend to be significantly underestimated (Wiedinmyer et al. 2014). The open waste burning by individuals and businesses is a significant source of air pollutants especially in developing countries (Wiedinmyer et al. 2014). Yet, 'backyard' burning of waste can be an issue also in developed economies. As open, uncontrolled combustion of domestic waste (i.e., trash burning of food items, packaging, and other residential items that occurs in homes) is a global phenomenon (Kodros et al. 2016), it is included in the questionnaire (Scenario 10).

Soil pollution is a serious environmental challenge. Most criminal activities contributing to land degradation involve trafficking in waste, which involves both the improper management (including collection, transport, storage, and disposal) as well as the illegal trade and movement of waste (INTERPOL and UNEP 2016). According to conservative estimates, there are three million sites in Europe that potentially suffer from soil pollution and 250,000 of these may require urgent action (Science Communication Unit 2013). While litter prevention 'is a very low

form of policing' Groombridge (2013, p. 404), the community policing concept includes proactive policing where the police identify 'social problems' such as litter with community members (Corsianos 2009, p. 119). Thus, the police have a role in fighting land pollution from littering to transnational waste trafficking, and a scenario involving disposing of a car battery to the side of a ditch is incorporated into the questionnaire (Scenario 6).

Pollution is potentially catastrophic for freshwater and marine ecosystems (Secretariat of the CBD and WHO 2015). While water quality is affected by human activities in general (INTERPOL and UNEP 2016), a proportion of water pollution stems from illegal activities. Yet, estimating the extent of water pollution crimes is difficult, as there is little research into the matter (Lynch et al. 2017). Liquid waste is frequently poured into streams or lakes in Europe, thus contaminating both local and possible downstream sites (Europol 2013). Therefore, a scenario involving witnessing pouring waste into a stream is included in the questionnaire (Scenario 7).

Hence, the questionnaire includes 8 green police misconduct scenarios: two scenarios of harming biodiversity by wildlife trafficking (one that includes a threatened species with regional importance and the other involving a globally known threatened species), three scenarios that influence negatively natural resources (forestry, fisheries, and minerals), as well as three scenarios damaging environmental quality (air, soil, and water). To enable comparing the results of the green police integrity survey with the traditional police integrity, the green police integrity questionnaire also includes scenarios from the general police integrity survey. Three scenarios are selected from the traditional instrument to illustrate the range of seriousness based on the results of a multi-country study of police integrity (Kutnjak Ivković and Haberfeld 2015). As respondents in almost every country studied evaluated the theft of knife from a crime scene as the most serious among the eleven scenarios (see Kutnjak Ivković and Haberfeld 2015), it is chosen to be included in this instrument as the illustration of one of the most serious scenarios. Police officers in the ten countries also mostly appeared to share an opinion about one of the least serious scenarios—the acceptance of gratuities—(see Kutnjak Ivković and Haberfeld 2015), that is also the least serious form of corruption according to the typology of police corruption by Roebuck and Barker (1974). Thus, this scenario is included in the current questionnaire as the illustration of the least serious scenario. A third classic scenario—which depicts a failure to execute an arrest warrant—is included to enable comparison with green integrity scenarios that include a decision not to act.

Every scenario is followed by seven questions measuring aspects of police integrity in these particular situations (see e.g., Kutnjak Ivković 2015). The first two questions ask about the police officers' own view and their perceptions of the views that the majority of other officers hold of the seriousness of each case. Thereafter, the questionnaire asked the respondents to assess whether that particular behavior would be seen as a violation of official rules in their agency. The following questions ask what discipline the respondents think such behavior should receive as well as what discipline they believe would actually follow in their police agency. The last two remaining questions inquire about the police officers' adherence to the code of silence by asking how likely the respondents, and in their opinion most of their fellow officers, would be to report a police officer who engaged in the behavior described in that scenario.

While the answers to the questions about the discipline such behavior should and would merit depend upon the legal norms in that particular country and they should fit the legal environment similarly to the general police integrity questionnaire (see e.g., Kutnjak Ivković 2015), there have been exceptions (see e.g., Vallmüür 2015) as at times not all disciplinary punishments that are available are included in the questionnaire. A constant practice where the options range from "no discipline" to "dismissal" (see Klockars et al. 2004) has been used in this study also. The answers to the remaining five questions use Likert-type scales from one to five (see Tables 1 and 2).

The Population and the Sample

All police officers covering public order police, criminal police, and integrated border administration functions in all four prefectures (excluding Jõhvi Police Station in the Eastern Prefecture due to administrative reasons) and in the central units of the Police and Border Guard Board (excluding the Central Criminal Police) were sent an e-mail invitation to participate in the survey in August 2018. The size of the population receiving the invitations containing a link to the web survey can be estimated at 2500 people (Police and Border Guard Board 2018b). A reminder e-mail was sent to the same list in the beginning of September 2018. To guarantee the full anonymity of respondents, no IP addresses were collected, but repeated answers from the same devices were disabled.

Altogether 204 respondents started the survey, about 50 did not complete the questionnaire.[3] The final sample includes responses from 155 respondents who have completed the questionnaire. However, 6 of them were not included in the analysis as they answered that they were not honest whilst filling out the questionnaire. Eventually, the response rate is between 6.2% (excluding partial completions) and 8.2% (including partial questionnaires). This response rate was expected as nonresponses are a typical concern in web surveys (Couper 2000). Arguably there is no reason to assume that those who chose not to participate in the survey are systematically different from respondents. However, stemming from the low response rate, this study does not encourage generalization.

The respondents came from all four prefectures: North (32.9%), South (25.5%), East (20.1%), West (18.1%); and from central units

---

[3] Of the 49 respondents who chose not to complete the survey, many did so relatively early (e.g., 15 quit after answering the first scenario, 5 more after the second scenario, 4 after the third, and another 4 after the fourth scenario which was the first green integrity scenario of the eight). This suggests that they decided to quit ahead of time and not to avoid answering particularly environmental crime scenarios or background questions.

Table 1 Scenario descriptions

Scenario number and type	Scenario description
Scenario 1 Classic scenario	A police officer is widely liked in the community. Local merchants and restaurant owners regularly show their appreciation for his attention by giving him gifts of food, cigarettes, and other items of small value
Scenario 2 Classic scenario	A police officer is aware that there is a felony warrant for a long-time friend of his. Although he sees his friend frequently over a period of more than a week and warns his friend of its existence, he does not arrest him
Scenario 3 Classic scenario	A police officer discovers a burglary of a hardware store. The display cases are smashed and many items have obviously been taken. While searching the store, he takes an expensive pocketknife and slips it into his pocket. He reports that the knife has been stolen during the burglary
Scenario 4 Natural resources—Forestry	During a night shift, a police officer in a patrol car notices a fully loaded timber truck turning to the highway from a state-owned forest. The police officer driving the car turns to his partner and tells him: 'Not our job—let us leave something for the environmental officials as well.' He keeps on driving and does not file a report about it. Evaluate the behavior of the police officer driving the patrol car
Scenario 5 Biodiversity—Regional	A police officer travels out of the EU and takes with him a container with half a kilo of live glass European Eels in his luggage
Scenario 6 Environmental quality—Soil	A police officer finds an old car battery at home, loads it into his car, and lifts it to the side of a ditch near a parking lot to dispose of it
Scenario 7 Environmental quality—Water	A police officer in a patrol car notices at night a septic tank truck releasing liquid into a stream. The police officer driving the car tells his partner: 'This is not our job—let us leave something for the environmental officials.' The police officer keeps driving without stopping and does not report the incident later. Evaluate the behavior of the police officer driving the patrol car
Scenario 8 Natural resources—Fisheries	A police officer has a hobby of recreational fishing that he practices in solitude when off duty. One weekend he uses his electric fishing gear to catch fish
Scenario 9 Biodiversity—Global	Police officer has a personal friend who has brought a kilo of powdered black rhino horn from his recent trip abroad. The police officer does not report his friend to the authorities. Evaluate the police officer's behavior
Scenario 10 Environmental quality—Air	On his day off, a police officer does spring cleaning of his home and burns his old furniture and car tires in the back yard
Scenario 11 Natural resources—Minerals	Late in the evening, a police officer driving a patrol car along a quiet road sees two men shoveling sand into a two-wheeled trailer backed to the local public beach. The police officer in the passenger seat wants to stop the car and investigate. His older partner tells him, 'We are patrolling for real crimes' and keeps on driving. Evaluate the behavior of the older partner

(3.4%). The most widely represented assignment was investigator (35.6%), followed equally by patrol (17.5%), and prevention (such as community policing officer, juvenile) (17.5%), thereafter other work line specialist e.g. detention house personnel or Information Bureau officials (13.4%), and lastly equally the managers of divisions, bureaus, or departments (8.1%) and the border administration (8.1%). However, for the purpose of simplicity, the respondents are referred to as 'police officers' when discussing the results of the survey.

The ranks were merged into three groups to add to the confidentiality. The most widely represented group was that ranging from Chief Constable and Border Guard Chief Inspector to

Table 2 Wording of the questions and possible answers

Question number	Wording of the question and possible answers
Question 1	How serious do you consider this behavior to be? Not at all serious Very serious 1 2 3 4 5
Question 2	How serious do most police officers in your agency consider this behavior to be? Not at all serious Very serious 1 2 3 4 5
Question 3	Would this behavior be regarded as a violation of official policy in your agency? Definitely not Definitely yes 1 2 3 4 5
Question 4	If an officer in your agency engaged in this behavior and was discovered doing so, what, if any, discipline do you think should follow? 1. None 4. Period of suspension without pay 2. Verbal reprimand 5. Demotion in rank 3. Written reprimand 6. Dismissal
Question 5	If an officer in your agency engaged in this behavior and was discovered doing so, what, if any, discipline do you think would follow? 1. None 4. Period of suspension without pay 2. Verbal reprimand 5. Demotion in rank 3. Written reprimand 6. Dismissal
Question 6	Do you think you would report a fellow police officer who engaged in this behavior? Definitely not Definitely yes 1 2 3 4 5
Question 7	Do you think most police officers in your agency would report a fellow police officer who engaged in this behavior? Definitely not Definitely yes 1 2 3 4 5

Police Captain and Border Guard Captain (65.8%). Ranks below these formed the second largest group (28.9%) and of respondents whose role is Police Major and Border Guard Major and upwards, formed a small proportion (5.4%) of the sample. The majority of the respondents (73.2%) reported having no subordinates, while about one fifth (19.5%) had six or more. Almost a third (30.2%) of the respondents reported beyond 20 years of service, more than a quarter (26.2%) reported 11–15 years, and 18.8% reported 5 years of service or less.

The majority of the respondents (89.9%) identified themselves as Estonians, 7.4% as Russians, and 2.7% as other. Considering 59.8% of the respondents were men and 40.3% were women, the large proportion of women may look unusual, compared to the proportion of women in other police agencies across the world (Vallès 2013), but it is expected in Estonia as women have formed a considerable proportion of the police force in Estonia historically (see e.g. Vallmüür 2016).

Results

Seriousness

The average seriousness the surveyed police officers assigned to the green police integrity scenarios varied on a 5-point scale from 3.44 to 4.61 when presenting their own views, and from 3.14 to 4.22 when judging how others would see these (see Table 3). One the other hand, seriousness the police officers who participated in the survey assigned to the classic police integrity scenarios varied from 3.96 to 4.87, giving these scenarios the overall 1st, 2nd, and 8th rank, and from 3.67 to 4.72, ranking 1st, 2nd, and 6th, when evaluating

Table 3 Results

Scenario number and description	Own seriousness			Others' seriousness			Mean difference	Violation of rules		
	M	SD	Rank	M	SD	Rank	(own-others)	M	SD	Rank
Scenario 1: free meals, gifts from merchants	3.96	1.31	8	3.67	1.15	6	0.29	4.51	0.86	4
Scenario 2: failure to arrest friend with warrant	4.69	0.73	2	4.38	0.88	2	0.31	4.89	0.44	2
Scenario 3: theft of knife from crime scene	4.87	0.60	1	4.72	0.70	1	0.15	4.97	0.16	1
Scenario 4: ignoring a timber truck	4.05	1.01	6	3.64	1.06	7	0.41	4.08	1.00	8
Scenario 5: trafficking live eels	3.44	1.35	11	3.18	1.33	10	0.26	3.53	1.30	11
Scenario 6: lifting a battery to the side of a ditch	4.04	1.04	7	3.50	1.09	9	0.54*	3.95	1.12	9
Scenario 7: ignoring septic tank truck	4.61	0.73	3	4.22	0.92	3	0.39	4.61	0.63	3
Scenario 8: fishing with electricity	4.19	1.10	4	3.84	1.19	4	0.36	4.36	0.90	5
Scenario 9: not reporting importing rhino horn	4.13	1.14	5	3.73	1.26	5	0.40	4.28	1.00	6
Scenario 10: burning car tires	3.50	1.24	10	3.14	1.20	11	0.36	3.62	1.21	10
Scenario 11: ignoring sand removal	3.91	1.01	9	3.60	1.06	8	0.32	4.13	0.93	7

Scenario number and description	Own willingness to report			Others' willingness to report			Mean difference
	M	SD	Rank	M	SD	Rank	(own-others)
Scenario 1: free meals, gifts from merchants	3.50	1.31	7–8	3.12	1.04	8	0.38
Scenario 2: failure to arrest friend with warrant	4.44	0.92	2	3.99	0.91	2	0.46
Scenario 3: theft of knife from crime scene	4.77	0.56	1	4.33	0.79	1	0.44
Scenario 4: ignoring a timber truck	3.64	1.18	6	3.15	1.17	6	0.49
Scenario 5: trafficking live eels	3.17	1.42	10	2.95	1.29	10	0.21
Scenario 6: lifting a battery to the side of a ditch	3.36	1.27	9	2.97	1.19	9	0.39
Scenario 7: ignoring septic tank truck	4.18	1.05	3	3.65	1.06	3	0.53*
Scenario 8: fishing with electricity	3.81	1.20	4	3.45	1.15	4	0.36
Scenario 9: not reporting importing rhino horn	3.77	1.28	5	3.37	1.26	5	0.40
Scenario 10: burning car tires	3.08	1.27	11	2.75	1.21	11	0.33
Scenario 11: ignoring sand removal	3.50	1.24	7–8	3.13	1.17	7	0.37

how most police officers in their agency would view these.[4] Hence, the green police integrity scenarios tended to be evaluated as somewhat less serious than the classic police integrity scenarios.

---

[4]These values were approximately expected as in the previous survey carried out in the police in Estonia in 2013 these seriousness scores ranged from 3.77 (SD = 1.39) to 4.89 (SD = 0.58) and from 3.28 (SD = 1.29) to 4.59 (SD = 0.77) respectively (see Vallmüür 2015).

Out of the two scenarios from the area of damaging biodiversity, the scenario describing a police officer not reporting a friend who has imported a kilo of black rhino horn (scenario 9) was evaluated as more serious (4.13; Table 3) and actually ranked fifth based on the seriousness assigned to it by the respondents and according to how they expect most of the police officers to view it. On the other hand, the scenario depicting a police officer travelling out of the EU himself/herself and taking in his/her luggage a container with half a kilo of live glass eels of the European eel (scenario 5) was assigned a seriousness that makes it the least serious scenario of all of the cases in the survey from the perspective of the respondents (3.44; Table 3). This can be explained by multiple respondents commenting in the questionnaire that either they, or most police officers, lack information about glass eels.

Among the three scenarios addressing negative influence on natural resources, the scenario depicting a police officer using his/her electric fishing equipment on one weekend for fishing (scenario 8) was considered the most serious (4.19, Table 3), making it the 4th most serious offense both according to the views of the respondents as well as by how they expected most of their colleagues to view such a situation. While viewed not as serious, the scenario depicting a police officer seeing during a night shift in a patrol car a timber truck turning to the highway from a state forest (scenario 4: 4.05; Table 3) ranked as the 6th most serious scenario overall. Finally, the 3rd scenario in this group, the scenario characterizing a police officer in a patrol car seeing late in the evening two men shoveling sand into a trailer (scenario 11) was evaluated to be somewhat less serious (3.91; Table 3) making it one of the least serious (9th) scenarios.

In the group of the scenarios addressing the damage to the environmental quality, the scenario describing a police officer in a patrol car seeing a septic tank truck releasing liquid into a stream (scenario 7) was assigned a seriousness that made it the third most serious scenario based on how the respondents viewed it (4.61; Table 3). In other words, the respondents evaluated this green police integrity scenario about as serious/slightly less serious than the scenarios describing the theft from a crime scene and a failure to execute an arrest warrant. The other two scenarios from this category of green police misconduct were not evaluated as serious. In particular, the scenario depicting a police officer lifting an old car battery to the side of a ditch (scenario 6) was evaluated in a way that made it the seventh most serious scenario according to the views of

the respondents (4.04; Table 3), and the scenario describing a police officer himself or herself polluting the air by burning old furniture and car tires (scenario 10) was evaluated in a way that made it the second least serious act (10th) based on how the police officers viewed it (3.50; Table 3).

The scenario describing the theft of knife from a crime scene (scenario 3), which was included in this questionnaire to illustrate the seriousness police officers assign to one of the most serious scenarios typically studied globally, was evaluated with the highest average score (4.87; Table 3). At the same time, the scenario depicting the acceptance of gratuities (scenario 1) which was included in the current questionnaire to illustrate the level of seriousness assigned to the scenario that is typically seen as one of the least serious ones, was evaluated as the lowest of the classic scenarios in this study (3.96; Table 3). However, when including the green police integrity scenarios, then the acceptance of gratuities ranked eighth in terms of how serious the respondents considered it to be and sixth when evaluating how serious most of the police officers would find it.

The classic police integrity scenario that describes a failure to execute an arrest warrant (scenario 2) that was included in the questionnaire to enable comparison with green integrity scenarios depicting a decision not to act was evaluated by the respondents in a way that assigns it the second highest seriousness from the point of view of the police officers who participated in the survey (4.69; Table 3). Considering the seriousness assigned to the case of choosing not to execute an arrest warrant issued for a friend, it is noteworthy that the scenario describing a police officer not reporting a friend who has imported a kilo of black rhino horn (scenario 9) was evaluated as less serious and ranked only 5th (4.13; Table 3). Whether the difference stems from an arrest warrant already being issued in one case or in principle a lesser importance awarded to wildlife trafficking can be determined by further research.

While the respondents expected most of their colleagues to view these scenarios less seriously in all scenarios (Table 3), the difference was meaningful only in one case, considering the rule of thumb that only the differences of 0.50 or larger are considered as meaningful as established by Klockars et al. (2006).

Violation of Rules

Each of the 11 scenarios would violate official rules in Estonia. Although the respondents tended to hold the view that such behaviors would be seen as violations in their agency, there were differences across the scenarios.

The average views of police officers on whether these situations would be seen as violations in their agency ranged in case of green police integrity scenarios from as low as 3.53 to 4.36 and in one case even to 4.61 (see Table 3). At the same time, the mean of the respondents evaluating the behavior being seen as a violation in their agency ranged in case of classic police misconduct scenarios from 4.51 to 4.97 (see Table 3). Thus, in case of seven out of the eight green integrity scenarios, compared to the least serious classic scenario, the respondents were, on average, less certain that the behavior would be seen as violation in their agency.

In the group of scenarios describing damage to biodiversity the respondents were on average rather certain that not reporting a friend trafficking rhino horn (scenario 9: 4.28; Table 3) would be seen as a violation in their agency. The confidence that a police officer trafficking live glass eels in his or her luggage (scenario 5: 3.53; Table 3) would be seen as a violation in their agency was lower among the two scenarios and the lowest overall.

Among the three scenarios depicting negative influence on natural resources the average belief that these behaviors would be seen as violations in their agency was relatively similar (see Table 3) ranging from 4.08 when evaluating choosing not to investigate a timber truck (scenario 4) through 4.13 judging not investigating sand shoveling to a trailer from a public beach (scenario 11) to 4.36 for a police officer fishing with his or her own electric fishing gear (scenario 8).

Out of the three scenarios from the area of polluting the environment, the scenarios describing a police officer burning car tires in his or her yard (scenario 10: 3.62; Table 3) and a police officer disposing of a car batter by lifting it to the side of the ditch (scenario 6: 3.95; Table 3), were the ones where the respondents were on average less confident that it would be seen as a violation in their agency. At the same time, the respondents were on average much more certain that not investigating a septic tank truck releasing liquid into a stream (scenario 7: 4.61; Table 3) would be seen as violations of official rules, making it the scenario with the highest average confidence of it being seen as a violation. The above suggests that while police officers are aware that they have an obligation of responding to environmental crimes of pollution when witnessing or suspecting these taking place, they are less aware about the requirement of not harming the environment by pollution when off-duty.

With the sole exception of the scenario describing a septic tank truck releasing liquid into a stream (Min = 2, Max = 5), answers to all of the green police integrity scenarios ranged across the full scale (Min = 1, Max = 5) when asked whether these behaviors would be seen as violations in their agency. At the same time, when evaluating whether behaviors described in the three classic scenarios would be seen as violations of policies in their organization, the answers of respondents did not range across the full scale. The answers remained solely at 'Definitely yes' side of the scale when evaluating the scenario describing theft of knife from a crime scene (scenario 3: Min = 4, Max = 5) and while the evaluations of the other two classic scenarios (scenarios 1&2: Min = 2, Max = 5) ranged considerably, not once was 'Definitely not' chosen in either one of these cases. Hence, in case of all but one green integrity scenarios there was at least one respondent who was certain these situations would not be seen as violations in that agency, while no surveyed police officers held such views in case of the classic police misconduct scenarios. Thus, not only are the ranges of average beliefs of the respondents about the scenarios being seen as violations in their agency quite different in case of green police integrity scenarios compared to the classic ones, but the scales of responses differ in seven cases out of the eight green integrity scenarios compared with even the least serious classic scenarios.

Appropriate and Expected Discipline

The answers for the preferred and expected disciplinary sanctions for each scenario ranged from 'none' to 'dismissal' suggesting that, for each and every case out of the eleven, there was at least one respondent who is of the opinion that for this behavior no discipline at all should or would follow or that dismissal should and would be meted out.

For the green integrity scenarios, as illustrated on Table 3, the modal response for both appropriate and expected discipline was without an exception either verbal reprimand or written reprimand. Verbal reprimand, the most lenient disciplinary option, was the most widely held preference and expectation in two scenarios.

At the same time, for the three classic police scenarios 'dismissal' was the modal discipline that was expected to be meted out by the organization in each case, and considered appropriate by the largest number of respondents in two scenarios out of the three. For the third and least serious classic scenario—acceptance of gratuities (scenario 1)—verbal reprimand, closely followed by written reprimand, was the discipline that the largest number of respondents found appropriate.

In the groups of scenarios describing harming the *biodiversity* as well as damaging *natural resources*, written reprimand was the modal preference and expectation for a discipline without an exception. Out of the three scenarios from the area of *polluting the environment*, two—a police officer disposing of a car battery by lifting it to the side of a ditch (scenario 6), and burning car tires in the yard (scenario 10)—were perceived by the largest groups of respondents to merit and receive a verbal reprimand. For the third scenario in this group—not investigating a septic tank

releasing water into a stream (scenario 7)—the modal preference and expectation was a written reprimand as in case of the rest of the green integrity scenarios.

When looking at the distribution of the most severe forms of discipline that the respondents supported and expected, a very obvious difference is apparent (see Fig. 1). Namely, across all of the green integrity scenarios only 1.3–19.5% of respondents were of opinion that a dismissal should follow and only 2.0–22.8% expected dismissal to follow. However, already for the least serious classic scenario—the acceptance of gratuities (scenario 1)—17.4% of respondents thought that a dismissal should follow and 32.2% expected it. But for the two more serious classic scenarios—failing to execute an arrest warrant (scenario 2) and theft from the crime scene (scenario 3) 50.3% and 84.6% of the police officers participating in the survey supported dismissal following such behaviors and 63.1% and 83.9% expected it to be meted out by their agency. Similarly, while across green police integrity scenarios 2.0–22.8% of police officers participating in the survey were of opinion that no discipline should follow and as many as 6.0–26.8% expected no discipline to follow, then in case of classic police integrity scenarios the proportions were only 0.7–6.7% and 0.7–4.0% respectively.

Thus, while for the classic scenarios the most serious discipline was supported and expected by up to 84.6% and 83.9% of respondents, then for all of the green integrity scenarios only the two most lenient discipline options were found appropriate and most likely to be meted out in their agency according to the largest groups of police officers participating in the survey.

Officers' Willingness to Report Misconduct

The average willingness to report the described behaviors ranged across the green police integrity scenarios on a 5-point scale from 3.08 to 4.18 (see Table 3). At the same time, the willingness to report classic forms of police misconduct ranged from 3.50 to 4.77 (see Table 3). Hence, the will-

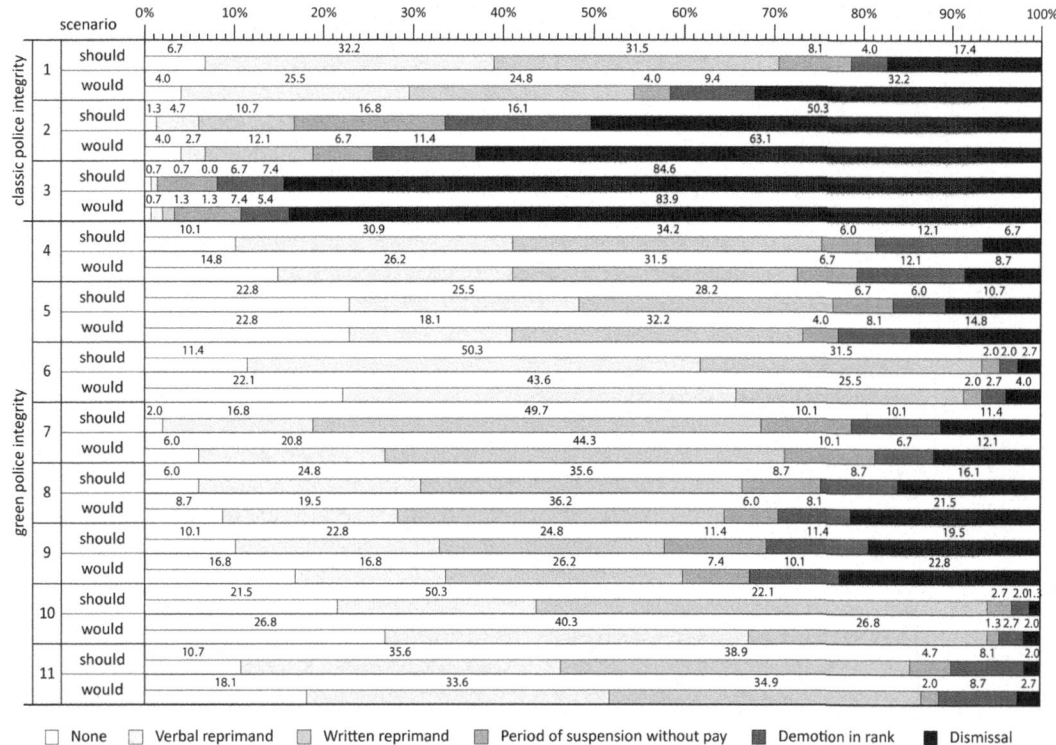

Fig. 1 Supported and expected discipline options by percentage

ingness to report green police integrity scenarios tended to be somewhat lower than in case of the classic police integrity scenarios.

Out of the two scenarios from the area of damaging biodiversity, the average willingness to report the case where a police officer did not report a friend that had imported rhino horn (Scenario 9) was higher (3.77; Table 3) ranking fifth with 18.1% (see Fig. 2) of respondents admitting they would not report it and 24.8% expecting their colleagues not to report such an act (3.37; Table 3). At the same time, the average willingness to report a police officer exporting live glass eels in the luggage (Scenario 5) was lower (3.17; Table 3) ranking tenth with 32.9% of respondents admitting that they would not have reported it and 34% of them believed that most of their colleagues would not report it either (2.95, Table 3).

Willingness to report situations asserting negative influence on natural resources was rather similar within that group of scenarios. The aver-

age willingness of respondents to report a police officer catching fish with electricity (Scenario 8) made it rank 4th (3.81, Table 3) with 13.4% admitting they would not report it and 18.8% expecting their colleagues not to report it (3.45; Table 3). The respondents' average willingness to report not investigating a suspicious timber truck (Scenario 4: 3.64; Table 3) and not investigating shoveling sand to a trailer from a beach (Scenario 11: 3.50; Table 3) were rather similar, ranking sixth and seventh-eighth respectively with 16.8% and 18.1% choosing not to report these acts. Notably, of the respondents 26.8% expected their colleagues not to report not investigating a suspicious timber truck (Scenario 4: 3.15; Table 3) and 28.9% believed that other police officers would not report not investigating shoveling sand to a trailer from a beach (Scenario 11: 3.13; Table 3).

Willingness to report the scenarios described in the group addressing polluting the environment differed considerably across these scenarios. Within that group the average willingness to

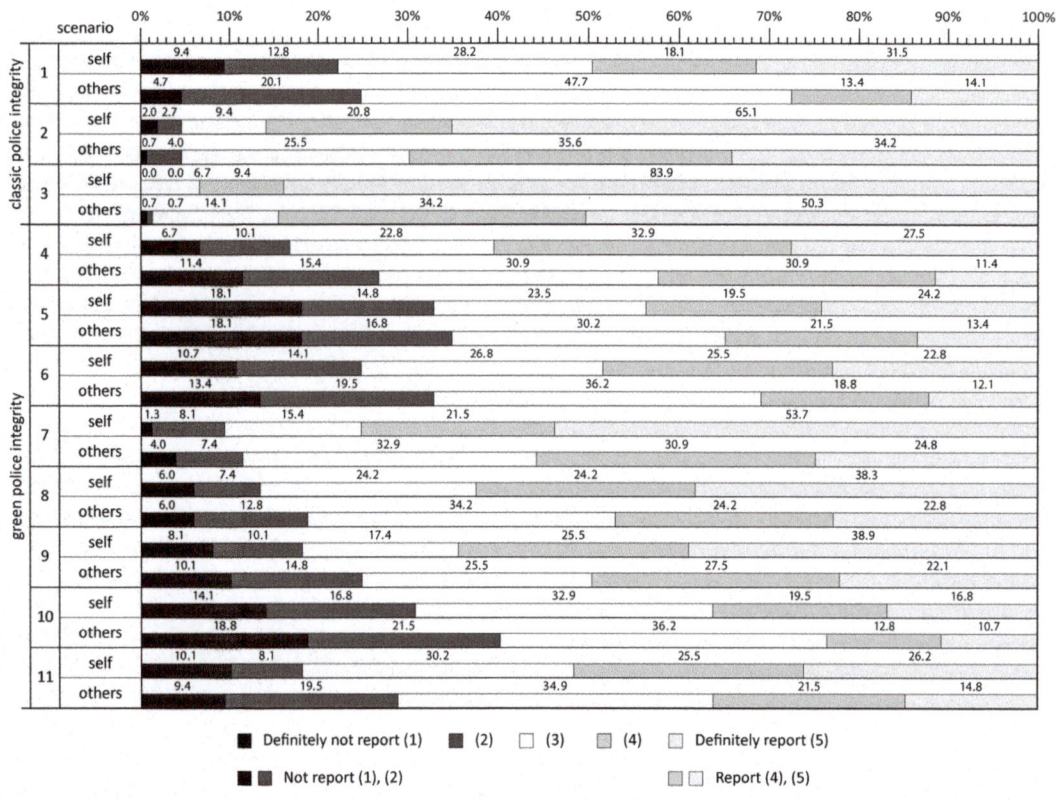

Fig. 2 Willingness to report by percentages

report was the lowest when evaluating a police officer burning car tires in the yard (Scenario 10) (3.08; Table 3) making it rank 11th with 30.9% of police officers answering that they would not have reported it. Furthermore, as many as 40.3% of respondents believed most of their colleagues would not report such an act (2.75; Table 3). The average willingness to report a police officer disposing of a car battery by lifting it to a ditch (Scenario 6), ranked 9th (3.36; Table 3) as 24.8% of police officers would not have reported it and 32.9% expected most of their colleagues to refrain from reporting it also (2.97; Table 3).

The scenario describing not investigating a suspicious septic tank truck (Scenario 7) was evaluated with the highest willingness to report among the green integrity scenarios ranking third overall (4.18; Table 3). The respondents, on average, expected their colleagues to be less willing to report this act (3.65; Table 3) to the extent that this scenario was also the only one of all of the

scenarios in the questionnaire, where the difference between own willingness to report and that expected from others was big enough (0.53) to be meaningful according to the rule of thumb principle. Only 9.4% of the police officers participating in the survey would not have reported it and 11.4% expected their colleagues not to. At the same time, 75.2% would have reported it, while 55.7% expected that their colleagues would.

Out of the classic police integrity scenarios the theft of knife from the crime scene (Scenario 3) was awarded the highest willingness to report (4.77; Table 3) making it rank first with no respondents saying that they would not report that situation (Min = 3, Max = 5), but it was the sole such rating across all of the scenarios. Also, only 1.3% of the respondents expected most police officers not to report it (4.33, Table 3). The willingness the police officers participating in the survey showed to report a police officer failing to execute an arrest warrant was high enough (4.44; Table 3) to give it the second ranking with only 4.7% of respondents claiming both not to report such an act and to expect most of their colleagues not to report it (3.99; Table 3). The willingness to report the third classic police integrity scenario— a police officer accepting gratuities (scenario 1)—was evaluated low enough (3.50; Table 3) to make it share the seventh-eighth rank with the act of not investigating shoveling sand to a trailer from the beach (scenario 11). As many as 22.1% of the respondents admitted they would not have reported it and 24.8% expected their colleagues not to report it either (3.12; Table 3).

In case of all green police integrity scenarios the answers of respondents ranged from 'Definitely not report' to 'Definitely report' both when judging how they would behave as well as when reflecting on how most of their colleagues would act. Furthermore, the above suggests that various green police integrity scenarios are covered by the blue code to a considerable extent. At the same time, classic scenarios tend to be less covered by the code of silence and, in case of one scenario, there were no respondents to answer that they would not report it. This suggests that while some police misconduct situations would not be covered by the code of silence among the surveyed police officers then none of the green police integrity scenarios would fall into that group.

Conclusion

The importance of the environment is formally recognized globally, but the scale of environmental crime is vast and expanding. While the necessity of the police in tackling environmental crime is growing, the theory of police integrity and its methodology had not studied the nature of green integrity in the police nor what characterizes police organizations that have high green integrity and how to create these. The purpose of the current chapter was to present a designated tool to study green integrity in the police and to expand the theory of police integrity with that of green police integrity.

The chapter presented a designated typology of scenarios to study green police integrity and addressed each of the four police integrity dimensions with a focus on green police integrity. The research tool for studying green integrity in the police was piloted in Estonia, where 149 police officers provided their views. The findings suggest the seriousness the respondents assigned to the green police integrity scenarios tended to be relatively low compared to the classic police integrity scenarios. However, the study does not allow concluding whether these rankings would be similar in the rest of the police organization in Estonia and in other countries. Prior comparative police integrity analysis (Kutnjak Ivković and Haberfeld 2015) has shown that the rankings of the seriousness are similar in countries with shared socio-economic traits. At the same time, it has been demonstrated that the seriousness police officers assign to the acts is, to a large extent, determined by the level of discipline the organization is expected to mete out on an offending police officer (see e.g., Klockars et al. 2004). Thus further research is needed to understand the determinants of the seriousness police officers assign to green crimes.

In this study, compared to the least serious classic scenario, the respondents were, on average, less certain that the behavior would be seen as violation in their agency in case of all green integrity scenarios with one exception. This suggests that the rules related to environmental crimes and to policing these may not have been introduced and taught to them as widely as rules related to classic police misconduct. This is further supported by the fact that the PBGB has no information about the knowledge on environmental crimes the police officers have prior to joining the PBGB as well as about introducing and teaching the rules related to environmental violations within the PBGB. At the same time, the PBGB explicitly requested carrying out the given survey also among their border administration functions, stating that environmental matters are important in their whole organization. This apparent discord between the interest as well as intended principles compared to past practices may suggest rather a lack of systematic preventive approach not willful organizational disregard. The framework provided in this chapter may be useful when reviewing these practices.

However, an aspect that needs considering, especially when establishing rules about environmental offenses that may appear distanced from classical crimes, is how the creation and relevance of these is perceived among the police officers. The manner the formal rules are created influences how supportively police officers view these—rules that are perceived as designed by administrators familiar with the specifics of law enforcement are viewed more favorably than rules imposed by detached administrators unaware of the specifics of law enforcement (Kutnjak Ivković 2015). Hence, special care should be taken particularly when creating any rules that would regulate policing environmental crimes or increasing the focus on environmental protection in the law enforcement as these subjects may be perceived as especially detached from the common practices of police officers.

The findings also suggest that, based on the experience of the respondents, environmental rules may not be treated as seriously in terms of enforcement as classic violations are. Namely, dismissal was the modal discipline that the respondents expected to be meted out by the organization for the three classic police scenarios. Furthermore, the largest number of police officers participating in the survey also considered dismissal to be the appropriate discipline in two scenarios out of the three. Curiously, for the green integrity scenarios the modal response for both appropriate and expected discipline was without an exception either verbal or written reprimand—the most lenient forms of discipline included in the questionnaire.

The findings may suggest that, according to the respondents, there is some organizational tolerance toward environmental misconduct. The support and expectation for relatively lenient discipline for the green integrity scenarios is not surprising by itself as the seriousness of the scenarios was evaluated comparatively low also. Namely, the police officers' opinions on preferred and anticipated discipline tend to be related to their evaluations of the seriousness of the act — typically, the more serious the behavior is perceived, the stricter is the discipline that is believed to be appropriate (Kutnjak Ivković and Klockars 2004). However, it is remarkable, that while for the least serious classic police integrity scenario a dismissal was expected to follow, then even for these green police integrity scenarios that were found to be more serious than this scenario, a written reprimand was expected to be meted out and supported by the largest group of the respondents. This further indicates that, based on the experience of the respondents, there may be some systematic tolerance for such behaviors.

As verbal reprimand was expected for two scenarios that characterized individual acts of air and soil pollution carried out by police officers while not on duty, it is possible there may be some general tolerance particularly toward these types of behaviors according to the police officers participating in the survey. At the same time, disposing of a car battery by lifting it to the side of the ditch was the only scenario, where the respondents considered it to be more serious than they expected their colleagues to view it to the extent that is considered meaningful. This suggests that the respondents may not be aware of the actual intolerance among their colleagues towards such behaviors.

The green police integrity scenarios were also more covered by the code of silence than the classic forms of police misconduct. The scenarios that were protected the most by the blue code depicted a police officer disposing of a car battery by lifting it to the side of a ditch, a police officer burning car tires in the yard, and curiously, the most protected act—a police officer exporting in luggage a container with live glass eels that constitutes illegal trafficking of protected species. This suggests that instances of individually illegally polluting the air and soil would be covered by the blue code relatively widely among the respondents. And so would be illegal trafficking of protected species, while fishing with electricity would be less protected. Discovering what causes these differences requires further research. Whether it stems from a high profile case of police officers fishing with electricity in the particular country, or it is a global tendency, or common to the countries with similar socio-economic background, remains to be discovered.

While this pilot study provided an overview of green police integrity among the police officers surveyed in Estonia, qualitative and comparative research is needed to provide insight into key determinants and causal links that would point to evidence based ways of creating law enforcement organizations with high green integrity. However, even individual country studies can provide a structured approach for practitioners to consider these matters.

Acknowledgements I gratefully acknowledge the support given by Prof. Sanja Kutnjak Ivković on this chapter in its various stages, the views of Prof. Maria R. Haberfeld, the feedback from Rocco Ots and Prof. Priit Suve on the scenarios, and preparing the figures for publication by Līva Breġe.

References

Almer, C., & Goeschl, T. (2011). The political economy of the environmental criminal justice system: A production function approach. *Public Choice, 148*, 611–630.

Andersen, J. P., & Papazoglou, K. (2015). Compassion fatigue and compassion satisfaction among police officers: An understudied topic. *International Journal of Emergency Mental Health and Human Resilience, 17*(3), 661–663.

Anderson, B., & Jooste, J. (2014). Wildlife poaching: Africa's surging trafficking threat. *Africa Security Brief, 28*, 1–8.

Anvelt, K. (2014, March 27) Piirivalvurid jäid salapüügiga vahele. [Border Guards got caught with illegal fishing]. Eesti Päevaleht. Retrieved September 7, 2018, from http://epl.delfi.ee/news/eesti/piirivalvurid-jaid-salapuugiga-vahele?id=68321273

Beaumont, N. J., Austen, M. C., Atkins, J. P., Burdon, D., Degraer, S., Dentinho, T. P., Derous, S., Holm, P., Horton, T., van Ierland, E., Marboe, A. H., Starkey, D. J., Townsend, M., & Zarzycki, T. (2007). Identification, definition and quantification of goods and services provided by marine biodiversity: Implications for the ecosystem approach. *Marine Pollution Bulletin, 54*(3), 253–265.

Beke, M., & Blomeyer, R. (2014). *Illegal, unreported and unregulated fishing: Sanctions in the EU Study.* Directorate-General for Internal Policies, Policy Department Structural and Cohesion Policies. Brussels: European Parliament. https://doi.org/10.2861/66959.

Blindell, J. (2006). 21st century policing: The role of police in detection, investigation and prosecution of environmental crime. *ACPR issues*, May, No 2. Payneham: Australasian Centre for Policing Research.

Boyd, D. R. (2012). *The environmental rights revolution. A global study of constitutions, human rights, and the environment.* Vancouver, BC: UBC Press.

Burns, K. (2017). Constitutions & the environment: Comparative approaches to environmental protection and the struggle to translate rights into enforcement. Environmental Law Review Syndicate. Retrieved July 21, 2018, from http://vjel.vermontlaw.edu/constitutions-environment-comparative-approaches-environmental-protection-struggle-translate-rights-enforcement/

Christy, B. (2016). Special Investigation: Inside the deadly rhino horn trade. *National Geographic.* October. Retrieved November 29, 2018, from https://www.nationalgeographic.com/magazine/2016/10/dark-world-of-the-rhino-horn-trade/

Civil Service Act. (2012). RT I, 06.07.2012, 1; 01.02.2018.

Code of Criminal Procedure. (2003). RT I 2003, 27, 166; 10.06.2018.

Code of Misdemeanor Procedure. (2002). RT I 2002, 50, 313; 09.01.2018.

Constitution of the Republic of Estonia. (1992). RT 1992, 26, 349; 06.05.2015.

Cooke, S. J., & Cowx, I. G. (2006). Contrasting recreational and commercial fishing: Searching for common issues to promote unified conservation of fisheries resources and aquatic environments. *Biological Conservation, 128*, 93–108.

Cooper, A., & Pilkey, O. (2014. December, 8) Bringing sand to the beach. *The Mark News.* Retrieved March 31, 2018, from http://www.themarknews.com/2014/12/08/bringing-sand-to-the-beach/

Corsianos, M. (2009). *Policing and gendered justice: Examining the possibilities.* Toronto, ON: University of Toronto Press.

Couper, M. P. (2000). Web surveys. A review of issues and approaches. *Public Opinion Quarterly, 64*, 464–494.

Edwards, S. M. (1996). Environmental criminal enforcement efforts by the States. In S. M. Edwards, T. D. Edwards, & C. B. Fields (Eds.), *Environmental crime and criminality: Theoretical and practical issues* (pp. 205–244). New York, NY: Garland Publishing.

Elliott, L. (2007). Transnational environmental crime in the Asia Pacific: An 'un(der)securitized' security problem? *The Pacific Review, 20*(4), 499–522.

Eurojust. (2014). *Strategic project on environmental crime. Report.* The Hague: Eurojust.

Europol. (2013). *Threat assessment 2013. Environmental Crime in the EU.* The Hague: Europol.

Eurostat. (2017). *GDP per capita in PPS.* Data from 1st December 2017. Retrieved April 14, 2018, from http://ec.europa.eu/eurostat/tgm/table.do?tab=table&init=1&plugin=1&language=en&pcode=tec00114

Eurostat. (2018). *Total and land area by NUTS 2 region.* Retrieved April 15, 2018, from https://data.europa.eu/euodp/data/dataset/HZKBS2y8ycdZijX0PMHPA

Figley, C. R. (1999). Police compassion fatigue (PCF): Theory, research, assessment, treatment, and prevention. In J. M. Violanti & D. Paton (Eds.), *Police trauma: Psychological aftermath of civilian combat* (pp. 37–53). Springfield, IL: Charles C Thomas.

Foley, J. A., DeFries, R., Asner, G. P., Barford, C., Bonan, G., Carpenter, S. R., Chapin, F. S., Coe, M. T., Daily, G. C., Gibbs, H. K., Helkowski, J. H., Holloway, T., Howard, E. A., Kucharik, C. J., Monfreda, C., Patz, J. A., Prentice, I. C., Ramankutty, N., & Snyder, P. K. (2005). Global consequences of land use. *Science, 309*, 570–574.

Font, T., & Lloret, J. (2014). Biological and ecological impacts derived from recreational fishing in mediterranean coastal areas. *Reviews in Fisheries Science & Aquaculture, 22*(1), 73–85.

Gibbs, C., & Boratto, R. (2017). *Environmental crime.* Oxford Research Encyclopedia of Criminology. https://doi.org/10.1093/acrefore/9780190264079.013.269.

Groombridge, N. (2013). Matter all over the place. Litter, criminology and criminal justice. In N. South & A. Brisman (Eds.), *Routledge International Handbook of Green Criminology* (pp. 394–408). London: Routledge.

Gould, L. A. (1997). Can an old dog be taught new tricks? Teaching cultural diversity to police officers. Policing: An International Journal of Police Strategies & Management, 20(2), 339–356.

Hayman, G., & Brack, D. (2002). *International Environmental Crime: the nature and control of environmental black markets.* Workshop Report. London: Royal Institute of International Affairs.

International Monetary Fund. (2017). *World Economic Outlook. Database—WEO Groups and Aggregates Information.* April 2017. Retrieved April 15, 2018, from https://www.imf.org/external/pubs/ft/weo/2017/01/weodata/groups.htm

INTERPOL. (2015). *Environmental crime and its convergence with other serious crimes.* Lyon: INTERPOL.

INTERPOL & UNEP. (2016). *Strategic report: Environment, peace and security—A convergence of threats.* INTERPOL and UNEP.

Kalmre, V. (2009, June 17). Kohus mõistis Aivar Otsaltile tingimisi vangistuse. [The Court sentenced Aivar Otsalt with conditional imprisonment] *Tartu Postimees.* Retrieved September 7, 2018, from https://tartu.postimees.ee/132970/kohus-moistis-aivar-otsaltile-tingimisi-vangistuse.

Klockars, C. B., & Kutnjak Ivković, S. (2004). Measuring police integrity. In A. R. Piquero, J. R. Greene, & M. J. Hickman (Eds.), *Police integrity and ethics* (pp. 3–20). Belmont, CA: Wadsworth/Thomson Learning.

Klockars, C. B., Kutnjak Ivković, S., Harver, W. E., & Haberfeld, M. R. (2000). *The measurement of police integrity. Research in brief. U.S. Department of Justice, Office of Justice programs, National Institute of Justice.* Washington, DC: Government Printing Office.

Klockars, C. B., Kutnjak, I. S., & Haberfeld, M. R. (2004). The contours of police integrity. In C. B. Klockars, I. S. Kutnjak, & M. R. Haberfeld (Eds.), *The contours*

of police integrity (pp. 1–18). Thousand Oaks, CA: Sage.

Klockars, C. B., Kutnjak Ivković, S., & Haberfeld, M. R. (2006). *Enhancing police integrity.* Dordrecht: Springer.

Kodros, K. J., Wiedinmyer, C., Ford, B., Cucinotta, R., Gan, R., Magzamen, S., & Pierce, J. R. (2016). Global burden of mortalities due to chronic exposure to ambient PM2.5 from open combustion of domestic waste. *Environmental Research Letters, 11*(12), 124022.

Kriminaalmenetluse seadustiku muutmise ja sellega seonduvalt teiste seaduste muutmise seadus [The Act amending the Code of Criminal Procedure and acts pertaining to this act]. (2011). RT I, 23.02.2011, 1; 01.09.2011.

Kutnjak Ivković, S. (2015). Studying police integrity). In S. Kutnjak Ivković & M. R. Haberfeld (Eds.), *Measuring police integrity across the world* (pp. 1–36). New York, NY: Springer.

Kutnjak Ivković, S., & Haberfeld, M. R. (2015). A comparative perspective on police integrity. In S. Kutnjak Ivković & M. R. Haberfeld (Eds.), *Measuring police integrity across the world* (pp. 329–368). New York, NY: Springer.

Kutnjak Ivković, S., & Klockars, C. B. (2004). Police integrity in Croatia. In C. B. Klockars, S. Kutnjak Ivković, & M. R. Haberfeld (Eds.), *The contours of police integrity* (pp. 56–74). Thousand Oaks, CA: Sage.

Law Enforcement Act. (2011). RT I, 22.03.2011, 4; 01.07.2018.

Lin, J. (2005). Tackling Southeast Asia's illegal wildlife trade. *Singapore Year Book of International Law, 9*, 191–208.

Lynch, M. J., Stretesky, P. B., & Long, M. A. (2017). State and green crimes related to water pollution and ecological disorganization: Water pollution from publicly owned treatment works (POTW) facilities across US states. *Palgrave Communications, 3*(17070).

May, C. (2017). *Transnational crime and the developing world.* Washington, DC: Global Financial Integrity.

Milfont, T. L. (2012). Cultural differences in environmental engagement. In S. Clayton (Ed.), *The Oxford handbook of environmental and conservation psychology* (pp. 181–202). Oxford: Oxford University Press.

Natali, L. (2013). The contemporary horizon of green criminology). In N. South & A. Brisman (Eds.), *Routledge International Handbook of Green Criminology* (pp. 73–84). London: Routledge.

National Audit Office of Estonia. (2016). *Politsei- ja Piirivalveameti moodustamise kulg ja tulemuslikkus. Kas ühendasutuse loomisega on saavutatud kokkuhoid ja teenuse kvaliteedi paranemine? Riigikontrolli aruanne Riigikogule 19. April 2016.* [The process and effectiveness of the formation of the Police and Border Guard Board. Has the creation of the merged agency achieved savings and increased the quality of service? Report of the National Audit Office of Estonia to the Parliament of Estonia]. Tallinn: Riigikontroll.

Nellemann, C., Henriksen, R., Kreilhuber, A., Stewart, D., Kotsovou, M., Raxter, P., Mrema, E., & Barrat,

S. (Eds.). (2016). *The rise of environmental crime—A growing threat to natural resources, peace, development and security. A UNEP-INTERPOL Rapid Response Assessment, United Nations Environment Programme and RHIPTO Rapid Response—Norwegian Center for Global Analyses.*

Norris, P., & Inglehart, R. (2011). *Sacred and secular: Religion and politics worldwide.* Cambridge: Cambridge University Press.

NZPA. (2012, October 1). Day in the life of … the Maritime Unit. *NZPA 45*(9). Retrieved March 24, 2018, from https://www.policeassn.org.nz/newsroom/publications/featured-articles/day-life-maritime-unit

Penal Code. (2001). RT I 2001, 61, 364; 15.07.2018.

Police and Border Guard Act. (2009). RT I 2009, 26, 159; 01.10.2017.

Police and Border Guard Board. (2014). *Korruptsioonialasest informatsioonist ja teenistujaga seotud erakorralistest juhtumitest teavitamise kord.* [The procedure of notifying about corruption related information and exceptional cases related to a staff member.] 29.05.2014 Directive of the Director General of the Police and Border Guard Board.

Police and Border Guard Board. (2018a). Police and Border Guard Board—in cooperation we create safety. Retrieved July 27, 2018, from https://www2.politsei.ee/en/organisatsioon/organization/.

Police and Border Guard Board. (2018b). *Response to the inquiry.* Retrieved September 6, 2018.

Prior, T., Giurco, D., Mudd, G., Mason, L., & Behrisch, J. (2012). Resource depletion, peak minerals and the implications for sustainable resource management. *Global Environmental Change, 22*(3), 577–587.

Roebuck, J. B., & Barker, T. (1974). A typology of police corruption. *Social Problems, 21*, 423–437.

Rudi, H. & Berendson, R. (2009, May 19). Kapo pidas kinni politseiprefekt Aivar Otsalti. [Estonian Internal Security Service detained Aivar Otsalt]. *Postimees.* Retrieved September 8, 2018, from https://www.postimees.ee/120941/kapo-pidas-kinni-politseiprefekt-aivar-otsalti.

Schandl, H., Fischer-Kowalski, M., et al. (2016). *Global material flows and resource productivity. Assessment report for the UNEP International Resource Panel.* Paris: U.N. Environment Programme.

Science Communication Unit. (2013). *Science for environment policy in-depth report: Soil contamination: Impacts on Human Health.* Report produced for the European Commission DG Environment, September 2013. Bristol: Science Communication Unit, University of the West of England.

Secretariat of the CBD & WHO (Secretariat of the Convention on Biological Diversity & World Health Organizaton). (2015). *Connecting global priorities: Biodiversity and human health. A state of knowledge review.* Secretariat of the Convention on Biological Diversity & World Health Organization. Retrieved April 3, 2018, from https://www.cbd.int/health/SOK-biodiversity-en.pdf.

SEG (Sustainable Eel Group). (2018, March, 9). *Criminals Trafficked 110 Million Eels to Asia so far this Season.* Retrieved March 14, 2018, from http://www.sustainableeelgroup.org/2018/03/09/criminals-trafficked-110-million-eels-to-asia-so-far-this-season/.

Smith, L. (2017, December 8). Trafficking makes eel 'as valuable as cocaine' Friday. *I News.* Retrieved March 14, 2018, from https://inews.co.uk/news/environment/trafficking-makes-eel-valuable-cocaine/.

South, N., Brisman, A., & Beirne, P. (2013). A guide to a green criminology. In N. South & A. Brisman (Eds.), *Routledge International Handbook of Green Criminology* (pp. 27–42). London: Routledge.

Statistics Estonia. (2017). Population by ethnic nationality, 1 January, years. Retrieved April 14, 2018, from https://www.stat.ee/34278.

Statistics Estonia. (2018). *Main indicators.* January 1. 2018 data. Retrieved April 14, 2018, from https://www.stat.ee/main-indicators.

Stein, F. M., Wong, J. C. Y., Sheng, V., Law, C. S. W., Schröder, B., & Baker, D. M. (2016). First genetic evidence of illegal trade in endangered European eel (Anguilla anguilla) from Europe to Asia. *Conservation Genetics Resources, 8*, 533. https://doi.org/10.1007/s12686-016-0576-1.

Sutherland, W. J., Barnard, P., Broad, S., Clout, M., Connor, B., Côté, I. M., Dicks, L. V., Doran, H., Entwistle, A. C., Fleishman, E., Fox, M., Gaston, K. J., Gibbons, D. W., Jiang, Z., Keim, B., Lickorish, F. A., Markillie, P., Monk, K. A., Pearce-Higgins, J. W., Peck, L. S., Pretty, J., Spalding, M. D., Tonneijck, F. H., Wintle, B. C., & Ockendon, N. (2017). A 2017 horizon scan of emerging issues for global conservation and biological diversity. *Trends in Ecology & Evolution, 32*(1), 31–40.

The Estonian Academy of Security Sciences. (2018). *Response to the inquiry.* Retrieved October 1, 2018.

The Scotsman. (2010, February 11). Tiree's stretches of pristine white sand have been targeted by thieves in midnight raids. *The Scotsman.* Retrieved March 31, 2018, from https://www.scotsman.com/news/tiree-s-stretches-of-pristine-white-sand-have-been-targeted-by-thieves-in-midnight-raids-1-790177.

Tomkins, K. (2005). Police, law enforcement and the environment. *Current Issues in Criminal Justice, 16*(3), 294–306.

Torres, A., Liu, J., Brandt, J., & Lear, K. (2017, September 7). The world is facing a global sand crisis. *The Conversation.* Retrieved March 31, 2018, from https://theconversation.com/the-world-is-facing-a-global-sand-crisis-83557.

United Nations. (2015). *Transforming our world: the 2030 agenda for sustainable development.* Resolution adopted by the United Nations General Assembly on 25 September 2015. New York: United Nations.

Vallès, L. (Ed.). (2013). *Women in police services in the EU. Facts and figures. 2012.* Generalitat de Catalunia: Institut de Seguretat Pública de Catalunia. Retrieved September 16, 2018, from http://ispc.gencat.cat/web/.

content/home/ms_-_institut_de_seguretat_publica_
de_catalunya/recerca/Estudis-ispc/women_in_police_
services/women_in_police_services_eu_2012.pdf

Vallmüür, B. (2015). Police integrity in Estonia. In
S. Kutnjak Ivković & M. R. Haberfeld (Eds.),
Measuring police integrity across the world (pp. 125–
152). New York, NY: Springer.

Vallmüür, B. (2016). Exploring gender-neutrality of
police integrity in Estonia. *Policing: An International
Journal of Police Strategies & Management, 39*(2),
401–415.

White, R. (2013). *Crimes against nature. Environmental
criminology and ecological justice.* Abingdon:
Routledge.

White, R. (2016). Building NESTs to combat environmental crime networks. *Trends in Organized Crime,
19*(1), 88–105.

Wiedinmyer, C., Yokelson, R. J., & Gullett, B. K. (2014).
Global emissions of trace gases, particulate matter,
and hazardous air pollutants from open burning of
domestic waste. *Environmental Science & Technology,
48*(16), 9523–9530.

World Bank. (2018). World Bank Country and Lending
Groups. Retrieved April 15, 2018, from https://
datahelpdesk.worldbank.org/knowledgebase/
articles/906519-world-bank-country-and-lending-
groups.

Wright, G. (2011). Conceptualising and combating transnational environmental crime. *Trends in Organised
Crime, 14*, 332–346.

Yeager, P. C., & Simpson, S. (2009). Environmental
crime. In M. H. Tonry (Ed.), *The Oxford handbook
of crime and public policy* (pp. 325–355). Oxford:
Oxford University Press.

Police Integrity and the Perceived Effectiveness of Policing: Evidence from a Survey Among Ugandan Police Officers

Natascha Wagner and Wil Hout

Introduction

As a key element of the 'strong arm' of the state, the police have generally been the subject of much academic research. The police face the so-called 'paradox of violence' of the democratic state: the police (next to the army) claim the monopoly on the legitimate use of violence, but also need to respect legal restraints on the actual use of its powers. As argued by Gary Marx (2001), 'a democratic society needs protection both by police and from police'. Given the role of police in society, the integrity of police officers is very important. Moreover, identification of the factors that promote police integrity and those that hinder it has considerable societal relevance.

Research on police integrity has grown substantially over the past two decades (see the overview of publications in Kutnjak Ivković 2015, pp. 18–30). The academic literature in this field received a major boost with the seminal work of Klockars et al. (2000), who developed a method for the measurement of police integrity built on hypothetical cases (vignettes) rather than attempts to ask police officers direct questions about their behavior. The advantage of the approach is that it reduces bias since the vignettes do not directly inquire about own behavior but ask for the assessment of the hypothetical behavior depicted in the cases. Moreover, the vignettes allow the presentation of a set of uniform cases to all study participants independent of their experience and (socio-economic) background. This method was underpinned by the so-called organizational theory of police integrity, consisting of four dimensions: organizational rules, techniques of controlling police misconduct, the police agencies' efforts of curtailing the 'code of silence' in the police force, and the influence of the social and political environment on the police force (Kutnjak Ivković 2015, pp. 5–11).

Previous studies have mainly focused on the *internal* validation of the vignette approach to police integrity. First, studies have demonstrated that more severe cases are judged more severely (e.g., Jenks et al. 2014, p. 330). Second, the vignettes have shown to be applicable across countries and contexts, subject to minor context-specific adjustments, thus yielding coherent results (Kutnjak Ivković and Haberfeld 2015, p. 334).

In order to add to the existing body of work evolving to a large extent around the internal consistency of the vignette approach, this chapter aims to assess the *external* validity of the vignettes. Thus, we link evaluative questions about the vignettes to the perceived institutional environment and perceptions of police effectiveness and assess to what extent they are related.

N. Wagner (✉) · W. Hout
International Institute of Social Studies, Erasmus University Rotterdam, Rotterdam, The Netherlands
e-mail: wagner@iss.nl; hout@iss.nl

© Springer Nature Switzerland AG 2019
S. Kutnjak Ivković, M. R. Haberfeld (eds.), *Exploring Police Integrity*,
https://doi.org/10.1007/978-3-030-29065-8_7

We consider the police officers' own perceptions of the situation and the work of the police as prime candidates for such an analysis.

This chapter uses questions about the perceptions of the institutional environment and police effectiveness among Ugandan police officers to contextualize the findings on police integrity measured by the vignettes. We have identified ten elements of the perceived institutional environment (e.g., similar treatment by age, gender, and socio-economic status; level of crime in the community) and police effectiveness (e.g., confidence in own and colleagues' work) and analyze the relationship of these elements with the evaluative responses to the vignette cases. Our data, collected in 2015 in an attempt to evaluate a police reform project (see, e.g., Hout et al. 2016, pp. 51–75), expressly contained questions about the wider environment of the Ugandan police force, as well as police officers' own assessments of their work situation and perceptions of the operations and effectiveness of the police organization. Thus, our research attempts to contribute to research in the tradition of the organizational approach to police integrity by focusing mainly on how police officers' perceptions of their institutional environment may impact on their position on various forms of police misconduct.

Next to adding to insights about the external validity of the vignettes, we make a methodological contribution to the literature on police integrity. While it is relevant to assess the hypothetical cases one by one and compare the assessments of police officers, we feel it is equally valuable to pool the outcomes and look at patterns underlying the ensemble of vignettes to contribute to a deeper understanding of the usefulness of vignettes.

Police Integrity and Perceptions of the Police Force

Research in the field of governance has led to the definition of integrity as 'the quality of acting in accordance with relevant moral values, norms, and rules' (Lasthuizen et al. 2011, p. 387), where integrity can be a quality both of individuals and organizations. Police integrity is commonly understood as 'the normative inclination among police to resist temptations to abuse the rights and privileges of their occupation' (Klockars et al. 2006, p. 1).

The literature on police integrity has hitherto focused mostly on the impact of various (socio-economic and experience-related) characteristics of police officers and the infrastructure and overall situation of the police agencies on the perceptions of seriousness of police misconduct and the perceptions of fellow officers' willingness to report (Kutnjak Ivković 2015, pp. 18–27). Research focusing on perceptions of the institutional environment in the police force has remained surprisingly scarce, although it is not difficult to argue that the way in which police officers perceive their environment may have an impact toward their attitudes on misconduct and their willingness to report acts of misconduct.

Several studies have demonstrated how differences at the macro-societal level impact on police officers' attitudes to corruption, the treatment of prisoners, and other forms of misconduct. For instance, Kutnjak Ivković et al. (2016a, b) report on research among the police in Croatia and show that features of society at large seem to play a role in officers' assessment of police misbehavior, although the impact of such community characteristics is limited by variations in organizational features of the police. Further, a study on police integrity in Russia finds a clear impact of the overall societal perception of corruption. The authors of that study (Cheloukhine et al. 2015, p. 179) conclude as follows:

> In the environment in which corruption is entrenched into everyday life and everything is for sale, the acceptance of kickbacks … and thefts from the crime scene … are the new 'normal.' In the situation in which planting of evidence on innocent people and falsification of official records to bust the arrest records are occurring on a regular basis, falsification of a police record … and a failure to exercise an arrest warrant on a friend … are also becoming the new 'normal.'

Comparative studies on police integrity corroborate the impact of the institutional environment and, in particular, of the social perception of corruption (e.g., Andreescu et al. 2012, pp. 198–199; Kutnjak Ivković and Haberfeld 2015). Further, comparative research on the treatment of suspect behavior and the use of force indicates how the culture of a police force seems to impact on the attitudes of police officers toward the use of force (Waddington et al. 2009, pp. 134–135). Finally, a team of French researchers demonstrated how the 'professional ideologies' of police officers (expressed in the three main positions that police activity should be mainly repressive or preventive or a combination of both) are impacting on their opinions on the role of the police (Coulangeon et al. 2012).

Relatively little research has so far been done on the perceptions of police officers regarding the police force and on how these perceptions affect police officers' attitudes toward misconduct and their willingness to report misconduct. Various studies have addressed the impact of the organizational culture and the code of silence on the perceptions of police officers about police integrity (e.g. Kucukuysal 2008; Kutnjak Ivković and Sauerman 2015), while others have analyzed the impact of different disciplinary environments on perceived disciplinary consequences of misconduct (e.g., Lee et al. 2013; Kutnjak Ivković and Khechumyan 2014; Cheloukhine et al. 2015; Kutnjak Ivković et al. 2016a, b; Kuo 2018). Further, a number of studies have focused on the impact of perceptions of disciplinary fairness (i.e., how fair do officers feel that the disciplinary consequences of their behavior are?) on the likelihood that misconduct will be reported and the code of silence will be broken (e.g. Kutnjak Ivković and Shelley 2010; Long et al. 2013; Kutnjak Ivković and Sauerman 2013; Porter et al. 2015). Wolfe and Piquero (2011) showed how different aspects of perceived organizational justice—broken down into distributive, procedural and interactional aspects—influence the incidence of police misconduct. Using a slightly different approach, Myhill and Bradford (2013) demonstrated how perceptions of organizational justice impact positively on police attitudes to serving the public. Finally, a study by Bucak (2012) has shown that police cynicism (understood as the pessimistic outlook of police officers towards their job) has an impact, albeit moderately, on police integrity.

The lack of attention to perceptions of police officers on the functioning of the police force, and particularly its effectiveness, has motivated the current study. We feel that a more profound analysis of police officers' perceptions of the effectiveness of their own work and its possible relationship with police integrity would contribute to a better understanding of the influence of the social and political environment on the police force (the fourth dimension highlighted in the organizational theory of police integrity). In a similar vein as Bucak (2012, pp. 44–49) we start from the hypothesis that the way in which police officers appreciate their work, and in particular the degree to which they believe that their work contributes to social values, impacts on the way they perform their duties. Thus, the perception of one's own work as being ineffective may lead to the acceptance of corruption and other forms of misconduct on the part of the police.

The Uganda National Police

Before moving on to our empirical analysis we present some background information about Uganda and its police force. Since 1986, Ugandan politics has been dominated by President Yoweri Museveni's National Resistance Movement (NRM), the political successor to the National Resistance Army (NRA), which prevailed in the Ugandan Bush War, the protracted civil war against the regime of Milton Obote (1980–1985). The Ugandan 'Movement System', which existed from 1986 until 2005, was envisaged to be a non-party political system, where representatives were elected on individual rather than party platforms. Museveni won the first Ugandan presidential elections in 1996 and was re-elected to the presidency in four subsequent national elections (2001, 2006, 2011 and 2016). Although Uganda has had multi-party elections since the mid-2000s, Museveni's regime has become increasingly authoritarian. Regime maintenance became an important objective, and this led to the search for instruments to broaden the regime's support base among the Ugandan population (Khisa 2014).

Increased opposition led the Museveni regime to mobilize political support for the NRM by using patronage-driven appointments and tolerating corruption, the rising costs of which have been labeled 'inflationary patronage' (Khisa 2014, pp. 32–36; Barkan 2011; cf. Tangri and Mwenda 2013). Decentralization has been an important instrument of patronage; the increase of the number of districts from around 40 in the mid-1990s to 111 since 2012 (Ministry of Trade, Industry and Cooperatives 2017) served as a means for the regime to appoint its supporters to local government positions (Golooba-Mutebi and Hickey 2013, pp. 16–17). Further, the NRM government became increasingly repressive, targeting independent media, the judiciary and opposition parties (Anderson and Fisher 2016). In recent decades, the Uganda National Police and the national army have been important instruments of the regime's attempts to maintain power. A former army commander, Major-General Mugisha Muntu, and current opponent of the Museveni regime, characterized the Uganda National Police recently as 'an extension of the ruling party' (Economist 2018).

The Ugandan police force was institutionalized in 1906 (Uganda Police Force 2007) and has officially been known as 'Uganda National Police' since April 2014 (Lumu 2014). It is divided functionally into 20 directorates based on tasks and geographically into regional and district offices, police stations and posts (Uganda Police 2015). Data about the police and policing activities is scant since the statistical capacity of the police is weak (Uganda Police Force 2007). In the early 2000s, Uganda had fewer than 15,000 police officers, with considerable year-to-year variation according to the available statistics (Commonwealth Human Rights Initiative 2006a, pp. 26–27). In 2007, the Ugandan police force experienced a major increase of personnel—it went from approximately 27,000 to 48,000 officers—and saw the creation of more directorates in preparation for the Commonwealth Heads of Government Meeting (Xinhua News Agency 2007). At the end of 2014, the Inspector General announced an increase of the police from roughly 40,000 to 65,000 officers (Kakamwa 2014).

Concerning crime statistics and the security environment in Uganda, 252,065 crimes were reported in 2017, resulting in a crime rate involving 667 victims per 100,000 Ugandans (Uganda Police 2017, p. 2). Public sector crime investiga-

tions have been declining over a range of years. The Ugandan police reported 37 cases of corruption in 2017, compared to 194 in 2016 and 413 in 2013 (Uganda Police 2013, p. 9, 2017, p. 8). Background information on the types of public sector corruption are not provided leaving it open whether corruption within the police is also included in these figures. The 2013 Crime Report indicated 19 cases in which police officers were under investigation of suspected crimes (Uganda Police 2013).

Uganda is in the top quintile of the most corrupt countries according to the 2018 Corruption Perceptions Index (Transparency International 2018) and the Ugandan police is regarded as particularly corrupt (Wambua 2015; Basheka 2013, pp. 72–74; Transparency International-Kenya 2013). Results of various surveys—including Uganda's National Service Delivery Study 2015 (Kato 2016) and older surveys carried out by the Commonwealth Human Rights Initiative (2006b) between 1998 and 2005—indicate that a majority of Ugandan citizens have consistently rated the police as the most corrupt institution in the country.

The characteristics of corruption and fraud in Uganda, and the perception of corruption within the Ugandan national police, make the country an interesting case to study police integrity in relation to the extent to which police officers themselves perceive their work as effective. We expect that, in particular, the high-corruption context of Uganda may reveal challenges to integrity and professionalism among the police.

Survey Set Up, Sampling, and Questionnaire

Our data are derived from interviews with police officers from 10 of the 143 Ugandan police districts (Uganda Police 2017, p. e, f). The survey districts are Bushenyi, Iganga, Jinja, Kabale, Kabarole, Tororo, Luwero, Mbarara, Mityana, and Soroti. On purpose, no single Northern Ugandan district was sampled because of the impact of the conflict between the Ugandan government and the Lord's Resistance Army rebels on the region. We employed the vignette cases along with questions about the perception of police work among 600 police officers in the 10 selected districts, sampling 60 officers within each district. The data collection was carried out by our local university partner, the Uganda Management Institute. The research team worked in close collaboration with the police. After authorization from the police headquarters, the local research team wrote a letter to the regional police officers informing them about the activities and asking for support. The research team then identified the study participants together with the police. The district-level sampling strategy was well respected with only some very minor deviations: in two districts only 59 officers could be interviewed, while in another two districts 61 officers were interviewed. Thus, the target sample of a total of 600 individuals was reached since officers that could not participate were replaced.

We organized the survey in groups of 30 officers. Survey activities took place at the local level. To this end we rented venues that where equipped with enough tables and chairs for 30 police officers. To reach the target number of 60 officers per district, at least two survey sessions took place in every district, one in the morning and one in the afternoon of the scheduled survey days.

In an introduction, the enumerators presented the survey to the participating police officers and allowed for questions. The survey was conducted in English since English is one of the two official languages in Uganda and widely spoken in public services and government. The survey consisted of a self-administered pen and paper questionnaire. Each police officer was provided enough personal space to ensure privacy and confidentiality. To further protect anonymity, we did not ask the officers to provide their names or addresses. All survey activities took place in April 2015.

In terms of sampling, we aimed at the representation of officers across all levels of rank. To this end, individual officers were selected in a stratified way. First, we purposively invited regional-level officers to participate in the survey because of their leading position. Second, we also purposively included the leading police officers of the district headquarters in the survey. Finally, we randomly sampled police stations within districts:

Half the officers in our sample come from small stations (with up to 10 officers) and 70% of them from mid-sized stations (with up to 25 officers). We introduced random participation at the police station level by randomly picking the day of the survey resulting in local participation based on availability or presence. At the local level we do not expect any systematic selection of participants into our sample since the police stations only have few officers. As motivated, we applied this sampling procedure to have a stratified sample of officers that represents the full spectrum of police work, functions, positions, and hierarchies.

The survey among police officers had two parts. In the first part, officers reported their basic socio-economic characteristics together with information about their work experience and some basic facts about the staffing and equipment of their police station. In the second and core part, officers were asked to review twelve vignette cases and questions about the perceived institutional environment and effectiveness of the police. The vignettes were adapted to the Ugandan context based on the earlier versions developed by Klockars et al. (2000, 2006) and Kutnjak Ivković (2005a, b). Adaptation to the local context was necessary since, for example, the offering of small gifts on holidays such as Christmas is not perceived as an indication of corruption. Furthermore, we wanted to test to what extent the police complaint form, introduced by the Ugandan police prior to our survey, was accepted among the police. Therefore, we included a case about the application of the form. Similarly, the peaceful monitoring of demonstrations and the professional clearing of potential conflicts, while accepting the right to demonstrate, was another aspect of policing that we considered necessary assessing in the specific Ugandan context. The complaint form as well as the monitoring of demonstrations were topics that were perceived as very relevant by the locals.

Thus, the cases that we deployed were co-developed with our local research partner, pretested with the police and adjusted to the local context. Importantly, on purpose we opted for the inclusion of case scenarios with cultural load. For example, the originally proposed case scenarios contain the case of a burglary in a jewelry shop (Klockars et al. 2000, 2006). Since jewelry shops are not common in local Uganda, there would not have been any value in presenting such a scenario. Consequently, we introduced a burglary in a general merchandise shop. We specified the goods relative to locally know units and products in an attempt to contextualize and to ensure that the police officers responding to the case had a good sense of the stolen value. Similarly, we included the category "Reported severe crimes against individuals not followed up upon" since this was identified by civil society organizations as a major problem in Uganda. Thus, we were taking a needs-based and context-specific approach when replacing existing and integrating new cases. We consider this the strength of our analysis since the vignettes are the result of an in-depth analysis of the local context and conditions prior to the implementation of the case scenarios at scale.

We presented the vignette cases in random order to avoid an order by severity. For the sake of exposition in this chapter, we have grouped the cases into six categories of two cases each: the first group focuses on the code of conduct among police officers, the second on bribery, the third on theft, the fourth on the refusal to register a complaint against the police, the fifth on severe crimes against individuals that are not followed up by the police, and the sixth on undue force used by the police against suspects and demonstrators (Table 1).

The wording of the vignette cases can be found in Appendix 2. Note that we implemented the vignettes in the context of an impact assessment of the Police Accountability and Reform Project (for detailed results see Hout et al. 2016, 2019; Wagner et al. 2019). Moreover, the original wording of the vignette cases allowed for the random variation of the gender of the portrayed police officers, perpetrators, and victims. The related gender dynamics are assessed in a separate article (Wagner et al. 2017). We show there that neither the randomly varying gender of the police officer nor the randomly varying gender of the victim depicted in the vignette cases are related to the judgment of police malpractice, or to suggested disciplinary measures. What we do find is that male respondents tend to be stricter in

Table 1 Grouping of the twelve vignette cases

Group 1: Code of conduct among the police officers
Case 1: Police mechanic repairing supervisor's car in exchange for holidays
Case 2: Police officer driving drunk and having an accident goes unreported by colleague
Group 2: Bribery
Case 3: Acceptance of freely offered meals and small gifts while on duty
Case 4: Speeding not reported in exchange for a bribe
Group 3: Theft
Case 5: Officer taking money from a lost wallet
Case 6: Police officer stealing goods when investigating a burglary
Group 4: Refusal to register complaints
Case 7: Refusal to register a complaint and humiliation of the complainant
Case 8: Refusal to register a complaint and a one-week detention for the complainant for false accusation
Group 5: Reported severe crimes against individuals not followed up upon
Case 9: Police officer refusing to register mistreatment of wife
Case 10: Reported murder not being followed up on
Group 6: Undue force used by the police
Case 11: Foot patrol torturing a thief
Case 12: Brutal strike down of a demonstration

their assessment of the hypothetical cases. Overall, the results show that gender perceptions do not differ between male and female police officers. Based on this finding, we do not expect that the survey experiment has any repercussions for the analysis at hand. Most importantly, since the gender variations were introduced randomly and balancing holds well across randomly introduced male and female gender attributes, we are methodologically on the safe side.

In our survey we obtained comprehensive answers to five of the original seven evaluative questions introduced by Klockars et al. The police officers answered the following questions for each case:

1. How serious do YOU consider this behavior to be? (Referred to as 'Own seriousness')

2. Do you think YOU would report a fellow police officer who engaged in this behavior? (Referred to as 'Own reporting')
3. How serious do MOST POLICE OFFICERS IN YOUR OFFICE consider this behavior to be? (Referred to as 'Colleagues' seriousness')
4. If an officer in your agency engaged in this behavior and was discovered doing so, what if any disciplinary measure do YOU think SHOULD follow? (Referred to as 'Disciplinary measure that should follow')
5. Would this behavior be regarded as a violation of official policy in your agency? (Referred to as 'Regarded as violation of official policy')

In line with the existing literature, the possible answer categories range from 1 to 5 on a Likert scale. Responses to questions 1 and 3 had the answer categories 'not at all serious' [1] to 'very serious' [5]. Questions 2 and 5 could be answered on a categorical scale from 'definitely not' [1] to 'definitely yes' [5]. Question 4 on disciplinary measures comprised six categories in ascending order of severity of the response: 'none' [1], 'verbal reprimand' [2], 'written reprimand' [3], 'period of suspension without pay' [4], 'demotion in rank' [5] and 'dismissal' [6].

In addition, information about the officers' perception of the institutional environment and police effectiveness was collected by using a set of ten Likert scale questions. The questions about the perceived institutional environment and police effectiveness include the following aspects:

1. What is the perceived crime level in the local community?
2. Do the police treat young people the same as older people?
3. Do the police treat poor people the same as rich people?
4. Do the police treat men the same as women?
5. What is the level of confidence in the officer's own work?
6. What is the level of confidence in the work of the police in general?
7. Do the police always have the duty to make people obey the law?
8. Do the police perform a good job in treating people fairly and with respect?

9. Do the police perform a good job in managing crime?
10. Are the police corrupt?

These questions were chosen because our survey was implemented in the context of Dutch policies and funding decisions focusing on rule of law and control of corruption initiatives in Uganda. The multi-facetted aspects of good governance to reduce corruption were the guiding principles for Dutch financial involvement. The above ten questions were selected to capture good governance at the level of the police. On purpose we focused on aspects of the perceived institutional environment and police effectiveness. Our approach is in line with Miles-Johnson and Pickering (2018) who assess police recruits' perceptions of trust in minority group members.

Our first four questions are motivated by the idea that police officers evaluate their work relative to the broader community they live and work in and the different groups that constitute that community. In addition, question 1 is motivated by the finding that police officers have positive perceptions of their work when crime is reduced (Bradford et al. 2013). Questions 5 and 6 are motivated by the fact that by and large the existing literature assesses confidence and relatedly trust in the police (Balliet and Van Lange 2013; Bradford 2014; Mastrofski et al. 2016) but the aspect of own confidence receives less attention. We argue that police officers can only view their role as positive if next to the perception of the police by the public, the officers themselves have confidence in their work and the work of their colleagues. In addition, existing evidence shows that police officers perceive a sense of effectiveness when they are perceived as upholding the law (Jenks et al. 2012). This rational motives question 7. Questions 8 and 9 are meant to capture procedural fairness and justice, as well as policing that is equitable across all members of society (Miles-Johnson 2016). Finally, question 10 asks for a self-assessment of the level of corruption at the police. Our approach is related to the work by Carr and Maxwell (2018) who assess officers' perceptions of organizational justice on officer trust in the public. Similar to our research they employ multiple perception questions. Yet, their focus is different since they consider the relationship with the supervisor, as well as distributive and procedural justice within the police force.

Individually and jointly our set of 10 questions allows us to assess perceptions of the institutional environment and effectiveness of the police. Thus, in our analysis we combine the information we have obtained from the vignette cases with the questions about perceived institutional environment and effectiveness to see how these perceptions affect police officers' attitudes toward misconduct and their willingness to report such behavior.

Descriptive Statistics

Background Characteristics of the Police Officers and the Districts

Descriptive statistics of the background characteristics of the respondents and related to district characteristics are presented in Table 2, Panel A.

The data on individual characteristics of the respondents provide an overview of the police officers included in our research. The average officer in the sample is almost 42 years old. Slightly less than a quarter of the respondents are female. Most of the officers are married (84%) and a similar percentage of the interviewees are head of a household (84%). They live in a household with, on average, almost 7 people. However, variation in household size is substantial (the standard deviation is 4). Almost half of the officers have completed secondary education, while 27% finished advanced secondary education and 25% have a higher education degree. Less than 3% have completed only primary education. Thus, our sample consists of prime-age individuals, who are predominately male and have a fairly high level of education relative to the overall population of Uganda. We control for all these aspects in the multivariate analysis to ensure that our findings are not influenced by variations in omitted background characteristics.

In terms of economic well-being, we observed the following. Around 60% of the respondents earn between UGX 300,000 and 500,000 on a monthly basis.[1] Another almost 25% of the sample earn UGX 500,000 and more. The average respondent owns 1.34 mobile phones and has almost 2 habitable rooms at home. The inclusion of these economic variables in the analysis ensures that our results of interest are not influenced by differences in income that might be related to differences in perceptions.

Sports activities are reported by 53% of the respondents and almost half of the respondents indicate being a member in a club or community organization. The latter two aspects serve as controls for the activity levels of the respondents and their readiness to actively engage in activities next to their work. We consider it necessary to control for these aspects since perceptions are linked to behavior not only at work but also in private life.

Work-related characteristics are presented in Panel B of Table 2. They form part of the second set of control variables. We collected information on the section of the police force the respondents are placed in, the length of their career as a police officer, and the infrastructure at their station (number of rooms, number of cars/motorcycles/bicycles). The average police officer has spent 18.8 years in service. Unsurprisingly, there is a considerable variation in this variable (the standard deviation is 10.5). The majority of the respondents, that is 46%, perform general duties. Officers working in the investigation section make up 26% of the sample. The remaining officers work for other sections, including traffic police and intelligence departments. The police stations they are placed in vary greatly in size: on average they have 12.8 rooms but the standard deviation is 9.3. Police motorcycles are the most common means of transport for the officers. The average station has 6.8 motorcycles, while it also possesses 1.5 cars and 2.1 bicycles.

Finally, Panel C of Table 2 presents some district-level characteristics. We selected the 600 respondents from 10 districts, while aiming to obtain pairs of two similar districts in the district selection. To assess the district socio-economic

[1] This roughly corresponds to a range of US$ 80 and 135 based on the UGX/US$ exchange rate of 0.00027 from January 31st, 2019. According to World Bank (2019) data, per capita gross national income in Uganda was US$ 50 per month in 2017.

Table 2 Descriptive statistics of the control variables

	Mean	Std. Dev.
Panel A: Individual level background characteristics		
Age	41.785	9.426
Gender (Female = 1)	0.228	
Marital status (Married = 1)	0.843	
Participant is the household head	0.843	
Household size	6.672	3.992
Education levels (Excluded category: Primary education)		
Secondary	0.455	
Advanced secondary	0.268	
Higher	0.248	
Income level (Excluded category: Income < 200,000UGX)		
Income 200,000–300,000UGX	0.115	
Income 300,000–500,000UGX	0.603	
Income 500,000–700,000UGX	0.140	
Income>700,000UGX	0.095	
# Habitable rooms	1.750	1.103
# Mobile phones owned	1.337	0.578
Does sport	0.525	
Member of a club/community organization	0.482	
Panel B: Work related covariates		
Number of years spent as police officer	18.800	10.556
Police rank (Excluded category: Low rank)		
High rank	0.060	
Medium rank	0.322	
Police section (Excluded category: Other sections and duties)		
Traffic	0.043	
Investigation	0.262	
Intelligence	0.063	
General duties	0.463	
# Rooms of police station	12.758	9.259
# Police cars at station	1.522	1.508
# Police motorcycles at station	6.762	12.557
# Police bicycles at station	2.147	5.361
Panel C: District-level control variables		
Population size (log)	12.941	0.242
Population growth	2.226	0.777
Poverty head count rate	22.310	8.539
Gini index	0.398	0.073
Share of the population belonging to the largest ethnicity	73.980	14.454
Police officers per 100,000 inhabitants	133.214	0.090
Crime rate	338.232	143.510
Homicide rate	8.629	3.910

Note: The sample consists of 600 police officers. Descriptive statistics of district-level control variables are calculated on the basis of 10 district-level observations

and crime related situation we collected district level administrative data for all 10 districts from the local administrations: The average district has roughly 420,000 inhabitants and grows at an annual rate of 2%, while about one-fifth of the population is living in poverty. The average Gini inequality index is 0.4 (District level administrative data). The districts are ethnically fairly homogeneous, as is shown by the finding that more than 70% of the population at district level belong to the district's main ethnic group. The number of police officers per 100,000 inhabitants is 133.[2] The crime rate is 338.2 and the homicide rate is 8.6 (District level administrative data). Similar to the individual-level characteristics, we control for the district-level characteristics in the multivariate analysis to avoid that our results are biased as a consequence of differences across districts.

Descriptive Statistics of the Outcome Variables Derived from the Vignette Cases

The descriptive statistics of the five outcome variables that we collected for the twelve vignette cases are presented in Table 3. This table presents the average for the five outcomes across all twelve cases, thus resulting from 7200 observations (12 cases*600 police officers). A detailed, case-by-case assessment is presented in Table 8 in Appendix 1. We present the simple averages resulting from the Likert scale answers.

We observe that the responses to all five questions range on average between 3.9 and 4.4, which suggests that the depicted cases of misbehavior are taken seriously by the officers. We find the lowest average Likert rating (3.9) for the evaluative question about the disciplinary measure

Table 3 Descriptive statistics of the outcome variable

	Mean	Std. Dev.
Own seriousness	3.974	1.546
Own reporting	4.154	1.289
Colleagues' seriousness	3.878	1.423
Disciplinary measure that should follow	3.852	1.514
Regarded as violation of official policy	4.398	1.199

Note: The sample consists of 7200 observations from 12 vignette cases responded to by 600 police officers

[2]In comparison, the average EU country had about 318 police officers per 100,000 inhabitants in 2016. The EU member state with the lowest number of officers is Finland, which had 137 officers per 100,000 inhabitants in 2016 (EuroStat 2016).

that should follow and the highest average rating (4.4) for the evaluative question whether the behavior is a violation of official policy. Moreover, we observe that the officers think that they themselves consider the depicted cases of misconduct slightly more seriously compared to their colleagues (Table 3).

Concerning the detailed descriptive statistics per case, our findings are in line with observations of other researchers in the field (cf. Kutnjak Ivković and Haberfeld 2015, pp. 340–346). We find that there is a sorting of assessments by case severity (see Table 8 in Appendix 1). The first two vignette cases, on police code of conduct, are judged rather mildly. Receiving holidays in exchange for repairing a supervisor's car is assessed moderately negatively (the average score is 3.72), although officers tend to be generally aware that such behavior violates official policy (average score of 4.24), which they would report (average score of 4.06). The misbehavior described in the second case, related to covering a drunk colleague who caused an accident, is by and large seen as a light offense.

Cases of bribery are depicted in the second group of vignettes. Case 3, on accepting gifts while on duty, receives the lowest Likert scores of all cases. All respondents score only slightly higher than the neutral position (a value of 3) when it comes to reporting a colleague. Case 4, related to the acceptance of bribes, is evaluated very critically, as indicated by the score of 4.4. Moreover, police officers tend to agree that this misbehavior should be subject to stringent disciplinary action (average score of 4.3).

The third group of cases contains incidences of theft. Case 5 (the misappropriation of money from a lost wallet) and case 6 (illegal enrichment when investigating a burglary) are judged quite harshly with scores of 4.0 and 4.5, respectively, and a great majority of respondents indicate they would report such misbehavior of a colleague. Case 6 is the instance of misbehavior that would require the toughest disciplinary response in the view of the police officers: the average score on the disciplinary action scale is 5.1.

Overall, the first six cases suggest that police officers have a clear idea about acceptable and non-acceptable police behavior: acceptance of bribes and theft are evaluated more critically than violations of the police force's code of conduct. In most cases, officers see themselves as more critical of misbehavior than their colleagues. Responses to the question whether particular forms of misbehavior violate official policy indicate the existence of a gap between formal rules and actual practices since on average they tend to receive the highest score within a case.

The next two cases depict situations in which police officers refuse to register complaints. The refusal to register a complaint and the humiliation of the complainant (case 7) is judged rather mildly (score of 3.6), but the arrest of a complainant on false grounds (case 8) is considered unacceptable by the majority of officers (score of 4.0). This is in line with our expectations and shows the internal coherence of the vignette cases.

Lastly, cases of reported severe crimes against individuals without adequate follow-up by the police (cases 9 and 10), and of the use of undue force (cases 11 and 12) are assessed seriously or very seriously. Case 9, which involves the refusal to register the mistreatment of a wife, is considered to be one of the most serious forms of police misbehavior (score of 4.3). Police officers agree that such misbehavior should be subject to strict disciplinary action (score of 4.0). Although the failure to follow up on a reported murder (case 10) is assessed as a serious form of misconduct (score of 3.9), police officers do not feel such behavior should be punished very severely (score of 2.7 on the disciplinary action scale). The two cases of undue police force are considered to be serious, as they are rated with a score of 3.9 (case 11) and 4.1 (case 12). In these instances, disciplinary action should be quite harsh, according to the average police officer, whose response leads to a score of 3.9 on the disciplinary action scale in both cases.

Descriptive Statistics of the Perceived Effectiveness of the Police

As initially motivated we want to study the vignette case assessments in relation to the perceived effectiveness of the police. To do so, we build on the ten Likert scale questions about the perceived institutional environment and police effectiveness that were introduced above in section "Descriptive Statistics". Table 4 presents the descriptive statistics related to the ten perception variables on the institutional environment and police effectiveness. All variables are measured on a five-point Likert scale, similar to the measurement of the responses to the vignette cases.

The first item among the perception variables inquiries about the level of crime in the local community and in Uganda as a whole. The average score of 2.5 on this item indicates that police officers perceive some problems with regard to the overall crime level in the country, while, at the same time, they consider the problems to be moderately important. The next aspect we consider refers to the question whether the police treat young people the same as old people. The average rating of 4.0 suggests that the majority of the police officers think that younger people are treated better. In contrast, they do not on average

Table 4 Descriptive statistics of the perception variables

	Mean	Std. Dev.
Perception components		
1. Perceived crime in community	2.540	1.236
2. Similar treatment: Young vs. old	4.038	1.095
3. Similar treatment: Poor vs. rich	3.565	1.296
4. Similar treatment: Men vs. women	3.808	1.203
5. Confidence in own work	4.582	0.835
6. Confidence in work of colleagues	4.428	0.889
7. Police: Duty to always enforce the law	4.715	0.701
8. Police treats people fairly and with respect	4.090	1.003
9. Police manages crime well	4.302	0.842
10. Police is corrupt	2.560	1.420
Average perception index	3.863	0.459
PCA perception index	0.000	1.820

Note: All variables are Likert scaled on a scale from 1 to 5 with 1 representing the category "Definitely not", "Not very good" and "Much worse" and 5 representing the category "Definitely yes", "Very good" and "Much better"

feel that there is a big discrepancy in the treatment of poor and rich individuals (average score 3.5). Police officers tend to perceive the treatment of men as slightly more favorable compared to the way women are treated (score of 3.8).

Confidence in the police officers' own work is high as shown by the average score of 4.6 on the fourth perception component. Police officers' confidence in the work of their fellow officers is also high, albeit 0.2 points lower than confidence in their own performance, suggesting that there is some sense of an *esprit de corps*. When it comes to the role of the police, the officers are very clear that it is *always* their duty to make people obey the law. This component obtains the highest overall score at 4.7. Moreover, the great majority of interviewed police officers think the police are doing a good job in treating people fairly and with respect (average score of 4.1).

Next we turn to the management of crime: the average score of 4.30 is even 0.2 points higher than the average on the fairness and respect question, which suggests that the officers have a high opinion about the quality of policing. Here one may see some tension with the observation by the Ugandan population that the police are the most corrupt institution in the country, which was reported above in section "The Uganda National Police". Item 9 of our perception variables addresses perceived corruption in the police force. In the light of the self-congratulatory attitude of police officers, it is not surprising that officers tend to downplay the seriousness of corruption. The statement 'The police are corrupt' receives an average score of 2.6, which suggests that, despite their positive assessment of the work of the police, officers seem to be moderately aware of problems with corruption in the police force.

Taken separately, the ten perception questions provide insight into how individual police officers perceive different dimensions of the institutional environment and police effectiveness in Uganda. The responses to the questions are interesting in themselves but they do not give us a complete picture of the perceived overall level of the institutional environment and police effectiveness. For this reason, the next step in the analysis is to correlate the ten questions in order to

assess to what extent they are related. Results of the correlation analysis are presented in Table 5.

Visual inspection of the correlation coefficients shows that most of the ten perception indicators are highly correlated. The correlations range between −0.353 and 0.571. Most items are positively correlated, but the perceived level of crime in the community and the perceived level of police corruption show negative correlations with the other variables. The magnitude of the pair-wise correlations and the fact that all but one are highly statistically significant, leads us to the conclusion that the chosen indicators of the perceived institutional environment and police effectiveness are jointly relevant. This result suggests that taken together the indicators may be used as a measurement of the self-assessed quality of work of the police.

On the basis of the results reported in Table 5, we include the indicators using two approaches. Firstly, we built an index that expresses the *average* score across all ten items. Secondly, we retrieved the first principal component of the variables and use this component score as indicator. The bottom two rows of Table 4 present the descriptive statistics using the two approaches. The average index of the ten perception variables is 3.9 with a standard deviation of 0.5. This indicates that the overall perception of police effectiveness borders on 'good' and is thus rather favorable. The average PCA index is 0.0 with a standard deviation of 1.8. The PCA index shows high variability since it is designed to accumulate maximum variability over the ten perception components. It ranges from a minimum of −6.8 to a maximum of 2.7. The next section contains a more detailed discussion of the findings of the multivariate analysis involving the responses to the questions on the perception of police effectiveness and the evaluative questions relating to the vignette cases.

Empirical Model

We set up a multivariate empirical model to analyze the relationship between the evaluative questions on police misbehavior and the measures of

Table 5 Pair-wise correlations of the perception variables

	Perceived crime in community	Similar treatment: young-old	Similar treatment: Poor-rich	Similar treatment: Men-women	Confidence in own work	Confidence in work of colleagues	Police: Duty to always enforce the law	Police treat people fairly	Police manage crime well	Police are corrupt
Perceived crime in community	1									
Similar treatment: Young-old	−0.142***	1								
Similar treatment: Poor-rich	−0.134***	0.463***	1							
Similar treatment: Men-women	−0.101**	0.485***	0.467***	1						
Confidence in own work	−0.074*	0.226***	0.159***	0.186***	1					
Confidence in work of colleagues	−0.130***	0.259***	0.317***	0.305***	0.404***	1				
Police: Duty to always enforce law	−0.010**	0.140***	0.099**	0.189***	0.170***	0.325***	1			
Police treat people fairly	−0.129***	0.267***	0.455***	0.280***	0.119**	0.301***	0.203***	1		
Police manage crime well	−0.195***	0.259***	0.384***	0.258***	0.192***	0.358***	0.231***	0.571***	1	
Police are corrupt	0.149***	−0.176***	−0.353***	−0.252***	−0.049	−0.231***	−0.170***	−0.221***	−0.218***	1

Note: Pair-wise correlations of the different components of the perception about the police. ***/**/* denotes statistical significance at a significance level of 1/5/10%, respectively

the perceived institutional environment and effectiveness of policing. The following model is used to estimate the evaluative response of every police officer i in district d responding to case c:

$$Y_{idc} = a_0 + a_1 Effect_{idc} + a_2 Socio_{idc}$$
$$+ a_3 Work_{idc} + a_4 District_{dc} + \lambda_c + \varepsilon_{idc},$$

where the outcome variable Y_{idc} represents one of the five evaluative responses to the vignettes cases. The coefficients of interest are collected in vector a_1. These are the coefficients associated with the individual components of the perceived institutional environment and police effectiveness, denoted as $Effect_{idc}$. In addition, we include a series of control variables: the individual characteristics of the respondents are collected in $Socio_{idc}$, the work-related characteristics in $Work_{idc}$ and the district characteristics are denoted by $District_{dc}$. For the estimation of this model we pool all vignette cases since our primary interest is not to assess differences across vignettes but to relate the average rating of the vignette responses across cases to the perceived institutional environment and police effectiveness. In order to account for the fact that the vignettes display cases of differing severity, we control for case specific effects λ_c, which implies that we include 11 case specific effects, leaving one case specific effect as the excluded category. Standard errors ε_{idc} are clustered at the individual level since the case-specific residual is likely to be correlated within officers' responses.

In addition, we estimate a model where we replace the matrix of the ten independent perceived institutional environment and police effectiveness measures with a single combined index. First we construct the average level of police effectiveness: $Effect_{idc1} + Effect_{idc2} + \ldots + Effect_{idc10})/10$. This index, based on the average across the individual items, gives equal weight to all its constituting components.

Second, we use a method that is considered superior and is based on the construction of an index using principal component analysis. In principal component analysis we employ an orthogonal transformation to convert our ten *correlated* effectiveness variables by means of a statistical procedure into linearly uncorrelated variables called principal components. This transformation is based on maximizing the variance in the first principal component, so that this first component reflects the internal structure of the police effectiveness variables in a way that best explains their variance and contains most of the information across the original components. We employ both the average index and the principal component index separately to gauge the robustness of the results. The index creation is supported by earlier research, which attempted to derive a scale of (seriousness of) police misconduct and indicated that the vignettes appear to represent a one- or two-dimensional space (cf. Jenks et al. 2014, p. 328; Lee et al. 2013, p. 390). Based on the existing literature, we opted for the inclusion of only one dimension since the average index is one-dimensional and we aimed for a straightforward and direct comparison of the results.

As an additional assessment of the robustness of our results, we estimate the three models that were outlined above with district fixed effects instead of including the district characteristics. Results of the latter three analyses are presented in Appendix 1 in Tables 9 (for model 1, using detailed perception components) and 10 (for model 2, using the average perception index, and model 3, applying the index derived from principal component analysis).

Results

The results of our analyses are presented in Tables 6 and 7. Next to the ten perception variables (Table 6) or the perception indices (Table 7), all regression analyses contain the above-mentioned individual, work-related, and district-specific control variables as well as the vignette fixed effects. These coefficient estimates are not presented for the sake of brevity and clarity of exposition.

We start by assessing the relationship between the evaluative responses to the vignette cases and

Table 6 Results with detailed perception components

	Own seriousness	Own reporting	Colleagues' seriousness	Disciplinary measure that should follow	Regarded as violation of official policy
Perception components					
1. Perceived crime in community	0.023 (0.034)	−0.036 (0.022)	−0.013 (0.030)	−0.014 (0.025)	−0.040 (0.029)
2. Similar treatment: Young vs. old	−0.069 (0.046)	0.043 (0.032)	−0.074** (0.036)	0.003 (0.031)	0.016 (0.026)
3. Similar treatment: Poor vs. rich	−0.011 (0.044)	0.032 (0.027)	0.055 (0.037)	−0.005 (0.030)	−0.012 (0.026)
4. Similar treatment: Men vs. women	0.054 (0.041)	0.124*** (0.038)	0.078** (0.037)	−0.011 (0.029)	−0.010 (0.026)
5. Confidence in own work	0.085 (0.058)	−0.002 (0.036)	0.042 (0.048)	0.027 (0.039)	0.088** (0.042)
6. Confidence in work of colleagues	0.005 (0.057)	0.091* (0.053)	−0.014 (0.046)	0.023 (0.040)	0.068* (0.036)
7. Police: Duty to always enforce the law	0.043 (0.062)	0.039 (0.035)	0.074 (0.059)	0.019 (0.056)	0.153*** (0.054)
8. Police treats people fairly and with respect	0.150*** (0.055)	0.034 (0.022)	0.161*** (0.050)	0.061 (0.040)	−0.054 (0.037)
9. Police manages crime well	−0.054 (0.058)	0.021 (0.030)	−0.010 (0.052)	−0.023 (0.045)	0.008 (0.043)
10. Police is corrupt	0.071** (0.031)	0.031 (0.040)	0.006 (0.027)	−0.012 (0.023)	0.064*** (0.025)

Note: OLS regression results. The regressions are based on 600 individuals and their responses to 12 cases resulting in 7200 observations. All regressions include case specific effects (not shown). Individual level socio-economic characteristics that are controlled for but coefficients are not shown: age, gender, marital status, whether the respondent is household head, education level (dummies for secondary, advanced secondary and higher education, excluded category: primary education), household size, income level (dummies), number of habitable rooms in the house, number of mobile phones owned, whether the person does sports and whether the person is a member of a community organization. Work related characteristics that are controlled for but coefficients are not shown: Years of service, rank (high rank and medium rank, low rank forms the excluded category), number of rooms of the police station, number of police cars, number of police motorcycles, number of police bicycles, Police section (traffic, investigation, intelligence, general duties, excluded category: Other sections and duties). District-level characteristics that are controlled for but coefficients are not shown: Population size (log), population growth, rate of police officers, crime rate, homicide rate, poverty head count, Gini coefficient, share of the population belonging to the main ethnicity of the district. Standard errors are clustered at the level of the individual respondent
***/**/* Denotes statistical significance at a significance level of 1/5/10 percent, respectively

the individual perception components. The results that are summarized in Table 6 show not only that the different evaluative responses capture different aspects of police integrity, but also that the perceptions of the institutional environment and police effectiveness contain a variety of elements. This implies that across the five evalu-ative responses we find correlations with differ-ent aspects of police effectiveness.

Column 1 of Table 6 displays the relationship between the response to the question 'How seri-ous do YOU consider this behavior to be?' and the ten perceived institutional environment and police effectiveness components. As can be seen,

Table 7 Results employing a perception index

	Own seriousness		Own reporting		Colleagues' seriousness		Disciplinary measure that should follow		Regarded as violation of official policy	
	Average	PCA	Average	PCA	Average	PCA	Average	PCA	Average	PCA
Average perception index	0.203**		0.378***		0.371***		0.088		0.144*	
	(0.091)		(0.065)		(0.079)		(0.062)		(0.087)	
PCA perception index		0.023		0.098***		0.104***		0.031**		0.026
		(0.023)		(0.016)		(0.020)		(0.016)		(0.021)

Note: Compare note to Table 6 for detailed information about the employed empirical specifications
***/**/* denotes statistical significance at a significance level of 1/5/10 percent, respectively

the perceived severity of misbehavior is associated significantly with the perception that the police treat people fairly and with the perceived corruption level. The coefficient estimate of 0.150 indicates considerable practical relevance: an increase of one standard deviation in the perceived fair treatment of people (sd = 1.003, see Table 4, row 8) explains almost 10% (=[0.150* 1.003]/1.546*100) of the standard deviation in the perceived severity of the misbehavior. Similarly, an increase of one standard deviation in the perceived corruption level (sd = 1.420, see Table 4, row 10), which reflects a decrease in perceived corruption, explains 6.5% (=[0.071* 1.420]/1.546*100) of the standard deviation in the perceived severity of the misbehavior. Taken together these two components of perceived police effectiveness explain more than 15% of the standard deviation of responses to the evaluative question about own seriousness. This is a sizeable effect and suggests that case evaluations are related to two aspects of perceived functioning of the police, namely the respectful treatment of people and the perceived level of corruption.

The likelihood that police officers would report the misbehavior of a fellow officer shows a statistically significant relationship to the confidence in the work of the colleagues (significant at the 10% level) and to the perceived discrepancy in the treatment of men and women (very strongly related and significant at the 1% level). A one standard deviation increase in the perceived discrepancy in the treatment of men and women (sd = 1.203, see Table 4, row 4) explains 11.6% (=[0.124*1.203]/1.289*100) of the standard deviation of the evaluative question about report a fellow police. Similarly 6.3% (=[0.091*0.889]/ 1.289*100) of the standard deviation in reporting is explained by a one standard deviation increase in the confidence that police officers have in the work of their colleagues (sd = 0.889, see Table 4, row 6). This shows that perceived police effectiveness, in particular related to the perception that both sexes are treated differently and the confidence in the performance of colleagues, seems to impact on officers' responses to the question about the reporting of misbehavior.

When we turn to the police officers' view of their colleagues and how serious they think most police officers in their office consider the depicted misbehavior to be, the outcome variable appears to be impacted by three variables of perceived police effectiveness. All are linked to the treatment of people. Firstly, the assessment of the seriousness of misbehavior as expected from colleagues seems to be associated negatively with the perceived favoring of young people. Secondly, colleagues' assessment of the seriousness appears to be associated positively with the perceived favoring of men, while, thirdly, it is associated positively with the fair and respectful treatment of people. While only the association with the third variable seems strong, we need to gauge the relationship relative to the measurement of the variables as presented in the descriptive statistics (Table 4). A one standard deviation increase in the first and second variable explain 5.7% (=[0.074*1.095]/1.423*100) and 6.6% (=[0.078*1.203]/1.423*100) in the standard deviation of the colleagues assessment, respectively. Taken together the three components of perceived police effectiveness explain 23.6% (=[0.074*1.095 + 0.078*1.203 + 0.161*1.003]/1.42 3*100) of the standard deviation of the evaluative question about colleagues' seriousness.

The fourth evaluative question deals with the disciplinary measure that should follow particular forms of misbehavior. No single component related to the perceptions of the institutional environment and police effectiveness appears to have any explanatory power vis-à-vis the imposition of disciplinary sanctions.

Finally, we assess whether police officers see the depicted forms of misbehavior as a violation of official policy in their agency. This evaluation appears to be correlated with four of the perceived institutional environment and police effectiveness components, namely confidence in own work, confidence in the work of colleagues, the perception that police officers always have the duty to enforce the law, and the perceived corruption level. Except for the confidence in the work of colleagues, coefficient estimates are statistically significant at the 1 or 5% level. Together they explain 27.7% (=[0.088∗0.835 + 0.068∗ 0.889+ 0.153∗0.701 + 1.42 ∗0.064]/1.199∗100) of the standard deviation in this outcome variable.

Our findings indicate that overall there is no doubt that the assessment of the vignette cases is not only linked to individual, work-related, and police infrastructure variables (which are not shown for the sake of brevity), but that the perceived institutional environment and police effectiveness variables have additional explanatory power for policy integrity. There is no single item that captures the perception of the institutional environment and police effectiveness fully, but seven of the ten perception variables seem to play a role in relation to different evaluative positions.

Linking the five evaluative responses to the vignette cases to the ten individual components of the perceived institutional environment and police effectiveness might be misleading. We might end up emphasizing only selected dimensions of the perceived institutional environment and police effectiveness despite the fact that we have shown in the pair-wise correlations that none of these components should be looked at individually since the majority are heavily interrelated and only represent different aspects of some larger underlying concept. For this reason we now turn to the assessment of the combined indices of the perceived institutional environment and police effectiveness. Results of the analyses are presented in Table 7. All five evaluative responses appear to be correlated positively with both effectiveness indices. Our results show that of the five evaluative variables, two are positively and statistically significantly correlated with both the *average* police effectiveness index and the PCA index, while two are only statistically significantly correlated with the average index and one is only statistically significantly correlated with the PCA index.

Looking into the analysis of the evaluative responses to the vignette cases one-by-one (Table 7), we find that for the assessment of the severity of the case a one standard deviation increase in the average index (sd = 0.459, see Table 4, row 11) explains 6% (=[0.203∗0.459]/

1.546∗100) of the standard deviation in the assessed severity of the case. We do not find a significant relationship between the PCA index and the severity of the case. When it comes to the reporting of a fellow police officer, we find a stronger relationship (0.378), which means that a one standard deviation increase in the average index (sd = 0.459, see Table 4, row 11) explains 13% (=[0.378∗0.459]/1.289∗100) of the standard deviation in the reporting of a fellow officer. We further find a statistically significant relationship with the PCA index. A one standard deviation increase in the PCA index (sd = 1.820, see Table 4, row 12) explains roughly 14% (=[0.098∗1.820]/1.289∗100) of the standard deviation in reporting. Thus, while the coefficient estimates differ for the different indices, both indices are similar in terms of explanatory power when it comes to the reporting outcome. This result stems from the fact that the indices also have different distributions as can be gauged from a comparison of the differences of the means and standard deviations. For the evaluative question about colleagues' seriousness we also find that both indices are statistically significant. Again they explain similar portions of the standard deviation in that question. The *average* index explains 12% (=[0.371∗0.459]/1.423∗100), while the PCA index accounts for 13% (=[0.104∗1.820]/1.423∗100). With respect to officers' position on disciplinary measures, only the PCA index is significantly related to the evaluative question. The PCA index explains about 4% (=[0.031∗1.820]/1.514∗100) of the standard deviation of the question about disciplinary measures. This finding is in line with the analysis of the one-by-one analysis of the perceived institutional environment and police effectiveness (Table 6). This showed that none of the perception variables was individually significant. The final evaluative question relates to the official policy in the agency. For this outcome only the average index has explanatory power.

Despite variations in the associations between police integrity and the presented indices, there is no doubt that the two aspects are related yet sensitive to the type of measurement and aggregation. By way of conclusion, we argue that different aspects of the perceived institutional environment and police effectiveness are related to different evaluative dimensions of police integrity. The relationship between the different aspects of police integrity and the index of perceived police effectiveness is sensitive to the construction of the index demonstrating that a summary index of perceived police effectiveness does not necessarily reflect the associations of its constituting components completely. Overall, we infer that the subjective perceptions of the institutional environment and police effectiveness undoubtedly feed into attitudes of police integrity suggesting that the vignettes can serve as a tool to channel and represent the individual subjective biases in a coherent form.

As indicated above, an additional robustness test is presented in Tables 9 and 10 in Appendix 1. In the analyses underlying these tables, the district control variables are replaced with district fixed effects. The results are almost identical to the findings presented earlier in this section, not only in terms of the direction of the effect and its statistical significance, but also in terms of magnitude. These additional tests make us confident about the reliability of our results.

Conclusion

In this chapter, we have attempted to contribute to the burgeoning literature on police integrity by assessing what is the relationship between Ugandan police officers' perceptions of the institutional environment and the effectiveness of policing on their evaluations of specific forms of police misbehavior. Using data collected in a survey involving 600 police officers in Uganda, we focused on 10 perception variables, which we analyzed separately and collectively. The results of our analyses show that there are indeed concrete signs that the perceived quality of the institutional environment and police effectiveness is impacting on evaluative dimensions of police

integrity. Our research shows that the perceived quality of the institutional environment and perceptions of police effectiveness are impacting the evaluations of police misbehavior. The perceptions that are most strongly linked to the evaluative questions about police integrity are the assessment of the differential gender treatment, police officers' confidence in the work of colleagues, the view that the police treat people fairly and with respect and the perceptions about corruption in the police force.

While all of these factors relate to several dimensions of police integrity, our results also demonstrate that there is not a one-to-one relationship between the assessed dimensions of the perceived environmental context and police effectiveness, on the one hand, and the evaluations of misbehavior by police officers, on the other. When combining the ten dimensions of the perceived institutional environment and police effectiveness in two indices (an average index and a principal-component index) and analyzing the relationship with the evaluative responses to the vignette cases, we find further evidence that the subjective perceptions of the institutional environment and police effectiveness feed into attitudes toward police integrity. At the same time, we find that the relationship between the evaluative questions about police integrity and the index of perceived police effectiveness is sensitive to the construction of the index. Thus, while the vignettes are meant as a tool to reduce subjective biases in the evaluation of police misbehavior, the assessment of the vignettes is not free of individual perceptions. This suggests that the vignettes can be seen as means to channel and represent the individual subjective biases in a coherent and comparable form.

We consider the results presented in this chapter only as a first attempt at linking police integrity to perceptions about the institutional environment and policing effectiveness. In particular, our research is aiming at complementing earlier studies on the impact of various factors on the attitudes of police officers to corruption and misconduct, such as the police's organizational culture and characteristics (Eitle et al. 2014; Kucukuysal 2008; Kutnjak Ivković and Sauerman 2015), their disciplinary environments (Lee et al. 2013; Kutnjak Ivković and Khechumyan 2014; Cheloukhine et al. 2015; Kutnjak Ivković et al. 2016a, b; Kuo 2018), disciplinary fairness and organizational justice (Kutnjak Ivković and Shelley 2010; Wolfe and Piquero 2011; Kutnjak Ivković and Sauerman 2013; Long et al. 2013; Myhill and Bradford 2013; Porter et al. 2015), individual and work related characteristics (Reynolds and Helfers 2018; Lee et al. 2013) as well as police cynicism (Bucak 2012).

Our results suggest new avenues for research into the relationship between the evaluative positions of police officers and perceptions of institutional environment and effectiveness. An obvious first step would be to theorize police effectiveness more thoroughly. As suggested by the results obtained in our principal component analysis, there appears to be an underlying dimension of police effectiveness in the perception variables (cf. Table 5). A more systematic review of the literature of public service effectiveness may bring out a wider range of indicators, and possibly also dimensions that would be useful in research on perceptions of police effectiveness.

Another way to enrich the analysis of police effectiveness could be the combination of research using vignettes of police integrity with client surveys at the level of police stations of units. In such client surveys, individual citizens who had contact with the police (either for solving their problems or because they were suspected of crimes or misdemeanors) could be asked to provide their assessment of the performance of the police. As a next step, average police station or unit level vignette scores could be associated with the perceptions of the public.

Finally, researchers could attempt to draw on different strands of research, such as for instance the studies done by Waddington et al. (2009) on police culture, to get better and more nuanced insight into the perceptions of police officers about what is considered to be effective policing. Such an approach may possibly build bridges to more detailed psychological research to better understand the perceptions of the police. If possible, officers could be requested for input at different stages of their career in order to incorporate the impact of socialization during years of service.

Appendix 1: Supplementary Tables

Table 8 Detailed descriptive statistics of the vignette cases

	Own seriousness	Own reporting	Colleagues' seriousness	Disciplinary measure that should follow	Regarded as violation of official policy
Group 1: Code of conduct among the police officers					
Case 1: Police mechanic repairing supervisor's car in exchange for holidays					
Mean	3.720	4.058	3.693	3.803	4.243
Std. Dev.	1.566	1.305	1.422	1.348	1.303
Case 2: Police officer driving drunk and having an accident goes unreported by colleague					
Overall mean	3.710	3.918	3.597	3.645	4.107
Std. Dev.	1.585	1.397	1.463	1.459	1.371
Group 2: Bribery					
Case 3: Acceptance of freely offered meals and small gifts while on duty					
Overall mean	3.533	3.165	3.445	3.150	3.955
Std. Dev.	1.534	1.552	1.500	1.399	1.488
Case 4: Speeding not reported in exchange for a bribe					
Mean	4.367	4.253	3.920	4.313	4.542
Std. Dev.	1.279	1.164	1.424	1.263	1.093
Group 3: Theft					
Case 5: Officer taking money from a lost wallet					
Mean	4.042	4.272	3.795	4.110	4.433
Std. Dev.	1.537	1.248	1.454	1.428	1.154
Case 6: Police officer stealing goods when investigating a burglary					
Mean	4.472	4.603	4.327	5.068	4.643
Std. Dev.	1.228	0.913	1.188	1.205	0.965
Group 4: Refusal to register complaints					
Case 7: Refusal to register a complaint and humiliation of the complainant					
Mean	3.622	4.033	3.542	3.478	4.313
Std. Dev.	1.663	1.232	1.476	1.300	1.235
Case 8: Refusal to register a complaint and a one-week detention for the complainant for false accusation					
Mean	4.010	4.473	3.970	4.122	4.563
Std. Dev.	1.593	1.043	1.424	1.239	1.059
Group 5: Reported severe crimes against individuals not followed up upon					
Case 9: Police officer refusing to register mistreatment of wife					
Mean	4.275	4.472	4.125	4.012	4.592
Std. Dev.	1.425	1.020	1.284	1.280	0.976
Case 10: Reported murder not being followed up on					
Mean	3.922	4.467	4.100	2.728	4.530
Std. Dev.	1.630	0.997	1.324	1.204	1.059
Group 6: Undue force used by the police					
Case 11: Foot patrol torturing a thief					
Mean	3.895	4.077	3.783	3.875	4.352
Std. Dev.	1.565	1.303	1.427	1.391	1.233
Case 12: Brutal strike down of a demonstration					
Mean	4.117	4.053	4.235	3.923	4.508
Std. Dev.	1.578	1.490	1.354	2.125	1.147

Note: The number of observations per case and response is 600

Table 9 Results with detailed perception components

	Own seriousness	Own reporting	Colleagues' seriousness	Disciplinary measure that should follow	Regarded as violation of official policy
Perception components					
1. Perceived crime in community	0.024 (0.034)	−0.036 (0.022)	−0.013 (0.030)	−0.015 (0.025)	−0.040 (0.029)
2. Similar treatment: Young vs. old	−0.067 (0.046)	0.045 (0.032)	−0.077** (0.037)	−0.001 (0.031)	0.020 (0.026)
3. Similar treatment: Poor vs. rich	−0.012 (0.044)	0.031 (0.027)	0.056 (0.037)	−0.003 (0.029)	−0.014 (0.025)
4. Similar treatment: Men vs. women	0.056 (0.041)	0.122*** (0.039)	0.076** (0.037)	−0.014 (0.029)	−0.006 (0.026)
5. Confidence in own work	0.082 (0.057)	−0.004 (0.037)	0.045 (0.049)	0.031 (0.039)	0.084** (0.041)
6. Confidence in work of colleagues	0.003 (0.057)	0.093* (0.053)	−0.013 (0.046)	0.025 (0.041)	0.065* (0.036)
7. Police: Duty to always enforce the law	0.046 (0.062)	0.038 (0.035)	0.071 (0.060)	0.015 (0.055)	0.157*** (0.054)
8. Police treat people fairly and with respect	0.149*** (0.055)	0.035 (0.022)	0.162*** (0.050)	0.062 (0.040)	−0.055 (0.036)
9. Police manage crime well	−0.058 (0.058)	0.023 (0.030)	−0.006 (0.052)	−0.017 (0.045)	0.002 (0.043)
10. Police are corrupt	0.072** (0.031)	0.028 (0.041)	0.004 (0.027)	−0.015 (0.023)	0.067*** (0.024)

Note: The regressions are based on 600 individuals and their responses to 12 cases resulting in 7200 observations. All regressions include case specific and district specific effects (not shown). Individual level socio-economic characteristics that are controlled for but coefficients are not shown: age, gender, marital status, whether the respondent is household head, education level (dummies for secondary, advanced secondary and higher education, excluded category: primary education), household size, income level (dummies), number of habitable rooms in the house, number of mobile phones owned, whether the person does sports and whether the person is a member of a community organization. Work related characteristics that are controlled for but coefficients are not shown: Years of service, rank (high rank and medium rank, low rank forms the excluded category), number of rooms of the police station, number of police cars, number of police motorcycles, number of police bicycles, Police section (traffic, investigation, intelligence, general duties, excluded category: Other sections and duties). Standard errors are clustered at the level of the individual respondent

***/**/* Denotes statistical significance at a significance level of 1/5/10 percent, respectively

Table 10 Results employing a perception index

	Own seriousness		Own reporting		Colleagues' seriousness		Disciplinary measure that should follow		Regarded as violation of official policy	
	Average	PCA	Average	PCA	Average	PCA	Average	PCA	Average	PCA
Average perception index	0.202**		0.377***		0.373***		0.091		0.141	
	(0.090)		(0.065)		(0.079)		(0.062)		(0.086)	
PCA perception index		0.021		0.097***		0.106***		0.033**		0.024
		(0.023)		(0.016)		(0.020)		(0.016)		(0.021)

Note: Compare note to Table 5 for detailed information about the employed empirical specifications
***/**/* Denotes statistical significance at a significance level of 1/5/10 percent, respectively.

Appendix 2: The 12 Vignette Cases

Group 1: Code of Conduct Among the Police Officers

Case 1: A police officer, who happens to be a very good auto mechanic, is scheduled to work during coming holidays. The supervisor offers to give him these days off, if he agrees to repair her/his personal car. Evaluate the supervisor's behavior.

Case 2: At 2:00 a.m., a police officer, who is on duty, is driving her/his patrol car on a deserted road. S/he sees a vehicle that has been driven off the road and is stuck in a ditch. S/he approaches the vehicle and observes that the driver is not hurt but is obviously drunk. S/he also finds that the driver is a police officer. S/he transports the driver home. Evaluate the behavior of the police officer on duty.

Group 2: Bribery

Case 3: A police officer routinely accepts free meals, cigarettes, and other items of small value from merchants on his duty. S/he does not solicit these gifts and is careful not to abuse the generosity of those who give gifts to her/him.

Case 4: A police officer stops a motorist for speeding. The officer agrees to accept a personal gift of half of the amount of the fine in exchange for not taking the offending motorist to court to answer to charges for the traffic offence.

Group 3: Theft

Case 5: A police officer finds a wallet in a parking lot. It contains an amount of money equivalent to a full day's pay for that officer. S/he reports the wallet as lost property but keeps the money for her/himself.

Case 6: A police officer discovers a burglary of a general merchandise shop. The display cases are smashed, and it is obvious that many items have been taken. While searching the shop, s/he takes 10 jerricans of cooking oil and 1 sack of posho of 100 kilograms worth about a month's pay for that officer. S/he reports that the items had been stolen during the burglary.

Group 4: Refusal to Register Complaints

Case 7: A formerly arrested man comes to the police station and wants to fill in a complaint form. He claims that he was not treated properly during his arrest. The police officer who is in charge laughs at him and sends him away.

Case 8: A men goes to a police station to register a complaint over one of their officers who had beaten and tortured him. At the station he finds a friend of the officer who tortured him. The friend refuses to register his complaint and instead decides to detain him for a weak over giving false information to the police. Evaluate the behavior of the friend.

Group 5: Reported Severe Crimes Against Individuals Not Followed Up Upon

Case 9: A women goes to the police station to report a case where her husband has been beating her for the last one year. She lost one of her teeth and has a damaged eye due to the beating. The police officer on duty thinks this is a mere family dispute and not a crime for the police to handle. S/he refuses to register the case.

Case 10: A police officer on duty receives a woman who wants to register a case of murder of her child by a neighbor. The officer registers the case and promises to follow up and arrest the suspect in a few hours' time. Two days down the road, the suspect has not been arrested and was sending messages threatening to harm the complainant. The woman went back to the same police station to report the scenario and the suspect was arrested and detained at the police station. However, the suspect was released immediately on account that there was not enough evidence to convict him. Evaluate the behavior of the police officer who first received the woman.

Group 6: Undue Force Used by the Police

Case 11: Two police officers on foot patrol surprise a man who is attempting to break into a shop. The man flees. They chase him for about ½ a kilometer before apprehending him by tackling him and wrestling him to the ground. After he is under control, both officers punch him a couple of times in the stomach and step on his back several times as punishment for fleeing and resisting.

Case 12: A sub-district has a challenge of water shortage for a period of four months. The area leader together with residents decide to petition national water for the poor services and failure to deliver. However, the situation continues for two more months. The area leader and the residents opt to stage a peaceful demonstration as a way of showing their dissatisfaction. No sooner had the demonstration started than the District Police Commander deployed a team of officers with teargas and firing of live ammunitions killing 20 of the demonstrators including the area leader. Evaluate the District Police Commander's behavior.

References

Anderson, D. M., & Fisher, J. (2016). Authoritarianism and the securitization of development: The case of Uganda. In T. Hagmann & F. Reyntjens (Eds.), *Development without democracy? Foreign aid and authoritarian regimes in Africa* (pp. 67–90). London: Zed Books.

Andreescu, V., Keeling, D. G., Vito, G. F., & Voinic, M. C. (2012). Romanian and American police officers' perceptions of professional integrity and ethical behavior. *Revista Romana de Sociologie, 23*(3/4), 185–207.

Balliet, D., & Van Lange, P. A. (2013). Trust, conflict, and cooperation: A meta-analysis. *Psychological Bulletin, 139*(5), 1090–1112.

Barkan, J. D. (2011). *Uganda: Assessing risks to stability*. Washington, DC: Center for Strategic and International Studies.

Basheka, B. C. (2013). Public administration and corruption in Uganda. In S. Vyas-Doorgapersad, T. Lukamba-Muhiya, & E. Peprah Ababio (Eds.), *Public administration in Africa: Performance and challenges* (pp. 45–81). Boca Raton: CRC.

Bradford, B. (2014). Policing and social identity: Procedural justice, inclusion and cooperation between police and public. *Policing and Society, 24*(1), 22–43.

Bradford, B., Jackson, J., & Hough, M. (2013). Police futures and legitimacy: Redefining "Good Policing". In J. Brown (Ed.), *Future of policing*. Abingdon: Routledge.

Bucak, S. (2012) *An Examination of Police Cynicism in Turkey and Its Impacts on Officers' Perception of Corruption*, PhD thesis, University of Chicago. Retrieved February 12, 2019, from https://indigo.uic.edu/handle/10027/9738.

Carr, J. D., & Maxwell, S. R. (2018). Police officers' perceptions of organizational justice and their trust in the public. *Police Practice and Research, 19*(4), 365–379.

Cheloukhine, S., Kutnjak Ivković, S., Haq, Q., & Haberfeld, M. R. (2015). Police integrity in Russia. In S. Kutnjak Ivković & M. R. Haberfeld (Eds.), *Measuring police integrity across the world: Studies from established democracies and countries in transition* (pp. 153–182). New York: Springer.

Commonwealth Human Rights Initiative. (2006a). *A review of the Uganda police force budget and its effects on crime management*. Retrieved February 12, 2019, from http://www.humanrightsinitiative.org/publications/police/uganda_report.pdf.

Commonwealth Human Rights Initiative. (2006b). *The police, the people, the politics: Police accountability in Uganda*. Retrieved February 12, 2019, from http://www.humanrightsinitiative.org/publications/police/uganda_country_report_2006.pdf.

Coulangeon, P., Pruvost, G., Roharik, I., & Matthews, T. (2012). Professional ideologies: A latent class analysis of police officers' opinions on the role of the police. *Revue Française de Sociologie (English Edition), 53*(3), 347–380.

Economist. (2018). *Uganda's politicised police force is not reducing crime'*. Retrieved February 12, 2019, from https://www.economist.com/middle-east-and-africa/2018/07/05/ugandas-politicised-police-force-is-not-reducing-crime.

Eitle, D., D'Alessio, S. J., & Stolzenberg, L. (2014). The effect of organizational and environmental factors on police misconduct. *Police Quarterly, 17*(2), 103–126.

EuroStat. (2016). *Police, court and prison personnel statistics*. Retrieved February 12, 2019, from https://ec.europa.eu/eurostat/statistics-explained/index.php?title=Police,_court_and_prison_personnel_statistics.

Golooba-Mutebi, F., & Hickey, S. (2013). *'Investigating the links between political settlements and inclusive development in Uganda: Towards a Research Agenda', ESID Working Paper 20*. Manchester: Effective States and Inclusive Development Research Centre.

Hout, W., Brouwers, R., Fisher, J., Namara, R., Schakel, L., & Wagner, N. (2016). *Policy review good governance: Democratisation, promotion of rule of law and control of corruption—Uganda field study*. Final Report for the Policy and Operations Evaluation

Department (IOB), Ministry of Foreign Affairs, The Netherlands.

Hout, W., Wagner, N., & Namara, R. (2019). Holding Ugandan police to account: Case study of the police accountability and reform project. In S. Bergh, S. Pellisserey, & C. Sathyamala (Eds.), *The state of accountability in the global south: Challenges and responses*. Cheltenham: Edward Elgar. forthcoming.

Jenks, D., Johnson, L. M., & Matthews, T. (2012). Examining police integrity: Categorizing corruption vignettes. In *International Police Executive Symposium, Geneva Centre for the Democratic Control of Armed Forces, Coginta–for Police Reforms and Community Safety*.

Jenks, D., Johnson, L. M., & Matthews, T. (2014). Examining police integrity: Categorizing corruption vignettes. In M. Guzman, A. M. Das, & D. Das (Eds.), *The evolution of policing* (pp. 317–331). Boca Raton: CRC.

Kakamwa, C. (2014). Uganda to increase size of police force, *New Vision*, 26 December.

Kato, J. (2016). 'Police most corrupt institution—UBOS', *Daily Monitor*, 22 June. Retrieved February 12, 2019, from http://www.monitor.co.ug/News/National/Police-most-corrupt-institution-UBOS/688334-3261630-3jq36az/index.html.

Khisa, M. (2014). Challenges to policy implementation in Uganda: Reflections on politics and the state. *Ugandan Journal of Management and Public Policy Studies, 8*(1), 28–43.

Klockars, C. B., Kutnjak Ivković, S., Harver, W. E., & Haberfeld, M. R. (2000). *The Measurement of Police Integrity*, Research in Brief, NCJ 181465, Rockville: National Institute of Justice.

Klockars, C. B., Kutnjak Ivković, S., & Haberfeld, M. R. (2006). *Enhancing police integrity*. Dordrecht: Springer.

Kucukuysal, B. (2008). *Determinants of Turkish police officers' perception of integrity: Impact of organizational culture*, PhD thesis, University of Central Florida. Retrieved February 12, 2019, from http://etd.fcla.edu/CF/CFE0002242/Kucukuysal_Bahadir_200807_PhD.pdf.

Kuo, S. Y. (2018). Police misconduct in Taiwan: comparing perceptions of the police and electronic gaming service workers. *Crime, Law and Social Change, 69*(5), 657–679.

Kutnjak Ivković, S. (2005a) Fallen Blue Knights: Controlling Police Corruption, Oxford: Oxford University Press.

Kutnjak Ivković, S. (2005b) Police (Mis) Behavior: A Cross-Cultural Study of Corruption Seriousness. *Policing: An International Journal of Police Strategies & Management, 28*(3), 546–566.

Kutnjak Ivković, S. (2015). Studying police integrity. In S. Kutnjak Ivković & M. R. Haberfeld (Eds.), *Measuring police integrity across the world: Studies from established democracies and countries in transition* (pp. 1–36). New York: Springer.

Kutnjak Ivković, S., & Haberfeld, M. R. (2015). A comparative perspective on police integrity. In S. Kutnjak Ivković & M. R. Haberfeld (Eds.), *Measuring police integrity across the world: Studies from established democracies and countries in transition* (pp. 329–368). New York: Springer.

Kutnjak Ivković, S., & Khechumyan, A. (2014). Measuring police integrity among urban and rural police in Armenia: From local results to global implications. *International Journal of Comparative and Applied Criminal Justice, 38*(1), 39–61.

Kutnjak Ivković, S., & Sauerman, A. (2013). Curtailing the code of silence among the South African police. *Policing: An International Journal of Police Strategies & Management, 36*(1), 175–198.

Kutnjak Ivković, S., & Sauerman, A. (2015). Threading the thin blue line: Transition towards democratic policing and the integrity of the South African police service. *Policing and Society, 25*(1), 25–52.

Kutnjak Ivković, S., & Shelley, T. O. (2010). The code of silence and disciplinary fairness. *Policing: An International Journal of Police Strategies & Management, 33*(3), 548–574.

Kutnjak Ivković, S., Cajner Mraović, I., & Borovec, K. (2016a). An empirical test of the influence of society at large on police integrity in a centralized police system. *Policing: An International Journal of Police Strategies and Management, 39*(2), 302–318.

Kutnjak Ivković, S., Haberfeld, M., Kang, W., Peacock, R., & Sauerman, A. (2016b). A multi-country comparative study of the perceived police disciplinary environments. *Policing: An International Journal of Police Strategies & Management, 39*(2), 338–353.

Lasthuizen, K., Huberts, L., & Heres, L. (2011). How to measure integrity violations: Towards a validated typology of unethical behavior. *Public Management Review, 13*(3), 383–408.

Lee, H., Lim, H., Moore, D. D., & Kim, J. (2013). How police organizational structure correlates with front-line officers' attitudes toward corruption: A multilevel model. *Police Practice and Research, 14*(5), 386–401.

Long, M. A., Cross, J. E., Shelley, T. O., & Kutnjak Ivković, S. (2013). The normative order of reporting police misconduct: Examining the roles of offense seriousness, legitimacy, and fairness. *Social Psychology Quarterly, 76*(3), 242–267.

Lumu, D. (2014). Uganda Police changes name, *New Vision*, Kampala. Retrieved February 12, 2019, from http://www.newvision.co.ug/news/654457-uganda-police-changes-name.html.

Marx, G. T. (2001). Police and democracy. In M. Amir & S. Einstein (Eds.), *Policing, security and democracy: Theory and practice* (Vol. 2). Huntsville: Office of International Criminal Justice. Retrieved February 12, 2019, from http://web.mit.edu/gtmarx/www/dempol.html.

Mastrofski, S. D., Jonathan-Zamir, T., Moyal, S., & Willis, J. J. (2016). Predicting procedural justice in police-citizen encounters. *Criminal Justice and Behavior, 43*(1), 119–139.

Miles-Johnson, T. (2016). Perceptions of group value: How Australian transgender people view policing. *Policing and Society, 26*(6), 605–626.

Miles-Johnson, T., & Pickering, S. (2018). Police recruits and perceptions of trust in diverse groups. *Police Practice and Research, 19*(4), 311–328.

Ministry of Finance, Planning and Economic Development. (2017). National Budget Framework Paper FY 2018/19-FY 2022/23. Retrieved February 12, 2019, from http://budget.go.ug/budget/content/national-budget-framework-paper-6.

Myhill, A., & Bradford, B. (2013). Overcoming cop culture? Organizational justice and police officers' attitudes toward the public. *Policing: An International Journal of Police Strategies & Management, 36*(2), 338–356.

Porter, L. E., Prenzler, T., & Hine, K. (2015). Police integrity in Australia. In S. Kutnjak Ivković & M. R. Haberfeld (Eds.), *Measuring police integrity across the world: Studies from established democracies and countries in transition* (pp. 67–96). New York: Springer.

Reynolds, P. D., & Helfers, R. C. (2018). Differences in perceptions of organizational fairness based on job characteristics among police officers. *American Journal of Criminal Justice, 43*(2), 371–388.

Tangri, R., & Mwenda, A. (2013). *The politics of elite corruption in Africa: Uganda in comparative african perspective*. London: Routledge.

Transparency International. (2018). *Corruption Perceptions Index 2018*. Retrieved February 12, 2019, from https://www.transparency.org/cpi2018.

Transparency International-Kenya. (2013). *The East African Bribery Index 2013*. Retrieved February 12, 2019, from http://tikenya.org/wp-content/uploads/2017/06/the-east-african-bribery-index-2013.pdf.

Uganda Police. (2013). *Annual Crime and Traffic/Road Safety Report*. Retrieved February 12, 2019, from http://www.upf.go.ug/download/publications(2)/Annual_Crime_and_Traffic_Road_Safety_Report_2013(2).pdf.

Uganda Police. (2015). *Directorates*. Retrieved February 12, 2019, from http://www.upf.go.ug/directorate.

Uganda Police. (2017). *Annual Crime Report 2017*. Retrieved February 12, 2019, from https://www.upf.go.ug/wp-content/uploads/2018/07/ANNUAL-CRIME-REPORT-2017.pdf.

Uganda Police Force. (2007). *Strengthening statistics for development planning. Sector strategic plan for statistics (2006/07–2010/11)*. Retrieved February 12, 2019, from http://www.ubos.org/onlinefiles/uploads/ubos/pdf%20documents/PNSD/UPF%20SSPS.pdf.

Waddington, P. A. J., Adang, O., Baker, D., Birkbeck, C., Feltes, T., Gerardo Gabaldón, L., Paes Machado, E., & Stenning, P. (2009). Singing the same tune? International continuities and discontinuities in how police talk about using force. *Crime, Law and Social Change, 52*(2), 111–138.

Wagner, N., Rieger, M., Bedi, A., & Hout, W. (2017). Gender and policing norms: Evidence from survey experiments among police officers in Uganda. *Journal of African Economies, 26*(4), 492–525.

Wagner, N., Hout, W., & Namara, R. (2019). *Improving police integrity in Uganda: Impact assessment of the police accountability and reform project*. Unpublished manuscript.

Wambua, P. M. (2015). *Police corruption in Africa undermines trust, but support for law enforcement remains strong*. Afrobarometer Dispatch 56.

Wolfe, S. E., & Piquero, A. R. (2011). Organizational justice and police misconduct. *Criminal Justice and Behavior, 38*(4), 332–353.

World Bank. (2019). *Data: Uganda*. Retrieved February 12, 2019, from https://data.worldbank.org/country/uganda.

Xinhua News Agency. (2007). *Ugandan police force undergoes massive overhaul ahead of Commonwealth Summit*, 1 July. Retrieved February 12, 2019, from http://en.people.cn/200707/02/eng20070702_389277.html.

A Complex Relation Between the Code of Silence and Education

Darko Datzer, Sanja Kutnjak Ivković,
Eldan Mujanović, and Skyler Morgan

Introduction

It is widely recognized that groups in certain occupations such as doctors, lawyers, and the military develop and sustain beliefs and values that can differ from those of the conventional society and form their own subcultures (Ritzer and Ryan 2011). The police profession is no different; the day a new recruit walks through the doors of the police academy, he leaves the society at large behind to enter a profession that not only gives him a job, but also defines who he is (Skolnick and Fyfe 1993; Skolnick 2002). As argued by Waddington (1999), the police subculture refers to accepted practices, rules, and principles of conduct that are situationally applied. Similarly, Prenzler (2009) considers police subculture to encompass group identities, values, attitudes, beliefs, traditions, unwritten codes, symbols, rituals, and habits.

D. Datzer (✉) · E. Mujanović
Faculty of Criminal Justice, Criminology
and Security Studies, University of Sarajevo,
Sarajevo, Bosnia and Herzegovina
e-mail: ddatzer@fkn.unsa.ba;
emujanovic@fkn.unsa.ba

S. Kutnjak Ivković · S. Morgan
School of Criminal Justice, Michigan State
University, East Lansing, MI, USA
e-mail: kutnjak@msu.edu; morga292@msu.edu

As an institution that has the legal right to use force (e.g., Klockars 1985), the police have contact with different parts of the society, from citizens who violate the traffic laws, public protesters, and marginalized groups, to white-collar offenders and habitual offenders. Their unique experiences bond police officers together and prompt them to form a police subculture. As Skolnick argues (2002, p. 8), "[l]oyalty to fellow officers is a key feature of the culture of policing, regardless of whether criminality is involved." Although loyalty is present in many occupational groups, Skolnick (2002) argues that demands placed on the police could result in an especially tight bond and shared sense of solidarity. Solidarity is a tool to hold the line, "coming together" in the face of danger, be it from criminals or the civil society (Crank 2004; Westmarland 2008).

The code of silence has emerged as a ubiquitous trait of the police subculture (Klockars et al. 2000; Kutnjak Ivković 2015b; Kutnjak Ivković et al. 2016; Kutnjak Ivković and Shelley 2010; Roberg et al. 2004). In the heat of the moment, police officers must make immediate decisions they may later regret and may want to keep quiet, so solidarity and secrecy serve as mechanisms to protect their actions from any control (Rothwell and Baldwin 2007). Although recent research raises the possibility that the code may be even stronger among civilian police staff than among sworn police officers (e.g., Rothwell and Baldwin 2007; Wright 2010), the code of silence is nevertheless

© Springer Nature Switzerland AG 2019
S. Kutnjak Ivković, M. R. Haberfeld (eds.), *Exploring Police Integrity*,
https://doi.org/10.1007/978-3-030-29065-8_8

present among police officers and remains an enormous obstacle to effective misconduct control (e.g., Christopher Commission 1991; Knapp Commission 1972; Mollen Commission 1994; Kutnjak Ivković 2005; Skolnick 2002).

The same code of kinship, as a "code" or "curtain" of silence, can sustain a subculture protecting the interests of members who violate the law and other legal rules. The vail of secrecy hides violation of legal rules and insulates the police from the outside attempts of controlling them. It helps them overcome what they perceive as unrealistic requirements of judicial due process and public accountability in doing their jobs (Crank 2004). The secrecy surrounding police misconduct may also exist to shield officers from bureaucratic rules and punitive discipline associated with military and quasi-military organizations (Kutnjak Ivković and Shelley 2005). Official rules regulating police behavior are constantly amended and added, resulting in an abundance of new rules regulating police conduct. Therefore, it is not uncommon that many police officers are not acquainted with many of those rules and standards (Roberg et al. 2004). Unless protected by the code, deviating from those rules puts police officers at risk to be formally disciplined, sometimes severely. It is not surprising that under such conditions some form of code of silence will evolve (Klockars et al. 2000). The code exists to "protect officers from individuals, entities, or processes that seek accountability from law enforcement agencies and/or their personnel" (Kutnjak Ivković and Shelley, 2010, p. 550).

As prior research indicates, the code of silence is not monolithic; its contours vary greatly across ranks, police agencies, and countries (see, e.g., Klockars et al. 2004; Kutnjak Ivković and Haberfeld 2015). Although the extant research has demonstrated that the code of silence could vary greatly, it did not explore whether the code of silence varies with the police officers' educational level.

This chapter explores the variation in the extent of the code of silence. Using the data recently collected in Bosnia and Herzegovina (BiH), we study not only the contours of the code

of silence, but also the effect of the police officers' education on their adherence to the code of silence. Our first hypothesis is that there is a positive relation between the adherence to the code of silence and education. Because BiH provides different avenues of obtaining academic and police education, we are able to study not only the influence of the level of education on the code of silence, but also the influence of the type of police officers' academic education on the code of silence. Accordingly, our second hypothesis is that, controlling for the level of education, there is a positive relation between the adherence to the code of silence and the type of education police officers received (ranging from a mostly police-related education to a more diverse and broader education).

The Code of Silence, Police Culture, and Police Integrity

The code of silence, the blue curtain of silence, or the wall of silence encompasses a set of informal rules within the police culture that openly prohibits police officers from reporting other police officers' misconduct (Klockars et al. 2000; Kutnjak Ivković 2015b; Kutnjak Ivković et al. 2016; Kutnjak Ivković and Shelley 2010; Roberg et al. 2004). The existence of such and informal code has numerous consequences. To begin, it allows police misconduct to continue. According to Skolnick and Fyfe (1993) and Skolnick (2002), breaking the rules is quite common among police officers. Consequently, police officers will not report misconduct of other police officers when they are engaged in misconduct themselves; "nobody wants to open a Pandora's box of snitching and counter-snitching" (Skolnick 2002, p. 12).

By pressuring police officers to stick to the code, the code prohibits revealing and sanctioning police misconduct within police agencies, giving the police officers who violate official rules a sense of empowerment and a reason to believe that police officers can count on fellow officers to "back up any story irrespective of the truthfulness"(Skolnick 2002, p. 8). Police code of silence, therefore, contributes toward diminishing police accountability. If corruption and other forms of misconduct are present within the police agencies and the public has the perception that little is done to reduce it, it comes as no surprise that the code of silence impacts public confidence in the police adversely. If the police are seen as unable to discipline their own, communities are reluctant to co-operate with the police. In such circumstances, citizens could turn to private security and engage in vigilante justice (Prenzler 2009).

If solidarity is a trait of police subculture, it comes as no surprise that those who dare to break the veil of secrecy might expect negative consequences. Norms of the subculture sustaining the code of silence are a result of socialization. As Stoddard (1968) noticed 50 years ago, "a new recruit can be socialized into accepting these illegal practices by mild, informal negative sanctions such as the withholding of group acceptance" (p. 203). In the case of non-conformity to subcultural norms and values by an honest police officer, this police officer could face years of ostracism, banishment from the police family, and much more serious ways of compelling into police subculture, such as "fists to face, nightsticks to ribs, and knees to groin" (Punch 2009, p. 73). Weisburd et al. (2001) documented that police officers who report fellow officers' misconduct might be chastised by the co-workers; "he [police officer who told on others] doesn't exist. He doesn't get backup. No one hangs out with him. As far as they're concerned, he's a bastard child in the department…" (Weisburd et al. 2001, p. 30).

The existence of unwritten, informal code of silence has been documented in police forces across the globe. The police code of silence "develops in virtually every police agency" (Klockars et al. 2000, p. 3). Nonetheless, its extent and behaviour it helps to cover vary. Based on the existing literature (e.g., Christopher Commission 1991; Mollen Commission 1994), the code of silence and police misconduct seem to be positively related: the stronger the code of silence, the more likely that serious misconduct could be found in the police agency.

Klockars and Kutnjak Ivković (2004) viewed the code of silence as an integral part of the theory of police integrity. The theory of police integrity recognizes four dimensions, all social and organizational in nature. The third dimension of theory of police integrity—the most important part of the theory of police integrity for the purposes of this study—refers to the code of silence (Klockars et al. 2000). In a police agency of low integrity, the code of silence is expected to be strong and its contours would protect many forms of police misconduct. In a police agency of high integrity, the code of silence is under control and covers only the least serious forms of police misconduct. As Klockars and colleagues argued (2000, p. 2), the code's strength and beneficiaries can vary from one police agency to another; "The Code may apply to only low-level corruption in some agencies and to the most serious corruption in others."

Indeed, in their initial study of 30 U.S. police agencies (Klockars et al. 2000, 2004), Klockars and colleagues (2000) found that indeed there is a substantial variation of the code of silence across the police agencies.

> … whom and what The Code covers can vary substantially not only *among* police agencies but also *within* police agencies. Particularly in large police agencies, the occupational culture of integrity may differ substantially among precincts, service areas, task forces, and work groups.

As part of their study, Klockars and colleagues (Klockars and Kutnjak Ivković 2004; Klockars et al. 2004, 2006) develop an accompanying methodological approach—a police officer survey. First questionnaire consisted of 11 hypothetical situations describing mostly examples of police corruption (Klockars et al. 2000), while the second questionnaire contained a range of examples of police misconduct, from police corruption to the use of excessive force, planting of evidence, and falsification of official documents (e.g., Klockars et al. 2004, 2006). Every scenario in both questionnaires was accompanied by a series of questions measuring the normative and proportionate reflections of police integrity (Kutnjak Ivković 2015b).

Since the initial study by Klockars et al. (2000), the police integrity theory and methodology have been used to measure police integrity in general and its constituting dimensions, including the code of silence, across many countries in the world (see, e.g., Klockars et al. 2004; Kutnjak Ivković and Haberfeld 2015). Some of these studies include traditional Western democracies (e.g., Kutnjak Ivković et al. 2016; Lim and Sloan 2016; Long et al. 2013; Rothwell and Baldwin 2007; Vallmuur 2015; Westmarland 2005), while others are countries in transition (e.g., Cheloukhine et al. 2015; Haberfeld 2004; Khechumyan and Kutnjak Ivković 2015; Kremer 2000; Kutnjak Ivković 2015a; Kutnjak Ivković and Khechumyan 2013; Kutnjak Ivković and Klockars 1998, 2000, 2004; Kutnjak Ivković and Sauerman 2013; Kutnjak Ivković and Shelley 2005, 2007, 2008a, b, 2010; Lobnikar and Mesko 2015; Pagon and Lobnikar 2000, 2004). Without any exceptions, the code of silence was detected in every country in which scholars tried to empirically assess the boundaries of the code of silence.

Klockars et al. (2004) provided a 14-country comparative analysis based on the first questionnaire. The most visible differences across all measures of integrity among the countries were detected in the area of willingness to report other officers' misconduct (Klockars et al. 2004). In five out of 14 countries (Croatia, Hungary, Pakistan, Poland, and South Africa), the code of silence seemed to be very strong as not a single incident out of 11 scenarios would be likely to be reported. On the other hand, the code of silence was much weaker in several other countries (e.g., Austria, Canada, Finland, the Netherlands, Sweden, and the United Kingdom). Klockars et al. (2004, p. 17) noted that, despite these differences in the countours of the code of silence across 14 countries, there were also similarities across the countries:

> ... in every one of the countries surveyed, an officer could accept free drinks to overlook a bar that remained open past the official closing time or strike a prisoner in confinement without assuming that his or her police colleagues who witnessed the offense would be sure to report it. In appears that there are few places in the world in which a police officer would turn in a fellow police officer who accepts free meals and discounts, or holiday gifts.

While the code seems to be strong and protecting such behavior evaluated as the least serious across most of these countries, the code seemed to be weaker and less likely to protect the behavior evaluated as the most serious. Indeed, there was a substantially greater degree of variation of the code across the countries when police officers evaluated the most serious forms of misconduct than then they evaluated the least serious forms of misconduct.

The subsequent ten-country analysis of police integrity based on the second version of the questionnaire (Kutnjak Ivković and Haberfeld 2015) revealed very similar results: the code of silence is a common feature across the countries (Kutnjak Ivković and Haberfeld 2015, p. 364):

> ...it should come as no surprise that the code of silence is present in each and every country. ... what seems to be protected by the code varies greatly across the ten countries. Yet, there are reverberating common themes. A police officer who accepts free meals and verbally abuses citizens would likely be protected by fellow police officers in any surveyed country. On the other hand, respondents indicated that stealing at the crime scene or abusing deadly force probably would not go unreported in most surveyed countries.

Across the countries, the highest probability of being reported was for the situations describing theft from a crime scene, unjustifiable use of deadly force, and falsification of the official report. On the other hand, the code of silence was the strongest for the least serious forms of misconduct, such as the acceptance of free meals and gifts from merchants and a verbal abuse of a citizen.

Although not investigated as thoroughly as elsewhere, the existence of the police code of silence in Bosnia and Herzegovina was addressed in a handful of existing studies. As part of a larger study dealing with police integrity, police officers in Bosnia and Herzegovina's capital Sarajevo were surveyed in 2003 (Kutnjak Ivković and Shelley 2005, 2008a, b). Sarajevo was chosen as case study, because it is a large police agency that has been trained by the international community and monitored extensively. As the presence of the code of silence has been empirically documented in many countries across the world (see, e.g., Klockars et al. 2004; Kutnjak Ivković and Haberfeld 2015), its presence in Bosnia and Herzegovina is not surprising. In the application of the first questionnaire, Kutnjak Ivković and Shelley (2005, 2008a, b) have shown not only that such a code indeed exists in BiH, but also that is follows a similar pattern detected in other countries: the less serious the behavior is perceived, the more likely that the code of silence would apply in such situations. The research suggests that behaviours which would most likely to be reported were theft from a crime scene and theft of money from a found wallet, while the lowest probability of being reported was for the use of excessive force, running off-duty security system business by police officer, and the acceptance of holiday gifts from merchants (Kutnjak Ivković and Shelley 2005, 2008a).

Another study, conducted by Maljević et al. (2006), also demonstrated the presence of the code of silence within the BiH police. While a small percentage of surveyed police officers reported accepting a bribe themselves, a substantial percentage of the officers seemed to be familiar with at least one case of corruption. At the same time, only about one-third of the respondents stated that they would report another officer for engaging in corruption and about one-quarter would try to stop the officer from engaging in misconduct (Maljević et al. 2006).

Because there are only a handful of studies exploring the code of silence in BiH, we also present the results of the studies focusing on other East-European countries in transition (Table 1). Several common conclusions appear. First, the code of silence is not a flat prohibition of reporting and varies across scenarios (e.g., Cheloukhine et al. 2015; Haberfeld 2004; Khechumyan and Kutnjak Ivković 2015; Kremer 2000; Kutnjak Ivković 2015a; Kutnjak Ivković and Khechumyan 2013; Kutnjak Ivković and Klockars 1998, 2000, 2004; Kutnjak Ivković and Shelley 2005, 2007, 2008a, b, 2010; Lobnikar and Mesko 2015; Pagon and Lobnikar 2000, 2004; Vallmuur 2015).

Second, when the contours of the code of silence differ greatly across countries, they follow a very distinct pattern. Simply put, the extent of the code is negatively related to the perceived seriousness evaluation (e.g., Cheloukhine et al. 2015; Haberfeld 2004; Khechumyan and Kutnjak Ivković 2015; Kremer 2000; Kutnjak Ivković

Table 1 Publications about the Code of Silence in Eastern Europe

Questionnaire 1	Questionnaire 2
Armenia (Kutnjak Ivković and Khechumyan 2013)	**Armenia** (Khechumyan and Kutnjak Ivković 2015)
Bosnia and Herzegovina (Kutnjak Ivković and Shelley 2005, 2008a, b)	
Croatia (Kutnjak Ivković and Klockars 1998, 2000, 2004)	**Croatia** (Kutnjak Ivković 2015a)
Czech Republic (Kutnjak Ivković and Shelley 2007, 2008a, b, 2010)	
	Estonia (Vallmuur 2015)
Hungary (Kremer 2000, 2004)	
Poland (Haberfeld 2004)	
Romania (Andreescu et al. 2012)	
	Russia (Cheloukhine et al. 2015)
Slovenia (Pagon and Lobnikar 2000, 2004)	**Slovenia** (Lobnikar and Mesko 2015)
Total: 8 countries	Total: 5 countries

2015a; Kutnjak Ivković and Khechumyan 2013; Kutnjak Ivković and Klockars 2004; Lobnikar and Mesko 2015; Pagon and Lobnikar 2000, 2004; Vallmuur 2015).

Third, the contours of the code are not uniform across East-European countries in transition. While the strength of the code was similar between Armenia and Croatia for the least serious behaviors, the code was much stronger for the most serious behaviors in Armenia than in Croatia (Kutnjak Ivković and Khechumyan 2013). Although both countries are classified as countries in transition from a totalitarian communist regime, democratization of the country—which includes the control of corruption—has taken larger strides in Croatia than in Armenia. Furthermore, the code of silence in Russia, a country located lower on the Transparency International Corruption Perceptions Index (hence perceived as more corrupt), than either Croatia or Armenia, seems to be even stronger (Cheloukhine et al. 2015, p. 176). In fact,

Cheloukhine et al. (2015, p. 176) argued that "the code of silence would protect almost all behaviors described in the [second] questionnaire."

Kutnjak Ivković and Shelley (2010) also compared the code of silence in BiH and the Czech Republic. The authors uncovered that the contours of the code varied across the rank in the Czech Republic, but not in BiH (Kutnjak Ivković and Shelley 2008a, b). In other words, the code of silence in BiH seemed to be more homogeneous than the one in the Czech Republic. Kutnjak Ivković and Shelley (2008b, p. 468) explained the potential reasons:

> …both countries approached democratization of the police from very similar starting points (having a strong militia serving the communist regime), but ended up traversing quite different paths toward democratic policing (peaceful disintegration in the CR and the war in BiH). The differences we report in this study may be related to the path traveled, namely the war (or the lack thereof) and the climate it creates. The existence of a more homogeneous code of silence among the line officers and supervisors in BiH is potentially a consequence of a stronger camaraderie among the police that developed during the war.

Fourth, police officers typically assume that they would be about as likely or even more likely to report than their fellow officers (e.g., Kutnjak Ivković 2015a; Kutnjak Ivković and Klockars 2000; Kutnjak Ivković and Shelley 2010; Lobnikar and Mesko 2015; Pagon and Lobnikar 2000; Vallmuur 2015). The results of the first survey from Armenia (Kutnjak Ivković and Khechumyan 2013) are an exception from this rule as they suggest the opposite: police officers from Armenia assumed that other officers would be more likely to say that they would report than the respondents themselves.

Code of Silence, Police Misconduct, and Police Education

Despite the large body of extant research exploring the code of silence and its contours, no prior study has provided an empirical assessment of the relation between the police officers' educational level and their (un)willingness to report

misconduct. As the twenty-first century has brought a widespread change in the nature and complexity of police work, police education, defined as "developing the ability to conceptualize and expand the theoretical and analytical learning process" (Kratcoski 2004, p. 104), has become even more important than ever. As Paoline et al. (2000, p. 585) argued, "[e]ducational experiences might result in a greater appreciation of the multiple functions that police perform in modern society, of limitations on police authority, and of the social, economic, and psychological forces that shape the problems and behavior of the people with whom they have contact." The U.S. Commission on Civil Rights (2000, p. 16) emphasized one more advantage of increased educational expectations: "a college degree requirement…would help restore public confidence in police with proper training who are less likely to succumb to temptations of deviant behavior."

The importance of police training and education originates from two needs: to professionalize the police and to change police attitudes. The idea can be traced back to August Vollmer, who thought that education would not only improve the professional behavior and increase the effectiveness or expertise of police, but also that it would upgrade the occupation of policing in the eyes of the public (Shernock 1992; Roberg and Bonn 2004). We argue that, because of its capacity to advance police officers' intellectual development by enhancing their knowledge of "concepts, terms, policies, practices and theories" (Haberfeld 2013, p. 34), advanced education will better prepare police officers to understand legal rules and anticipate the consequences of their violations. At the same time, higher education will enable them to be more critical of instances of police misconduct they witness and be less likely to tolerate such behavior in silence. Thus, higher education may increase or qualitatively affect police officers' recognition and assessment of wrongdoing, and it may affect the increase in the perceived responsibility for action. At the same time, higher education might weaken the bonds to the police culture and make more educated police officers less tied by the cultural norms (Reuss-Ianni 1983) and, potentially, more likely to report misconduct.

Scholars exploring the potential influence of general education/police education on police performance and attitudes examined a range of issues, from the way police relate to citizens, their communication skills, and daily commitment to policing, to their attitudes toward police work and supervisors' evaluations (Paoline and Terrill 2007), but none of them examined the relation between education and the code of silence. The early studies from the 1980s were confounded by the fact that there were very few police officers with any type of higher education (Sherman and Blumberg 1981). Over the past 30 years, there has been a significant shift in police education with a drastic increase of police officers with higher educational degrees, including baccalaureate degrees, master's degrees, and even doctoral degrees. Linked to this shift in higher education among police officers, there has been an increased interest among scholars to study the potential influence of higher education on police officers' values and behavior. The general assumption was that the overall performance of officers with a higher education will surpass the performance of officers with only a high-school diploma.

Early research on the connection between higher education and police performance produced mixed results. Some scholars reported differences in police performance based on the police officers' education (college-educated police officers had higher performance ratings and fewer disciplinary actions than high-school educated police officers; Finnegan 1976; Cascio 1977), while others found no significant differences in the police use of deadly force across different educational backgrounds (Sherman and Blumberg 1981). Sherman and Blumberg (1981) elaborated on their negative findings by contextualizing them. First, at the time the data were collected in the 1970s (Sherman and Blumberg 1981), there were very few police officers with 4-year degrees both in their sample and in the population of police officers in the United States. Consequently, because of the small number of educated police officers in their study, Sherman

and Blumberg (1981) uncovered many results with differences that, although suggestive, were not statistically significant. Secondly, Sherman and Blumberg (1981) argued that the college-level education for police officers at the time was so similar to the training at the academy that there would likely be no differences between the college-educated and academy-trained police officers in their attitudes. Because of these issues, Sherman and Blumberg (1981) warned the readers that their findings on higher education and the use of deadly force among police officers should be taken with caution and argued that the effect of education will remain unclear until the number of police officers with college degrees increases. Indeed, while college-level education has become more common among police officer over time, a shift occurred in the nature of education offered to police officers at universities (toward more academic education in the university setting).

Since the early 1990s, there has been a more uniform consensus in the literature that police education is associated with higher police performance, attitudes of high integrity, and less police misconduct measured through citizen complaints, views about ethical conduct, and rule-violations (Kappeler and Sapp 1992; Shernock 1992).[1] Education can affect police officers' moral reasoning. College education can yield a shift in police officers' reasoning from conventional moral reasoning with the empahsis on loyalty to specific people and social systems to the more universal or principled moral reasoning with the empahsis on more abstract thinking and universal priniciples of protecting human rights. Because of this more abstract way of thinking, college-educated police officers are assumed to have significantly higher probability

---

[1]Methodologically, scholars have approached studying the influence of higher education on police officers in many different ways. The methodological approaches have included surveys (Chapman 2012; Johnson 2012; Paoline et al. 2015; Telep 2011; Worden 1990), citizen complaints (Hassell and Archbold 2010; Lersch and Kunzman 2001; Manis et al. 2008), and police use of force reports (Lim and Lee 2015). Also, a few authors have used a mixed methods approach, including interviews and observations (Paoline and Terrill 2007; Rydberg and Terrill 2010).

to report and prevent misconduct of other, less educated police officers (Braback 1984). If a college education makes officers more ethical, it is reasonable to expect that college-educated officers would also be less supportive of the abuse of police authority. While Shernock's study (1992) has indeed showed that higher education plays a certain role in developing a consciousness, the study did not find that police officers with higher education would be more or less willing to report fellow officer's misconduct.

On the other hand, Worden's study (1990) showed that college-educated police officers are more amenable to legal restrictions than officers without a degree. This finding can be explained in the way that higher education may imply greater likelihood of appreciating the role of police in a democratic society and a greater likelihood of recognizing the need to operate within the parameters set by the rule of law. College educated police officers are more able to see the restrictions on police practices as necessary and legitimate, so they have a greater respect for legal norms and, in turn, may be less likely to tolerate practices that violate these rules. Telep (2011) examined the effect of higher education on police officer's perceptions of abuse of authority. Compared to other studies (Lersch and Kunzman 2001; Manis et al. 2008), Telep took a more inclusive approach to education and showed that education matters; compared to the officers with no college education, police officers with any type of higher education (some college and above) were less supportive of the abuse of authority. Furthermore, Chapman's study of the self-reported use of force in minority communities (2012) also showed that, while education and attitudes toward the use of force were not related for detectives, patrol officers' education was strongly correlated to their perceptions of the use of force, both perceived frequency of force and perceived severity of force.

Other scholars have used interviews and observations as a methodological approach in studying the connection between police education and police misconduct (Paoline and Terrill 2007; Rydberg and Terrill 2010). Paoline and Terrill (2007) reported that, compared to the

police officers without a 4-year degree, officers with a 4-year degree used significantly less physical force. In addition, Paoline and Terrill (2007) found that officers with any type of college education, be it a 4-year degree or 2-year degree, used significantly less verbal force than police officers with only a high school degree (Paoline and Terrill 2007). Likewise, Rydberg and Terrill (2010) used interviews and observations to look at the influence of higher education on arrest and the use of force. The findings from Rydberg and Terrill's study (2010) suggested that higher education had no influence on either the police officers' decision to arrest or search, but significantly reduced the likelihood of the use of force (Rydberg and Terrill 2010). Similarly, McElvain and Kposowa (2008, p. 515) documented that "college-educated officers were more than 30% less likely to shoot than their counterparts without college education."

Finally, scholars have utilized official agency records, from citizen complaints and discipline records to the use of force reports, to assess the potential relation between education and police misconduct. Studies in which complaints have been the source of data about police misconduct showed mixed results about the connection between level of education and misconduct. Manis et al. (2008) explored the influence of Mid-western police officers' education level on police misconduct. To assess potential differences in the frequency of police misconduct, Manis et al. (2008) looked at all of the formal complaints and informal complaints from 2002 to 2005 in a Mid-western police police department. The results showed significant differences in the frequency of formal complaints, but no differences in the frequency of informal complaints (Manis et al. 2008). More specifically, compared to the police officers without a 4-year degree, police officers with a 4-year degree had significantly fewer formal complaints. In addition, Manie and colleagues (2008) reported that the degree type (criminal justice or non-criminal-justice) had no influence on the frequency of both informal and formal complaints.

Lersch and Kunzman (2001) also relied on complaints, filed between 1995 to 2000, as the source of data in their study of a Southern police department. Unlike Manie and colleagues (2008), Lersch and Kunzman (2001) explored not only the frequency with which complaints were filed, but also the rates at which they were sustained. The results indicate that, compared to the officers with only a high-school education, officers with 2 years of college education had both fewer complaints filed and fewer complaints sustained (Lersch and Kunzman 2001). Interestingly, the effects of the 4 years of college education were not as consistent; compared to the officers with only a high-school education, officers with 4 years of college eduction were less likely to have a complaint filed, but were about equally likely to have a complaint sustained (Lersch and Kunzman 2001). On the other hand, Hassell and Archbold (2010) found that the level of education explained neither the nature of informal complains, disposition of formal complaints, nor the type of discipline imposed on the police officers.

Similar to complaints, Lim and Lee (2015) used the police use of force reports from a police department in Texas for their methodological approach. Unlike other studies, Lim and Lee (2015) looked at the effects of supervisor education and training on police officers' use of force. The authors found that supervisors' education and training on the use of force were directly related to the police officers' use of force practices. At the same time, Lim and Lee (2015) also reported that the police officers' own level of education was negatively related to the higher levels of force used.

Police Education in BiH

In 1992, Bosnia and Herzegovina proclaimed independence from the former Yugoslavia, immediately followed by the war that ended with the Dayton Peace Accord in 1995. BiH is a member of the Council of Europe since 2002 and is a potential candidate for the membership in the European Union and the North Atlantic Treaty Organization (NATO).

Since BiH has received a status of a potential candidate country for the accession to the European Union, creating a democratic police has become one of the top priorities in the country's political agenda. It comes as no surprise that the Council of Ministers of Bosnia and Herzegovina has declared "the professional, effective and efficient delivery of police services is key to facing security challenges " (2015, p. 6). The fight against corruption is also considered a top priority, for which developing an accountable police is essential. Controlling the code of silence is one of the critical elements of the accountable police.

BiH is composed of two entities, the Federation of Bosnia and Herzegovina and Republika Srpska, as well as the Brcko District. The Federation consists of 10 cantons. As a consequence of the Dayton Peace Accord, the police in BiH are decentralized and include police agencies at the cantonal level (first level), entity level (second level), and state level (third level). Republika Srpska has a unified police agency, while the organization of the police in the Federation of BiH is more complex. In particular, there are ten Cantonal police agencies within the Federation, each accountable to its own Cantonal Ministry of the Interior (there are no cantons in Republika Srpska). The entity-level policing includes Ministry of the Interior of Republika Srpska and the Federation Ministry of the Interior. The third police agency at the entity level is the Police of Brcko District. Finally, there are three police agencies at the state or national level: State Investigation and Protection Agency (SIPA), State Border Police of BiH, and Directorate for Coordination of Police Bodies.

Police Education Before the Reform

The police high school in former Socialist Republic of Bosnia and Herzegovina was founded in 1970. Prior to this date, the police had been trained through six-months courses. After 1970, students of the newly founded police high school, who were male and elementary-school graduates, spent 4 years in the high school. In 1986, the length of the program was shortened to 2 years, thereby shifting the recruitment focus to high-school students who have completed 2 years of high-school education in any high school and offering the police high-school curriculum for the last 2 years of their high-school education (Spahić 2005).

A completion of the police high-school program was one way of becoming a police officer. Since the dropout rates from the police high school were high (up to 30%), a deficit of personnel that resulted was compensated through a year-long courses for graduates of other high schools. After the war broke in 1992, two institutions authorized to train police personnel existed: the (old) one that was physically transferred from Sarajevo to Bugojno but formally continued to have the headquarters in Sarajevo and the (new) one that was formed in Banja Luka. Both had 4-year curricula for regular students and also organized several-months long crash courses about police work for graduates of other high schools.

The war ended with a peace accord, negotiated by the international community. Immediately after the war, the police were seen as one of three sectors most vital to democratization (Aitchison 2007). With many of the police officers suspected of committing war crimes or other crimes, and/or being perceived as instruments of political power, it came as no surprise that the international community, heavily present in the country, insisted that the reforms be made. The General Framework Agreement for Peace, ending the war, provided International Police Force (IPTF) under the UN authority. After a year, IPTF was followed by the European Union Police Mission (EUPM).

The peace agreement gave the authority to the international police forces to engage in the vetting of the BiH police as a three-stage process: registration, screening, and in-depth background checks (e.g., housing status, criminal records, academic credentials). In addition, the international police forces required BiH police officers to go through a compulsory training in human rights, public order, and crime-related topics (United Nations Security Council 2002). As a result of the vetting process, burdened with many difficulties, the police in BiH were heavily downsized to about 16,000 (from about 32,750 in 1996; Wisler 2007, p. 259).

The compulsory training, organized by the international police forces, provided trainees with certificates of completion that satisfy one of the requirements of the vetting process. This training was compulsory for *all* police officers, including both new recruits and existing officers. This one-month course comprised of a "week-long human dignity course and a three-week transition course" (United Nations Security Council 2002).

Structural police reforms took place after 2003, when the European Union exhibited a greater interest in re-designing the police in BiH through the accession process. Rationalizing the police services and developing a single police structure, which were the objectives of the international-community driven reforms, has not been established (Celador 2009; Juncos 2011). In fact, the outcome seems to be exactly the opposite: an increasing number of police agencies.

Police Education in the Federation of Bosnia and Herzegovina

The Federation of Bosnia and Herzegovina introduced a new law on police in 1996 that created another avenue of becoming a police officer. In addition to the opportunity of attending the police high school, candidates could become police officers after a completion of the 3–6 months-long police course. Under the 1996 Bonn-Petersburg Agreement, the Federation of Bosnia and Herzegovina agreed to develop new training standards and curricula, which, eventually, led toward the establishment of the Police Academy in Sarajevo. The 1998 Law on the Police officially introduced the new police academy and abolished the police high school. The last-year students at the now closing police high school were allowed to continue their education at the newly established police academy. The duration of the police training at the new police academy was prescribed to be 12 months, including 8 months of theoretical work and 4 months of field work. Courses covered human rights, communication skills, criminal law, psychology, and foreign languages (Spahić 2005).

Police Education in Republika Srpska

In 1992, the police high school was founded in Republika Srpska. The high school maintained a 4-year curriculum. In addition, the high school also organized shorter police courses for graduates of other high schools who wanted to become police officers. Because of the on-going war in the early 1990s and the increased need for a large number of police officers, these six-month long or even shorter courses that would train high-school graduates in the basics of police work were viewed as critical (Nikač et al. 2012).

Two years after the beginning of police reform in Federation of Bosnia and Herzegovina, Republika Srpska also signed an agreement with the UN on police restructuring, reform, and democratization. Pursuant to this agreement, the Republika Srpska Police Academy was founded in 1999 and the police high school was abolished at the same time. The Police Academy provides a year-long training to high-school graduates who plan to become police officers.

Police Education for State Agencies

Although the Dayton Peace Accord originally decentralized police agencies in BiH, the international community supported the establishment of the state-level police agencies as well. First, the State Border Service was formed (later renamed the Border Police) in 2000, followed by the State Investigation and Protection Agency in 2002 and the Directorate for Coordination of Police Bodies in 2008. In 2004, national agencies have become a part of the national Ministry of Public Security.

The personnel for these state agencies was either transferred from entities' police agencies (including cantons) or the Brčko police, or was selected by filling out vacancies. When citizens apply to fill positions in one of these state agencies, some agencies (such as the Border Police) would organize their own year-long training, while other agencies (such as the State Investigation and Protection Agency) would utilize resources of entities' police academies. Either way, candidates for the positions would have to have some type of police training before they commence their work. According to the ICMPD and TC Team Consult (2004), in just few years after its establishment, the Border Police had almost 90% of its police officers receiving the basic or transitional training.

The Law on Directorate for the Coordination of Police Bodies and Police Support Agencies in BiH (2008) assigned the primary role of providing police education for state-level police agencies to the newly established Agency for Education and Professional Training. In 2009, the Agency for Education and Professional Training has begun its work; all police officer and junior police inspector candidates at state level had to complete the appropriate training at the Agency.

Methodology

Questionnaire

This study utilizes the second police integrity questionnaire (Klockars et al. 2006) to measure the code of silence. The questionnaire contains descriptions of 11 hypothetical scenarios, incorporating examples of police corruption (6 scenarios), use of excessive force (4 scenarios), and other forms of police misconduct (4 scenarios). In addition, we have added three scenarios that were also used in the Croatian study (Kutnjak Ivković 2009). One of these new scenarios is originally coming from the first police corruption questionnaire (Klockars et al. 2000) and describes the acceptance of a bribe from a motorist caught speeding. As one of the most frequent forms of corruption in Eastern Europe (e.g., Frič and Walek 2001), we reasoned that this is the scenario that should be added to the police integrity questionnaire. The remaining two scenarios describe failures to react, a behavior that was mostly omitted from the police integrity questionnaire. One of the new scenarios describes the police officers' failure to include the label of a hate crime into the crime report. In the other scenario, a police officer fails to react when he notices juveniles writing graffiti on the wall (Kutnjak Ivković 2009).

Each scenario is followed by a series of seven identical questions. These questions targeted the respondents' evaluations of misconduct serious-ness, views about rule-violations, opinions about expected and appropriate discipline, as well as their willingness to report misconduct. As this chapter focuses on the code of silence, we will primarily rely on the questions about the respon-dents' willingness to report. The question was asking the respondents to assess how likely the respondents were to report behavior described in the questionnaire ("Do you think you would report a fellow police officer who engaged in this behavior?"). The respondents could select an answer from a 5-point Likert scale, ranging from 1 = "definitely would not report" to 5 = "defi-nitely would report."

To increase the chances that police officers would answer truthfully, Klockars et al. (2006) included very few demographic questions. They included questions about the length of the respon-dents' service, rank, assignment, and supervisory position. We added a question measuring the respondents' educational level and gender.

Sample

This chapter is based on the data collected in Bosnia and Herzegovina. In summer of 2017, we surveyed police officers across both cantonal and entity levels during their roll-calls. First, a list of all police entities (14) in Bosnia and Herzegovina was assembled. Because this research project explores police officers' views about misconduct by police officers who do typical police work, such as patroling the beat and investigating crimes, police agencies that have more special-ized tasks (e.g., Border Police) are excluded from our sampling frame. We randomly selected 7 police entities and then composed the list of police administrations within each police entity. Then, we randomly selected 4 to 5 police agen-cies from each of the 7 entities from the list. All organizational units (police stations, criminal investigation departments, traffic police depart-ments) within each police agency were then con-sidered tertiary sampling units. We also randomly selected the day when the questionnaire was dis-tributed, making it the final stage of sampling procedure.

We surveyed all police officers in these selected police agencies during night roll-calls.[2] Out of 1,040 potential respondents, 1,006 agreed to par-ticipate, resulting in the response rate of 96%. About one-half of our respondents are coming from the Federation (54%), about one-third (35.2%) from the Republika Srpska, about one-tenth (8.7%) from the Brcko District, and a few (2%) from the state police. Although not designed to be proportionate, the distribution of our sample corresponds well with the distribution of the police population in 2001[3] and 2017 (Table 2), with the majority coming from the Federation, about one-third from the Republika Srpska, and less than 10% from the Brcko District and the state police.

In terms of their demographic characteristics, most of the respondents are experienced police officers with over 15 years of experience (64.5%, Table 3). At the same time, most of them are non-supervisors (85%, Table 3). The most frequent assignments are patrol (48.0%) and investigation (17.1%, Table 3). About three-quarters (70.4%, Table 3) of the respondents are high-school gradu-ates, while most of the other respondents have a bachelor's degree (22.2%, Table 3) and very few respondents have advanced degrees (1.5%). Finally, about one-tenth of the respondents (9.7%, Table 3) are women. The percentage of women in our sample closely matches the percentage of women in the population. In particular, about 14.7% of police personnel are women (Agency for Statistics of Bosnia and Herzegovina).

Lastly, we asked the respondents whether other police officers and the respondents them-selves were telling the truth when filling out the questionnaire. About one-third of the respon-dents assumed that others would lie (33.4%, Table 3). Answers by the respondents who either

---

[2] We considered distributing the questionnaires during the morning roll calls, but decided against it. While morning roll calls would have both officers who have just finished their shift and officers who are starting their shifts, the officers who are about to leave and go home would be very unlikely to participate in the survey. Hence, we decided to survey during evening roll calls.

[3] In 2001, there were 15,491 police officers in the country, out of which 42.8 percent were in the Republika Srpska, 53.1 percent in the Federation, 2 percent in the Brcko District, and 2 percent in the state police agencies (2001 Yearbook of the United Nations, 2001, p. 335).

Table 2 Sample and Population Distributions

| | Sample | | 2001[a] | | 2017[b] | |
	Number	Percent	Number	Percent	Number	Percent
Federation	544	54.1%	8241	53.2%	7687	56.2%
Republika Srpska	354	35.2%	6630	42.8%	5236	38.3%
District Brcko	88	8.7%	310	2.0%	245	2.0%
State police	20	2.0%	310	2.0%	498	3.6%
Total	1006	100.0%	15,491	100.0%	13,666	100.0%

[a]Source: 2001 Yearbook of the United Nations, 2001, p. 335
[b]Source: Bosnia's answers to the Questionnaire Information requested by the European Commission to the Council of Ministers of Bosnia and Herzegovina for the Preparation of the Opinion on the Application of Bosnia and Herzegovina for Membership of the European Union, 2018, available at http://www.dei.gov.ba/dei/direkcija/sektor_strategija/Upitnik/odgovoriupitnik/Archive.aspx?langTag=en-US&template_id=120&pageIndex=3

Table 3 Respondents' Demographic Characteristics

	Number	Percent
Length of service		
Below 5 years	135	13.7%
6–15 years	216	21.8%
Over 15 years	638	64.5%
Supervisory position		
Supervisors	142	15.0%
Non-supervisors	802	85.0%
Assignment		
Patrol	457	48.0%
Detective/investigative	163	17.1%
Traffic	82	8.6%
SWAT	32	3.4%
Community policing	25	2.6%
Communications	38	4.0%
Administrative	20	2.1%
Other	136	14.3%
Education		
Police high school	325	37.9%
Non-police high school	262	30.5%
Police associate's degree	25	2.9%
Non-police associate's degree	20	2.3%
Police B.A.	129	15.0%
Non-police B.A.	72	8.4%
Non-police M.A./Ph.D.	13	1.5%
Other	12	1.4%
Gender		
Male	871	90.3%
Female	94	9.7%
Others told the truth		
Yes	651	66.6%
No	327	33.4%
Respondent told the truth		
Yes	902	93.3%
No	65	6.7%

said that they lied or did not answer this question were excluded from the analyses.

Analytical Strategy

The purpose of this chapter is to explore the relation between the respondents' education and the adherence to the code of silence. Our variables measuring of the code of silence for each scenario will be the respondents' own willingness to adhere to the code. The respondents could have selected one answer on a 5-point scale.

We will test the potential relation between the respondents' education and their own willingness to report in several steps. In sum, before the police education reform at the end of 1990s in the Federation of Bosnia and Herzegovina and Republika Srpska, there were two basic ways of becoming a police officer. First, a citizen would have have attended a police high school. Second, a citizen, who is a high school graduate, could have attended short course on police work, ranging from about a month to 6 months. Before the reform at state level police forces at the end of 2000s, one could have entered police agency through the transfer from other police agencies or by attending a year-long basic police training.

In the first step, we will look into the relation between the respondents' *educational level* and the code of silence. We anticipate that the respondents who have attained a higher educational level will be less likely to say that they would adhere to the code of silence than the respondents who have only a lower educational level. The rationale is that higher education will better prepare the respondents to understand legal rules and the consequences of their violations, thus enabling them to be more critical of police misconduct and more likely to be willing to report it. Comparing and contrasting potential differences in the expressed willingness to report across educational levels (e.g., B.A. vs. M.A., M.A. vs. Ph.D.) with fine granularity is not feasible because the overwhelming majority of our respondents (70%) have only a high-school education and too few respondents in our sample have any education beyond a B.A. degree (1.5%).

In the second step, we will explore the potential relation between the *type of their education* (e.g., police, non-police) and the code of silence. The type of education—police-related academic education and non-police academic education—is about equally split in the sample: 56.6% of the respondents had a police-related academic education, while 43.4% had non-police related academic education.[4] Unlike police officers whose academic education was more general, police officers whose academic education was primarily police-related have been exposed to, and socialized into, a police culture for a longer period of time and much earlier in their lives and, in turn, are probably more likely to adhere to the norms of the police culture. Hence, we anticipate that the respondents who have obtained a police-related academic education (e.g., police high school, police college B.A. degree) would be more likely to say that they would adhere to the code of silence than the respondents who have non-police related academic education (e.g., regular high school, a B.A. degree at a university).

In the third step, we will explore a *potential interactional effect between the educational level and type of education* on the respondents' expressed willingness to report. In particular, we will divide respondents into four categories: (1) police high-school education ("police lower"), (2) other high school education ("other lower"), (3) police B.A. degree ("police higher"), and (4) other B.A. or higher degrees ("other higher"). We expect that the respondents with the highest level of education and less exposure to police-related academic education ("other higher") would be most likely to say that they would report than the respondents with the lower level of education and more exposure to the police-related academic education ("police lower").

Expressed Own Willingness to Report

Respondents' Educational Level and Own Willingness to Report

We have dichotomized the respondents' educational level into two categories: high-school education and higher education (associates' degree, B.A. degree, M.A. degree, or Ph.D.). We will first compare the respondents' expressed willingness to report and their educational status. Then, because educational level and supervisory position are strongly related (Chi-square = 86.3, p < .001),[5] we will control for the supervisory status by analyzing the relation between education and the code of silence separately for non-supervisors and supervisors.

Although we expected that the more educated respondents would be less likely to adhere to the code of silence, the results clearly show that this is not the case for the majority of the scenarios (Tables 4 and 5). The educational level was not significantly related to the expressed willingness

---

[4]We asked the respondents about the highest academic level they have achieved. Potentially, a respondent could have attended a police high school and then obtained a non-police B.A. degree. Similarly, a respondents could have attended a regular high school and then obtained a police B.A. degree. Although the respondent in both cases was exposed to both types of education, we classfiy them based on the highest and more recent educational experience.

[5]The binominal analysis of educational level (dichotomized to high-school and above high school) and supervisory position (dichotomized as yes and no) revealed that only 6.9% of the respondents with the high-school education are supervisors, while the percentage of the respondents with the more advanced degrees who are supervisors is 31.6%. Put differently, only one-third of supervisors (33.1%) have high-school education, while two-thirds (66.9%) of supervisors have a higher education. On the other hand, three-quarters of non-supervisors (75.6%) have the high-school education and one-quarter of non-supervisors (24.4%) have a higher education.

Table 4 Respondents' Own Willingness to Report: Non-Supervisors

	High School Mean	Higher education Mean	Difference	T-test
Scenario 1: Free Meals, Gifts from Merchants	2.96	2.82	+.14	.988
Scenario 2: Fail to Arrest Friend with Warrant	4.18	4.26	−.08	−.698
Scenario 3: Theft of Knife from Crime Scene	4.42	4.50	−.08	−.748
Scenario 4: Unjustifiable Use of Deadly Force	4.20	4.30	−.10	−.829
Scenario 5: Supervisor: Holiday Off for Errands	3.33	3.34	−.01	−.077
Scenario 6: Officer Strikes Prisoner Who Hurt Partner	2.79	2.66	+.13	.946
Scenario 7: Verbal Abuse of Motorist	2.60	2.32	+.28	2.081*
Scenario 8: Cover-Up of Police DUI Accident	2.73	2.62	+.11	.732
Scenario 9: Auto-Body Shop 5% Kickback	3.81	3.73	+.08	.584
Scenario 10: False Report on Drug on Dealer	3.93	3.75	+.18	1.382
Scenario 11: Sgt. Fails to Halt Beating	3.25	2.95	+.30	2.116*
Scenario 12: Failure to Report Hate Crime	3.18	2.91	+.27	2.033*
Scenario 13: Bribe from Speeding Motorist	4.00	4.07	−.07	−.556
Scenario 14: Failure to React to Graffiti	3.36	3.15	+.21	1.562

* $p < .05$

Table 5 Respondents' Own Willingness to Report: Supervisors

	High School Mean	Higher education Mean	Difference	T-test
Scenario 1: Free Meals, Gifts from Merchants	3.44	3.71	−.27	−.865
Scenario 2: Fail to Arrest Friend with Warrant	4.44	4.66	−.22	−1.023
Scenario 3: Theft of Knife from Crime Scene	4.72	4.86	−.14	−1.010
Scenario 4: Unjustifiable Use of Deadly Force	4.64	4.54	−.10	.560
Scenario 5: Supervisor: Holiday Off for Errands	3.54	3.73	−.19	−.657
Scenario 6: Officer Strikes Prisoner Who Hurt Partner	3.44	2.99	+.45	1.429
Scenario 7: Verbal Abuse of Motorist	3.00	2.90	+.10	.339
Scenario 8: Cover-Up of Police DUI Accident	3.00	2.81	+.19	.610
Scenario 9: Auto-Body Shop 5% Kickback	4.08	4.20	−.12	−.497
Scenario 10: False Report on Drug on Dealer	4.44	4.39	+.05	.220
Scenario 11: Sgt. Fails to Halt Beating	3.62	3.61	+.01	.027
Scenario 12: Failure to Report Hate Crime	3.82	3.43	+.39	1.343
Scenario 13: Bribe from Speeding Motorist	4.54	4.70	−.16	−.956
Scenario 14: Failure to React to Graffiti	3.82	3.42	+.40	1.504

to report in the majority of scenarios. In fact, educational level was significantly related to the respondents' expressed willingness to report in only 3 out of 14 scenarios for non-supervisors (Table 4). In the three scenarios with statistically significant differences for non-supervisors, the respondents who have a higher education were more likely to say that they would report (i.e., had higher means) than the respondents with only a high-school education. Furthermore, the differences between the means for high-school educated respondents and the means for respondents with higher education tended to be rather small, typically below 0.20 on a 5-point scale

Table 6 Respondents' Own Willingness to Report: Non-Supervisors

	Police education	Non-police education		
	Mean	Mean	Difference	T-test
Scenario 1: Free Meals, Gifts from Merchants	2.78	3.10	−.32	−2.64**
Scenario 2: Fail to Arrest Friend with Warrant	4.06	4.37	−.31	−3.17**
Scenario 3: Theft of Knife from Crime Scene	4.34	4.57	−.23	−2.88**
Scenario 4: Unjustifiable Use of Deadly Force	4.09	4.40	−.31	−3.30**
Scenario 5: Supervisor: Holiday Off for Errands	3.18	3.52	−.34	−2.80**
Scenario 6: Officer Strikes Prisoner Who Hurt Partner	2.63	2.93	−.30	−2.47*
Scenario 7: Verbal Abuse of Motorist	2.44	2.64	−.20	−1.70
Scenario 8: Cover-Up of Police DUI Accident	2.56	2.88	−.32	−2.69**
Scenario 9: Auto-Body Shop 5% Kickback	3.70	3.90	−.20	−1.80
Scenario 10: False Report on Drug on Dealer	3.73	4.08	−.35	−3.24**
Scenario 11: Sgt. Fails to Halt Beating	3.04	3.36	−.32	−2.68**
Scenario 12: Failure to Report Hate Crime	2.98	3.29	−.31	−2.69**
Scenario 13: Bribe from Speeding Motorist	3.91	4.17	−.26	−2.47*
Scenario 14: Failure to React to Graffiti	3.14	3.52	−.38	−3.19**

$* p < .05; ** p < .01$

from 1 to 5.[6] At the same time, the level of education and the code of silence were not related for supervisors as there were no scenarios with statistically significant differences across educational levels for supervisors (Table 5).[7]

Respondents' Type of Education and Own Willingness to Report

In addition to the level of education, we also incorporated the type of education into our question. As described above, at each educational level, the respondents could have obtained education in a police-related academic institution (e.g., police college) or a general academic institution (e.g., university). About one-half (56.6%) of the respondents had a police-related academic education, while the other half (43.4%) had a general academic education.

Type of education seems to be strongly related to the respondents' expressed willingness to report misconduct for non-supervisors (Table 6): in 12 out of 14 scenarios, where were statistically significant differences between the respondents who had a police-related academic education and the respondents who had a general academic education. Although the differences were not large (i.e., above .50), nevertheless, they form a unified picture: in all scenarios with statistically significant differences, the line officers who had a general academic education were more likely to say that they would report than the line officers who had a police-related academic education (Table 6).

On the other hand, type of academic education and the respondents' willingness to report did not seem to be related for supervisors (Table 7). In no scenarios there were statistically significant differences (Table 7) and in only three scenarios (Table 7) there were potentially marginally significant differences. To take into account the possibility that our sample of supervisors is relatively small and hence affecting the power of t-test, we also looked at the size of differences. In 8 out of 14 scenarios (57%), the actual differences between the means for supervisors with a general

---

[6]Klockars et al. (2006) consider differences of .50 on a 5-point scale to be large and substantively important.

[7]This is partly a consequence of the test power. Specifically, while the differences between the means were in three cases larger for supervisors than for non-supervisors, they were not statistically signfiicant because of the much smaller number of supervisors (N = 118) than non-supervisors (N = 689) in the sample and affecting the power of the test.

Table 7 Respondents' Own Willingness to Report: Supervisors

	Police Education Mean	Non-Police Educ. Mean	Difference	T-Test
Scenario 1: Free Meals, Gifts from Merchants	3.59	3.69	−.10	−.33
Scenario 2: Fail to Arrest Friend with Warrant	4.58	4.60	−.02	−.10
Scenario 3: Theft of Knife from Crime Scene	4.84	4.78	+.06	.53
Scenario 4: Unjustifiable Use of Deadly Force	4.51	4.68	−.17	−.95
Scenario 5: Supervisor: Holiday Off for Errands	3.68	3.67	+.01	−.03
Scenario 6: Officer Strikes Prisoner Who Hurt Partner	2.94	3.44	−.48	−1.61
Scenario 7: Verbal Abuse of Motorist	2.81	3.16	−.35	−1.21
Scenario 8: Cover-Up of Police DUI Accident	2.66	3.18	−.52	−1.75 (.08)
Scenario 9: Auto-Body Shop 5% Kickback	4.08	4.31	−.23	−.95
Scenario 10: False Report on Drug on Dealer	4.30	4.60	−.30	−1.76 (.08)
Scenario 11: Sgt. Fails to Halt Beating	3.49	3.80	−.31	−1.13
Scenario 12: Failure to Report Hate Crime	3.53	3.61	−.08	−.30
Scenario 13: Bribe from Speeding Motorist	4.69	4.58	+.11	.70
Scenario 14: Failure to React to Graffiti	3.59	3.49	+.10	.39

academic education and the supervisors with the police-related academic education were very small (below .10 on a 5-point scale from 1 to 5), indicating that the differences are not substantively important.

Respondents' Educational Level/Type of Education and Own Willingness to Report

The next set of analyses explore the effect of the educational level and type of education at the same time. To assess the interactional effect of educational level and type of education, we reclassified the respondents into four categories: police high-school education ("police lower" or category 1), other high school education ("other lower" or category 2), police B.A. degree ("police higher" or category 3), other B.A. or higher degrees ("other higher" or category 4). Out of the officers in our sample, 38.4% were in "police lower" category, 31.0% in the "other lower" category, 18.2% in the "police higher" category, and 12.4% were in the "other higher category."

A one-way ANOVA analyses revealed that there is a strong interactional effect of educational level and type of education on the line offi-

cers' expressed willingness to report (Table 8). In 12 out of 14 scenarios there were statistically significant differences across the four categories of line officers. In 8 scenarios (Scenario 1: Free Meals, Gifts from Merchants; Scenario 4: Unjustifiable Use of Deadly Force; Scenario 5: Supervisor: Holiday Off for Errands; Scenario 6: Officer Strikes Prisoner Who Hurt Partner; Scenario 8: Cover-Up of Police DUI & Accident; Scenario 11: Sgt. Fails to Halt Beating; Scenario 12: Failure to Report Hate Crime; Scenario 13: Bribe from Speeding Motorist) these differences were quite large (above .50). In addition, there were 3 scenarios with the differences approaching the cut-off point (Scenario 2: Fail to Arrest Friend with Warrant; Scenario 9: Auto-Body Shop 5% Kickback; Scenario 10: False Report of Drug on Dealer). The F-test just indicates that at least some of the differences were statistically significant, but does not reveal which of the pairs have means that are statistically significant. The post-hoc analyses revealed interesting patterns (Table 8).

First, when the level of education is controlled for, the type of education mattered only at the college level. Specifically, the most frequent pair with significant differences (10 scenarios with statistically significant differences) included

Table 8 Respondents' Own Willingness to Report: Non-Supervisors

	Police lower (1) Mean	Other lower (2) Mean	Police higher (3) Mean	Other higher (4) Mean	F-test
Scenario 1: Free Meals, Gifts from Merchants	2.86 (2)	3.08 (3)	2.55 (1)	3.20 (4)	3.39* (2 v. 3, 3 v. 4)
Scenario 2: Fail to Arrest Friend with Warrant	4.06 (1)	4.33 (3)	4.08 (2)	4.51 (4)	3.57* (1 v. 4, 3 v. 4)
Scenario 3: Theft of Knife from Crime Scene	4.34 (1.5)	4.53 (3)	4.34 (1.5)	4.72 (4)	3.12* (1 v. 4, 3 v. 4)
Scenario 4: Unjustifiable Use of Deadly Force	4.09 (2)	4.34 (3)	4.08 (1)	4.60 (4)	4.22** (1 v. 4, 3 v. 4)
Scenario 5: Supervisor: Holiday Off for Errands	3.21 (2)	3.47 (3)	3.09 (1)	3.69 (4)	3.11* (3 v. 4)
Scenario 6: Officer Strikes Prisoner Who Hurt Partner	2.70 (2)	2.91 (3)	2.40 (1)	3.01 (4)	2.96* (2 v. 3, 3 v. 4)
Scenario 7: Verbal Abuse of Motorist	2.54 (3)	2.68 (4)	2.16 (1)	2.53 (2)	2.57 (.053) (2 v. 3)
Scenario 8: Cover-Up of Police DUI Accident	2.64 (2)	2.83 (3)	2.31 (1)	3.07 (4)	3.99** (2 v. 3, 3 v. 4)
Scenario 9: Auto-Body Shop 5% Kickback	3.75 (2)	3.88 (3)	3.56 (1)	3.99 (4)	1.62
Scenario 10: False Report on Drug on Dealer	3.79 (2)	4.10 (4)	3.56 (1)	4.03 (3)	4.06** (2 v. 3, 3 v. 4)
Scenario 11: Sgt. Fails to Halt Beating	3.14 (2)	3.39 (4)	2.73 (1)	3.28 (3)	4.16** (2 v. 3, 3 v. 4)
Scenario 12: Failure to Report Hate Crime	3.08 (2)	3.30 (4)	2.69 (1)	3.23 (3)	4.16** (2 v. 3, 3 v. 4)
Scenario 13: Bribe from Speeding Motorist	3.93 (2)	4.09 (3)	3.83 (1)	4.41 (4)	3.09* (1 v. 4, 3 v. 4)
Scenario 14: Failure to React to Graffiti	3.20 (2)	3.56 (4)	2.99 (1)	3.39 (3)	4.06** (2 v. 3)
Average mean	3.38	3.61	3.17	3.69	

* $p < .05$; ** $p < .01$

"police higher" (3) and "other higher" (4) educational categories (Table 8). In all of these scenarios, the respondents with other higher education (4) seemed more likely to say that they would report than the respondents with police-related higher education (3). In other words, the type of education mattered a lot at the higher educational level (3 vs. 4 in 11 out of 14 scenarios), while it did not matter at all at the lower educational level (1 vs. 2 in 0 out of 14 scenarios; Table 8).

Put differently, the average mean across 14 scenarios for the respondents with police higher education (3) was 3.17, while it was 3.69 for the respondents with the other higher education (4), resulting in a large difference of 0.52. On the other hand, the average mean across 14 scenarios for the respondents with police lower education (1) was 3.38, while it was 3.61 for the respondents with other lower education (2), resulting in a difference of only 0.23 or about one-half the difference of the means of the college-educated group.

Second, when the type of education is controlled for, the level of education did not matter; there were no statistically significant findings when we compared the respondents' willingness to report across the two educational levels for the same type of education (i.e., "police lower" (1) v. "police higher" (3) and "other lower" (2) and "other higher"(4)). Similarly, the comparison of the average mean across 14 scenarios showed

Table 9 Respondents' Own Willingness to Report: Supervisors

	Police Lower (1)	Other Lower (2)	Police Higher (3)	Other Higher (4)	
	Mean	Mean	Mean	Mean	F-Test
Scenario 1: Free Meals, Gifts from Merchants	3.63 (3)	3.13 (1)	3.57 (2)	3.97 (4)	.97
Scenario 2: Fail to Arrest Friend with Warrant	4.46 (2)	4.40 (1)	4.64 (3)	4.70 (4)	.51
Scenario 3: Theft of Knife from Crime Scene	4.79 (2)	4.60 (1)	4.86 (3)	4.87 (4)	.83
Scenario 4: Unjustifiable Use of Deadly Force	4.50 (1)	4.87 (4)	4.52 (2)	4.59 (3)	.60
Scenario 5: Supervisor: Holiday Off for Errands	3.38 (1)	3.80 (3)	3.82 (4)	3.60 (2)	.62
Scenario 6: Officer Strikes Prisoner Who Hurt Partner	3.50 (3.5)	3.33 (2)	2.70 (1)	3.50 (3.5)	2.30 (.08)
Scenario 7: Verbal Abuse of Motorist	2.91 (3)	3.13 (4)	2.76 (1)	3.17 (2)	.54
Scenario 8: Cover-Up of Police DUI Accident	2.83 (2)	3.29 (4)	2.58 (1)	3.13 (3)	1.18
Scenario 9: Auto-Body Shop 5% Kickback	4.04 (1)	4.13 (3)	4.10 (2)	4.40 (4)	.45
Scenario 10: False Report on Drug on Dealer	4.33 (2)	4.60 (3.5)	4.28 (1)	4.60 (3.5)	.86
Scenario 11: Sgt. Fails to Halt Beating	3.46 (1)	3.87 (4)	3.50 (2)	3.77 (3)	.44
Scenario 12: Failure to Report Hate Crime	3.83 (4)	3.79 (3)	3.38 (1)	3.53 (2)	.65
Scenario 13: Bribe from Speeding Motorist	4.54 (2)	4.53 (1)	4.76 (4)	4.60 (3)	.54
Scenario 14: Failure to React to Graffiti	3.83 (4)	3.80 (3)	3.47 (2)	3.33 (1)	.84
Average mean	3.86	3.95	3.78	3.98	

small differences; the average mean across 14 scenarios for the respondents with police lower education (1) was 3.38 and it was 3.17 for the respondents with the police higher education (3), resulting in a difference of −0.21. Along the same lines, the average mean across 14 scenarios for the respondents with other lower education (2) was 3.61 and it was 3.69 for the respondents with other higher education (4), resulting in the mean difference of only −0.08.

Third, there were differences across the levels and types of education. Specifically, the second most frequent pair with statistically significant differences included "other lower" (2) and "police higher" (3) groups (Table 8). In 8 out of 14 scenarios, the respondents who attended a general high school (2) were more likely to say that they would report than the respondents who had a B.A. from the police college (3) (Table 8). Although

there were no statistically significant differences within the type of education at the high-school level (i.e., 1 vs. 2 in Table 9), attending a general high school yielded attitudes more critical of the code of silence than obtaining the police B.A.

The results for supervisors are not supportive of the general assessment that there is an interactional effect of the level and type of education on the respondents' willingness to report (Table 9). To begin, there were no scenarios with statistically significant differences, which can partly be a result of a more limited power of the test because of the smaller subsample. To potentially address the issue of test power, we also explored the actual differences in means. There were only 4 out of 14 scenarios with differences of above the .50 threshold (Scenario 1: Free Meals, Gifts from Merchants; Scenario 6: Officer Strikes Prisoner Who Hurt Partner; Scenario 8: Cover-Up of Police DUI Accident; Scenario 14: Failure to React to Graffiti), suggesting that these differences are of substantive importance. Put differently, there were no large differences in the majority of the scenarios (10 out of 14). Furthermore, in these 4 scenarios with large differences, no clear pattern is emerging. Finally, we also compared the average means for the four groups. They are all closely tied (there is only a 0.20 difference on a 5-point scale between the largest and smallest mean), providing further evidence that neither the level of education nor the type of education matter for supervisors' expressed willingness to report.

Conclusion

Most of the research on the relation between police education and police misconduct has been included the U.S.-based studies (e.g., Hassell and Archbold 2010; Lersch and Kunzman 2001; Lim and Lee 2015; Manis et al. 2008; Paoline and Terrill 2007; Rydberg and Terrill 2010). The problem with such studies is that the U.S. system of police education is relatively homogeneous as it requires future police officers, regardless of the level of their academic education, to attend a police academy. The educational system in BiH is more heterogeneous and provides opportunities to test not only the potential differences between the levels of education, but also the potential differences between the specific types of education.

Our results show that the *level* of academic education matters relatively little for the respondents' willingness to adhere to the code of silence. In the overwhelming majority of the scenarios (11 out of 14), whether officers were only high-school graduates or college graduates did not result in different levels of expressed willingness to report. The result was strong and persisted even when we controlled for the supervisory level. However, before we concluded our exploration of the issue, we have also explored the potential interaction between the level of academic education and type of education.

The results of our analysis of the potential effect of *type* of education on the code of silence

paint a very uniform picture: with a few exceptions, the type of education was directly related to the line officers' expressed willingness to report misconduct (while it did not matter for the supervisor expressed willingness to report). In 12 out of 14 scenarios, line officers who obtained academic education at non-police institutions (regular high school, college) were much less likely to say that they would adhere to the code than the line officers whose education was obtained primarily at the police institutions (police high school, police academy). Put differently, we could detect almost no difference between the respondents who obtained their education at two different academic levels but within the same type of education (e.g., police high school v. police academy).

Our final exploration targeted a potential interaction effect between the *level* of education and *type* of education. Among the four groups of respondents, respondents who have other college-level education (higher non-police education) seem to express the greatest willingness to dispose of the cultural norms and report police misconduct. This is visible in the majority of the scenarios when their expressed willingness to report is compared to the expressed willingness to report by the respondents who are either graduates of police high school (lower police education) or police academy (higher police education). On the other hand, the type of education did not matter for the respondents who were only high-school graduates, as the respondents who were police high-school graduates expressed similar levels of unwillingness to report as did the respondents who were graduates of other high schools.

In the end, education did matter, but the relation between education and the code of silence seems more complex than is typically anticipated. In fact, prior research did not find a clear and consistent relation between education and police misconduct. Lersch and Kunzman (2001) found that the effects of the 4-year college education resulted in a fewer complaints filed, but education did not have an effect on the number of complaints sustained. Similarly, Manis et al. (2008) reported that education had an effect on frequency of formal complaints, but not on the frequency of informal complaints. In addition,

Rydberg and Terrill (2010) reported that education had an effect on the likelihood of the use of force, but not on the decision to arrest or search. Furthermore, Chapman (2012) found that education was related to the patrol officers' attitudes toward the use of force, but that education was not related to the detectives' attitudes.

Our study provides more insights into why the educational effects on police misconduct are not uniform and straightforward. A key may lie not only in the level of education, but a combination of the level of education and the type of education. In particular, being educated at the police institution for several years, either at the police high school or the police academy, provided stronger socialization effects than being educated at a university and then attending a course to become a police officer. The level of education did not matter when the respondents spent several years getting their education at the police institutions. It did not matter also whether the respondents were educated at a regular high school or college. However, once the respondents have reached a higher-educational level, the type of their education started to matter, as the respondents who attended a university appeared less likely to adhere to the code of silence than the respondents who attended the police academy.

Further highlighting the complexity of the relation between education and police misconduct/police integrity, our findings indicate that neither the type nor the level of education mattered for the supervisors' willingness to report. In other words, the supervisors' code of silence seems to be much more homogeneous and resistant toward educational effects than line officers' code. While all four groups of supervisors had higher average means than the four respective groups of line officers, the size of the differences between the supervisors' and line officers' means was particularly pronounced for supervisors who were primarily educated at police institutions as they were much more likely to say that they would report than their line officers. Clearly, socialization into a supervisory role carries a somewhat different set of cultural values and norms than being just a line officer. Such a finding points toward a need for a further exploration of police culture(s).

References

Agency for Statistics of Bosnia and Herzegovina. (2013). *Women and men in Bosnia and Herzegovina.* Sarajevo: Agency for Statistics of Bosnia and Herzegovina.

Aitchison, A. (2007). Police reform in Bosnia and Herzegovina: State, democracy and international assistance. *Policing and Society, 17*(4), 321–343.

Andreescu, V., Keeling, D. G., Vito, G. F., & Voinic, M. C. (2012). Romanian and American police officers' perceptions of professional integrity and ethical behavior. *Revista Romana De Sociologie, 23*(3–4), 185–207.

Braback, M. (1984). Ethical characteristics of whistle blowers. *Journal of Research in Personality, 18,* 41–53.

Cascio, W. F. (1977). Formal education and police officer performance. *Journal of Political Science and Administration, 5*(1), 89–96.

Celador, G. C. (2009). Becoming 'European' through police reform: a successful strategy in Bosnia and Herzegovina? *Crime. Law and Social Change, 51*(2), 231–242.

Chapman, C. (2012). Use of force in minority communities is related to police education, age, experience, and ethnicity. *Police Practice and Research, 13*(5), 421–436.

Cheloukhine, S., Kutnjak Ivković, S., Haq, Q., & Haberfeld, M. R. (2015). Police integrity in Russia. In S. Kutnjak Ivković & M. Haberfeld (Eds.), *Police integrity across the world.* New York: Springer.

[Christopher Commission]. Independent Commission on the Los Angeles Police Department. (1991). *Report of the independent commission on the Los Angeles police department.* Los Angeles: Author.

Council of Ministers of Bosnia and Herzegovina. (2015). *Reform Agenda for Bosnia and Herzegovina 2015–2018.* Retrieved from https://europa.ba/wp-content/uploads/2015/09/Reform-Agenda-BiH.pdf

Crank, J. P. (2004). *Understanding police culture.* New York: Routledge.

Finnegan, J. C. (1976). A study of relationships between college education and police performance in Baltimore, Maryland. *The Police Chief, 43,* 60–62.

Frič, P., & Walek, C. (2001). *Crossing the thin blue line.* Prague: Transparency International CR.

Haberfeld, M. R. (2004). The heritage of police misconduct: The case of the Polish police. In C. B. Klockars, S. Kutnjak Ivković, & M. R. Haberfeld (Eds.), *The contours of police integrity* (pp. 95–210). Thousand Oaks, CA: Sage.

Haberfeld, M. R. (2013). *Critical issues in police training* (2nd ed.). Upper Saddle River, NJ: Prentice Hall.

Hassell, K. D., & Archbold, C. A. (2010). Widening the scope on complaints of police misconduct. *Policing: An International Journal of Police Strategies & Management, 33*(3), 473–489.

International Centre for Migration Policy Development (ICMPD) and TC Team Consult. (2004). *Final assessment report: Financial, Organisational and Administrative Assessment of the BiH Police Forces and the State Border Service.* Vienna: International Centre for Migration Policy Development.

Johnson, R. R. (2012). Police officer job satisfaction: A multidimensional analysis. *Police Quarterly, 15*(2), 157–176. https://doi.org/10.1177/1098611112442809.

Juncos, A. E. (2011). Europeanization by decree? The case of police reform in Bosnia. *JCMS: Journal of Common Market Studies, 49*(2), 367–389.

Kappeler, V. E., & Sapp, A. D. (1992). Police officer higher education, citizen complaints and departmental rule violations. *American Journal of Police, 11*(2), 37–54.

Khechumyan, A., & Kutnjak Ivković, S. (2015). Police integrity in Armenia. In S. Kutnjak Ivković & M. Haberfeld (Eds.), *Police integrity across the world.* New York: Springer.

Klockars, C. (1985). *The Idea of Police.* Newbury Park, CA: Sage.

Klockars, C. B., & Kutnjak Ivković, S. (2004). Measuring police integrity. In M. J. Hickman, A. R. Piquero, & J. R. Greene (Eds.), *Police integrity and ethics* (pp. 1.1–1.20). Belmont, CA: Wadsworth.

Klockars, C. B., Kutnjak Ivković, S., Harver, W. E., & Haberfeld, M. R. (2000). *The measurement of police integrity.* Washington, DC: National Institute of Justice.

Klockars, C. B., Kutnjak Ivković, S., & Haberfeld, M. R. (2004). Contours of police integrity. In C. B. Klockars, S. Kutnjak Ivković, & M. R. Haberfeld (Eds.), *The contours of police integrity* (pp. 1–18). Thousand Oaks, CA: Sage.

Klockars, C. B., Kutnjak Ivković, S., & Haberfeld, M. R. (2006). *Enhancing police integrity.* Dordrecht: Springer.

[Knapp Commission]. Commission to Investigate Allegations of Police Corruption and the City's Anti-Corruption Procedures. (1972). *Report on police corruption.* New York: G. Braziller.

Kratcoski, P. (2004). Police education and trainng in a global society: A guest editor's introduction. *Police Practice and Research: An International Journal, 5*(2), 103–105.

Kremer, F. (2000). Comparing supervisor and line officer opinions about the code of silence: The case of Hungary. In M. Pagon (Ed.), *Policing in Central and Eastern Europe: Ethics, integrity, and human rights* (pp. 211–219). Ljubljana: College of Police and Security Studies.

Kremer, F. (2004). Police integrity in Hungary. In C. B. Klockars, S. Kutnjak Ivković, & M. R. Haberfeld (Eds.), *The contours of police integrity* (pp. 116–130). Thousand Oaks, CA: Sage.

Kutnjak Ivković, S. (2005). *Fallen Blue Knights: Controlling police corruption.* New York: Oxford University Press.

Kutnjak Ivković, S. (2009). The Croatian police, police integrity, and transition toward democratic policing. *Policing: An International Journal of Police Strategies & Management, 32*(3), 459–488.

Kutnjak Ivković, S. (2015a). Police integrity in Croatia. In S. Kutnjak Ivković & M. R. Haberfeld (Eds.), *Measuring police integrity across the world* (pp. 97–123). Dordrecht: Springer.

Kutnjak Ivković, S. (2015b). Studying police integrity. In S. Kutnjak Ivković & M. R. Haberfeld (Eds.), *Measuring police integrity across the world* (pp. 1–36). Dordrecht: Springer.

Kutnjak Ivković, S., & Haberfeld, M. R. (2015). A comparative perspective on police integrity. In S. Kutnjak Ivković & M. R. Haberfeld (Eds.), *Measuring police integrity across the world* (pp. 329–368). Dordrecht: Springer.

Kutnjak Ivković, S., & Khechumyan, A. (2013). The state of police integrity in Armenia: Findings from the police integrity survey. *Policing, 36*(1), 70–90.

Kutnjak Ivković, S., & Klockars, C. B. (1998). The code of silence and the Croatian police. In M. Pagon (Ed.), *Policing in Central and Eastern Europe: Organizational, managerial, and human resource aspects* (pp. 329–347). Ljubljana: College of Police and Security Studies.

Kutnjak Ivković, S., & Klockars, C. B. (2000). Comparing police supervisor and line officer opinions about the code of silence: The case of Croatia. In M. Pagon (Ed.), *Policing in Central and Eastern Europe: Ethics, integrity, and human rights* (pp. 183–195). Ljubljana: College of Police and Security Studies.

Kutnjak Ivković, S., & Klockars, C. B. (2004). Police integrity in Croatia. In C. B. Klockars, S. Kutnjak Ivković, & M. R. Haberfeld (Eds.), *The contours of police integrity* (pp. 56–74). Thousand Oaks, CA: Sage.

Kutnjak Ivković, S., & Sauerman, A. (2013). Curtailing the code of silence among the South African Police. *Policing: An International Journal of Police Strategies and Management, 36*(1), 175–198.

Kutnjak Ivković, S., & Shelley, T. O. (2005). The Bosnian police and police integrity: A continuing story. *European Journal of Criminology, 2*(4), 428–464.

Kutnjak Ivković, S., & Shelley, T. O. (2007). Police integrity and the Czech police officers. *International Journal of Comparative and Applied Criminal Justice, 31*(1), 21–49.

Kutnjak Ivković, S., & Shelley, T. O. (2008a). The contours of police integrity across Eastern Europe: The case of Bosnia and Herzegovina and the Czech Republic. *International Criminal Justice Review, 18*(1), 59–82.

Kutnjak Ivković, S., & Shelley, T. O. (2008b). The police code of silence and different paths toward democratic policing. *Policing and Society, 18*(4), 445–473.

Kutnjak Ivković, S., & Shelley, T. O. (2010). The code of silence and disciplinary fairness. *Policing: An International Journal of Police Strategies & Management, 33*(3), 548–574.

Kutnjak Ivković, S., Haberfeld, M. R., & Peacock, R. (2016). Decoding the code of silence. *Criminal Justice Policy Review, 27*, 1–18.

Lersch, K. M., & Kunzman, L. L. (2001). Misconduct allegations and higher education in a southern sheriff's department. *American Journal of Criminal Justice: AJCJ, 25*(2), 161–172.

Lim, H., & Lee, H. (2015). The effects of supervisor education and training on police use of force. *Criminal Justice Studies, 28*(4), 444–463.

Lim, H., & Sloan, J. J. (2016). Police officer integrity: A partial replication and extension. *Policing: An International Journal of Police Strategies & Management, 39*(2), 284–301.

Lobnikar, B., & Mesko, G. (2015). Police integrity in Slovenia. In S. Kutnjak Ivković & M. Haberfeld (Eds.), *Police integrity across the world.* New York: Springer.

Long, M., Cross, J. E., Shelley, T. O., & Kutnjak Ivković, S. (2013). The normative order of reporting police misconduct: Examining the roles of offense seriousness, legitimacy, and fairness. *Social Psychology Quarterly, 76*(3), 242–267.

Maljević, A., Datzer, D., Muratbegović, E., & Budimlić, M. (2006). *Overtly about police corruption.* Sarajevo: Association of Criminalists in Bosnia and Herzegovina.

Manis, J., Archbold, C. A., & Hassell, K. D. (2008). Exploring the impact of police officer education level on allegations of police misconduct. *International Journal of Police Science and Management, 10*(4), 509–523.

McElvain, J. P., & Kposowa, A. J. (2008). Police officer characteristics and the likelihood of using deadly force. *Criminal Justice and Behavior, 35*(4), 505–521.

[Mollen Commission] New York City Commission to Investigate Allegations of Police Corruption and the Anti-Corruption Procedures of the Police Department. (1994). *Commission report.* New York: Author.

Nikač, Ž., Simić, B., Đurovski, M., & Pavlović, G. (2012). Uporedni prikaz policijske obuke i obrazovanja u Republici Srbiji, Makedoniji i Republici Srpskoj (A comparative overview of police training and education in the Republic of Serbia, Macedonia and the Republic of Srpska). *Bezbjednost- Policija- Građani (Safety - Police - Citizens), 8*(3–4), 37–56.

Pagon, M., & Lobnikar, B. (2000). Comparing Supervisor and Line Officer opinions about the code of silence: The case of Slovenia. In M. Pagon (Ed.), *Policing in Central and Eastern Europe: Ethics, integrity, and human rights* (pp. 197–209). Ljubljana: College of Police and Security Studies.

Pagon, M., & Lobnikar, B. (2004). Police integrity in Slovenia. In C. B. Klockars, S. Kutnjak Ivković, & M. R. Haberfeld (Eds.), *The contours of police integrity* (pp. 212–231). Thousand Oaks, CA: Sage.

Paoline, E. A., & Terrill, W. (2007). Police education, experience, and the use of force. *Criminal Justice and Behavior, 34*(2), 179–196.

Paoline, E. A., Myers, S. M., & Worden, R. E. (2000). Police culture, individualism, and community policing: Evidence from two police departments. *Justice Quarterly, 17*(3), 575–605.

Paoline, E. A., Terrill, W., & Rossler, M. T. (2015). Higher education, college degree major, and police occupational attitudes. *Journal of Criminal Justice Education, 26*(1), 49–73. https://doi.org/10.1080/105 11253.2014.923010.

Prenzler, T. (2009). *Police corruption: Preventing misconduct and maintaining integrity.* Boca Raton, FL: CRC.

Punch, M. (2009). *Police corruption. Deviance, accountability and reform in policing.* Cullompton: Willan.

Reuss-Ianni, E. (1983). *Two cultures of policing: Street cops and management cops.* New York: Transaction.

Ritzer, G., & Ryan, J. M. (2011). *The concise encyclopedia of sociology.* Oxford: Wiley-Blackwell.

Roberg, R., & Bonn, S. (2004). Higher education and policing: Where are we now? *Policing: An International Journal of Police Strategies & Management, 27*(4), 469–486.

Roberg, R., Crank, J., & Kuykendall, J. (2004). *Policija i društvo [Police and Society].* Sarajevo: Embassy of the United States of America, Office of Public Affairs.

Rothwell, G. R., & Baldwin, J. N. (2007). Whistle-blowing and the code of silence in police agencies policy and structural predictors. *Crime & Delinquency, 53*(4), 605–632.

Rydberg, J., & Terrill, W. (2010). The effect of higher education on police behavior. *Police Quarterly, 13*(1), 92–120.

Sherman, L. W., & Blumberg, M. (1981). Higher education and police use of deadly force. *Journal of Criminal Justice, 9*(4), 317–331.

Shernock, S. (1992). The effects of college education on professional attitudes among police. *Journal of Criminal Justice Education, 3*(1), 71–92.

Skolnick, J. H. (2002). Corruption and the blue code of silence. *Police Practice and Research, 3*(1), 7–19.

Skolnick, J. H., & Fyfe, J. (1993). *Above the law: Police and the excessive use of force.* New York: The Free Press.

Spahić, T. (2005). Bosna i Hercegovina: O reformskim tokovima u obuci i novim izazovima (Bosnia and Herzegovina: On reform paths in training and new challenges). In T. Spahić (Ed.), *Policijska obuka u Evropi: Jedinstvo u raznolikosti (Police Training in Europe: Unity in Diversity)* (pp. 118–127). Holzkirchen: Felix-Verlag.

Stoddard, E. R. (1968). The informal "Code" of police deviancy: A group approach to "Blue-Coat Crime". *The Journal of Criminal Law, Criminology, and Police Science, 59*(2), 201–213.

Telep, C. W. (2011). The impact of higher education on police officer attitudes toward abuse of authority. *Journal of Criminal Justice Education, 22*(3), 392–419.

U.S. Commission on Civil Rights. (2000). *Police practices and civil rights in New York City.* Washington, DC: Author.

United Nations Security Council. (2002). *Report of the Secretary-General on the United Nations Mission in Bosnia and Herzegovina no. S/2002/1314.* New York.

Vallmuur, B. (2015). Police integrity in Estonia. In S. Kutnjak Ivković & M. Haberfeld (Eds.), *Police integrity across the world.* New York: Springer.

Waddington, P. A. (1999). Police (canteen) culture: An appreciation. *British Journal of Criminology, 39*(2), 287–309.

Weisburd, D., Greenspan, R., Hamilton, E., Bryant, K. A., & Williams, H. (2001). *The abuse of police authority: A National Study of Police Officers Attitudes*. Washington, DC: Police Foundation.

Westmarland, L. (2005). Police ethics and integrity: Breaking the blue code of silence. *Policing and Society, 15*(2), 145–165.

Westmarland, L. (2008). Police cultures. In T. Newburn (Ed.), *Handbook of policing* (pp. 253–280). Cullompton: Willan.

Wisler, D. (2007). The international civilian police mission in Bosnia and Herzegovina: From democratization to nation-building. *Police Practice and Research, 8*(*3*), 253–268.

Worden, R. E. (1990). A badge and a baccalaureate: Policies, hypotheses, and further evidence. *Justice Quarterly, 7*(3), 565–592.

Wright, B. (2010). Civilianising the 'blue code'? An examination of attitudes to misconduct in the police extended family. *International Journal of Police Science and Management, 12*(3), 339–356.

Part III

Expanding the Police Integrity Methodology

Public Views About Police Misconduct and Police Integrity in a Comparative Perspective

Sanja Kutnjak Ivković, Irena Cajner Mraović,
Vladimir Božović, Barbara Prprović,
and Nikolina Nemec

Introduction

This chapter utilizes the police integrity theory and methodology originally developed by Klockars and Kutnjak Ivković (Klockars and Kutnjak Ivković 2004; Klockars et al. 1997, 2006) to assess public opinion about both police misconduct and the police. The original theory and methodology were developed primarily with the police and police officers in mind (Klockars and Kutnjak Ivković 2004; Klockars et al. 1997, 2006). Indeed, many empirical studies that followed included police officers as respondents and focused on police officers' assessments of

S. Kutnjak Ivković
School of Criminal Justice, Michigan State University, East Lansing, MI, USA
e-mail: kutnjak@msu.edu

I. C. Mraović
Department of Croatian Studies, University of Zagreb, Zagreb, Croatia

City Assembly of the City of Zagreb, Zagreb, Croatia

V. Božović
Department of Public Security at the Ministry of Interior, Belgrade, Serbia
e-mail: vladimir.bozovic@mup.gov.rs

B. Prprović (✉)
Croatian Red Cross Society, Čakovec, Croatia

N. Nemec
Department of Tourism, Entrepreneurship, and Development Projects, Ludbreg, Croatia

police integrity (for an overview, see, e.g., Klockars et al. 2004; Kutnjak Ivković and Haberfeld 2015; Kutnjak Ivković 2015), Shortly after the questionnaire was designed and used to survey U.S. police officers (Klockars et al. 1997), Klockars et al. (2002) envisioned a way in which a similar tool can be used for a public opinion survey. In particular, they have adjusted the original police corruption questionnaire to make it more suitable for the survey of general public. Despite these adjustments, the police integrity methodology has rarely been used to assess the public views about police misconduct. Even less frequent are the comparative studies of public opinion, allowing for in-depth cross-cultural comparisons of public views about police integrity and police misconduct.

This chapter focuses on public views about police misconduct and police integrity in two countries: Croatia and Serbia. Three decades ago, Croatia and Serbia were parts of the same country—the former Yugoslavia. Since the early 1990s and the dissolution of the former Yugoslavia, the ensuing transitional processes in the two countries took different turns and created separate and distinct political and social cultures in Croatia and Serbia. Using the police integrity survey methodology, this chapter compares and contrasts the public assessments of misconduct seriousness, appropriate discipline, and willingness to report. It also compares the perceptions of the public in these two countries in regard how

© Springer Nature Switzerland AG 2019
S. Kutnjak Ivković, M. R. Haberfeld (eds.), *Exploring Police Integrity*,
https://doi.org/10.1007/978-3-030-29065-8_9

the police in their country would evaluate misconduct seriousness, discipline that the police in their country would mete out, as well as the police officers' willingness to report misconduct in their country.

Public Views About Police Integrity

Although primarily developed to assess the level of police integrity in a police agency, the theory of police integrity and accompanying methodology (Klockars and Kutnjak Ivković 2004; Klockars et al. 1997, 2006) could be adjusted to serve as a measure of the public views of both police misconduct and the police. In particular, the citizens' own assessment of misconduct seriousness, appropriate discipline for misconduct, and their willingness to report could be used as a basis of their own views about police misconduct. On the other hand, a comparison of their own views of these measures with their estimates of how police officers would assess these behaviors can be utilized as their evaluations of the police.

Public Views About Police Integrity and Police Misconduct

The police integrity methodology opened possibilities and indeed resulted in many scholarly works assessing police integrity within police agencies across the world (see, e.g., Klockars et al. 2004; Kutnjak Ivković 2015; Kutnjak Ivković and Haberfeld 2015). While the study of police integrity through the opinions of police officers is widespread, as Table 1 shows, only a handful of studies explored public views about police misconduct and integrity (Bjerregaard and Lord 2004; Klockars and Kutnjak Ivković 1999; Klockars et al. 2002; Kutnjak Ivković 2004; Kutnjak Ivković and Klockars 2002; Kutnjak Ivković et al. 2002a, b, 2004; Meyer et al. 2013; Pagon et al. 2000; Rothwell and Baldwin 2006, 2007a, b; White 2008).

Following the design of the original police corruption questionnaire (Klockars and Kutnjak Ivković 2004; Klockars et al. 1997, 2000), to go beyond police corruption as the only gain-motivated opposite of police integrity, the second version of the questionnaire—the police integrity questionnaire—expanded its inquiry to the issues of police integrity at large (Klockars et al. 2004). However, all 14 studies on public views relied on the first questionnaire—the police corruption questionnaire (Table 1), while only one study (Kutnjak Ivković et al. 2002a) used both the police corruption questionnaire and the police integrity questionnaire. In other words, a true exploration of police integrity—that is, explorations via the police integrity questionnaire—is in its nascent stage.

Extant research explored public views of police misconduct in four countries (Table 1): Croatia (Klockars and Kutnjak Ivković 1999; Kutnjak Ivković 2004; Kutnjak Ivković and Klockars 2002; Kutnjak Ivković et al. 2002a, b, 2004; Pagon et al. 2000), Slovenia (Pagon et al. 2000; Kutnjak Ivković et al. 2002b), South Africa (Meyer et al. 2013), and the United States (Bjerregaard and Lord 2004; Klockars and Kutnjak Ivković 1999; Klockars et al. 2002; Kutnjak Ivković 2004; Kutnjak Ivković et al. 2002b; Rothwell and Baldwin 2006, 2007a, b; White 2008).

Of the 14 studies exploring public views, the overwhelming majority (11 out of 14; Table 1) relied on college students to represent public views. To make the student sample more similar to the general population in terms of their familiarity with police work, some of the scholars purposely selected students majoring in fields other than criminal justice or similar (see, e.g., Kutnjak Ivković and Klockars 2002; Kutnjak Ivković et al. 2002a, b; Kutnjak Ivković et al. 2004). Studies comparing the views of college students who are criminal justice majors with the views of college students majoring in other disciplines (e.g., Bjerregaard and Lord 2004) reported that the major is not a strong predictor of their evaluation of misconduct as seriousness. Similarly, Klockars et al. (2002, p. 190) found no statistically significant differences in the estimates of seriousness for criminal justice majors and other majors. The remaining studies (Rothwell and Baldwin 2006, 2007a, b) relied on civilian

Table 1 Studies exploring public views on police integrity

Study	Country	Sample	Questionnaire	Own assessment	Estimates of police assessment	Comparison with police	Cross-Country comparisons
Klockars and Kutnjak Ivković (1999)	Croatia, USA	504 Croatian college students; 1649 Croatian police officers; 375 U.S. college students; 3235 U.S. police officers	Police corruption	Seriousness	No	Yes	Yes (Croatia and U.S.A.)
Pagon et al. (2000)	Slovenia	254 Slovenian college students; 767 Slovenian police officers	Police corruption	Seriousness, discipline, willingness to report	Yes (seriousness, discipline, willingness to report)	Yes	No
Klockars et al. (2002)	U.S.A.	375 U.S. college students; 3235 U.S. police officers	Police corruption	Seriousness, discipline, willingness to report	No	Yes	No
Kutnjak Ivković and Klockars (2002)	Croatia	504 Croatian college students; 379 Croatian high-school students; 223 Croatian police-college students	Police corruption	Seriousness, discipline, willingness to report	Yes (seriousness, discipline, willingness to report)	No	No
Kutnjak Ivković et al. (2002a)	Croatia	854 Croatian college students	Police corruption; police integrity	Seriousness, discipline, willingness to report	Yes (seriousness, discipline, willingness to report)	No	No
Kutnjak Ivković et al. (2002b)	Croatia, Slovenia (U.S.A.)	504 Croatian college students; 1649 Croatian police officers; 215 Slovenian college students; 696 Slovenian police officers	Police corruption	Seriousness	No	Yes	Yes (Croatia, Slovenia, U.S.A.)

(continued)

Table 1 (continued)

Study	Country	Sample	Questionnaire	Own assessment	Estimates of police assessment	Comparison with police	Cross-Country comparisons
Bjerregaard and Lord (2004)	U.S.A.	443 U.S. college students	Police corruption	Seriousness	No	Yes (U.S. police officers)	No
Kutnjak Ivković (2004)	Croatia, U.S.A.	504 Croatian college students; 1649 Croatian police officers; 375 U.S. college students; 3235 U.S. police officers	Police corruption	Seriousness	No	Yes	Yes (Croatia and U.S.A.)
Kutnjak Ivković et al. (2004)	Croatia	534 Croatian college students (1996); 511 Croatian college students (2001); 1649 Croatian police officers; 379 Croatian high-school students; 223 Croatian police-college students (1995); 271 Croatian police-college students (2001)	Police corruption	Seriousness	No	Yes	No
Rothwell and Baldwin (2006)	U.S.A.	168 U.S. civilian employees; 197 U.S. police officers	Police corruption	Willingness to report	No	Yes	No
Rothwell and Baldwin (2007a)	U.S.A.	168 U.S. civilian employees; 197 U.S. police officers	Police corruption	Willingness to report	No	Yes	No
Rothwell and Baldwin (2007b)	U.S.A.	168 U.S. civilian employees; 197 U.S. police officers	Police corruption	Willingness to report	No	Yes	No
White (2008)	U.S.A.	265 U.S. college students; 3235 U.S. police officers	Police corruption	Seriousness, discipline, willingness to report	No	Yes	No
Meyer et al. (2013)	South Africa	186 SA college students; 160 SA police officers	Police corruption	Seriousness, discipline, willingness to report	No	Yes	No

employees ("employees from Georgia state, county, and city governments," Rothwell and Baldwin 2006, p. 226).

The police integrity methodology allows for the exploration of several different measures of police integrity: perceptions of misconduct seriousness, assessments of whether the behavior violates official rules, views about appropriate and expected discipline, and estimates of willingness to report misconduct. Most of these questions come in pairs, in which the first question is asking for the respondents' own views (hence the respondents' own evaluations of police integrity; Table 1) and the second question is asking the respondents to estimate the views of the majority of police officers from their agency (hence the respondents' assessment of the police; Table 1).

Regardless of whether seriousness was the only measure used in the study (e.g., Bjerregaard and Lord 2004; Klockars and Kutnjak Ivković 1999; Kutnjak Ivković 2004; Kutnjak Ivković et al. 2002b) or only one of the several measures used (e.g., Klockars et al. 2002; Kutnjak Ivković and Klockars 2002; Kutnjak Ivković et al. 2002a; Meyer et al. 2013; Pagon et al. 2000; White 2008), the results uniformly show that citizens evaluate police misconduct to vary greatly in terms of its seriousness. While the acceptance of holiday gifts and the acceptance of gratuities in general are typically perceived as the least serious forms of misconduct in the police corruption questionnaire, stealing money from a found wallet and stealing a watch from the crime scene are evaluated as the most serious forms (e.g., Klockars and Kutnjak Ivković 1999; Kutnjak Ivković and Klockars 2002; Kutnjak Ivković et al. 2002a). These relative perceptions of seriousness are consistent across countries as well (e.g., Klockars and Kutnjak Ivković 1999; Kutnjak Ivković and Klockars 2002; Kutnjak Ivković et al. 2002a; Meyer et al. 2013; Pagon et al. 2000).

Similarly, the views about appropriate discipline differed across scenarios (e.g., Kutnjak Ivković and Klockars 2002; Kutnjak Ivković et al. 2002a; Meyer et al. 2013). Although the preferred discipline was not the same across different countries, common elements emerged. Citizens perceived that accepting holiday gifts and accepting discounts on the beat should result in the most lenient discipline, if any discipline at all (e.g., no discipline or a public reprimand in Croatia: Kutnjak Ivković et al. 2002a; Kutnjak Ivković and Klockars 2002 and South Africa: Meyer et al. 2013), while accepting a bribe from a speeding motorist and stealing from a crime scene should result in the harshest discipline (e.g., suspension or fine in Croatia: Kutnjak Ivković et al. 2002a; Kutnjak Ivković and Klockars 2002 and suspension without pay or dismissal in South Africa: Meyer et al. 2013).

Finally, citizens also expressed a substantial degree of heterogeneity in their assessment of willingness to reporting misconduct (e.g., Kutnjak Ivković and Klockars 2002; Kutnjak Ivković et al. 2002a; Meyer et al. 2013; Pagon et al. 2000; Rothwell and Baldwin 2006, 2007a, b). Citizens' expressed willingness to report seems to be directly related to their estimates of misconduct seriousness (e.g., Kutnjak Ivković et al. 2002a). While the acceptance of holiday gifts and discount meals on the beat are evaluated as the least serious, at the same time, they seem to be the most likely to be protected by the code of silence (e.g., Kutnjak Ivković and Klockars 2002; Kutnjak Ivković et al. 2002a; Meyer et al. 2013). On the other hand, citizens evaluated stealing from a crime scene, stealing found property, and accepting a bribe from a speeding motorist as the most serious and, hence, seemingly the least likely to be protected by the code of silence (e.g., Kutnjak Ivković and Klockars 2002; Kutnjak Ivković et al. 2002a; Meyer et al. 2013).

Public Views About the Police

A few studies (3 out of 14; Table 1) also used the questions tapping into the respondents' views of the police and thus allowed us to glean how citizens assess that the police would evaluate police misconduct.

In the Croatian study (Kutnjak Ivković et al. 2002a) in which both the police corruption and police integrity questionnaires were used, the authors found that the relative order of seriousness (i.e., inter-scenario ranking based on seriousness estimates) is quite similar between the respondents' own evaluations of seriousness and how they assume that police officers would evaluate these same scenarios (Kutnjak Ivković et al. 2002a). Yet, the authors reported large differences between the citizens' views and their estimates of police officers' views (Kutnjak Ivković et al. 2002a). Regardless of whether the respondents filled out the police corruption questionnaire or the police integrity questionnaire, the students expected that police officers would evaluate each and every scenario as significantly less serious than they did themselves (Kutnjak Ivković et al. 2002a, p. 317). Similarly, students reported that the police officers would be much more likely to adhere to the code of silence then they themselves were reportedly willing to do (Kutnjak Ivković et al. 2002a, p. 318). Finally, while students thought that some discipline would be appropriate for the behaviors described in each and every scenario, they anticipated that the police would discipline in only 4 out of 11 scenarios in both the police corruption questionnaire and the police integrity questionnaire (Kutnjak Ivković et al. 2002a). When they did anticipate some discipline, students expected harsh discipline (e.g., more serious than a warning) in only one scenario per questionnaire—theft from a crime scene in the police corruption questionnaire and abuse of deadly force in the police integrity questionnaire (Kutnjak Ivković et al. 2002a, p. 318).

The results of the Croatian study (Kutnjak Ivković and Klockars 2002), involving a heterogeneous sample of students, revealed that the respondents' evaluations depended upon their prior theoretical or practical knowledge of policing. In particular, regular college students, college students from the Police College, and students from the Police High School evaluated misconduct seriousness in very similar terms (Kutnjak Ivković and Klockars 2002, p. 287). Yet, their evaluations of how police officers would assess the seriousness were strongly related to their experience (Kutnjak Ivković and Klockars 2002, p. 287):

> While college students assumed that, compared to them, police officers would underestimate the seriousness in the majority of the cases (8 out of 11),

> Police High School students and Police College students did so in only one or two cases … and in fact assumed that police officers would evaluate these cases in quite a similar way as they did.

Similar results were reported for the explorations of the code of silence. In particular, regular college students expected the code to be stronger among police officers than among the college students in a number of scenarios, while the students from both the Police College and the Police High School expected the police officers to share the code (i.e., express similar level of willingness to report as they do; Kutnjak Ivković and Klockars 2002, p. 288).

Cross-Cultural Comparisons of Public Views of the Police Integrity and the Police

The overall number of studies exploring public views about police integrity and the police is low. Among them, the number of studies that provide a cross-cultural comparison is even lower (3 out of 14 studies; Table 1). There are two common features across these studies. First, they all rely on the police corruption questionnaire and do not use the police integrity questionnaire (Table 1). Second, they explore only one measure of police integrity—evaluations of seriousness (3 out of 3 studies; Table 1).

In the earliest study, conducted by Klockars and Kutnjak Ivković (1999), the authors compared the respondents' own estimates of seriousness in two markedly different countries—the United States and Croatia. Although the differences in the U.S. college students' and Croatian college students' evaluations of misconduct seriousness were statistically significant in the majority of the scenarios, the authors reported that these differences were of substantive importance in only two of the scenarios (i.e., differences in the means exceeded .50 on a 5-point Likert scale; Klockars and Kutnjak Ivković 1999, p. 102). In both scenarios, Croatian students evaluated the scenarios as more serious than the U.S. counterparts did.

Kutnjak Ivković (2004) expanded the comparison further by exploring relative assessments of scenario seriousness. In particular, Kutnjak Ivković (2004) studied how the assessment of seriousness for one scenario compared to the assessment of seriousness for the other scenarios in the questionnaire. To ease the cross-country comparisons, the scenarios were ranked from the scenarios evaluated to be the least serious to the scenarios evaluated to be the most serious. The comparison yielded a high correlation of perceptions of scenario seriousness, revealing a great deal of similarity in the relative assessments of seriousness between the college students from Croatia and the United States (Kutnjak Ivković 2004).

In another project, Kutnjak Ivković et al. (2002b) compared perceptions of seriousness across three countries: Croatia, Slovenia, and the United States. The results showed that in the majority of scenarios (9 out of 11; Kutnjak Ivković et al. 2002b, p. 302), there were statistically significant differences between the absolute assessments of misconduct seriousness by the Croatian college students and Slovenian college students. On the other hand, only one scenario—running an off-duty security system business—reached the threshold of having substantively important differences as well (Kutnjak Ivković et al. 2002b). Very similar results were obtained when the assessments of college students from Croatia and Slovenia were compared to the assessments of college students from the United States (Kutnjak Ivković et al. 2002b). At the same time, the comparison revealed a great degree of similarity between the rankings based on the answers provided by the college students from all three countries (Kutnjak Ivković et al. 2002b).

Public Views and Support for the Police in Croatia and Serbia

In the late 1980s, Croatia and Serbia were parts of the same country—the former Yugoslavia—and were policed by the same militia. In the 1990s, both countries were involved in armed conflicts. Since the early 1990s, Croatia has gained independence, joined the European Union, and became a NATO member. Over the last several years, Serbia has been negotiating the EU membership. Therefore, the transitional paths pursued by the two countries have been evolving quite differently over the past quarter century.

In both countries, the police have being transitioning from the former communist militia and are now defined as public service agencies (e.g., Croatian Police Law 2000, 2011; Serbian Law on Police 2005, 2016). However, an open question remains about the degree to which the police adhere to the rule of law. According to Freedom House, in terms of the overall adherence to the political rights and civil liberties, Croatia has a high score of 87 out of 100 in 2016 and, in general, is considered to respect citizens' political rights and civil liberties (Freedom House 2017). In 2016, Serbia was also considered "free" and had a similar, but somewhat lower score (78 out of 100; Freedom House 2017). Among all the measures of political rights and civil liberties, the rule of law remains one of the more challenging issues in both countries (Croatia's score for the adherence to the rule of law is 11/16 and Serbia's respective score is 10/16; Freedom House 2017). Functioning of the government was an additional challenge for Serbia (Serbia' score is 7/12 in 2016, while Croatia's respective score is 10/12; Freedom House 2017).

World Bank publishes the Worldwide Governance Indicators (2017), which capture six dimensions of governance (voice and accountability[1]; political stability and lack of violence/terrorism[2]; government effectiveness[3];

---

[1]Voice and accountability "captures perceptions of the extent to which a country's citizens are able to participate in selecting their government, as well as freedom of expression, freedom of association, and a free media" (World Bank 2017).

[2]Political Stability and Absence of Violence/Terrorism "measures perceptions of the likelihood of political instability and/or politically-motivated violence, including terrorism" (World Bank 2017).

[3]Government effectiveness "captures perceptions of the quality of public services, the quality of the civil service and the degree of its independence from political pressures, the quality of policy formulation and implementation, and the credibility of the government's commitment to such policies" (World Bank 2017).

Table 2 Quality of Governance by Country

		Croatia			Serbia			Diff.	Diff.
	Year	# of Sources	Score	% Rank	# of Sources	Score	% Rank	score	rank
Voice and accountability	2005	11	0.43	62.02	9	−0.17	44.23	+0.60	+17.79
	2010	12	0.43	60.19	13	0.27	55.92	+0.16	+4.27
	2015	12	0.50	64.53	11	0.23	56.16	+0.27	+8.37
Political stability/ absence of terrorism	2005	6	0.43	59.42	6	−0.76	24.64	+1.19	+34.78
	2010	7	0.58	65.88	7	−0.44	30.81	+1.02	+35.07
	2015	9	0.58	63.33	8	0.23	55.71	+0.35	+7.62
Government effectiveness	2005	8	0.48	68.29	7	−0.31	44.88	+0.79	+23.41
	2010	9	0.63	70.33	9	−0.05	51.67	+0.68	+18.66
	2015	10	0.51	71.63	9	0.11	58.17	+0.40	+13.46
Regulatory quality	2005	10	0.49	65.20	8	−0.55	29.90	+1.04	+35.30
	2010	10	0.56	69.86	10	−0.02	52.63	+0.58	+17.23
	2015	12	0.36	64.90	11	0.14	56.73	+0.22	+8.17
Rule of Law	2005	12	0.09	55.50	10	−0.91	19.14	+1.00	+36.36
	2010	13	0.17	60.19	14	−0.40	41.71	+0.57	+18.48
	2015	14	0.20	62.50	13	−0.09	54.33	+0.29	+8.17
Control of corruption	2005	10	0.14	58.54	9	−0.38	44.39	+0.52	+14.15
	2010	11	−0.03	57.62	12	−0.29	49.05	+0.26	+8.57
	2015	13	0.20	63.46	12	−0.24	50.96	+0.44	+12.50

*Source: Worldwide Governance Indicators (2017), available at http://info.worldbank.org/governance/wgi/index.aspx#reports

regulatory quality[4]; rule of law[5]; and control of corruption[6]). Croatia and Serbia have had their indicators reported in 2005, 2010, and 2015 (Table 2). In all six dimensions of governance measured by the World Bank (2017), Croatia's scores are higher[7] (see Table 2) and the country's relative ranking is higher (see Table 2), indicating better functioning government. For about

one-half of these dimensions (political stability and absence of violence/terrorism, regulatory quality, and the rule of law) the differences between the two countries—both in terms of the score and ranking—were the largest in the earliest time period (2005) and the smallest in the most recent time period (2015). However, as Figs. 1, 2, and 3 indicate, this gap is primarily closing as a consequence of Serbia's improvement. In the most recent time period, the three critical dimensions for police integrity—control of corruption, rule of law, and government effectiveness—still show differences between the two countries, although the differences are not as large as they had been in the earliest time periods (Figs. 1, 2, and 3; Table 2).

Both countries are listed on the Transparency International Corruption Perceptions Index (CPI) as well.[8] This index evaluates countries based on how clean/corrupt the country is perceived

[4]Regulatory quality "captures perceptions of the ability of the government to formulate and implement sound policies and regulations that permit and promote private sector development" (World Bank 2017).

[5]Rule of law "captures perceptions of the extent to which agents have confidence in and abide by the rules of society, and in particular the quality of contract enforcement, property rights, the police, and the courts, as well as the likelihood of crime and violence" (World Bank 2017).

[6]Control of corruption "captures perceptions of the extent to which public power is exercised for private gain, including both petty and grand forms of corruption, as well as "capture" of the state by elites and private interests" (World Bank 2017).

[7]Each dimension is evaluated on a scale from −1 to +1 for each country (with higher numbers indicating better governance).

[8]In 1999–2000, Serbia was listed under "Yugoslavia." In 2003–2005, it was listed under "Serbia & Montenegro." From 2006, it is listed as "Serbia."

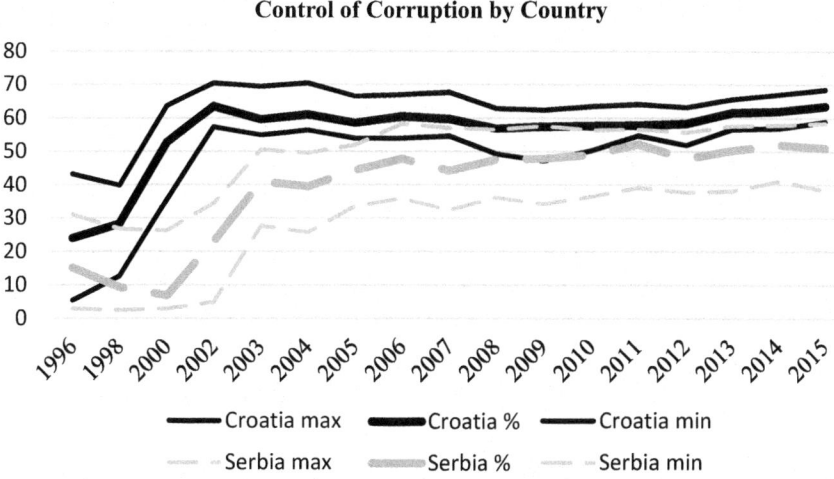

Fig. 1 Control of Corruption by Country. *Source: Worldwide Governance Indicators (2017), available at http://info.worldbank.org/governance/wgi/index.aspx#reports

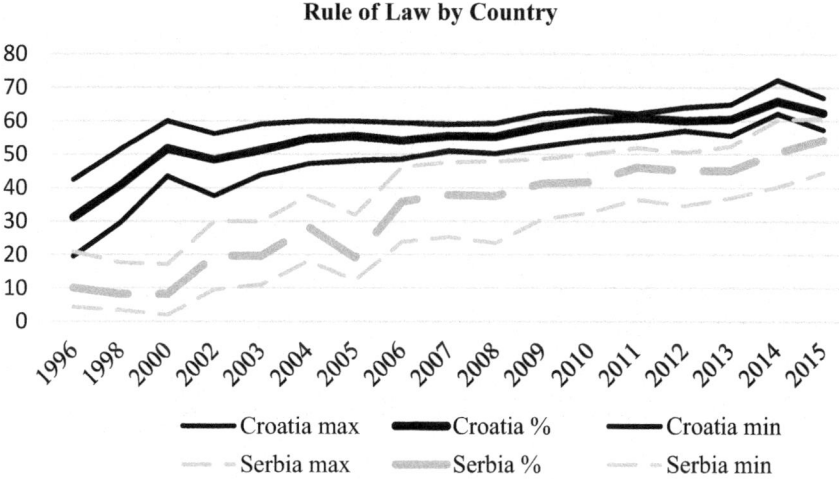

Fig. 2 Rule of Law by Country. *Source: Worldwide Governance Indicators (2017), available at http://info.worldbank.org/governance/wgi/index.aspx#reports

to be (Transparency International 2017). The Transparency International CPI covers a longer time period and provides more frequent data points (Table 3). Regardless of the measure used (e.g., score, rank, percent of countries with lower scores; Table 3), Croatia's measures indicate that the country is perceived as less corrupt than Serbia. The differences were particularly large in the early 2000s (Table 3).

If public opinion about the police and police integrity is based on the quality of governance and the lack of corruption, we would expect that in the

early periods the public in Croatia would be substantially more supportive of the government in general and the police in particular than the public in Serbia. However, we would expect more similar levels of public support for the police in the 2010s. World Values Survey (2017) included both countries only in the 1996 administration of the survey (Table 4). These 20-year old data indicate that the Croatian public showed substantially more support for the police, armed forces, the national government, and the church than the Serbian public did (the differences in the percent-

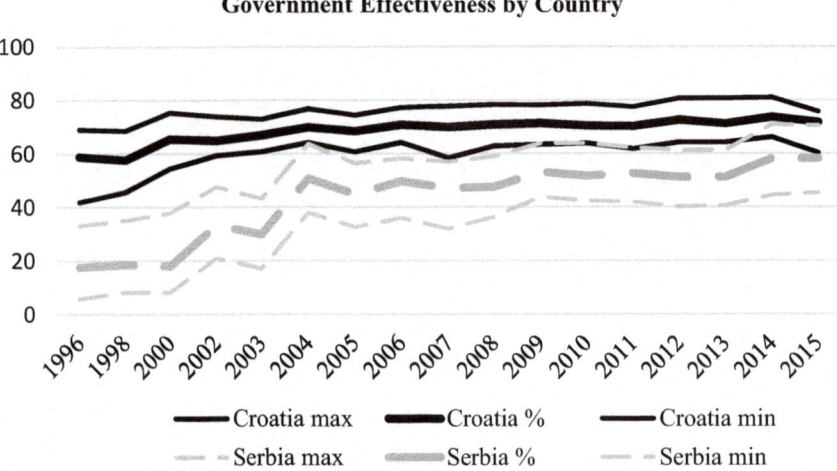

Fig. 3 Government Effectiveness by Country. *Source: Worldwide Governance Indicators (2017), available at http://info.worldbank.org/governance/wgi/index.aspx#reports

Table 3 Transparency International Corruption Perception Index by Country

	Croatia			Serbia			Diff. in scores
	Score	Rank	% Countries with lower scores	Score	Rank	% Countries with lower scores	
1999	2.7/10	74/99	25.3%	2.0/10	90/99	9.1%	+0.7
2000	3.7/10	51/90	43.3%	1.3/10	89/90	1.1%	+2.4
2001	3.9/10	47/91	48.4%	N/A	N/A	N/A	
2002	3.8/10	51/102	50.0%	N/A	N/A	N/A	
2003	3.7/10	59/133	55.6%	2.3/10	106/133	20.3%	+1.4
2004	3.5/10	67/145	53.8%	2.7/10	97/145	33.1%	+0.8
2005	3.4/10	70/158	55.7%	2.8/10	97/158	38.6%	+0.6
2006	3.4/10	69/163	57.7%	3.0/10	90/163	44.8%	+0.4
2007	4.1/10	64/179	64.2%	3.4/10	79/179	55.9%	+0.7
2008	4.4/10	62/180	65.5%	3.4/10	85/180	52.8%	+1.0
2009	4.1/10	66/180	63.3%	3.5/10	83/180	53.9%	+0.6
2010	4.1/10	62/178	65.2%	3.5/10	78/178	56.2%	+0.6
2011	4.0/10	66/182	63.7%	3.3/10	86/182	52.7%	+0.7
2012	46/100	62/174	64.4%	39/100	80/174	54.0%	+17
2013	49/100	57/175	67.4%	42/100	72/175	58.9%	+7
2014	48/100	61/174	64.9%	41/100	78/174	55.2%	+7
2015	51/100	50/167	70.1%	40/100	71/167	57.5%	+11
2016	49/100	55/176	68.8%	42/100	72/176	59.1%	+7

*Source: Transparency International Corruption Perceptions Index (2017), available at https://www.transparency.org/news/feature/corruption_perceptions_index_2016

ages of the respondents showing "a great deal" and "quite a lot" of support between the two countries were in the access of +15%; Table 3). On the other hand, the level of support for the courts, the parliament, and political parties was more similar across the two countries (the differences in the percentages of the respondents showing "a great deal" and "quite a lot" of support between the two countries were below 10%; Table 3). Unlike Croatia, Serbia was again included in the 2006 administration of the World Values Survey (Table 3); the 2006 data suggested that the level of support for the government, in particular the police, legal system, and parliament, has

Table 4 Confidence in the Governmental Institutions by Country

	Year	Country	Great deal (1)	Quite a lot (2)	1 + 2	Not very much	None at all	DK/no answer
Police	1996	Croatia	14.3%	45.1%	59.4%	32.5%	6.1%	2.0%
		Serbia	11.2%	32.0%	43.2%	34.9%	18.9%	3.0%
	2006	Serbia	3.9%	30.1%	34.0%	41.1%	22.1%	2.9%
Armed forces	1996	Croatia	27.9%	49.4%	77.3%	15.7%	5.4%	1.6%
		Serbia	23.0%	36.9%	59.9%	26.4%	10.9%	2.7%
	2006	Serbia	9.5%	41.0%	50.5%	32.9%	14.3%	2.4%
Legal system	1996	Croatia	9.3%	40.3%	49.6%	40.5%	6.4%	3.5%
		Serbia	12.0%	31.2%	43.2%	38.7%	15.5%	2.6%
Courts	2006	Serbia	2.4%	25.2%	27.6%	44.1%	25.2%	3.1%
National government	1996	Croatia	12.5%	38.0%	50.5%	34.5%	11.9%	3.1%
		Serbia	8.8%	24.1%	32.9%	37.0%	23.0%	7.1%
	2006	Serbia	1.6%	23.2%	24.8%	46.7%	25.2%	3.2%
Parliament	1996	Croatia	9.4%	30.4%	39.8%	41.6%	13.8%	4.7%
		Serbia	7.3%	21.9%	29.2%	36.6%	25.5%	8.8%
	2006	Serbia	0.9%	19.0%	19.9%	46.2%	30.6%	3.2%
Political parties	1996	Croatia	3.2%	17.9%	21.1%	53.1%	19.8%	6.0%
		Serbia	2.1%	13.8%	15.9%	41.5%	34.3%	8.3%
	2006	Serbia	0.9%	11.6%	12.5%	48.4%	35.9%	3.2%
Church	1996	Croatia	21.7%	34.4%	56.1%	28.3%	13.4%	2.3%
		Serbia	8.4%	27.6%	36.0%	34.2%	23.9%	5.9%
	2006	Serbia	15.7%	43.7%	59.4%	24.8%	12.0%	3.8%

∗Source: World Values Survey (2017), available at http://www.worldvaluessurvey.org/WVS DocumentationWV5.jsp

decreased, while the level of support for the religious institutions has increased (Table 3).

Similarly, the percentage of Croatian respondents participating in the 1996 International Crime Victimization Survey who said that the police were doing a good job in controlling crime was higher than the percentage of Serbian respondents (55.9% vs. 38.8%; Kutnjak Ivković 2008). Unfortunately, neither country was included in the more recent administrations of the ICVS. The substantial support for the Croatian police measurable in the mid-1990s surveys was associated with the overlap between the police and defense role that the police had played in the early 1990s (Kutnjak Ivković 2000; Kutnjak Ivković et al. 2002a). With the passage of time, the level of confidence in the Croatian police has started to decline. For example, while more than 60% of the Croatian respondents in the 1995 World Values Survey expressed a lot of confidence in the police, only about 46% did so in the 1999 European Values Survey (Kutnjak Ivković et al. 2002a, p. 313).

When the respondents were asked to assess how corrupt certain governmental organizations are, the results of the 2013 Transparency International Global Corruption Barometer suggested that the police in Croatia were viewed as less corrupt than the police in Serbia. Specifically, about one-half of the respondents in Croatia (51%; Table 5) and two-thirds (69%) of the respondents in Serbia evaluated the police to be "corrupt or extremely corrupt" (Transparency International 2013). Yet, among the nine governmental institutions included in the study, the police were considered to be among the less corrupt parts of the government in both countries (ranked as #6 in Croatia and 6.5 in Serbia; Table 5).

The experience with police bribery seems to be different as well. In 2013, about 3% of the Croatian respondents captured by the Transparency International Global Corruption Barometer (2013) reported paying a bribe to a police officer in the last year, while about 17% of the respondents in Serbia reported the same.

Table 5 Perceptions of Corruption of Governmental Institutions by Country

	Croatia		Serbia	
	Corrupt or extremely corrupt	Rank	Corrupt or extremely corrupt	Rank
Police	51%	6	69%	6.5
Military	24%	8	34%	8
Parliament/legislature	63%	4	69%	6.5
Judiciary	70%	2	82%	1
Political parties	72%	1	80%	3
Educational system	50%	7	70%	5
Medical and health services	61%	5	81%	2
Public servants	64%	3	78%	4

* Source: Transparency International (2013), available at https://www.transparency.org/gcb2013/country/?country=serbia

Table 6 Perceptions of Changes in Corruption by Country

	Croatia	Serbia
Stayed the same	51%	37%
Decreased	29%	55%
Increased	21%	8%

*Source: Transparency International (2013), available at https://www.transparency.org/gcb2013/country/?country=serbia

A couple of years later, one out of ten households in Croatia and one out of five households in Serbia reported paying a bribe when accessing basic services (Transparency International 2016, p. 17).

About one-half of Croatian citizens (51%) and, surprisingly, only about one-third of Serbian citizens (39%) thought that corruption is "one of the three biggest problems facing the country" (Transparency International 2016, p. 8). In 2013, the majority of the citizens surveyed in Croatia thought that the level of corruption remained the same in the last 3 years, while the majority of the citizens surveyed in Serbia thought that it has decreased somewhat (Table 6; Transparency International 2013). In 2016, about one-half of the citizens in both countries (57% in Croatia and 45% in Serbia; Transparency International 2016, p. 13) assessed their government's efforts in dealing with corruption negatively.

Methodology

Questionnaire

We used the police integrity questionnaire (Klockars et al. 2006) to measure public opinion about police and police misconduct. The questionnaire has 11 hypothetical scenarios describing police corruption (5 scenarios), use of excessive force (4 scenarios), and other forms of misconduct (2 scenarios). They are designed to present police officers with realistic scenarios that they may encounter on their beat (e.g., Klockars et al. 2006; Kutnjak Ivković 2015).

As we were about to survey the police officers in Croatia, we expanded the original police integrity questionnaire (Kutnjak Ivković 2009). We purposely added one scenario, the scenario that describes the acceptance of a bribe from a motorist caught speeding, from the police corruption questionnaire (Klockars et al. 2000). We reasoned that this is one of the critical forms of corruption in Eastern Europe (see, e.g., Frič & Walek 2001) and, hence, should be included in our study of police integrity. We also felt that the police integrity questionnaire focuses almost exclusively on police misconduct that occurs through active decision-making by the police officers and does not provide sufficient focus on the failure to react. Hence, we added two scenarios covering this topic. The first scenario outlines a partial failure to react, in which a police officer fails to record that the crime is a hate crime and instead enters it into the official form as a "regular" crime. The second scenario indicates a complete failure to react: it is a case in which a police officer decides not to intervene, that is, fail to intervene, when he notices juveniles writing graffiti on a wall (Kutnjak Ivković 2009).

In sum, the extended version of the police integrity questionnaire has 14 scenarios, of which 6 address police corruption, 4 use of excessive force, and 4 other forms of police misconduct. Scenarios dealing with police corruption were designed to match the police corruption typology developed by Roebuck and Barker (1974). In particular, there was one scenario addressing corruption of authority (Scenario 1: Free Meals/Gifts from Merchants), one scenario describing opportunistic theft (Scenario 3: Theft of Knife from Crime Scene), two scenarios featuring internal corruption (Scenario 5: Supervisor Offers Holiday for Errands; Scenario 8: Cover-Up of Police DUI & Accident), one scenario with a kickback (Scenario 9: Auto-Body Shop 5% Kickback), and one scenario with a shakedown (Scenario 13: Bribe from Speeding Motorist). These scenarios range substantially in their characteristics and, as empirical studies suggest, range in the perceived seriousness (e.g., Kutnjak Ivković 2015; Kutnjak Ivković and Haberfeld 2015).

The use of force scenarios were designed in a way that touches upon different parts of the use of force continuum. In particular, the verbal abuse scenario (Scenario 7- Verbal Abuse "Arrest an Asshole Day") is considered to be on the low end of the use of force continuum[9] because it depicts the (ab)use of verbal commands. On the opposite end of the use of force continuum is the (ab)use of deadly force (Scenario 4: Unjustifiable Use of Deadly Force). There is also a scenario between these two ends of the scale (Scenario 6: Officer Strikes Prisoner Who Hurt Partner), describing the use of excessive force in a retalia-

tory capacity. The fourth scenario that belongs to this category is also located somewhere between the two ends of the continuum, but it is different from other scenarios because it describes police misconduct by a supervisor (Scenario 11: Sgt. Fails to Halt Beating).

The remaining four scenarios are classified as "other forms of police misconduct." Three of them describe a failure to perform an official duty, either completely (Scenario 2: Failure to Arrest Friend with Warrant; Scenario 14: Failure to React to Graffiti) or partly (Scenario 12: Failure to Report Hate Crime). The last scenario in the group describes an intentional act of planting evidence and falsifying the official records (Scenario 10: False Report on Drug Dealer). This scenario, involving planting drugs on a known drug dealer and then falsifying official records to cover this activity, fits well the definition of noble-cause corruption (i.e., violations of procedural rules to obtain a morally high end).

The description of each scenario in the questionnaire was followed by seven identical questions. Four questions inquired about the respondents' own views and evaluations, while three additional questions probed the respondents' views of the police.

The respondents were first asked to assess how serious each misbehavior is. The possible answers to the question regarding seriousness ranged on a 5-point Likert scale from 1 = "not at all serious" to 5 = "very serious." The respondents were then asked whether they think that the behavior violates official rules. Possible answers were only three options: "yes," "no," and "I don't know" (Klockars et al. 2006, p. 141).

The next question focuses on the respondents' views of appropriate discipline for misconduct. To make the options more realistic for the respondents, we relied on the countries' available disciplinary options as prescribed by the respective laws (i.e., discipline that may legally be meted out for such behavior). Accordingly, the disciplinary options in the two countries do not match completely. The Croatian version of the questionnaire had 7 possible answers: 1 = none, 2 = written reprimand; 3 = fine up to 10% of salary; 4 = fine up to 20% of salary; 5 = no advancement in service for 2–4 years; 6 = reassignment into a

---

[9] Some authors argue that the use of force continuum does not involve any activities that do not create a physical contact between the police and the citizen. We follow the more dominant view that the use of force continuum starts with verbal commands.

lower-ranked assignment; and 7 = dismissal. The Serbian version of the questionnaire had 10 disciplinary options: 1 = none; 2 = written reprimand; 3 = fine up to 10% of salary; 4 = fine up to 20% of salary; 5 = fine up to 30% of salary; 6 = fine up to 40% of salary; 7 = reassignment into a lower-ranked assignment; 8 = no advancement in service for 2–4 years; 9 = demotion; 10 = dismissal. For the purpose of our analyses, we condensed these options by recoding the answers into four categories: 1 = none; 2 = written reprimand; 3 = some discipline other than dismissal; 4 = dismissal. Finally, the last question seeking the respondents' personal evaluations focused on their willingness to report misconduct. The respondents could have selected an answer from a 5-point Likert scale, ranging from 1 = "definitely would not report" to 5 = "definitely would report." There were also parallel questions asking the respondents to assess how police officers would view these behaviors.

To maximize the likelihood that the respondents would provide honest answers, we followed the police integrity methodology tradition (see, Klockars et al. 2006) and asked only two demographic questions. The first question asked the respondents about their gender, while the second question sought to elicit their vicarious knowledge about policing (whether somebody in the family is employed by the Ministry of the Interior).

In the tradition of the police integrity research methodology (see, Klockars et al. 2006), we reserved the last two questions in the entire survey for the questions about the truthfulness of their responses. In particular, we asked the respondents whether they anticipate that most police officers would provide honest answers to our questions and also whether the respondents themselves answered honestly. The answers by the respondents who did not answer affirmatively that they had provided honest answers were eliminated from further analyses.

The Samples

We used the same sampling strategy in both countries and surveyed college students attending the oldest, most prominent, and largest university in each country (University of Zagreb in Croatia and University of Belgrade in Serbia). We wanted to eliminate the possibility that the students, because of their major, would be more knowledgeable about policing and/or laws than the educated general public. Hence, we excluded schools such as Law, Sociology, Political Science, Criminology, Social Work, and similar disciplines from our sampling frame. Instead, we focused on schools from the STEM and similar fields. Thus, samples in both Croatia and Serbia are convenience samples of students from purposely selected schools. The samples were collected in 2016 during regular classes.

The Croatian sample includes 382 college students studying at the University of Zagreb. The Croatian students were surveyed at the Faculty of Physical Education (44.9%), the Faculty of Veterinary Medicine (18.9%), the Faculty of Mechanical Engineering (18.9%), and the Faculty of Transportation Engineering (17.3%; Table 7). The Serbian sample includes 404 college students studying at the University of Belgrade. The Serbian students in our sample were studying STEM disciplines: the Faculties of Mathematics (25.2%), Geography (10.9%), Chemistry (27.5%), and Biology (36.4%; Table 7).

In terms of their demographic characteristics (Table 8), respondents were similar along the dimension of family employed by the police, yet dissimilar along the dimension of gender. In particular, the percent of the respondents who had a family member employed in the police was

Table 7 Universities and Schools/Departments

	Frequency	Percent
University of Zagreb		
Kinesiology	171	44.9%
Veterinary medicine	72	18.9%
Mechanical engineering	72	18.9%
Transport and traffic sciences	66	17.3%
Total	*381*	*100.0%*
University of Belgrade		
Mathematics	102	25.2%
Geography	44	10.9%
Chemistry	111	27.5%
Biology	147	36.4%
Total	*404*	*100.0*

Table 8 Respondents' Demographic Characteristics

	Croatia		Serbia			
	Frequency	Percent	Frequency	Percent	Chi-square	Phi
Gender					84.49***	.330
Male	252	66.8%	135	33.8%		
Female	125	33.2%	264	66.2%		
Family employed by the police					3.32	−.065
Yes	21	5.6%	36	9.0%		
No	357	94.4%	366	91.0%		
Most police would answer honestly					8.62**	.105
Yes	75	19.8%	49	12.2%		
No	303	80.2%	354	87.8%		
Respondent answered honestly					.991	.036
Yes	363	96.0%	379	94.5%		
No	15	4.0%	22	5.5%		

similar in both countries—fewer than 10% of the respondents had family member(s) employed by the police (Table 8). On the other hand, while over two-thirds of the respondents in the Croatian sample are male (66.8%; Table 8), the same is true of only about one-third of the respondents in the Serbian sample (33.8%). Because prior research indicated that men and women may have somewhat different views about the police (e.g., confidence in the police, support for the police), we will control for gender in our analyses.

When explicitly asked whether they had provided honest answers while filling-out the questionnaire, the overwhelming majority of the respondents in both samples—over 95%—answered affirmatively (Table 8); the differences between two samples are very small (1%) and are not statistically significant. The situation is radically different with respect to the question about the police officers' likelihood of answering honestly; the overwhelming majority of the respondents in both countries (over 80%; Table 8), answered negatively (i.e., they anticipated that police officers would not provide honest answers). The respondents from the Croatian sample were more likely to say that the police officers would provide honest answers than the respondents from the Serbian sample (Table 8).

To control for potential gender effects in the cross-country comparisons, we have performed a linear regression of own estimates for each scenario with country and gender as independent variables.[10] For these measures, like seriousness, appropriate discipline, and willingness to report, we report means in the tables. These means were obtained by estimating a regression model in which gender is a control variable, thus addressing the issue of gender discrepancy across the two samples.

Results

Public Opinion About Police Misconduct

Public Evaluations of Misconduct Seriousness

The respondents from both countries exhibited a great deal of variability in how they perceived these forms of police misconduct. In particular, respondents' evaluations of seriousness varied greatly across scenarios, with the means ranging across the 5-point scale from the mid-point of the scale (about 3 for the lowest scores) to the serious end of the scale (close to 5 for the highest scores;

---

[10]Because the purpose of this chapter is compare country effects and not gender effects, we include gender in the analyses, but report just the means for seriousness by country and the corresponding values of *t*-tests.

Table 9 Respondents' Views of Misconduct Seriousness

	Croatia		Serbia			
	Mean	Rank	Mean	Rank	Difference	T-test
Police corruption						
Scenario 1: Free Meals/Gifts from Merchants	2.70	1	2.86	1	−.16	−1.77a
Scenario 3: Theft of Knife from Crime Scene	4.60	13	4.32	14	+.28	+3.83***
Scenario 5: Supervisor Offers Holiday for Errands	3.65	7	3.60	8	+.05	+.58
Scenario 8: Cover-Up of Police DUI & Accident	3.74	8	3.48	7	+.26	+2.67**
Scenario 9: Auto-Body Shop 5% Kickback	4.08	11	4.20	12	−.12	−.572
Scenario 13: Bribe from Speeding Motorist	3.86	9	3.92	10	−.06	−.397
Use of excessive force						
Scenario 4: Unjustifiable Use of Deadly Force	4.61	14	4.30	13	+.31	+2.84**
Scenario 6: Officer Strikes Prisoner Who Hurt Partner	3.32	4	3.32	5	.00	.03
Scenario 7: Verbal Abuse "Arrest an Asshole Day"	3.07	3	3.16	4	−.09	−.69
Scenario 11: Sgt. Fails to Halt Beating	3.36	5	2.95	2	+.41	+3.91***
Other forms						
Scenario 2: Failure to Arrest Friend with Warrant	4.35	12	4.13	11	+.22	+2.85**
Scenario 10: False Report on Drug Dealer	4.05	10	3.69	9	+.36	+3.76***
Scenario 12: Failure to Report Hate Crime	3.54	6	3.33	6	+.21	+2.25**
Scenario 14: Failure to React to Graffiti	2.82	2	3.14	3	−.32	−1.84a

Table 9). The respondents from two countries agreed both that the same two scenarios (Scenario 1: Free Meals/Gifts from Merchants; Scenario 14: Failure to React to Graffiti) were the least serious and that the same two scenarios (Scenario 3: Theft of Knife from Crime Scene; Scenario 4: Unjustifiable Use of Deadly Force; Table 9) were the most serious in the questionnaire.

Among scenarios describing various forms of police corruption, the respondents from both countries tended to regard opportunistic thefts (Scenario 3: Theft of Knife from Crime Scene), kickbacks (Scenario 9: Auto-Body Shop 5% Kickback) and shakedowns (Scenario 13: Bribe from Speeding Motorist) as the most serious. Indeed, as Roebuck and Barker (1974) argued, these are the behaviors to which most police agencies will react negatively and, if some discipline were to follow, that discipline would be harsh. On the other hand, respondents from both countries viewed corruption of authority— accepting small gifts from merchants (Scenario 1: Free Meals/Gifts from Merchants)—as the least serious form of corruption. Finally, respon-

dents from both countries consistently assessed the seriousness of the two scenarios dealing with internal corruption (Scenario 5: Supervisor Offers Holiday for Errands; Scenario 8: Cover-Up of Police DUI & Accident) to be between these extremes (Table 9).

Among the four scenarios describing the use of excessive force, the respondents from both countries evaluated the abuse of deadly force (Scenario 4: Unjustifiable Use of Deadly Force) as the most serious. Specifically, while the mean values for the other three scenarios describing the use of excessive force and/or verbal abuse (Scenario 6: Officer Strikes Prisoner Who Hurt Partner; Scenario 7: Verbal Abuse "Arrest an Asshole Day;" Scenario 11: Sgt. Fails to Halt Beating) are clustered together, within .30 point difference, the abuse of deadly force scenario is far removed from this cluster by one whole point on a 5-point scale (Table 9). It is particularly surprising that the verbal abuse of a citizen—a behavior on the lowest end of the use of force continuum—is not farther removed from the two scenarios describing the use of actual physical force (Scenario 6: Officer

Strikes Prisoner Who Hurt Partner; Scenario 11: Sgt. Fails to Halt Beating; Table 9). In fact, verbal abuse of a citizen (Scenario 7: Verbal Abuse "Arrest an Asshole Day") has been evaluated at the same level of seriousness or even as slightly more serious than a supervisor's failure to stop the use of physical force (Scenario 11: Sgt. Fails to Halt Beating) in Serbia.

Finally, among the four scenarios describing the other forms of police misconduct, both groups of respondents evaluated a failure to execute an arrest warrant on a friend (Scenario 2: Failure to Arrest Friend with Warrant) and planting drugs and falsifying an official record (Scenario 10: False Report on Drug Dealer) as substantially more serious than omitting to classify a crime as hate crime (Scenario 12: Failure to Report Hate Crime) or failing to react to graffiti (Scenario 14: Failure to React to Graffiti).

The evaluations provided by the respondents from the two countries were also similar in another way, along the metric of relative seriousness. Based on the mean values for each scenario, we ranked the scenarios for each country from the one with the lowest mean to the one with the highest mean. A bivariate correlation of the ranking from each country indicates that these relative rankings are very closely connected (Spearman's rho = .956, p < .001).

An exploration of potential cross-country differences yielded the big picture: in about one-half of the scenarios (7 out of 14 scenarios; Table 9), there are statistically significant differences between the evaluations of seriousness by our Croatian and Serbian samples. In all of these scenarios with statistically significant differences (Scenario 2: Failure to Arrest Friend with Warrant; Scenario 3: Theft of Knife from Crime Scene; Scenario 4: Unjustifiable Use of Deadly Force; Scenario 8: Cover-Up of Police DUI & Accident; Scenario 10: False Report on Drug Dealer; Scenario 11: Sgt. Fails to Halt Beating; Scenario 12: Failure to Report Hate Crime; Table 9), respondents from Croatia evaluated the behaviors as more serious. The differences are statistically significant among all three forms of police misconduct—police corruption, use of excessive force, and other forms of police misconduct (Table 9). However, while statistically

significant, none of these differences are very large (all are below the cut-off of .50) and, hence, are not perceived to be substantively important (e.g., Klockars et al. 2006).

Public Views About Appropriate Discipline

Disciplinary scales were not identical across the countries. Accordingly, we recoded the answers to create similar categories, as described in the methodology section. The scale common to both countries ranged from 1 = no discipline to 4 = dismissal.

The results show that the choice of the preferred discipline varied across scenarios. The mean values for appropriate discipline by the Croatian respondents varied from about 1.77 for a failure to react to graffiti (Scenario 14: Failure to React to Graffiti) to 3.55 for the theft from a crime scene (Scenario 3: Theft of Knife from Crime Scene), or a spread of 1.78. At the same time, the range of means is somewhat narrower for the Serbian respondents with a spread of being (only) 1.26: the mean values ranged from about 2.01 for the same scenario describing a failure to react to graffiti (Scenario 14: Failure to React to Graffiti) to about 3.27 for the scenario describing the abuse of deadly force (Scenario 4: Unjustifiable Use of Deadly Force; Table 10).

According to the respondents from both countries, among the scenarios describing various forms of corruption, the same three scenarios (Scenario 3: Theft of Knife from Crime Scene; Scenario 9: Auto-Body Shop 5% Kickback; Scenario 13: Bribe from Speeding Motorist) would merit the harshest discipline. The mean values for these scenarios are around 3 out of 4 in both countries, indicating that many of the respondents thought that some discipline other than dismissal should be appropriate for such behaviors. On the other hand, the mean values for the rest of police corruption scenarios (particularly for the scenario describing the acceptance of gratuities) are lower in both countries, suggesting that the respondents perceived that such behaviors deserve milder discipline.

Among the scenarios illustrating the use of excessive force, the abuse of deadly force (Scenario 4: Unjustifiable Use of Deadly Force) is the only scenario in which the respondents from both countries thought that some discipline or even dismissal would be appropriate (Table 10). In the rest of the use of excessive force scenarios (Scenario 6: Officer Strikes Prisoner Who Hurt Partner; Scenario 7: Verbal Abuse "Arrest an Asshole Day;" Scenario 11: Sgt. Fails to Halt Beating), the respondents from both countries thought that less severe discipline would be more appropriate (Table 10). The mean values of about 2 imply that this discipline would be consistent with the severity of a written reprimand.

Finally, among the four scenarios describing other forms of police misconduct, a failure to execute an arrest warrant on a friend (Scenario 2: Failure to Arrest Friend with Warrant) is the only scenario in which the means suggest that harsher discipline or, potentially even a dismissal, may be viewed as the appropriate discipline (Table 10). On the other hand, all of the other scenarios in this group (Scenario 10: False Report on Drug Dealer; Scenario 12: Failure to Report Hate Crime; Scenario 14: Failure to React to Graffiti)

are not perceived to merit harsh discipline by the respondents from both Croatia and Serbia.

Furthermore, similarities in the assessments of appropriate discipline for such behaviors carry over into the relative assessments as well. Specifically, the bivariate correlation of the scenario rankings for each country based on the harshness of the appropriate discipline (Table 10) showed a very strong correlation in the rankings by the two countries (Spearman's rho = .931, p < .001), indicating that the relative perceptions of appropriate discipline are very similar as well.

Cross-country comparisons resulted in differences as well. In the majority of the scenarios (9 out of 14 or about two-thirds), there were statistically significant differences across the two countries (Table 10). However, these differences were not large enough to quality as substantively important differences in any of the scenarios (e.g., Klockars et al. 2006).

The directions of the differences were split between the two countries: in about one-half (5 out of 9 scenarios), the respondents from Serbia advocated for somewhat harsher discipline than

Table 10 Respondents' Views about Appropriate Discipline

	Croatia		Serbia			
	Mean	Rank	Mean	Rank	Difference	T-test
Police corruption						
Scenario 1: Free Meals/Gifts from Merchants	2.11	3	2.41	6	−.30	−4.454∗∗∗
Scenario 3: Theft of Knife from Crime Scene	3.55	14	3.23	12	.32	6.334∗∗∗
Scenario 5: Supervisor Offers Holiday for Errands	2.45	7	2.67	8.5	−.22	−3.221∗∗
Scenario 8: Cover-Up of Police DUI & Accident	2.64	8	2.55	7	.09	1.393
Scenario 9: Auto-Body Shop 5% Kickback	3.10	11	2.96	10	.14	2.259∗
Scenario 13: Bribe from Speeding Motorist	3.04	10	3.02	11	.02	.272
Use of excessive force						
Scenario 4: Unjustifiable Use of Deadly Force	3.50	13	3.27	14	.23	3.606∗∗∗
Scenario 6: Officer Strikes Prisoner Who Hurt Partner	2.18	4	2.34	5	−.16	−2.243∗
Scenario 7: Verbal Abuse "Arrest an Asshole Day"	1.97	2	2.17	2	−.20	−2.970∗∗
Scenario 11: Sgt. Fails to Halt Beating	2.29	6	2.24	3	.05	.672
Other forms						
Scenario 2: Failure to Arrest Friend with Warrant	3.32	12	3.25	13	.07	1.323
Scenario 10: False report on Drug Dealer	2.87	9	2.67	8.5	.20	2.744∗∗
Scenario 12: Failure to Report Hate Crime	2.24	5	2.30	4	−.06	−.912
Scenario 14: Failure to React to Graffiti	1.77	1	2.01	1	−.24	−3.687∗∗∗

the Croatian respondents did (Table 10). These scenarios were typically evaluated to be on the least serious side (e.g., Scenario 1: Free Meals/Gifts from Merchants; Scenario 7: Verbal Abuse "Arrest an Asshole Day;" Scenario 14: Failure to React to Graffiti; Table 10). On the other hand, in about one-half (4 out of 9 scenarios) of the scenarios, the respondents from Croatia advocated for somewhat harsher discipline than the Serbian respondents did (Table 10). By contrast, these scenarios tended to include some of the most serious scenarios (e.g., Scenario 3: Theft of Knife from Crime Scene; Scenario 4: Unjustifiable Use of Deadly Force; Scenario 9: Auto-Body Shop 5% Kickback; Table 10).

Public Assessments of Own Willingness to Report

The respondents' expressed willingness to report misconduct in both countries varied substantially across behaviors. On the one end of the scale are the scenarios describing the behavior that had the highest chances of not being reported, such as the acceptance of gratuities (Scenario 1: Free Meals/

Gifts from Merchants) and failing to react to juveniles spotted writing the graffiti (Scenario 14: Failure to React to Graffiti). On the other end of the scale are the scenarios with the highest chances of being reported, such as stealing from a crime scene (Scenario 3: Theft of Knife from Crime Scene) and the unjustified use of deadly force (Scenario 4: Unjustifiable Use of Deadly Force; Table 11). In both countries, the respondents' expressed willingness to report was very closely associated with their perceptions about misconduct seriousness (Spearman's rho = .972, $p < .001$ for Croatia; Spearman's rho = .964, $p < .001$ for Serbia).

Among the scenarios describing police corruption, one scenario stood out in both countries: the respondents from both Croatia and Serbia said that they would be most likely to report a police officer who stole from a crime scene (Scenario 3: Theft of Knife from Crime Scene; Table 11). That is the only scenario placed well into the reporting side of the scale (the end of scale had a value of 5), whereas other scenarios are around the midpoint of the scale (value of 3)

Table 11 Respondents' Own Willingness to Report

	Croatia		Serbia			
	Mean	Rank	Mean	Rank	Difference	T-test
Police corruption						
Scenario 1: Free Meals/Gifts from Merchants	1.97	1	2.16	1	−.19	−2.020*
Scenario 3: Theft of Knife from Crime Scene	4.02	13	3.81	13.5	.21	1.991*
Scenario 5: Supervisor Offers Holiday for Errands	2.71	6	2.82	6.5	−.11	−.991
Scenario 8: Cover-Up of Police DUI & Accident	3.18	8.5	2.89	8	.29	2.624**
Scenario 9: Auto-Body Shop 5% Kickback	3.56	12	3.49	12	.07	.677
Scenario 13: Bribe from Speeding Motorist	3.18	8.5	3.44	11	−.04	−2.320*
Use of excessive force						
Scenario 4: Unjustifiable Use of Deadly Force	4.24	14	3.81	13.5	.43	4.280***
Scenario 6: Officer Strikes Prisoner Who Hurt Partner	2.61	4	2.77	4	.16	−1.364
Scenario 7: Verbal Abuse "Arrest an Asshole Day"	2.67	5	2.82	6.5	−.15	−1.251
Scenario 11: Sgt. Fails to Halt Beating	2.54	3	2.56	3	−.02	−.145
Other forms						
Scenario 2: Failure to Arrest Friend with Warrant	3.48	11	3.33	10	.15	1.410
Scenario 10: False Report on Drug Dealer	3.47	10	3.11	9	.36	3.039**
Scenario 12: Failure to Report Hate Crime	2.88	7	2.80	4	.08	.707
Scenario 14: Failure to React to Graffiti	2.04	2	2.31	2	−.27	−2.673**

or into the non-reporting side of the scale. The exact opposite is the treatment for the acceptance of gratuities (Scenario 1: Free Meals/Gifts from Merchants), regarding which the respondents from both countries seemed least likely to say that they would report a police officer who accepted free meals and small gifts from merchants.

Similarly to police corruption, the respondents from both countries singled out only one scenario dealing with the use of excessive force (Scenario 4: Unjustifiable Use of Deadly Force). Not surprisingly, the respondents from both Croatia and Serbia were the most likely to say that they would report a police officer who had abused deadly force (Table 11). Although this scenario has been perceived as the most likely to be reported in the whole questionnaire, the mean values are not close to the reporting side of the scale (value of 5). In fact, they are even below 4 in Serbia (Table 11). The remaining three scenarios describing various other incidents with the use of force and/or verbal abuse of citizens (Scenario 6: Officer Strikes Prisoner Who Hurt Partner; Scenario 7: Verbal Abuse "Arrest an Asshole Day;" Scenario 11: Sgt. Fails to Halt Beating) all have means in the non-reporting side of the scale, suggesting that the respondents in both countries would be unlikely to report police officers who engaged in such behaviors.

Finally, among the other forms of misconduct (Scenario 2: Failure to Arrest Friend with Warrant; Scenario 10: False Report on Drug Dealer; Scenario 12: Failure to Report Hate Crime; Scenario 14: Failure to React to Graffiti), the mean values are around the mid-point or in the non-reporting side of the scale (Table 11). Although there is some variation across these scenarios in the respondents' expressed willingness to report, the conclusion in both countries is the same: quite likely, these kinds of behaviors will be protected by the code of silence.

In addition, cross-country comparisons have revealed other similarities. In particular, the way that the respondents assessed how likely they were to report for one scenario compared to the other scenarios—that it, the relative measure of their willingness to report (i.e., rankings)—seems to be very similar across the two countries. A

bivariate correlation of the ranking from each country suggests that the relative rankings are highly correlated (Spearman's rho = .960, $p < .001$).

Cross-country comparisons revealed differences as well. The findings imply that the respondents from Serbia evaluated the scenarios in the questionnaire on a somewhat narrower scale (from 2.16 to 3.81) than the respondents from Croatia did (from 1.97 to 4.02). Furthermore, in about one-half of the scenarios (7 out of 14 scenarios; Table 11), there are statistically significant differences between the respondents' expressed willingness to report between the two countries, but the conclusion is not straightforward. In four out of seven scenarios (Scenario 3: Theft of Knife from Crime Scene; Scenario 8: Cover-Up of Police DUI & Accident; Scenario 4: Unjustifiable Use of Deadly Force; Scenario 10: False Report on Drug Dealer), some of which have been evaluated as the most serious misbehaviors (such as stealing from a crime scene, abusing deadly force, and falsifying the official reports), the Croatian respondents seemed more willing to say that they would report. By contrast, in three out of seven scenarios (Scenario 1: Free Meals/Gifts from Merchants; Scenario 13: Bribe from Speeding Motorist; Scenario 14: Failure to React to Graffiti), two of which are evaluated as the least serious in the group, the respondents from Serbia seemed more likely to say that they would report. However, the size of the differences between the means for the Croatian and Serbian respondents was in not large in any of the scenarios, thus failing to reach the level of substantively significant differences (e.g., Klockars et al. 2006).

Public Opinion About Police Integrity

Our cross-country comparisons of the results from the two samples focus on three elements of public opinion about the police: the respondents' estimates of police officers' assessments of seriousness, the respondents' perceptions of discipline that a police agency would mete out for misconduct, and the respondents' estimates of police officers' willingness to report. The data are presented by the type of police misconduct, while controlling for the respondents' gender.

Public Estimates of the Police Officers' Evaluations of Misconduct Seriousness

While the respondents from both countries assumed that the police officers' assessments of misconduct seriousness would vary across the scenarios, the extent of this variation was not large. Among scenarios describing various forms of police corruption, the respondents from both countries assumed that police officers would evaluated an opportunistic theft (Scenario 3: Theft of Knife from Crime Scene) and a kickback (Scenario 9: Auto-Body Shop 5% Kickback) as the most serious and the acceptance of gratuities (Scenario 1: Free Meals/Gifts from Merchants) as the least serious. However, the values of the actual means suggested that the respondents from both Croatia and Serbia assumed that only an opportunistic theft (Scenario 3: Theft of Knife from Crime Scene) would be evaluated by police officers in their countries as serious (the mean is well above the midpoint of 3.0 in Croatia and barely above the mid-point in Serbia; Table 12).

According to our respondents from both countries, the police would probably not evaluate as serious all other forms of corruption, including some serious forms of police corruption such as accepting a bribe from a motorist caught speeding (Scenario 13: Bribe from Speeding Motorist) and a kickback (Scenario 9: Auto-Body Shop 5% Kickback).

According to our respondents from both countries, police officers in their countries would find the abuse of deadly force (Scenario 4: Unjustifiable Use of Deadly Force) as the most serious form of the use of excessive force in the questionnaire (Table 12). Although this finding is by no means surprising, what is surprising is that the mean values for this scenario are not closer to 5, the end point of the scale. In fact, the mean value in Croatia is about 4 (4.14; Table 12), while in Serbia it is even below 4 (3.70; Table 12). All other scenarios describing the abuse of excessive force and/or verbal abuse (Scenario 6: Officer Strikes Prisoner Who Hurt Partner; Scenario 7: Verbal Abuse "Arrest an Asshole Day;" Scenario 11: Sgt. Fails to Halt Beating), some of which include direct or vicarious responsibility to physically

Table 12 Respondents' Estimates of Police Officers' Assessments of Seriousness

	Croatia		Serbia			
	Mean	Rank	Mean	Rank	Difference	T-test
Police corruption						
Scenario 1: Free Meals/Gifts from Merchants	2.27	3	2.18	3	.09	1.043
Scenario 3: Theft of Knife from Crime Scene	3.56	13	3.17	12	.39	2.496*
Scenario 5: Supervisor Offers Holiday for Errands	2.57	6	2.54	8	.03	.231
Scenario 8: Cover-Up of Police DUI & Accident	2.60	9	2.43	6.5	.17	1.777a
Scenario 9: Auto-Body Shop 5% Kickback	3.03	11	2.97	11	.06	.596
Scenario 13: Bribe from Speeding Motorist	2.59	8	2.43	6.5	.16	1.317
Use of excessive force						
Scenario 4: Unjustifiable Use of Deadly Force	4.14	14	3.70	14	.44	4.697***
Scenario 6: Officer Strikes Prisoner Who Hurt Partner	2.18	2	2.24	5	−.06	−.388
Scenario 7: Verbal Abuse "Arrest an Asshole Day"	1.98	1	1.90	1	.08	.957
Scenario 11: Sgt. Fails to Halt Beating	2.37	4	2.14	2	.23	2.258*
Other forms						
Scenario 2: Failure to Arrest Friend with Warrant	3.33	12	3.24	13	.09	.535
Scenario 10: False Report on Drug Dealer	3.01	10	2.77	10	.24	2.289*
Scenario 12: Failure to Report Hate Crime	2.58	7	2.62	9	.04	.272
Scenario 14: Failure to React to Graffiti	2.40	5	2.22	4	.18	1.989*

injuring a citizen, are perceived to be evaluated by the police officers as very mild: the mean values are all below 3, the mid-point of the scale (Table 12). According to the respondents from both countries, even a direct act of striking a handcuffed arrestee (Scenario 6: Officer Strikes Prisoner Who Hurt Partner) is not going to be viewed by the police as something serious.

Just like it was the case for scenarios describing police corruption and excessive force, the respondents assumed that police officers would not perceive as very serious neither of the four scenarios describing other forms of police misconduct (Table 12). The respondents assumed that failing to execute an arrest warrant (Scenario 2: Failure to Arrest Friend with Warrant) would be evaluated as the most serious in the group. However, as the analysis moves from the relative assessments of seriousness (i.e., how it compares to the other scenarios in the same group) to the more absolute assessments of seriousness (i.e., what the mean value is), the results indicate that the respondents in both countries assumed that police officers would not evaluate neither of these four behaviors as very serious (the mean values are close or below the mid-point of 3; Table 12). The mean values were at or below the median even in the scenario including noble-cause planting of evidence and falsification of official documents (Scenario 10: False Report on Drug Dealer; Table 12).

Another dimension of similarity between the estimates of police officers' evaluations of seriousness across the two countries is the way the scenarios are ranked in each country. Based on the mean values for each scenario, we ranked the scenarios for each country from the one with the lowest mean to the one with the highest mean. These two rankings are very similar, as a bivariate correlation of the rankings indicated (Spearman's rho = .928, p < .001).

Finally, a cross-country exploration yielded a few differences. The bottom line is that the estimates of how police officers would evaluate these scenarios in terms of their seriousness were mostly similar across the two countries. In other words, there were statistically significant differences in only about one-third of the scenarios (5

out of 14 or 35.7%; Table 12), but the differences did not reach the point of substantive importance (above the cut-off of .50; Klockars et al. 2006). In all five scenarios, the respondents from Croatia expected that police officers would evaluate them as more serious than the respondents from Serbia did (Table 12). Most of these scenarios (Scenario 3: Theft of Knife from Crime Scene; Scenario 4: Unjustifiable Use of Deadly Force; Scenario 10: False Report on Drug Dealer) describe the most serious forms of misconduct both in general and in their own subcategory.

Public Views About Expected Discipline

Although the respondents' opinions about discipline they expect police agencies to mete out varied across the scenarios (Table 13), the spread is not very large (below 2 on a 4-point scale). Specifically, the mean values for the expected discipline varied from about 3 (3.18 for Croatian respondents and 3.07 for Serbian respondents; Table 13) for an abuse of deadly force (Scenario 4: Unjustifiable Use of Deadly Force) to about 1.5 (1.42 for Croatian respondents and 1.59 for Serbian respondents; Table 13) for the verbal abuse of a citizen (Scenario 7: Verbal Abuse "Arrest an Asshole Day"). The spread is somewhat larger in Croatia (59% or 1.76 points out of 3.00 points on the scale) than in Serbia (49% or 1.48 points out of 3.00 points on the scale).

The only police corruption scenario in the questionnaire in which the respondents from both countries expected police agencies to react by meting out some harsher discipline is the scenario describing an opportunistic theft (Scenario 3: Theft of Knife from Crime Scene). Even in the scenarios describing an acceptance of a bribe (Scenario 13: Bribe from Speeding Motorist) or a kickback (Scenario 9: Auto-Body Shop 5% Kickback), the mean values are below or close to the midpoint of the scale of 2.5 (Table 13), suggesting that the respondents in both countries expected some form of milder discipline. In the remaining three scenarios (Scenario 1: Free Meals/Gifts from Merchants; Scenario 5: Supervisor Offers Holiday for Errands; Scenario 8: Cover-Up of Police DUI & Accident; Table 13), the means are at or even below 2, indicating that

Table 13 Respondents' Estimates of Expected Discipline

	Croatia		Serbia			
	Mean	Rank	Mean	Rank	Difference	T-test
Police corruption						
Scenario 1: Free Meals/Gifts from Merchants	1.64	3	1.75	3	.11	−1.724a
Scenario 3: Theft of Knife from Crime Scene	2.95	13	2.65	13	.30	4.066***
Scenario 5: Supervisor Offers Holiday for Errands	1.81	6	2.03	8	−.22	−3.087**
Scenario 8: Cover-Up of Police DUI & Accident	1.96	8	1.90	7	.06	.874
Scenario 9: Auto-Body Shop 5% Kickback	2.42	10	2.33	11	.09	1.111
Scenario 13: Bribe from Speeding Motorist	2.46	11	2.32	10	.14	1.824a
Use of excessive force						
Scenario 4: Unjustifiable Use of Deadly Force	3.18	14	3.07	14	.11	1.628
Scenario 6: Officer Strikes Prisoner Who Hurt Partner	1.73	5	1.79	4	.06	.823
Scenario 7: Verbal Abuse "Arrest an Asshole Day"	1.42	1	1.59	1	−.17	−2.844**
Scenario 11: Sgt. Fails to Halt Beating	1.92	7	1.80	5	.12	1.531
Other forms						
Scenario 2: Failure to Arrest Friend with Warrant	2.64	12	2.49	12	.15	1.925a
Scenario 10: False Report on Drug Dealer	2.26	9	2.04	9	.22	2.726**
Scenario 12: Failure to Report Hate Crime	1.72	4	1.84	6	.12	1.772a
Scenario 14: Failure to React to Graffiti	1.43	2	1.64	2	−.21	−3.441**

the respondents expected very mild discipline for such behaviors, if not no discipline at all.

The respondents in both countries expected some harsher discipline only in the scenarios describing the abuse of deadly force (Scenario 4: Unjustifiable Use of Deadly Force). In the rest of the scenarios describing use of excessive force and/or verbal abuse (Scenario 6: Officer Strikes Prisoner Who Hurt Partner; Scenario 7: Verbal Abuse "Arrest an Asshole Day;" Scenario 11: Sgt. Fails to Halt Beating), the respondents thought that either no discipline or very mild discipline, such as a reprimand, would follow. Even administering a dose of street justice would not likely be disciplined severely by the police (Table 13).

Failing to execute an arrest warrant on a friend (Scenario 2: Failure to Arrest Friend with Warrant) is the only scenario from the group of other forms of misconduct that would likely lead toward harsher discipline (Table 13). In all other scenarios, including noble-cause corruption (Scenario 10: False Report on Drug Dealer), the respondents in both countries expected very mild discipline or no discipline at all (Table 13).

These similarities in the expected discipline could be noticed in the relative assessments as well. In particular, the bivariate correlation suggest a very strong correlation between the rankings of the scenarios based on the harshness of the discipline in the two countries (Spearman's rho = .965, p < .001).

The results show very few statistically significant differences in expected discipline across the countries (Table 13). There were statistically significant differences in the respondents' assessments of expected discipline in only 5 out of 14, or about one-third of the scenarios (Table 13). At the same time, these differences tended to be rather small and, as such, are not considered to be of substantive importance (e.g., Klockars et al. 2006). The differences do not paint a uniform picture. On the one hand, in three scenarios—one from each type of police misconduct—respondents from Serbia were statistically more likely to expect harsher discipline (corruption: Scenario 5: Supervisor Offers Holiday for Errands; excessive force: Scenario 7: Verbal Abuse "Arrest an Asshole Day;" other forms: Scenario 14: Failure to React to Graffiti) than the Croatian respondents did (Table 13). On the other hand, in two scenarios (Scenario 3: Theft of Knife from Crime Scene; Scenario 10: False Report on Drug Dealer), both of which are evaluated to be among the most serious ones, the respondents from Croatia expected more severe discipline than the respondents from Serbia did (Table 13).

Public Estimates of the Police Officers' Willingness to Report

The respondents' estimates of police officers' willingness to report misconduct share a common characteristic across the two countries: with one exception (Scenario 4: Unjustifiable Use of Deadly Force), the respondents in both countries believed that the code of silence would protect all forms of misconduct described in the questionnaire (Table 14). In other words, in all other scenarios the mean values are all below the mid-point of the scale (3) and into the non-reporting side. Even for the most serious scenario in which the respondents were most likely to say that the police officers would report (Scenario 4: Unjustifiable Use of Deadly Force), the means

are barely across the mid-point and into the reporting side of the scale. Simply put, the respondents in both countries assumed that the strong code of silence would prevent police officers from reporting anything but the abuse of deadly force.

In all six scenarios describing police corruption (Scenario 1: Free Meals/Gifts from Merchants; Scenario 3: Theft of Knife from Crime Scene; Scenario 5: Supervisor Offers Holiday for Errands; Scenario 8: Cover-Up of Police DUI & Accident; Scenario 9: Auto-Body Shop 5% Kickback; Scenario 13: Bribe from Speeding Motorist), the respondents' answers indicated that they would not believe that the police officers from their respective countries would report any of these behaviors. This finding is particularly striking when the nature of police corruption described in some of the scenarios is taken into account: stealing from a crime scene (Scenario 3: Theft of Knife from Crime Scene) and accepting bribes (Scenario 13: Bribe from Speeding Motorist) and kickbacks (Scenario 9: Auto-Body Shop 5% Kickback) are traditionally

Table 14 Respondents' Estimates of Police Officers' Willingness to Report

	Croatia		Serbia			
	Mean	Rank	Mean	Rank	Difference	T-test
Police corruption						
Scenario 1: Free Meals/Gifts from Merchants	1.60	2	1.66	1	−.06	−.771
Scenario 3: Theft of Knife from Crime Scene	2.78	13	2.55	13	.23	2.480*
Scenario 5: Supervisor Offers Holiday for Errands	1.93	7	2.16	9	−.23	−2.551*
Scenario 8: Cover-Up of Police DUI & Accident	1.82	6	1.88	6	−.06	−.728
Scenario 9: Auto-Body Shop 5% Kickback	2.42	11	2.31	11	.11	1.207
Scenario 13: Bribe from Speeding Motorist	1.98	8	1.97	7	.01	.082
Use of excessive force						
Scenario 4: Unjustifiable Use of Deadly Force	3.34	14	3.28	14	.06	.586
Scenario 6: Officer Strikes Prisoner Who Hurt Partner	1.61	3	1.77	4	−.16	−1.855*
Scenario 7: Verbal Abuse "Arrest an Asshole Day"	1.47	1	1.67	2	−.20	−2.641**
Scenario 11: Sgt. Fails to Halt Beating	1.71	5	1.81	5	.10	1.135
Other forms						
Scenario 2: Failure to Arrest Friend with Warrant	2.45	12	2.36	12	.09	.995
Scenario 10: False Report on Drug Dealer	2.26	10	2.28	10	−.02	−.251
Scenario 12: Failure to Report Hate Crime	2.04	9	2.14	8	−.10	−.108
Scenario 14: Failure to React to Graffiti	1.69	4	1.73	3	−.04	−.491

perceived as very serious forms of corruption for which police agencies are expected to react. As expected, the code of silence is the strongest for the least serious forms of corruption such as the acceptance of gratuities (Scenario 1: Free Meals/ Gifts from Merchants) and internal corruption (5: Supervisor Offers Holiday for Errands; Scenario 8: Cover-Up of Police DUI & Accident; Table 14).

Among all scenarios addressing the use of excessive force (Scenario 4: Unjustifiable Use of Deadly Force; Scenario 6: Officer Strikes Prisoner Who Hurt Partner; Scenario 7: Verbal Abuse "Arrest an Asshole Day;" Scenario 11: Sgt. Fails to Halt Beating), only for the abuse of deadly force—the most severe force that there is—did the respondents assume that police officers would be somewhat more likely to report (Table 14). In all other scenarios, be they an instance of verbal abuse (Scenario 7: Verbal Abuse "Arrest an Asshole Day") or physical abuse (Scenario 6: Officer Strikes Prisoner Who Hurt Partner), respondents were uniform in assuming that police culture would tolerate such behaviors in silence (all mean values are below 2; Table 14).

In no scenario describing other forms of police misconduct (Scenario 2: Failure to Arrest Friend with Warrant; Scenario 10: False Report on Drug Dealer; Scenario 12: Failure to Report Hate Crime; Scenario 14: Failure to React to Graffiti) did the respondents estimate that police officers would report such behavior: all means are well below the mid-point of 3 and into the non-reporting side. According to our respondents, while it seems somewhat more likely that the police officers would report a failure to execute an arrest warrant on a friend (Scenario 2: Failure to Arrest Friend with Warrant) or planting of evidence and falsifying official documents (Scenario 10: False Report on Drug Dealer) than failing to report a hate crime (Scenario 12: Failure to Report Hate Crime) or failing to react to the juveniles writing graffiti (Scenario 14: Failure to React to Graffiti), the fact, nevertheless, remains that the code of silence would probably cover all of these behaviors.

Furthermore, when we rank-ordered scenarios based on the perceived strength of the code of silence for each country, the results show that these rankings are quite similar, as evinced by a very high correlation between these two rankings (Spearman's rho = .978, p < .001).

Finally, a comparison across countries yielded relatively few differences. In particular, we detected statistically significant differences in only 4 out of 14 scenarios (or 28.6% of all scenarios). Moreover, in all these scenarios, the differences were really small (all below 0.25 on a 5-point scale) and were substantively unimportant (e.g., Klockars et al. 2006). In the majority of these scenarios (3 out of 4), the respondents from Serbia were statistically significantly less likely to say that the police officers would adhere to the code of silence than were the respondents from Croatia did (Table 14).

Conclusion

Although the transitional processes in Croatia and Serbia are distinguishable both by the rate and extent of progress, recent indices (e.g., Transparency International 2013; World Bank 2017; World Values Survey 2017) suggest that the differences now are not as large as they were in the 1990s. Consistent application of the rule of law remains a challenge in both countries. On the other hand, Serbia is perceived to be more corrupt than Croatia and, consequently, opinion polls conducted in two countries suggest that the Serbian public perceives the police to be more corrupt than the Croatian public does.

Unlike the existing studies of more general support for the police, our study provides an in-depth exploration of a specific topic—public views of police misconduct and the police. We explored how respondents assessed seriousness of misconduct, appropriate and expected discipline such misconduct deserves, and how likely it is that such misconduct will be tolerated in silence. Unlike prior comparative studies of public views that relied on the police corruption questionnaire (e.g., Klockars and Kutnjak Ivković 1999; Kutnjak Ivković 2004; Kutnjak Ivković et al. 2002b), our study used the more comprehensive police integrity questionnaire, further extended with three additional scenarios.

The results of our study indicate that in about half of the scenarios the Croatian respondents evaluated police misconduct, particularly police corruption, as somewhat more serious than the Serbian respondents, although the differences were not large. Our results are similar to the results of the earlier study comparing the estimates of seriousness provided by Croatian and U.S. respondents (Klockars and Kutnjak Ivković 1999), in which the authors reported statistically significant, but relatively small, differences between the assessments of seriousness in the majority of the scenarios. Even in countries as diverse as the United States and Croatia, Klockars and Kutnjak Ivković (1999) detected large differences in only a small proportion of all scenarios. Similarly, a study comparing the public views from Croatia, Slovenia, and the United States (Kutnjak Ivković et al. 2002b) indicated many statistically significant, but few substantively large differences. In particular, there was only one scenario in which the differences in seriousness evaluations between the Slovenian and Croatian respondents were substantively large (Kutnjak Ivković et al. 2002b). Of course, it should not be surprising that a comparison of two relatively similar countries—Slovenia and Croatia—did not yield large differences in many scenarios.

At the same time, relative assessments of seriousness—how serious scenarios are evaluated compared to other scenarios—were quite similar across our samples from Croatia and Serbia, as were their relative assessment of appropriate discipline and willingness to report misconduct. These results fit well with extant research (e.g., Kutnjak Ivković 2004; Kutnjak Ivković et al. 2002b). Regardless of whether the comparison included just two countries (the United States and Croatia; Kutnjak Ivković 2004) or three countries (the United States, Croatia, and Slovenia; Kutnjak Ivković et al. 2002b), the results suggest a substantial degree of homogeneity in relative assessment of seriousness.

The respondents' views about the appropriate discipline suggested more disagreement as to what the appropriate discipline should be. Out of 9 scenarios with statistically significant but smaller differences, Croatian respondents thought that harsher discipline should be appropriate in about one-half of these scenarios, while Serbian respondents thought that harsher discipline should be appropriate in the other half of the scenarios with differences. This comparison revealed two sets of similarities as well. First, with the exception of the abuse of deadly force, the respondents from both countries thought that mild discipline or no discipline should follow. In the countries in which police corruption remains to be a challenging topic, it should come as no surprise that the respondents did not think that police misconduct should be disciplined severely. Second, their relative assessment of appropriate discipline was rather similar as well, indicating a relatively homogeneous view of appropriate discipline.

One of the challenges of dealing with corruption and other forms of police misconduct is to entice both citizens and police officers to report misconduct. Our results reveal that, with two exceptions (abuse of deadly force, stealing from a crime scene), the surveyed citizens from both countries would not be very likely to report police misconduct. In about one-half of the scenarios there were statistically significant differences, but they were not large. Regardless, it was not obvious that the respondents from one country would be more likely to report than the respondents from the other country, as the respondents from Croatia were more likely to say that they would report in about half of the scenarios with statistical differences and the respondents from Serbia were more likely to say that they would report in the other half of the scenarios with differences. The fact remains that the surveyed citizens are not quite willing to report most forms of police misconduct and would rather tolerate it in silence. This, in turn, allows police misconduct to continue.

When the respondents from both countries evaluated the police (i.e., how serious the police would evaluate these behaviors, what discipline would follow, and how likely the police are to adhere to the code of silence), they did not portray police agencies as police agencies of high integrity. In particular, citizens from both countries assumed that the police officers in their countries would evaluate only stealing from a crime scene and abusing deadly force as serious forms of police misconduct, while they assumed that all other forms of behavior described in the questionnaire, some of which include physical injuries of a citizen and severe forms of corruption, would not be evaluated as serious by the police. In about one-third of the scenarios there were statistically significant (but not substantively important) differences and, in these scenarios, the Croatian respondents thought that the police officer in their country would evaluate these behaviors as more serious.

The results about the discipline they expect their police would mete out are very similar to the findings about seriousness. Specifically, the respondents from both countries expected more severe discipline only for a theft from a crime scene and the abuse of deadly force. All other forms of misconduct, in their view, would yield either no discipline or very mild discipline. In about one-third of the scenarios with differences, the results did not create a clear picture as to whether the respondents from one country would expect harsher discipline.

Lastly, the code of silence is perceived to be very strong in both countries. The respondents from both countries expected that the police officers in their countries would tolerate all but one form of police misconduct. Only the abuse of deadly force—the most severe form of use of force resulting in a deadly consequence—is expected to be somewhat less likely to be tolerated in silence.

Taking together, these results suggest the public lack of confidence in the police willingness and ability to do something about all but most serious forms of police misconduct. At the same time, while the respondents themselves evaluated a number of different forms of police misconduct as serious, they did not think that harsh discipline should be used for almost any of the scenarios nor they showed willingness to report many of these forms of police misconduct. The latter findings suggest that citizenry in both countries sets a relatively low bar for discipline standards, conveying indirectly to the police that they do not favor an environment in which celerity and sever-

ity of discipline are both favored and expected. Such a state of affairs appears to work through the fourth dimension of the theory of police misconduct (Klockars and Kutnjak Ivković 2004) by sending the police a clear signal that society remains fairly tolerant of corruption and other forms of misconduct.

References

Bjerregaard, B., & Lord, V. B. (2004). An examination of the ethical and value orientation of criminal justice students. *Police Quarterly, 7*(2), 262–284.

Freedom House (2017). *Freedom in the world.* Retrieved from https://freedomhouse.org/report/freedom-world/2016/croatia

Frič, P., & Walek, C. (2001). Crossing the Thin Blue Line: An International Annual Review of Anti-Corruption Strategies in the Police. Prague, The Czech Republic: Transparency International Č R.

Klockars, C. B., & Kutnjak Ivković, S. (1999). The measurement of police delinquency. In W. Laufer & F. Adler (Eds.), *The criminology of criminal law. Advances in criminological theory* (Vol. 8, pp. 87–106). New Brunswick, NJ: Transaction.

Klockars, C. B., & Kutnjak Ivković, S. (2004). Measuring police integrity. In A. R. Piquero, J. R. Greene, & M. J. Hickman (Eds.), *Police integrity and ethics.* Belmont, CA: Wadsworth.

Klockars, C. B., Kutnjak Ivković, S., Harver, W. E., & Haberfeld, M. R. (1997). *The Measurement of police integrity.* Final report submitted to the U.S. Department of Justice, Office of Justice Programs, National Institute of Justice.

Klockars, C. B., Kutnjak Ivković, S., Harver, W. E., & Haberfeld, M. R. (2000). *The Measurement of police integrity.* Research in brief. U.S. Department of Justice, Office of Justice Programs, National Institute of Justice. Washington, DC: Government Printing Office.

Klockars, C. B., Haberfeld, M. R., Kutnjak Ivković, S., & Uydess, A. (2002). A minimum requirement for police corruption. In R. A. Silverman, T. P. Thornberry, B. Cohen, & B. Krisberg (Eds.), *Crime and justice at the millennium: Essays by and in honor of Marvin E Wolfgang.* Berlin: Springer.

Klockars, C. B., Kutnjak Ivković, S., & Haberfeld, M. R. (Eds.). (2004). *The contours of police integrity.* Newbury Park, CA: Sage.

Klockars, C. B., Kutnjak Ivković, S., & Haberfeld, M. R. (2006). *Enhancing police integrity.* New York: Springer.

Kutnjak Ivković, S. (2000). Challenges of policing democracies: The Croatian experience. In D. Das & O. Marenin (Eds.), *Challenges of policing democra-*

cies: *A world perspective* (pp. 45–85). Newark, NJ: Gordon and Breach.

Kutnjak Ivković, S. (2004). Evaluating the seriousness of police misconduct: A cross-cultural comparison of police officer and citizen views. *International Criminal Justice Review, 14*, 25–48.

Kutnjak Ivković, S. (2008). A comparative study of public support for the police. *International Criminal Justice Review, 18*(4), 406–434.

Kutnjak Ivković, S. (2015). Studying police integrity. In S. Kutnjak Ivković & M. Haberfeld (Eds.), *Police integrity across the world*. New York: Springer.

Kutnjak Ivković, S., & Haberfeld, M. R. (Eds.). (2015). *Police integrity across the world*. New York: Springer.

Kutnjak Ivković, S., & Klockars, C. B. (2002). Public views about police corruption: The case of Croatia. In M. Pagon (Ed.), *Policing in central and Eastern Europe: Deviance, violence, and victimization* (pp. 283–296). Ljubljana: College of Police and Security Studies.

Kutnjak Ivković, S., Cajner-Mraovic, I., Klockars, C. B., & Ivanusec, D. (2002a). Public perceptions about police misconduct in Croatia. In M. Pagon (Ed.), *Policing in Central and Eastern Europe: Deviance, violence, and victimization* (pp. 311–328). Ljubljana: College of Police and Security Studies.

Kutnjak Ivković, S., Pagon, M., Klockars, C. B., & Lobnikar, B. (2002b). A comparative view of public perceptions of police corruption. In M. Pagon (Ed.), *Policing in central and Eastern Europe: Deviance, violence, and victimization* (pp. 297–310). Ljubljana: College of Police and Security Studies.

Kutnjak Ivković, S., Cajner-Mraovic, I., & Ivanusec, D. (2004). The measurement of seriousness of police corruption. In G. Mesko, M. Pagon, & G. Dobovsek (Eds.), *Dilemmas of contemporary criminal justice* (pp. 300–311). Ljubljana: Faculty of Criminal Justice, University of Maribor.

Kutnjak Ivković, S. (2009). The Croatian police, police integrity, and transition toward democratic policing. Policing: *An International Journal, 32*(3), 459–488.

Law on Police. (2005). Službeni glasnik RS, 101/05.

Law on Police. (2016). Beograd: Službeni glasnik RS, 6/2016.

Meyer, M., Steyn, J., & Gopal, N. (2013). Exploring the public parameter of police integrity. *Policing: An International Journal of Police Strategies and Management, 36*(1), 140–156.

Pagon, M., Kutnjak Ivković, S., & Lobnikar, B. (2000). Police integrity and attitudes toward police corruption: A comparison between the police and the public. In M. Pagon (Ed.), *Policing in central and Eastern Europe: Ethics, integrity, and human rights* (pp. 383–396). Ljubljana: College of Police and Security Studies.

Police Law. (2000). Zagreb, Croatia: Narodne novine 129/01.

Police Law. (2011). Zagreb, Croatia: Narodne novine 34/11.

Roebuck, J. B., & Barker, T. (1974). A typology of police corruption. *Social Problems, 21*, 423–437.

Rothwell, G. R., & Baldwin, J. N. (2006). Ethical climates and contextual predictors of whistle-blowing. *Review of Public Personnel Administration, 26*(3), 216–244.

Rothwell, G. R., & Baldwin, J. N. (2007a). Whistle-blowing and the code of silence in police agencies, policy and structural predictors. *Crime & Delinquency, 53*(4), 605–632.

Rothwell, G. R., & Baldwin, J. N. (2007b). Ethical climate theory, whistle-blowing, and the code of silence in police agencies in the state of Georgia. *Journal of Business Ethics, 70*(4), 341–361.

Transparency International. (2013). *Global Corruption Barometer*. Retrieved from https://www.transparency.org/gcb2013/country/?country=serbia

Transparency International. (2016). *People and corruption: Europe and Central Asia*. Retrieved from https://www.transparency.org/whatwedo/publication/people_and_corruption_europe_and_central_asia_2016

Transparency International. (2017). *Corruption perceptions index*. Retrieved from https://www.transparency.org/news/feature/corruption_perceptions_index_2016#table

White, D. A. (2008). *Assessing the differences in opinion regarding gratuities in law enforcement. ProQuest Dissertations and Theses, 139-n/a*. Retrieved from http://ezproxy.msu.edu/login?url=http://search.proquest.com/docview/304836939?accountid=12598. (304836939).

World Bank. (2017). *Worldwide governance indicators*. Retrieved from http://info.worldbank.org/governance/wgi/index.aspx#reports.

World Values Survey. (2017). *Documentation*. Retrieved from http://www.worldvaluessurvey.org/WVSDocumentationWV5.jsp

Similar, Different or Somewhere in Between? The Police Officer and Citizen Views on Police Misconduct

Hyeyoung Lim

Introduction

Klockars, Kutnjak Ivković, and Haberfeld (2004) state that "police integrity is a belief rather than a behavior" and this belief is morally changed by their moral attitudes (p. 2). The emphasis on "personal belief" steered the studies on police corruption toward measuring individual officers' perceptions of wrongdoing and misconduct. The most commonly used inventory on police integrity is the one designed by Carl B. Klockars and Sanja Kutnjak Ivković in 1997 and expanded by Klockars and his colleagues (see Klockars and Kutnjak Ivković 2004; for convenience, hereafter referred to as the "Police Integrity Scale"). The scale contains 11 hypothetical scenarios that assess individual officers' perceptions of, and tolerance for, police misconduct. Each scenario is followed by seven questions, "crucial to the organizational/occupational-culture theory of police corruption and practical police administration" (Klockars 1999, p. 3). Since the release of the first data collected from a national sample of 30 agencies across the United States in 1999, the Police Integrity Scale has been utilized across the globe, in countries such as in Armenia, Australia, Croatia, Estonia, Russia, South Africa, South Korea, and Thailand (see Klockars et al. 2004; Kutnjak Ivković and Haberfeld 2015).

Most existing studies on police integrity, particularly the studies that used this scale, typically have focused on agency-level findings by aggregating the responses from individual officers. When Klockars and his colleagues conducted the first study, they purposefully did not collect individual-level data (e.g., race, gender) to prevent identification of their respondents; the only individual-level characteristic included in the original dataset is *police rank* (see Klockars 1999).

The purposes of the current study are to compare the *personal integrity* of police officers by rank and to compare the view of police officers with the views of university students regarding seriousness of police misconduct. The current study identifies how police officers' viewpoints on misconduct differ by their rank, categorized into three groups, *high*, *middle*, and *line level*. Also, the students' perceptions are compared across their academic majors, contrasting *criminal justice majors* and *non-criminal justice majors*. The working supposition behind this comparison was predicated upon the assumption that police officers are recruited from the communities they serve and thus should hold similar views to the students, at least at the line officers' level. The other supposition was predicated on the notion that the supervisory views and attitudes might have been already altered by

H. Lim (✉)
Department of Criminal Justice, University of Alabama at Birmingham, Birmingham, AL, USA
e-mail: hyeyoung@uab.edu

organizational subculture related to their supervisory position and legal responsibilities, thus, resulting in much larger differences in the views of police integrity between students and supervisors than between students and line officers.

Literature Review

The Views of the Police Officers on Police Misconduct

Walker (2006) states that "[police integrity] is a fundamental principle of a democratic society that the police should be held to account for their actions" (p. 1). What the police do and how they perform relies heavily on both agency-level integrity and personal-level integrity. According to Klockars et al. (2004), police integrity is "the normative inclination among police to resist temptations to abuse the rights and privileges of their occupation" (p. 2). That is, "integrity is the inclination to resist—[belief]—rather than the actual resistance to temptation—[behavior]" (Klockars et al. 2004, p. 3). This belief is affected by police moral attitudes or ethical standpoint, so assessing individual officers' moral belief is critical throughout their career, especially in the process of recruitment. Kleinig (1996) stated that individual moral demand is reconfigured by group culture so one of the most difficult situations police officers face is ordering of individual integrity and group loyalty.

The studies on police integrity and accountability have been focused on three levels of influencing factors: individual level (*rotten apples*), organizational level (*rotten barrels*), and ecological level (*rotten orchards*) factors. A relatively small number of studies have examined the relation between police integrity and individual-level factors, including age, gender, education, and length of service. Lim and Sloan (2016) examined individual officers' race, rank, level of education, total years of service in policing, and length of service at the current agency to identify how those factors affect officers' willingness to report a fellow officer's misconduct. They found that the level of education, rank, and total years

of service in policing were significantly related to individual officers' willingness to comrades (Lim and Sloan 2016). Another study found that there are moral differences across gender and race within a police department (Hickman et al. 2015). In addition, Fyfe and Kane (2006) found that highly-educated police officers were less likely to be fired for misbehavior, and Harris (2010) found that the longer officers serve in policing, the less likely they are to be terminated for misconduct.

Second, many studies have examined how a "rotten barrel" spoils "the apples." For example, Lee et al. (2013) examined how departmental deviant subculture affects line officers' attitudes toward police corruption by measuring the deviant subculture with individual officers' willingness to report their fellow officers' misconduct. Lee et al. (2013) found a strong relationship between a departmental deviant subculture and individual officers' attitudes toward police corruption. Lim and Sloan (2016) also found statistically significant relationships between the perceived deviant climate in their agency and police supervisors' willingness to report their fellow officers' misconduct such as accepting gratuities, filing a false report, abusing authority, and using excessive force. In addition, Eitle et al. (2014) found that organizational and environmental factors such as agency size, in-service training, and the presence of the Internal Affairs Unit have strong effects on police misconduct.

Last, utilizing an ecological approach to explain police deviant behaviors in geographic territories, available evidence also indicates that community/neighborhood contextual and cultural factors affect police integrity (Kane 2002; Klinger 1997; Kutnjak Ivković 2009; Sun et al. 2008). Klinger (1997) proposed an "ecology of patrol" model to explain how neighborhood contextual factors affect police behavior and found that officers developed distinct neighborhood-level perceptions of normal crime which affect police activities. Several studies have found that police officers tend to use higher levels of coercive force in disadvantaged neighborhoods (Morabito 2007; Smith 1986; Terrill and Reisig 2003) and in high violent crime areas

(Lawton 2007; Fridell and Lim 2016; Lim et al. 2014). Evidence also indicated that geographic ecological factors affected officer arrest decisions as well as incident reporting (Smith 1986; Morabito 2007).

Most of these studies, however, focused on police use-of-force regardless of whether the force used was excessive or not. Thus, it is unclear if those studies actually examined police misconduct, applying the ecological approach. Lim and Sloan (2016), however, tested how neighborhood violent crime rates affect police supervisors' willingness to blow the whistle and found that the relationship was not statistically significant.[1]

The purpose of the current study is not to examine all three-levels of factors affecting police integrity, but rather to compare the *personal integrity* of police officers by rank, as well as to compare the views expressed by police officers with the views expressed by university students on how serious they think the described police misconduct is. Kutnjak Ivković (2005) first examined the difference of the personal integrity between supervisors and line officers and whether the difference is similar or different across countries by analyzing the nationally sampled data in the U.S.A., Croatia, and Finland. She found that line officers tended to consider the described vignette behaviors less seriously than supervisors did, and the differences across 11 scenarios were statistically significant except two cases in Finland (C3 Bribe from speeding motorist and C7 Supervisor: Holiday for tune-up; see Appendix: *The Measurement of Police Integrity* for the detail descriptions of all scenarios). Although the rankings and mean values were somewhat different across nations because of "the legal, social, political, and disciplinary environments" as well as police culture, it was clear that supervisors' personal integrity was more likely higher than the line officers' personal integrity (Kutnjak Ivković 2005, p. 560).

Schafer and Martinelli (2008) also studied 478 first-line supervisors' perception of police integrity with the data collected at a single municipal police department in the United States. The results showed that the first-line supervisors (sergeants and lieutenants) considered the vignette behaviors more seriously than the nationally sampled officers in Klockars et al. (2000)'s study. Schafer and Martinelli (2008) reported that female and African-American supervisors tend to consider police misconduct more seriously and are more willing to report their fellow officers' misbehaviors while the level of education, service length, and years as a supervisor were not made a significant difference on their perception of police integrity.

While Schafer and Martinelli (2008) compared the personal integrity of the first-line supervisors with the nationally sampled police officers in Klockars et al.'s study (2000), Vito, Wolfe, Higgins, and Walsh (2011) examined management cops' views on the vignette behaviors using the Police Integrity Scale. Vito et al. (2011) administered the survey questionnaire to a total of 208 police managers (sergeants (53.4%) and middle managers including lieutenants (46.6%), two majors and a chief) attending the administrative training course of the Southern Police Institute (SPI) at the University of Louisville from 2005 to 2007. Vito et al. (2011) compared the personal integrity of sergeants and middle managers with the mean values and rankings from the nationally sampled police officers in the U.S., Croatia, and Finland from Kutnjak Ivković (2005). In the comparison among sergeants, middle managers, and the U.S. line officers, Vito et al. (2011) found that their rankings on the five vignette behaviors out of the 11 were somewhat different: C11 *Theft from found wallet*, C9 *Drink to ignore late bar closing*, C6 *Auto repair shop 5% kickback*, C7 *Supervisor: holiday for tune-up*, and C10 *Excessive force on car thief*. Across police ranks, their rankings on the rest of the six behaviors were the same, although the mean values of the U.S. line officers were .05–1.18 lower than the mean scores of the sergeants or middle managers at the SPI. Among supervisors across countries, the perceptions of the sergeants and

---

[1] The unit of analysis in the study of Lim and Sloan (2016) was police department including county-level law enforcement agencies (Sheriff and Constable), so the agency-level violent crime rates were analyzed.

middle managers at the SPI were very similar with the views of the nationally sampled supervisors in the U.S., but differed from the views of the supervisors in Croatia and Finland. Overall, the average mean values from the sampled supervisors at the SPI were slightly higher than the mean values from the nationally sampled supervisors.

The comparison between police supervisors and line officers concerning their personal integrity, especially how seriously they consider police misconduct, has been examined not only in the United States but also in other countries. In most of the existing studies, however, other than line officers, all other position ranks were categorized as a "supervisor" or "management cops," and the perceived views of sergeants and lieutenants were compared with the perceptions of line officers. In other words, there is a paucity of more refined comparisons of police officers' personal integrity by their position rank. To bridge this research gap, the current study examines police integrity by the three position ranks, *high-rank*, *middle-rank*, and *line officers*. It also compares the results with the finding reported in the existing studies (Schafer and Martinelli 2008 and Vito et al. 2011). In addition, the current study investigates the extent to which the views of police officers by the three position ranks are different or similar to the views of the university students.

The Views of the Public on Police Misconduct

The reality of studying the way the public perceives police misconduct is that the spotlight has been on police brutality or police use-of-excessive force against racial/ethnic minorities, especially against young African-American males. Evidence indicates that highly publicized police brutality events affect citizens' attitudes toward the police (Weitzer 2002). Weitzer (2002) tracked public attitudes toward the LAPD and NYPD before and after the highly-publicized events in New York City (e.g., the killing of Amadou Diallo and Patrick Dorismond). He found that citizens' unfavorable attitudes toward the police were signifi-

cantly increased after the highly-publicized events. With the growing number of 'habitual social networkers,' media coverage and headline news spread rapidly, shortening the public reaction time (see Edison Research 2010; Lim 2015). The effect of media on citizens' attitudes toward the police has been found significant in multiple studies (Dowler and Zawilski 2007; Lee et al. 2015; Lim 2015; Schuck and Rosenbaum 2005; Weitzer 2002). Using Albert Bandura's social learning theory, Lim (2015) measured the media effect by asking how frequently students hear or read about police misconduct through media and examined how the negative symbolic model, *media*, affects their attitudes toward the police. She found that the negative symbolic model influences students' levels of trust in police and their perception of biased policing, especially those who have not had direct contact with the police.

In 2015, Gallup reported that the combined percentage (18%) of those expressing very little or no confidence in the police was the highest since its first poll in 1993, although the majority of Americans remain confident in the police over a 22 year-period, ranging from 52 to 64%. Jones (2015) argues that this trend may be caused by the actions of the police in certain cities (e.g., Ferguson, MO, North Charleston, SC). Democrats (−13%), postgraduates (−11%), individuals aged 18–28 years old (−7%), men (−7%), those with an annual household income $75K or more (−7%), and Hispanics (−8%) showed the largest loss of trust in police in that year (Jones 2015). In 2016, however, a Gallup poll found that three in four of those surveyed (76%) said that they have 'a great deal of respect' for their local police officers (see McCarthy 2016). In the following year, 2017, it was found that Americans' confidence in the police was back at its historical average, 57%, but the confidence levels remained low among Blacks (30%), Hispanics (45%), Democrats (44%), and younger Americans (18–34 years old, 44%) (Norman 2017). These results suggest a critical issue in the relationship between the police and the community they serve: the public respect the police, but do not trust them.

Klockars et al. (2001) were the first to examine whether university students' opinions about police corruption scenarios differ from the corresponding views expressed by the police. In light of the several limitations in comparison between a national sample of police officers across the United States ($n = 3235$) and a sample of students enrolled at the University of Delaware ($n = 375$), Klockars et al. (2001) considered the perceived views of university students "as a rough indicator of middle-class public perceptions of police integrity" (p. 190). The survey results students revealed that students' perceptions about police misconduct seriousness were significantly different from the police, except in the scenario describing the use of excessive force. The students tended to rate nine out of the remaining ten scenarios less seriously than the police officers did. The only exception was the evaluation for a scenario describing a cover-up of a police officer's DUI and accident. Klockars et al. (2001) also found that students' rates on appropriate disciplines were significantly different from the police officers' on all the scenarios. In fact, their rates in the scenarios describing an off-duty security system business, cover-up of police DUI accident, and excessive force on car thief were higher than the police officers' rates were. That is, students through that more severe discipline would be appropriate for these types of police misconduct. Regarding willingness to report, there were no statistical differences for two scenarios, but for the remaining scenarios, students seemed to be less willing to report police misconduct than police officers were. Overall, Klockars et al. (2001) found that students perceived police misconduct less seriously, tended to approve of less severe discipline, and were less willing to report police misconduct.

While Klockars et al. (2001) compared the perceived perceptions of police misconduct between the police and the university students enrolled in introductory sociology or criminal justice courses, Bjerregaard and Lord (2004) examined whether criminal justice students' ethical attitudes, value orientations, and behaviors differ from those expressed by non-criminal justice majors. With a sample of 443 students (238 criminal justice majors and 205 non-criminal justice majors), Bjerregaard and Lord (2004) measured *value orientations* with four scale variables (trustworthiness (14 items), altruism (14 items), acceptance of authority (10 items), and needs determinism (7 items)), *likelihood of engagement* with the three variables (serious ethical violations (5 scenarios), moderate ethical violations (4 scenarios), and less serious violations (6 scenarios)), and perceptions of the seriousness of ethical violations with the 11 scenarios of Klockars et al. (2000). In particular, Bjerregaard and Lord (2004) categorized the ten vignette behaviors described in the Police Integrity Scale into three categories: *taking gratuities* (C2 Free meals, discounts on beat, C3 Bribe from speeding motorist, C4 Holiday gifts from merchants, C6 Auto repair shop 5% kickback, and C9 Drink to ignore late bar closing), *abuse of authority* (C7 Supervisor: Holiday for tune-up and C8 Cover-up of police DUI accident), and *criminal behavior* (C5 Crime scene theft of watch, C10 Excessive force on car thief, and C11 Theft from found wallet). They found that the criminal justice majors interested in law enforcement considered *taking gratuities* more seriously than both the criminal justice majors not interested in law enforcement and non-criminal justice majors. The students' perceptions of the other variables, *abuse of authority* and *criminal behavior*, however, did not vary significantly across the students' major and their occupational interests. Besides, the overall ratings of students on the three categories were lower than the ratings by the national sample of police officers in the study of Klockars et al. (2000): In a 5-point Likert scale, the students' ratings were 1–1.31 points lower than the police officers' ratings.

Overall, a relatively small number of studies have examined the perceptions of the public on police integrity and compared them with police officers' views. In this regard, the current study not only compares police officers' perceptions by rank but also contrasts them with the views of the public represented by university students. In addition, the study assess the extent of variation among university students' perceived perceptions on police misconduct by their major, *criminal justice major vs. non-criminal justice major*.

Methods

Data

This study uses three data sets: (1) Police Corruption in 30 Agencies in the United States, 1997 (ICPSR version; hereafter referred to as "Klockars (1999) data"), (2) Police Integrity Survey in Texas, collected from 2008 to 2010 at the Bill Blackwood Law Enforcement Management Institute of Texas (LEMIT) (hereafter referred to as "Lim (2010)—Officer Data"), and (3) Surveys on Citizen Attitudes toward Police, collected in different time periods at three 4-year public universities located in Midwestern and Southern regions of the United States (hereafter referred to as "Lim (2017)—Student Data"). The middle-rank officers' views were also compared with the studies of Schafer and Martinelli (2008) and Vito et al. (2011).

First, this study uses a secondary dataset collected by Klockars and his colleagues from 30 different police agencies in the United States using a convenience sampling method to examine "[individual] officers' perception of and tolerance for corruption" (Klockars 1999, p. 1). This dataset and its measurement have been widely used to study police integrity since its distribution by the Inter-University Consortium for Political and Social Research (ICPSR) in 1999 (see Klockars et al. 2000, 2004 and Kutnjak Ivković and Haberfeld 2015). In 30 U.S. law enforcement agencies, the data were collected from 3235 officers using a convenience sampling method.

The missing values, ranging from 23 (.71%) to 48 (1.48%) cases in a variable, were replaced by the median. For the purpose of this study, the responses from police chiefs/sheriffs (32 cases), sergeants (369 cases), lieutenants (119 cases), and line officers (2037 cases) were included. As a result, a total of 2557 cases remained for the final analyses. The average service length of the remaining officers was 6–10 years, and most of the officers (61.1%) worked at a very large police agency (over 500 sworn officers).

The second data set was collected from June 1, 2009 to March 12, 2010 in Texas using a survey questionnaire of police integrity, containing 17 scenarios of police misconduct—the original 11 scenarios (Klockars 1999) plus five revised and one modified-scenarios developed by Klockars et al. (2006). The survey was administered to 553 officers enrolled in specialized training programs at the Bill Blackwood Law Enforcement Management Institute of Texas (LEMIT).[2] The participants from municipal, county, state, and federal law enforcement agencies in Texas were asked to complete and return the survey questionnaire voluntarily during their enrolled training programs. After respondents who did not provide information about the ranks were excluded from the analysis, a total of 401 cases were retained for further data analyses: 291 chief/sheriff/constables, 40 sergeants, 43 lieutenants, and 27 line officers. Approximately 50% of the participants had over 20 years in service, and 144 officers (35.9%) were from state police agencies.

Lastly, a survey questionnaire was developed based on the Police-Public Contact Survey (PPCS) and the Police Integrity Scale (ten out of 11 scenarios were included to ask how seriously students consider each police misconduct)[3] as well as theories of social threat, social distance, and procedural justice to examine university students' attitudes toward the police. The survey was administered at three 4-year public universities located in the Midwest and Southern regions of the United States between Spring 2013 and Spring 2017.[4] For the current study, the partial data measured with the Police Integrity Scale were used to examine how university students view the seriousness of police misconduct and how similar or different it is from police officers'

---

[2]Its partial data were used in the study of Lim and Sloan (2016).

[3]The scenario of C10 "Excessive force on car thief" was excluded because the newly developed survey questionnaire for university student populations includes three items related to police use-of excessive force against racial/ethnic minorities. These three items were not used as a proxy measure of C10 in the current study because the original case description of C10 did not reflect the racial aspects of police use-of-force.

[4]The partial data were used in the studies of Lee et al. (2015) and Lim (2015).

own views. After replacing one to three missing responses per case with the median value, 1221 cases were retained for the current study. The average student age was 21, and their academic standings were freshmen (207, 17.0%), sophomore (223, 18.3%), junior (377, 30.9%), senior (397, 32.5%), and graduate students (17, 1.4%). Among them, 539 students were either criminal justice majors or minors, and 663 students (54.3%) were males.

The present study only compares participants' own views of police misconduct because of the data limitation of the third dataset that only contained students' own perceptions of the given scenarios of police misconduct and did not ask students to assess how most police officers would evaluate the same scenarios.

Variables

Dependent variables. The dependent variable in this study is the seriousness of police misconduct. Participants were asked to rate how seriously they consider each of the 11 cases of police misconduct on a 5-point Likert scale ("not at all serious" = 1 to "very serious" = 5). These 11 scenarios were labeled as C1 Business to C11 Wallet (see Appendix: The Measurement of Police Integrity for the detail descriptions of all scenarios).

Independent variables. The primary independent variables were the groups by police rank and dataset, entitled Klockars (1999) data, Lim (2010) data, and Lim (2017) data for convenience. Also, the mean scores of each study were expressed as $\bar{x}_K$ = a mean of Klockars (1999) data, $\bar{x}_{L_1}$ = a mean of Lim (2010) data, and $\bar{x}_{L_2}$ = a mean of Lim (2017) data, while $\bar{x}_{KL_1}$ and $\bar{x}_{KL_2}$ were represented the mean of the means (the average mean score of the two studies). In addition, $\bar{x}_{all}$ represents the grand mean of the three datasets.

All group variables are dichotomized (0 and 1). A study by Klockars (1999) was set as a reference group to examine the differences among the

datasets, and the responses in the three studies were also compared by officer rank—high, middle, and line—and by student major–criminal justice major and non-criminal justice major. chief of police, sheriff, and constable including assistant and deputy chiefs, sheriffs, and constables were considered as high-rank officers. For purposes of comparison with previous studies, the current study considers sergeants and lieutenants as middle-rank officers (see Schafer and Martinelli 2008 and Vito et al. 2011). Lastly, the students' views on the seriousness of police misconduct were grouped by their academic majors, *criminal justice majors* vs. *non-criminal justice majors.*

Analytic Strategies

For the purpose of this study, univariate and bivariate analyses were utilized to examine group differences. Independent t-test was mainly used to test group differences, and effect sizes via correlation coefficients (r) were also calculated to verify statistical significance. Because statistical significance depends upon sample size, conducting an effect size test was necessary to check how important the obtained effects are. The effect size is an objective and standardized measure of observed effects (Field 2005; Schmidt and Hunter 2015), verifying the statistically significant findings from independent t-tests.

Findings

Univariate analyses were conducted to describe the three datasets. As shown in Table 1, the three datasets show both similarities and differences. In terms of police officers' perceptions of each case, Texan police officers viewed police misconduct more seriously than the officers from across the nation did. On the other hand, university students evaluated some of the police misbehaviors (e.g., C4 Holidays, C6 Auto, C7 Supervisor, and C9 Bar) less seriously than police officers did. Both police officers and students, however, rated the three cases—C3 Speeding, C5 Burglary, and C11 Wallet—among the top four most serious cases of police misconduct (median = 5), and C1

Table 1 Descriptive statistics

Case	Klockars (1999) Officer Data (N = 2557)			Lim (2010) Officer Data (N = 401)			Lim (2017) Student Data (N = 1221)		
	Mean	Median	Std.	Mean	Median	Std.	Mean	Median	Std.
C1 Business	1.44	1	.92	1.82	1	1.15	1.55	1	1.04
C2 Meals	2.54	2	1.34	3.23	3	1.28	2.56	2	1.25
C3 Speeding	4.91	5	.40	4.99	5	.10	4.38	5	.90
C4 Holidays	2.80	3	1.38	3.40	3	1.28	2.09	2	1.16
C5 Burglary	4.95	5	.35	4.99	5	.12	4.74	5	.69
C6 Auto	4.45	5	.94	4.81	5	.48	3.81	4	1.18
C7 Supervisor	4.14	4	1.07	4.41	5	.87	3.03	3	1.17
C8 Alcohol	2.99	3	1.39	3.75	4	1.14	4.13	4	1.04
C9 Bar	4.51	5	.94	4.84	5	.45	3.86	4	1.06
C10 Brutality	4.00	5	1.26	4.66	5	.71	–	–	–
C11 Wallet	4.83	5	.59	4.98	5	.17	4.55	5	.80

Std. = standard deviation

Business case was rated as the least serious misbehavior (median = 1) across the three groups.

Officers' Own Views of Police Misconduct Seriousness by Rank

High-rank officers. The perceptions of the high-rank officers on the seriousness of each vignette misconduct were compared across the two studies (Klockars (1999) data and Lim (2010) data) to identify similarities and differences. There were 32 high-rank officers who described themselves as Chiefs, Sheriffs, and/or assistant/deputy chief or sheriffs in the Klockars (1999) data, while 291 high-rank officers from 401 law enforcement agencies including Constables were in the Lim (2010) officer data (see Table 2). The average scores for each scenario were compared first, followed by the comparison of the mean differences that sought to examine any statistical significances through independent t-tests. The findings from the independent t-tests were verified by correlation coefficients, *r*.

Table 2 displays the mean values of each study, t-values, effect sizes, ranges (a minimum and a maximum score per case), the mean of the two studies, and the case rank (the lower number represents the misconduct evaluated as less serious).

In general, the average scores of how seriously high-rank officers viewed each vignette were higher than the overall mean scores shown in Table 1. These gaps were bigger in the Klockars (1999) data than in the Lim (2010) data, but the difference may have resulted from the unbalanced sample sizes by rank in both studies (32 vs. 2525 and 291 vs. 401). The results from independent t-tests found statistically significant group differences, except for the three misconduct cases (C1 Business, C4 Holidays, and C7), but each effect size per case was small, less than .30.

Similarly, like the overall ratings shown in Table 1, in most of the cases (the exception of C7 Supervisor), the high-rank officers in Texas had slightly higher standards on police misconduct than the chiefs from the 30 nationally-sampled agencies did. It would be more convenient to identify these gaps by checking the data distributions via *ranges* or *minimum/maximum values*. For example, in the Klockars (1999) data, the high-rank officers rated the C5 Burglary case from 1 to 5 (*range* = 4), while the high-rank officers in Texas considered the same misconduct as serious to very serious, 3–5 (*range* = 2). The mean scores of C3 Speeding in both studies were subtly different ($\bar{x}_K = 4.81$, $\bar{x}_{L_1} = 4.99$) and were not statistically significant, but the effect size was significant (Es = .184, *p* < .01; see Table 2). Based on the mean of the means, the C3 Speeding ($\bar{x}_{KL_1} = 4.91$) case was considered the most seri-

Table 2 High-rank officers' (Chief/Sherriff/Constable) own views on the seriousness

Case	Klockars (n = 32)	Lim (n = 291)	T-value[a]	Effect size[b]	Klockars (range)	Lim (range)	Overall mean	Rank
C1 Business	1.62	1.81	−.87	.049	1–5	1–5	1.72	11
C2 Meals	3.22	3.37	−.52	.036	1–5	1–5	3.37	10
C3 Speeding	4.91	4.99	−1.14	.143*	3–5	4–5	4.99	1
C4 Holidays	3.47	3.43	.16	−.009	1–5	1–5	3.45	8
C5 Burglary	4.81	4.99	−1.26	.184**	1–5	3–5	4.90	3
C6 Auto	4.63	4.82	−1.46	.115*	2–5	2–5	4.73	5
C7 Supervisor	4.63	4.39	1.37	−.076	2–5	1–5	4.51	6
C8 Alcohol	3.13	3.74	−2.87**	.158**	1–5	1–5	3.44	9
C9 Bar	4.66	4.85	−1.61	.121*	3–5	1–5	4.76	4
C10 Brutality	4.22	4.74	−2.64**	.225**	1–5	1–5	4.48	7
C11 Wallet	4.91	4.97	−.96	.92	3–5	3–5	4.94	2

*p < .05, **p < .01, ***p < .001
[a]Klockars's study was coded as 0 and Lim's study was coded as 1
[b]According to Cohen's rules of thumb to interpret effect sizes by correlation coefficients, $r = .10$ means a small effect which explain 1% of the total variance); $r = .30$ is a medium effect that explains 9% of the total variance; and $r = .50$ represent a large effect size which counts for 25% of the variance

ous police misconduct case by the high-rank officers, and C11 Wallet case ($\bar{x}_{KL_1} = 4.94$) was ranked as the second most serious case, followed by C5 Burglary case ($\bar{x}_{KL_1} = 4.90$).

Middle-rank officers. Sergeants' and lieutenants' own views on the seriousness of police misconduct in both studies were also compared in the same manner. Except for C2 Meal case ($\bar{x}_K = 3.17$, $\bar{x}_{L_1} = 3.05$), the mean values by the middle-rank officers in Texas on the police misconduct were slightly higher than in Klockars (1999) data. Most of these cases resulted in statistically significant differences. Like the high-rank officers in Table 2, there were no statistically significant differences between the groups in a few cases (C1 Business, C4 Holidays, C7 Supervisor; Table 3).

Independent t-tests found that the other seven cases of misconduct were significantly different by the study groups, but only four were confirmed for their statistical significances by the effect size tests: C1 Business (t = −3.38, Es = .168, p < .01), C8 Alcohol (t = −3.41, Es = .130, p < .01), C10 Brutality (t = −2.86, Es = .099, p < .05), and C11 Wallet (t = −4.94, p < .001; Es = .086, p < .05). The middle-rank

officers in both studies ranked C3 Speeding and C5 Burglary cases as the most serious cases of police misconduct ($\bar{x}_{KL_1} = 4.98$). C11 Wallet case ($\bar{x}_{KL_1} = 4.95$) was ranked as the second most serious case.

Line officers. There was a relatively small number of line officers in Lim's data, so independent t-tests, as well as correlation analyses, could not be conducted. Instead, to show the group differences, Hedges' g values were calculated based on group means, standard deviations, and sample sizes. Cohen's d is appropriate when two groups' sample sizes and standard deviations are similar, and Hedges' g values provide a measure of weighted effect size when two groups' sample sizes are different, especially where sample sizes are less than 20 ("Effect size calculator for T-test," 2017; see Cohen 1988). Hedges' g is interpreted in the same manner as Cohen's d: small effect = .2, medium effect = .5, and large effect = .8.

Except for two cases, C3 Speeding and C5 Burglary, which had a standard deviation of zero, Hedges' g values were calculated for the remaining nine cases. As shown in Table 4, C3 Burglary (Es = .364), C9 Bar (Es = .270), C11 Wallet

Table 3 Middle-rank officers' (Sergeants' and Lieutenants) own views on the seriousness

Case	Klockars (n = 488)	Lim (n = 83)	T-value[a]	Effect size[b]	Klockars (range)	Lim (range)	Overall mean	Rank
C1 Business	1.47	1.94	−3.32***	.166**	1–5	1–5	1.71	11
C2 Meals	3.17	3.05	.80	−.033	1–5	1–5	3.11	10
C3 Speeding	4.96	5.00	−3.18**	.055	1–5	5–5	4.98	1
C4 Holidays	3.30	3.48	−1.17	.049	1–5	1–5	3.39	9
C5 Burglary	4.96	5.00	−2.82**	.049	1–5	5–5	4.98	1
C6 Auto	4.74	4.78	−.62	.026	1–5	3–5	4.76	5
C7 Supervisor	4.53	4.54	−.09	.004	1–5	3–5	4.54	6
C8 Alcohol	3.27	3.72	−3.18**	.121**	1–5	1–5	3.50	8
C9 Bar	4.72	4.84	−2.23*	.064	1–5	3–5	4.78	4
C10 Brutality	4.32	4.59	−2.86**	.093*	1–5	1–5	4.46	7
C11 Wallet	4.89	5.00	−4.92***	.085*	1–5	5–5	4.95	3

*p < .05, **p < .01, ***p < .001
[a]Klockars's study was coded as 0 and Lim's study was coded as 1
[b]According to Cohen's rules of thumb to interpret effect sizes by correlation coefficients, r = .10 means a small effect which explain 1% of the total variance); r = .30 is a medium effect that explains 9% of the total variance; and r = .50 represent a large effect size which counts for 25% of the variance

Table 4 Line officers' own views on the seriousness

Case	Klockars (n = 2037)	Lim (n = 27)	Hedges' g^{ab}	Klockars (range)	Lim (range)	Mean	Rank
C1 Business	1.43	1.48	.058	1–5	1–4	1.46	11
C2 Meals	2.38	2.22	.120	1–5	1–5	2.30	10
C3 Speeding	4.90	5.00	–	1–5	5–5	4.95	2
C4 Holidays	2.67	2.82	.109	1–5	1–5	2.75	9
C5 Burglary	4.95	5.00	–	1–5	5–5	4.98	1
C6 Auto	4.38	4.74	.364	1–5	3–5	4.56	5
C7 Supervisor	4.04	4.22	.185	1–5	2–5	4.13	6
C8 Alcohol	2.93	3.89	.760	1–5	2–5	3.41	8
C9 Bar	4.46	4.68	.270	1–5	3–5	4.57	4
C10 Brutality	3.92	4.07	.132	1–5	2–5	4.00	7
C11 Wallet	4.81	4.96	.328	1–5	4–5	4.89	3

*p < .05, **p < .01, ***p < .001
[a]Klockars's study was coded as 0 and Lim's study was coded as 1
[b]According to Cohen, Cohen's d and Hedges' g are similarly interpreted: small effect = .2, medium effect = .5, and large effect = .8

(Es = .328) cases had a small effect, and C8 Alcohol case had a medium effect ($\bar{x}_K = 2.93$, $\bar{x}_{L_1} = 3.89$, Es = .760). Like middle-rank police officers, line officers also viewed C5 Burglary as the most serious case of police misconduct, but all police officers regardless of their rank considered C3 Speeding, C5 Burglary, and C11 Wallet cases as the top three most serious cases of police misconduct.

Students' Own Views on the Seriousness of Police Misconduct by Academic Major

University students' perceptions of the ten vignette police misbehaviors were also measured. Because Lim measured students' views on police use of excessive force (C10 Brutality) with a set of questions, the current study only included the ten scenarios (see Table 1). As shown in Table 5, students ranked C5 Burglary ($\overline{x}_{L_2} = 4.74$), C11 Wallet ($\overline{x}_{L_2} = 4.55$), and C3 Speeding ($\overline{x}_{L_2} = 4.39$), as the top three most serious cases of police misconduct.

The results also suggest that, although the students' views did not differ significantly in most scenarios, students' views on police misconduct were different by their academic major, *criminal justice majors vs. non-criminal justice majors*, in several scenarios (Table 5). For example, CJ majors considered C3 Speeding ($t = -3.16$, $r = .09$, $p < .01$), C4 Holidays ($t = -4.97$, $Es = 0.14$, $p < .001$), and C9 Bar ($t = -2.90$, $Es = .08$, $p < .01$) cases as more serious than non-CJ majors did, although the effect size was very small. On the other hand, CJ majors viewed C8 Alcohol ($t = 3.77$, $Es = .11$, $p < .01$) case as less serious than non-CJ majors did, although the effect size was small.

Group Comparisons

Table 6 shows mean values by police rank and academic major. Table 6 also includes two additional research studies by Schafer and Martinelli (2008) and Vito et al. (2011). As shown in Table 6, the views of police officers on each misconduct case across ranks and research studies were some-what similar, while students' views were clearly different from officers' views on some, but not all cases of police misconduct. For example, students' perceptions were similar to those expressed by line officers in regard to C4 Holidays (the mean scores ranged from 2.12 to 2.67; less serious), but middle to high-rank officers considered that behavior as somewhat more serious (the mean scores ranged from 3.30 to 3.48). However, students considered C8 Alcohol case as more serious than line officers did, yet C9 Bar case as less seriously than police practitioners did. There was a big gap between students' and police officers' views regarding the C7 Supervisor case: the mean value was 3.03 among students (2.98 from the CJ students; 3.06 from the non-CJ students) and 4.24 among police officers (ranged from 4.04 to 4.63; see Tables 1 and 6).

To better identify group differences and similarities, mean scores were rank-ordered in Table 7. One the one hand, C5 Burglary was ranked as the most serious case of police misconduct across the research studies, except for the high-rank officers from the nationally sampled agencies, who rated the case as a top three. C3 Speeding and C11 Wallet were also ranked as the top three most serious cases across all research studies. On the other hand, C1 Business and C2 Meals were typically ranked among the least serious cases. C10 Brutality was ranked quite differ-

Table 5 Students' own views on the seriousness

Case	CJ (n = 539)	Non-CJ (n = 682)	T-test[a]	Effect size[b]	CJ (range)	Non-CJ (range)	Mean	Rank
C1 Business	1.51	1.58	1.27	.036	1–5	1–5	1.55	10
C2 Meals	2.60	2.52	−1.11	.032	1–5	1–5	2.56	8
C3 Speeding	4.47	4.30	−3.16**	.089**	1–5	1–5	4.39	3
C4 Holidays	2.28	1.95	−4.97***	.142**	1–5	1–5	2.12	9
C5 Burglary	4.76	4.71	−1.40	.039	1–5	1–5	4.74	1
C6 Auto	3.77	3.84	.99	.028	1–5	1–5	3.81	6
C7 Supervisor	2.98	3.06	1.23	.035	1–5	1–5	3.02	7
C8 Alcohol	4.00	4.23	3.77***	.107**	1–5	1–5	4.12	4
C9 Bar	3.96	3.79	−2.90**	.082**	1–5	1–5	3.88	5
C10 Brutality	–	–	–	–	–	–	–	–
C11 Wallet	4.59	4.51	−1.58	.045	1–5	1–5	4.55	2

*$p < .05$, **$p < .01$, ***$p < .001$
[a]Criminal justice majors were coded as 1, and non-criminal justice majors were coded as 0
[b]According to Cohen's rules of thumb to interpret effect sizes by correlation coefficients, $r = .10$ means a small effect which explain 1% of the total variance); $r = .30$ is a medium effect that explains 9% of the total variance; and $r = .50$ represent a large effect size which counts for 25% of the variance

Table 6 Mean values of seriousness by groups

Case	High-rank (Chief)		Middle-rank (Sergeant/Lieutenant)				Line officer		Student	
	Klockars (n = 32)	Lim (n = 291)	Klockars (n = 488)	Lim (n = 85)	S&M[a] (N = 478)	Vito et al.[a] (N = 208)	Klockars (n = 2037)	Lim (n = 27)	CJ (n = 539)	Non-CJ (n = 682)
C1 Business	1.62 (1)	1.81 (2)	1.47 (2)	1.94 (2)	1.63 (2)	1.77 (2)	1.43 (1)	1.48 (2)	1.51 (2)	1.58 (2)
C2 Meals	3.22 (3)	3.37 (3)	3.17 (3)	3.05 (3)	3.35 (3)	3.38 (3)	2.38 (2)	2.22 (2)	2.60 (3)	2.52 (3)
C3 Speeding	4.91 (5)	4.99 (5)	4.96 (5)	5.00 (5)	4.96 (5)	4.97 (5)	4.90 (5)	5.00 (5)	4.47 (5)	4.30 (4)
C4 Holidays	3.47 (3)	3.43 (3)	3.30 (3)	3.48 (4)	3.48 (4)	3.46 (4)	2.67 (3)	2.82 (3)	2.28 (2)	1.95 (2)
C5 Burglary	4.81 (5)	4.99 (5)	4.96 (5)	5.00 (5)	5.00 (5)	4.99 (5)	4.95 (5)	5.00 (5)	4.76 (5)	4.71 (5)
C6 Auto	4.63 (5)	4.82 (5)	4.74 (5)	4.78 (5)	4.60 (5)	4.80 (5)	4.38 (4)	4.74 (5)	3.77 (4)	3.84 (4)
C7 Supervisor	4.63 (5)	4.39 (4)	4.53 (5)	4.54 (5)	4.57 (5)	4.55 (5)	4.04 (4)	4.22 (4)	2.98 (3)	3.06 (3)
C8 Alcohol	3.13 (3)	3.74 (4)	3.27 (3)	3.72 (4)	3.89 (4)	3.78 (4)	2.93 (3)	3.89 (4)	4.00 (4)	4.23 (4)
C9 Bar	4.66 (5)	4.85 (5)	4.72 (5)	4.84 (5)	4.75 (5)	4.75 (5)	4.46 (5)	4.68 (5)	3.96 (4)	3.79 (4)
C10 Brutality	4.22 (4)	4.74 (5)	4.32 (4)	4.59 (5)	4.62 (5)	4.64 (5)	3.92 (4)	4.07 (4)	–	–
C11 Wallet	4.91 (5)	4.97 (5)	4.89 (5)	5.00 (5)	4.96 (5)	4.96 (5)	4.81 (5)	4.96 (5)	4.59 (5)	4.51 (5)

[a]The studies by Schafer and Martinelli (2008) and Vito et al. (2011) were included in this Table for reference purpose. The mean values of both Sergeant and Middle Manager shown in Table 6 in Vito et al.'s study were summed and divided by 2 to be consistent with the current study (see Vito et al. 2011, p. 157)

Table 7 Case rankings based on the mean values

Case	High-rank officer		Middle-rank officer		S&M (N = 478)	Vito et al. (N = 208)	Line officer		Student	
	Klockars (n = 32)	Lim (n = 291)	Klockars (n = 488)	Lim (n = 85)			Klockars (n = 2037)	Lim (n = 27)	CJ (n = 539)	Non-CJ (n = 682)
C1 Business	11	11	11	11	11	11	11	11	10	10
C2 Meals	9	10	10	10	10	10	10	10	8	8
C3 Speeding	1	1	1	1	2	2	2	1	3	3
C4 Holidays	8	9	8	9	9	9	9	9	9	9
C5 Burglary	3	1	1	1	1	1	1	1	1	1
C6 Auto	5	4	4	5	6	4	5	4	6	5
C7 Supervisor	5	7	6	7	7	7	6	6	7	7
C8 Alcohol	10	8	9	8	8	8	7	8	4	4
C9 Bar	4	5	5	4	4	5	4	5	5	6
C10 Brutality	7	6	7	6	5	6	8	7	–	–
C11 Wallet	1	3	3	1	2	3	3	3	2	2

ently by groups of police officers: high-rank officers rated it as the sixth or the seventh, middle-rank officers ranked it the fifth to the eighth, and line officers ranked it as the seventh or the eighth. This finding reflects a long-lasting critical and complicated issue in policing, *police use of force.*

Finally, effect sizes of the group comparisons in the three studies were calculated to identify robust statistical significances of each group's view on misconduct. As shown in Table 8, there were significant differences between the views on high-rank officers and middle-rank officers on C1 Business (*Es* = .113, *p* < .001), C7 Supervisor (*Es* = .070, *p* < .05), C8 Alcohol (*Es* = .125, *p* < .01), C10 Brutality (*Es* = .166, *p* < .01), and C11 Wallet (*Es* = .077, *p* < .05) cases, but the effect sizes were small (less than .30). Line officers had different opinions in regard to all cases of misconduct from high- and middle-rank officers, except the C5 Burglary case. In particular, their views on C2 Meals (*Es* = .252, *p* < .01) and C10 Brutality (*Es* = .208, *p* < .01) cases showed slightly higher effect sizes than for the other vignette misconduct (*Es* < .20) (see Table 8).

The students' considerations of the ten cases of police misconduct differed from police practitioners' evaluations. The views of students on police integrity significantly differed from the perceptions of police officers across all three ranks, except for C1 Business with middle-rank officers. The effect sizes between high-rank officers and students were of medium size on C4 Holidays (*Es* = .417, *p* < .01), C6 Auto (*Es* = .350, *p* < .01), C7 Supervisor (*Es* = .449, *p* < .01), and C9 Bar (*Es* = .373, *p* < .01), and were small for the rest of the cases. In particular, students' perceptions were different from middle-rank officers' views on six out of ten cases: C3 Speeding (*Es* = .338), C4 Holidays (*Es* = .428), C6 Auto (*Es* = .396), C7 Supervisor (*Es* = .554), C8 Alcohol (*Es* = .306), and C9 Bar (*Es* = .394). Lastly, focusing on the comparison between students and line officers, most of the cases yielded a small effect, while three cases, C3 Speeding (*Es* = .365, *p* < .01), C7 Supervisor (*Es* = .396, *p* < .01), and C8 Alcohol (*Es* = .410, *p* < .01), had medium effects.

Discussion

This study compares police officers' views on police misconduct by police officers' occupational rank, and police officers' views with university students' views. The current study found both similarities and differences across three studies by police rank, and students' academic majors.

First, all four groups—high, middle, line-level police officers, and students—shared the common ground on C1 Business ($\bar{x}_{all} = 2$, except line officers in Klockars (1999) data), C3 Speeding ($\bar{x}_{all} = 5$, except Non-CJ students), C5 Burglary ($\bar{x}_{all} = 5$), and C11 Wallet ($\bar{x}_{all} = 5$) cases (the mean values, rounded to the nearest hundredth, are shown in Table 6). These four cases were all related to monetary gain, but the differencing factor is whether the gain was illegal. Regarding the C1 Business case, running a private business and taking advantage of being a police officer mostly depended on the departmental policies. That consideration explains why police officers and students ranked the case as the least serious among cases of police misconduct and show a general consensus in regard to it, although their responses varied from 1 to 5 (see Tables 1, 2, 3, 4, and 5). On the other hand, C3 Speeding (*accepting of a personal gift of half of the amount of the fine*), C5 Burglary (*taking a watch, worth about 2 days' pay*), and C11 Wallet (*keeping the money equivalent to a full-day's pay*) cases, describing an officer's illegal monetary gain on crime scenes by abusing police authority or by falsifying a report, were clearly identified by all participants as ethical violations ($\bar{x}_{all} = 5$; See Table 6).

Second, the current study found some similarities in how police officers of various ranks view cases of police misconduct. The perceptions of the high-rank officers—Chiefs, Sheriffs, and Constables—were very similar to the perceptions of the middle-rank officers—sergeants and lieutenants—across all 11 cases, as revealed by the univariate analyses from Table 6. These results were confirmed by the bivariate analyses, with six out of 11 cases displaying no statistically different differences between groups. The other five

Table 8 Effect sizes on group comparisons

| Case | High-rank officer vs. | | | | | | Middle-rank officer vs. | | | | Line officer vs. | |
| | Middle-rank | | Line officer | | Student | | Line officer | | Student | | Student | |
	T-test[a]	ES[b]	T-test[a]	ES[b]	T-test[a]	ES[b]	T-test[a]	ES[b]	T-test[a]	ES[b]	T-test[a]	ES[b]
C1 Business	3.27***	.113***	5.41***	.130**	3.42***	.092**	2.45**	.050**	−.155	.004	−3.37***	.060**
C2 Meals	1.38*	.079*	12.69***	.252**	10.15***	.250**	12.71***	.240**	9.25***	.214**	−4.01***	.070**
C3 Speeding	.80	.027	5.85***	.066***	21.80***	.288***	4.36***	.067**	20.78***	.338**	19.02***	.365**
C4 Holidays	1.13	.038	9.84***	.189**	16.99***	.417**	10.31***	.197**	19.13***	.428**	12.88***	.211**
C5 Burglary	.12	.004	1.33	.023	9.17***	.148**	1.47	.026	9.94***	.177**	9.81***	.197**
C6 Auto	1.47	.047	11.53***	.150**	22.28***	.350**	11.01***	.161**	22.37***	.390**	14.27***	.252**
C7 Supervisor	−1.99*	.070*	6.66***	.117**	22.83***	.449**	12.46***	.192**	32.89***	.554**	24.73***	.396**
C8 Alcohol	3.88***	.125**	10.20***	.181**	−6.29***	.169**	6.22***	.120**	−12.54***	.306**	−27.70***	.410**
C9 Bar	2.23*	.068	10.64***	.132**	23.85***	.373**	7.99***	.124**	21.43***	.394**	16.03***	.275**
C10 Brutality	5.59***	.166**	15.86***	.208**	–	–	8.41***	.144**	–	–	–	–
C11 Wallet	2.75**	.077*	8.29***	.090**	16.09***	.230**	3.99***	.065**	12.24***	.231**	10.12***	.186**

*$p < .05$, **$p \le .01$, ***$p \le .001$

[a]ES = effect size, r

[b]According to Cohen's rules of thumb to interpret effect sizes by correlation coefficients, $r = .10$ means a small effect which explain 1% of the total variance); $r = .30$ is a medium effect that explains 9% of the total variance; and $r = .50$ represent a large effect size which counts for 25% of the variance

cases, C1 Business, C7 Supervisor, C8 Alcohol, and C10 Brutality, and C11 Wallet, were slightly more seriously considered by middle-rank officers. Although independent t-tests found statistical differences between the viewpoints of high- and middle-rank officers, the effect sizes were relatively small, ranging from .08 to .17 (see Table 8). Unlike the commonality of the viewpoints between high- and middle-rank officers, the perceptions of line officers were quite different from both high- and middle-rank officers in all but one case, C5 Burglary (see Table 8).

The concept of cultural schisms in police departments, *management cops* and *street* cops, proposed by Reuss-Ianni (1983), might well explain these similarities and differences in the perceived perceptions on police misconduct among police officers. High- and middle-rank police officers are more likely characterized as *management cops* who pledge "to formal bureaucratic structures and rigid lines of authority and decision-making," while line officers are the *street cops*, "[who] treasure the latitude given street-smart cops to intelligently improvise responses to events" (Herbert 1998, p. 343). Reuss-Ianni (1983) neither distinguished this cultural schism based on police positions or ranks nor clearly explained the features of the schism (see Bittner 1984); however, the schism clearly distinguishes among police officers' roles, responsibilities, and oriented interests by their rank position. Thus, high- and middle-rank officers, *management cops*, share viewpoints on police misconduct most strongly amongst themselves than they do with line officers, *street cops*.

Third, line officers' perceptions in ten out of 11 cases of police misconduct were significantly different from the views of high- and middle-rank officers. The effect sizes of the differences ranged from .090 to .252 for the comparison between high-rank officers and line officers and from .050 to .240 for the comparison between middle-rank officers and line officers. The effects were small, but the differences were statistically significant. Vito et al. (2011) found no difference between management cops and street cops in regard to the seriousness of police misconduct, but the current study found that their views were significantly different depending on the nature of police misconduct. The current study also found that line officers tend to consider C2 Meals (*free meals, discounts on the beat*), C4 Holidays (*holiday gifts from merchants*), and C10 Brutality (*excessive force on car thief*) cases as less serious than high- and middle-rank officers do. The average mean differences ranged from .47 to .81 (see Tables 2, 3, and 4). These findings also clearly demonstrate the presence of different viewpoints between management cops and street cops on gratuities and police use of excessive force. Middle-rank or first-line supervisors play significant roles in shaping their subordinate officer conduct. Studies have found that police supervision and the qualification of supervisors significantly affect officer conduct and decision-making (see Engel and Worden 2003; Lee et al. 2015; Lim and Lee 2015; Schafer and Martinelli 2008). More consideration should be given to the roles of middle-rank officers in the efforts of organizational changes (Schafer and Martinelli 2008).

Last, university students' perceptions of police misconduct were significantly different from all police rank groups, and the magnitude of the effects varied. The different viewpoint on C7 Supervisor (*holiday for a tune-up*) between students and middle-rank officers had the largest effect size, accounting for about 25% of the total variance. Students perceived the C7 case as less serious than middle-rank officers did, with the mean difference between the two groups of 1.52 (3.02 vs. 4.54). This difference could be related to students' lack of awareness of workplace ethics professional job experiences. In addition, for seven out of ten cases in the Police Integrity Scale, the mean scores of students' views were lower than the mean values of all three police rank groups. The three cases in which the mean values were higher for students than they were for police groups were C1 Business, C2 Meals, and C8 Alcohol. Although these cases were ranked as the least serious cases of police misconduct, the current study found that students perceived those forms of police misconduct as more serious than police officers did (see Table 6). Moreover, students' views were considerably different from the views of the police on

C2 Meals and C4 Holidays. For these two cases, students' views were closer to line officers' views than to the views of the management cops (high- and middle-rank officers), although the differences between students' and line officers' perceived views were statistically different, with small effect sizes.

On the other hand, the views of line officers and students were not akin to those expressed high-rank officers, with one notable exception— C5 Burglary—the top-ranked scenario across all groups. There was no statistical difference in the C5 Burglary case among police officers regardless of their rank positions, while students' view was significantly different from the views of all police rank groups (see Table 8). The mean of students' view was lower ($\bar{x} = 4.74$) than the mean values of the police groups, $\bar{x} = 4.95$ for high-rank officers and $\bar{x} = 4.99$ for middle-rank officers and line officers. The results of the current study clearly reveal expectation gaps between the police and the public in regard to various aspects of police integrity.

The present study has several limitations. First, the data used in this study were collected at different time periods and places. The Klockars (1999) data were collected across the United States in 1997, Lim's police supervisor data were obtained in Texas from June 2009 to March 2010, and Lim's student data were collected at three 4-year public universities located in Midwestern and Southern regions of the United States from Spring 2013 to Spring 2017. Because generations and cultures affect individuals' perceptions, future studies should consider these gaps to conduct a more accurate comparison. Second, generalizing the outcomes of the current study is restricted because the three data sets were collected using different sampling methods. Third, the current study only examined how serious the participants considered scenario-based police misconduct, so the results might not thoroughly reflect or represent their integrity or ethical standpoint.

Finally, individual-level (rotten apples) and ecological-level (rotten orchards) studies on police integrity have been under-researched. In addition, the Police Integrity Scale has limita-

tions in terms of its ability to cover all types of police misconduct. For example, Stinson et al. (2013) analyzed 221 drug-related police corruption cases, derived from published online news articles. They found that police officers were involved in various criminal offenses including drug/narcotic offense, robbery, burglary, forcible rape, destroying evidence, and false reporting. Stinson et al. (2013) also found that drug trafficking was "the most recurrent pattern of drug-related police corruption" and that older officers and those who work at a larger agency were less likely to lose their job after being arrested for a drug-related police corruption (p. 501). Future studies should seek to develop additional realistic scenarios to examine officer's moral beliefs, the organizational climate, and police discipline, as well as the public expectation on police misconduct.

Conclusion

As an exploratory study that compares the perceptions of police misconduct between the police and the public, whether their viewpoints are similar, different, or somewhere in between, the current study clearly demonstrates the existence of perceptual gaps and indirectly explains why Americans respect the police but do not trust them. The study also demonstrates the similarity and dissimilarity of the viewpoints among police officers by their rank, especially between management cops and street cops, as well as the positional standpoints of middle-rank officers in between high-rank officers and line officers. In conclusion, knowing, learning, understanding, and accepting the gaps and differences would promote further development of a true melting-pot culture and would build up trust and confidence in American society.

Finally, the additional important facet of this study is in identifying an interesting research venue that needs to be further explored, more explicitly the similarities between students' and line officers' perceptions of misconduct. The study has documented that there is a much larger gap in the attitudes between students and supervisors than between students and line officers. It seems that the police officer views tend to change as officers ascend in ranks and responsibilities, a transformation that is presumably influenced by the organizational subculture that generates changes in these perceptions and attitudes.

Appendix: The Measurement of Police Integrity

C1 Off-duty Security System Business: An officer runs his own private business in which he sells and installs security devices, such as alarms, special locks, etc. He does this work during his off-duty hours.

C2 Free Meals, Discounts on Beat: An officer routinely accepts free meals, cigarettes, and other items of small value from merchants on his beat. He does not solicit these gifts and is careful not to abuse the generosity of those who give gifts to him.

C3 Bribe from Speeding Motorist: An officer stops a motorist for speeding. The officer agrees to accept a personal gift of half of the amount of the fine in exchange for not issuing a citation.

C4 Holiday Gifts from Merchants: An officer is widely liked in the community, and on holidays local merchants and restaurant and bar owners show their appreciation for his attention by giving him gifts of food and liquor.

C5 Crime Scene Theft of Watch: An officer discovers a burglary of a jewelry shop. The display cases are smashed and It is obvious that many Items have been taken. While searching the shop, he takes a watch, worth about 2 days pay for that officer. He reports that the watch had been stolen during the burglary.

C6 Auto Repair Shop 5% Kickback: A police officer has a private arrangement with a local auto body shop to refer the owners of the cars damaged in the accidents to the shop. In exchange for each referral, he receives a payment of 5% at the repair bill from the shop owner.

C7 Supervisor: Holiday for Tune-up: A police officer, who happens to be a very good auto mechanic, is scheduled to work during the coming holidays. A supervisor offers to give him these days off if he agrees to tune-up his supervisor's personal car. Evaluate the SUPERVISOR'S behavior.

C8 Cover-up of Police DUI Accident: At 2 A.M., an officer, who is on duty, is driving his patrol car on a deserted road. He sees a vehicle that has been driven off the road and is stuck in a ditch. He approaches the vehicle and observes that the driver is not hurt but is obviously intoxicated. He also finds that the driver is a police officer. Instead of reporting this accident and offense he transports the driver to his home.

C9 Drink to Ignore Late Bar Closing: An officer finds a bar on his beat which is still serving drinks a half hour past its legal closing time. Instead of reporting this violation, the police officer agrees to accept a couple of free drinks from the owner.

C10 Excessive Force on Car Thief: Two officers on foot patrol surprise a man who is attempting to break into an automobile. The man flees. They chase him for about two blocks before apprehending him by tackling him and wrestling him to the ground. After he is under control both officers punch him a couple of times in the stomach as punishment for fleeing and resisting.

C11 Theft from Found Wallet: An officer finds a wallet in a parking lot. It contains the amount of money equivalent to a full-day's pay for that officer. He reports the wallet as lost property but keeps the money for himself.

References

Bittner, E. (1984). The broken badge: Reuss-Ianni and the culture of policing. *American Bar Foundation Research Journal, 9*(1), 206–213.

Bjerregaard, B., & Lord, V. B. (2004). An examination of the ethical and value orientation of criminal justice students. *Police Quarterly, 7*(2), 262–284.

Cohen, J. (1988). *Statistical power analysis for the behavioral sciences* (2nd ed.). Hillsdale, NJ: Lawrence Erlbaum Associates.

Dowler, K., & Zawilski, V. (2007). Public perceptions of police misconduct and discrimination: Examining the impact of media consumption. *Journal of Criminal Justice, 35*(2), 193–203.

Edison Research. (2010). *The social habit – frequent social networkers*. Retrieved from http://www.edison-research.com/the_social_habit_frequent_social_networkers_in_america/

Effect Size Calculator for T-test. (2017, May 15). Retrieved from http://www.socscistatistics.com/effectsize/Default3.aspx

Eitle, D., D'Alessio, S. J., & Stolzenberg, L. (2014). The effect of organizational and environmental factors on police misconduct. *Police Quarterly, 17*(2), 103–126.

Engel, R. S., & Worden, R. E. (2003). Police officers' attitudes, behavior, and supervisory influences: An analysis of problem solving. *Criminology, 41*, 131–166.

Field, A. P. (2005). *Discovering statistics using SPSS* (2nd ed.). London, UK: Sage.

Fridell, L., & Lim, H. (2016). Assessing the racial aspects of police force using the implicit- and counter-bias perspectives. *Journal of Criminal Justice, 44*, 36–48.

Fyfe, J., & Kane, R. (2006). *Bad cops: A study of career-ending misconduct among New York City police officers*. Washington, DC: The US Department of Justice. Retrieved from www.ncjrs.gov/pdffiles1/nij/grants/215795.pdf.

Harris, C. J. (2010). Problem officers? Analyzing problem behavior patterns from a large cohort. *Journal of Criminal Justice, 38*(2), 216–225.

Herbert, S. (1998). Police subculture reconsidered. *Criminology, 36*(2), 343–369.

Hickman, M. J., Piquero, A. R., Powell, Z. A., & Greene, J. (2015). Expanding the measurement of police integrity. *Policing: An International Journal of Police Strategies and Management, 39*(2), 246–267.

Jones, J. M. (2015, June 19). *In U.S., Confidence in police lowest in 22 years*. Retrieved from http://www.gallup.com/poll/183704/confidence-police-lowest-years.aspx

Kane, R. J. (2002). The social ecology of police misconduct. *Criminology, 40*(4), 867–896.

Kleinig, J. (1996). *Ethics of policing*. London, UK: Cambridge University Press.

Klinger, D. A. (1997). Negotiating order in patrol work: An ecological theory of police response to deviance. *Criminology, 35*(2), 277–306.

Klockars, C. B. (1999). *Police corruption in thirty agencies in the United States, 1997*. ICPSR version. Washington, DC: U.S. Department of Justice, National Institute of Justice [producer], 1997. Ann Arbor, MI: Inter-university Consortium for Political and Social Research [distributor], 1999. https://doi.org/10.3886/ICPSR02629.v1

Klockars, C. B., Kutnjak Ivković, S., Harver, W. E., & Haberfeld, M. R. (2000). *The measurement of police integrity*. NIJ Research in Brief (Document No.

NCJ 181465). Washington, DC: U.S. Department of Justice, National Institute of Justice.

Klockars, C. B., Haberfeld, M. R., Kutnjak Ivković, S., & Uydess, A. (2001). A minimum requirement for police corruption. In R. A. Silverman, T. P. Thornberry, B. Cohen, & B. Krisberg (Eds.), *Crime and justice at the millennium: Essays by and in Honor of Marvin E. Wolfgang* (pp. 173–196). Dordrecht, The Netherlands: Springer.

Klockars, C. B., & Kutnjak Ivković, S. (2004). Measuring Police Integrity. In A. R. Piquero, J. R. Greene, & M. J. Hickman (Eds.), *Police Integrity and Ethics* (pp. 1.3–1.20). Belmont, CA: Wadsworth Publishing.

Klockars, C. B., Kutnjak Ivković, S., & Haberfeld, M. R. (2004). The contours of police integrity. In C. B. Klockars, S. Kutnjak Ivković, & M. R. Haberfeld (Eds.), *The contours of police integrity* (pp. 1–18). Thousand Oaks, CA: Sage.

Klockars, C. B., Kutnjak Ivković, S. K., & Haberfeld, M. R. (2006). *Enhancing police integrity*. Dordrecht, The Netherlands: Springer.

Kutnjak Ivković, S. (2005). Police mis(behavior): A cross-cultural study of corruption seriousness. *Policing: An International Journal of Police Strategies & Management, 28*(3), 546–566.

Kutnjak Ivković, S. (2009). Rotten apples, rotten branches, and rotten orchards: A cautionary tale of police misconduct. *Criminology & Public Policy, 8*(4), 777–785.

Kutnjak Ivković, S., & Haberfeld, M. (2015). *Measuring police integrity across the world*. New York: Springer.

Lawton, B. A. (2007). Levels of nonlethal force: An examination of individual, situational, and contextual factors. *Journal of Research in Crime and Delinquency, 44*(2), 163–184.

Lee, H., Lim, H., Moore, D. D., & Kim, J. (2013). How police organizational structure correlates with front-line officers' attitudes toward corruption: A multilevel model. *Police Practice and Research: An International Journal, 14*(5), 386–401.

Lee, J., Lim, H., & Lee, H. (2015). Differential social distance and confidence in the police. *International Journal of Police Science and Management, 17*(3), 147–154.

Lim, H. (2015). Social modeling effects on perception of the police: Focus on indirect police contact experience among college students. *Policing: An International Journal of Police Strategies and Management, 38*(4), 675–689.

Lim, H., & Lee, H. (2015). The effect of supervisor education and training on police use of force. *Criminal Justice Studies, 28*(4), 444–463.

Lim, H., & Sloan, J. J. (2016). Police office integrity: A partial replication and extension. *Policing: An International Journal of Police Strategies and Management, 39*(2), 284–301.

Lim, H., Fridell, L. A., & Lee, H. (2014). The impact of supervision and neighborhood context on police use of less-lethal force: A multi-level analysis. *Journal of Police Studies, 14*(2), 155–182.

McCarthy, J. (2016, October 24). *Americans' respect for police surges*. Retrieved from http://www.gallup.com/poll/196610/americans-respect-police-surges.aspx

Morabito, M. S. (2007). Horizons of context: Understanding the police decision to arrest people with mental illness. *Psychiatric Services, 58*(12), 1582–1587.

Norman, J. (2017, July 10). *Confidence in police back at historical average*. Retrieved from http://www.gallup.com/poll/213869/confidence-police-back-historical-average.aspx

Reuss-Ianni, E. (1983). *Two cultures of policing: Street cops and management cops*. New Brunswick, NJ: Transaction, Inc..

Schafer, J. A., & Martinelli, T. J. (2008). First-line supervisor's perceptions of police integrity. *Policing: An International Journal of Police Strategies and Management, 31*(2), 305–323.

Schmidt, F. L., & Hunter, J. E. (2015). *Methods of meta-analysis: Correcting error and bias in research findings* (3rd ed.). Thousand Oaks, CA: Sage.

Schuck, A. M., & Rosenbaum, D. P. (2005). Global and neighborhood attitudes toward the police: Differentiation by race, ethnicity and type of contact. *Journal of Quantitative Criminology, 21*(4), 391–418.

Smith, D. A. (1986). The neighborhood context of police behavior. In A. J. Reiss & M. Tonry (Eds.), *Communities and crime* (pp. 313–341). Chicago, IL: University of Chicago Press.

Stinson, P. M., Liederbach, J., Brewer, S., Schmalzried, H. D., Mathna, B. E., & Long, K. L. (2013). A study of drug-related police corruption arrests. *Policing: An International Journal of Police Strategies and Management, 36*(3), 491–511.

Sun, I. Y., Payne, B. K., & Wu, Y. (2008). The impact of situational factors, officer characteristics, and neighborhood context on police behavior: A multi-level analysis. *Journal of Criminal Justice, 36*(1), 22–32.

Terrill, W., & Reisig, M. D. (2003). Neighborhood context and police use of force. *Journal of Research in Crime and Delinquency, 40*(3), 291–321.

Vito, G. F., Wolfe, S., Higgines, G. E., & Walsh, W. F. (2011). Police integrity: Rankings of scenarios on the Klockars scale by "management cops.". *Criminal Justice Review, 36*(2), 152–164.

Walker, S. (2006). *Police accountability: Current issues and research needs*. National Institute of Justice (NIJ) policing Research workshop, Washington, DC.

Weitzer, R. (2002). Incidents of police misconduct and public opinion. *Journal of Criminal Justice, 30*(5), 397–408.

Slovenian Resident and Police Officer Evaluations of the Harm Caused by Different Types of Police Deviance

Branko Lobnikar, Gorazd Meško, Aljaž Hölzl, and Kaja Prislan

Introduction

Efforts to develop a professional, legitimate, and accountable police service are present in all contemporary societies. There are few, if any, countries that can be fully satisfied with the level of professionalism of its police service, its level of legitimacy within the society, and with the outcomes the police deliver in terms of security while respecting the rule of law and individual liberties (Meško and Klemenčič 2007).

The challenges posed to the police organization are even greater in emerging democracies. While Slovenia was an emerging democracy in the early 1990s, today Slovenia is a modern Central-European democracy, independent since 1991. With a population of approximately two million and a GDP of 23,596 USD per capita in 2017, it is considered quite a successful transitional country from a former socialist republic to a functional democracy. After gaining independence in 1991, Slovenia soon became a member of the United Nations and joined other major international political, security, and economic organizations such as the Council of Europe (in 1993), the European Union (in 2004), NATO (in 2004), and

the Organization for Economic Cooperation and Development (OECD in 2010). In 2007, Slovenia joined the Euro Zone.

The Slovenian police service employs approximately 8800 personnel, or one police officer for every 267 inhabitants. Since 1991, Slovenian police went through several police reforms, introduced to adhere closer to the Western/democratic style of policing. The initial reforms were symbolic yet important: renaming the militia (*milica*) into the police (*policija*) and changing the insignias. The Constitution of the Republic of Slovenia of 1991 (Constitution 1991) not only explicitly prohibited members of the police and armed forces from being members of any political party, but also put strong emphasis on the protection of human rights. New criminal procedure legislation of 1995 strengthened judicial control over police powers through strict warrant requirements and wide judicial powers to exclude illegally obtained evidence (Grilc and Klemenčič 2006). A landmark institutional reform came with the adoption of the new Police Act (1998). It created the General Police Directorate as an autonomous body within the Ministry of the Interior. The Act also significantly changed basic police powers and introduced civilian oversight in the resolution of complaints involving police ill-treatment. Early in 2013, new police legislation was adopted (Police Tasks and Powers Act 2013). The new legislation stresses decentralization, reinforces

B. Lobnikar (✉) · G. Meško · A. Hölzl · K. Prislan
Faculty of Criminal Justice and Security, University of Maribor, Maribor, Slovenia
e-mail: branko.lobnikar@fvv.uni-mb.si; gorazd.mesko@fvv.uni-mb.si; aljaz.holzl@gmail.com; kaja.prislan@fvv.uni-mb.si

© Springer Nature Switzerland AG 2019
S. Kutnjak Ivković, M. R. Haberfeld (eds.), *Exploring Police Integrity*,
https://doi.org/10.1007/978-3-030-29065-8_11

cooperation between the police and the local community, and emphasizes the roles of problem solving and community policing in local policing, merging with intelligence-led policing in crime investigation. Over the course of the last two decades, the pluralization of police institutions has also occurred, introducing municipal wardens as additional public policing stakeholders in local communities. All changes cumulated in the transformation of the police training in Slovenia and the strengthening of the required educational level for the entry-level police work. Starting with 2013, police officers in Slovenia need to have at least a college education.

Surveys on police corruption and integrity of the Slovenian police started soon after the Slovenian independence. The first paper on police deviance was published by Meško (1994). Analyzing police culture, the author dicussed some forms of deviance within the police organization, not only those defined as criminal offences, but also other forms of police deviance such as aggressiveness, sleeping on duty, alcoholism, or drug addiction. Since the mid-1990s, papers and articles on dark sides of policing—police misconduct and police deviance—have become a part of the critical criminological analysis of the Slovenian policing. At the end of the 1990s, studies in this field have shifted from studying individuals' integrity (or corruption as its antipode) to studying organizational-cultural factors of police integrity (e.g., Pagon et al. 1998).

The purpose of this chapter is to analyze the perceptions concerning different forms of police deviance. This study was conducted among police officers and residents. The empirical part of the chapter studies the seriousness evaluations of individual examples of police deviance conducted among Slovenia's residents and police officers. In addition, the chapter compares and contrasts police officer and resident views of misconduct seriousness and analyzes potential differences in the assessments provided by the two groups of respondents.

Police Deviance and Police Integrity

Because it affects the legitimacy of the police, police deviance is one of the topical issues that has been addressed by researchers focusing on the field of policing. Although researchers had been tackling this issue from the very early stages of the professionalization of the police profession, the interest in this topic has been reinvigorated, as greater emphasis has been placed on the democracy, transparency, and fairness (justice) of contemporary police organizations (e.g. Son and Rome 2004; Kane 2005; Garcia 2005; Gau and Brunson 2010). Studies of police deviance have intensified since the mid-twentieth century, when, apart from police corruption, the issues of police discrimination (Legewie 2016) and brutality (Worden 2015) also became pertinent.

Ethical behavior and high integrity of police officers on the one hand and deviant behavior on the other hand are two opposite outcomes of work behavior (Pagon and Lobnikar 2000, 2004). There is an expectation that police officers will impartially enforce the law and that their decisions will be open to scrutiny. Unfortunately, the history of policing has revealed that this is often a myth and that officers engage in a range of activities that break the disciplinary code and sometimes even the criminal law (e.g. Punch 2000; Newburn 1999; Kane 2002; Klockars et al. 2004; Donner et al. 2016; Albrecht 2017). Because of the inconsistent reporting and difficulties with its detection, the actual level of police deviance cannot be assessed. Consequently, the researchers have tended to focus on evaluating the public and police officer perceptions about deviance seriousness, as well as of their willingness to report them.

Police deviance is not a uniform phenomenon. There are different categories and typologies that vary in terms of the seriousness and substance of deviant behavior. For a misbehavior to be considered police misconduct, the officer must have used his/her employment status to engage in job-specific malpractice. This definition includes both legal (for example, unprofessional or unethical) and illegal activities (Kane 2002). Barker and Carter (1991) emphasize that it is difficult to define all phenomena and methods related to police deviance. However, they pinpoint two predominant categories of deviant behavior. The first category emerges in relation to the police profession (i.e., professional deviance), which includes all acts, both criminal and non-criminal, committed by police officers in the course of their work. This type of deviance is exhibited in the form of police officers' misbehavior at work and corruption within the police organization, and is mainly linked to the status of police officers as employees of an organization and less so to the exercise of their tasks. The second category represents the abuse of power, including, for instance, physical abuse (officers using excessive force), psychological abuse (officers discriminating against or disrespecting individuals involved in police proceedings), and abuse of the law (officers violating constitutionally enshrined basic human rights and fundamental freedoms, without using physical force or psychological abuse). The most severe type of police officers' abuse of power stems from their right to take someone's life (Kotnik 1993).

Punch (2000) distinguishes between three broad categories of police deviance: *corruption* (the conventional understanding of taking something, against one's duty, to do or not to do something in exchange for money or gifts from an external corrupter), *misconduct* (similarly to other workers, the police break their own internal rules and procedures; they sleep on duty, report sick when they are healthy, are 'creative' with expense declarations, etc.), and *police crime* (police officers not only accept bribes, but also break the law in other serious ways, that is, by using excessive force, by becoming involved in drug dealing, theft and burglary, and violating a person's rights). However, there is a great deal of overlap between the categories (e.g., corruption and crime).

In Slovenia, studies on police deviance start with the study by Meško (1994) on police personality characteristics and police officers' attitudes towards marginal social groups. The most intriguing finding relates to the positive attitudes displayed by police officers toward criminals and the negative attitudes displayed toward victims of crime. Lobnikar et al. (2004) conducted a survey about the frequency and causes of violence and aggressive behavior at the workplace. They found that victimization of Slovenian police officers can, above all, be accounted for by social undermining by peers and superiors. Therefore, the authors conclude that social undermining most probably leads to victimization at workplace. Among demographic factors of victimization, gender affiliation is the most recurrent one, which is particularly true of sexual harassment, where gender is the main descriptive variable. In the study on deviance and police organizational culture in Slovenia (Banutai et al. 2011), the main contributors to deviant behavior in Slovenia was the lack of support by supervisors, low organizational commitment, and weak police-citizens relationships.

If police deviance represents one side of the coin, police integrity denotes the opposite side. The management and accountability of the police, police integrity, and related issues are important aspects of contemporary policing (Lim and Sloan 2016). Integrity is associated with such virtues as purity, solidarity, involvement, sincerity, and scrupulousness (Kaptein 2001). Delattre (1996) defines integrity as the settled dispositions, the resolve and determination, and the established habit of doing right where there is no one to make you do it but yourself. According to Vicchio (1997), integrity is central to the mission of democratic policing. Furthermore, police integrity denotes a series of concepts and beliefs, the combination of which represents the framework for the functioning of police organizations, as well as for the professional and personal ethics of individual police officers (which, among others, includes honesty and fairness, honor, morals, loyalty, respect of fundamental principles, and commitment to the common mission).

Pagon et al. (2003) describe integrity as the symmetry between individuals' moral beliefs and convictions and their conduct. Individuals possessing a high degree of integrity will do what they believe to be morally right and not what other people believe they should do regardless of potential repercussions. Klockars et al. (2000, 2004) define police integrity as normative inclination among the police to resist temptations to abuse the rights and privileges of their occupation. They further claim that integrity is a belief rather than a behavior. At an individual level, it is an opinion, while at the group level, it is a norm. Hence, the idea of police integrity is morally charged and police conduct is, at least to a certain degree, right or wrong. Finally, a characteristic of integrity is that it is virtually inseparable from moral attitudes because it combines a belief with an inclination to behave in accordance with that belief (Klockars et al. 2004). Police officers with a high degree of integrity are expected not to act contrary to moral and ethical standards, and should not look the other way when their colleagues act illegally, but clearly express and defend their positions (Šumi 2008; Šumi et al. 2012).

Studying police integrity is especially important because of the specificity of police work and the ability of the police to encroach upon individuals' rights and freedoms. Two decades ago, research in this field has shifted from studying individuals' integrity (or corruption as its antipode) to studying organizational-cultural factors of police integrity (e.g., Pagon et al. 1998). The first Slovenian study we present here is on the perceptions of police manager integrity. The study was carried out in 2010 on a sample of 768 police officers (Šumi et al. 2012). The instrument Perceived Leader Integrity Scale (PLIS) was used for measuring management integrity. The study is important for the Slovenian police because the use of a PLIS questionnaire enables accurate measurement of how police officers evaluate their supervisors' integrity. The results show that the perceived index of integrity of Slovenian police managers is rather high: an average of 5.52 (S.D. 1.33) was calculated on the scale form 1 (low) to 7 (high). Further analysis revealed that the best predictors for the perception of a high level of integrity were the work and management experience of managers and their educational level. More experienced managers who also have a higher education level received higher marks for leader integrity by their subordinated police officers.

The second study was conducted in late 1990s. Klockars et al. (2000) developed a survey instrument that measures the extent of police integrity. Their questionnaire includes descriptions of 11 hypothetical scenarios, the majority of which address various forms of police corruption, from the acceptance of gratuities and gifts to opportunistic thefts and shakedowns. The study results (Pagon et al. 1998, 2000; Pagon and Lobnikar 2004) showed that police officers in Slovenia have a high level of integrity. The study, conducted among police officers (767) and students (254) as the comparison group, found that in most cases police officers had a higher level of integrity than students did, both in terms of their moral standards and their behavioral intentions. Moreover, the police officers were the most frequently willing to report the most serious police misconduct, such as theft of watch from crime scene, theft from a found wallet, and bribe from speeding motorist. The two cases in which the police officers were the least willing to report were off-duty security system business and accepting holiday gifts from local merchants. The regression analyses revealed the officers' own perception of the seriousness of corrupt behavior was the most significant determinant of their willingness to report corruption, accounting for as much as 43.6% of the variance. The respondents' organizational attributes (e.g., assignment, rank) and their beliefs about appropriate discipline accounted for additional 11.4% and 9.4% of the variance, respectively. Although some aspects of the code were detected, the authors concluded that police officers in Slovenia possess high integrity (Pagon and Lobnikar 2004; Kutnjak Ivković et al. 2000; Haberfeld, Klockars, Kutnjak Ivković, Pagon, 2000).

The second wave of the integrity study from 2011 revealed that the majority of the respondents recognized scenarios they evaluated as violations of the official rules (Lobnikar and Meško 2015). Three scenarios (cover-up of fellow police officer driving under influence accident, taking free meals and gifts from merchants, and failing to report hate crime) feature some variations in answers, while there were more scenarios in which the respondents' assessment of whether the described behavior qualifies as a violation of official rules were almost unanimous (e.g., theft of knife from crime scene, false report on drug dealer). The respondents' labelling of a particular behavior as rule-violating is closely related to how serious they evaluated the behavior to be; if they thought that the behavior tended to be more serious, they were more likely to say that it violated official rules. The respondents' evaluations of scenario seriousness suggest that the scenarios were generally evaluated to be on the serious side; means were clustered between the midpoint of the scale and the "very serious" end of the scale.

Influence of Police Deviance on the Perception of the Legitimacy of the Police

The emergence of police deviance depends on various factors, related not only to individual characteristics, but also to organizational and community influences. Kutnjak Ivković (2005, 2009a) and Wolfe and Piquero (2011) find that police deviance is predominantly dependent on the organizational-level influences such as education and training, policy, recruitment, and internal organizational justice. Important community or environmental factors include, for example, the level of social disorganization, and the mobility of residents (Terrill and Reisig 2003; Kane 2002; Weitzer 1999), while individual factors predominantly refer to the general individual characteristics and traits of police officers such as officer race, education, age, and past behavior (e.g., documented traffic offenses) (Kane and White 2009; Greene et al. 2004; McElvain and Kposowa 2004). In last two decades, when discussing the main reasons for the occurrence of police deviance, there has been a shift from focusing on individual factors to recognizing the importance of organizational issues (Klockars et al. 2004, 2006).

At the same time, residents' perceptions of police deviance are mostly affected by the circumstances and conditions related to the perceptions of

crime and disorder, as well as by the media reports of individual incidents (Chermak et al. 2006). A study carried out by Son and Rome (2004), for instance, shows that certain types of deviance are frequently detected by both residents and police officers, however, they are evaluated as less serious (e.g. minor gratuities, sleeping on the job, unnecessary speeding). In general, residents tend to evaluate police deviance as a more frequent phenomenon in comparison to police officers, who tend to believe that these are rare and isolated cases that do not reflect the actual extent of integrity in the police (Son and Rome 2004; Porter et al. 2015; Cheloukhine et al. 2015; Liqun 2015; Oberwittler and Roché 2018).

Police officers in Australia (Porter et al. 2015) understood the serious nature of different types of ethics violations and expressed willingness to report violations, although willingness to report was correlated with the degrees of perceived seriousness. As with the results of similar surveys (e.g., in Slovenia, Lobnikar and Meško 2015), the respondents tended to have a lower view of the integrity of their colleagues when compared to their own. In contrast to Australia, police in Russia did not perceive the behaviors described in the research scenarios as very serious (Cheloukhine et al. 2015).

Liqun (2015) concluded that, compared to the concepts such as public opinion about the police and legitimacy of police work, confidence in the police is the preferred choice when we survey the citizenry about the level of support for the police. Yet, confidence in the police is an attitude, the result of a more in-depth reflection on the role and position of the police in a modern society. Therefore, it is necessary to understand the concept of legitimacy from the point of view of confidence in police work.

Legitimacy is the fundamental concept for the democratic functioning of authorities. It is based on the people's perceptions of the way institutions perform their mission in society and the way they exercise their powers (Jackson et al. 2015; Tyler 2011). Various studies find that the evaluation of the legitimacy of policing is most strongly correlated with the trust in police work, the assessment of procedural justice, and perceptions of police effectiveness (e.g. Tyler 2011; Reisig et al. 2012; Trinkner et al. 2016; Tankebe et al. 2016). Citizens' attitude toward authorities and law obedience depends on their perception of the legitimacy of police work (Cohen-Charash and Spector 2001; Colquitt et al. 2001), which is why contemporary police organizations have been focusing on maintaining and strengthening public support to policing.

Trust and legitimacy are generated through just, community-oriented, and inclusive policing (Trinkner et al. 2016). Therefore, police officers' deviant behavior represents a strong impediment to public trust and confidence. One could claim that police officers' deviance is one of the main sources of mistrust in the police and, consequently, one of the factors weakening the legitimacy of police organizations (Semukhina and Reynolds 2014). Furthermore, public beliefs and opinions regarding the prevalence of police officers' deviant behavior produces the same effect, regardless of the actual degree of deviance within the police and the opinions about deviant behaviors held by police officers themselves.

Studies on police legitimacy in Slovenia show that public opinion is formed on the basis of previous experience (Sotlar et al. 2015). Perceptions of police officers' deviance influence the perception of police legitimacy. They affect the performance and effectiveness of policing (maintaining law and order, addressing crime) because they influence public attitudes toward the police, thus determining their willingness to cooperate with the police (Miller and Davis 2008). Furthermore, they also affect the relationships and general conditions within a police organization (Hunter 1999). Therefore, perceptions of police officers' integrity represent an important aspect of assessing the police and shape attitudes toward police organizations.

Research findings indicate that personal experiences of policing have a significant effect on citizens' general assessment of the police (Tyler and Fagan 2008). While there is some debate over the effect of positive contacts with the police, researchers agree that unpleasant experiences tend to increase unfavorable opinions (Tyler 2006). As Sunshine and Tyler (2003) emphasized, citizens think about the police in ways that have to do with the values and norms that sustain social life and look to the police to protect and strengthen social values. When the community is seen as morally deteriorating, public satisfaction with the police may be affected negatively. So, public trust in policing is shaped by evaluations of the extent to which the police typify community morals and values (Sunshine and Tyler 2003). The key to public support for the police is the view among members of the public that they share moral solidarity, or a set of common moral values, with the police (Lobnikar et al. 2015).

Different types of deviant behavior occur in almost all professions and organizations. However, police deviance raises the highest degree of concern because it refers to deviant behaviors of those who are supposed to prevent such phenomena and who have access to all kinds of confidential personal data, as well as the right to use means of restraint. Therefore, the abuse of power, brutality, and corruption continue to be in the focus of public and media attention. In contemporary societies, the police still are a primary institution through which the state maintains law and order and provides security to its residents. To continuously gain and maintain the trust of individuals and society as a whole, police officers must perform their tasks responsibly and by observing a high degree of professional ethics and personal integrity. Because police officers' deviant behavior may be expressed in different ways (e.g., in the form of corruption, abuse or misapplication of police powers, omission of activities or conducts, gaining occasional benefits, and covering up errors), the perception of the seriousness of individual types must be analyzed in addition to the prevalence of police deviance. This chapter presents the results of a study on perceived police deviance, conducted on a sample of Slovenian police officers and a sample of Slovenia's residents.

Methods, Data Collection and Description of the Sample

Questionnaire

Klockars and Kutnjak Ivković (2004) developed a survey instrument that measures the extent of police integrity. Their questionnaire incorporates descriptions of 11 hypothetical scenarios, the overwhelming majority of which address various types of police corruption. The questionnaire has been used to survey police officers in a number of countries across the world, from the United States, England, and Canada to Japan and Pakistan (see Klockars et al. 2004). Out of the East-European countries in transition, it has been used in Croatia, Slovenia, Bosnia and Herzegovina, Poland, Hungary, and the Czech Republic (see Klockars et al. 2004; Kutnjak Ivković and Shelley 2005).

The second version of their questionnaire includes scenarios covering a variety of types of police misconduct ranging from police corruption and the use of excessive force to the planting of evidence and verbal abuse (Klockars et al. 2006). In consultation with the Croatian Police, Kutnjak Ivković (2009b) added three scenarios to the questionnaire. The first additional scenario describes the failure to note on the police report that a crime could be classified as a hate crime, while the second scenario focuses on the acceptance of a bribe from a motorist caught speeding. Finally, the third scenario describes the failure to intervene when a police officer sees juveniles writing graffiti on a wall. These three additional scenarios were also used in the Slovenian version of the questionnaire.

Each scenario is followed by the same set of questions, used both in the first and the second version of the questionnaire (Kutnjak Ivković 2009b). Two questions evaluate the level of offense seriousness ("*How serious the respondent consider the described behavior to be*"). In the first question, the respondent is asked to assess how serious he or she personally evaluates the described behavior, while in the next question the respondent is asked to evaluate how serious most police officers would consider the described

behavior. The questions and scenarios were the same for police officers and residents. The last part of the questionnaire contains a few demographic questions.

Sample

In the first half of 2016, an online survey (using online survey platform www.1ka.si) was used to gather information from Slovenia's residents. Researchers invited adults (age 14 and above) from Slovenia via the Internet (Facebook, Twitter) and via direct e-mailing to participate in the survey. We relied on the snowball method (anyone who participated in the survey was asked to provide a link to an online survey to their acquaintances). The participation was voluntary and no compensation was offered for participation. The analysis was conducted on the responses provided by a sample of 338 residents. Table 1 presents the demographic data for the resident sample.

Most respondents form the citizen subsample were male, more than one-half had completed at least secondary school. Most were either employed or were students. In addition, just over one-half of them lived in an urban environment. When respondents were presented with questions related to the police, most of them (47%) stated that their contacts with the police were rare. Twenty-two percent of the respondents were in

Table 1 Demographic characteristics of the resident sample

		Residents	
		n	%
Gender	Male	198	59
	Female	140	41
Education	Primary school	10	2.9
	High school	171	50.6
	College	34	10.1
	BA and more	123	36.4
Status	Employed or self-employed	49.0%	
	Students	42.0%	
	Unemployed	7.0%	
	Retirees	2.0%	
Place of living	Urban	53.0%	
	Rural	47.0%	

contact with the police occasionally or a few times per year, while 7% of respondents said such contacts were frequent and 9% reported their contacts with the police were very frequently. On the other hand, 16% of respondents did not have any contact with the police at all.

The data obtained by surveying the residents were compared with the data gathered from police officers, collected in 2011 within the scope of a study conducted by Lobnikar and Meško (2015). Data from the police sample were obtained from 550 police officers from all three levels of police organization (national, regional, and local). In the area of each police administration, various police stations were selected. A total of 1000 questionnaires were sent to the selected police stations on a given date with the prior consent of the police management. The questionnaires were submitted to police officers working their shift, together with a return mail envelope and a cover letter describing the main purpose of the survey. Police officers were asked to fill in the questionnaire, seal the envelope, and return it to the research institution. Anonymity was guaranteed to police officers and residents. Their participation was voluntary.

The vast majority of the surveyed police officers were male, and were employed in a medium-sized department. Most of them had work experience of 11–20 years, while a little less than three-quarters of them worked in the police operations. The demographic structure is presented in Table 2.

Police officers and residents were asked to evaluate the seriousness of individual types of described behaviors, after which residents were asked to assess how police officers working in their local community would evaluate the same types of behavior. The police subsample respondents were asked to evaluate how serious they perceive the behaviors described in scenarios. Two questions probed the respondents about the seriousness of the behavior; the first question sought their own evaluations of seriousness, while the second question asked about their estimates of how the majority of the police officers in their agency would evaluate the behavior. The aim of asking police officers how they think other police officers would evaluate the serioussnes of

Table 2 Demographic characteristics of the police officer sample

		Police (%)
Gender	Male	88.5
	Female	11.5
Size of department	Small police department (up to 25 officers)	25.3
	Medium-sized department (with 26–75 police officers)	47.3
	Department with more than 75 police officers	31.0
Years of service	Up to 10 years	22.4
	Between 11 and 20 years	42.2
	More than 20 years	36.4
Rank	Police officers (from junior to senior police officers)	81.7
	Various inspector ranks	18.3
Task	Public order officers	18.1
	Crime investigation officers	12.5
	Dispatchers	7.0
	Traffic officers	8.6
	Community policing officers	22.1
	Shift commander/ administration	31.5
Position	Non-managerial duties	73.3
	Managerial duties	26.5

a particular scenario was to avoid self-serving bias. All respondents (residents and police officers) were offered answers on a 5-point scale, ranging from "not at all serious" to "very serious." In the analysis we calculated statistically significant differences between the answers provided by the police officers and those given by the residents concerning the seriousness of the described behaviors. Beside the t-test, Cohen's "d" test[1] was applied because of the difference in the size of the two samples.

---

[1]One type of effect size, the standardized mean effect, expresses the mean difference between two groups in standard deviation units. Typically, this is reported as Cohen's d. Though the values calculated for effect size are generally low, they share the same range as standard deviation (−3.0 to 3.0) and can thus be quite large. Interpretation depends on the research question. The meaning of effect size varies according to context. The standard interpretation offered by Cohen is: .8 = large; .5 = moderate; .2 = small (https://researchrundowns.com/quantitative-methods/effect-size/).

Results

Residents' Own Evaluations of Seriousness

We present the results of the analysis of the responses provided by police officers and residents regarding their evaluations of the seriousness posed by different types of deviant behavior. For each of the fourteen examples of police officers' deviant behavior, police officers and residents included in the sample were asked the following question: *In your opinion, how serious is the described behavior?*

We first examine how the residents evaluated the described behaviors. As shown in Table 3, residents believed that the acceptance of free meals and gifts from merchants (as a form of corruption of authority) was the least serious. Nevertheless, an extensive distribution of answers shows that opinions regarding the acceptance of gratuities, gifts, and other benefits awarded to police officers are diverging. The same applies to not reacting to graffiti, evaluated as less serious by a third of all residents, while a third of residents believed it to be extremely serious.

On the other hand, residents found the theft of a knife from the crime scene (a form of an oppor-

Table 3 A comparison of the residents' and police officers' own evaluations of seriousness

Scenario number and description	A: Residents' own evaluations of seriousness		Very serious (4 + 5)	B: Police officers' own evaluations of seriousness		Very serious (4 + 5)	Cohen's d	t-test
	Mean	SD	(%)	Mean	SD	(%)	test	
Scenario 1—free meals, gifts from merchants	2.84	1.30	33	3.64	1.27	58	0.90 Large	9.03*
Scenario 2—failure to arrest friend with warrant	4.38	1.02	85	4.76	0.66	95	0.44 Small	6.74*
Scenario 3—theft of knife from crime scene	4.55	0.91	91	4.87	0.57	97	0.42 Small	6.44*
Scenario 4—unjustifiable use of deadly force	4.43	1.01	84	4.55	0.86	87	0.13 Very small	1.89
Scenario 5—supervisor: holiday off for errands	3.72	1.37	62	4.45	0.92	85	0.62 Medium	9.49*
Scenario 6—officer strikes prisoner who hurt partner	3.87	1.28	69	4.13	1.14	77	0.21 Small	3.15*
Scenario 7—verbal abuse "Arrest asshole day"	3.49	1.40	57	3.66	1.28	59	0.13 Very small	1.85
Scenario 8—cover-up of police DUI accident	3.99	1.28	72	2.87	1.40	35	0.83 Large	11.95*
Scenario 9—auto-body shop 5 percent kickback	3.95	1.31	72	4.63	0.96	90	0.59 Medium	8.89*
Scenario 10—false report on drug on dealer	4.42	1.05	86	4.67	0.81	92	0.27 Small	3.98*
Scenario 11—supervisor fails to halt beating	3.58	1.47	62	4.34	1.10	81	0.58 Medium	8.77*
Scenario 12—failing to report hate crime	3.97	1.14	71	4.01	1.02	71	0.04 Very small	0.54
Scenario 13—bribe from speeding motorist	4.25	1.19	81	4.85	0.63	96	0.63 Medium	9.80*
Scenario 14—not reacting to graffiti	3.13	1.32	39	4.13	1.01	75	0.85 Large	12.71*

*p < .001; Scale: 1—not serious; 5 extremely serious

tunistic theft) to be the most inappropriate behavior. This act was evaluated at the very top of the scale of serious violations. Unjustifiable and excessive use of deadly force (a form of a direct criminal activity) is viewed as the second most serious scenario. False report on a drug dealer and failure to arrest a friend with a warrant were also ranked as the police officers' most serious and inappropriate behaviors.

The results clearly show that residents have little or no tolerance toward most of the described types of police officers' deviance. In general, residents did not find the described behaviors acceptable, indicating that the majority of residents expressed a high degree of intolerance toward any type of police officers' deviant behavior.

Police Officers' Own Evaluations of Seriousness

Next, let us discuss the results of the analysis applied to the answers provided by police officers (Table 3). The police officers' evaluations of scenario seriousness suggest that the scenarios were generally evaluated to be on the serious side (mean values are clustered between the midpoint of the scale and the serious end of the scale; Table 3). However, these evaluations ranged in terms of their seriousness from the scenario evaluated as the least serious (the scenario describing the cover up of police DUI), to the scenario evaluated as the most serious (the scenario describing the theft of a knife from the crime scene).

Based on the police officers' evaluations, the scenarios fall into three categories of perceived seriousness. First, the three forms of police misbehavior (free meals and gifts from merchants, cover-up of police DUI accident, and verbal abuse) were not considered as very serious by the Slovenian police officers. The example of covering up for an intoxicated police officer was the only scenario with the mean value lower than 3. Second, police officers considered five scenarios (not noticing ethnically motivated crime, doing nothing when juveniles observed draw graffiti, excessive force—punching a suspect, supervisor's failure to prevent beating a suspect, and supervisor's abuse of power) to be of an intermediate level

of seriousness. Third, the most serious scenarios have mean values substantially closer to 5 (the "extremely serious" end of the scale). These forms of police misbehavior are related to plain violations of criminal law and include cases involving opportunistic theft (theft of a knife from the crime scene), a behavior illustrating a failure to execute an arrest warrant on a friend, and the acceptance of a bribe. All three described behaviors constitute violations of official rules, wherein police officers do something they were not supposed to do (e.g., steal a knife from the crime scene) or fail/omit to do something they were supposed to do (e.g., fail to arrest a friend). The same group of scenarios could also be complemented by the example of shooting a runaway suspect and taking a 5% off the repair bill from a local auto body shop owner.

Comparing Residents' and Police Officers' Own Evaluations of Seriousness

A comparison of the mean values of the residents' and police officers' own evaluations of seriousness suggests that in eleven out of fourteen scenarios there were statistically significant differences (Table 3; see also Fig. 1) and in seven scenarios these differences were on the larger side ("medium" or "large" in Table 3).

In the overwhelming majority of the scenarios with statistically significant differences (eleven out of twelve), police officers evaluated these scenarios as more serious than residents did. In other words, police officers tend to perceive these forms of police deviance as more serious than citizens do. In only one scenario, describing the cover-up of police DUI, police officers evaluated the scenario as less serious than residents (Table 3).

Comparing Residents' Own Evaluations of Seriousness with Residents' Estimates of Police Officer Evaluations of Seriousness

Apart from evaluating the described examples of police officers' inappropriate behavior, residents were also asked to evaluate *the degree of serious-*

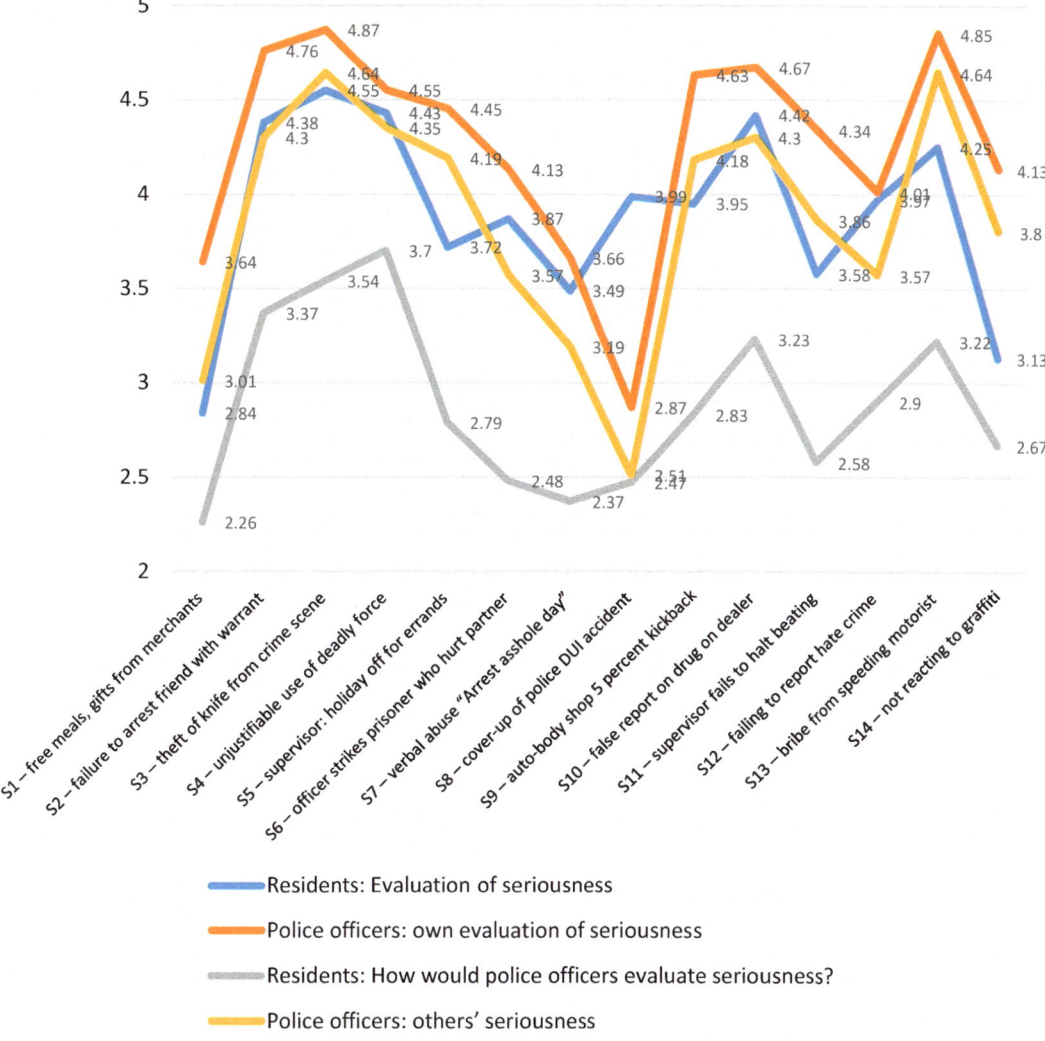

Fig. 1 Differences in perceptions of seriousness—comparison of mean values

ness that would be attributed to the described behaviors by the majority of police officers working in their place of residence (Table 4). On the one hand, residents believe that police officers would consider free meals and gifts from merchants as the least serious, followed by verbal abuse and the use of excessive force in which an officer strikes an offender. On the other hand, residents believe police officers would consider unjustifiable and excessive use of deadly force to be the most serious behavior, followed by theft of a knife from the crime scene and a failure to arrest friend with a warrant.

Further, in the analysis of residents' estimates of police officer seriousness, we compared the residents' own evaluations of seriousness with the residents' estimates of police officer evaluations of seriousness (Table 4). The results lead us to conclude that in all 14 scenarios the residents thought that police officers would regard cases of police deviance as less serious than the residents themselves did. In all fourteen scenarios, the differences were statistically significant. In addition, these differences are also large, in many scenarios exceeding 1.00 on a 5-point scale (Table 4).

Table 4 A comparison of the residents' own evaluations of seriousness and estimates of police officers' evaluations of seriousness

Scenario number and description	A: Residents' own evaluations of seriousness		Very serious (4 + 5)	C: Residents' estimates of police officer evaluations of seriousness		Very serious (4 + 5)	Cohen's d	t-test
	Mean	SD	(%)	Mean	SD	(%)	test	
Scenario 1—free meals, gifts from merchants	2.84	1.30	33	2.26	1.24	17	0.17 Very small	5.86*
Scenario 2—failure to arrest friend with warrant	4.38	1.02	85	3.37	1.28	49	0.87 Large	8.04*
Scenario 3—theft of knife from crime scene	4.55	0.91	91	3.54	1.37	55	0.86 Large	11.25*
Scenario 4—unjustifiable use of deadly force	4.43	1.01	84	3.70	1.22	62	0.65 Medium	7.42*
Scenario 5—supervisor: holiday off for errands	3.72	1.37	62	2.79	1.41	32	0.67 Medium	8.69*
Scenario 6—officer strikes prisoner who hurt partner	3.87	1.28	69	2.48	1.33	25	1.06 Large	13.84*
Scenario 7—verbal abuse "Arrest asshole day"	3.49	1.40	57	2.37	1.33	24	0.82 Large	10.66*
Scenario 8—cover-up of police DUI accident	3.99	1.28	72	2.47	1.33	21	1.16 Large	15.13*
Scenario 9—auto-body shop 5 percent kickback	3.95	1.31	72	2.83	1.38	34	0.82 Large	10.34*
Scenario 10—false report on drug on dealer	4.42	1.05	86	3.23	1.34	44	0.99 Large	12.85*
Scenario 11—supervisor fails to halt beating	3.58	1.47	62	2.58	1.33	27	0.71 Medium	9.27*
Scenario 12—failing to report hate crime	3.97	1.14	71	2.90	1.26	32	0.89 Large	11.57*
Scenario 13—bribe from speeding motorist	4.25	1.19	81	3.22	1.43	47	0.78 Medium	10.17*
Scenario 14—not reacting to graffiti	3.13	1.32	39	2.62	1.25	24	0.39 Small	5.15*

*$p < .001$; Scale: 1—not serious; 5 extremely serious

Following the rule-of-thumb established by Klockars et al. (2006), we would consider all of these differences to be meaningful as well because they all exceed the .50 threshold. Put differently, residents think that the police officers are much more tolerant of their own deviance than the residents seem to be. To minimize the effect of self-serving bias, we also compare the residents' estimates of police officers' evaluations of seriousness with the police officers' estimates of other police officers' evaluations of seriousness.

Comparing Police Officers' Own Evaluations of Seriousness with Police Officers' Estimates of Other Police Officer Evaluations of Seriousness

A comparison of the police officers' own estimates of seriousness and how serious they estimated that other police officers in the agency would evaluate the same scenarios revealed several findings (Table 5). For every scenario, the respondents evaluated scenarios as more serious

Table 5 A comparison of the police officers' own evaluations of seriousness and estimates of other police officers' evaluations of seriousness

Scenario number and description	A: Police officers' own evaluations of seriousness		Very serious (4 + 5)	C: Police officers' estimates of other police officer evaluations of seriousness		Very serious (4 + 5)	
	Mean	SD	(%)	Mean	SD	(%)	t-test
Scenario 1—free meals, gifts from merchants	3.64	1.27	58	3.01	1.15	34.2	14,21*
Scenario 2—failure to arrest friend with warrant	4.76	0.66	95	4.3	0.84	85.7	15,60*
Scenario 3—theft of knife from crime scene	4.87	0.57	97	4.64	0.75	93.3	10,07*
Scenario 4—unjustifiable use of deadly force	4.55	0.86	87	4.35	0.96	82	8,20*
Scenario 5—supervisor: holiday off for errands	4.45	0.92	85	4.19	0.98	76.3	8,43*
Scenario 6—officer strikes prisoner who hurt partner	4.13	1.14	77	3.57	1.21	55.1	14,96*
Scenario 7—verbal abuse "Arrest asshole day"	3.66	1.28	59	3.19	1.24	40.6	13,77*
Scenario 8—cover-up of police DUI accident	2.87	1.40	35	2.51	1.25	21.7	9,74*
Scenario 9—auto-body shop 5 percent kickback	4.63	0.96	90	4.18	0.99	78.4	12,32*
Scenario 10—false report on drug on dealer	4.67	0.81	92	4.3	1.00	82.4	12,24*
Scenario 11—supervisor fails to halt beating	4.34	1.10	81	3.86	1.22	66.4	13,57*
Scenario 12—failing to report hate crime	4.01	1.02	71	3.57	1.12	54.1	12,66*
Scenario 13—bribe from speeding motorist	4.85	0.63	96	4.64	0.78	90.9	7,51*
Scenario 14—not reacting to graffiti	4.13	1.01	75	3.8	1.07	62.2	11,243*

*p < .001; Scale: 1—not serious; 5 extremely serious

than they thought the other police officers would; the means for their evaluations of own seriousness were always statistically significantly higher than the means for others' estimates of seriousness.

Following the rule-of-thumb established by Klockars et al. (2006), we consider the differences of .50 or larger to be meaningful. Such meaningful differences were found in only two scenarios (free meals, gifts from merchants; officer strikes prisoner who hurt partner). The police officers appear to have considered themselves to be stricter compared to their colleagues, but the differences in most cases are not very large (if we take into account the rule set by Klockars et al. (2006)). Still, the differences were all statistically significant.

Comparing Residents' and Police Officers' Estimates of Police Officers' Evaluations of Seriousness

A comparison of the mean values of the police officers' estimated evaluations of seriousness provided by residents and police officers reveals that in thirteen out of fourteen scenarios (Table 6; see also Fig. 1), the residents believed that the police officers would evaluate the described scenarios as less serious and more acceptable than what police officers perceived to be the case. In 13 out of 14 scenarios, these differences were not only statistically significant (Table 6), but also large, well above the rule-of-thumb threshold established by Klockars et al. (2006). In fact, in 9

out of 14 scenarios, the differences exceeded the value on 1.0 on a 5-point scale (Table 6), suggesting quite different views of how police officers might evaluate these scenarios. Unlike police officers, residents were particularly unlikely to assume that police officers would evaluate the offering of holiday off for errands, the auto-body shop kickback, and a bribe from a speeding motorist as serious as serious.

Table 6 A comparison of the residents' and police officers' estimates of police officer evaluations of seriousness

Scenario number and description	C: Residents' estimates of police officer evaluations of seriousness		Very serious (4 + 5) (%)	D: Police officers' estimates of other police officer evaluations of seriousness		Very serious (4 + 5) (%)	Cohen's d test	t-test/p
	Mean	SD		Mean	SD			
Scenario 1—free meals, gifts from merchants	2.26	1.24	17	3.01	1.15	34.2	0.62 Medium	9.16*
Scenario 2—failure to arrest friend with warrant	3.37	1.28	49	4.3	0.84	85.7	0.86 Large	13.06*
Scenario 3—theft of knife from crime scene	3.54	1.37	55	4.64	0.75	93.3	0.99 Large	15.44*
Scenario 4—unjustifiable use of deadly force	3.70	1.22	62	4.35	0.96	82	0.59 Medium	8.82*
Scenario 5—supervisor: holiday off for errands	2.79	1.41	32	4.19	0.98	76.3	1.14 Large	17.42*
Scenario 6—officer strikes prisoner who hurt partner	2.48	1.33	25	3.57	1.21	55.1	0.86 Large	12.55*
Scenario 7—verbal abuse "Arrest asshole day"	2.37	1.33	24	3.19	1.24	40.6	0.64 Medium	9.31*
Scenario 8—cover-up of police DUI accident	2.47	1.33	21	2.51	1.25	21.7	0.03 Non	0.45
Scenario 9—auto-body shop 5 percent kickback	2.83	1.38	34	4.18	0.99	78.4	1.12 Large	16.92*
Scenario 10—false report on drug on dealer	3.23	1.34	44	4.3	1.00	82.4	0.90 Large	13.56*
Scenario 11—supervisor fails to halt beating	2.58	1.33	27	3.86	1.22	66.4	0.22 Small	14.66*
Scenario 12—failing to report hate crime	2.90	1.26	32	3.57	1.12	54.1	0.56 Medium	8.25*
Scenario 13—bribe from speeding motorist	3.22	1.43	47	4.64	0.78	90.9	1.23 Large	19.12*
Scenario 14—not reacting to graffiti	2.62	1.25	24	3.8	1.07	62.2	1.01 Large	14.95*

*p < .001; Scale: 1—not serious; 5 extremely serious

Discussion

Police organizations are striving to recruit personnel with the highest degree of integrity and robust moral values. However, even if one assumes that the police manage to obtain personnel with adequate characteristics and virtues, this does not guarantee success because subsequent pressures and unpredictable situations experienced by police officers could lead to an inappropriate, unethical or even criminal act. In this case, the resulting consequences are much broader because they affect not only police officers' lives and careers, but also the rights and well-being of the public, and the reputation and respect enjoyed by the police organization as a whole. Police officers' deviant behaviors are often subject to extensive media coverage. There is a great need for evaluating the way the public perceives police officers' integrity and their perception regarding the seriousness of police deviance. The results presented in this chapter provide important insights because they focus on the degree of police officers' integrity, the type of behavior they would find acceptable, their evaluation of a given situation, as well as the residents' evaluation of the same issues. These findings enable us gauge the extent of alignment between police officers' and residents' beliefs and values, an important step toward an objective assessment of the legitimacy of any police organization.

Both groups of respondents were presented with the same questions. When evaluating the seriousness of deviant behaviors, police officers evaluated all behaviors but one as more serious than the residents did. Results show that police officers mostly evaluate themselves and their colleagues as morally responsible individuals. Police officers were also asked to assess the degree of seriousness that their colleagues would attribute to the described behaviors (Lobnikar and Meško 2015). Results show that most police officers believe their colleagues would consider such behaviors as serious, while the residents' opinion indicated quite the opposite. Residents were also asked about their trust in, and satisfaction with, the police. On average, they expressed a moderate degree of trust

in the police, while most respondents were relatively unsatisfied with police work. These views should be considered in the interpretation of research results because they could also affect their evaluation of police officers' deviance or ethical stance.

The analysis of answers provided by residents with respect to police officers generally depicts a bleaker picture. Residents hold very unfavorable opinions regarding all types of police deviance. At the same time, results show that residents do not believe that police officers considers such behaviors unacceptable. There is a considerable gap between the results of police officers evaluating deviant behaviors in the police and the opinions residents expressed regarding police officers' self-evaluation. Residents believe that police officers would evaluate the majority of scenarios depicting less serious violations as acceptable. Their opinion converges with police officers' opinion only in regard to three particularly serious violations of police integrity. It appears that residents believe that police officers consider most cases, absent those involving severe violations of the law or moral and ethical standards of the police, as acceptable and as a part of their daily work.

A comforting sign is that both groups of respondents have a similarly critical opinion with respect to the described types of police officers' deviant behaviors, particularly those belonging to the group of serious violations. However, both groups considered certain acts such as gratuities and benefits provided to police officers acceptable and almost self-evident. Whereas it is true that they could reflect good relationships between officers and local residents, such practices may have much broader implications. For instance, if a police officer deals in a police procedure with a person providing such gratuities, that person could expect the officer to abandon or otherwise modify the necessary measures in light of such a good relationship. Unlike residents, police officers considered the scenario involving a cover-up of an accident caused by an intoxicated colleague currently not on duty, thus helping him avoid punishment, as the least serious violation. This is a textbook example of the code of silence.

It indicates the existence of a police culture that supports solidarity among its members materially beyond acceptable collegial behavior.

To strengthen the confidence of the people of Slovenia in the police and ensure the highest level of accountability, civilian oversight in the resolution of complaints of ill-treatment by the police was introduced by the Police Act of 1998. Following the ruling of the European Court of Human Rights in the cases of *Rehbock vs. Slovenia* (in 2000) and *Matko vs. Slovenia* (in 2006), a Department for the Prosecution of Officials with special authorizations within the Office of the State Prosecutor General was established in 2007. This step took investigations of police officers suspected of committing criminal offenses out of the hands of the police organization. To reinforce accountability of the police, the new police legislation was adopted in Slovenia in 2013. The issue of integrity is explicitly pointed out in paragraph 17 of Police Tasks and Powers Act (2013), where it is stated that police officers in performing police tasks shall observe the code of professional conduct and strengthen police integrity. Paragraph 31 of the Organization and Work of Police Act (2013) addresses integrity and internal security within the police. According to this paragraph, the police shall ensure internal security by applying internal security procedures so as to prevent, detect, evaluate, and analyze potential risks threatening the internal security of the police, and implement measures to reduce the risks of degrading the integrity of police employees and police units. To do so, the police make provisions to ensure the organizational and personal integrity of employees, and have their own code of ethics. The internal security within the police is a condition facilitating a lawful, professional, and smooth performance of police tasks, and ensuring the security of police employees and safe use of technical means and equipment, facilities, premises, and the environs. The types and methods of implementing the procedures and measures are prescribed by the Minister upon a proposal of the Director General of the Police.

The process of dealing with complaints against the work of police officers is defined in Chapter IV—Complaints Against the Work of Police Officers in Organization And Work Of The Police Act (2013). A person who disagrees with an action of a police officer or thinks a police officer failed to act while performing police tasks, which could constitute a violation of human rights or fundamental freedoms, is entitled to file a complaint. Complaints could be considered in a conciliation procedure or, absent successful conciliation, before a panel. In a conciliation procedure, a complaint is considered in the police unit within which the complainant's human rights or fundamental freedoms were allegedly violated. A conciliation procedure is a meeting between the head of police unit to which the police officer against whom the complaint was made is assigned and the complainant. At the conciliation procedure meeting, the complainant is informed of its rights, and about the course of the complaint procedure. Police powers and the conduct of the police officer in the incident is explained and, if the complaint is justified, the complainant is informed of the measures that have been or will be taken (e.g., apology, written or oral caution to the police officer, proposal for the initiation of disciplinary procedure, minor offence proceedings or criminal proceedings). In some cases, a complaint is considered directly before a panel.[2] The Ministry of the Interior designates a rapporteur to establish the facts of the complaint. A rapporteur may enter police premises related to examining the complaint, examine the complaint concerning a police unit, examine documents, interview the complainant and the police officer against whom the complaint was made, as well as obtain information from, and the opinions of, specialist police service. The Minister of the Interior appoints a panel consisting of three members, the authorized representative of the Minister as the head of the panel and two representatives of the public as panel members. At the panel meeting, the rapporteur report the findings. The complainant and the police officer express their views on the content of the complaint and facts related to the complaint and,

---

[2] For more detail see chapter IV. *Complaints against the Work of Police Officers* in Police Tasks and Powers Act (2013).

through the head of the panel, pose questions to the invitees or propose that additional evidence be presented. On the basis of established facts and circumstances, the panel votes to decide on the merits of the complaint. A decision is adopted by a simple majority vote. When voting is concluded, the head of the panel immediately informs everybody present of the decision of the panel; the decision of the panel is final (Police Tasks and Powers Act 2013).

In contemporary society, the focus ought to be on policing by consent, rather than on policing by the imposition and enforcement of regulations using superior force alone. As Haberfeld (1997) noticed, the concept of police-community relations is not a new one for any democratic society. When Sir Robert Peel undertook reform of the London police with the Metropolitan Police Act of 1829, he emphasized that the police should work in cooperation with the people and the members of the office should protect the rights, serve the needs, and earn the trust of the population they police. This impetus remains unaltered to the present day. Sustained legitimacy, skilled professionalism, and effective accountability must exist before policing can be considered democratic; and all three are interdependent. Professional behavior and accountability sustain legitimacy; accountability helps professionalize the police; legitimacy grants the police a necessary degree of professional autonomy (Caparini and Marenin 2004). However, even a professional and accountable police force will not become legitimized if it fails in its major functions of maintaining order, neutrally enforcing laws, and providing security and protecting people and their property without discrimination or bias. Tyler's (2011) model of social regulation puts procedural justice and legitimacy center-stage. On the one hand, the police need to control the population. On the other hand, the police need to win the "hearts and minds" of individuals trough legitimate use of power.

There are numerous strategies aimed at preventing police deviance, including education and training of police officers and residents regarding accountability, clear and consistent disciplinary

proceedings, administrative supervision, dealing with complaints, introducing community policing in daily policing, training in the field of ethics and integrity, inclusion of the general public, and transparency and efficient control over the exercise of police tasks and powers (Kutnjak Ivković et al. 2016). Efforts to manage police corruption and other types of police misconduct are most likely to be successful if they are directed at changing perceptions and moral beliefs about the seriousness of corruption. The results reveal that police leaders have to foster the desired character development and moral habits of police officers. Leadership based on rules and punishment requires a great deal of time to produce desirable outcomes. However, this does not suffice. Police leaders must also demonstrate the same level of commitment when it comes to the communication regarding police integrity with the general public. A high degree of police officers' integrity is a necessary, albeit not a sufficient condition for the legitimacy of policing. Residents must also believe that police officers are honest and fair, and that the integrity of policing guides their daily police activities. Results presented in this chapter show that police leaders in Slovenia still have a great deal of work to do along this dimension.

References

Albrecht J. F. (2017). Criminological explanations for police deviance. In *Police brutality, misconduct, and corruption*. Springer Briefs in Criminology. Cham: Springer.

Banutai, E., Šifrer, J., & Meško, G. (2011). Deviance and police organisational culture in Slovenia. In G. Meško, A. Sotlar, & J. Winterdyk (Eds.), *Policing in Central and Eastern Europe - Social control of unconventional deviance: Conference proceedings* (pp. 379–400). Ljubljana: Faculty of Criminal Justice and Security.

Barker, T., & Carter, D. L. (1991). *Police deviance*. Cincinnati, OH: Anderson.

Caparini, M., Marenin, O. (2004). *Transforming police in Central and Eastern Europe – Process and progress*. DCAF – Geneva Centre for the Democratic Control of Armed Forces.

Cheloukhine, S., Kutnjak Ivković, S., Haq, Q., & Haberfeld, M. (2015). Police integrity in Russia. In S. Kutnjak Ivković & M. Haberfeld (Eds.), *Measuring police integrity across the world*. New York: Springer.

Chermak, S., McGarell, E., & Gruenewald, J. (2006). Media coverage of police misconduct an attitudes toward police. *Policing: An International Journal, 29*(2), 261–281.

Cohen-Charash, Y., & Spector, P. E. (2001). The role of justice in organizations: A metaanalysis. *Organizational Behavior and Human Decision Processes, 86*(6), 278–321.

Colquitt, J. A., Conlon, D. E., Wesson, M. J., Porter, C., & Ng, K. Y. (2001). Justice at the millennium: A meta-analytic review of 25 years of organizational justice research. *Journal of Applied Psychology, 86*(3), 425–445.

Constitution. (1991). Official Gazette RS Nos. 33/91-I, 42/97, 66/2000, 24/03, 69/04, 68/06, and 47/13.

Delattre, E. J. (1996). *Character and cops: Ethics in policing* (3rd ed.). Washington, DC: The AEI Press.

Donner, K., Maskaly, J., & Fridell, L. (2016). Social bonds and police misconduct: An examination of social control theory and its relationship to workplace deviance among police supervisors. *Policing: An International Journal of Police Strategies & Management., 39*(2), 416–431. https://doi.org/10.1108/PIJPSM-10-2015-0109.

Garcia, V. (2005). Constructing the 'other' within police culture: an analysis of a deviant unit within the police organization. *Police Practice and Research, 6*(1), 65–80. https://doi.org/10.1080/15614260500047283.

Gau, J. M., & Brunson, R. K. (2010). Procedural justice and order maintenance policing: A study of inner-city young men's perceptions of police legitimacy. *Justice Quarterly., 27*(2), 255–279. https://doi.org/10.1080/07418820902763889.

Greene, J. R., Piquero, A. R., Hickman, M. J., & Lawton, B. A. (2004). *Police integrity and accountability in Philadelphia: Predicting and assessing police misconduct.* Washington, DC: National Institute of Justice.

Grilc, J., & Klemenčič, G. (2006). *Preiskava stanovanje in drugih prostorov – analiza prakse in odprta vprašanja,* Ljubljana: Faculty of Criminal Justice and Security Studies. (Search of premises – analysis of practice and outstanding legal issues)

Haberfeld, M. R. (1997). Poland: "the police are not the public and the public are not the police": Transformation from militia to police. *Policing: An International Journal of Police Strategies & Management, 20*(4), 641–654.

Haberfeld, M. R., Klockars, C. B., Kutnjak Ivković, S., & Pagon, M. (2000). Police officer perceptions of the disciplinary consequences of police corruption in Croatia, Poland, Slovenia, and the United States. *Police Practice & Research, 1*(1), 41–72.

Hunter, R. D. (1999). Officer opinions on police misconduct. *Journal of Contemporary Criminal Justice, 15*(2), 155–170.

Jackson, J., Hough, M., Bradford, B., & Kuha, J. (2015). Empirical legitimacy as two connected psychological states. In G. Meško & J. Tankebe (Eds.), *Trust and legitimacy in criminal justice* (pp. 137–160). London: Springer.

Kane, R. J. (2002). The social ecology of police misconduct. *Criminology, 40*, 867–896.

Kane, R. J. (2005). Compromised police legitimacy as a predictor of violent crime in structurally disadvantaged communities. *Criminology., 23*(2), 469–498.

Kane, R. J., & White, M. D. (2009). Bad cops: A study of career-ending misconduct among New York City police officers. *Criminology and Public Policy, 8*, 735–767.

Kaptein, M. (2001). Integrity management of police organizations. *Policing: An International Journal of Police Strategies & Management., 24*(3), 281–300.

Klockars, C. B., & Kutnjak Ivković, S. (2004). Measuring police integrity. In M. Hickman, A. R. Piquero, & J. R. Greene (Eds.), *Police integrity and ethics* (pp. 3–20). Belmont, CA: Wadsworth Publishing.

Klockars, C. B., Kutnjak Ivković, S., Harver, W. E., Haberfeld, M. R. (2000). *The measurement of police integrity.* Washington, DC: National Institute of Justice, Research in Brief

Klockars, C. B., Kutnjak Ivković, S., & Haberfeld, M. R. (Eds.). (2004). *The Contours of Police Integrity* (pp. 1–18). Thousand Oaks: Sage.

Klockars, C. B., Kutnjak Ivković, S., & Haberfeld, M. R. (2006). *Enhancing Police integrity.* New York: Springer.

Kotnik, S. (1993). Thomas Barker, David Carter: Police deviance. *Journal of Criminal Investigation and Criminology, 44*(2), 414–417.

Kutnjak Ivković, S. (2005). *Fallen blue knights: Controlling police corruption.* Oxford, UK: Oxford University Press.

Kutnjak Ivković, S. (2009a). Rotten apples, rotten branches, and rotten orchards. *Criminology and Public Policy, 8*, 777–785.

Kutnjak Ivković, S. (2009b). The Croatian police, police integrity, and transition toward democratic policing. *Policing: An International Journal of Police Strategies and Management, 32*(3), 459–488.

Kutnjak Ivković, S., & Shelley, T. O. (2005). The Bosnian police and police integrity: A continuing story. *European Journal of Criminology, 2*(4), 428–454.

Kutnjak Ivković, S., Klockars, C. B., Lobnikar, B., & Pagon, M. (2000). Police integrity and the Code of Silence: A case of the Slovenian Police Force. In G. Meško (Ed.), *Corruption in Central and Eastern Europe at the turn of millennium* (pp. 85–102). Ljubljana: College of Police and Security Studies.

Kutnjak Ivković, S., Cajner Mraović, I., & Borovec, K. (2016). Does community policing matter for police integrity? *Revija za kriminalistiko in kriminologijo, 67*(4), 313–325.

Legewie, J. (2016). Racial profiling and use of force in police stops: How local events trigger periods of increased discrimination. *American Journal of Sociology., 122*(2), 379–424. https://doi.org/10.1086/687518.

Lim, H., & Sloan, J. J. (2016). Police officer integrity: A partial replication and extension. *Policing: An International Journal of Police Strategies &*

Management, 39(2), 284–301. https://doi.org/10.1108/PIJPSM-10-2015-0127.

Liqun, C. (2015). Differentiating confidence in the police, trust in the police, and satisfaction with the police. *Policing: An International Journal of Police Strategies & Management, 38*(2), 239–249. https://doi.org/10.1108/PIJPSM-12-2014-0127.

Lobnikar, B., & Meško, G. (2015). Perception of police corruption and the level of integrity among Slovenian police officers. *Police Practice & Research: An International Journal, 16*(4), 341–353.

Lobnikar, B., Pagon, M., & Ovsenik, M. (2004). The frequency and the causes of violence and aggressive behavior at the workplace: The case of Slovenian police. *Organizacija: revija za management, informatiko in kadre, 37*(6), 371–378.

Lobnikar, B., Sotlar, A., & Modic, M. (2015). Do we trust them?: Public opinion on police work in plural policing environments in Central and Eastern Europe. In G. Meško, J. Tankebe (Eds.) *Trust and legitimacy in criminal justice: European perspectives* (pp. 189–202). Springer.

Matko vs. Slovenia. (2006). *European Court of Human Rights*, 2 November 2006, No. 43393/98. Retrieved from http://sim.law.uu.nl/sim/caselaw/Hof.nsf/2422ec00f1ace923c1256681002b47f1/90a62d83069411f7c125721700466c54?OpenDocument

McElvain, J. P., & Kposowa, A. J. (2004). Police officer characteristics and internal affairs investigations for use of force allegations. *Journal of Criminal Justice, 32*, 265–279.

Meško, G. (1994). Policijska subkultura [Police subculture]. *Revija za kriminalistiko in kriminologijo, 45*(2), 143–149.

Meško, G., & Klemenčič, G. (2007). Rebuilding legitimacy and police professionalism in an emerging democracy: The Slovenian experience. In T. R. Tyler (Ed.), *Legitimacy and criminal justice*. New York: Russell Sage.

Miller, J., & Davis, R. C. (2008). Unpacking public attitudes to the police: Contrasting perceptions of misconduct with traditional measures of satisfaction. *International Journal of Police Science & Management, 10*(1), 9–22.

Newburn, T. (1999). *Understanding and preventing police corruption: lessons from the literature*. Police Research Series. Barry Webb (ed.) London: Home Office, Policing and Reducing Crime Unit, Research, Development and Statistics Directorate.

Oberwittler, D., & Roché, S. (Eds.). (2018). *Police-citizen relations across the world*. London: Routledge. https://doi.org/10.4324/9781315406664.

Organisation and Work of the Police Act. (2013). Official Gazette of the RS, No. 15/2013 Retrieved from https://www.policija.si/images/stories/Legislation/pdf/OrganisationAndWorkOfThePoliceAct.pdf

Pagon, M., & Lobnikar, B. (2000). Comparing supervisor and line officer opinions about the code of silence: The case of Slovenia. In M. Pagon (Ed.), *Policing in Central and Eastern Europe. Ethics, integrity, and*

human rights (pp. 197–209). College of Police and Security Studies: Ljubljana.

Pagon, M., & Lobnikar, B. (2004). Police integrity in Slovenia. In C. B. Klockars, S. Kutnjak Ivković, & M. R. Haberfeld (Eds.), *The contours of police integrity*. Thousand Oaks: Sage.

Pagon, M., Kutnjak Ivković, S., & Klockars, C. (1998). The measurement of police integrity in Slovenia. *Crime control policies: political rhetoric or empirical reality?* (p. 221). Academy of Criminal Justice Sciences, Annual Meeting, Albuquerque, New Mexico, March 10–14.

Pagon, M., Kutnjak Ivković, S., & Lobnikar, B. (2000). Police integrity and attitudes toward police corruption: A comparison between the police and the public. In M. Pagon (Ed.), *Policing in Central and Eastern Europe. Ethics, integrity, and human rights* (pp. 383–396). College of Police and Security Studies: Ljubljana.

Pagon, M., Kutnjak Ivković, S., & Lobnikar, B. (2003). Policijska integriteta in stališča do policijske korupcije: primerjava med policisti in študenti [Police integrity and perceptions of police corruption: Comparison between police officers' and students]. In V. M. Pagon, G. Meško, & B. Lobnikar (Eds.), *Etika, integriteta in človekove pravice z vidika policijske dejavnosti [Ethics, integrity and human rights in policing]* (pp. 149–162). Ljubljana: College of Police and Security Studies.

Police Act. (1998). Official Gazette of the RS, No. 49/98.

Police Tasks and Powers Act. (2013). Official Gazette of the RS, No. 15/2013. Retrieved from https://www.policija.si/images/stories/Legislation/pdf/Police_Tasks_and_Powers_Act_EN.pdf

Porter, L., Prenzler, T., & Hine, K. (2015). Police integrity in Australia. In S. Kutnjak Ivković & M. Haberfeld (Eds.), *Measuring police integrity across the world*. New York: Springer.

Punch, M. (2000). Police corruption and its prevention. *European Journal on Criminal Policy and Research, 8*, 301–324.

Rehbock vs. Slovenia. (2000). European Court of Human Rights, 28 November 2000, No. 29462/95. Retrieved from http://sim.law.uu.nl/sim/caselaw/Hof.nsf/1d4d0dd240bfee7ec12568490035df05/5a19b8f46cf8347ac12569a700378430?OpenDocument

Reisig, M. D., Tankebe, J., & Meško, G. (2012). Procedural justice, police legitimacy, and public cooperation with the police among young Slovene adults. *Journal of Criminal Justice & Security, 14*, 147–164.

Semukhina, O., & Reynolds, K. M. (2014). Russian citizens' perceptions of corruption and trust of the police. *Policing and Society., 24*(2), 158–188. https://doi.org/10.1080/10439463.2013.784290.

Son, I. S., & Rome, D. M. (2004). The prevalence and visibility of police misconduct: A survey of citizens and police officers. *Police quarterly, 7*(2), 179–204.

Sotlar, A., Modic, M., & Lobnikar, B. (2015). Javno mnenje o institucijah pluralne policijske dejavnosti v Sloveniji [Public opinion about institutions of plural policing]. In G. Meško, K. Eman, & B. Flander (Eds.), *Oblast, legitimnost in družbeno nadzorstvo [Power, legitimacy and social control]* (pp. 159–187). Ljubljana: Faculty of Criminal Justice and Security, University of Maribor.

Šumi, R. (2008). Strateški načrt krepitve integritete policistov [Strategic plans for police integrity reinforcement]. *Varnost, 56*(2), 1–4.

Šumi, R., Lobnikar, B., Banutai, E., & Rančigaj, K. (2012). Integriteta policijskih vodij in njihova skrb za skupnost. [Integrity of police leaders and their care for the community]. *Varstvoslovje: revija za teorijo in prakso varstvoslovja., 14*(1), 60–74.

Sunshine, J., & Tyler, T. (2003). The role of procedural justice and legitimacy in shaping public support for policing. *Law and Society Review, 37*(3), 513–547.

Tankebe, J., Reisig, M., & Wang, X. (2016). A multi-dimensional model of police legitimacy: A cross-cultural Assessment. *Law and Human Behaviour, 40*(1), 11–22.

Terrill, W., & Reisig, M. D. (2003). Neighborhood context and police use of force. *Journal of Research in Crime and Delinquency, 40*, 291–321.

Trinkner, R., Tyler, T. R., & Golf, P. A. (2016). Justice from within: The relations between a procedurally just organizational climate and police organizational efficiency, endorsement of democratic policing, and offi-

cer well-being. *Psychology, Public Policy, and Law, 22*(2), 158–172.

Tyler, T. R. (2006). *Why people obey the law*. Princeton: Princeton University Press.

Tyler, T. (2011). Trust and legitimacy: Policing in the USA and Europe. *European Journal of Criminology, 8*(4), 254–266.

Tyler, T. R., & Fagan, J. (2008). Legitimacy and cooperation: Why do people help the police fight crime in their communities? *Ohio State Journal of Criminal Law, 6*(21), 231–275.

Vicchio, S. J. (1997, July 14–16), *Ethics and police integrity. Keynote address*. Washington, DC: National Institute of Justice, National Symposium on Police Integrity. Retrieved from http://www.fbi.gov/leb/july972.htm

Weitzer, R. (1999). Citizens' perceptions of police misconduct: Race and neighborhood context. *Justice Quarterly, 16*, 819–846.

Wolfe, S. E., & Piquero, A. R. (2011). Organizational justice and police misconduct. *Criminal Justice and Behavior, 38*(4), 332–353.

Worden, R. E. (2015). The "causes" of police brutality. Theory and evidence on police use of force. In E. R. Maguire & D. E. Duffee (Eds.), *Criminal justice theory: Explaining the nature and behavior of criminal justice* (pp. 149–204). New York: Routledge.

Exploring Gender Differences in the Australian Context: Organizational and Cultural Dimensions of Ethical Attitudes

Louse E. Porter and Tim Prenzler

Women in Policing

Professional, organized, public sector policing as we know it today is little more than 200 years old, with its origins in late-eighteenth and early-nineteenth century Britain. For about half of that time police work was exclusively male. Limited openings were made for women in a small number of departments internationally from the early-twentieth century. Female police were first appointed in a sprinkling of locations in the early decades of the twentieth century, including Portland Oregon in 1908, Los Angeles in 1910 and Toronto in 1913; with some expansion during the First World War (Brown and Heidensohn 2000; Jackson 2006). Large scale improvements in the recruitment, deployment, and promotion of women from the 1960s occurred in response to changing social attitudes, buoyed by the second wave of feminism, and also with a significant boost in most cases from anti-discrimination and public sector equity legislation, introduced on a piecemeal basis, mainly in democratic countries, from the 1970s (Jones 1986; Martin 1990).

Despite significant progress in equity in the past 50 years, policing remains universally a male-dominated occupation. In many non-democratic and developing countries, where figures are available, it is often the case that women constitute less than 10% of personnel, with smaller numbers at higher ranks and specialist units (Gaanderse and Valasek 2011; Natarajan 2008; Prenzler and Sinclair 2013). However, even in the United States, Canada, and many European countries in recent years, women have made up less than 20% of officers in most departments (Cordner and Cordner 2011; Institute for Public Security of Catalonia 2013; Prenzler and Sinclair 2013; Ward and Prenzler 2016). Only a few jurisdictions, most notably in the United Kingdom, northern Europe, and Australia, have achieved representation over 25%, including a few cases with overall numbers above 20% in management.

The male-dominated nature of policing has deep roots in social myths about gender and police work. The initial exclusion of women was based on the dominant idea that women's natural place was in the home and in nurturing roles, reinforced by the assumption that women were incapable of dealing with violent offenders and the associated physical demands of policing (Martin and Jurik 2007). Hence, pioneering women police were largely confined to welfare-oriented patrol work directed towards female offenders, female victims, and children. They also often served as assistants to detectives, interviewing female suspects, sometimes acting undercover when a female identity was required,

L. E. Porter (✉) · T. Prenzler
School of Criminology and Criminal Justice at Griffith University, Brisbane, Australia
e-mail: l.porter@griffith.edu.au; t.prenzler@griffith.edu.au

© Springer Nature Switzerland AG 2019
S. Kutnjak Ivković, M. R. Haberfeld (eds.), *Exploring Police Integrity*,
https://doi.org/10.1007/978-3-030-29065-8_12

and often simply serving as typists and administrative assistants.

The initial opening of employment positions followed from the intense lobbying efforts of middle and upper class women's advocacy groups—'the women police movement' within the first wave of feminism—but with mixed views about full gender equity. World War One marked a major turning point, when female officers were engaged in many locations to address labor shortages, help manage increased social problems involving women and children, and contribute to the control of women suspected of passing on venereal diseases. The inter-war years and Great Depression involved considerable stasis, followed by slightly enlarged opportunities under the social conditions generated by World War Two. Normally, only unmarried women were recruited for much of this pioneering period. The officers were usually organized in separate sections, not included in the standard rank structure and not sworn in. In the 1950s and 1960s, the initial breakouts from these units often simply involved an extension of gendered nurturing roles, with women assigned to school traffic duties and juvenile aid units (Heidensohn 1992; Prenzler 2015).

False assumptions about women's incapacity were emblematic of a lack of science in many aspects of police work. It was not until the 1970s that innovative research in the United States showed that female police were generally as capable as their male colleagues and were, in fact, better in some areas such as public service and de-escalating conflict (Lunneborg 1989). The research also showed public support for female officers (Lunneborg 1989). More recently, ongoing problems of police corruption and misconduct, and the systemic problems of excessive force and neglect of victims of crime, have motivated calls for greater numbers of female officers (National Center for Women and Policing 2002). This position has also been supported by judicial inquiries showing much lower rates of corruption among female officers (e.g., Christopher 1991; Robertson and Bazley 2007; Wood 1997) and research showing that female officers attract less complaints, are less likely to resort to force and

less likely to engage in excessive force (e.g., Lonsway et al. 2002; Porter and Prenzler 2015; see the following section for detail).

The formal integration of women in police organizations—mainly from the 1960s and 1970s—involved their inclusion in mixed patrol teams, swearing in, adoption of uniforms and rank, and access to pension plans. A mixture of motives lay behind this expansion. In some cases, police unions advocated, and even litigated, for equality and enlarged roles for women, based in part on positive experiences with serving female officers (Prenzler 2015). In other cases, female officers were utilized to address shortages of qualified applicants. However, equity legislation was arguably the main driver of change. Anti-discrimination laws required the removal of all non-relevant barriers to employment, including gender quotas and marriage bars. In many cases, police managers simply ignored these requirements, until forced by litigation. In other cases, most notably in the United States, police departments were obliged to accept recruitment quotas for women (and other minority groups) under consent decrees (Martin and Jurik 2007).

The movement of women into mainstream policing frequently entailed the exposure of female officers to intense sexual harassment, ostracism, and subversion on-the-job. Full-time employment and rigid shift structures militated again mothers who needed to negotiate flexible employment options. In addition, anti-discrimination obligations were often undermined by the introduction of military-style obstacle course tests in recruitment, and the operation of a 'Boys' Club' in deployment and promotion decisions (Dick and Cassell 2002; Dick and Hyde 2006; Langan et al. 2016; Silvestri 2003). In some locations, a second wave of legislation in the form of public sector equity Acts forced police managers to report on equity targets and programs, and actively support women (and other equity target groups), through measures such as focused recruitment drives, pre-application orientation sessions, the inclusion of women on selection panels, changes to language and selection criteria, equity education, and sexual harassment support programs (Prenzler and Sinclair 2013).

From a broad feminist perspective, policing was just one occupation among many that men monopolized for income, pensions, power, and prestige. This patriarchal process involved confining women to poorly paid service occupations and unpaid home duties in the nuclear family supporting a dominant male. At the same time, scholars have shown that the battle over the employment of women police was also part of a particular conflict over the nature of police work. For example, Appier's (1993) research highlighted the contrast between the 'preventive-protective' model of policing, advocated by the women police movement, and the dominant 'punitive' or 'crime control' model traditionally applied in male-dominated policing systems. The confinement of women police in small units in quasi-social work and secretarial roles represented a victory for the repressive control model. The 'war on crime' analogy privileged arrest and force as the main policing tactics. It supported the militarized structure and culture of police organizations, and provided an ideological justification for the exclusion of 'the weaker sex'. To have women perform regular police duties also undermined the heroic warrior identity of policing as a dangerous and physically demanding occupation that required exclusively male traits of courage and strength (Balkin 1988).

An overlapping explanation for male resistance to women police concerned the protection of corruption. For example, Hunt's (1990) participant observation study of a U.S. police force showed how female officers disrupted established corruption networks that relied on group participation, solidarity, and secrecy. In particular, Hunt focused on how the organizational culture was suffused with binary oppositions about acceptable and unacceptable behaviors, persons and values—framed within a basic male/female dichotomy. The dominant culture encouraged, respected, and supported summary 'street justice', arrest and force as primary responses to crime; as well as promoting on- and off-duty practices of excessive drinking, swearing and lewd jokes, defiance of departmental rules, casual sex, disdain for management, acceptance of bribes and gratuities, racism, sexism, and homophobia

(Hunt 1990). These practices were defined and celebrated as 'male'. The despised opposites of these were considered 'female' and 'feminine': respect for legal due process rights, respect for suspects, concern for the welfare of suspects and victims, tolerance, crime prevention, education, and showing emotion (Hunt 1990).

Hunt's (1990) study was undertaken in a department that was subject to a court order to employ female officers. The increased presence of women working in a range of normal duties entailed a profound threat to the whole identity of the majority of male officers and to the way they had been 'doing business' for decades. Of particular note was the way in which female officers were seen as the 'moral woman' who would not conform to, and threatened to reveal, the secret world of interconnected male camaraderie and corruption (see also Prenzler 2015).

There is also a body of research that examines how women adapt to the intense macho culture of policing. A number of responses and strategies are apparent. In some cases women may attempt to adopt a masculine persona, although this runs the risk of being labelled as unfeminine, 'butch' and/or 'dykes' (Rabe-Hemp 2008a). Conforming to the dominant culture can extend to over-compensating and using excessive force, and participating in corruption (Novak et al. 2008). Given their extreme minority status, a more common coping mechanism involves keeping a low profile, avoiding trouble, and lowering career expectations. Wexler (1985), for example, described a 'neutral-impersonal style' adopted by many female officers, and Jacobs (1987) utilized the concept of the 'professional officer' style. In such cases, when faced with continuing hostility, women will often resign prematurely, especially when they begin having children and find they are not able to fit back into shift patterns. Others will apply for traditional roles in areas such as victim support or juvenile justice, or administrative positions with regular hours (Rabe-Hemp 2008a). Even in formally integrated police agencies, some will accept the view that women have a limited, gender-specific, role, and should not be represented equally across all areas of police work (Niland 1996). Other women are more defiant and will take on the challenge of being 'twice as good' as their male counterparts to obtain promotion and specialist deployments (Rabe-Hemp 2008a).

The issue of the lower propensity toward violence and corruption among female police (see below) presents something of a dilemma for policy makers, especially when justifications are sought for proactive measures to enhance equity. Better policing has been used repeatedly as a rationale for more female officers and this has been extended to better protection by police for women and girls from domestic violence and sexual assault, especially in developing nations (Natarajan 2008; National Center for Women and Policing 2002; United Nations 2009). However, this approach has also been criticized in terms of 'gender essentialism': the perpetuation of stereotypes about intrinsic male and female qualities, and exploitation of women to address organizational deficits (Valenius 2007). The inclusion of women because they are seen as more moral, more responsible, and less violent may mean that they feel pressured into a 'civilizer' role, including feeling they are meant to act as chaperones to males, when this is not what they sought from employment in policing. Employing more women for this purpose can also be seen as simply a lazy way of improving police conduct, when managers need to more decisively address issues of deficient organizational practices.

Gender and Ethics: In the Field

This section looks more closely at research on gender differentials in police performance in the area of integrity, focusing on studies utilizing behavioral indicators including officially recorded use-of-force data, recorded fatalities and injuries, citizen complaints, observation data, and litigation. The broad assumption behind these studies is that fewer complaints and less force, including injurious and fatal force, are positive indicators. At the same time, it must be kept in mind that some force at some time is likely to be necessary for effective policing and that police who do their job conscientiously may also attract unwarranted complaints.

The available studies reviewed did not include higher rates of adverse conduct indicators for women, while a small number of studies have made a primary finding of no significant gender differences. In the latter case, Crawford and Burns (1998) and Hoffman and Hickey (2005) found no gender differences in U.S. officers' use of force. Similarly, in an observation study, Paoline and Terrill (2005, p. 24) found no significant gender differences in levels of 'verbal and physical coercion' (see also Hassell and Archbold 2010; Terrill and Mastrofski 2002).

The majority of studies, however, have made at least one finding indicating that female officers use less force—and often much less force—than their male counterparts, including when controlling for factors such as age, experience, and arrest activity. For example, Hoffman and Hickey (2005) found that women had a lower rate of weapon use, when all weapon types were combined. Bazley et al. (2007) found that the male mean for the number of use of force reports submitted was significantly higher, at 45.47, than the female mean of 34.17, and that males deployed a wider range of types of force. Williams and Hester's (2003) analysis of force reports in a Florida sheriff's department showed that 4% of female officers used force compared to 17% of males (see also Brandl and Stroshine 2013).

Surveys of arresting officers in U.S. police departments by Garner et al. (2002) and Schuck and Rabe-Hemp (2005) found that women used less force than men. In a large survey of Brazilian police, approximately 25% of female officers reported using force 'often' and 4% 'very often', compared to 34% and 10% of males respectively (Skogan 2013). These findings are supported by systematic observation studies. Paoline and Terrill (2005) found that male officers used more physical force against male suspects. In South Australia, Braithwaite and Brewer (1998) observed that male officers were twice as likely as female officers to engage in threatening behavior and make physical contact with members of the public. According to Rabe-Hemp's (2008b) observations in two U.S. departments, female officers 'were over 27 percent less likely than male officers … to exhibit extreme controlling behaviors such as threats, physical restraint, searches, and arrest in their interactions with citizens' (p. 429; also Sun et al. 2008). More generally, observational research and surveys of citizens indicate that female officers appear to be more respectful and less aggressive, and more effective in diffusing conflict (Bloch and Anderson 1974; Grennan 1987; Sherman 1975; Sichel et al. 1978).

These findings extend to fatalities and injuries caused by police actions. In U.S. studies, Boylen and Little (1990) and Brown and Langan (2001) found that female officers, proportionately, were much less likely to kill offenders. McElvain and Kposowa's (2008) study of a county sheriff's department showed that male officers were three times more likely than female officers to be involved in fatal shootings (also Horvath 1987). Hoffman and Hickey (2005) found a lower rate of injuries to suspects arrested by women (1.2 per 100 arrests) compared to men (1.7 per 100 arrests). In Queensland, Australia, a study found that males made up 85% of general duties officers but 91% of 57 cases of police vehicle pursuits resulting in death or injury (Criminal Justice Commission 1998).

Complaints constitute another area of research where gender differences are commonly found. Both Lersch (1998) and Harris (2010) found women were underrepresented in complaints data. Similarly, the Queensland Criminal Justice Commission (1996) analyzed 3 years of complaints against officers at ranks most likely to be involved in front-line policing. Women attracted fewer complaints overall, with a wider margin for more serious 'misconduct' matters: 11.7 per 100 female officers and 17.2 per 100 males. In the same department, similar proportions of misconduct complaints were found later by Waugh et al. (1998) and, more recently, Porter and Prenzler (2015) who analyzed 6 years of force-related complaint data and found that women made up 26.7% of officers and 16.0% of officers subject to demeanor-related complaints.

The study referred to above by the National Center for Women and Policing included an analysis of gender in police civil liability cases in two departments (Lonsway et al. 2002). In the LAPD,

over a 10-year period, the ratio of male to female patrol officers was 4:1, while the ratio of payouts for excessive force claims in lawsuits was 23:1. Males accounted for US$63.4 million and females US$2.8 million. Payouts for fatalities involved a ratio of 31:1 (Lonsway et al. 2002). In Cincinnati, between 1990 and 2000, women accounted for 17.1% of patrol officers but were responsible for just 7.7% of a total $1.7 million in losses in excessive force cases and wrongful deaths settled out of court (Lonsway et al. 2002). In an earlier report, *Equality Denied: The Status of Women in Policing, 2001*, the Centre drew a clear association between the male dominance of policing and diverse forms of damaging misconduct:

> The continued under-representation of women in policing is a significant contributing factor to the widespread excessive force and corruption scandals plaguing law enforcement today, scandals that are costing the US taxpayers tens of millions of dollars annually in liability lawsuit payouts for injuries and wrongful deaths of citizens (National Center for Women and Policing 2002, p. 3).

Finally, findings from two major corruption inquiries should be mentioned. The high profile 'Christopher Commission' into the LAPD, following the Rodney King beating, recorded the following in relation to gender and excessive force (Christopher 1991, pp. 83–84):

> Virtually every indicator examined by the Commission establishes that female LAPD officers are involved in excessive use of force at rates substantially below those of male officers. There were no female officers among the 120 officers with the most use of force reports. Female officers accounted for 3.4 percent of the officers involved in or at the scene of incidents underlying the 83 most serious lawsuits against the LAPD resolved from 1986 through 1990.

In New South Wales, Australia, the major Wood Royal Commission of Inquiry found widespread and entrenched corruption in the Force. According to the report, 'This royal commission and similar inquiries have found relatively few women police involved in corrupt practices. Where it has emerged it has largely related to process corruption or "secondary corruption" involving protection of other officers from internal investigations' (Wood 1997, p. 43).

Gender and Ethics: Survey Research

The above studies show that female police officers may behave differently to male officers in some circumstances. As noted, gender differences in underlying ethical orientation, or integrity, have been suggested. This section reviews studies that have explored gender differences in ethical perceptions through survey research, utilizing the police integrity survey methodology of Klockars et al. (2000), or similar scenario based questioning. That methodology draws on a theory of police integrity that focuses on officers' perceptions of seriousness of a variety of ethical violations (or near violations) as a measure of integrity (rather than directly measuring police misconduct). The methodology also adopts an organizational perspective, measuring perceptions of discipline and policy, as well as the code of silence.

Seriousness Perceptions

Studies have looked at officers' views of specific behavioral scenarios as well as broadly at personal views of seriousness (combining judgements across multiple scenarios). Regarding the latter, while some have found that females had higher seriousness ratings than male officers (e.g. Andreescu et al. 2012, Romania), others have not found significant gender differences (Charles 2009, USA; Kucukuysal 2008, Turkey; Pagon et al. 2004, Slovenia; Porter et al. 2015, Australia). Studies that have compared seriousness perceptions across individual scenarios have shown varied results in terms of both the presence and direction of gender differences for specific behaviors.

Only two studies reviewed found male officers to have a greater perception of seriousness than female officers on any scenario behaviors. Wagner et al. (2016) found male officers in Uganda viewed theft from a crime scene and a supervisor offering leave in exchange for servicing a car more seriously than did female officers. Similarly, Pagon et al. (2004) found male Slovenian police officers saw a supervisor granting leave in exchange for errands as more serious than did female officers, in addition to receiving gratuities from local business owners.

The remaining studies have found that female officers viewed scenarios more seriously than males, although the extent of these differences varies. In Australia, Waugh et al. (1998) found no gender differences in seriousness perceptions for police recruits and a difference for new officers on only one scenario (females viewed performing a registration check to obtain the details of an attractive woman more seriously than males). In the U.S.A., McDevitt et al. (2011) found female officers saw covering up an officer's illegal behavior more seriously than males, but only in medium sized agencies, not in large agencies. In Sweden, Levander and Ekenvall (2004, p. 256) found a difference only for excessive force, which they concluded could be due to females' "softer attitude" or gendered social desirability responding. Similarly, Pagon et al. (2004) found excessive force, as well as covering up officers' illegal behavior, were the only scenarios less acceptable to female officers in Slovenia.

Further studies have found gender differences in seriousness perceptions across a larger range of scenarios. Most consistently is that females view excessive force more seriously than males (Andreescu et al. 2012; CMC 2010; Huon et al. 1995; Vallmüür 2016). However, differences have also been found for using the position of a police officer to gain personal advantage (Andreescu et al. 2012; CMC 2010; Huon et al. 1995; Vallmüür 2016), rudeness (Huon et al. 1995; Vallmüür 2016), falsifying reports (CMC 2010; Vallmüür 2016), cheating at the police academy (Huon et al. 1995), and ignoring or accepting drugs (CMC 2010).

Studies have also asked officers to rate the seriousness perceptions of other officers in their department. In Australia, female recruits, new officers (CMC 2010), and established officers (Porter et al. 2015) had significantly more cynical views about the ethics of other officers in general. Huon et al. (1995) also found female officers to rate the seriousness perceptions of other officers lower than males on a range of specific scenarios. Pagon et al. (2004) showed a similar difference in

Slovenia, both on average, and for several specific scenarios. In Estonia, however, Vallmüür (2016) found no gender differences in perception of the cultural norms.

Perceptions of Violations

Only three studies could be located that found gender differences in officers' perception of whether behaviors constituted a violation of their agency's policy. Results were varied. In Uganda, Wagner et al. (2016) found male police officers were more likely to view behavior as a violation than were females. In Slovenia, Pagon et al. (2004) showed male officers were more likely to see acceptance of gratuities as a violation than were female officers, while the opposite was found for covering up an officer's illegal behavior. In Estonia, Vallmüür (2016) showed that women were more likely to see rudeness and excessive force as a violation. However, men more consistently saw unjustified deadly force (shooting an unarmed suspect) as a violation. Over all, though, there is little evidence of gender differences in officers' understanding of policy violations.

Disciplinary Views

Where studies have found gender differences in the disciplinary response expected to follow the scenarios, these differences have been consistent. It would seem that female officers have more favorable, or less punitive, views of the likely organizational response. This has been shown both at the broad level (CMC 2010; Pagon et al. 2004; Porter et al. 2015) as well as with respect to specific behaviors (Pagon et al. 2004). It is unclear whether this indicates a positive view—that they see the organization as more supporting and less punitive—or a negative view—that they are cynical regarding the organizational commitment to responding to misbehavior and disciplining officers.

Findings regarding views of appropriate discipline are more varied. Studies that have compared a composite score of appropriate discipline across a number of scenarios have tended to find no significant gender differences (Andreescu et al. 2012; Pagon et al. 2004; Wagner et al. 2016). However, female officers have been found to have more severe views of the disciplinary response to specific scenarios of operating an off-duty business and excessive force (Andreescu et al. 2012), covering up an officer's illegal behavior (Pagon et al. 2004; Wagner et al. 2016), and receiving kickbacks (Vallmüür 2016). In contrast, female officers have been found to have a more lenient response to theft (Pagon et al. 2004; Wagner et al. 2016), covering for an officer's illegal behavior (McDevitt et al. 2011), exchanging leave for favors (Pagon et al. 2004), and shooting an unarmed suspect (Vallmüür 2016).

The Code of Silence

Several studies have failed to find gender differences in officers' willingness to act in response to misconduct (e.g. Waugh et al. 1998; CMC 2010), including when willingness to report was averaged across scenarios (Andreescu et al. 2012; Pagon et al. 2004; Porter et al. 2015). However, other studies, when looking at specific forms of behavior, have found some differences: in some cases female officers are more willing to report than men, in other cases the relationship is reversed. For example, Pagon et al. (2004) showed female Slovenian officers were significantly more willing to report three scenarios: two involved excessive force; the other was covering for an officer's illegal behavior. In Estonia, Vallmüür (2016) also showed female officers more willing to report a supervisor ignoring the use of excessive force, as well as officer rudeness. In addition, Andreescu et al. (2012) showed that female police recruits in Romania were significantly more likely to report three scenarios (off-duty business, theft, and kickbacks), and that in eight of the ten scenarios, a smaller proportion of females than males were unwilling to report. An explanation offered by Huon, et al. (1995, p. 19) is that female officers are an "outgroup" who have not "been accepted into the 'brother-hood'", thus shielding women from the negative impact of police culture and preserving their integrity.

In contrast, Levander and Ekenvall (2004) sur-veyed Swedish officers and found that gender tended not to influence officers' willingness to report, except for a scenario of covering up an officer's illegal behavior, which females were less willing to report. In Estonia, Vallmüür (2016) reported females less likely to report theft, and in Australia, the CMC (2010) showed new female officers were less likely to act in response to two scenarios involving officer deception. More widespread gender differences have been found in Uganda, where Wagner et al. (2016) reported female officers were less inclined to report half of their 12 scenarios, and in Slovenia (Lobnikar et al. 2016) where female officers were less likely to report 11 of the 14 scenarios measured. Wagner, et al. concluded that the differences were particularly evident for more serious behav-ior, which also seems largely the case in the Slovenian study. Lobnikar et al. (2016) and Wagner et al. (2016) both suggest that women may choose not to report misconduct through fear of negative consequences regarding their career opportunities, due to their unequal status in the organizational hierarchy (discussed earlier in this chapter). Andreescu, et al. (2012, p.13) also discuss that female officers "want to be accepted as equals by their male colleagues. And in order to fit in, women are expected not to vio-late the widely accepted gender norms … [by] being disloyal to the 'brotherhood'". Thus, will-ingness to report may be influenced by perceived social expectations and norms.

Some studies have explored gender differ-ences in officers' perceptions regarding the will-ingness of other officers to report misconduct. Significant differences consistently support the view that females are more pessimistic about police culture than male officers. Porter et al. (2015) showed that Australian female officers, when averaged across 11 scenarios, judged the willingness of others to report lower than did male officers. While Pagon et al. (2004) found no significant difference at the aggregate level (aver-aged across all scenarios), they did find females were less inclined than males to believe other officers would report rudeness, theft, and kick-backs. Vallmüür (2016) showed the same result for rudeness, theft, use of force, and leave in exchange for errands. McDevitt et al. (2011) sim-ilarly found females (but only in larger agencies) less likely to believe officers would report all three of the scenarios measured: kickbacks, cov-ering for an officer's illegal behavior, and lying about evidence.

The theory of police integrity (Klockars et al. 2000) recognizes that officers' integrity can be influenced by perceptions of informal norms and some studies have explored this in relation to gender. Lobnikar et al. (2016) found that female officers' willingness to report was more highly correlated with their views of what other officers' think or would do, than their own perceptions of seriousness of the infraction. They concluded that the perceptions of others were more impor-tant to females than males. However, Pagon et al. (2004) concluded the opposite from multivariate models: "females paid much less attention to social clues in deciding whether to report police misconduct or not than did males" (p. 15).

Present Study

The above review highlights that the issue of gen-der in policing, as it relates to ethical behavior, is not straightforward. Female officers have strug-gled to be accepted into policing, and while opportunities for women have improved, there is still evidence that their position may be fragile and unequal to males. Efforts to increase female representation in policing have often cited the argument of improving police culture and, thus, behavior. While studies typically show that female officers may exhibit less indicators of problematic behavior in the field, surveys of their ethical beliefs do not show consistent differences to male officers. In Australia, Porter et al. (2015) found gender differences across some of the integrity constructs, but did not go further to explore how these differed according to the spe-cific nature of the scenarios, and did not explore gender differences as predictors of integrity. They concluded that "further research could attempt to unpack the relationships between the integrity constructs for males and females to understand whether there are gender differences in the relative importance of, for example, police culture versus personal views" (p. 93). The aim of the remainder of this chapter is to explore the differences between male and female Australian officers on the constructs of integrity and how their views of the organizational and cultural norms effect their hypothetical behavior.

Method

This chapter explores the ethical perceptions of a sample of Australian police officers using survey data collected in 2013 via a survey designed by Klockars et al. (2006). These data were first described in Porter et al. (2015), which provides a detailed description of the methodology employed. The method will be summarized here, followed by new analysis of gender differences across the survey constructs.

Sample

The sample for this study is drawn from police officers in two policing jurisdictions of Australia. Australian policing is decentralized, comprising eight jurisdictions. Policing is primarily organized at the state/territory level, with seven police agencies representing the Northern Territory and the six states of New South Wales, Queensland, South Australia, Tasmania, Victoria and Western Australia. In addition, the Australian Federal Police have a national function enforcing federal law, as well as a local policing function within the Australian Capital Territory. The size of these eight jurisdictions varies geographically, as well as by population and police numbers, with the largest police service comprising almost 17,000 sworn police officers and the smallest comprising approximately 1200 sworn officers. The two agencies sampled in this research included one

large and one smaller size agency (agencies elected to remain anonymous).

A total of 856 Australian police officers responded to the survey. However, a small proportion (1.29%) confessed that they had not answered the questions honestly and so their data were removed from the sample. Further, 112 respondents did not disclose their gender, leaving a total of 744 usable responses for the current analysis: 532 males (62.15%) and 212 females (24.77%). The gender proportion is consistent with the approximate proportion of female officers in Australian policing agencies, as noted earlier in the introduction to this chapter. However, the sample is slightly skewed towards more experienced officers, with over two-thirds having more than 10 years of experience, and almost half in supervisory positions. The majority of the sample (around three-quarters) occupied middle ranks of senior constables or sergeants/senior sergeants, with smaller proportions of constables as well as high ranking officers.

Table 1 shows the characteristics of the sample by gender. While gender proportions were comparable across ranks, there were significant associations between gender and supervisory status as well as length of service. Males were more likely to be supervisors and to have served longer.

Materials

The survey presented eleven scenarios describing unethical behavior of a police officer (see appendix A). Each scenario was followed by the same seven questions that measured four constructs: perceptions of seriousness, violation of policy, disciplinary response, and willingness to report the officer in question.

Perception of seriousness. Two questions asked respondents about their perception of seriousness. The first question asked 'How serious do you consider this behavior to be?' The second question asked 'How serious would most police officers in your agency consider this behavior to be?' Both questions were followed by a

Table 1 Sample demographics by gender

		Female n = 212	Male n = 532	Total N = 744	χ^2	df	p
Rank	Recruit/constable	17 (10.43%)	45 (10.04%)	62 (10.15%)	6.999	3	0.072
	Senior constable	73 (44.79%)	166 (37.05%)	239 (39.12%)			
	Sergeant/Snr. Sgt.	60 (36.81%)	167 (37.28%)	227 (37.15%)			
	Inspector to Chief Superintendent/ Commander	13 (7.98%)	70 (15.63%)	83 (13.58%)			
	Total	*163 (100%)*	*448 (100%)*	*611 (100%)*			
Supervisor	Non-supervisor	131 (62.68%)	255 (48.76%)	386 (52.73%)	11.612	1	0.001
	Supervisor	78 (37.32%)	268 (51.24%)	346 (47.27%)			
	Total	*209 (100%)*	*523 (100%)*	*732 (100%)*			
Length of service	Up to 10 years	69 (34.67%)	137 (26.30%)	206 (28.61%)	17.715	2	<0.001
	11–20 years	78 (39.20%)	159 (30.52%)	237 (32.92%)			
	Over 20 years	52 (26.13%)	225 (43.19%)	277 (38.47%)			
	Total	*199 (100%)*	*521 (100%)*	*720 (100%)*			

five-point scale with anchor points labelled as 1 = 'not at all serious' and 5 = 'very serious'.

Violation of policy. A single item asked respondents 'Would this behavior be regarded as a violation of official policy in your agency?' This was followed by a five-point scale with anchor points labelled as 1 = 'definitely not' and 5 = 'definitely yes'.

Disciplinary response. Respondents were asked to indicate their views of the most likely and most appropriate disciplinary response: 'If an officer in your agency engaged in this behavior and was discovered doing so, what, if any, discipline do you think *should* follow?'; 'If an officer in your agency engaged in this behavior and was discovered doing so, what, if any, discipline do you think *would* follow?' Response options for both questions were ordered as follows: 1 = 'None'; 2 = 'Verbal reprimand'; 3 = 'Written reprimand'; 4 = 'Period of suspension without pay'; 5 = 'Demotion in rank'; 6 = 'Dismissal'.

Willingness to report. Respondents were asked about their own hypothetical willingness to report the scenario: 'Do you think you would report a fellow police officer who engaged in this behavior?' They were also asked their perception of other officers' willingness: 'Do you think most police officers in your agency would report a fellow police officer who engaged in this behavior?' Responses were on a five-point scale with anchor

points labelled as 1 = 'definitely not' and 5 = 'definitely yes'.

Design/Analysis

The responses of female and male officers were first compared on each item across the eleven scenarios individually. Mean scores on each construct (item) were also calculated for males and females. This shows whether there are gender differences broadly on the constructs, and where these vary according to the type of behavior described.

In order to gauge how officers viewed themselves in relation to the perceived cultural norms, measures of 'self-other difference' were created by subtracting responses on the items concerning 'most officers' from the items asking about 'you.' This was performed for the two items measuring seriousness perceptions, with a positive self-other difference indicating that the respondents thought they viewed the scenario as more serious than most officers, and a negative self-other difference indicating that they saw the scenario as less serious than most officers. The same calculation was performed for the two willingness to report items. Again a positive self-other difference indicates officers would be more willing than most to report, while a negative difference indicates they would be less willing to report than most.

An index of 'disciplinary fairness' was calculated in a similar way. The respondents' perception of the disciplinary response that *should* happen was subtracted from the perceived disciplinary response that *would* happen. A difference of zero indicates fairness (the response that would occur is no different to the response that should occur), a positive score indicates expected harsher discipline would occur than should occur, and a negative score indicates a more lenient disciplinary response would occur than should.

All gender comparisons were explored controlling for supervisory status, due to the significant association between gender and supervisory status (noted above in the sample section), and that previous literature has highlighted that supervisory status can affect ethical attitudes. Gender differences were, therefore, explored using two-way ANOVAs (limited to analyzing only main effects) comparing the difference in means between females and males for each scenario controlling for supervisory status. The estimated marginal means (i.e. controlling for supervisory status) of the gender comparisons are reported[1]. Given the number of comparisons made, the probability of a type one error is inflated and caution should be taken in interpreting significance levels. Partial eta squared (η^2_p) is calculated to measure the size of the effects.

Multiple regression was used to explore social and organizational culture predictors of officers' willingness to report the scenarios (own willingness). Responses on the constructs of interest were averaged across all 11 scenarios to provide a composite index. Regressions were conducted separately for females and males to compare the models, controlling for supervisory status (0 = non supervisor and 1 = supervisor).

Results

The results of the analyses are organized into four parts. First, gender differences on the items representing personal views are presented, fol-

lowed by gender differences on items representing participants' views of the culture. This is followed by a section exploring how participants relate to the culture, or their perceived cultural 'fit'. Finally, the effects of perceptions of culture on personal views is explored.

Personal Views

This section explores gender differences in the personal views of the participants regarding the seriousness of scenarios, whether each constitutes a policy violation, the appropriate disciplinary response, and whether they would be willing to report each scenario.

Perceptions of Seriousness

Table 2 shows the gender comparison of officers' perceptions of the seriousness of the 11 scenarios. Female and male officers had similar views of the relative seriousness of the scenarios, as shown by broad similarity on the rank ordering of the mean ratings. The rudeness scenario (scenario 7) was seen as the least serious, with a mean rating just above the midpoint of the scale for females (mean = 3.14) and just below the midpoint of the scale for males (mean = 2.98). Theft from a crime scene (scenario 3) was viewed as most serious by all officers. The mean seriousness ratings of the scenarios were also similar across many of the scenarios. Males and females differed significantly on only three of the eleven scenarios; females viewed the two force related scenarios (scenario 6, where officers punch the fleeing suspect, and scenario 11, where a supervisor ignores the beating of a suspect in custody) and the discount for a referral as significantly more serious than did males (scenario 9). When seriousness ratings were averaged across all 11 scenarios, females had a significantly higher average seriousness rating (4.42) than males (4.32). All effect sizes were small, however.

Violation

There were very few gender differences in officers' understanding of whether the scenarios constituted a policy violation (Table 3). Both

---

[1]The differences in means by supervisory status (main effect) are not reported as these were not of interest.

Table 2 Estimated marginal means, standard errors, and ANOVA main effect results for the comparison of male and female officers' own perceptions of seriousness, controlling for supervisory status

	Serious own	Female			Male			F	df	p	η^2_p
		Rank	Mean	S.E.	Rank	Mean	S.E.				
1	Gratuities	2	3.51	0.08	2	3.45	0.05	0.37	1728	.542	
2	Omits-warrant	6	4.65	0.05	7	4.56	0.03	2.63	1729	.105	
3	Theft	11	4.94	0.02	11	4.94	0.01	0.02	1729	.885	
4	Shooting	8	4.87	0.03	10	4.89	0.02	0.24	1729	.625	
5	Leave/errands	3	4.02	0.07	3	3.92	0.04	1.77	1729	.183	
6	Force–punch	5	4.49	0.07	4	4.25	0.04	8.61	1729	.003	0.01
7	Rudeness	1	3.14	0.08	1	2.98	0.05	2.86	1729	.091	
8	Omits–DUI	4	4.47	0.06	5	4.38	0.04	1.84	1729	.169	
9	Discount for referral	10	4.89	0.03	8	4.80	0.02	5.54	1729	.019	0.01
10	Evidence	9	4.88	0.03	9	4.85	0.02	0.57	1729	.428	
11	Omits-force	7	4.73	0.06	6	4.51	0.04	3.21	1727	.001	0.01
	Average seriousness		4.42	0.03		4.32	0.02	6.70	1729	.010	0.01

Table 3 Estimated marginal means, standard errors, and ANOVA main effect results for the comparison of male and female officers' perceptions of violation, controlling for supervisory status

	Violation	Female			Male			F	df	p	η^2_p
		Rank	Mean	S.E.	Rank	Mean	S.E.				
1	Gratuities	3	4.51	0.06	3	4.56	0.04	0.51	1728	.477	
2	Omits-warrant	7	4.86	0.04	4	4.80	0.02	1.69	1729	.194	
3	Theft	11	4.98	0.01	11	4.98	0.01	0.27	1728	.869	
4	Shooting	4	4.71	0.04	5	4.82	0.03	5.26	1729	.022	0.01
5	Leave/errands	2	4.33	0.06	2	4.35	0.04	0.06	1729	.800	
6	Force–punch	5	4.82	0.03	6	4.88	0.02	2.80	1729	.095	
7	Rudeness	1	4.18	0.06	1	4.32	0.04	3.91	1729	.048	0.01
8	Omits–DUI	6	4.85	0.03	7	4.89	0.02	1.34	1729	.247	
9	Discount for referral	10	4.97	0.02	9	4.95	0.01	0.59	1729	.444	
10	Evidence	9	4.96	0.02	10	4.96	0.01	0.16	1729	.690	
11	Omits-force	8	4.95	0.02	8	4.92	0.02	1.14	1727	.287	

female and male officers rated each of the scenarios as at least 4, on average, on the five point scale, recognizing that each violated official policy of their organization. Only two significant gender differences were found. For both the rudeness scenario (scenario 7) and the shooting scenario (scenario 4), female officers' ratings were significantly lower than were males', showing that they were less likely to consider these as violations, although effect sizes were small.

Appropriate Discipline

Female and male officers had similar views on the appropriate disciplinary response to each scenario; that is, what discipline *should* follow (Table 4). Males were significantly harsher than females regarding their suggested discipline for

ignoring an officer's DUI (scenario 8), shooting (scenario 4), and theft (scenario 3). The effect sizes of these differences were small, though. Indeed, looking at the modal discipline category selected for each scenario, the majority of males and females were in agreement on ten of the scenarios. After averaging the disciplinary responses across all scenarios, there was no significant difference between females and males on ratings of the discipline that should occur.

Willingness to Report

There were few significant differences between female and male officers in the degree to which they were willing to report each scenario (Table 5). Females were significantly more willing to report three scenarios: ignoring a friend's

Table 4 Estimated marginal means, standard errors, and ANOVA main effect results for the comparison of male and female officers' perceptions of the disciplinary response that should follow each scenario, controlling for supervisory status

		Female				Male				F	df	p	η^2_p
		Rank	Mean	S.E.	Mode	Rank	Mean	S.E.	Mode				
1	Gratuities	2	2.56	0.07	Verbal reprimand	2	2.62	0.04	Verbal reprimand	4.88	1727	.485	
2	Omits–warrant	6	4.12	0.09	Suspension	4	4.00	0.06	Suspension	1.15	1728	.284	
3	Theft	11	5.50	0.06	Dismissal	11	5.67	0.03	Dismissal	6.49	1729	.011	0.01
4	Shooting	8	5.14	0.08	Dismissal	10	5.46	0.05	Dismissal	11.77	1716	.001	0.02
5	Leave/errands	3	3.09	0.08	Written reprimand	3	3.22	0.05	Written reprimand	1.76	1726	.185	
6	Force–punch	4	4.01	0.10	Suspension	5	4.14	0.06	Suspension	1.30	1726	.254	
7	Rudeness	1	2.37	0.05	Verbal reprimand	1	2.31	0.03	Verbal reprimand	1.42	1729	.233	
8	Omits–DUI	5	4.02	0.09	Suspension	6	4.24	0.05	Suspension	4.78	1725	.029	0.01
9	Discount for referral	9	5.16	0.08	Dismissal	8	5.21	0.05	Dismissal	0.25	1728	.620	
10	Evidence	10	5.22	0.07	Dismissal	9	5.38	0.04	Dismissal	3.77	1728	.053	
11	Omits–force	7	4.71	0.09	Dismissal	7	4.66	0.06	Reduction in rank	0.19	1726	.666	
	Average		4.17	0.04			4.26	0.03		3.07	1729	.080	

Table 5 Estimated marginal means, standard errors, and ANOVA main effect results for the comparison of male and female officers' own willingness to report the scenarios, controlling for supervisory status

		Female			Male						
	Willing own	Rank	Mean	S.E.	Rank	Mean	S.E.	F	df	p	η^2_p
1	Gratuities	2	3.42	0.09	2	3.37	0.06	0.23	1727	.633	
2	Omits-warrant	7	4.52	0.07	7	4.34	0.04	5.34	1728	.021	0.01
3	Theft	10	4.86	0.04	10	4.82	0.02	0.75	1729	.386	
4	Shooting	11	4.88	0.03	11	4.92	0.02	1.22	1728	.271	
5	Leave/errands	3	3.76	0.08	3	3.81	0.05	0.26	1729	.600	
6	Force–punch	4	4.17	0.08	4	3.94	0.05	4.97	1729	.026	0.01
7	Rudeness	1	3.08	0.09	1	2.92	0.06	2.31	1729	.126	
8	Omits–DUI	5	4.21	0.08	5	4.09	0.05	1.88	1729	.171	
9	Discount for referral	8	4.78	0.05	8	4.68	0.03	3.51	1729	.062	
10	Evidence	9	4.81	0.05	9	4.69	0.03	4.63	1729	.032	0.01
11	Omits-force	6	4.42	0.08	6	4.31	0.05	1.57	1727	.210	
	Average		4.26	0.05		4.17	0.03	2.92	1729	.088	

warrant (Scenario 2), excessive force on a fleeing suspect (scenario 6), and falsifying evidence (scenario 10). However, the effect sizes were small. When averaged across all 11 scenarios, no significant gender difference was apparent in willingness to report.

Perceptions of Culture

This section explores gender differences in the perception of the organizational and social culture. Perception of the social culture is explored through views of how serious most officers would view the scenarios and the willingness of most officers to report each scenario. Perception of the organizational culture is explored through views of the likely disciplinary response to the scenarios.

Perceptions of Others' Seriousness Views

Females and males differed to a greater extent on their views of the normative cultural values, that is, the seriousness perceptions of 'most officers' (Table 6). Across all scenarios, females had a lower opinion of most officers' perceptions than did the male officers. This difference was significant for eight of the 11 scenarios, but with small effect sizes. The exceptions were scenario 2 (ignoring a friend's warrant), scenario 6 (exces-

sive force on fleeing suspect) and scenario 4 (shooting). When perception of others' seriousness was averaged across the eleven scenarios, females' ratings were also significantly lower than males', although the effect size was small.

Perceptions of Others' Willingness to Report

Table 7 shows that there were also gender differences when officers considered how willing 'most officers' would be to report the scenarios. Females consistently showed a lower opinion of most officers' willingness to report; their average ratings on this item were significantly lower than those of males for each of the scenarios with small to medium effect sizes. When ratings were averaged across all eleven scenarios, a significant gender difference was maintained with an effect size of .04.

Likely Disciplinary Response

The views regarding what disciplinary response *would* follow each scenario are shown in Table 8. On average, males tended to expect harsher discipline than females on almost all scenarios. The exception to this was scenario 2 where the officer ignores a friend's warrant. The ANOVAs showed these differences in mean responses were significant across eight of the eleven scenarios with small to medium effect sizes. However, the modal disciplinary response for each scenario

Table 6 Estimated marginal means, standard errors, and ANOVA main effect results for the comparison of male and female officers' perceptions of how serious most officers view the scenarios to be, controlling for supervisory status

	Serious most	Female			Male						
	Scenario	Rank	Mean	S.E.	Rank	Mean	S.E.	F	df	p	η^2_p
1	Gratuities	2	3.03	0.08	2	3.33	0.05	10.72	1727	.001	0.02
2	Omits-warrant	7	4.44	0.05	7	4.46	0.03	0.20	1727	.654	
3	Theft	10	4.76	0.03	10	4.84	0.02	4.84	1727	.028	0.01
4	Shooting	11	4.81	0.03	11	4.88	0.02	3.34	1728	.068	
5	Leave/errands	3	3.54	0.07	3	3.76	0.04	6.90	1727	.009	0.01
6	Force–punch	4	3.94	0.07	4	4.08	0.04	2.80	1726	.094	
7	Rudeness	1	2.65	0.08	1	2.96	0.05	11.25	1728	.001	0.02
8	Omits–DUI	5	3.97	0.06	5	4.23	0.04	12.58	1728	<.001	0.02
9	Discount for Referral	8	4.58	0.04	8	4.72	0.03	7.46	1727	.006	0.01
10	Evidence	9	4.63	0.04	9	4.77	0.03	7.86	1728	.005	0.01
11	Omits-force	6	4.22	0.06	6	4.39	0.04	5.28	1725	.022	0.01
	Average		4.05	0.04		4.22	0.02	16.73	1728	<.001	0.02

Table 7 Estimated marginal means, standard errors, and ANOVA main effect results for the comparison of male and female officers' perceptions of how willing most officers would be to report the scenarios, controlling for supervisory status

	Willing most	Female			Male						
		Rank	Mean	S.E.	Rank	Mean	S.E.	F	df	p	η^2_p
1	Gratuities	2	2.71	0.08	2	3.16	0.05	24.66	1726	<.001	0.03
2	Omits-warrant	7	3.92	0.07	7	4.12	0.05	6.91	1727	.009	0.01
3	Theft	10	4.38	0.05	10	4.58	0.03	11.56	1728	.001	0.02
4	Shooting	11	4.67	0.04	11	4.87	0.02	18.04	1727	<.001	0.02
5	Leave/errands	3	3.06	0.08	3	3.49	0.05	21.32	1728	<.001	0.03
6	Force–punch	4	3.37	0.08	4	3.67	0.05	9.55	1727	.002	0.01
7	Rudeness	1	2.47	0.08	1	2.82	0.05	13.18	1728	<.001	0.02
8	Omits–DUI	5	3.44	0.07	5	3.85	0.05	21.95	1727	<.001	0.03
9	Discount for referral	8	4.15	0.06	8	4.46	0.04	20.66	1727	<.001	0.03
10	Evidence	9	4.24	0.07	9	4.47	0.04	11.60	1726	.001	0.02
11	Omits-force	6	3.70	0.07	6	4.08	0.05	18.11	1725	<.001	0.02
	Average		3.65	0.05		3.96	0.03	32.18	1728	<.001	0.04

was the same for females and males on all but four scenarios. Averaging across all eleven scenarios, females showed significantly lower ratings of expected discipline than males.

Cultural Alignment

With gender differences shown in how officers' perceive their culture, this section explores gender differences in participants' social and organizational cultural alignment. Alignment with the social culture is explored through the differences between the officers' own seriousness perceptions and their perceptions of others' seriousness, as well as differences between their own willingness to report and the perceived willingness of other officers to report. The degree of these self-other differences is also compared between female and male officers. Alignment with the organization is explored through the perceptions of disciplinary fairness (i.e., whether the expected disciplinary response is viewed as appropriate).

Table 8 Estimated marginal means, standard errors, and ANOVA main effect results for the comparison of male and female officers' perceptions of the disciplinary response that would follow each scenario, controlling for supervisory status

		Female				Male							
		Rank	Mean	S.E.	Mode	Rank	Mean	S.E.	Mode	F	df	p	η^2_p
1	Gratuities	3	2.69	0.08	Written reprimand	2	2.85	0.05	Written reprimand	3.19	1727	.075	
2	Omits-warrant	4	3.92	0.09	Suspension	4	3.90	0.06	Written reprimand	0.03	1727	.874	
3	Theft	10	5.10	0.07	Dismissal	10	5.51	0.04	Dismissal	25.65	1728	<.001	0.03
4	Shooting	11	5.17	0.07	Dismissal	11	5.57	0.05	Dismissal	20.21	1717	<.001	0.03
5	Leave/errands	2	2.58	0.08	Verbal reprimand	3	2.96	0.05	Written reprimand	15.86	1725	<.001	0.02
6	Force–punch	5	3.93	0.09	Suspension	6	4.55	0.06	Suspension	32.65	1723	<.001	0.04
7	Rudeness	1	2.47	0.05	Verbal reprimand	1	2.52	0.03	Verbal reprimand	0.98	1728	.323	
8	Omits–DUI	6	4.10	0.09	Suspension	5	4.53	0.05	Dismissal	17.74	1723	<.001	0.02
9	Discount for referral	8	4.91	0.08	Dismissal	8	5.16	0.05	Dismissal	6.45	1726	.011	0.01
10	Evidence	9	4.97	0.07	Dismissal	9	5.37	0.05	Dismissal	20.91	1727	<.001	0.03
11	Omits-force	7	4.56	0.08	Suspension	7	4.89	0.05	Dismissal	12.14	1725	.001	0.02
	Average		4.04	0.05			4.34	0.03		33.21	1729	<.001	0.04

Table 9 Estimated marginal means, standard errors, and ANOVA main effect results for the comparison of self-other difference in serious perceptions (own-most) by gender, controlling for supervisory status

		Female			Male			Male female difference			
	Serious diff	Mean	S.E.	d[a]	Mean	S.E.	d[a]	F	df	p	η^2_p
1	Gratuities	0.47***	0.06	0.42	0.12**	0.04	0.10	21.67	1727	<.001	0.03
2	Omits-warrant	0.22***	0.04	0.32	0.10***	0.03	0.13	6.45	1727	.011	0.01
3	Theft	0.18***	0.03	0.44	0.10***	0.02	0.29	6.32	1727	.012	0.01
4	Shooting	0.06**	0.02	0.13	0.01	0.01		5.98	1728	.015	0.01
5	Leave/errands	0.48***	0.05	0.49	0.16***	0.03	0.16	27.52	1727	<.001	0.04
6	Force–punch	0.54***	0.06	0.55	0.18***	0.04	0.18	29.76	1726	<.001	0.04
7	Rudeness	0.48***	0.05	0.41	0.02	0.03		53.03	1728	<.001	0.07
8	Omits–DUI	0.50***	0.05	0.56	0.14***	0.03	0.17	34.73	1728	<.001	0.05
9	Discount for referral	0.30***	0.04	0.51	0.08***	0.02	0.15	28.84	1727	<.001	0.04
10	Evidence	0.26***	0.04	0.46	0.09***	0.02	0.15	14.85	1728	<.001	0.02
11	Omits-force	0.50***	0.05	0.64	0.12***	0.03	0.15	37.76	1725	<.001	0.05

[a]Effect size of self-other difference
*Mean self-other difference significant at $p < .05$ (paired samples t-test)
**Mean self-other difference significant at $p < .01$ (paired samples t-test)
***Mean self-other difference significant at $p < .001$ (paired samples t-test)

Differences in Seriousness Perceptions

Table 9 shows the degree of difference between officers' own seriousness rating for each scenario and their beliefs about how others would rate each. There were differences between the mean 'self' and 'other' ratings for both males and females; on average, both females and males thought they were more ethical than most officers. However, these differences were more pronounced for females than males.

Female officers, particularly, saw themselves differently to most officers, with paired t-tests revealing statistically significant differences between their ratings of their own and most officers' seriousness perceptions on all scenarios, with effect sizes (Cohen's d) ranging from .13 to .64. The greatest differences female officers perceived between their own judgements and those of most officers were for the two scenarios involving the use of force (scenario 6 and 11). Differences on nine of the eleven scenarios showed effect sizes greater than .4. In contrast, while male officers, on average, also thought they held different seriousness perceptions to most officers, with statistically significant differences on nine of the eleven scenarios, Cohen's d effect sizes were very small (all less than .3).

Finally, the ANOVAs showed that, compared to males, female officers saw themselves as more different from the majority regarding their seriousness perceptions on all scenarios, with effect sizes (partial eta squared) ranging from .01 to .07. Thus, female officers perceived a significantly greater divide between their own and normative values than did males, with six of the differences approaching or equivalent to a medium effect size. The perception of self-other difference was particularly larger for females than males for the rudeness scenario (scenario 7).

Differences in Willingness to Report

On average, both male and female officers believed they were significantly more likely than most to report each scenario (Table 10). For male officers, paired t-tests showed this view of the self as more willing to report was significant across all scenarios, with the difference ranging from .05 for scenario 5 (exchanging leave for errands) to .32 for scenario 4 (shooting). However, Cohen's d showed the effect sizes of these differences to be small.

Female officers showed greater perceived differences between their own and others' willingness to report than did male officers. Table 10

Table 10 Estimated marginal means, standard errors, and ANOVA main effect results for the comparison of self-other difference in willingness to report (own-most) by gender, controlling for supervisory status

		Female			Male			Male-female difference			
		Mean	S.E.	d#	Mean	S.E.	d#	F	df	p	η^2_p
1	Gratuities	0.71***	0.08	0.55	0.21***	0.05	0.18	31.18	1726	<.001	0.04
2	Omits-warrant	0.61***	0.06	0.61	0.21***	0.04	0.23	31.85	1727	<.001	0.04
3	Theft	0.49***	0.05	0.77	0.25***	0.03	0.39	19.73	1728	<.001	0.03
4	Shooting	0.21***	0.03	0.35	0.05***	0.02	0.11	24.69	1727	<.001	0.03
5	Leave/errands	0.70***	0.07	0.59	0.32***	0.04	0.28	20.90	1728	<.001	0.03
6	Force–punch	0.79***	0.07	0.65	0.28***	0.05	0.23	34.95	1727	<.001	0.05
7	Rudeness	0.61***	0.07	0.46	0.10*	0.04	0.09	36.45	1728	<.001	0.05
8	Omits–DUI	0.77***	0.07	0.69	0.24***	0.04	0.22	39.22	1727	<.001	0.05
9	Discount for referral	0.62***	0.05	0.83	0.21***	0.03	0.29	51.62	1727	<.001	0.07
10	Evidence	0.56***	0.05	0.78	0.21***	0.03	0.29	32.39	1726	<.001	0.04
11	Omits-force	0.71***	0.06	0.68	0.23***	0.04	0.21	39.31	1725	<.001	0.05

[a]Effect size of self-other difference
*Mean self-other difference significant at p < .05 (paired samples t-test)
***Mean self-other difference significant at p < .001 (paired samples t-test)

shows that the average difference in female officers' ratings of themselves and others ranged from .21 for scenario 4 (shooting) to .79 for the use of force against a fleeing suspect. The majority of the effect sizes were medium to large. The differences in female officers' self-other perceptions were particularly large for scenario 9 (discount for referral; d = .83), scenario 10 (falsifying evidence; d = .78), and scenario 3 (theft from a crime scene; d = .77).

The final three columns of Table 10 show the results of ANOVAs comparing the difference scores (controlling for supervisor status) and their effect sizes. Female officers consistently showed a significantly greater degree of perceived difference between themselves and most officers, regarding their willingness to report the scenarios, compared to male officers. Eight of these differences were approaching, or equivalent to, medium effects, with the largest effect being for the discount for referrals (scenario 9). Stated another way, male officers, on average, conveyed a larger degree of similarity to (or fit with) the majority culture regarding reporting of unethical behavior.

Fairness of Discipline

The difference between the officers' perception of the discipline that *would* and *should* occur

shows the degree of officers' agreement (or alignment) with the organizational response to the scenarios, and is considered as a proxy for views on the fairness of discipline. The first four columns of Table 11 describe the mean fairness scores of female officers. Paired t-tests showed significant differences between female officers' ratings of what would and should occur on seven scenarios. Females believed that the response to two scenarios—gratuities (scenario 1) and rudeness (scenario 7)—would be significantly higher than it should be (representing harsh discipline) with small effect sizes (d = .3). In contrast, female officers on average thought that the discipline would be too lenient (lower than what should occur) for scenario 2 (ignoring a friend's warrant), with a small effect size; scenarios 9 (discount for referral) and 10 (planting evidence), with a medium effect size (d < .6); and scenarios 3 (theft) and 5 (exchanging leave for errands), with a large effect size (d > .8).

The second four columns of Table 11 show the mean fairness scores for male officers. While female officers tended to believe discipline would be lenient, the male officers most often viewed discipline to be harsh. Like female officers, male officers rated scenario 1 (gratuities) and scenario 7 (rudeness) as receiving harsh discipline; effect

Table 11 Estimated marginal means, standard errors, and ANOVA main effect results for the difference between the discipline perceived 'would' and 'should' occur (would—should) by gender, controlling for supervisory status

Fairness	Female				Male				Male-female difference			
	Rank	Mean	S.E.	d^a	Rank	Mean	S.E.	d^a	F	df	p	η^2_p
1. Gratuities	11	0.14*	0.08	−0.31	9	0.24***	0.05	−0.43	1.32	1727	.252	
2. Omits-warrant	5	−0.20**	0.07	0.38	3	−0.10*	0.04	0.21	1.53	1727	.217	
3. Theft	2	−0.41***	0.07	0.86	2	−0.16***	0.04	0.43	13.34	1728	<.001	0.02
4. Shooting	8	0.03	0.07		6	0.09**	0.04	−0.25	1.07	1714	.302	
5. Leave/errands	1	−0.50***	0.07	1.00	1	−0.25**	0.04	0.50	8.56	1725	.004	0.01
6. Force—punch	7	−0.07	0.09		11	0.41***	0.06	−0.64	20.84	1723	<.001	0.03
7. Rudeness	9	0.09*	0.04	−0.32	7	0.22***	0.03	−0.72	6.17	1728	.013	0.01
8. Omits-DUI	10	0.09	0.08		10	0.29***	0.05	−0.53	4.89	1723	.027	0.01
9. Discount for referral	3	−0.26***	0.06	0.58	4	−0.05	0.04		9.16	1726	.003	0.01
10. Evidence	4	−0.24***	0.05	0.55	5	−0.01	0.03		12.86	1727	<.001	0.02
11. Omits-force	6	−0.15	0.08		8	0.22***	0.05	−0.41	16.03	1725	<.001	0.02

[a]Effect size of would-should difference

*Mean would-should difference significant at p < .05 (paired samples t-test)

**Mean would-should difference significant at p < .01 (paired samples t-test)

***Mean would-should difference significant at p < .001 (paired samples t-test)

sizes of these differences were slightly larger for males than females (d = .43 to .72). However, male officers saw a further four scenarios as receiving harsh discipline; scenario 4 (shooting) and scenario 11 (ignoring beating of suspect), with small effect sizes (d < .5); and scenarios 8 (ignoring DUI) and 6 (force against fleeing suspect), with medium effect sizes (d = .53 to .64). Like female officers, males saw discipline to be significantly lenient for scenario 2 (ignoring a friend's warrant), scenarios 3 (theft) and scenario 5 (exchanging leave for errands), with small to medium effect sizes.

The final four columns of Table 11 show the results of the ANOVAs testing how different female and male officers were in their fairness scores (controlling for supervisory status). While both males and females tended towards a perception of leniency on scenarios 3 (theft), 5 (leave for errands), 9 (discount for referral), and 10 (evidence), females had a significantly greater perception of leniency for these behaviors than did males. Conversely, while both females and males tended to perceive scenarios 7 (rudeness) and 8 (ignores DIU) as receiving somewhat harsher discipline than they should, males had a significantly greater perception of harshness for these scenarios than did females. Interestingly, the use of force scenarios (scenarios 6 and 11) show a gender difference not only in magnitude of fairness perception but also in direction, with female

officers on average thinking the response would be more lenient than it should be and male officers thinking it would be harsher than it should be; these differences between males and females were both statistically significant.

Predicting Personal Attitudes from Perceptions of Culture

The analyses above shows the range of gender differences in officers' own perceptions and their perceptions of, and alignment to, the culture. This section explores the relationship between these for males and females. Regressions were performed to test whether perceptions of the social culture (perceptions of most officers' seriousness and willingness to report) and organizational culture (likely disciplinary response) are significant predictors of officers' hypothetical behavior (willingness to report). Regressions were performed separately for males and females, with constructs averaged across the 11 scenarios and controlling for supervisory status (Table 12).

For females, the model was significant and explained 37% of the variance in willingness to report. Supervisory status predicted willingness to report. However, of the culture measures, only the perception of others' willingness to report was significant. The more likely female officers thought others would report, the more likely they

Table 12 Predicting willingness to report for females and males

	Females			Males		
	B	S.E.	Beta	B	S.E.	Beta
Intercept	2.152	0.281		0.818	0.222	
Supervisor	0.322	0.068	0.263***	0.232	0.047	0.163***
Discipline would	−0.07	0.053	−0.086	−0.049	0.044	−0.042
Seriousness most	0.176	0.108	0.151	0.399	0.077	0.277***
Willingness most	0.419	0.084	0.477***	0.445	0.059	0.412***
R	0.618			0.667		
R^2	0.382			0.444		
Adjusted R^2	0.370			0.440		
S.E.	0.472			0.534		
F	31.387			103.546		
Sig.	<.001			<.001		

***Significant at p < .001

said they would report. Expected discipline was not significant, neither were perceptions of other's seriousness views.

Results were slightly different for male officers. The model was significant, accounting for 44% of the variance. Supervisory status and perception of others' willingness to report were significant. In contrast to the model for females, perceptions of others' seriousness was also significant. Expected discipline was not significant.

Discussion

This chapter has explored gender differences in policing with respect to ethical attitudes and behavior. In the main, the findings support the larger literature, although gender differences were not consistently large across all constructs and all forms of behavior. This shows the importance of exploring specific ethical attitudes in detail. However, where differences were evident, these were more favorable to female officers, supporting previous studies of police ethical perceptions and behavior.

There were few gender differences in personal ethical views. The seriousness with which males and females viewed the individual scenarios was largely consistent, with the main exception being that women viewed the use of force more seriously than males (which is consistent with a number of previous studies reviewed earlier). However, a gender difference in seriousness remained significant when aggregated across the scenarios. There were also very few differences in understanding whether the scenarios constituted a violation (also consistent with prior literature), and in willingness to report them. Officers also had similar views on what would be an appropriate disciplinary response. Again, though, in the aggregate, females suggested lower discipline than males, which is consistent with previous studies (CMC 2010; Pagon et al. 2004; Porter et al. 2015). Thus, while, on average, females tended to view behavior more seriously, they had a broadly more lenient view of the appropriate response.

The findings, particularly in relation to views of force, are consistent with evidence regarding officer behavior. For example, female officers are less likely to use force in dealing with suspects, and much less likely to attract complaints of excessive force. Women are also more likely to show empathy and respect to suspects and victims of crimes, and provide assistance (Corsianos 2009; Eagly et al. 2000; Rabe-Hemp 2008b). Female officers also attract less misconduct complaints generally, and this picture of lower levels of participation in misconduct is supported by the findings of some corruption enquiries. The findings do not necessarily entail 'gender essentialism' in assuming all women are intrinsically 'ethical' (Valenius 2007), in part because the numbers clearly show that women police account for a proportion of adverse data. The situation is roughly consistent with the 'gender gap' in crime rates internationally, and other diverse sources on gender differences in aggression (Archer 2004; Heidensohn and Silvestri 2012).

Gender differences were far more evident when exploring officers' perceptions of the social and organizational culture, as well as the alignment between their personal and cultural perceptions. Males tended to expect harsher discipline than females on almost all scenarios, and be more inclined to believe that discipline would be unfairly harsh, compared to females. The largest and most consistent difference evident in the integrity constructs, however, was how officers viewed themselves in comparison to other officers—the social culture. While it has been shown that officers tend to view themselves more favorably in comparison to their colleagues (Porter et al. 2015; Porter and Prenzler 2016a), female officers consistently had a lower opinion of both the perceptions and behavior of other officers—more so than men. In addition, compared to males, females saw themselves as more different to the majority. As noted earlier in this chapter, the majority of officers, including in Australia, are male. Therefore, when asked to comment on the majority culture, it is possible that officers are considering male culture. This could potentially explain why females see a greater difference to themselves; partly, they *are* different to males in some of their ethical views, as noted above, and partly they may *feel* more different because they are the 'outgroup' (as proposed by Huon et al. 1995). As noted earlier in this chapter, being a member of the outgroup could have positive or negative effects. Huon et al. (1995) proposed the outgroup may be 'protected' from the unethical culture. Indeed, Porter and Prenzler (2016a) found that a greater perceived self-other difference decreased the odds of not reporting infractions. However, they also cautioned that such a perceived difference could have negative impacts in the long term, through mechanisms that encourage the minority to adopt, or conform to, the majority position, in order to fit in (see also Andreescu et al. 2012).

The impact of perceived norms on officers' hypothetical willingness to report the scenarios was explored, and a gender difference was observed. For both males and females, perceptions of the social culture was a more important predictor than perceptions of the organizational culture; the disciplinary response expected did not significantly predict willingness to report (when controlling for the other variables). Males and females were also similar in that their willingness to report was significantly predicted by their perceptions of others' willingness to report. However, males' willingness to report was also predicted by their perceptions of others' seriousness views, while this was not the case for females. Thus, while perceptions of social norms were important to both, there was a subtle difference between the importance of the behavioral norm (also termed a descriptive norm) and the attitudinal norm (also termed an injunctive norm). For females, only the behavioral norm was important regarding their own hypothetical behavior. For males, however, both the behavior and attitudes of others were important predictors of their own behavior. This may offer further support for the view of Huon et al. (1995) noted above, in that females may be somewhat 'protected' from the effects of the perceived attitudinal norm (what others think). In contrast, though,

the behavioral norm is clearly important. Female officers may wish to conform to the behavioral norm to fit in, as suggested by Andreescu et al. (2012), or for fear of reprisal, as noted by Wagner et al. (2016). However, given that perceptions of the behavioral norm were also significant for male officers, this may not be a gender issue, but one of normative police culture in general. The results add to those of Lobnikar et al. (2016) and Pagon et al. (2004) to refine our understanding of the effects of cultural perceptions for males and females.

Given that females seem to hold somewhat more ethical views (at least for some forms of behavior), and that cultural norms influence officers' behavioral intentions, there may be support for the argument that employing more female officers could enhance the integrity of a police service (by improving the cultural norm). However, given that women still appear in adverse indicators of police conduct, simply employing them in larger numbers in order to sanitize and humanize police forces will not fix the problem (Rabe-Hemp 2008a, b; Wood 1997). Women are susceptible to organizational influences and to temptations and opportunities for misconduct and corruption in the complex and often fraught task environment of policing. Female recruits still need to be carefully selected, with close attention to integrity issues and personality; and they need to be trained through an intensive ethical development, and physical skills development, program. Throughout their careers they need to be subject to the same comprehensive integrity management framework as their male counterparts, including complaint profiling and early intervention (Porter and Prenzler 2016b). Effective integrity management processes also need to take into account other factors that influence police behavior, including the age, education, and experience of officers (Bolger 2015; Paoline and Terrill 2007). Indeed, in the present study, supervisory status was a significant predictor of willingness to report regardless of gender.

Scenarios

Number	Label	Scenario
1	Gratuities	A police officer is widely liked in the community. Local business owners regularly show their appreciation for his attention by giving him gifts of food, cigarettes, and other items of small value
2	Omits-warrant	A police officer is aware that there is an arrest warrant for a long time friend of his. Although he sees his friend frequently over a period of more than a week and warns his friend of its existence, he does not arrest him or pass on information about his friend's whereabouts to other police
3	Theft	A police officer discovers a burglary of a hardware store. The display cases are smashed and many items have obviously been taken. While searching the store, he takes an expensive pocket knife and slips it into his pocket. He reports that the knife has been stolen during the burglary
4	Shooting	An officer, who was severely beaten by a person resisting arrest, has just returned to duty. On patrol, the officer approaches a person standing in a dimly lit alley. Suddenly, the person throws a gym bag at the officer and begins to run away. The officer fatally shoots the person, striking him in the back. It was later determined that the person was unarmed
5	Leave/errands	A police officer is scheduled to work during coming holidays. The supervisor offers to give him these days off, if he agrees to run some personal errands for the supervisor. Evaluate the SUPERVISOR'S behavior
6	Force-punch	In responding with her male partner to a fight in a bar, a young, female officer receives a black eye from one of the male combatants. The man is arrested, handcuffed, and, as he is led into the cells, the male member of the team punches him very hard in the kidney area saying, "hurts, doesn't it"
7	Rudeness	A police officer stops a motorist for speeding. As the officer approaches the vehicle, the driver yells, "What the hell are you stopping me for?" The officer replies, "Because today is 'Arrest an Arsehole Day'"
8	Omits-DUI	At 2 A.M. a police officer, who is on duty, is driving his patrol car on a deserted road. He sees a vehicle that has been driven off the road and is stuck in a ditch. He approaches the vehicle and observes that the driver is not hurt but is obviously intoxicated. He also finds that the driver is a police officer. Instead of reporting this accident and offense he transports the driver to his home
9	Discount for referral	A police officer has a private arrangement with a local Smash Repairer to refer the owners of cars damaged in accidents to the shop. In exchange for each referral, he receives a payment of 5% of the repair bill from the shop owner
10	Evidence	A police officer arrests two drug dealers involved in a street fight. One has a large quantity of heroin on his person. In order to charge them both with serious offences, the officer falsely reports that the heroin was found on both men
11	Omits-force	A police sergeant, without intervening, watches officers under his supervision repeatedly strike and kick a man arrested for child abuse. The man has previous child abuse arrests. Evaluate the SERGEANT'S behavior

References

Andreescu, V., Keeling, D. G., Voinic, M. C., & Tonea, B. N. (2012). Future Romanian law enforcement: Gender differences in perceptions of police misconduct. *Journal of Social Research & Policy, 3*(1), 97–113.

Appier, J. (1993). Preventive justice. *Women & Criminal Justice, 4*(1), 3–36.

Archer, J. (2004). Sex differences in aggression in real-world settings: A Meta-analytic review. *Review of General Psychology, 8*(4), 291–322.

Balkin, J. (1988). Why policemen don't like policewomen. *Journal of Police Science and Administration, 16*(1), 29–38.

Bazley, T., Lersch, M., & Mieczkowski, T. (2007). Officer force versus suspect resistance: A gendered analysis of officers in an urban police department. *Journal of Criminal Justice, 35*(2), 183–192.

Bloch, P., & Anderson, D. (1974). *Policewomen on patrol: Final report.* Washington, DC: Police Foundation.

Bolger, P. (2015). Just following orders: A Meta-analysis of the correlates of American police officer use of force decisions. *American Journal of Criminal Justice, 40*(3), 466–492.

Boylen, M., & Little, R. (1990). Fatal assaults on United States law enforcement officers. *The Police Journal, 63*(1), 61–77.

Braithwaite, H. & Brewer, N. (1998). Differences in the Conflict Resolution Tactics of Male and Female Police Patrol Officers. *International Journal of Police Science & Management, 1*(3), 276–287.

Brandl, S., & Stroshine, M. (2013). The Role of officer attributes, job characteristics, and arrest activity in explaining police use of force. *Criminal Justice Policy Review, 24*(5), 551–572.

Brown, J., & Heidensohn, F. (2000). *Gender and policing: Comparative perspectives.* Houndmills: Macmillan.

Brown, J., & Langan, P. (2001). *Policing and homicide, 1976-98.* Washington, DC: US Department of Justice.

Charles, S. (2009). *Professional integrity, modern racism, self-esteem, and universality-diversity orientation of police officers in a large urban police agency.* Unpublished thesis, Fordham University. AAI3361463.

Christopher, W. (1991). *Report of the Independent Commission on the Los Angeles Police Department.* Los Angeles: Independent Commission on the LAPD.

CMC. (2010). *The ethical perceptions and attitudes of Queensland Police Service recruits and first year constables, 1995–2008.* Brisbane: CMC.

Cordner, G., & Cordner, A. (2011). Stuck on a plateau? Obstacles to the recruitment, selection, and retention of women police. *Police Quarterly, 14*(3), 207–226.

Corsianos, M. (2009). *Policing and gendered justice.* Toronto: University of Toronto Press.

Crawford, C., & Burns, R. (1998). Predictors of the police use of force: The Application of a continuum perspective in Phoenix. *Police Quarterly, 1*(4), 41–63.

Criminal Justice Commission. (1996). *Gender and ethics in policing.* Brisbane: Author.

Criminal Justice Commission (1998). *Police pursuits in Queensland resulting in death or injury.* Brisbane: CJC.

Dick, P., & Cassell, C. (2002). Barriers to managing diversity in a UK constabulary: The Role of discourse. *Journal of Management Studies, 39*(7), 953–976.

Dick, P., & Hyde, R. (2006). Line manager involvement in the career development of part-time police officers: Can't manage, won't manage? *British Journal of Guidance and Counselling, 34*(3), 365–364.

Eagly, A., Wood, W., & Diekman, A. (2000). Social role theory of sex differences and similarities: A Current appraisal. In T. Eckes & H. Trautner (Eds.), *The Developmental social psychology of gender* (pp. 123–174). New York: Taylor & Francis.

Gaanderse, M., & Valasek, K. (2011). *The Security sector and gender in West Africa.* Geneva: Geneva Center for the Democratic Control of Armed Forces.

Garner, J., Maxwell, C., & Heraux, C. (2002). Characteristics associated with the prevalence and severity of force used by the police. *Justice Quarterly, 19*(4), 705–747.

Grennan, S. (1987). Findings on the role of officer gender in violent encounters with citizens. *Journal of Police Science and Administration, 15*(1), 78–85.

Harris, J. (2010). Problem officers? Analyzing problem behavior patterns from a large cohort. *Journal of Criminal Justice, 38*(2), 216–225.

Hassell, K., & Archbold, C. (2010). Widening the scope of complaints of police misconduct. *Policing: An International Journal of Police Strategies and Management, 33*(3), 473–489.

Heidensohn, F. (1992). *Women in control? The Role of women in law enforcement.* Oxford: Clarendon.

Heidensohn, F., & Silvestri, M. (2012). Gender and crime. In M. Maguire, R. Morgan, & R. Reiner (Eds.), *The Oxford handbook of criminology* (pp. 336–369). Oxford: Oxford University Press.

Hoffman, P., & Hickey, E. (2005). Use of force by female police officers. *Journal of Criminal Justice, 33*(2), 145–151.

Horvath, F. (1987). The Police use of deadly force: A Description of selected characteristics of intra-state incidents. *Journal of Police Science and Administration, 15*(3), 226–238.

Hunt, J. (1990). The Logic of sexism among police. *Women and Criminal Justice, 1*(2), 3–30.

Huon, G. F., Hesketh, B. L., Frank, M. G., McConkey, K. M., & McGrath, G. M. (1995). *Perceptions of ethical dilemmas: Ethics and policing study 1.* Australasian Centre for Policing Research.

Institute for Public Security of Catalonia. (2013). *Women in police services in the EU, facts and figures – 2012.* Author: Barcelona.

Jackson, L. (2006). Women police: Gender, welfare and surveillance in the twentieth century. Manchester: Manchester University Press

Jacobs, P. (1987). How female police officers cope with a traditionally male position. *Sociology and Social Research, 72*(1), 4–6.

Jones, S. (1986). *Policewomen and equality: Formal policy v informal practice?* Houndmills: Routledge.

Klockars, C. B., Kutnjak Ivković, S., & Haberfeld, M. R. (2000). *The contours of police integrity*. Thousand Oaks, CA: Sage Publications.

Klockars, C. B., Kutnjak Ivković, S., & Haberfeld, M. R. (2006). *Enhancing police integrity*. New York, NY: Springer.

Kucukuysal, B. (2008). *Determinants of Turkish police officers' perception of integrity: Impact of organizational culture*. Doctoral dissertation, University of Central Florida.

Langan, D., Sanders, C., & Agocs, T. (2016). Canadian police mothers and the boys' club: Pregnancy, maternity leave, and returning to work. *Women & Criminal Justice,* 1–15, https://doi.org/10.1080/08974454.2016.1256254

Lersch, K. (1998). Exploring gender differences in citizen allegations of misconduct: An Analysis of a municipal police department. *Women and Criminal Justice, 9*(4), 69–79.

Levander, M. T., & Ekenvall, B. (2004). Homogeneity in moral standards in Swedish police culture. In C. B. Klockars, S. Kutnjak Ivković, & M. R. Haberfeld (Eds.), *The contours of police integrity* (pp. 251–264). Thousand Oaks, CA: Sage Publications.

Lobnikar, B., Prislan, K., Čuvan, B., & Meško, G. (2016). The code of silence and female police officers in Slovenia: Gender differences in willingness to report police misconduct. *Policing: An International Journal of Police Strategies & Management, 39*(2), 387–400.

Lonsway, K., Wood, M., Fickling, M., de Leon, A., Moore, M., Harrington, P., Smeal, E., & Spillar, K. (2002). *Men, women, and excessive force: A tale of two genders*. Beverly Hills: National Center for Women and Policing.

Lunneborg, P. (1989). *Women police officers: Current career profile*. Springfield, IL: Charles C Thomas.

Martin, S. (1990). *On the move: The status of women in policing*. Washington, DC: Police Foundation.

Martin, S., & Jurik, N. (2007). *Doing justice, doing gender: Women in legal and criminal justice occupations*. Thousand Oaks, CA: Sage.

McDevitt, J., Posick, C., Zschoche, R., Rosenbaum, D. P., Buslik, M., & Fridell, L. (2011). *Police integrity, responsibility, and discipline. Topical report*. Washington, DC: National Institute of Justice.

McElvain, J., & Kposowa, A. (2008). Police officer characteristics and the likelihood of using deadly force. *Criminal Justice and Behavior, 35*(4), 505–521.

Natarajan, M. (2008). *Women police in a changing society: Back door to equality*. Aldershot: Ashgate.

National Center for Women and Policing. (2002). *Equality denied: The status of women in policing, 2001*. Washington, DC: National Center for Women and Policing.

Niland, C. (1996, July). *The impact of police culture on women and their performance in policing*. Paper presented at the First Australasian Women in Policing Conference, Sydney.

Novak, K., Brown, R., & Frank, J. (2008). Women on patrol: An Analysis of differences in officer arrest behavior. *Policing: An International Journal of Police Strategies and Management, 34*(4), 566–587.

Pagon, M., Lobnikar, B., & Anelj, D. (2004). Gender differences in leniency towards police misconduct. In G. Mesko, M. Pagon, & B. Dobovsek (Eds.), *Policing in Central and Eastern Europe-dilemmas of contemporary criminal justice* (pp. 1–16). Ljubljana: Faculty of Criminal Justice, University of Maribor.

Paoline, E., & Terrill, W. (2005). Women police officers and the use of coercion. *Women and Criminal Justice, 15*(3–4), 97–119.

Paoline, E., & Terrill, W. (2007). Police education, experience, and the use of force. *Criminal Justice & Behavior, 34*(2), 179–196.

Porter, L. E., & Prenzler, T. (2015). Police officer gender and excessive force complaints: An Australian study. *Policing & Society.* https://doi.org/10.1080/10439463.2015.1114616.

Porter, L. E., & Prenzler, T. (2016a). The code of silence and ethical perceptions: Exploring police officer unwillingness to report misconduct. *Policing: An International Journal of Police Strategies and Management, 39*(2), 370–386.

Porter, L. E., & Prenzler, T. (2016b). Corruption prevention and complaint management. In T. Prenzler (Ed.), *Policing and security in practice: Challenges and achievements* (2nd ed., pp. 130–148). Houndmills: Palgrave-Macmillan.

Porter, L. E., Prenzler, T., & Hine, K. (2015). Police integrity in Australia. In S. Kutnjak Ivković & M. R. Haberfeld (Eds.), *Measuring police integrity across the world* (pp. 67–96). New York, NY: Springer.

Prenzler, T. (2015). *One hundred years of women police in Australia*. Brisbane: Australian Academic Press.

Prenzler, T., & Porter, L. E. (2016). Improving police behavior and police-community relations through innovative responses to complaints. In S. Lister & M. Rowe (Eds.), *Accountability in policing: Contemporary debates* (pp. 49–68). Abingdon: Routledge.

Prenzler, T., & Sinclair, G. (2013). The Status of women police officers: An International review. *International Journal of Law, Crime, and Justice, 41*(2), 115–131.

Rabe-Hemp, C. (2008a). Survival in an 'all boys club': Policewomen and their fight for acceptance. *Policing: An International journal of Police Strategies and Management, 31*(2), 251–270.

Rabe-Hemp, C. (2008b). Female officers and the ethic of care: Does officer gender impact police behaviors? *Journal of Criminal Justice, 36*(5), 426–434.

Robertson, J., & Bazley, M. (2007). *Report of the commission of inquiry into police conduct* (Vol. 1). Wellington: Authors.

Schuck, A., & Rabe-Hemp, C. (2005). Women police: The use of force by and against female officers. *Women and Criminal Justice, 16*(4), 91–117.

Sherman, L. (1975). An Evaluation of policewomen on patrol in a suburban police department. *Journal of Police Science and Administration, 3*(4), 434–438.

Sichel, J., Friedman, L., Quint, J., & Smith, M. (1978). *Women on patrol: A Pilot study of police performance in New York City.* New York: Vera Institute of Justice.

Silvestri, M. (2003). *Women in charge: Policing, gender and leadership.* Collumpton: Willan.

Skogan, W. (2013). Use of force and police reform in Brazil: A national survey of police officers. *Police Practice and Research: An International Journal, 14*(4), 319–329.

Sun, I., Payne, B., & Wu, Y. (2008). The Impact of officer characteristics, and neighbourhood context on police behavior: A Multilevel analysis. *Journal of Criminal Justice, 36*, 22–32.

Terrill, W., & Mastrofski, S. (2002). Situational and officer-based determinants of police coercion. *Justice Quarterly, 19*(2), 215–249.

United Nations (2009). *2009 World Survey of the Role of Women in Economic Development.* New York: United Nations.

Valenius, J. (2007). A few kind women: Gender essentialism and Nordic peace keeping operations. *International Peacekeeping, 14*(4), 510–523.

Vallmüür, B. (2016). Exploring gender-neutrality of police integrity in Estonia. *Policing: An International Journal of Police Strategies & Management, 39*(2), 401–415.

Wagner, N., Rieger, M., Bedi, A. S., & Hout, W. (2016). Are women better police officers? Evidence from survey experiments in Uganda. *ISS Working Paper Series/ General Series, 615*(615), 1–34.

Ward, A., & Prenzler, T. (2016). Good practice case studies in the advancement of women in policing. *International Journal of Police Science and Management, 18*(4), 242–250.

Waugh, L., Ede, A., & Alley, A. (1998). Police culture, women police and attitudes towards misconduct. *International Journal of Police Science & Management, 1*(3), 288–300.

Wexler, J. (1985). Role styles of women police officers. *Sex Roles, 12*(7/8), 749–755.

Williams, J. J. & Hester, G. (2003). Sheriff law enforcement officers and the use of force. *Journal of Criminal Justice, 31*(4), 373–381.

Wood, J. (1997). *Royal commission into the New South Wales Police Service: Final report.* Sydney: NSW Government Printer.

Part IV

Exploring Validity and Reliability of Police Integrity Methodology

Improving the Measurement of Police Integrity: An Application of LTM to the Klockars et al. (1997) Scales

Jon Maskály, Christopher M. Donner, and Tiffany Chen

Introduction

Recent events highlight the consummate need for police agencies to bolster the perceived legitimacy of the police in the eyes of their constituents. One of the means through which this can be accomplished is by holding officers who engage in misconduct accountable for their actions (Palmiotto 2001). This puts police executives in an awkward position because it is incumbent upon them to prevent misconduct—or bolster the integrity—of officers (Kutnjak Ivković 2005). However, just as with crime in general (Mosher et al. 2010), research consistently suggests only a small fraction of instances of police misconduct are reported (e.g., Long et al. 2013). Despite being unaware of all instances of misconduct, the legitimacy of the police is eroded by any act of misconduct.

For agencies to effectively understand, and subsequently address misconduct, they need an alternative mechanism for assessing levels of police integrity (Klockars et al. 2004). To fill this gap, Klockars et al. (1997) developed a methodology for studying police integrity by asking officers to rate a series of vignettes. This methodology—including the measures—are largely recognized as being the best way to study police integrity (Rosenbaum 2016). The methodology has been used in many studies in the United States and a swath of countries around the world, and the methodology is extremely robust to social and political variations (see generally, Kutnjak Ivković and Haberfeld 2015).

While there are some strengths to the method, one of the limitations in the measurement is how police integrity is rarely studied as a construct. Except a handful of studies, most scholars examine the 11 scenarios—across each of the domains measured—rather than treating police integrity as a latent construct. The difference in the statistical treatment of these approaches may seem trivial at first. However, latent constructs are intentionally designed to be more parsimonious, to partial out shared variance, and to analyze unique variance while controlling for error variance (Brown 2014). This allows scholars to more precisely understand the nuances of police integrity measured by the Klockars et al. (1997) scale. Furthermore, while there are some ways to perform this operation, modern psychometric techniques (i.e., item response theory) permit us to thoroughly—and simultaneously—examine person- and item-level variation in police integrity (De Ayala 2009).

J. Maskály (✉)
School of Economic, Political, and Policy Sciences, University of Texas, Dallas, TX, USA

C. M. Donner
Department of Criminal Justice and Criminology, Loyola University, Chicago, IL, USA
e-mail: cdonner@luc.edu

T. Chen
University of Texas, Dallas, TX, USA
e-mail: tiffany.chen2@utdallas.edu

© Springer Nature Switzerland AG 2019
S. Kutnjak Ivković, M. R. Haberfeld (eds.), *Exploring Police Integrity*,
https://doi.org/10.1007/978-3-030-29065-8_13

The purpose of this chapter is to examine the properties of the latent construct(s) captured using the initial data collected by Klockars et al. (1997). To strengthen our understanding of the potential results from our study (i.e., item-difficulty, invariance), we first conduct a thorough review of the literature. In this review, we focus first on those studies that attempt to measure police integrity as a latent construct. Second, we review the bulk of the literature which uses the Klockars et al. (1997) methodology looking at individual items, noting both the consistency and inconsistency of findings in regards to the strengths and weaknesses of the items. This approach allows us to see where there may be differential degrees of validity in the data or, conversely, whether the differences are attributable to context as theory would suggest (Klockars et al. 2004). This process is repeated for each of the dimensions captured in the survey.

Following the literature review, we develop valid and reliable latent constructs of each of the five of the dimensions measured,[1] while considering the potential inter-relationships between the constructs. The analysis proceeds in three phases. First, we use a modern psychometric approach and reassess the validity of the measures using an item response theory approach. Second, we estimate the correlation between the various sub-constructs of integrity. Third, we examine the measurement invariance of police integrity between large and smaller police organizations looking for evidence of differential item function. Finally, we conclude with a discussion of the implications of the results as they relate to the future measurement of police integrity using the first version of the Klockars et al. methodology, as well as potential challenges to the theoretical model of police integrity.

Literature Review

Klockars et al. Scale

With the amount of discretion involved in policing, there are bound to be abuses of authority and instances of misconduct. This has been a hot topic among researchers over the past few decades, and it has continued to gain popular interest as some high profile cases involving police misconduct have circulated in the news. Because measuring police integrity creates validity concerns due to the complexity and sensitive nature of the issue, Klockars et al. (1997) devised a scale of 11 hypothetical case scenarios to assess officers' perceived seriousness of various forms of misconduct, their expected disciplinary action, and whether they and others would be willing to report such violations. As this scale had been administered in surveys to numerous police agencies over time, a second version of the questionnaire was developed by Klockars et al. (2004) to address issues that arose, specifically forms of misconduct that were not for any particular gain. Since then, scholars have used the first or second questionnaire, or a combination of the two to measure police integrity as it pertains to their specific context and culture. These scales have been used to measure police integrity domestically (e.g., Chappell and Piquero 2004; Kutnjak Ivković et al. 2012, 2015, 2018; Klockars et al. 1997; McDevitt et al. 2011; Rothwell and Baldwin 2006, 2007; Wolfe and Piquero 2011), internationally (e.g., Alain 2004; Chattha and Kutnjak Ivković 2004; Cheloukhine et al. 2015; Edelbacher and Kutnjak Ivković 2004; Haberfeld 2004; Kutnjak Ivković 2012, 2015; Kutnjak Ivković and Klockars 2004; Kutnjak Ivković and Sauerman 2012; Kutnjak Ivković and Shelley 2005; Johnson 2004; Kang and Kutnjak Ivković 2015; Khechumyan and Kutnjak Ivković 2015; Kremer 2004; Levander and Ekenvall 2004; Newham 2004; Lobnikar

---

[1]While we would have liked to include all seven dimensions, the two dimensions related to the discipline a person *should* receive and the discipline a person *would* receive for engaging in this behavior presented unique problems. Specifically, the results from the model indicated serious violation of the assumptions with the model, which suggests the need for additional work to develop the constructs being measured. These problems stem from differences between organizations, whereby some organizations have the ability—and willingness—to use some types of disciplinary procedures that are not available or widely employed in others.

and Mesko 2015; Pagon and Lobnikar 2004; Phetthong and Kutnjak Ivković 2015; Porter et al. 2015; Punch et al. 2004; Puonti et al. 2004; Sauerman and Kutnjak Ivković 2015; Tasdoven and Kaya 2014; Vallmuur 2015; Westmarland 2004; Wright 2010), and cross-culturally (Andreescu et al. 2012; Huberts et al. 2003; Kutnjak Ivković 2004; Kutnjak Ivković and Haberfeld 2015; Kutnjak Ivković and Shelley 2008; Khruakham and Lee 2013). The domestic studies have rarely deviated from the items used in the first (Klockars et al. 1997) and second (Klockars et al. 2004) versions of the questionnaire with the exception of two studies (Rothwell and Baldwin 2006, 2007), where modifications were necessary to measure whistle-blowing among civilian employees. The majority of international and cross-cultural studies have utilized the original items as well; however, there have been a handful of studies that added or made revisions to the items of measurement. These adjustments were necessary for the scale to be relevant in the cultures of Armenia (e.g., Khechumyan and Kutnjak Ivković 2015), Australia (e.g., Porter et al. 2015), Croatia (e.g., Kutnjak Ivković 2012), England (e.g., Wright 2010), Hungary (e.g., Kremer 2004), Pakistan (e.g., Chattha and Kutnjak Ivković 2004), Russia (e.g., Cheloukhine et al. 2015), Slovenia (Lobnikar and Mesko 2015), South Africa (e.g., Kutnjak Ivković and Sauerman 2012), and Sweden (e.g., Levander and Ekenvall 2004).

Most studies that utilize the scales created by Klockars et al. (1997) and Klockars et al. (2004) have the same objectives and have taken similar approaches to evaluating police agencies by focusing on the individual items of the scales. The results from the individual items are assumed to create a comprehensive evaluation of police integrity, but there is a reason to believe that this is not the case. Because police integrity is a multifaceted and complex idea, it is necessary to explore its measurement as a latent construct, which only a handful of studies have attempted. This is possible by looking at information on how respondents assess the seriousness of vignettes and their willingness to report fellow officers' misbehavior.

Offense Seriousness

The first version of the scale was followed by seven questions with the first two asking about the seriousness of each case scenario. Respondents were asked their personal views of each case and their perceptions of other officers in their agency regarding each scenario. Rather than asking respondents to rank-order the seriousness of individual items, there have been a handful of studies that utilized latent factor analyses to assess and interpret seriousness. Chappell and Piquero (2004), for example, used five of the case scenarios from the first version of the scale and created three sub-constructs (gifts, theft, and force) and measures of social learning constructs (peer associations, definitions, reinforcement), with the ultimate objective of establishing social learning as a theoretical explanation for police misconduct. Similarly, Wolfe and Piquero (2011) utilized the first version of the scale to control for deviant police peer associations. Respondents were asked to evaluate the seriousness of the case scenarios, but the responses were coded in such a way that peer associations could be measured as well. The items were then combined to create the sub-constructs of minor deviant peers and serious deviant peers. These variables were found to be significant predictors of code of silence attitudes and noble cause corruption beliefs, which will be discussed later.

Rather than explaining the theoretical basis of police misconduct, Jenks et al. (2012) conducted a latent factor analysis on the eleven case scenarios from the first version of the questionnaire to assess whether behaviors typically perceived as corruption are represented by the measurement. They found that each of the vignettes measured police integrity to varying degrees, and, in regards to the seriousness of events, accepting gratuities and having an off-duty business were not considered to be corrupt. More specifically, these items could only account for 10.4% of the variance and are therefore not indicative of corruption. It is important to note, however, that Jenks et al. (2012) later refer to these same items as conflict of interest behaviors and less serious integrity violations, as to acknowledge their importance in the police deviance literature. This study demonstrated the way the original scenarios have been utilized to measure police integrity is limited and incomplete.

As previously mentioned, the bulk of the literature involving the first version of the scale has looked at individual case items to examine the overall integrity of the organization of interest. In most studies, respondents are asked to evaluate the seriousness of each vignette and to assess their perceptions of how their peers would evaluate the same items. Findings from the original Klockars et al. (1997) study demonstrated how the scenarios were essentially divided into those considered not very serious, those at an intermediate level of seriousness, and those that were very serious. More specifically, the off-duty business, receipt of gratuities, and covering up a DUI were not considered serious. Excessive force following a foot pursuit, time off in exchange for personal favors, and accepting drinks in exchange for ignoring bar closing times were considered an intermediate level of seriousness. Stealing from a found wallet, accepting bribes, and stealing from a crime scene were considered the most serious violations. Subsequent studies have found that respondents rank order the scenarios very similarly (Kutnjak Ivković 2012; Kutnjak Ivković et al. 2012; Vito et al. 2011). Interestingly, this holds true with cross-cultural comparisons (Andreescu et al. 2012; Huberts et al. 2003; Kutnjak Ivković 2004; Kutnjak Ivković and Haberfeld 2015; Kutnjak Ivković and Shelley 2008; Khruakham and Lee 2013). What differs is the extent of seriousness of the items, but the rank ordering remains consistent across various agencies and countries.

Policy Violation

Although originally included as a survey item, Klockars et al. (1997) spend very little time discussing the results pertaining to this question. Instead, they primarily focus on the seriousness and reporting survey items. Subsequent research, however, has devoted attention to this interesting question, which taps into a respondent's perception as to whether the misconduct behavior constitutes a policy violation within his/her respective agency (e.g., Kutnjak Ivković and Khechumyan 2014; Vito et al. 2011). Overall, it is quite clear—as would be expected—that those behaviors deemed more serious are more likely to be identified as a policy violation.

Utilizing a sample of sworn police personnel from the State of Kentucky, Vito and colleagues (2014) found that 90% or higher of the sample rated six of the eleven misconduct scenarios as "definitely yes" a violation of agency policy. This includes 99.6% of the sample indicating a policy violation for theft of a watch from a crime and 99.2% of the sample reporting a policy violation for theft from a found wallet. At the other end of the spectrum, however, 61.3% said that covering up a fellow officer's DUI accident was a violating of agency policy and only 58.5% stated that it was a policy violation to accept holiday gifts from local merchants.

Similarly, in a comparison of four U.S. cities ("Rainless West," Charleston, Charlotte, and St. Petersburg), research from Kutnjak Ivković et al. (2013) demonstrated that misconduct acts generally perceived as less serious were less likely to be identified as a policy violation. For example, covering up a fellow officer's DUI accident yielded an affirmative response from 68% of Charlotte officers to 85% of Charleston officers. However, when it came to falsely reporting a suspect's drug possession, 95% or higher of all four samples indicated such an act constituted a policy violation. This line of research has also been explored with police agencies outside of the United States (e.g., Kutnjak Ivković and Shelley 2005). While there is noticeably more variation in policy violation perception among these non--U.S. agencies, the same general trend— more serious acts identified as violations—is seen when examining police officers in Armenia (Kutnjak Ivković and Khechumyan 2014), Bosnia (Kutnjak Ivković and Shelley 2005), and Czechoslovakia (Kutnjak Ivković and Shelley 2007).

Willingness to Report

Perhaps the most important questions following the eleven vignettes from the first version ask *whether the respondent would report another officer* who engaged in the behavior and *whether most officers in his/her agency would report another officer* for the same behavior. These questions seek to address what is referred to as the "Code of Silence" or the "Blue Curtain," an informal protection and environment that discourages the reporting of misconduct committed by colleagues (e.g., Skolnick 2002). Respondents from the original study stated they would not report other officers for the minor violations, including working an off-duty business, accepting gratuities, or a DUI cover-up. They did, however, say they would report officers who engaged in stealing from a crime scene or a found wallet, accepting bribes, or using excessive force (Klockars et al. 1997). Latent factor analyses revealed deviant peers to be a significant predictor of code of silence attitudes (Wolfe and Piquero 2011). Having associations with individuals regarded as deviant peers increases the influence of the police subculture that discourages reporting the misconduct of fellow officers. This influence was found to be offset if officers believed their agency to be organizationally just. When officers are not as committed to the code of silence, they are more likely to perceive the presence of organizational justice within their agencies. As Wolfe and Piquero (2011) have noted, further analysis is needed to fully explore the relationship between organizational justice, deviant peer associations, and the code of silence.

The remaining individual-item studies again revealed a few compelling trends in their findings. A strong correlation was found between perceived seriousness of the violation and willingness to report, where the code of silence was stronger for minor violations and weaker for more serious ones (Andreescu et al. 2012; Alain 2004; Kutnjak Ivković et al. 2015, 2018; Kutnjak Ivković and Shelley 2005; Klockars et al. 2004; Levander and Ekenvall 2004; Lobnikar and Mesko 2015; Long et al. 2013; Pagon and Lobnikar 2004; Phettong and Kutnjak Ivković

2015; Porter et al. 2015; Punch et al. 2004; Westmarland 2004). Also, officer reluctance to report was strongly correlated with the perception that other officers belonging to the same agency would not report the incident either (Kutnjak Ivković et al. 2018; Kutnjak Ivković and Sauerman 2012). There were also agencies that demonstrated a strong code of silence regardless of the perceived seriousness of the violation (Chattha and Kutnjak Ivković 2004; Cheloukhine et al. 2015; Haberfeld 2004; Kang and Kutnjak Ivković 2015; Khechumyan and Kutnjak Ivković 2015; Vallmuur 2015). This is indicative that the agencies with these findings have overall lower levels of police integrity. More importantly, the code of silence was found to exist in varying degrees among all agencies regardless of the context or culture (Andreescu et al. 2012; Chattha and Kutnjak Ivković 2004; Cheloukhine et al. 2015; Haberfeld 2004; Huberts et al. 2003; Kutnjak Ivković 2015; Kutnjak Ivković and Haberfeld 2015; Kutnjak Ivković et al. 2012, 2015; Kutnjak Ivković and Sauerman 2012; Kutnjak Ivković and Shelley 2005, 2008; Kang and Kutnjak Ivković 2015; Khechumyan and Kutnjak Ivković 2015; Klockars et al. 1997; Lobnikar and Mesko 2015; Phetthong and Kutnjak Ivković 2015; Punch et al. 2004; Rothwell and Baldwin 2007; Tasdoven and Kaya 2014; Wolfe and Piquero 2011; Wright 2010). Lastly, younger officers with fewer years of experience were less likely to report misconduct than their more senior counterparts (Porter et al. 2015; Rothwell and Baldwin 2006, 2007; Tasdoven and Kaya 2014).

Current Study

The current study adds to the existing literature by enhancing the conceptualization and measurement of police integrity using methodology developed by Klockars et al. (1997). The unique contribution of this study is that we overcome three limitations of prior research on police integrity.

First, many prior studies have assessed police integrity with the use of single item indicators within individual vignettes or attitudinal assessments—or both. This is a methodological limitation that has been criticized by scholars in the past (e.g., Taylor and Hale 1986) on the grounds that single-item indicators only capture a narrow range of information and are prone to higher levels of error.[2] We overcome this limitation by conceptualizing police integrity as a *latent trait*, which is measured by several indicators in the Klockars et al. (1997) scenarios. Specifically, we use item-response theory (IRT) to assess the probability that an officer would respond to an item in such a way that suggests s/he has integrity. Instead of focusing on the scale as whole—as is the case when using classical psychometric techniques—we focus on how each item performs independently as a measure of police integrity.

Second, it is necessary to identify potential factors that may vary how the items measure police integrity. Specifically, this variation is called differential item functioning (DIF). Further progression in our understanding of police integrity requires the development of robust measures, which means measures that function appropriately across various domains. In other words, we need to ensure that measures of police integrity are *invariant* across appropriate groups, something for which IRT methods are particularly suitable (De Ayala 2009). While there are several factors that could be the source of invariance, we focus on the size of the police organization because it is associated with several other factors that could potentially influence officer integrity. Specifically, larger organizations tend to have more infrastructure in place for independently assessing allegations of police misconduct, tend to have more direct supervision of subordinates; however, these organizations also tend to have more opportunities for engaging in misconduct (Eitle et al. 2014; Marché 2009). Conversely, larger police organizations are typically more heterogeneous, which can lead to breakdowns in

informal social control mechanisms (Maguire 1997; Maskály et al. 2017). Given the competing effects of organizational size on police misconduct, we remain agnostic about the precise effect of organization size and instead examine whether there is an effect. If indeed there is an organizational effect on the measurement of police integrity, this effect will then be interpreted.

Third, we look at the relationship between the attitudinal dimensions that are captured using the Klockars et al. (1997) data. Recall there are as many as seven different measures associated with each vignette; however, due to data issues we are limited to assessing only five. We assert that each of these taps a different dimension of police integrity, and the relationships each of these dimensions of police integrity have are important to understand for empirical, theoretical, and policy reasons. The relationship between the dimensions may even provide evidence for both the convergent and discriminant validity of the measures.

Method

Data/Sample

This study uses data originally collected by Klockars et al. (1997) from thirty police departments throughout the United States. There were a total of 3232 completed questionnaires, representing a response rate of 55.5%. The demographic characteristics of the sample are presented in Table 1. To assuage the concerns of the officers completing the surveys that individual respondents could be identified, the principal investigators only collected a limited number of demographic information and the agencies sampled were never identified. These decisions, however, result in two important limitations. First, we are unable to assess how representative the sample of officers who responded to the survey are compared to the population of officers working in these agencies. Second, we cannot assess how representative these officers—and agencies—are of policing in the United States. Despite these two limitations, we feel confident that these data

---

[2]There are scholars who now suggest that the use of single-item indicators is appropriate in certain situations (e.g., relevancy and adequacy of the measure; Fuchs and Diamantopoulos 2009).

Table 1 Respondent demographics

	% of Respondents
Years as police officer[a]	
Less than 1 year	4.08
1–2 years	7.67
3–5 years	15.32
5–10 years	24.04
11–15 years	16.15
16–20 years	13.86
Over 20 years	17.42
Years at current station[b]	
Less than 1 year	4.39
1–2 years	9.16
3–5 years	16.31
5–10 years	23.36
11–15 years	15.53
16–20 years	13.21
Over 20 years	15.90
Rank[c]	
Recruit	1.73
Officer/Deputy	64.24
Detective	11.76
Corporal	1.79
Sergeant	11.42
Lieutenant	3.68
Captain/Major/Colonel	2.60
Chief/Sherriff	0.99
Other	0.06
Current assignment[d]	
Patrol	64.00
Detective/Investigations	14.70
Special Operations	10.37
Communications	0.31
Administrative	5.94
Other	4.95
Supervisory status[e]	
Non-Supervisor	79.12
Supervisor	19.59
Agency type	
Very Large Municipal Police (N > 500)	59.84
Large Municipal Police (201 < N < 500)	7.77
Medium Municipal Police (76 < N < 200)	9.03
Small Municipal Police (25 < N < 75)	6.65
Very Small Municipal (N < 25)	2.88
Sherriff	1.86
County Police	11.97

[a]Missing values = 1.45%
[b]Missing values = 2.13%
[c]Missing values = 1.73%
[d]Missing values = 1.73%
[e]Missing values = 1.30%

are appropriate for this study of assessing measurement validity, especially given that patterns in the data have been largely replicated by prior studies using this instrument and methodology (e.g., Klockars et al. 2004; Westmarland 2004).

The questionnaire asked officers to rate eleven different vignettes depicting police integrity on five different dimensions. From this, we developed five measures that are used in the current analyses. The eleven scenarios are presented in abbreviated form in Table 2, along with descriptive statistics for each dimension. Each scenario was initially rated on a Likert scale, using either five or six points, with higher values depicting higher levels of integrity. The first four dimensions capture information about the respondent's level of integrity directly (e.g., how seriously do you think this is, would you report this) and indirectly (e.g., how serious do most officers think this is, would most officers report this). This indirect method may be a better indicator of a respondent's attitudes as it reduces social desirability bias (Fisher 1993). The fifth dimension asked respondents to identify if each of these scenarios was a policy violation within their organization.[3]

Missing Data

Almost all of the questionnaires contained *some* missing data (96.5%), but no single questionnaire was missing more than 3% of the data. The data were inspected looking for patterns in the missing data to determine if certain items or respondents were consistently missing. Ultimately, we found no statistical pattern in the missing data. Therefore, to retain maximum sample size, ten data sets were simulated using a chained equations approach. All of the current analyses were performed on all eleven data sets—the ten imputed datasets plus the original. The use of

---

[3]Because we do not know who the agencies are or what their policies were, we are not sure that all vignettes depict something against department policy. However, because many departments prohibit the actions in all of these scenarios, and most agencies prohibit all of the most serious scenarios, we make the assumption that this is a violation of the policy in the respondent's agency.

Table 2 Descriptive statistics for items and dimensions

		Own seriousness	Most officers seriousness	Policy violation	Would YOU report	Would OTHERS report
1	Owning security business on the side (**M**)	1.46 (0.95)	1.48 (0.88)	1.73 (1.22)	1.37 (0.93)	1.46 (0.91)
2	Accepting free meals/gifts from business (**M**)	2.59 (1.34)	2.31 (1.18)	3.88 (1.42)	1.93 (1.27)	1.83 (1.09)
3	Taking a gift in lieu of citation (**S**)	4.90 (0.46)	4.78 (0.58)	4.95 (0.38)	4.17 (1.28)	3.91 (1.18)
4	Accepting food/liquor from residents (**M**)	2.85 (1.39)	2.63 (1.28)	3.89 (1.39)	2.36 (1.42)	2.28 (1.25)
5	Stealing from burglary scene (**S**)	4.99 (0.42)	4.86 (0.52)	4.95 (0.37)	4.52 (1.08)	4.32 (1.05)
6	Body shop kickback scheme (**S**)	4.47 (0.93)	4.24 (1.01)	4.77 (0.68)	3.93 (1.37)	3.69 (1.26)
7	Supervisor preferential scheduling (**M**)	4.15 (1.07)	3.94 (1.11)	4.41 (0.99)	3.43 (1.47)	3.27 (1.35)
8	Not reporting crash of drunk officer (**M**)	3.02 (1.39)	2.85 (1.28)	4.12 (1.25)	2.33 (1.45)	2.28 (1.26)
9	Taking drinks from bar violating law (**M**)	4.51 (0.93)	4.26 (1.04)	4.80 (0.67)	3.71 (1.43)	3.46 (1.33)
10	Punching suspect who flees from officers (**S**)	4.02 (1.25)	3.68 (1.27)	4.71 (0.78)	3.37 (1.52)	3.05 (1.38)
11	Stealing money from lost wallet (**S**)	4.82 (0.61)	4.67 (0.77)	4.91 (0.48)	4.20 (1.28)	3.94 (1.26)
	SCALE RANGE	*1–5*	*1–5*	*1–5*	*1–5*	*1–5*
	LOW ANCHOR	*Not at all serious*	*Not at all serious*	*Definitely not*	*Definitely not*	*Definitely not*
	HIGH ANCHOR	*Very serious*	*Very serious*	*Definitely yes*	*Definitely yes*	*Definitely yes*

multiple imputation is the best way to deal with missing data issues (Allison 2002). As a result of this procedure, all parameter estimates were derived using Rubin's Rules, which involves pooling estimates across models (Rubin 1987).

Analytical Plan

We employ modern psychometrics techniques, notably *latent trait models* (LTM; i.e., item response theory) to estimate the latent ability of the officers that responded to the vignettes. We estimate models for each of the six dimensions described above. After determining the measurement properties of each of these dimensions, we estimate the officer's level of integrity—denoted as Θ—on each dimension using the expected A Posteriori (EAP) method (Mislevy and Stocking

1989; Uebersax 1993). We then assess the bivariate relationship between each of these dimensions using correlation. These analyses are designed to assess the potential overlap between the various factors captured by each of the constructs. Finally, we assess the invariance property of the LTM by looking for differential item functioning (DIF) between respondents from large departments (i.e., N > 500) compared to those from all other departments.

Results

We began by estimating the number of parameters that would best represent the psychometric traits of each construct.[4] However, we determined

---

[4] The first parameter is the *b* parameter, called difficulty

that the polytomous response options violated one of the underlying assumptions of the LTM (i.e., ordered thresholds).[5] These thresholds should be ordered on the difficulty parameter along the X-axis as shown in the left panel of Fig. 1, which represents respondents' perceptions of seriousness for accepting free meals and gifts. In the context of this study, this would mean that a person with less integrity should be more likely to endorse the *not at all serious* response option rather than any of the others. However, this requirement of the model was exceptionally problematic, as shown in the right panel of Fig. 1, which represents respondents' perceptions of accepting free drinks from a bar that is operating illegally. When the data were examined in more detail, there was a clear break in the response categories. Specifically, most respondents endorsing the lower end of the spectrum (i.e., categories one or two on a five point Likert scale) felt differently than those who responded with a higher value. This trend is seen with the strong floor and ceiling effects noted in the mean values presented in Table 2. Therefore, we recoded all variables such that for all items values of one and two were coded as 0 (no integrity), and all higher values coded as 1 (integrity).[6]

Item Unidimensionality

When estimating LTMs, it is necessary to determine if all items are capturing one underlying latent trait—in this case, police integrity—or if multiple traits are captured with the items (De Ayala 2009). This process is done by fitting a model to all the items and then examining correlations in the residuals by looking for Q_3 statistics larger than ± 0.2 (Yen 1993).[7] Items that exceed this threshold violate the underlying assumptions of the LTM and are said to be misfitting. The results suggested that there were, in fact, two traits being captured with each of the six dimensions. One trait captured integrity as it relates to minor forms of police misconduct and the other more serious forms of misconduct. This pattern is depicted in the pattern of results in Table 2, whereby there is less variation in the more serious forms of misconduct compared to minor forms.

This pattern, however, was not universal as there were certain items (e.g., Item 1: owning a security business on the side; Item 10: punching a suspect who flees from officers) that were problematic. Item 1 was problematic in that it *only* measures the same latent trait as other items in the *policy violation* dimension, but not the others. This may suggest that Item 1 is capturing something that is normative or permitted by policy for some of the respondents. Item 10 consistently loaded on the serious misconduct trait for all dimensions *except* for on the dimension for *would others report*. This may suggest that officers believe that others within their organization do not see the actions depicted in this vignette as a serious form of misconduct. Further, during the initial development of the police integrity measure by Klockars et al. (1997), these two scenarios as a way to assess the honesty of the respondents. Specifically, in many departments, it is normative for officers to work off-duty and

---

parameter, estimates the location on Θ (the abscissa) where a respondent is more likely to endorse one response category. The second parameter is the *a* parameter, called the discrimination parameter, which is the slope of the curve at the location of the *b* parameter. This parameter allows for understanding how well an item can identify a person with a certain level of the latent trait. The steeper the slope, the more discriminating the item. The final parameter is the *c* parameter, called the pseudo-chance parameter, which estimates uncertainty in respondents' answers. In other words, some respondents have a non-zero probability of endorsing a category, regardless of their level on Θ.

[5] Thresholds refer to the location where the curve from one response option (e.g., strongly disagree) cross over with the response curve for another response option (e.g., disagree). If *L* equals the number of response options. There are always *L*-1 thresholds.

[6] Some scholars are reticent to use dichotomous items due to the loss of information (Brown 2006); however, here the respondents' answers suggested a natural dichotomy in the data. The reason for this is unclear, but may have something to do with the ambiguity of the items and differences in department policy that are not captured here.

---

[7] Technically the maximum tolerance is derived $Q3 = -1/(L - 1)$, where L is the number of items. This would yield a maximum Q_3 value of $|0.10|$, but de Ayala (2009) suggests that using $|.20|$ value reduces the chances of making a Type I error, especially with large samples.

Fig. 1 Response characteristic curves of correctly and
incorrectly functioning items

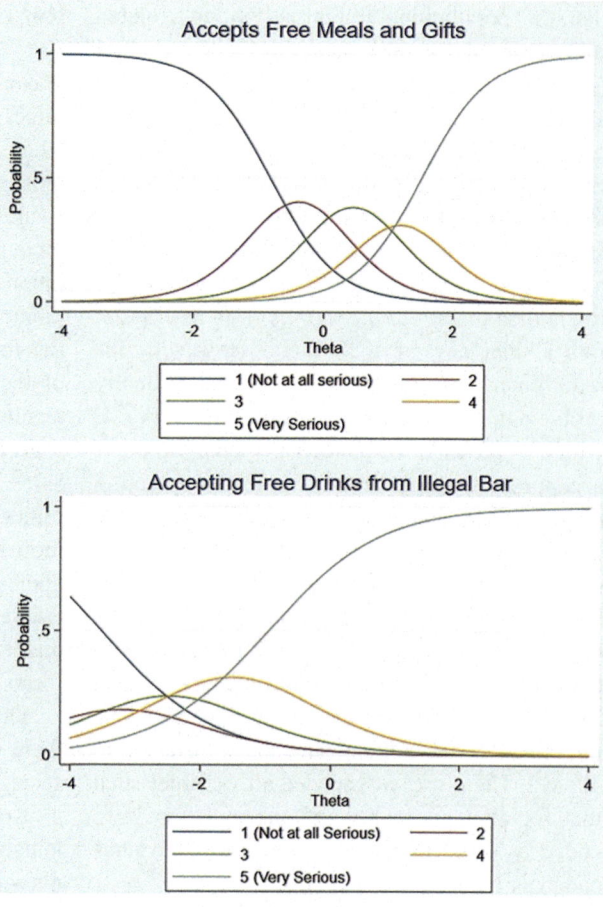

thus this may not be a good measure of police integrity. Given that one in three officers reported that this was a violation of department policy; we decided to include this as a measure of integrity. Interestingly, in only two departments (n = 23) did all officers indicate this was not a policy violation whereas there was some degree of variability about this in other departments (M = 72.37%, SD = 14.74, 38.98–95.00%). Similarly, the measure of excessive force was included as a measure of the blue code of silence, with only one department (n = 5) all reporting this would definitely be a policy violation, with some degree of variability in the remaining departments (M = 75.45%, SD = 15.41, 33.33–96.36%). These decisions have been described in more detail in other publications (e.g., Kutnjak Ivković 2015). To make the results more meaningful and easily assimilated, the structure of the latent traits was forced

to fit despite slight item misfit ($Q_3 < |.30|$). Specifically, those items in Table 2 with an *M* refer to minor misconduct and those with an *S* refer to serious misconduct.

Latent Trait Model Analyses

All models were estimated using IRT Pro 3.0. The results from the final models are in Tables 3 and 4 and are divided by trait and severity, and they will be discussed as such below. Recall that the number of parameters estimated per model varies according to the number of parameters needed to explain best the psychometric properties of the latent trait being measured. All latent trait models (LTM) must estimate a *difficulty* parameter (**b**). This parameter describes the estimated level of police integrity that an officer

Table 3 Latent trait estimates (LTM) for constructs of police integrity

	Own perception of seriousness			Others perceptions of seriousness				Policy violation		
	Minor misconduct		Serious Misconduct	Minor misconduct			Serious misconduct	Minor misconduct		Serious misconduct
	a	b	b	a	b	c	b	a	b	b
Owns side business	0.61	3.35	–	0.80	3.28	0.04	–	0.38	3.71	–
Accepts free meals	1.93	0.07	–	1.95	0.47		–	1.56	–1.18	–
Gifts of food & liquor	2.34	–0.19	–	2.55	0.03		–	12.34	–0.78	–
Supervisor scheduling	1.55	–2.07	–	1.57	–1.80		–	0.92	–3.27	–
Fellow officer DUI	1.12	–0.52	–	1.05	–0.30		–	1.03	–2.12	–
Free drinks from bar	1.86	–2.22	–	1.65	–2.03		–	1.34	–3.31	–
Speeding bribe	–	–	–2.89	–	–	–	–2.84	–	–	–2.84
Burglary theft	–	–	–2.95	–	–		–2.89	–	–	–2.88
Body shop kickback	–	–	–1.92	–	–		–1.80	–	–	–2.31
Punch fleeing suspect	–	–	–1.21	–	–		–1.02	–	–	–2.04
Found property theft	–	–	–2.56	–	–		–2.31	–	–	–2.69

Table 4 LTM estimates for additional constructs of police integrity

	Would report fellow officer			Others would report fellow officer		
	Minor misconduct		Serious misconduct	Minor misconduct		Serious misconduct
	a	b	b	a	b	b
Owns side business	1.09	2.39	–	0.92	2.40	–
Accepts free meals	2.57	0.75	–	2.09	0.96	–
Gifts of food and liquor	2.38	0.31	–	2.13	0.39	–
Supervisor scheduling	2.23	–0.73	–	1.86	–0.75	–
Fellow officer DUI	1.78	0.39	–	1.77	0.42	–
Free drinks from bar	3.59	–0.83	–	2.72	–0.78	–
Speeding bribe	–	–	–1.20	–	–	–1.23
Burglary theft	–	–	–1.48	–	–	–1.58
Body shop kickback	–	–	–0.97	–	–	–0.98
Punch fleeing suspect	–	–	–0.54	–	–	–0.39
Found property theft	–	–	–1.16	–	–	–1.12

must possess before s/he has a $p \geq .50$ of endorsing the item, which is the minimum average level of integrity for officers who endorsed this particular item considering their responses to all items in the measure. The value of this parameter can range from $-\infty$ to $+\infty$, but tends to be between -4 and $+4$. If the psychometric properties of the items are more complicated, the next parameter added to the model is the *discrimination* parameter (**a**). This parameter represents the slope of the ogive at the difficulty parameter (i.e., $p = .50$). In practice, this value will always be positive with values greater than 1 representing items with acceptable levels of discrimination (De Ayala 2009). If these two parameters cannot explain the psychometric properties, the *pseudo-chance* parameter (**c**) is estimated. This parameter represents the minimum probability that a respondent has of endorsing an item regardless of his/her level of police integrity. When this parameter is needed, the values tend to be rather small, although they could theoretically be as high as 1.0. Because psychometrics are relatively new in the field of criminology, Fig. 2 depicts a hypothetical item with each of the three parameters labeled.

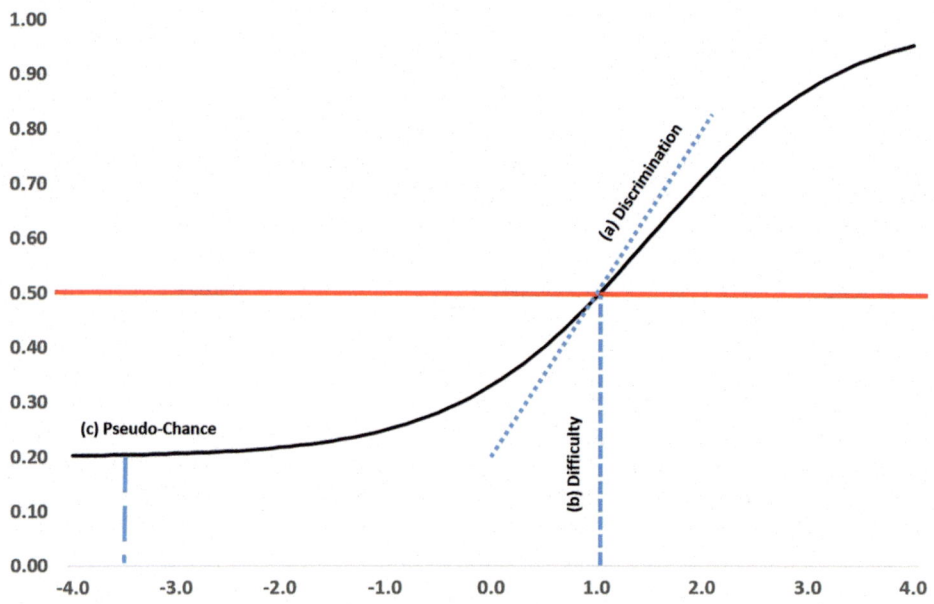

Fig. 2 Hypothetical item characteristic curve with parameter estimates labeled

Own Perception of Seriousness

The first latent trait created was based on the respondents' assessment of the seriousness of the particular scenario. The parameter estimates for minor misconduct are shown in the top half of the leftmost panel of Table 3. These results suggest certain behaviors are very easy for officers to endorse, regardless of their personal levels of integrity. Accepting free drinks from a bar that is operating illegally (b = −2.22) and doing personal favors for a supervisor in exchange for preferential scheduling (b = −2.07) are two acts that most officers indicate are rather serious. Although both difficulty estimates are negative, these items are not necessarily poor indicators of police integrity. Rather, these coefficients suggest that officers with lower levels of police integrity are still likely to see these behaviors as serious. Alternatively, we see that not arresting a fellow officer involved in a DUI crash (b = −0.52), accepting gifts from neighborhood residents (b = −0.19), and accepting free meals at a restaurant (b = 0.07) are serious violations for officers with average police integrity.[8] We also see that an

officer owning a side business that installs security systems is only seen as seriously concerning by those officers with the highest level of police integrity (b = 3.35). Furthermore, all misconduct acts apart from owning a side business are capable of adequately discriminating those officers who have integrity from those who do not.

Finally, we look at the test information function (TIF), which graphically plots the function:

$$I(\Theta) = a_i^2 p_i(\Theta) q_i(\Theta)$$

where a represents the discrimination parameter, p_i represents the probability of endorsing item i and q_i represents the probability of not endorsing item i.[9] The test information for all six minor misconduct acts is presented in Fig. 4. Higher information values indicate the measures ability to reliably measure police integrity at the given level, whereas low values indicate a potentially inconsistent measurement of the trait at that level. Looking at the TIF in the upper left-hand panel of Fig. 4, we see the measure of respondents' perception of seriousness is capable of identifying those officers with below average police integrity.

---

[8] Recall that these coefficients can be interpreted like z-scores and therefore a 0 indicates an average level of the trait.

[9] This measure is analogous to the reliability coefficients in classical test theory.

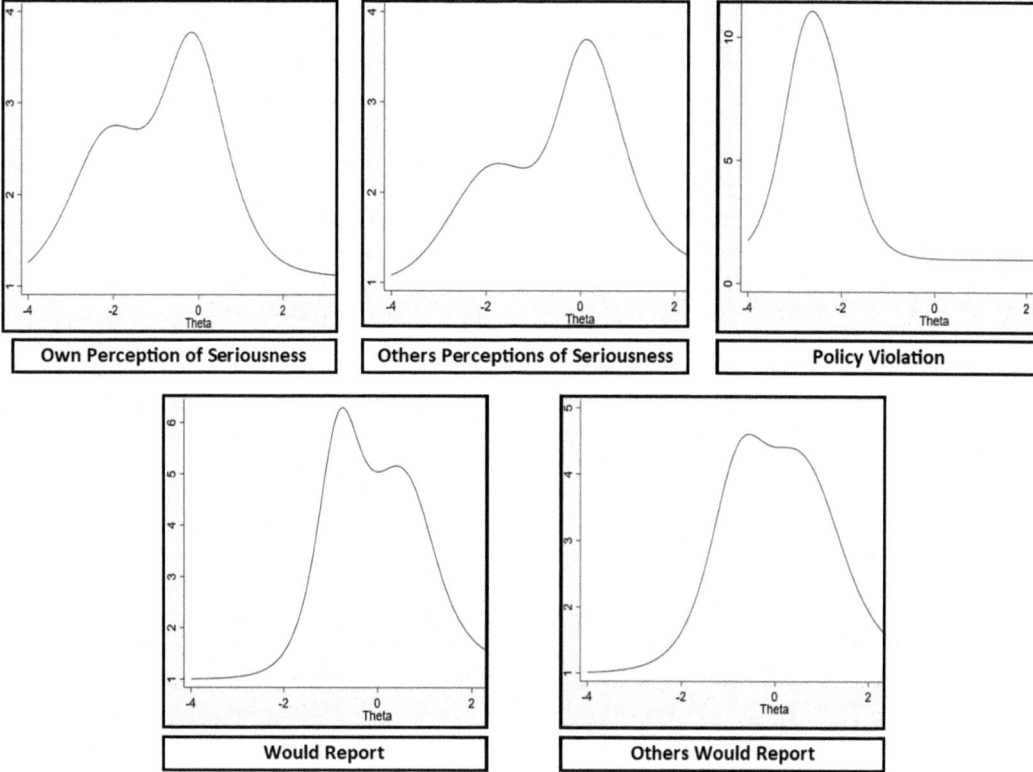

Fig. 3 Test information functions for integrity constructs related to minor misconduct

Next, we look at how the serious misconduct items measure police integrity.[10] Unlike for minor misconduct, there was no need to estimate the discrimination parameter because all items had a similar ability to discriminate those who have integrity from those who do not because respondents were almost universally likely to indicate these behaviors as problematic. One curious finding is that officers find it easier to report the misconduct acts of theft or receiving a kickback as being more serious ($-2.95 < b < -1.92$) compared to unnecessary use of force ($b = -1.21$). Additionally, when looking at the TIF in the upper left-hand panel of Fig. 5, we see that this measure does not reliably capture information from those with higher levels of police integrity on the serious misconduct measure.

Others Perception of Seriousness

We now turn to the middle panel of Table 3 to look at respondents' perceptions of how serious other officers would find these types of behaviors. Again, starting with the minor forms of misconduct, we see that some acts are easier (accepting free drinks from the illegal bar; $b = -2.03$) for respondents to identify as serious for others in their organization compared to others (own a side business; $b = 3.28$). Particularly interesting, while respondents indicate that it is easier for them to identify many of these scenarios as troubling, the items are ordered in the same way for both others in the organization and for

---

[10]One thing that is important to note, while we are referring to these latent traits as police integrity, the measures are not on the same scale. In other words, we cannot directly compare the results from one construct to another without putting them both on the same metric.

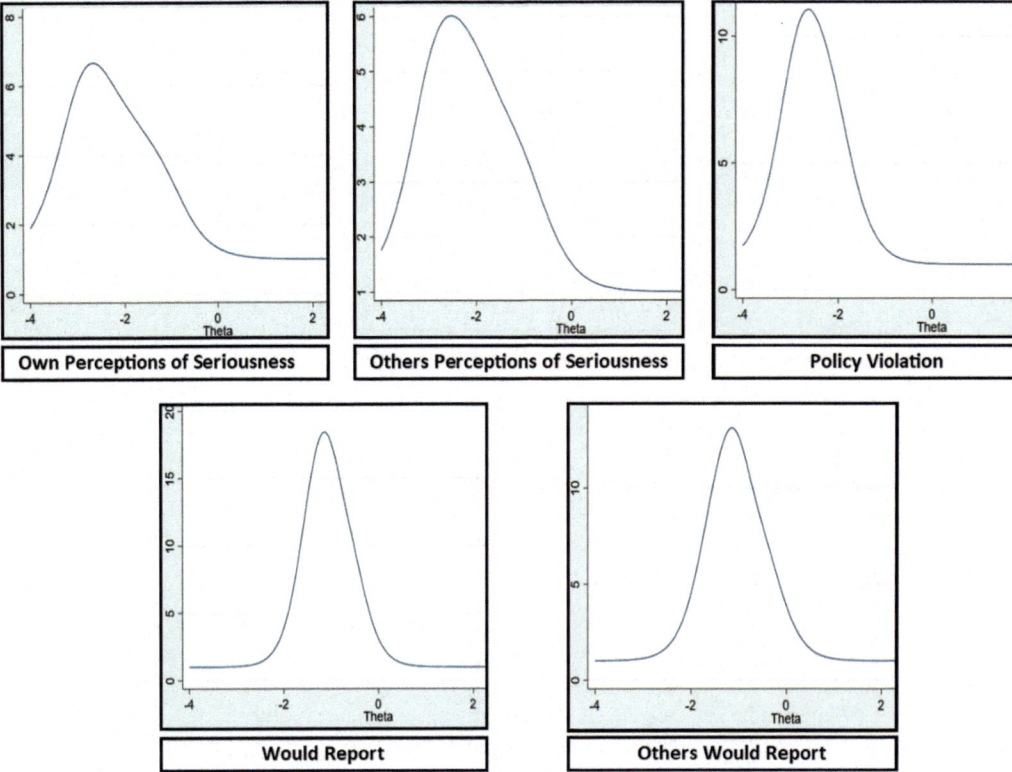

Fig. 4 Test information functions for integrity constructs for more serious misconduct

individual perception. Owning a security business was, again, the only item that did not adequately discriminate between those with and without integrity. Furthermore, this model was the only model that needed a pseudo-chance parameter, which was rather small (c = 0.04). This means that there was a 4% chance that respondent would express concern with an item, regardless of his/her level of integrity. The need for this parameter here is not entirely surprising given that respondents were asked to infer the beliefs of others, although it is curious that, despite being asked to do this for multiple behaviors, this was the only one that needed it. Finally, when looking at the TIF in the upper middle panel of Fig. 3, we see that this measure captures good information from those respondents with slightly lower than average police integrity. Conversely, unlike the measure for own perceptions of seriousness, this measure more reliably captures information from those with slightly higher than average police integrity.

The same trends are largely observed when looking at the serious forms of misconduct in the bottom of the middle panel in Table 3. The items are rank ordered in the same way and officers are universally more likely than not to see these behaviors as problematic. We see the strong break between acts of graft and the use of unnecessary force. Unlike with minor misconduct, it was unnecessary to estimate additional parameters for this model. Further, this measure only reliably captures information from those with lower than average police integrity, although it does slightly better for those closer to—although still below—the mean.

Policy Violation

Next, we examine respondents to report whether engaging in these behaviors would be a policy violation. The results for the minor forms of misconduct are particularly interesting because while

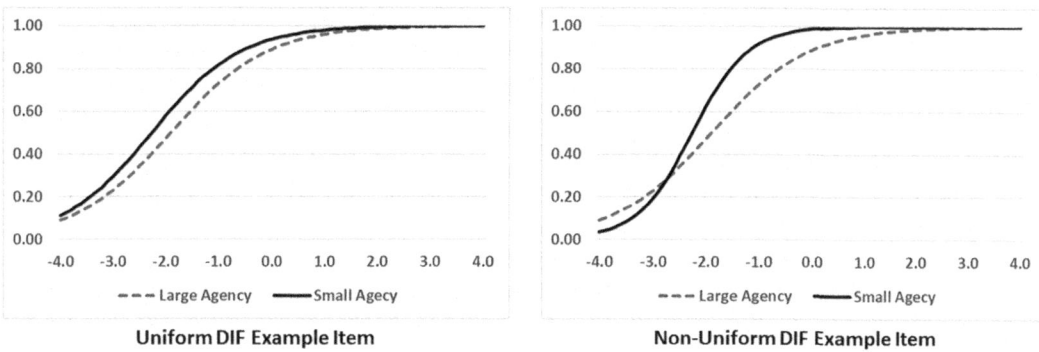

Fig. 5 Depiction of uniform and non-uniform differential item functioning

most respondents saw these behaviors as not necessarily that serious, and thought most others in their organization would as well, more respondents identified these as policy violations. Specifically, two findings stand out. First, respondents were more likely to identify accepting free meals from a restaurant as a policy violation than accepting gifts of food and liquor from community residents, which is opposite from perceptions of own seriousness and others seriousness. Secondly, as seen by the reduced magnitude of the coefficients, these items are less able to discriminate between those officers with and without integrity. This may suggest that these items are not good for measuring police integrity, which is supported by the TIF in the upper right panel of Fig. 3.

For serious forms of misconduct, the difficulty estimates follow the same familiar pattern as with perceptions of own seriousness and others seriousness. Participants almost universally identify these as policy violations, which would suggest they have integrity. In fact, the TIF for the serious forms of misconduct—shown in Fig. 4—looks very similar to the TIF for minor forms of misconduct. In other words, our ability to measure integrity is equally as weak for both minor and more serious misconduct.

Would Report

Another dimension of police integrity revolves around whether officers are willing to report observed instances of misconduct. The results for minor misconduct are presented in the top middle panel of Table 4. The general pattern of results indicates that officers must have a relatively high level of integrity before expressing a willingness to report minor misconduct of fellow officers. However, it is worth noting that the ordering of the measures remains consistent as with prior constructs. Specifically, we see that even officers with below average integrity will report a fellow officer for accepting free drinks from a bar ($b = -0.83$) and supervisors giving out preferential scheduling ($b = -0.73$).

Conversely, officers need a higher amount of integrity before reporting a fellow officer than they do to express the same scenario is a serious form of misconduct. The only exception to this pattern comes from those officers who own a security business on the side. The results here suggest that officers need less integrity to report a fellow officer for this behavior than they do to suggest that owning a side business is a serious problem. This finding is curious because logic dictates officers should be more willing to report those behaviors they see as serious. This same general pattern is seen for the serious forms of misconduct. The TIF for minor misconduct, shown in the bottom middle panel of Fig. 3, suggests that these items do a reasonable job of measuring integrity for respondents with integrity estimates between -1.75 and $+1.5$. Nevertheless, the same latent trait accurately measures a much narrower group of respondents for serious misconduct. As shown in the bottom middle panel of Fig. 4, this measure really only does well for those with integrity estimates between -2 and -0.25.

Others Would Report

The final latent trait looks at respondents' perceptions of the willingness of other officers to report misconduct; these results are presented in the top half of the right panel of Table 4. The results follow the same pattern as observed in prior constructs. The same is true for the results presented in the bottom of the right panel of Table 4 for the serious forms of misconduct. The data suggest a difference between own perceptions and others' perceptions measures for both seriousness and willingness to report. For seriousness, respondents with lower levels of integrity saw misconduct as more serious than they thought most other officers in their department would. With two exceptions (accepting free meals and punching a suspect who fled from the police), this pattern was not present for willingness to report. Instead, these estimates are within the standard error of one another, meaning that respondents' felt their willingness to report misconduct was the same as most other officers in their department. In both exceptions, respondents require lower levels of integrity before being willing to report these forms of misconduct. The TIF, shown in the bottom right panel of Fig. 3, shows that this measure also does reasonably well at measuring integrity, for minor misconduct, for those respondents with estimates between −2 and +1.5. While the TIF for the serious forms of misconduct, shown in the bottom right panel of Fig. 4, suggest we are only adequately measuring those with integrity estimates between −2 and +0.25.

Inter-Construct Correlations

One of the key questions of the current study centers on the relationships between the various constructs. To examine these relationships, we estimated ability estimates for each participant based on his/her responses to the items using the EAP method (Thissen et al. 1995). We then estimated the pairwise correlations between these constructs (see Table 5). All correlations were significant except for two, which are shown in

red in the table. Due to the sample size (N = 3232), it was necessary to look beyond the statistical significance of these relationships and instead look at the substantive significance of the relationships. It is necessary to determine if the latent traits being measured are capturing the same underlying dimension—police integrity—or if various dimensions are being captured. One way of assessing this is to look at test-retest coefficients to determine if the trait is being reliably measured with both methods.[11] Prior research suggests that the magnitude of the correlations should be 0.70 or higher (Thornberry and Krohn 2000).

Using this criterion, shown in blue in Table 5, we see that only four coefficients meet this threshold. Respondents' perceptions of seriousness are highly correlated with how serious most others in the organization would report the behavior to be for both minor (r = .77) and serious forms of misconduct (r = .77). Similarly, respondents' willingness to report is correlated with others' willingness to report both minor (r = .76) and serious misconduct (r = .79). However, if we relax the criterion to 0.60 (see generally, Crocker and Algina 2008), shown in orange in Table 5, there are another five coefficients that are substantively significant. A respondents' perception of seriousness is positively correlated with his/her willingness to report misconduct for minor misconduct (r = 0.68). Others' perceptions and others' willingness to report are highly correlated for both minor (r = 0.66) and serious misconduct (r = 0.61). Finally, a respondents' willingness to report minor misconduct is correlated with his/her willingness to report serious misconduct (r = 0.68) as is the willingness of others to report both types of misconduct (r = 0.66). These estimates suggest that these measures are currently tapping a similar construct in the mind of respondents' and the differences may be indicative of a way to enhance the measures of police integrity.

---

[11]While most of the time this method is used with a temporal break in between, it is consistent with logic that different methods should exert the same level of correlation.

Table 5 Correlation matrix for latent traits captured in the various integrity measures

Factor	1	2	3	4	5	6	7	8	9	10
Own seriousness minor (**1**)	**1.00**									
Own seriousness major (**2**)	0.45	**1.00**								
Others seriousness minor (**3**)	0.77	0.38	**1.00**							
Others seriousness major (**4**)	0.36	0.77	0.46	**1.00**						
Policy violation minor (**5**)	0.48	0.24	0.44	0.21	**1.00**					
Policy violation major (**6**)	0.22	0.54	0.22	0.51	0.31	**1.00**				
Would report minor (**7**)	0.68	0.42	0.59	0.38	0.31	0.21	**1.00**			
Would report major (**8**)	0.46	0.58	0.39	0.55	0.19	0.35	0.68	**1.00**		
Others would report minor (**9**)	0.52	0.32	0.66	0.42	0.30	0.20	0.76	0.52	**1.00**	
Others would report major (**10**)	0.36	0.49	0.45	0.61	0.17	0.34	0.58	0.79	0.66	**1.00**

All coefficients, except those in red, are significant at $p < .001$

Examining Measurement Invariance Property

One key consideration when designing measurement is that the measure needs to be consistent. Having a measure that consistently operates with different populations of police officers is imperative for enhancing our understanding of police integrity. In the context of the concept of police integrity, and considering the methodology employed by the principal investigators, agency size was an important factor to examine for measurement invariance. There are inherent differences between large and small departments, especially regarding the availability of resources to control misconduct and enhance police integrity. Thus, an integrity measure that does not function the same in small and large police departments has a limited ability for furthering our understanding of police integrity.

Measures that function differently are said to exhibit *differential item functioning* (DIF), of which there are two types: *uniform* and *non-uniform*. Here, uniform DIF refers to situations where respondents from small departments are consistently differently measured than respondents from large departments. Non-uniform DIF refers to situations where the likelihood of endorsing an item is different for respondents from small departments *at a given integrity level* compared to those from large departments. An example of both uniform and non-uniform DIF is displayed in Fig. 5.

The results of the analyses indicate that DIF is present, especially for the minor forms of misconduct across all six traits. For the respondents' perceptions of seriousness, these estimates are presented in the left panel of Table 6. Focusing on the respondent's views of seriousness, four items exhibit DIF—all of which are uniform. Respondents from large police departments, compared to smaller departments, need higher levels of integrity before expressing that accepting free meals ($b_{Large} = 0.38$; $b_{Small} = -0.35$), receiving gifts from neighborhoods residents ($b_{Large} = 0.03$; $b_{Small} = -0.48$), and letting a fellow officer off for a DUI ($b_{Large} = -0.43$; $b_{Small} = -0.64$) are serious concerns. Only in small agencies do respondents need more integrity than respondents in large agencies to say that owning a secu-

Table 6 DIF estimates minor misconduct latent traits

	Own perception of seriousness						Others perceptions of seriousness							
	Large agencies		Small agencies		DIF X²	DIF Type	Large agencies			Small agencies			DIF X²	DIF type
	a	b	a	b			a	b	c	a	b	c		
Owning side business	0.72	2.76	0.55	3.90	36.78	U	1.33	2.46	0.06	0.44	4.78	0.02	28.24	U
Accepts free meals	1.76	0.38	2.04	−0.35	52.33	U	1.70	0.94		2.25	−0.05		52.71	U
Gifts of food & liquor	2.08	0.03	2.42	−0.48	8.26	U	2.11	0.32		2.38	−0.35		19.08	U
Supervisor scheduling	1.47	−2.07	1.77	−2.02	–	–	1.78	−1.58		1.41	−2.09		6.03	NU
Fellow officer DUI	1.19	−0.43	1.10	−0.64	22.88	U	1.21	−0.21		1.06	−0.41		43.47	U
Free drinks from bar	1.68	−2.27	2.41	−2.08	–	–	1.68	−1.97		1.95	−1.94		–	–

rity business on the side is problematic ($b_{Large} = 2.76$; $b_{Small} = 3.90$), although both require a substantial amount of integrity.

The right panel of Table 6 shows DIF results for respondents' perceptions of other officers in the organization. A similar pattern to the individual perceptions was observed. However, two additional findings are worth noting here. First, the item asking about supervisor scheduling displays DIF when asking about the perceptions of others in the department, but not for the respondents' own perception. These results indicate that supervisors engaging in preferential scheduling is seen as a more serious integrity problem by most officers in small departments than in large departments ($b_{Large} = -1.58$; $b_{Small} = -2.09$). This difference, though, is not uniform across integrity levels. Respondents with low levels of integrity see this as more problematic in small departments than large departments.

The second interesting finding is the value of the pseudo-chance (**c**) parameter. The estimate is three times larger in large departments (c = 0.06) compared to small departments (c = 0.02). This suggests that there is more ambiguity for respondents from large departments knowing how most other officers feel about certain types of misconduct. On a certain level, this is quite logical because those from large department simply cannot know the feelings of most other officers in their organization—unlike an officer who works in a department of ten officers.

In looking at the results for the policy violation trait (Table 7, left panel), we see that respondents from small departments are more likely to say these misconduct behaviors are policy violations for four of the five DIF items. The only exception is that officers from large departments, regardless of integrity level, are more likely to report that owning a side security business is a policy violation ($b_{Large} = 2.46$; $b_{Small} = 4.79$). Additionally, while there is no DIF for accepting free drinks from an illegal bar, it is interesting that this item requires the least amount of integrity to identify as a policy violation for those in large agencies. On the other hand, preferential scheduling from a supervisor is the easiest to identify as a policy violation in small agencies.

Table 7 DIF estimates minor misconduct for additional latent traits

| | Policy violation | | | | | |
| | Large agencies | | Small agencies | | DIF | DIF |
	a	b	a	b	X²	type
Owning side business	1.33	2.46	0.44	4.79	60.80	U
Accepts free meals	1.70	0.94	2.25	−0.05	74.32	U
Gifts of food & liquor	2.11	0.32	2.38	−0.35	23.11	U
Supervisor scheduling	1.78	−1.58	1.41	−2.09	6.42	U
Fellow officer DUI	1.21	−0.21	1.06	−0.41	27.86	U
Free drinks from bar	1.68	−1.97	1.95	−1.94	–	–

Next, we turn to the respondents' willingness to report minor misconduct, which is presented in the left panel of Table 8. The results are not entirely consistent between large and small agencies. Some items (e.g., accepting free meals, and accepting gifts of food and liquor) are more likely to be reported by officers from small agencies, regardless of their level of integrity. The remaining items showing DIF suggest that officers from large agencies are more likely to report these instances of misconduct than are officers from smaller departments, regardless of integrity level. The differences here suggest that there may be fundamental differences in what kinds of misconduct may be normative—or tolerated—in different sized agencies.

The final DIF analysis, for minor misconduct, is presented in right panel of Table 8. This shows whether respondents feel as though most other officers in their organization would report the misconduct (Table 9). Officers in small agencies—regardless of integrity level—are more likely to indicate other officers would report owning a side business, accepting free meals, accepting free food and gifts, and preferential scheduling by a supervisor. However, officers from large departments are more likely to indi-

Table 8 DIF estimates minor misconduct for additional latent traits

	Would report						Others would report					
	Large agencies		Small agencies		DIF X²	DIF Type	Large agencies		Small agencies		DIF X²	DIF type
	a	b	a	b			a	b	a	b		
Owns side business	1.12	2.30	1.11	2.42	18.23	U	0.87	2.52	1.01	2.23	11.57	U
Accepts free meals	2.18	1.04	3.14	0.43	46.52	U	1.74	1.38	2.46	0.55	59.56	U
Gifts of food and liquor	2.14	0.49	2.66	0.07	26.15	U	1.81	0.64	2.44	0.09	35.17	U
Supervisor scheduling	2.06	−0.73	2.47	−0.73	–	–	1.84	−0.68	1.85	−0.87	39.46	U
Fellow officer DUI	2.01	0.35	1.67	0.41	30.27	U	1.94	0.41	1.75	0.42	–	–
Free drinks from bar	3.72	−0.86	3.75	−0.77	10.84	U	3.08	−0.79	2.71	−0.46	26.50	U

Table 9 DIF estimates for more serious misconduct

	Would report			
	Large agencies b	Small agencies b	DIF X²	DIF type
Speeding bribe	−1.22	−1.06	4.24	NU
Burglary theft	−1.51	−1.46	–	–
Body shop kickback	−1.00	−0.93	–	–
Punch fleeing suspect	−0.53	−0.55	–	–
Found property theft	−1.16	−1.16	–	–

cate that most other officers would be willing to report officers who accept free drinks from bars. Each of these cases exhibits uniform DIF. It is interesting to note the differences between the respondents' willingness to report and their assessment of most others' willingness to report. Typically, respondents indicate that they are much more willing to report misconduct than are their colleagues.

Discussion

The initial development of the measure of police integrity by Klockars et al. (1997) represents a major milestone in our ability to explain—and

hopefully control—police misconduct. The results from this study do two key things to help advance this cause. First, consistent with other methods, it is clear we can measure police integrity; however, it would seem that there are several dimensions of police integrity that, while related, are independent of one another. Second, we identify specific ways in which these measures can be further enhanced to bolster our understanding of police integrity. This second point is where we focus most of our attention by discussing four specific issues that were identified.

First, it may be time to reconsider some of the long held beliefs that we have about the best ways to measure attitudinal indicators. Traditionally, social scientists are encouraged to use the most *informative* level of measurement, which are continuous (i.e., interval/ratio). As long as continuous data meet certain assumptions (e.g., normally distributed, sufficient sample size) the data can be easily and meaningfully analyzed using powerful parametric statistical techniques (Allen and Yen 2002). However, getting this type of data is often not practical in the social sciences, and instead we rely on the next best alternative—ordinal measures. These measures allow us to rank order the attributes of a variable without knowing the precise distance between the attributes, and this is why Likert scales have become so popular (Oppenheim 2000).

There is a growing number of scholars who are critical of the appropriateness of ordinal measures and highlight the challenges associated with their continued use (e.g., Ogden and Ho 2011). Some of these limitations were quite apparent in the current data set. Specifically, we saw evidence that there were clear breaks between those respondents with high levels of integrity and those with lower levels of integrity. The strong floor or ceiling effects noted in the items suggests participants may have arbitrarily rated an item as a four versus a five—for example. In other words, respondents were making a distinction without a difference in the substantive trait of interest. The results here would suggest that simplifying the measurement scheme, even as a dichotomous response as we did here, may be more useful for measuring police integrity. However, the scale could also be trichotomized to allow participants a category to express indecision.

There are benefits to simplifying the measurement scheme. It would be very easy to classify officers who definitively exhibit the underlying trait (i.e., finding it serious, acceptable, a violation of policy, would report it, etc.). This simplified measurement scheme also reduces the cognitive load on respondents, which reduces the amount of measurement error. Furthermore, this change would allow scholars to develop still more scenarios to better capture all dimensions of the latent traits. Recall that for minor forms of misconduct these items were able to capture information on a decent spectrum of the latent trait; however, there is a need to enhance the amount of information captured. This will require additional items that make it easier to determine where a particular respondent falls on the latent trait. For serious forms of misconduct, there is also a need for additional scenarios. Because most officers see these behaviors as problematic, we are unable to see how much integrity officers have for serious forms of misconduct.

This problem, for both minor and serious forms of misconduct, can be readily solved with the addition of extra scenarios presenting relevant and clear scenarios of misconduct. Specifically, there were certain items included in the initial instrument that were problematic from a psycho-metric perspective, and, thus, imbue error into any subsequent analysis. Two specific items that were problematic are owning a side business and accepting free drinks from a bar operating past closing time. In many agencies, officers are prohibited from working outside of policing or are restricted to the types of businesses in which they can work. As currently worded, this item may not capture police integrity because some officers are permitted to engage in this behavior. Furthermore, there are some places in the United States—and around the world for that matter—where alcohol establishments do not have mandatory closing times. These items could be reworked to ensure that each measure better taps into police integrity—no matter the origin of the officer. Some of this work, at the very least, has been undertaken with the revamped version of the police integrity scale by Klockars et al. (2004).

Another potential issue that arises from the use of current, and subsequently developed, vignettes is the lack of verisimilitude, which can increase error (see generally, Bornstein 1999). The argument is that vignettes are not adequate representations of reality and respondents may not respond in the same way to a contrived scenario. Additionally, respondents may lack sufficient contextual information to make an accurate determination about their true sentiments. One potential solution to this would be the development of videotaped scenarios, potentially using body worn or dash cameras, where the scenarios are acted out for the officers. The additional information (e.g., how serious was the crash the drunk officer was involved in?) may make it easier for respondents to make an accurate assessment of their sentiments while still standardizing the scenarios.

Second, the way in which the initial measures were designed by Klockars et al. (1997) where officers were asked to rate their own perceptions and those of most others in their organization may be particularly useful for studying police integrity. Asking respondents about sensitive issues raises realistic concerns about the potential for a social desirability bias in the respondents' answer (Tourangeau and Yan 2007). However, the correlation between respondents' feelings of seriousness and those of most others was highly correlated. The similarity in the measures is evidence that there is a social desirability bias when asking about the respondent's perceptions directly, but is reduced when asking about the perceptions of others. Recall that Table 3 shows that respondents were generally more likely to report instances of misconduct sooner compared to others in their organization. The use of others may represent the respondents' true sentiments, which are often quite close to their own. In essence, asking about others provides respondents a way to express themselves more honestly without the risk of losing face. Additionally, these results could be evidence of a self-serving bias whereby respondents are accurately reporting the beliefs of most others in their organization and change their views to make themselves look better. Determining which of these two explanations is correct requires more psychometric work, but the results may well provide evidence of a way to reduce the social desirability of responses from measures of police integrity.

Third, it is important to begin examining the relationships between the various domains police integrity. The correlation matrix, presented in Table 5, suggests that the various questions in the survey are capturing different elements of police integrity. While many of these elements are not strongly related, the magnitude of the relationships suggests it may be important to look at these constructs in more detail. The reason for this is unclear, but we know these multiple dimensions of police integrity are not orthogonal to one another. Subsequent research should examine this issue in more detail. It may be that these are different forms of integrity or that responses might be dependent upon one another in some sort of sequence (i.e., logical or temporal).

Finally, this research provides evidence of measurement invariance in police integrity between larger agencies (N > 500) and smaller agencies. In other words, the level of police integrity it takes to see the behaviors depicted in the vignettes as concerning varies by department size. Although this difference is largely only true for minor forms of misconduct. The implications of this finding is that scholars wishing to compare

the results from larger and smaller departments will need to equate the results. Parameters from latent trait models are person-free (i.e., measurement works regardless of who you measure) and item-free (i.e., what items you use to measure the same latent trait), but this assumption only holds if the invariance assumption holds where there is no evidence of differential item function (De Ayala 2009). This is one of the reasons we vigorously test the invariance assumption as a product of agency size in this study.

Due to the fact that these data were collected in such a way to maximize confidentiality of the respondents, we cannot look at potential reasons for the DIF reported here; however, we have two likely sources that subsequent research should consider. The first place to explore is departmental policy. Due to inherent differences in resource and staffing availability of larger departments (Pfeffer and Salancik 2003), there may be differences in mechanisms to control the behavior of officers. In other words, these officers may have different external factors that are regulating the behavior. The second potential place for scholars to look is at cultural differences in the organizations. Due to the inherently heterogeneous nature of larger departments, integrity may be eroded because there is less trust, sharing, and informal social control in these types of organizations (Maskály et al. 2017). These cultural differences represent internal factors to bolster the integrity of officers.

Conclusion

By societal mandate, the police are responsible for enforcing laws and maintaining public order. However, they are entrusted to do so while adhering to moral, legal, and administrative codes of conduct. Thus, when the police commit workplace misconduct, whether it be crime scene theft, excessive force, or covering up for a fellow officer's misconduct, it can result in a myriad of adverse consequences, such as the erosion of police legitimacy, the weakening of police-community relationships, and liability lawsuits. As such, this issue has been—and continues to be—a genuine concern for society. One of the continuing challenges, though, has been how to best measure misconduct/integrity. This chapter has sought to shed light on this challenge. We examined the properties of the latent constructs of police integrity using data collected by Klockars et al. (1997) to bolster our understanding of the measurement of police integrity. We used latent trait modeling to reassess the validity of the measures, estimated the correlation between the various sub-constructs of police integrity, and examined measurement invariance of police integrity. Our research confirms the validity and reliability of the Klockars et al. (1997) methodology, but our results also indicate that our work is not done. We call on future researchers to continue to refine the measurement of police integrity so that police administrators may be better position to implement policies and practices to reduce police misconduct.

References

Alain, M. (2004). An exploratory study of Quebec's police officers' attitudes toward ethical dilemmas. In C. B. Klockars, S. Kutnjak Ivković, & M. R. Haberfeld (Eds.), *The contours of police integrity* (pp. 40–55). Thousand Oaks, CA: Sage.

Allen, M. J., & Yen, W. M. (2002). *Introduction to measurement theory*. Long Grove, IL: Waveland Press.

Allison, P. D. (2002). Missing data: Quantitative applications in the social sciences. *British Journal of Mathematical and Statistical Psychology, 55*(1), 193–196.

Andreescu, V., Keeling, D. G., Vito, G. F., & Voinic, M. C. (2012). Romanian and American police officers' perceptions of professional integrity and ethical behavior. *Revista Romana de Sociologie, 23*(3/4), 185–207.

Bornstein, B. H. (1999). The ecological validity of jury simulations: Is the jury still out? *Law & Human Behavior, 23*, 75–91.

Brown, T. A. (2006). *Confirmatory factor analysis for applied research*. New York: Guilford Press.

Brown, T. A. (2014). *Confirmatory factor analysis for applied research*. Guilford Publications.

Chappell, A. T., & Piquero, A. R. (2004). Applying social learning theory to police misconduct. *Deviant Behavior, 25*, 89–108.

Chattha, Z. N., & Kutnjak Ivković, S. (2004). Police misconduct: The Pakistani paradigm. In C. B. Klockars, S. Kutnjak Ivković, & M. R. Haberfeld (Eds.), *The contours of police integrity* (pp. 175–194). Thousand Oaks, CA: Sage.

Cheloukhine, S., Kutnjak Ivković, S., Haq, Q., & Haberfeld, M. R. (2015). Police integrity in Russia. In S. Kutnjak Ivković & M. R. Haberfeld (Eds.), *Measuring police integrity across the world: Studies from established democracies and countries in transition* (pp. 153–181). New York: Springer.

Crocker, L., & Algina, J. (2008). *Introduction to classical & modern test theory*. Mason, OH: Cengage.

De Ayala, R. J. (2009). *The theory and practice of item response theory*. New York: Guilford Publications.

Edelbacher, M., & Kutnjak Ivković, S. (2004). Ethics and the police: Studying police integrity in Austria. In C. B. Klockars, S. Kutnjak Ivković, & M. R. Haberfeld (Eds.), *The contours of police integrity* (pp. 19–39). Thousand Oaks, CA: Sage.

Eitle, D., D'Alessio, S. J., & Stolzenberg, L. (2014). The effect of organizational and environmental factors on police misconduct. *Police Quarterly, 17*(2), 103–126.

Fisher, R. J. (1993). Social desirability bias and the validity of indirect questioning. *Journal of Consumer Research, 20*(2), 303–315.

Fuchs, C., & Diamantopoulos, A. (2009). Using single-item measures for construct measurement in management research: Conceptual issues and application guidelines. *Die Betriebswirtschaft, 69*(2), 195.

Haberfeld, M. R. (2004). The heritage of police misconduct: The case of the Polish police. In C. B. Klockars, S. Kutnjak Ivković, & M. R. Haberfeld (Eds.), *The contours of police Integrity* (pp. 195–211). Thousand Oaks, CA: Sage.

Huberts, L., Lamboo, T., & Punch, M. (2003). Police integrity in the Netherlands and the United States: Awareness and alertness. *Police Practice and Research, 4*(3), 217–232.

Jenks, D., Johnson, L. M., & Matthews, T. (2012). Examining police integrity: Categorizing corruption vignettes. In *International Police Executive Symposium, Geneva Centre for the Democratic Control of Armed Forces, Coginta—for Police Reforms and Community Safety*.

Johnson, D. T. (2004). Police integrity in Japan. In C. B. Klockars, S. Kutnjak Ivković, & M. R. Haberfeld (Eds.), *The contours of police integrity* (pp. 130–160). Thousand Oaks, CA: Sage.

Kang, W., & Kutnjak Ivković, S. (2015). Police integrity in South Korea. In S. Kutnjak Ivković & M. R. Haberfeld (Eds.), *Measuring police integrity across the world: Studies from established democracies and countries in transition* (pp. 241–267). New York: Springer.

Khechumyan, A., & Kutnjak Ivković, S. (2015). Police integrity in Armenia. In S. Kutnjak Ivković & M. R. Haberfeld (Eds.), *Measuring police integrity across the world: Studies from established democracies and countries in transition* (pp. 37–65). New York: Springer.

Khruakham, S., & Lee, J. (2013). Cross-nation comparison of the intolerance to police misconduct: Findings from a Thai police cadet survey. *International Journal of Police Science & Management, 15*(3), 237–245.

Klockars, C. B., Kutnjak Ivković, S., Harver, W. E., & Haberfeld, M. R. (1997). *The measurement of police integrity* (pp. 65–70). Washington, DC: National Institute of Justice.

Klockars, C. B., Kutnjak Ivković, S., & Haberfeld, M. R. (2004). Police integrity in the United States of America. In *The contours of police integrity* (pp. 265–282). Thousand Oaks, CA: Sage.

Kremer, F. (2004). Police integrity in Hungary: How the police have adapted to political transition. In C. B. Klockars, S. Kutnjak Ivković, & M. R. Haberfeld (Eds.), *The contours of police integrity* (pp. 116–129). Thousand Oaks, CA: Sage.

Kutnjak Ivković, S. (2004). Evaluating the seriousness of police misconduct: A cross-cultural comparison of police officer and citizen views. *International Criminal Justice Review, 14*, 25–48.

Kutnjak Ivković, S. (2005). Police (mis) behavior: A cross-cultural study of corruption seriousness. *Policing: An International Journal of Police Strategies & Management, 28*(3), 546–566.

Kutnjak Ivković, S. (2012). Exploring the relation between police integrity and rank: A Croatian example. *International Criminal Justice Review, 22*(4), 372–396.

Kutnjak Ivković, S. (2015). Police integrity in Croatia. In S. Kutnjak Ivković & M. R. Haberfeld (Eds.), *Measuring police integrity across the world: Studies from established democracies and countries in transition* (pp. 97–123). New York: Springer.

Kutnjak Ivković, S., & Haberfeld, M. R. (2015). A comparative perspective on police integrity. In S. Kutnjak Ivković & M. R. Haberfeld (Eds.), *Measuring police integrity across the world: Studies from established democracies and countries in transition* (pp. 329–368). New York: Springer.

Kutnjak Ivković, S., & Khechumyan, A. (2014). Measuring police integrity among urban and rural police in Armenia: From local results to global implications. *International Journal of Comparative and Applied Criminal Justice, 38*(1), 39–61.

Kutnjak Ivković, S., & Klockars, C. B. (2004). Police integrity in Croatia. In C. B. Klockars, S. Kutnjak Ivković, & M. R. Haberfeld (Eds.), *The contours of police integrity* (pp. 56–74). Thousand Oaks, CA: Sage.

Kutnjak Ivković, S., & Sauerman, A. (2012). The code of silence: Revisiting South African policeintegrity. *South African Crime Quarterly, 40*, 15–24.

Kutnjak Ivković, S., & Shelley, T. O. (2005). The Bosnian police and police integrity: A continuing story. *European Journal of Criminology, 2*(4), 428–464.

Kutnjak Ivković, S., & Shelley, T. O. (2007). Police integrity and the Czech police officers. *International Journal of Comparative and Applied Criminal Justice, 31*(1), 21–49.

Kutnjak Ivković, S., & Shelley, T. O. (2008). The contours of police integrity across Eastern Europe: The case of Bosnia and Herzegovina and the Czech Republic. *International Criminal Justice Review, 18*(1), 59–82.

Kutnjak Ivković, S., Haberfeld, M., & Peacock, R. (2012). Rainless west: The integrity survey's role in agency accountability. *Police Quarterly, 16*(2), 148–176.

Kutnjak Ivković, S., Haberfeld, M. R., & Peacock, R. (2015). Police integrity in the United States. In S. Kutnjak Ivković & M. R. Haberfeld (Eds.), *Measuring police integrity across the world: Studies from established democracies and countries in transition* (pp. 295–327). New York: Springer.

Kutnjak Ivković, S., Haberfeld, M., & Peacock, R. (2018). Decoding the code of silence. *Criminal Justice Policy Review, 29*(2), 172–189.

Levander, M. T., & Ekenvall, B. (2004). Homogeneity in moral standards in Swedish police culture. In C. B. Klockars, S. Kutnjak Ivković, & M. R. Haberfeld (Eds.), *The contours of police integrity* (pp. 251–264). Thousand Oaks, CA: Sage.

Lobnikar, B., & Mesko, G. (2015). Police integrity in Slovenia. In S. Kutnjak Ivković & M. R. Haberfeld (Eds.), *Measuring police integrity across the world: Studies from established democracies and countries in transition* (pp. 183–211). New York: Springer.

Long, M. A., Cross, J. E., Shelley, T. O., & Kutnjak Ivković, S. (2013). The normative order of reporting police misconduct: Examining the roles of offense seriousness, legitimacy, and fairness. *Social Psychology Quarterly, 76*(3), 242–267.

Maguire, E. R. (1997). Structural changes in large municipal police organizations during the community policing era. *Justice Quarterly, 14*, 547–576.

Marché, G. E. (2009). Integrity, culture, and scale: an empirical test of the big bad police agency. *Crime, Law and Social Change, 51*(5), 463–486.

Maskály, J., Donner, C. M., & Fridell, L. (2017). Police CEOs and subordinates' perceptions of workplace misconduct: Examining the effect of demographic similarity on attitudinal congruence. *Policing: An International Journal of Police Strategies & Management, 40*(1), 57–70.

McDevitt, J., Posick, C., Zschoche, R., Rosenbaum, D. P., Buslik, M., & Fridell, L. (2011). *Police integrity, responsibility, and discipline.* Washington, DC: National Institute of Justice.

Mislevy, R. J., & Stocking, M. L. (1989). A consumer's guide to LOGIST and BILOG. *Applied Psychological Measurement, 13*, 57–75.

Mosher, C. J., Miethe, T. D., & Hart, T. C. (2010). *The mismeasure of crime.* Thousand Oaks, CA: Sage.

Newham, G. (2004). Out of step: Integrity and the South African police service. In C. B. Klockars, S. Kutnjak Ivković, & M. R. Haberfeld (Eds.), *The contours of police integrity* (pp. 232–250). Thousand Oaks, CA: Sage.

Ogden, J., & Ho, J. (2011). How meaningful are data from Likert scales? An evaluation of how ratings are made and the role of the response shift in the socially disadvantaged. *Journal of Health Psychology, 17*, 350–361.

Oppenheim, A. N. (2000). *Questionnaire design, interviewing and attitude measurement* (2nd ed.). London: Bloomsbury Academic.

Pagon, M., & Lobnikar, B. (2004). Police integrity in Slovenia. In C. B. Klockars, S. Kutnjak Ivković, & M. R. Haberfeld (Eds.), *The contours of police integrity* (pp. 212–231). Thousand Oaks, CA: Sage.

Palmiotto, M. (2001). *Police misconduct: A reader for the 21st century* (pp. 344–354). Upper Saddle River, NJ: Prentice Hall.

Pfeffer, J., & Salancik, G. R. (2003). *The external control of organizations: A resource dependence perspective.* Stanford: Stanford University Press.

Phetthong, N., & Kutnjak Ivković, S. (2015). Police integrity in Thailand. In S. Kutnjak Ivković & M. R. Haberfeld (Eds.), *Measuring police integrity across the world: Studies from established democracies and countries in transition* (pp. 269–293). New York: Springer.

Porter, L. E., Prenzler, T., & Hine, K. (2015). Police integrity in Australia. In S. Kutnjak Ivković & M. R. Haberfeld (Eds.), *Measuring police integrity across the world: Studies from established democracies and countries in transition* (pp. 67–96). New York: Springer.

Punch, M., Huberts, L. W. J. C., & Lamboo, M. E. D. (2004). Integrity perceptions and investigations in the Netherlands. In C. B. Klockars, S. Kutnjak Ivković, & M. R. Haberfeld (Eds.), *The contours of police integrity* (pp. 161–174). Thousand Oaks, CA: Sage.

Puonti, A., Vuorinen, S., & Kutnjak Ivković, S. (2004). Sustaining police integrity in Finland. In C. B. Klockars, S. Kutnjak Ivković, & M. R. Haberfeld (Eds.), *The contours of police integrity* (pp. 95–115). Thousand Oaks, CA: Sage.

Rosenbaum, D. P. (2016). Special issue on police integrity: an introduction. *Policing: An International Journal of Police Strategies & Management, 39*(2).

Rothwell, G. R., & Baldwin, J. N. (2006). Ethical climates and contextual predictors of whistle-blowing. *Review of Public Personnel Administration, 26*(3), 216–244.

Rothwell, G. R., & Baldwin, J. N. (2007). Whistle-blowing and the code of silence in police agencies: Policy and structural predictors. *Crime & Delinquency, 53*(4), 605–632.

Rubin, D. B. (1987). *Multiple imputation for nonresponse in surveys.* New York: Wiley.

Sauerman, A., & Kutnjak Ivković, S. (2015). Police integrity in South Africa. In S. Kutnjak Ivković & M. R. Haberfeld (Eds.), *Measuring police integrity across the world: Studies from established democracies and*

countries in transition (pp. 213–239). New York: Springer.

Skolnick, J. (2002). Corruption and the blue code of silence. *Police Practice and Research, 3*(1), 7–19.

Tasdoven, H., & Kaya, M. (2014). The impact of ethical leadership on police officers' code of silence and integrity: Results from the Turkish national police. *International Journal of Public Administration, 37*(9), 529–541.

Taylor, R. B., & Hale, M. (1986). Testing alternative models of fear of crime. *The Journal of Criminal Law and Criminology (1973-), 77*(1), 151–189.

Thissen, D., Pommerich, M., Billeaud, K., & Williams, V. S. (1995). Item response theory for scores on tests including polytomous items with ordered responses. *Applied Psychological Measurement, 19*(1), 39–49.

Thornberry, T. P., & Krohn, M. D. (2000). The self-report method for measuring delinquency and crime. *Criminal Justice, 4*(1), 33–83.

Tourangeau, R., & Yan, T. (2007). Sensitive questions in surveys. *Psychological Bulletin, 133,* 859–883.

Uebersax, J. S. (1993). Statistical modeling of expert ratings on medical treatment appropriateness. *Journal of the American Statistical Association, 88*(422), 421–427.

Vallmuur, B. (2015). Police integrity in Estonia. In S. Kutnjak Ivković & M. R. Haberfeld (Eds.), *Measuring police integrity across the world: Studies from established democracies and countries in transition* (pp. 125–152). New York: Springer.

Vito, G. F., Wolfe, S., Higgins, G. E., & Walsh, W. F. (2011). Police integrity: Rankings of scenarios on the Klockars scale by "management cops". *Criminal Justice Review, 36*(2), 152–164.

Westmarland, L. (2004). Policing integrity: Britain's thin blue line. In C. B. Klockars, S. Kutnjak Ivković, & M. R. Haberfeld (Eds.), *The contours of police integrity* (pp. 75–94). Thousand Oaks, CA: Sage.

Wolfe, S. E., & Piquero, A. R. (2011). Organizational justice and police misconduct. *Criminal Justice and Behavior, 38*(4), 332–353.

Wright, B. (2010). Civilianizing the 'blue code'? An examination of attitudes to misconduct in the police extended family. *International Journal of Police Science & Management, 12*(3), 339–356.

Yen, W. M. (1993). Scaling performance assessments: Strategies for managing local item dependence. *Journal of Educational Measurement, 30*(3), 187–213.

The Speed of Progress: Comparing Citizen Perceptions of Police Corruption in Croatia over Time

Sanja Kutnjak Ivković, Irena Cajner Mraović, and Dorotea Sudar

Introduction

Development of the police integrity theory and the accompanying methodology (Klockars and Kutnjak Ivković 2004; Klockars et al. 1997, 2006) provided scholars and police administrators with a tool with which to assess empirically the level of police integrity in a police agency. In ideal circumstances, the methodology could be used to measure the effects of agency reforms addressing police misconduct, both short-term and long-term, by first assessing police integrity before the reforms have been promulgated, and then assessing it in the aftermath of the reforms. Although the tools required for such assessments are available (Klockars et al. 2006), they have not been used in a systematic way beyond the initial U.S. project implemented by Klockars and colleagues (2006).

Since the development of the theory and accompanying methodology in the mid-1990s

(see, e.g., Klockars and Kutnjak Ivković 2004; Klockars et al. 1997), research studies have covered 30 countries (see Kutnjak Ivković 2015). The overwhelming proportion of these studies were cross-sectional studies, providing a snapshot and exploring the contours of police integrity at a specific time (see Kutnjak Ivković 2015). Only a handful of studies (e.g., Klockars et al. 2006; Kutnjak Ivković 2009) compared the results from the same agencies over time.

While the original study was designed as a survey of police officers, the police integrity study methodology could be adjusted to allow for a public survey soliciting public views about police integrity, as well as their assessments of police officers' views on police integrity. Although Klockars and colleagues have applied this methodology to survey college students in the late 1990s (Klockars et al. 2001), the large body of extant research on police integrity almost exclusively limits the scope of its inquiry to police officers and rarely includes the public (e.g., Kutnjak Ivković and Klockars 2002; Kutnjak Ivković et al. 2002a, b; Pagon et al. 2000). No study to date has used this methodology to assess changes in public opinion over time.

Over the past two decades, Croatia has undergone through systematic and extensive changes to its political and economic system in preparation to join the European Union in 2013. This chapter seeks to explore changes in the public

S. Kutnjak Ivković
Michigan State University School of Criminal Justice, East Lansing, MI, USA
e-mail: kutnjak@msu.edu

I. Cajner Mraović
Department of Croatian Studies, University of Zagreb, Croatia; City Assembly of the City of Zagreb, Zagreb, Croatia

D. Sudar (✉)
Center for Croatian Studies, University of Zagreb, Zagreb, Croatia

© Springer Nature Switzerland AG 2019
S. Kutnjak Ivković, M. R. Haberfeld (eds.), *Exploring Police Integrity*,
https://doi.org/10.1007/978-3-030-29065-8_14

opinion over two decades (1996–2016). The surveys of Croatian college students were performed in 1996 and 2016. Using the six scenarios common to the two surveys, this chapter analyzes changes in public views of police misconduct and public perceptions of police assessments of police misconduct.

Exploring Public Views of Police Integrity

The theory of police integrity (e.g., Klockars and Kutnjak Ivković 2004; Klockars et al. 1997, 2006) has been developed to explain factors critical for a police agency to establish or maintain high integrity. The accompanying methodology—the questionnaire containing scenarios describing hypothetical examples of police misconduct—has been firmly established as an effective empirical tool to measure the level of police integrity in a police agency. The bulk of the extant research has explored police views of police integrity (see, e.g., Kutnjak Ivković et al. 2004; Kutnjak Ivković and Haberfeld 2015). Only a handful of studies used the same methodology to explore public views about police integrity, although they did not measure temporal changes.

A typical approach in the study of public opinions about police integrity has been to rely on a sample of college students, sometimes majoring in fields that would provide students with neither knowledge of policing/laws nor experience with police agencies (e.g., internships). Kutnjak Ivković et al. (2002a) surveyed college students attending classes at the University of Zagreb, Croatia, and asked them to evaluate scenarios describing police misconduct, as well as to assess how police officers would evaluate the described misconduct. The results showed that college students were able to distinguish across different examples of police misconduct, assessing an opportunistic theft as the most serious and the acceptance of gratuities as the least serious form of misconduct. At the same time, college students also estimated that police officers would be less likely to evaluate the described instances of misconduct than they were

(Kutnjak Ivković et al. 2002a). Differences in the respondents' views of appropriate and expected discipline were even larger: while the students thought that each form of misconduct should result in some discipline, they assumed that police would issue no discipline in 7 out of 11 scenarios (Kutnjak Ivković et al. 2002a). Finally, the students perceived the code of silence among the police to be extremely strong—they did not think that the police would report any of the forms of misconduct in the questionnaire (Kutnjak Ivković et al. 2002a).

Meyer et al. (2013) surveyed a convenience sample of the first-year social studies students at University of KwaZulu-Natal in South Africa and a sample of the police officers from the South African Police Service. Although the focus on their paper is primarily on the student-police differences in assessments of seriousness, appropriate discipline, and willingness to report, the paper also contains the results of the student survey. The results show that the overwhelming majority of the students (over 94%) viewed theft from a crime scene and acceptance of a bribe from a speeding motorist as very serious forms of police misconduct, while only a minority of the students evaluated acceptance of free meals and discounts, holiday gifts, and running an off-duty business as very serious forms of police misconduct (Meyer et al. 2013). Although the students evaluated the behaviors described in the majority of the scenarios as very serious, they thought that dismissal is an appropriate discipline only in one scenario—that in which a police officer steals from a crime scene. In most other scenarios, some as serious as accepting a bribe from a motorist or stealing money from a found wallet, students did not think that dismissal would be appropriate. Finally, although the majority of the students stated that they would report a police officer who engaged in the behavior described in seven out of 11 scenarios, there were still four scenarios in which the majority of the students in the sample would have preferred not to report such behavior.

Bjerregaard and Lord (2004) sought to explore not only how college students view police integrity, but also to measure potential differences between students pursuing a criminal justice major and students pursuing other majors. However, the choice of major was unrelated to the students' perceptions of seriousness of ethical violations (Bjerregaard and Lord 2004). In addition to college students, Kutnjak Ivković and Klockars (2002) included students studying at the Police High School and Police College. Compared to regular college students (sampled to exclude law school and criminal justice programs), both of these groups have either additional experience in policing or familiarity with police processes and procedures. Despite their differential familiarity with policing, all three groups expressed very similar views across groups about misconduct seriousness and their willingness to report it, as well as their views about appropriate discipline for such misconduct (Kutnjak Ivković and Klockars 2002).

A few studies took a comparative approach and contrasted seriousness evaluations across countries (e.g., Klockars and Kutnjak Ivković 1999; Kutnjak Ivković 2004; Kutnjak Ivković et al. 2002b). When college students from Croatia and the United States were asked to assess the seriousness of the same 11 scenarios, statistically significant differences surfaced in eight out of 11 scenarios, though these differences or substantive importance in only two scenarios (Klockars and Kutnjak Ivković 1999; Kutnjak Ivković 2004). In both of these scenarios, Croatian students evaluated the behavior as more serious than the U.S. students did. A comparison of estimates of seriousness provided by college students from two neighboring countries, Croatia and Slovenia, once again reached levels of statistically significance for many scenarios, yet those differences were substantively small in all but the scenario describing the police officer's engagement in off-duty business (Kutnjak Ivković et al. 2002b).

Exploring Public Views of Police Officer Integrity

A few studies also compared citizen views with their perceptions of the police officer views (e.g., Kutnjak Ivković and Klockars 2002; Kutnjak Ivković et al. 2002a, b; Pagon et al. 2000). Based

on a survey of college students, Kutnjak Ivković and colleagues (2002a, b) reported that in all scenarios students estimated that police officers would evaluated police misconduct as less serious. Because of the self-serving bias, it is quite reasonable to expect that the respondents would present themselves as "better"—which in this context means evaluating misconduct as more serious—than others. However, the size of the differences in their opinions and the heterogeneity of the size of these differences across different measures of integrity suggest that these differences are not only a consequence of the self-serving bias, but also negative views of the police. In particular, the students' own evaluations of seriousness in this study were typically 1 point higher on a 5-point scale than what they though police evaluations of seriousness would be (Kutnjak Ivković et al. 2002a, p 317).

The differences were even more obvious when their own views about appropriate discipline were compared to their views about discipline they expected the police to mete out; Kutnjak Ivković and colleagues (2002a, p. 318) wrote: "While the college students thought that some discipline is appropriate in every case… and in the majority of the cases opted for some discipline…, they anticipated that the police would issue no discipline at all in the seven cases, and would issue a public warning in the additional three cases." In other words, while the respondents argued that some discipline is appropriate for almost every example of police misconduct described in the questionnaire, they thought that the police would mete out no discipline in most of the cases. Finally, the negative view of the police agency's integrity is further expressed in the comparison of the views about the respondents' own expressed willingness to report and the estimated police officers' willingness to report. Simply put, college students expected that the code of silence among the Croatian police is very strong (Kutnjak Ivkovic et al. 2002a, b).

Similar results, documenting shared public perception of a strong code of silence among the police, were also reported in a paper analyzing the views of the Slovenian students (Pagon et al. 2000). In a comparative paper, Pagon et al. (2000) not only compared the police officer views across three countries (Croatia, Slovenia, the United States), but also compared the Slovenian police officer views with the Slovenian college student views. They reported that the police officers' and the students' own expressed willingness to report, as well their estimates of most police officers' willingness to report, were both statistically different in the majority of the scenarios. Pagon and colleagues (2000, p. 392) found that the difference between the respondents' own willingness to report and the estimated police officers' willingness to report was much larger for students than it was for police officers. Accordingly, Pagon and colleagues (2000, p. 392) concluded that, "police officers have significantly more faith in other police officers, when it comes to reporting corrupt behaviors, than do the students."

Finally, a study by Kutnjak Ivković and Klockars (2002) added more insights because it not only compared students' own evaluations with their predictions of the police officers' evaluations, but also compared college students' views about the police with the views held by the students who were in the early stages of learning how to become police officers (i.e., students the Police High School and students from the Police College). The fact that the students at the Police High School and Police College had more familiarity or more extensive experience with policing than the college students did was reflected in their views of the police. Specifically, although their own evaluations of misconduct seriousness were quite similar, their views about police evaluations of seriousness were quite different. In eight out of 11 scenarios, college students' estimates of the police officers' evaluations of police misconduct were much less serious than the Police High School and Police College students' estimates of the police officers' evaluations of police misconduct (Kutnjak Ivković and Klockars 2002). A similar conclusion was drawn about the respondents' views about expected discipline; college students were again more likely to anticipate that discipline would be less severe than either the students at the Police High School or students at the Police College did. Finally, while students at the Police High School and Police

College anticipated that police officers would be as likely to say that they would report as they themselves would, college students once again expected the code of silence to be stronger among the police than among them (Kutnjak Ivković and Klockars 2002).

Changes in Public and Police Views About Police Integrity over Time

Klockars et al. (2006, p. 137) argued that repeated surveys of police integrity could be used to test the reliability of the initial findings:

> The simplest way to employ a second survey as a test of the reliability of the earlier inquiry is what is sometimes called a "test-retest" strategy. It involves distributing a second survey after sufficient time has passed for respondents to forget the answers they had given on a first survey and then comparing the results. If answers to the same question on both surveys are identical, or differ only in ways that are explainable by some obvious event, it is evidence that respondents are answering honestly.

Klockars et al. (2006) went beyond merely testing the reliability of the initial findings. Rather, they used the survey to assess the potential changes in police officer views. In their study, Klockars et al. (2006) retested the Charlotte-Mecklenburg Police Department, Charleston Police Department, and St. Petersburg Police Department. Five scenarios were included in both test- and retest surveys, some in the original, others in a modified form (Klockars et al. 2006, p. 142). The reexamination included all questions or measures of police integrity. To eliminate the effect of noise, Klockars et al. (2006, p. 142) considered as substantial only the results with sizeable differences (i.e., a one-half point differential on a 5-point scale).

A comparison of the test/retest findings over time revealed literally no change in the survey results in the Charleston Police Department and the Charlotte-Mecklenburg Police Department over time (Klockars et al. 2006, p. 142). Yet, the results for the St. Petersburg Police Department indicated significant shift in the respondents' answers, but only regarding one scenario, pertaining to the acceptance of gratuities

(Klockars et al. 2006, p. 142). The retest survey was part of a larger study of police integrity in these police agencies, so the researchers have had extensive knowledge of these police agencies and were quite familiar with the changes in their official rules and police cultures (Klockars et al. 2006). Indeed, the results in St. Petersburg resonated with real-life events: "[i]t is possible that the new chief's tightening up on discipline, his emphasis on integrity, and the exam question [on the sergeant's exam about a hypothetical scenario in which a new sergeant overhears police officers talking about availability of free meals] may have had an impact on the responses to this question" (Klockars et al. 2006, p. 146).

Kutnjak Ivković (2009) compared the results of the two police integrity surveys of the Croatian police, collected 13 years apart. Despite the time difference, representative samples of Croatian police officers expressed many similarities in the way they were able to recognize and label corrupt behaviors as rule violations (Kutnjak Ivković 2009). While the evaluations of misconduct seriousness were also very similar across the two sweeps of the survey, the respondents' expected harsher discipline and expressed willingness to report were quite different in 2008 than they were in 1995 (Kutnjak Ivković 2009). Kutnjak Ivković (2009, p. 477) elaborated, "[t]hese results [the code of silence being narrower in 2008] persist throughout the scenarios, regardless of how serious the scenario was evaluated to be or how likely the respondents were to view it as a violation of official rules." Furthermore, dismissal was an expected discipline in a much larger number of scenarios in 2008. The possible explanation for the shift in perceptions was related to the events in the society at large (Kutnjak Ivković 2009, p. 480):

> Police officers surveyed in 1995 had been through recent war experiences together with many other officers from their respective police stations, often saving each other's lives and sharing the hardship of an armed conflict; the resulting connections and loyalty were likely somewhat akin to close kinship. By contrast, because of the sheer passage of time, during which there were many retirements and steady downsizing of the Croatian police, police officers surveyed 13 years later, in 2008, have been functioning in much less closely connected units in which the relationships, though still characterized by some degree of loyalty and solidarity, cannot really compare with the relationships that prevailed in the mid-1990s, solidified by war camaraderie.

In their study of police integrity in South Africa, Kutnjak Ivković and Sauerman (2012) focused their attention on a temporal comparison in the coverage of the code of silence. They used the same technique as Klockars et al. (2006). In particular, they compared the respondents' answers about willingness to report for the six scenarios included in both surveys. Their results indicated that the respondents' stated willingness to report changed to a certain degree, implying that the code of silence in South Africa seemed to be narrower in 2010/2011 than it was in 2005 (Kutnjak Ivković and Sauerman 2012). On the other hand, the respondents' evaluations of others' perceived willingness to report largely remained similar across time. Put differently, while there seems to have been a shift in the respondents' own perceptions, their assessments of the police culture within which they operated remained stable.

Finally, Khechumyan and Kutnjak Ivković (2015) also compared the extent of the code of silence in two sweeps of the police integrity survey in Armenia. The 5-year gap between the two surveys (2008/2009–2013) was sufficient to suggest that the code of silence might have weakened. On the other hand, they found that the respondents from both administrations of the survey shared the same tendency—they underestimated others' willingness to report.

Kutnjak Ivković et al. (2004) explored the changes in the views expressed by college students and students at a police college surveyed over a 5-year time period (1995 and 2001). The study did not capture all elements of police integrity; it focused only on the respondents' views about misconduct seriousness. The respondents' assessments of seriousness "were remarkably similar in all eleven cases" (Kutnjak Ivković et al. 2004, p. 307). While the results for the students at the police college were also similar across time in the majority of the scenarios, they differed in the only scenario describing the use of excessive force (Kutnjak Ivković et al. 2004, p. 307). In particular, the 2001 sample evaluated the use of excessive force as more serious. This change was attributed to the novel regulation restricting the use of force and the sample composition (fewer police officers in the more recent sample; Kutnjak Ivković et al. 2004, p. 307).

Methodology

Questionnaire

To assess potential changes in the public perception of corruption in Croatia over time, we used two different versions of the questionnaire. Both questionnaires contain hypothetical scenarios describing police misconduct. Because the project started as a way to measure the opposite of police corruption (Kutnjak Ivković 2015), the first, police corruption questionnaire (Klockars and Kutnjak Ivković 1995, Klockars and Kutnjak Ivković 2004; Klockars, Kutnjak Ivković, and Haberfeld 2004) contains nine scenarios describing various forms of police corruption, one scenario describing an off-duty employment, and one scenario describing the use of excessive force. Scenarios provide descriptions of various forms of police corruption, based on the typology of police corruption provided by Roebuck and Barker (1974). All corruption scenarios include illegal gain (Kutnjak Ivković 2015), defined in relative terms for purposess of both cross-cultural applications (Kutnjak Ivković 2015) and longitudinal studies (e.g., "two-day pay" instead of "$50").

To address the potential criticism that police integrity might be more than a tendency to resist corruption and that the police corruption questionnaire deals almost exclusively with corruption, Klockars and colleagues developed another questionnaire that provides a broader coverage of police integrity (Klockars et al. 2006). The second questionnaire, the police integrity questionnaire, contains 11 scenarios describing various forms of police misconduct (Klockars et al. 2006). Specifically, of the 11 scenarios, five scenarios describe corruption (Scenarios 1, 3, 5, 8, and 9), four scenarios describe the use of excessive force (Scenarios 4, 6, 7, and 10), and two scenarios describe other forms of police misconduct (Scenarios 2 and 10).

To allow for comparisons over time (i.e., the test-retest measure), the police integrity questionnaire was designed purposely in a way that partly overlaps with the police corruption questionnaire (Klockars et al. 2006). In particular, five police corruption scenarios from the police corruption questionnaire were included in the police integrity questionnaire (Klockars et al. 2006). Two scenarios (Cover-Up of Police DUI Accident; Auto-Body Shop 5% Kickback) were identical in both questionnaires (Table 1). In two additional scenarios (Theft of Knife from Crime Scene; Supervisor: Holiday Off), the wording of the scenario is very similar and only one item was changed. In the scenario describing the theft of knife from a crime scene, the item that has been stolen is different; it is "a watch, worth about two day pay" in the police corruption scenario and "an expensive pocket knife" in the police integrity questionnaire (Table 1). In the scenario describing a supervisor who demands a favor in exchange for receiving days off during holidays, the specific favor that the police officer has to do in exchange is different: it is tuning-up a supervisor's personal car in the police corruption questionnaire, while it is running some personal errands for the supervisor in the police integrity questionnaire (Klockars et al. 2006; Kutnjak Ivković 2015). Finally, there were two scenarios describing the acceptance of gratuities in the police corruption scenario. Only one of these two scenarios was included in the police integrity questionnaire, albeit with somewhat changed wording (Table 1).

In preparation for the administration of the police integrity survey among Croatian police officers and with consultation with the Croatian police, three scenarios were added to the questionnaire (Kutnjak Ivković 2009). The first added scenario (Scenario 12) describes the failure to note on the report that a crime could be classified as a hate crime. The second added scenario (Scenario 13) originates in the police corruption questionnaire and has been taken verbatim from it (Scenario 3 in the first questionnaire). The rationale for its inclusion is that the scenario describing the acceptance of a bribe from a motorist caught speeding captures a form of

Table 1 Scenario descriptions

Form of corruption	Questionnaire 1	Questionnaire 2
Corruption of authority	**Scenario 4:** *A police officer is widely liked in the community, and on holidays local merchants and restaurant and bar owners show their appreciation for his attention by giving him gifts of food and liquor*	**Scenario 1:** *A police officer is widely liked in the community. Local merchants and restaurant owners regularly show their appreciation for his attention by giving him gifts of food, cigarettes, and other items of small value*
Opportunistic theft	**Scenario 5:** A police officer discovers a burglary of a jewelry shop. The display cases are smashed and it is obvious that many items have been taken. While searching the shop, he takes a *watch, worth about two day pay* for that officer. He reports that the watch had been stolen during the burglary	**Scenario 3:** A police officer discovers a burglary of a hardware store. The display cases are smashed and many items have obviously been taken. While searching the store, he takes an *expensive pocket knife* and slips it into his pocket. He reports that the knife has been stolen during the burglary
Internal corruption	**Scenario 7:** A police officer, who happens to be a very good auto mechanic, is scheduled to work during the coming holidays. A supervisor offers to give him these days off, if he agrees to *tune-up his supervisor's personal car*. Evaluate the SUPERVISOR'S behavior	**Scenario 5:** A police officer is scheduled to work during coming holidays. The supervisor offers to give him these days off, if he agrees to *run some personal errands for the supervisor*. Evaluate the SUPERVISOR'S behavior
Internal corruption	**Scenario 8:** At 2 A.M. a police officer, who is on duty, is driving his patrol car on a deserted road. He sees a vehicle that has been driven off the road and is stuck in a ditch. He approaches the vehicle and observes that the driver is not hurt but is obviously intoxicated. He also finds that the driver is a police officer. Instead of reporting this accident and offense he transports the driver to his home	**Scenario 8:** At 2:00 A.M. a police officer, who is on duty, is driving his patrol car on a deserted road. He sees a vehicle that has been driven off the road and is stuck in a ditch. He approaches the vehicle and observes that the driver is not hurt but is obviously intoxicated. He also finds that the driver is a police officer. Instead of reporting this accident and offense, he transports the driver to his home
Kickback	**Scenario 6:** A police officer has a private arrangement with a local auto body shop to refer the owners of the cars damaged in the accidents to the shop. In exchange for each referral, he receives a payment of 5% of the repair bill from the shop owner	**Scenario 9:** A police officer has a private arrangement with a local auto body shop to refer the owners of cars damaged in accidents to the shop. In exchange for each referral, he receives a payment of 5% of the repair bill from the shop owner
Shakedown	**Scenario 3:** A police officer stops a motorist for speeding. The officer agrees to accept a personal gift for half of the amount of the fine in exchange for not issuing a citation	**Scenario 13:** A police officer stops a motorist for speeding. The officer agrees to accept a personal gift for half of the amount of the fine in exchange for not issuing a citation

police corruption frequently experienced in East-European countries, according to Fric and Walek (2001). This scenario was included in the police integrity questionnaire in the unchanged format (Table 1). The third added scenario (Scenario 14) focuses on a failure to act; it describes the failure to intervene when the police officer sees juve-

niles writing graffiti on a wall (Kutnjak Ivković 2009).

In the end, of the six scenarios included in both surveys, the wording of three scenarios (accepting bribe from a speeding motorist; autobody shop 5% kickback; cover-up of police DUI accident) was identical in both surveys. In two scenarios (theft from a crime scene; internal corruption with a supervisor), the description of the behavior is identical, but there was a change in the gain (Table 1). Finally, the corruption of authority scenario has been modified between the two surveys. The police corruption questionnaire had two scenarios dealing with corruption of authority: Scenario 2 describes the acceptance of gratuities on a regular basis ("A police officer routinely accepts free meals, cigarettes, and other items of small value from merchants on his beat. He does not solicit these gifts and is careful not to abuse the generosity of those who give gifts to him.") and Scenario 4 describes the acceptance of small gifts during holidays ("A police officer is widely liked in the community, and on holidays local merchants and restaurant and bar owners show their appreciation for his attention by giving him gifts of food and liquor."). The police integrity questionnaire has one scenario dealing with corruption of authority ("A police officer is widely liked in the community. Local merchants and restaurant owners regularly show their appreciation for his attention by giving him gifts of food, cigarettes, and other items of small value."). This scenario is a modified version of Scenario 4 from the police corruption questionnaire; it shifts the frequency of these gifts from only occurring during holidays to a more regular occurrence.

Upon reading the description of each scenario, the respondents were asked to evaluate the describe behavior using seven questions. The wording of these questions was identical in both questionnaires. The questions in both the police corruption questionnaire and the police integrity questionnaire were initially designed for police officers, so we had to make some minor adjustment to the questions to make them more applicable to citizens. The first two questions asked about the perceived seriousness of misconduct. The first question asked about the respondents' own assessment of seriousness and the second question asked the respondents to assess how they thought the majority of police officers would evaluate the scenario. In the police officer survey, the second question asked about "most police officers in your agency," while in the public sur-

vey, it asked about "most police officers." The respondents could have selected an answer from a 5-point Likert scale, ranging from 1 = "not at all serious" to 5 = "very serious." The identical modification in the wording of the question was made for the two parallel questions tapping into willingness to report. The respondents could have selected an answer from a 5-point Likert scale, ranging from 1 = "definitely would not report" to 5 = "definitely would report."

The third question in the questionnaire explored the respondents' familiarity with official rules. In the version of the questionnaire for police officers, it inquired about a potential "violation of official policy in your agency" (Klockars et al. 2006). In the version of the questionnaire for the public, the part "in your agency" has been deleted. The police corruption questionnaire used the 5-point Likert scale for this question, ranging from 1 = "definitely not" to 5 = "definitely yes." However, as Klockars and colleagues argued (2006, p. 141), "[t]his range of choices complicated interpreting officer responses because the meaning of responses other than '1' or '5' was somewhat unclear." Consequently, the police integrity questionnaire had three options: "yes," "no," and "I don't know" (Klockars et al. 2006, p. 141). We recoded the answers on the police integrity questionnaire to match the answers on the police integrity questionnaire (1 and 2 = "no," 3 = "I don't know," and 4 and 5 = "yes").

Finally, the questionnaires had two questions measuring the views about discipline that the respondents perceived is appropriate for such misconduct and the corresponding discipline the respondents expect the police to mete out. These two questions are dependent upon the country's legal system (see, e.g., Kutnjak Ivković 2015, p. 16) and, hence, can vary greatly across legal systems (Klockars, Kutnjak Ivković, and Haberfeld 2004). Legal norms can also vary across time, particularly in a country in transition undergoing reforms. The police corruption questionnaire was used in Croatia in the mid-1990s; it reflected disciplinary options at the time ("no discipline," "public reprimand," "fine," "period of suspension," and "dismissal"). The police integrity questionnaire was used in Croatia in the

2000s; it contained somewhat different disciplinary options ("no discipline," "written reprimand," "fine in the amount of 10% of the employee's salary," "fine in the amount of 20% of the employee's salary," "no promotion in rank for 2–4 years," "no advancement in service for 2–4 years," "reassignment into a lower-ranked assignment," and "dismissal"). Both scales have common ends ("no discipline" and "dismissal"). The 1990s version had three additional choices, while the 2000s one had six additional choices. Some of the choices were very similar ("public reprimand" in the 1990s and "written reprimand" in the 2000s), so we recoded the variable into four categories: "no discipline," "reprimand," "some other discipline," and "dismissal."

The questionnaire concluded with just a few demographic questions. To prevent potential identification of respondents and entice them to participate in the survey, the original idea was to have only a minimal number of demographic questions. As both questionnaires were designed to survey police officers, demographic questions focused on their job-related characteristics (e.g., length of service, supervisory position, type of assignment, size of police agency). These questions were inappropriate for a public opinion survey, so we developed new demographic questions. The police corruption questionnaire had questions focusing on student experience (e.g., year in school, major) and potential police-related experience (e.g., whether they have served as police officers, whether they plan to become police officers). The police integrity questionnaire had just two questions, inquiring about respondents' gender and whether somebody in the family is employed by the Ministry of the Interior. The last two questions in both questionnaires asked the respondents whether they have answered honestly while filling out the questionnaire and whether they think that most police officers would have done the same.

The Samples

We used the same methodological approach for the two surveys: we collected convenience sam-

ples of surveyed college students at University of Zagreb.[1] To avoid participation of students with levels of knowledge more extensive than those of an otherwise educated citizen—students studying law/criminal justice and/or students who may have worked as police officers—we selected students pursuing majors which traditionally do not lend themselves to such background knowledge or experiences (e.g., engineering, veterinary medicine, education).

In 1996, we surveyed 504 college students studying at the University of Zagreb. Copies of the police corruption questionnaires were distributed during regular classes to students enrolled in the School of Educational Studies (44.6%), the School of Physical Education (31.0%), the School of Electrical Engineering (11.9%), and the School of Veterinary Medicine (12.5%). About 40% were first- or second-year students (Kutnjak Ivković and Klockars 2002, p. 286). None of the students had served as police officers and almost no students planned to become police officers (1.4%; Kutnjak Ivković and Klockars 2002, p. 286).

In 2016, we surveyed 382 college students studying at the University of Zagreb. Copies of the police integrity questionnaire were distributed during regular classes to college students enrolled in the School of Physical Education (44.8%), the School of Veterinary Medicine (18.8%), the School of Mechanical Engineering (18.8%), and the School of Transportation Engineering (17.5%). About two-thirds were male students (66.8%) and one-third were female students. When asked whether any member of the respondents' family is employed by the Ministry of the Interior, only very few (5.6%) answered affirmatively.

The last question in both questionnaires asked the respondents whether they have answered honestly while filling out the questionnaire. The overwhelming majority of students in both samples answered affirmatively (94.4% in 1996 and 96% in 2016). The analyses that follow exclude

---

[1]These are not longitudinal random samples, but two cross-sectional convenience samples. Thus, we use just the basic statistical tools and draw tentative conclusions.

the respondents who explicitly stated that they had not answered honestly.

Changes in the Croatian Society and the Police

In 1996, at the time the first survey was carried out, Croatia has just begun to recover from the recent war in which the police performed both the military and the police role (Kutnjak Ivković 2000). The war had many negative consequences, including the relaxation of official rules and the strengthening of the code of silence among the police (see, e.g., Kutnjak Ivković 2004a). In the late 1990s, various changes affecting the society at large, from economic and legal to organizational and social, started to take place (Kutnjak Ivković 2000; Kutnjak Ivković 2004a; 2015).

Legal reforms included the enactment of the new Criminal Code (1997), the Criminal Procedure Code (1997, 2008), and the Police Law (2000, 2011). These laws were critical for the change of the police role and functions. The police have officially been defined as the "public service within the Ministry of the Interior entrusted to perform the tasks enumerated by the law" (Article 2, Police Law 2000). The new laws regulated police rights and duties, as well as streamlined the promotion and discipline of the police (Kutnjak Ivković 2015). As Kutnjak Ivković (2015) argues, each new version of the laws was more detailed and sophisticated, but the issue of the frequency with which these laws were actually enforced persisted. The results of empirical studies show that, while the respondents in the 1995 survey of police officers expected no discipline or very mild discipline even for the most serious violations (Kutnjak Ivković 2004a), the results of the 2008/2009 survey of the police indicated that the police expected harsher discipline, including five scenarios in which they expected to be dismissed if they had engaged in such behavior (Kutnjak Ivković 2015). The code of silence also seems to be weakening over time as well (e.g., Kutnjak Ivković 2004a; 2015).

Government has tried to address widespread corruption in the society. Reforms have been conducted, but the strongest push to deal with corruption came from the European Union, through the obstacles Croatia faced to its ascension toward EU membership. While the government has been pushing for the reforms, the top-level governmental officials, including former Prime Minister Ivo Sanader, have been indicted in the 2010s and tried for high-level corruption. In 2013, two top police administrators have been removed from their posts because of police misconduct. In particular, the heads of the Vukovar-Srijemska Police Administration were arrested for corruption and the head of the Splitsko-Dalmatinska Police Administration was removed from the post for abuse of his official position. Not surprisingly, the majority of the citizens surveyed as part of the 2010 Transparency International survey (2010, p. 47) evaluated the government's efforts to deal with corruption as ineffective. Furthermore, they believed that the level of corruption in the country has *increased* in the last 3 years (Transparency International 2010). The very next year, an UNODC study showed that the situation with corruption has not improved: about one-half of the respondents perceived that the level of corruption had remained the same in the last 2 years, while about one-third of the respondents thought that the level of corruption had *increased* (UNODC 2011, p. 44).

The fact is that corruption remains to be a part of everyday life in Croatia. Derenčinović (2000) pointed out that more than 30% of the respondents in his study reported paying a bribe to a police officer. Similar findings surfaced in the 2001 International Crime Victimization Survey: about 15% of the citizens participating in the study stated that a police officer asked them to pay a bribe last year (Kutnjak Ivković 2009). The results of the 2010 UNODC survey were no different; 12% of the citizens participating in the study reported giving public officials money, gifts, or favors on at least one occasion during last year (UNODC 2011, p. 16).

The country's ranking on the Transparency International Corruption Perception Index (CPI) reflects the fact that changes have been made in the earlier period, followed by relative stagnation. In 1999, Croatia's CPI score was 2.7 out of 10. By 2008, about a decade later, the score had increased substantially to 4.4 (Transparency International 2008), implying that the country is perceived as less corrupt. As it turns out, the score remained relatively stable, without further improvement. In 2010, it actually decreased to 4.1 (Transparency International 2010), with further slight decline to 4.0 in 2011 (Transparency International 2011). Most recently, the score was 51 out of 100 in 2015 (Transparency International 2016) and 49 out of 100 in 2016.

Croatia has experienced considerable challenges in its fight against corruption and organized crime (Nacional Survey 2008), resulting in the decline in the level of public support for the police (Kutnjak Ivković 2008). The post-war surveys in the 1990s suggested an unprecedented level of support for the police (see, Kutnjak Ivković 2008), with 60% of the citizens in the World Values Survey showing support for police (Kutnjak Ivković and Klockars 2002). This support reflected gratitude to the police for the military function it had performed during the war, especially in its early stages. However, as the time passed and the government was not as successful in dealing with corruption as had been expected, public opinion about the police worsened. Indeed, the respondents in Derenčinović (2000) evaluated the police as the second most corrupt profession and the fourth most corrupt governmental institution.

Results

Differences in Public Opinion About Police Corruption

To assess any potential differences in the public attitudes toward corruption over time, we compare the responses about police corruption by the respondents from the 1996 sample to those from the 2016 sample. In the process, we analyze their views about misconduct seriousness, their assessment whether the described behavior violates the rules, their views about appropriate discipline, and their willingness to report misconduct.

First, we explore the respondents' evaluations of seriousness (Table 2). In the majority of the scenarios, both samples evaluated scenarios as serious (mean values are in above the scale midpoint of 3.0, toward the serious side of the scale; Table 2). In about one-half of the scenarios (Scenario 2: Gifts from Merchants; Scenario 4: Auto-Body Shop 5% Kickback; Scenario 6: Cover-Up of Police DUI Accident), there are statistically significant differences (Table 2); and in two of these scenarios, the differences are also substantively large. In all the scenarios with statistically significant differences, the 2016 respondents evaluated misconduct as more serious than the 1996 respondents did.

To explore whether the change in views could be attributed to the changes in the wording of the scenarios (see Methodology), we analyze the scenarios that were identical in both surveys separately from those in which the wording was

Table 2 Respondents' own evaluations of seriousness

	1996 Sample		2016 Sample			
	Mean	Rank	Mean	Rank	Difference	T-test
Scenario 1: Bribe from speeding motorist	3.89	5	3.93	4	−.04	−.459
Scenario 2: Gifts from merchants	1.83	1	2.74	1	−.91	−11.389***
Scenario 3: Theft from crime scene	4.57	6	4.66	6	−.09	−1.585
Scenario 4: Auto-body shop 5% kickback	3.41	2	4.15	5	−.74	−9.508***
Scenario 5: Supervisor	3.71	4	3.74	2	−.04	−.466
Scenario 6: Cover-up of police DUI accident	3.45	3	3.83	3	−.39	−4.576***

$*p < .05$; $**p < .01$; $***p < .001$

Table 3 Violation of official rules

	1996 Sample			2016 Sample				
	Yes (%)	No (%)	Don't know (%)	Yes (%)	No (%)	Don't know (%)	Chi-square	Phi
Scenario 1: Bribe from speeding motorist	88.0	6.2	5.8	88.0	5.0	7.0	.966	.034
Scenario 2: Gifts from merchants	10.7	78.3	10.9	30.3	32.0	37.7	187.96***	.466
Scenario 3: Theft from crime scene	93.4	3.4	3.2	97.2	1.1	1.7	6.76*	.088
Scenario 4: Auto-body shop 5% kickback	51.4	25.5	23.1	74.7	5.8	19.6	67.39***	.279
Scenario 5: Supervisor	60.3	21.6	18.1	56.1	15.2	28.7	15.91***	.136
Scenario 6: Cover-up of police DUI accident	65.9	17.1	17.1	75.2	7.7	17.1	16.66***	.139

$* p < .05$; $** p < .01$; $*** p < .001$

modified. We first focus on the three identical scenarios (Scenario 1: Bribe from Speeding Motorist; Scenario 4: Auto-Body 5% Kickback; Scenario 6: Cover-Up of Police DUI). In two of the three scenarios (Scenario 4: Auto-Body 5% Kickback; Scenario 6: Cover-Up of Police DUI), the 2016 respondents evaluated misconduct as more serious than the 1996 respondents did (Table 2), indicating that any changes in seriousness evaluations did not stem from the change in wording. Among the three gently modified scenarios (Scenario 2: Gifts from Merchants; Scenario 3: Theft from Crime Scene; Scenario 5: Supervisor), statistically significant differences were found in only one (Scenario 2: Gifts from Merchants), or about one-third of the gently modified scenarios (Table 2).

Second, we study the respondents' views whether the behavior described in the scenario violates official rules (Table 3). In five out of six scenarios, the majority of respondents in both samples evaluated these behaviors as rule violations. Only in the scenario describing the acceptance of gratuities (Scenario 2: Gifts from Merchants) did a minority of the respondents evaluate the described case of police misconduct as a violation of official rules.

In the majority of the scenarios (five out of six or 83%; Table 3), there were statistically significant differences between the two samples in the respondents' assessments of whether the behavior violates official rules (and in four out of five

scenarios the differences were also large and substantively important[2]). In the only scenario with no statistically significant differences (Scenario 1: Bribe from Speeding Motorist), the overwhelming majority of the respondents—88 percent in both samples—evaluated this behavior as a violation of the official rules, thus leaving very little room for potential disagreement. Such views should not be surprising because this is one of the most serious forms of corruption, potentially punishable by a prison sentence.

Among the three identical scenarios (Scenario 1: Bribe from Speeding Motorist; Scenario 4: Auto-Body 5% Kickback; Scenario 6: Cover-Up of Police DUI), the differences in the respondents' views about rule violations were significant in two scenarios (67%; Table 3). In both of these scenarios (Scenario 4: Auto-Body Shop 5% Kickback; Scenario 6: Cover-Up of Police DUI Accident), the 2016 respondents were more likely to evaluate these behaviors as violations of official rules than the 1996 respondents were (Table 3). While about one-half (51.4%) of the 1996 respondents evaluated a 5% kickback as a rule-violating behavior, the same was true of about three-quarters (74.7%) of the 2016 respondents (Table 3). Similarly,

---

[2]Klockars et al. (2006) defined as substantive differences those that, in addition to being statistically significant, exceed .50 for a mean value on a 5-point scale and 10% for a percentage.

Table 4 Respondents' own willingness to report

	1996 Sample		2016 Sample			
	Mean	Rank	Mean	Rank	Difference	T-test
Scenario 1: Bribe from speeding motorist	2.77	5	3.16	3	−.39	−3904***
Scenario 2: Gifts from merchants	1.40	1	1.94	1	−.54	−7.931***
Scenario 3: Theft from crime scene	3.91	6	4.01	6	−.10	−1.195
Scenario 4: Auto-body shop 5% kickback	2.62	4	3.53	5	−.91	−9.567***
Scenario 5: Supervisor	2.52	2	2.70	2	−.18	−1.965a
Scenario 6: Cover-up of police DUI accident	2.54	3	3.18	4	−.64	−6.614***

$* p < .05; ** p < .01; *** p < .001$

while about two-thirds (65.9%) of the 1996 respondents viewed that the cover-up of police DUI accident is a rule violation, this view was shared by about three-quarters (75.2%) of the 2016 respondents (Table 3).

Statistically significant differences surfaced in connection with all the three modified scenarios (Scenario 2: Gifts from Merchants; Scenario 3: Theft from Crime Scene; Scenario 5: Supervisor). In both Scenario 2 (Gifts from Merchants) and Scenario 3 (Theft from Crime Scene), the 2016 respondents were more likely to recognize these behaviors are rule violating than the 1996 respondents were, although the differences were not very pronounced percentage-wise for Scenario 3 (97.2% v. 93.4%; Table 3), casting doubt on their substantive importance. The issue is more complex for the last scenario in the group, Scenario 5 (Supervisor). The percent of the 1996 respondents who evaluated the behavior as rule-violating is somewhat higher than the percent of the 2016 respondents (60.3% v. 56.1%). At the same time, the 2016 respondents were less likely to say that this is not a violation of the official rules and more likely to say that they do not know whether this is a violation than the 1996 respondents were (Table 3).

Third, we examine the respondents' willingness to report misconduct (Table 4). In the overwhelming majority of the scenarios, the respondents in both samples would be reluctant to report police corruption. With the exception of Scenario 3, describing an opportunistic theft, the mean values are all below 3.0 (the mid-point of the scale) and/or barely reach into the reporting side of the scale.

There were statistically significant differences across the two samples in four out of six scenarios (or 67%); the detected differences were substantively important in three out of four scenarios (Table 4). In addition, there was one more scenario with marginally significant differences. In all these scenarios with statistically significant differences, the 2016 respondents were more likely to say that they would report than the 1996 respondents were.

The differences across time were statistically significant in all three identical scenarios (Scenario 1: Bribe from Speeding Motorist; Scenario 4: Auto-Body 5% Kickback; Scenario 6: Cover-Up of Police DUI), and were substantively important in two of them. In these scenarios, the 1996 respondents were more likely to say that they would not report than the 2016 respondents were (Table 9). In some of these scenarios, such as Scenario 4 (Auto-Body 5% Kickback), the differences between the 1996 and 2016 means were as large as 1 on a 5-point scale (Table 4).

The situation is not as clear-cut regarding the three modified scenarios (Scenario 2: Gifts from Merchants; Scenario 3: Theft from Crime Scene; Scenario 5: Supervisor). In one scenario (Scenario 2: Gifts from Merchants), the 2016 respondents were less likely to say that they would not report than the 1996 respondents were (Table 4). On the other end, there were no statistically significant differences across time in the respondents' likelihood of reporting an opportunistic theft (Scenario 3: Theft from Crime Scene). Finally, the differences were marginally significant for the scenario describing internal corruption involving a supervisor (Scenario 5: Supervisor). In this scenario,

Table 5 Respondents' views about appropriate discipline

	1996 Sample				2016 Sample					
	None (%)	Rep. (%)	Other (%)	Dismissal (%)	None (%)	Rep. (%)	Other (%)	Dismissal (%)	Chi-square	Phi
Scenario 1: Bribe from speeding motorist	2.4	15.3	70.9	11.4	7.1	9.7	57.7	25.4	45.06***	.230
Scenario 2: Gifts from merchants	74.7	14.9	9.4	1.0	30.6	30.9	35.1	3.4	171.18***	.447
Scenario 3: Theft from crime scene	1.0	3.8	60.0	35.2	0.8	1.4	38.8	58.9	48.86***	.238
Scenario 4: Auto-body shop 5% kickback	18.9	20.5	53.4	7.2	7.2	8.9	49.7	34.2	121.93***	.376
Scenario 5: Supervisor	18.9	35.8	40.8	4.6	18.6	29.3	42.3	9.9	11.38*	.115
Scenario 6: Cover-up of police DUI accident	13.3	39.0	41.7	6.0	12.3	20.4	55.5	11.8	39.72***	.215

$* p < .05; ** p < .01; *** p < .001$

the 2016 respondents were also marginally less likely to say that they would not report than the 1996 respondents were (Table 4).

Fourth, we analyze the respondents' views about appropriate discipline (Table 5). There was only one scenario in 1996 in which the majority of the respondents thought that no discipline was appropriate (Scenario 2: Gifts from Merchants; Table 5). There was no such scenario in 2016, although the percent of the respondents who said that such behavior should not be disciplined is a strong minority (about 30%; Table 5). While the respondents thought that some discipline should be appropriate for almost all behaviors described in the scenarios, with one exception (Scenario 3 for 2016 respondents), the majority of the respondents in both 1996 and 2016 did not think that dismissal should be the appropriate choice for the behaviors described in any of the scenarios.

In a nutshell, there were statistically significant and large differences in all six scenarios (Table 5), with the 2016 respondents expressing to a larger extent than the 1996 respondents that somewhat harsher discipline would be more appropriate. However, a more detailed inquiry provides a more complex and nuanced picture. In the three identical scenarios (Scenario 1: Bribe

from Speeding Motorist; Scenario 4: Auto-Body 5% Kickback; Scenario 6: Cover-Up of Police DUI), the 2016 respondents were more likely to advocate for harsher discipline, particularly dismissal than the 1996 respondents were (Table 5). In some of these scenarios, such as Scenario 4 (Auto-Body 5% Kickback), the differences were quite large: while only 7% of the 1996 respondents thought that dismissing a police officer who engaged in a kickback should merit dismissal, 34% of the 2016 respondents thought the same (Table 5). In sum, the 2016 respondents were less likely than the 1996 respondents to perceive that no discipline or milder discipline would be appropriate for the behaviors described in the identical scenarios.

In the case of three modified scenarios (Scenario 2: Gifts from Merchants; Scenario 3: Theft from Crime Scene; Scenario 5: Supervisor), the situation was not as straightforward. In particular, in the scenario describing the acceptance of gratuities (Scenario 2: Gifts from Merchants), the differences were not in the dismissal side of the scale, but on the opposite end. While about three-quarters (74.7%) of the 1996 respondents thought that the police officer who accepts gratuities should not be disciplined, this view was shared by only about one-third (30.6%) of the

Table 6 Respondents' views of police officer estimates of seriousness

	1996 Sample		2016 Sample			
	Mean	Rank	Mean	Rank	Difference	T-test
Scenario 1: Bribe from speeding motorist	2.57	3	2.48	2	.08	.983
Scenario 2: Gifts from merchants	1.62	1	2.18	1	−.56	−8.249***
Scenario 3: Theft from crime scene	3.59	6	3.51	6	.08	.996
Scenario 4: Auto-body shop 5% kickback	2.60	4	2.91	5	−.31	−4.001***
Scenario 5: Supervisor	2.97	5	2.57	3	.40	3.705***
Scenario 6: Cover-up of police DUI accident	2.50	2	2.58	4	−.08	−.998

* $p < .05$; ** $p < .01$; *** $p < .001$

2016 respondents (Table 5). On the other hand, the discourse regarding appropriate discipline for an opportunistic theft (Scenario 3: Theft from Crime Scene) was in the domain of dismissal. Whereas the majority of the 2016 respondents (58.9%) thought that a police officer who steals from a crime scene should be fired, only about one-third (35.2%) of the 1996 respondents shared this view (Table 5). Finally, the differences in Scenario 5 (Supervisor) were spread out across both reprimand and dismissal. Regardless, the 2016 respondents seemed less likely to advocate for reprimand and were more likely to advocate for a more severe discipline, including dismissal (Table 5).

Differences in Public Opinion About the Police

Our interest lies not only in exploring how public views of police corruption have changed over time, but also in studying changes in how they perceive that police view police corruption. To that end, several questions in the questionnaire asked the respondents to assess how police officers would evaluate police corruption. These questions target perceived police officers' estimates of seriousness and willingness to report, as well as the respondents' perceptions of the potential discipline that police would mete out for such violations.

First, we explore the respondents' assessments of police officers' evaluations of misconduct seriousness (Table 6). The results show that there were statistically significant differences between

the 1996 respondents' assessments of police officers' evaluations of seriousness and the 2016 respondents' assessments in about one-half of the scenarios (Table 6). Out of these differences, however, the only large and substantively important difference arose in connection with Scenario 2. Regardless of whether scenarios involve no differences or statistically significant differences between the two samples, there was one common theme across the two samples: the respondents did not perceive that police officers would evaluate these behaviors as very serious (in only one scenario out of six featured the mean value above 3.0, the mid-point of the scale; Table 6).

Among the three identical scenarios (Scenario 1: Bribe from Speeding Motorist; Scenario 4: Auto-Body 5% Kickback; Scenario 6: Cover-Up of Police DUI), there was only one scenario (Scenario 4: Auto-Body 5% Kickback) with statistically significant differences. The 2016 respondents were more likely to estimate that police officers would evaluate the acceptance of a kickback as a serious form of misconduct than the 1996 respondents were (Table 6). The perceived police evaluations of seriousness were very similar for the other two scenarios (Table 6).

The situation with the three modified scenarios (Scenario 2: Gifts from Merchants; Scenario 3: Theft from Crime Scene; Scenario 5: Supervisor) is more complicated. When confronted with the scenario describing the acceptance of gratuities (Scenario 2: Gifts from Merchants), the 1996 respondents were more likely to assess that police officers would not evaluate this behavior as a serious form of misconduct than the 2016 respondents were. On the

Table 7 Respondents' views of police officer estimates of willingness to report

	1996 Sample		2016 Sample			
	Mean	Rank	Mean	Rank	Difference	T-test
Scenario 1: Bribe from speeding motorist	2.06	3	1.96	4	.10	1.272
Scenario 2: Gifts from merchants	1.45	1	1.59	1	−.14	−2.533*
Scenario 3: Theft from crime scene	2.97	6	2.73	6	.24	2.910*
Scenario 4: Auto-body shop 5% kickback	2.23	5	2.40	5	−.17	−2.295*
Scenario 5: Supervisor	2.17	4	1.91	3	.26	3.407*
Scenario 6: Cover-up of police DUI accident	1.81	2	1.83	2	.02	−.220

$* p < .05$; $** p < .01$; $*** p < .001$

Table 8 Respondents' views about expected discipline

	1996 Sample				2016 Sample					
	None (%)	Rep. (%)	Other (%)	Dismissal (%)	None (%)	Rep. (%)	Other (%)	Dismissal (%)	Chi-square	Phi
Scenario 1: Bribe from speeding motorist	14.9	26.4	50.5	8.2	25.3	27.0	36.4	11.4	23.155***	.165
Scenario 2: Gifts from merchants	74.0	16.1	9.3	0.6	59.9	25.1	13.0	1.9	20.533***	.154
Scenario 3: Theft from crime scene	4.4	12.3	59.1	24.2	10.3	17.3	44.7	27.7	23.741***	.166
Scenario 4: Auto-body shop 5% kickback	25.9	26.5	42.5	5.0	24.6	25.8	37.3	12.3	15.562**	.135
Scenario 5: Supervisor	44.9	29.2	22.7	3.2	51.7	25.1	20.9	2.2	4.213	.070
Scenario 6: Cover-up of police DUI accident	31.6	32.0	33.4	3.0	41.8	25.8	28.0	4.4	12.121**	.118

$* p < .05$; $** p < .01$; $*** p < .001$

other hand, the 1996 respondents were more likely to state that police officers would evaluate a case of internal corruption involving a supervisor (Scenario 5: Supervisor) as more serious than the 2016 respondents were (Table 6). Finally, there were no statistically significant differences in regard to the scenario describing an opportunistic theft (Scenario 3: Theft from Crime Scene).

Second, we also focused on the respondents' assessments of the code of silence among the police (Table 7). Although we found statistically significant differences in the majority of the scenarios (four out of six or 67%), they are not large and substantively important. The means for both samples indicate that the respondents estimated

that the code of silence would cover these behaviors (the mean values are all below the mid-point of 3). Furthermore, the direction of the differences is unclear. In particular, in about one-half of these scenarios with differences, the 2016 respondents were more likely to perceive that the code was weaker than the 1996 respondents were, while in the other one-half of the scenarios, it was *vice versa* (Table 7).

In the three identical scenarios (Scenario 1: Bribe from Speeding Motorist; Scenario 4: Auto-Body 5% Kickback; Scenario 6: Cover-Up of Police DUI), we found no statistically significant differences between the two samples in their estimates of the code of silence. In the only scenario with differences (Scenario 4: Auto-Body 5% Kickback), albeit not very large, the 1996 respondents were more likely to say that the police code of silence would protect the acceptance of a kickback than the 2016 respondents were (Table 7).

There were statistically significant differences in all three modified scenarios (Scenario 2: Gifts from Merchants; Scenario 3: Theft from Crime Scene; Scenario 5: Supervisor). While these differences are statistically significant, they are not very large. The 1996 respondents were more likely to anticipate a stronger code of silence than the 2016 respondents were in only one scenario (Scenario 2: Gifts from Merchants). By contrast, in the other two scenarios, the 1996 respondents were more likely to anticipate that the code would be less likely to protect such behavior than the 2016 respondents were (Table 7).

Third, we explored the respondents' perceptions about the police disciplinary environments (Table 8). There are statistically significant differences in the overwhelming majority of scenarios (five out of six or 83%, Table 8), and in about one-half of them, the 2016 respondents expected more serious discipline and in just about one-half of them, the 1996 respondents expected more serious discipline (Table 8).

The common features across the two samples imply that dismissal is not the discipline that the respondents in either sample expected that the police would mete out for any of these behaviors (Table 8). Even in the scenario evaluated to be the most likely to result in a dismissal (Scenario 3: Theft from Crime Scene), only about one-quarter of the respondents in both samples expected it (Table 8). In fact, the majority of the respondents

in both samples either expected no discipline or discipline not more serious than a reprimand in the majority of the scenarios (four out of six scenarios for the 1996 sample and four to five out of six scenarios for the 2016 sample; Table 8).

In the three identical scenarios (Scenario 1: Bribe from Speeding Motorist; Scenario 4: Auto-Body 5% Kickback; Scenario 6: Cover-Up of Police DUI), the 2016 respondents either expected harsher discipline, such as dismissal in one scenario (Scenario 4: Auto-Body 5% Kickback), or are more likely to expect any discipline (Scenario 1: Bribe from Speeding Motorist). On the other hand, the 2016 respondents were more likely to expect no discipline for a cover-up of police DUI accident (Scenario 6) than the 1996 respondents were (41.8% v. 31.6%, Table 8).

In the case of three modified scenarios (Scenario 2: Gifts from Merchants; Scenario 3: Theft from Crime Scene; Scenario 5: Supervisor), the results are split. In one scenario (Scenario 5: Supervisor), there were no statistically significant differences at all. In another scenario (Scenario 2: Gifts from Merchants), the 2016 respondents were more likely to expect some discipline than the 1996 respondents were, while in the remaining modified scenario (Scenario 3: Theft from Crime Scene), the 2016 respondents were more likely to expect no discipline or just a reprimand than the 1996 respondents were (Table 8).

Differences in Differences

In addition, our plan was also to compare whether there are any differences across time in the differ-

Table 9 Respondents' own estimates and their views of police officer estimates of seriousness (1996 sample)

	Own		Police officer			
	Mean	Rank	Mean	Rank	Difference	T-test
Scenario 1: Bribe from speeding motorist	3.89	5	2.57	3	1.32	19.447***
Scenario 2: Gifts from merchants	1.83	1	1.62	1	.208	4.366***
Scenario 3: Theft from crime scene	4.57	6	3.59	6	.974	18.209***
Scenario 4: Auto-body shop 5% kickback	3.41	2	2.60	4	.809	14.752***
Scenario 5: Supervisor	3.71	4	2.97	5	.732	12.758***
Scenario 6: Cover-up of police DUI accident	3.45	3	2.50	2	.948	15.841***

$* p < .05; ** p < .01; *** p < .001$

Table 10 Respondents' own estimates and their views of police officer estimates of seriousness (2016 sample)

	Own		Police officer			
	Mean	Rank	Mean	Rank	Difference	T-test
Scenario 1: Bribe from speeding motorist	3.93	4	2.48	2	1.442	19.120***
Scenario 2: Gifts from merchants	2.74	1	2.18	1	.556	7.012***
Scenario 3: Theft from crime scene	4.66	6	3.51	6	1.144	18.442***
Scenario 4: Auto-body shop 5% kickback	4.15	5	2.91	5	1.235	18.615***
Scenario 5: Supervisor	3.74	2	2.57	3	1.177	10.465***
Scenario 6: Cover-up of police DUI accident	3.83	3	2.58	4	1.253	17.493***

$* p < .05; ** p < .01; *** p < .001$

Table 11 Respondents' views about appropriate and expected discipline (1996 sample)

	Appropriate discipline				Expected discipline					
	None (%)	Rep. (%)	Other (%)	Dismissal (%)	None (%)	Rep. (%)	Other (%)	Dismissal (%)	Chi-square	Phi
Scenario 1: Bribe from speeding motorist	2.4 17.7	15.3	70.9	11.4	14.9 41.3	26.4	50.5	8.2	127.44*** Difference: 23.6%	.504
Scenario 2: Gifts from merchants	74.7 89.6	14.9	9.4	1.0	74.0 90.1	16.1	9.3	0.6	314.34*** Difference: 0.5%	.792
Scenario 3: Theft from crime scene	1.0	3.8	60.0 35.2	35.2	4.4	12.3	59.1 24.2	24.2	178.71*** Difference: 11.3%	.596
Scenario 4: Auto-body shop 5% kickback	18.9 39.4	20.5	53.4	7.2	25.9 52.4	26.5	42.5	5.0	360.17*** Difference: 13.0%	.849
Scenario 5: Supervisor	18.9 54.7	35.8	40.8	4.6	44.9 74.1	29.2	22.7	3.2	208.32*** Difference: 19.4%	.644
Scenario 6: Cover-up of police DUI accident	13.3 52.3	39.0	41.7	6.0	31.6 63.6	32.0	33.4	3.0	288.33*** Difference: 11.3%	.758

$* p < .05; ** p < .01; *** p < .001$

ences between public and public assessment of police views on police corruption (i.e., comparing their own views with their estimates of police officers' views). We explored these differences in differences using three measures: seriousness, discipline, and willingness to report. At the outset, we expected that the respondents' own views would be more "positive"—indicating a higher degree of integrity—than the views they would expect police officers to have. The rationale is based on self-serving bias, that is, a psychological phenomenon that leads to us evaluate our own conduct or performance more positively than those of others.

First, a comparison of seriousness evaluations for each sample showed identical results: as expected, in each of the six scenarios, in both samples, the respondents' own evaluation of seriousness significantly exceeded their evaluations of the seriousness with which police officers would view the respective scenarios (Tables 9 and 10). The only scenario with statistically significant, albeit moderate differences was Scenario 2 (Gifts from Merchants). Some scenarios generated smaller differences than others. For example, the difference of the means between own and estimated police officers' estimates of seriousness is the smallest (.208 in 1996 and .556 in 2016) for

Table 12 Respondents' views about appropriate and expected discipline (2016 sample)

	Appropriate discipline				Expected discipline					
	None (%)	Rep. (%)	Other (%)	Dismissal (%)	None (%)	Rep. (%)	Other (%)	Dismissal (%)	Chi-square	Phi
Scenario 1: Bribe from speeding motorist	7.1 16.8	9.7	57.7	25.4	25.3 52.3	27.0	36.4	11.4	138.55*** Difference: 35.5%	.631
Scenario 2: Gifts from merchants	30.6 61.5	30.9	35.1	3.4	59.9 85.0	25.1	13.0	1.9	43.05*** Difference: 23.5%	.348
Scenario 3: Theft from crime scene	0.8	1.4	38.8	58.9 58.9	10.3	17.3	44.7	27.7 27.7	98.10*** Difference: 31.2%	.526
Scenario 4: Auto-body shop 5% kickback	7.2 16.1	8.9	49.7	34.2	24.6 50.4	25.8	37.3	12.3	167.54*** Difference: 34.3%	.396
Scenario 5: Supervisor	18.6 47.9	29.3	42.3	9.9	51.7 76.8	25.1	20.9	2.2	100.70*** Difference: 28.9%	.534
Scenario 6: Cover-up of police DUI accident	12.3 32.7	20.4	55.5	11.8	41.8 67.6	25.8	28.0	4.4	150.32*** Difference: 34.9%	.650

$* p < .05;$ $** p < .01;$ $*** p < .001$

the scenario describing the acceptance of gratuities (Scenario 2: Gifts from Merchants), while it is the largest (1.32 in 1996 and 1.44 in 2016) for the scenario describing the acceptance of a bribe from a motorist caught speeding (Scenario 1: Bribe from Speeding Motorist; Tables 9 and 10).

When we explored the differences between the two samples (i.e., differences in differences), we noticed that the differences between own and estimated police officer views increased over time for each and every scenario (i.e., the difference in means in 1996 v. the difference in means in 2016). In particular, the differences in differences were the smallest, about .12 to .20 (Tables 9 and 10), for two most serious scenarios (Scenario 1: Bribe from Speeding Motorist; Scenario 3: Theft from Crime Scene). On the other hand, the differences in differences were the largest (.45) for the scenario of internal corruption involving a supervisor (Scenario 5: Supervisor). The remaining three scenarios (Scenario 2: Gifts from Merchants; Scenario 4: Auto-Body 5% Kickback; Scenario 6: Cover-Up of Police DUI) featured differences of about .30 to .35 (Tables 9 and 10).

Second, a comparison of the views about appropriate and expected discipline indicated very similar findings. Specifically, there were statistically significant differences in most of the scenarios (five out of six for 1996 and six out of six for 2016; Tables 11 and 12); as expected, the respondents in both samples thought that the appropriate discipline should be harsher than the discipline they expect the agency to mete out. In Scenario 3 (Theft from Crime Scene), we compared their views on dismissal, while in all other scenarios we compared their choices for mild, if any discipline (encompassing options of no discipline and reprimand merged together).

There was a substantial range in the mean differences between appropriate and expected discipline for each sample. For the 1996 sample, it ranged from as little as a 11% difference for Scenario 6 (Cover-Up for Police DUI Accident) and Scenario 3 (Theft from Crime Scene) to as much as a 23.6% difference for Scenario 1 (Bribe from Speeding Motorist; Table 11). On the other hand, the range was smaller for the 2016 sample. However, at the same time, most

Table 13 Respondents' own willingness to report and their views of police officer willingness to report (1996 sample)

	Own		Police officer			
	Mean	Rank	Mean	Rank	Difference	T-test
Scenario 1: Bribe from speeding motorist	2.77	5	2.06	3	.71	9.925***
Scenario 2: Gifts from merchants	1.40	1	1.45	1	−.05	−1.255
Scenario 3: Theft from crime scene	3.91	6	2.97	6	.94	14.275***
Scenario 4: Auto-body shop 5% kickback	2.62	4	2.23	5	.39	6.181***
Scenario 5: Supervisor	2.52	2	2.17	4	.35	5.658***
Scenario 6: Cover-up of police DUI accident	2.54	3	1.81	2	.73	12.096***

$*p < .05; **p < .01; ***p < .001$

Table 14 Respondents' own willingness to report and their views of police officer willingness to report (2016 sample)

	Own		Police officer			
	Mean	Rank	Mean	Rank	Difference	T-test
Scenario 1: Bribe from speeding motorist	3.16	3	1.96	4	1.20	15.018***
Scenario 2: Gifts from merchants	1.94	1	1.59	1	.35	4.935***
Scenario 3: Theft from crime scene	4.01	6	2.73	6	1.28	15.378***
Scenario 4: Auto-body shop 5% kickback	3.53	5	2.40	5	1.13	14.670***
Scenario 5: Supervisor	2.70	2	1.91	3	.79	10.175***
Scenario 6: Cover-up of police DUI accident	3.18	4	1.83	2	1.35	17.177***

$*p < .05; **p < .01; ***p < .001$

of the differences between the appropriate and expected discipline were larger, in excess of 30% (Table 12).

Differences in differences between the views about appropriate and expected discipline increased over time for all scenarios (i.e., the difference in means in 1996 v. the difference in means in 2016). Specifically, the difference in difference was the smallest for the scenario describing a case of internal corruption involving a supervisor (Scenario 5: Supervisor), while it was the largest for the scenario describing a police DUI cover-up (Scenario 6: Cover-Up of Police DUI). A common feature is that, regardless of whether it was an identical or modified scenario, compared to the 1996 respondents, the 2016 respondents viewed that the police agencies were more likely to mete out discipline they would perceive to be too lenient compared to the discipline they thought was appropriate (Tables 11 and 12).

Third, a comparison of own and estimated police officer willingness to report showed similar results for the two samples. In particular, the overwhelming majority of the scenarios showed statistically significant and large differences (five out of six scenarios for 1996 and six out of six scenarios for 2016; Tables 13 and 14). In all scenarios with statistically significant differences, respondents perceived that police officers would be more likely to stick to the code of silence than the respondents themselves would (Tables 13 and 14). There was substantial variation in the size of the differences, from as little as .35 for Scenario 5 in 1996 and Scenario 2 in 2016, to as much as .94 for Scenario 3 in 1996 and 1.35 for Scenario 6 in 2016. The range of differences was larger in 2016 than it was in 1996. In particular, the largest difference between own and estimated police officer willingness to report was exactly 1 in 2016 (difference in means of .35 for Scenario 2 v. 1.35 for Scenario 6; Table 14) and only .35 in 1996 (difference in means of .35 for Scenario 5 v. .94 for Scenario 3; Table 13).

When we explored the differences between the two samples (i.e., differences in differences), we noticed that the differences between own and estimated police officer adherence to the code of silence increased over time for all scenarios (i.e., the difference in means in 1996 v. the difference in means in 2016). In particular, the differences in differences were the smallest for the most serious scenarios (Scenario 3: Theft from Crime Scene) and were only about .35 (Tables 13 and 14). Differences in differences were the largest (.85) for the scenario describing another serious form of corruption—a kickback (Scenario 4: Auto-Body 5% Kickback). As a rule, it seems that the differences in differences were larger for identical scenarios (Scenario 1: Bribe from Speeding Motorist; Scenario 4: Auto-Body 5% Kickback; Scenario 6: Cover-Up of Police DUI) than for the modified scenarios (Scenario 2: Gifts from Merchants; Scenario 3: Theft from Crime Scene; Scenario 5: Supervisor). Regardless of whether it was an identical or modified scenario, their common feature is that, compared to the 1996 respondents, the 2016 respondents viewed police officers as more likely to support the code of silence than they would support the code themselves.

Conclusion

Croatia's path toward democracy and democratic policing has been complex (Kutnjak Ivković 2004a). Corruption was and remains one of its serious challenges. Although various indicators suggest that the situation has improved in the 2010s compared to the mid-1990s, the progress in dealing with corruption has been only partial and it does not seem to continue at the same rate of speed.

We have used the police integrity methodology to assess changes in the public views of police corruption and the police. Two surveys of the Croatian college students, spread two decades apart, provided an opportunity to explore the degree to which respondents' evaluations of corruption seriousness, views about appropriate discipline, and willingness to report misconduct may have changed over time.

In a nutshell, our results indicate that the college students who evaluated police corruption in 2016 had somewhat different views than the college students who did the same in 1996. The differences in the views were not equally distributed across all measures of police corruption. The largest and strongest divergence of opinions surfaced in regard to the views of appropriate discipline for misconduct and the greatest convergence of opinions was related to the respondents' evaluations of seriousness.

A comparison of seriousness assessments over time yielded statistically significant differences in the majority of the scenarios, but those differences were large and substantively important in only two scenarios. College students evaluated misconduct as serious both in 1996 and 2016. The fact that evaluations of seriousness are more similar than dissimilar is not really surprising. Prior research on the Croatian college students, spanning a 5-year period from 1996 to 2001, concluded that the evaluations of seriousness were very similar (Kutnjak Ivković et al. 2004, p. 307). The only exception was a scenario describing the use of excessive force, perceived as much more serious in 2001 than in 1996 (Kutnjak Ivković et al. 2004, p. 307). The authors attributed that change to the changes in legal regulation of the police implemented at the time (Kutnjak Ivković et al. 2004, p. 307).

The conclusions we drew on the basis of student survey results—largely the absence of many large differences in the public evaluations of corruption—mirror those evaluating changes in the evaluation of corruption seriousness provided by the police (Kutnjak Ivković 2009). Rather, the results of the comparison across two samples of police officers revealed that the same types of corruption were perceived as the most serious and the least serious (Kutnjak Ivković 2009). Kutnjak Ivković (2009) concluded that this lack of substantial differences probably derived from the common understanding of police misconduct seriousness.

Our results show large temporal differences in the respondents' familiarity with official rules in a substantial proportion of scenarios. For most of them, the students surveyed in 2016 were more likely to label the described behaviors as rule violations than the students surveyed in 1996 were. A parallel survey of police officers covering 13 years, 1995–2008/2009, pointed toward a different set of conclusions; the results suggested the presence of many similarities across scenarios (Kutnjak Ivković 2009) and more mixed results. Specifically, in several scenarios, the police officers surveyed in 2008/2009 were somewhat more likely to evaluate behaviors as rule violations, while in other scenarios, police officers surveyed in 1995 were more likely to recognize them as rule violations.

Some of the largest differences we encountered between the two student samples related to their perceptions of appropriate discipline. Statistically significant and large differences appeared in each and every scenario, with the 2016 respondents supporting harsher discipline. The 2016 respondents seemed less likely to advocate for no discipline or only a reprimand and were more likely to advocate for a more severe discipline, including dismissal. These results fit well with the existing study of the change in the police views over time (Kutnjak Ivković 2009). Compared to their colleagues surveyed in 1995, police officers surveyed in 2008/2009 both supported and also expected more severe discipline. While dismissal was a preferred discipline for only one scenario in 1995, it was a preferred discipline for six scenarios in 2008/2009 (Kutnjak Ivković 2009). One of the potential explanations for such a large change over time, documented for both police offices and students, is a gradual disappearance of the war-related mentality, in accordance with which only the most serious misconduct was disciplined. Indeed, available statistical data on the actual disciplinary processes support this view. Based on the disciplinary data from 1992 to 1999, we can conclude that the more serious charges constituted a larger proportion of the disciplinary cases at the beginning of the period (thus suggesting that only the most serious cases were disciplined), while the less serious

charges have become more predominant toward the end of the period as the "war-is-over" mentality started to develop (Kutnjak Ivković 2004a).

Lastly, we also examined the respondents' willingness to report misconduct, a critical step in a society resolved to deal with corruption. The results show large differences in about one-half of the scenarios, suggesting that the code of silence among college students was not as strong in 2016 as it was in 1996. These findings mirror the results of a comparable study on police officers (Kutnjak Ivković 2009) that reported a weakening of the code of silence among police officers. While the close camaraderie among the police, developed during the war and weakening over time since, was a compelling explanation for the differences in police estimates of the code of silence, the same argument could not be used to explain the differences in the public views of the code. The more relevant argument would likely rely on the changes in the society at large. In other words, the weakening of the code of silence among college students could be taken as a positive effect of the societal resolve to fight corruption.

Public views of the police have changed to a certain degree as well. While the changes in the respondents' own views are relatively straightforward, changes in their views about the police are more complex. In some cases, the 1996 respondents evaluated the police as perceiving scenarios as more serious, more likely to result in a harsher discipline, and more willing to report. On the other hand, in other cases, the 2016 respondents were the ones who thought that the police would evaluate the scenarios as more serious, expect harsher discipline, and would be more willing to report. The absence of clear-cut changes is not particularly surprising in the Croatian conditions. When the society sends mixed messages about corruption and the police—stricter laws and emphasis on the reform, yet top police administrators and politicians are largely not disciplined and/or punished for corruption—it is by no means surprising that there is no systematic improvement in the way citizens evaluate the police.

References

Bjerregaard, B., & Lord, V. B. (2004). An examination of the ethical and value orientation of criminal justice students. *Police Quarterly, 7*(2), 262–284.

Code of Criminal Procedure. (1997). Zagreb, Croatia: Narodne novine 110/97.

Code of Criminal Procedure. (2008). Zagreb, Croatia: Narodne novine 152/08.

Criminal Code. (1997). Zagreb, Croatia: Narodne novine 110/97.

Derenčinović, D. (2000). *Kaznenopravni sadrzaji u suprotstavljanju korupciji.* Doctoral Dissertation, University of Zagreb, Zagreb, Croatia.

Frič, P., & Walek C. (2001). *Crossing the Thin Blue Line.* Prague: Prague, Czech Republic: Transparency International CR.

Khechumyan, A., & Kutnjak Ivković, S. (2015). Police integrity in Armenia. In S. Kutnjak Ivković & M. Haberfeld (Eds.), *Police integrity across the world.* New York: Springer.

Klockars, C., & Kutnjak Ivković, S. (1995). A Cross-Cultural Study of Police Corruption. The 47th Annual Meeting of the American Society of Criminology, Boston, Massachusetts, November 1995.

Klockars, C. B., & Kutnjak Ivković, S. (1999). The measurement of police delinquency. In W. Laufer & F. Adler (Eds.), *The criminology of criminal Law. Advances in criminological theory* (Vol. 8, pp. 87–106). Transaction: New Brunswick, NJ.

Klockars, C. B., & Kutnjak Ivković, S. (2004). Measuring police integrity. In A. R. Piquero, J. R. Greene, & M. J. Hickman (Eds.), *Police integrity and ethics.* Belmont, CA: Wadsworth Publishing.

Klockars, C. B., Kutnjak Ivković, S., Harver, W. E., & Haberfeld, M. R.. (1997). *The measurement of police integrity.* Final report submitted to the U.S. Department of Justice, Office of Justice Programs, National Institute of Justice.

Klockars, C. B., Haberfeld, M. R., Kutnjak Ivković, S., & Uydess, A. (2001). A minimum requirement for police corruption. In R. A. Silverman, T. P. Thornberry, B. Cohen, & B. Krisberg (Eds.), *Crime and justice at the millennium: Essays by and in honor of Marvin E. Wolfgang.* New York: Springer.

Klockars, C. B., Kutnjak Ivković, S., & Haberfeld, M. R. (2006). *Enhancing police integrity.* New York: Springer.

Klockars, C. B., Kutnjak Ivković, S., & M. R. Haberfeld (Eds.). (2004). *The Contours of Police Integrity.* Newbury Park, CA: Sage Publication.

Kutnjak Ivković, S. (2000). Challenges of Policing Democracies: The Croatian Experience. In Das, D. and O. Marenin (Eds.). *Challenges of Policing Democracies: A World Perspective* (pp. 45–85). Newark, NJ: Gordon and Breach Publishers.

Kutnjak Ivković, S. (2004). Evaluating the seriousness of police misconduct: A cross-cultural comparison of police officer and citizen views. *International Criminal Justice Review, 14*, 25–48.

Kutnjak Ivković, S. (2004a). Distinct and different: Transformation of the Croatian police. In M. Caparini & O. Marenin (Eds.), *Transforming police in Central and Eastern Europe.* Muenster, Germany/Somerset, NJ: Lit Verlag/Transaction Publishers.

Kutnjak Ivković, S. (2008). A comparative study of public support for the police. *International Criminal Justice Review, 18*(4), 406–434.

Kutnjak Ivković, S. (2009). The Croatian police, police integrity, and transition toward democratic policing. *Policing: An International Journal of Police Strategies and Management, 32*(3), 459–488.

Kutnjak Ivković, S. (2015). Police integrity in Croatia. In S. Kutnjak Ivković & M. Haberfeld (Eds.), *Police integrity across the world.* New York: Springer.

Kutnjak Ivković, S., & Haberfeld M. R., (Eds.) (2015). *Police Integrity across the World.* New York; Springer.

Kutnjak Ivković, S., & Klockars, C. B. (2002). Public views about police corruption: The case of Croatia. In M. Pagon (Ed.), *Policing in Central and Eastern Europe: Deviance, violence, and victimization* (pp. 283–296). College of Police and Security Studies: Ljubljana, Slovenia.

Kutnjak Ivković, S., & Sauerman, A. (2012). The Code of silence: Revisiting South African police integrity. *South African Crime Quarterly, 40*(June), 15–24.

Kutnjak Ivković, S., Cajner-Mraović, I., Klockars, C. B., & Ivanusec, D. (2002a). Public perceptions about police misconduct in Croatia. In M. Pagon (Ed.), *Policing in central and Eastern Europe: Deviance, violence, and victimization* (pp. 311–328). College of Police and Security Studies: Ljubljana, Slovenia.

Kutnjak Ivković, S., Pagon, M., Klockars, C. B., & Lobnikar, B. (2002b). A comparative view of public perceptions of police corruption. In M. Pagon (Ed.), *Policing in Central and Eastern Europe: Deviance, violence, and victimization* (pp. 297–310). College of Police and Security Studies: Ljubljana, Slovenia.

Kutnjak Ivković, S., Cajner-Mraović, I., & Ivanusec, D. (2004). The measurement of seriousness of police corruption. In G. Mesko, M. Pagon, & G. Dobovsek (Eds.), *Dilemmas of contemporary criminal justice* (pp. 300–311). Ljubljana, Slovenia: Faculty of Criminal Justice, University of Maribor.

Meyer, M., Steyn, J., & Gopal, N. (2013). Exploring the public parameter of police integrity. *Policing: An International Journal of Police Strategies and Management, 36*(1), 140–156.

Pagon, M., Kutnjak Ivković, S., & Lobnikar, B. (2000). Police integrity and attitudes toward police corruption: A comparison between the police and the public. In M. Pagon (Ed.), *Policing in Central and Eastern Europe: Ethics, integrity, and human rights* (pp. 383–396). College of Police and Security Studies: Ljubljana, Slovenia.

Police Law. (2000). Zagreb, Croatia: Narodne novine 129/01.

Police Law. (2011). Zagreb, Croatia: Narodne novine 34/11.

Roebuck, J. B., & Barker, T. (1974). A typology of police corruption. *Social Problems, 21*, 423–437.

Transparency International. (2008). *Global corruption barometer*. Available at http://archive.transparency.org/policy_research/surveys_indices/cpi/2008.

Transparency International. (2010). *Global corruption barometer*. Available at http://www.transparency.org/content/download/57371/917572/version/2/file/Barometer_2010_web

Transparency International. (2011). *Corruption Perceptions Index*. Available at http://www.transparency.org/policy_research/surveys_indices/cpi

Transparency International. (2016). *Corruption Perceptions Index*. Available at https://www.transparency.org/cpi2015/#results-table

UNODC. (2011). *Corruption in the Western Balkans: Bribery as experienced by the population*. Available at http://www.unodc.org/documents/data-and-analysis/statistics/corruption/Western_balkans_corruption_report_2011_web.pdf

The Effects of Ethics Training on Police Integrity

Filip Van Droogenbroeck, Bram Spruyt,
Sanja Kutnjak Ivković, and M. R. Haberfeld

Introduction

Police integrity is defined as "the normative inclination among police to resist temptations to abuse the rights and privileges of their occupation" (Klockars et al. 2006, p. 1). The definition implies that police integrity is a belief or views held by the police rather than the actual behavior (Klockars et al. 2006). In other words, the emphasis in this definition is on the *inclination* to resist temptations, rather than the actual behavior. The expectation is that, because of the relation between police integrity and morality, police officers who evaluate something as morally wrong should also be more likely to behave in accordance with such beliefs, be it by reporting misconduct themselves or supporting discipline for police misconduct (Kutnjak Ivković 2015b). Indeed, Klockars et al. (2006, p. 2) argued that,

F. Van Droogenbroeck · B. Spruyt (✉)
Sociology Department, Vrije Universiteit Brussel,
Brussels, Belgium
e-mail: filip.van.droogenbroeck@vub.be;
bram.spruyt@vub.be

S. Kutnjak Ivković
Michigan State University, School of Criminal
Justice, East Lansing, MI, USA
e-mail: kutnjak@msu.edu

M. R. Haberfeld
John Jay College of Criminal Justice,
City University of New York,
New York, NY, USA
e-mail: makih@sprynet.com

"[j]ust as a belief in honesty inclines one to avoid lying and a belief in fidelity obliges one to be faithful, integrity requires not only a belief that certain behaviors are right or wrong but also actions that are in accord with those beliefs."

A police agency plays a critical role in shaping both police officers' attitudes and behavior. There are several different dimensions along which the police agency can do so. One such dimension is the way in which the official rules are created and communicated to the police officers (Klockars et al. 2000, 2004, 2006; Kutnjak Ivković 2015b). The so-called first dimension of the theory of police integrity (Klockars et al. 2000, 2004, 2006; Kutnjak Ivković 2015b) puts emphasis not only on the police agency's obligation to develop policies and formal rules, but also on the police agency's communication of these rules and their rationale to the police officers. Another dimension is the creation of organizational activities that permit the detection, investigation, and discipline of police misconduct (Klockars et al. 2000, 2004, 2006; Kutnjak Ivković 2015b). This second dimension of the theory of police integrity (Klockars et al. 2000, 2004, 2006; Kutnjak Ivković 2015b) discusses the police agency's obligation to create and maintain a range of such activities, including internal investigations, inspections, integrity testing, review of citizen complaints, and application of discipline. The third dimension incorporates the police agency's responsibility in circumscribing the code of silence (Klockars et al. 2000, 2004,

2006; Kutnjak Ivković 2015b). Thus, the third dimension of the theory of police integrity (Klockars et al. 2000, 2004, 2006; Kutnjak Ivković 2015b) focuses on the police agency's efforts at dealing with the informal prohibition in the police culture of reporting misconduct of fellow police officers (Klockars et al. 2000, 2004, 2006; Kutnjak Ivković 2015a, b).

Hence, one way in which a police agency can shape police officers' attitudes and behaviors is to engage in the implementation of the activities included in the first dimension of the theory—teaching and communicating the official rules and norms of the police agency to the police officers. This chapter explores whether police integrity can be taught or cultivated through a police integrity training. Specifically, we explore whether a 1-day training called the *Holocaust, Police, and Human Rights (HPM)* program has an impact on the police officers' responses to three types of police misconduct. This training takes place in the Holocaust Remembrance Museum in Belgium (Kazerne Dossin 2019), and is adapted to members of the Belgian federal police. The main focus of the training lies on teaching the participants the causes and mechanisms of group violence, while, at the same time, reminding them that police officers have individual responsibility to act when they witness misconduct. We investigate both the immediate and long-term effects of this training on evaluations of police integrity provided by 200 members of the Belgian police.

Training Police Integrity

Ethics Training

The goal of police training is to teach a specific method of performing a task or responding to a given situation. Training is focused on how to most effectively accomplish a task whenever a particular situation arises and usually involves two stages. First, prescribed procedures are presented and explained. Second, these procedures are practiced until they become second nature. Hence, training is experiential and goal-oriented.

The skills associated with most training programs include the ability to determine whether or not the circumstances warrant following a prescribed course of action, the physical and verbal skills associated with those actions, and the cognitive abilities needed to recall what steps should be followed and in what order for each of the situations covered in the training program (Timm and Christian 1991).

Ethics training, in most cases, is a standalone module that does not penetrate into all the other aspects of police work (e.g., Haberfeld 2018). Despite some proclamations that ethics are part of the overall departmental training, it is rather rare to see this theme being weaved into all the other training modules. This creates an artificial separation between the concepts of ethical policing and everyday police actions; ethics training remains very much peripheral to the entire training concept. This state of affairs is more indicative of police agencies with decentralized nature, like the United States, and less so in centralized police agencies (Haberfeld 2018).

While most of the decentralized nations vary immensely in their efforts to instill ethics training, resulting in no real mandatory standards, as Klockars et al. (2006) found in their integrity research, the centralized police agencies in other areas of the world have a more standardized approach. Research by Klockars et al. (2006) revealed that three municipal agencies have relied on different sources to provide the basic police training: while the Charlotte-Mecklenburg Police Department runs its own training academy, St. Petersburg Police Department sends its recruits to a regional training academy, and the Charleston Police Department relies on the state police academy. A common feature across these police agencies is that the police ethics is taught in separate modules that last a few hours. In fact, Klitzman (2015) found differences among a number of U.S. police academies in their integrity training sessions. Some of these differences were reflected to different levels of knowledge of the code of ethics. However, the study found almost no differences between the academies in the development pattern of recruits' moral reasoning skills which, according to Klitzman, points to the importance of the selection process that proceeds the training (2015). In other words, the relatively limited impact of ethics training on police officers may be partly explained by the police officers' held preexisting attitudes.

In decentralized countries, such as the United States, private consulting companies, such as the Blue Courage (2019), might offer modules that range in length and content based on the financial resources of a police agency. Such modules can range from a few hours to a few days (e.g., Blue Courage 2019). On the other hand, centralized police agencies, such as Croatia or Poland, provide the same training to all employees of their nationalized police agencies. In addition, the European Union Agency for Law Enforcement Training CEPOL offers modules that last between 4 and 6 days (European Union Agency for Law Enforcement Training—CEPOL 2019).

As the Czech National Police struggled with issues of economic corruption, especially within its traffic enforcement unit, Haberfeld (2002) has been invited to create an ethics training module. When the author introduced the training module to the police trainers and asked them to incorporate one ethical scenario into each of their basic academy training 33 modules, the trainers refused to engage in this exercise claiming that ethics cannot be possibly incorporated into all the other training modules, as it should be a standalone component (Haberfeld 2002). After an extensive debate, the basic training was eventually changed to incorporate this specific exercise (Haberfeld 2002). According to Jonstone (2017) who studied the Czech police years later, the Czech police still have problems with investigations of major cases of corruption.

In the Belgian context, which is the focus of this chapter, police officers can receive ethics training through two pathways. First, trainees receive ethics training during their general obligatory training in the police academies. Police academies are legally required to include a course on police integrity in their curriculum. The regulations specify the objectives of the ethics training. These include: becoming familiar with police integrity, the code of ethics, police misconduct, police organizational values and their

discretionary power (Maesschalck and De Schrijver 2015). Second, members of the police can choose ethics training programs as part of their continuing professional development. One of them is the Holocaust, Police, and Human rights training, which is the subject of this chapter.

Effect of Ethics Training on Attitudes and Behavior

Antrobus et al. (2019) found some limited positive effects of the training on both officer attitudes and actual on-the-job behavior. The evaluators' ratings of procedurally just behaviors in public interactions were generally higher for the experimental group in which officers received the training modules than the control group that was not exposed to the training (Antrobus et al. 2019). In their study of ethics training offered by the Australian police agencies, Prenzler and Ronken (2016) note that, in order for ethics training to be effective, it needs to clarify expectations and assist in managing ethical dilemmas, such as how to reject gratuities without causing offense. Research has also shown that attitudes toward certain behaviors can indeed be influenced and changed as a function of training (e.g., Conti and Nolan 2005). However, these changes, as a consequence of ethics training, are more likely to serve in restraining the professional vision of incoming officers and the traditional model of police officers as law enforcers rather than peace generators is reinforced (Conti and Nolan 2005).

In reality, the effects of training on police attitudes and behaviors are still quite under-researched as a topic; Skogan et al. (2015, p. 320) describe the state of affairs:

> We know virtually nothing about the short- or long-term effects associated with police training of any type. A committee established by the National Research Council to evaluate the state of policing in the United States found that there were "scarcely more than a handful of studies" on the effects of training, and that police training and education were being offered without scientific evidence of their likely effects. The panel concluded "[T]he committee cannot overstate the importance of

developing a comprehensive and scientifically rigorous program to learn what is and is not effective in the education and training of police officers" (Skogan and Frydl 2004, p. 154).

One of the critical answers related to the in-service training is whether police administrators can devise a module that will effectively change the officers' attitudes and behavior. The answer to this question is probably directly related to the type of misconduct (e.g., corruption for gain, noble cause corruption, conduct unbecoming, use of excessive force). Based on decades of research of police ethics, Caldero and his colleagues (Caldero 2014; Crank and Caldero 2004), concluded that, if police misconduct is a function of the lack of awareness (e.g., cultural sensitivity) and the lack of knowledge (e.g., familiarity with the official rules, incorrect use of technology, severity of the expected discipline), behavior is amenable to change through the in-service-training. On the other hand, if the misconduct is purely of the for-gain nature or intentionally done (e.g., theft at the crime scene, use of excessive force), it is probably not going to be influenced by the in-service efforts to the same degree.

However, training alone is but one component that may work toward the establishment of integrity in any police agency. The influence of training is strongly affected by the departments' recruitment, screening, and selection efforts that proceeded it and the socialization efforts by peers and superiors that follow it, as well as a variety of less obvious organizational, political, and economic factors (Klockars et al. 2006).

Measuring Police Integrity

Police Integrity Measurements

As police integrity is defined as the normative *inclination* to resist temptations (Klockars et al. 2000, 2004, 2006), a methodological approach seeking to measure police integrity empirically could focus on the assessments of police officers' *attitudes*, rather than their actual behavior. The benefit of such an approach is that police officers are more likely to agree to participate in the study

and do so truthfully. At the same time, police administrators are more likely to allow the survey to be carried out in their police agencies (see, e.g., Klockars et al. 2000).

To provide the tools that would enable an empirical measurement of police integrity, Klockars et al. (2000, 2004, 2006) have developed two questionnaires. The first questionnaire was developed in the mid-1990s (e.g., Klockars et al. 2000; Klockars and Kutnjak Ivković 2004) and the second questionnaire was developed in the late 1990s (e.g., Klockars et al. 2006). Both questionnaires are built on the same basic principles. First, the questionnaires inquire about the police officers' attitudes. Second, they include about a dozen or so short vignettes describing hypothetical examples of police misconduct. Third, the questionnaires greatly limit the number of demographic questions to minimize the chances of breaking anonymity.

The questionnaires contain short vignettes containing hypothetical examples of police misconduct. The examples are associated with the functions of a line officer walking the beat (Kutnjak Ivković 2015b). Klockars et al. (2006, p. 16) explained that, "[i]n designing the scenarios we sought to describe incidents that were not only plausible and common forms of police misconduct … but ones that were uncomplicated by details that might introduce ambiguity into either the interpretation of the behavior or the motive of the officer depicted in the scenario." At the same time, the selection of the scenarios is such that they are suitable to be used across modern, industrialized societies. Consequently, the questionnaire is amenable to comparative research.

The first questionnaire, developed in the mid-1990s, includes 11 scenarios, mostly describing examples of police corruption (e.g., Klockars and Kutnjak Ivković 2004; Klockars et al. 2000). The selection of the scenarios was based on the typology of police corruption by Roebuck and Barker (1974). Because it started as a project measuring the opposite of police corruption (Kutnjak Ivković 2015b), the first questionnaire—called the police corruption questionnaire—focuses on the resistance to temptations of primarily one category—illegal gain (Kutnjak Ivković 2015b).

The second questionnaire, developed in the late 1990s, also includes 11 scenarios, but, in addition to the police corruption scenarios, also contains scenarios describing the use of excessive force, planting of evidence, and other forms of police misconduct (e.g., Klockars et al. 2006). In that sense, the second questionnaire—called the police integrity questionnaire—is more encompassing and includes abuses motivated by a range of motives (see, e.g., Klockars et al. 2000, 2006).

To enable a comparison across the two questionnaires as a test-retest reliability measure, Klockars et al. (2006) kept the five scenarios from the first questionnaire describing a range of police corruption in the second questionnaire as well. While a few scenarios were identical, others were only slightly changed. The outline of the scenarios was very similar across the two versions of the questionnaire (e.g., theft from a crime scene), but specific details have changed (e.g., theft of a watch in the police corruption questionnaire and theft of a knife in the police integrity questionnaire).

Measuring Police Integrity over Time

Although both the police corruption questionnaire and the police integrity questionnaire have been available for over two decades and have been widely used by scholars across the world (for an overview, see Kutnjak Ivković 2015b; Kutnjak Ivković and Haberfeld 2019), our search of police integrity studies published in English revealed no longitudinal studies of police integrity. In other words, there were no existing studies that measured the effect of social, political, economic, or organizational changes on individual police officers' attitudes over time. In that sense, our study—a longitudinal study of police integrity—makes a unique contribution to the extant research on police integrity. While there were no longitudinal studies that we could find in our literature search, there were a few cross-sectional surveys collected over a period of time that relied on nationwide representative samples (Kutnjak Ivković and Klockars 2004; Kutnjak Ivković 2009, 2015a; Pagon and Lobnikar 2004;

Lobnikar and Meško 2015) or samples that constitute over 75% of the population (e.g., Klockars et al. 2006). Because of this methodological approach (i.e., a representative sample or a population), these studies provide an aggregate agency assessments and could be used as a measure of the degree to which police agency attitudes have changed over time. Such studies have been conducted in Croatia (Kutnjak Ivković 2009, 2015a; Kutnjak Ivković and Klockars 2004), Slovenia (Pagon and Lobnikar 2004; Lobnikar and Meško 2015), and the United States (Klockars et al. 2006).

There are two common features across these studies (Klockars et al. 2006; Kutnjak Ivković 2009, 2015a; Kutnjak Ivković and Klockars 2004; Lobnikar and Meško 2015; Pagon and Lobnikar 2004). First, the data were collected at two time periods, although the length of time between the two administrations of the survey ranged from 2 years (e.g., Klockars et al. 2006) to over a decade (e.g., Kutnjak Ivković 2009, 2015a; Lobnikar and Meško 2015; Pagon and Lobnikar 2004). Second, the police corruption questionnaire was used for the first administration of the survey and the police integrity questionnaire was used for the second administration of the survey. Because the two questionnaires overlap only partly, the long-term comparisons are limited to the five scenarios that are either identical or mildly modified in the second questionnaire.[1]

The police corruption questionnaire was distributed in the mid-1990s at the 30 U.S. police agencies (Klockars et al. 2000). However, as part of a larger study on enhancing police integrity (Klockars et al. 2006), the police integrity questionnaire was distributed in the late 1990s in only 3 out of the 30 police agencies (Charleston Police Department; Charlotte-Mecklenburg Police Department; St. Petersburg Police Department). The results showed that police officer views on police integrity in the Charleston Police

---

[1]In the police integrity questionnaire, two scenarios describing the acceptance of gratuities from the police corruption scenarios were merged into one. This is the only scenario out of the five scenarios that has been systematically altered.

Department and the Charlotte-Mecklenburg Police Department have not substantively changed over time and remained very similar to the views expressed a couple of years earlier (Klockars et al. 2006). On the other hand, there was a substantial change in the police officer views in the St. Petersburg Police Department, but only in one scenario—the scenario describing the acceptance of gratuities (Klockars et al. 2006). Klockars et al. (2006) indicated that such a change in views is not surprising, having in mind several recent events in the police agency that could have positively influenced police officer views about the acceptance of gratuities (e.g., the appointment of a new police chief who put more emphasis on discipline, inclusion of a question about the acceptance of gratuities posted on the recent sergeant's exam).

The two Croatian police surveys relied on representative samples of the Croatian police collected in 1995 (e.g., Kutnjak Ivković and Klockars 2004) and 2008 (e.g., Kutnjak Ivković 2009, 2015a). Unlike the U.S. study (Klockars et al. 2006), the longer passage of time in the Croatian study created more opportunities for substantial changes in the police officer views. Although the study did not compare the results of the two surveys using statistical tools, even a cursory exploration lead Kutnjak Ivković (2009) to conclude that the police and organizational cultures have changed: not only has the code of silence become weaker in the later period, but also police officers have started to expect harsher discipline to be meted out by police agencies. Such results should not surprising having in mind the fact that, during the 13 years that lapsed between the two surveys, the transformations of the society at large and the police in particular have been taking place (e.g., Kutnjak Ivković 2009).

While the authors of the two Slovenian studies did not directly compare the results (Pagon and Lobnikar 2004; Lobnikar and Meško 2015), the authors used the same measures (mean values) for the two administrations of the survey. Because the earlier study, conducted in the late 1990s (Pagon and Lobnikar 2004), utilized the police corruption questionnaire, and the later study,

conducted in the 2011 (Lobnikar and Meško 2015), utilized the police integrity questionnaire, there are only five scenarios suitable for the exploration over time. A comparison revealed that the assessments of misconduct seriousness and the respondents' expressed willingness to report were almost identical for the most serious form of police corruption (theft from a crime scene) described in the five scenarios. For the remaining three identical and/or very similar scenarios (kickback, internal corruption, and cover-up of police DUI), the respondents surveyed in 2011 evaluated these behaviors as somewhat more serious and were also more likely to say that they would report than the respondents surveyed in the late 1990s. However, the differences were not large and would probably not be considered to be of substantive importance. Finally, the views were the most dissimilar about the scenarios involving the acceptance of gratuities.[2] While it is possible that the Slovenian police have become less tolerant of the acceptance of gratuities, this large difference in the views can be potentially attributed to the fact that the scenario describing the acceptance of gratuities was the most dissimilar across the two versions of the questionnaire.

While these studies are useful because they offer interesting insights in how police agencies change at the aggregate level, they do not offer any information about how individual police officers' views change over time. To entice police officers to participate in the surveys and answer questions honestly, Klockars et al. (2000, 2004, 2006) kept the demographic questions to a minimum to avoid potential identification of police officers. However, the current longitudinal study went a step forward by measuring the same questions among the same respondents before and after they have attended a training in police integrity. In other words, this study is one of the first studies of police integrity using the Klockars

---

[2]The mean for seriousness evaluations by the respondents surveyed in 2011 was 1.64 points higher (3.64 v. 2.00) than it was in the late 1990s. Similarly, the mean for the respondents' willingness to report in the 2011 survey was 1.10 points higher (2.76 v. 1.66) than it was in the late 1990s.

et al. methodology (Klockars et al. 2006) that is able to describe *within subject* changes over time.

Methodology

Ethics Training

Kazerne Dossin is a Holocaust Remembrance Museum in the city of Mechelen, Belgium (Kazerne Dossin 2019). Its core mission is to cultivate insight into both the causes and the prevention of collective violence. The training uses the case of the Holocaust to draw participants' attention to timeless mechanisms of collective violence. Since 2014, the Museum organizes the Holocaust, Police and Human Rights (HPM) training as part of the learning trajectories it provides. In addition to the program for police officers, the Museum also includes tracks for secondary school pupils, journalists, and other groups.

The HPM training focuses on the members of the federal police of Belgium (see Kazerne Dossin 2019). The training lasts 1 day and includes a Museum visit, followed by a workshop focused on human rights and ethical awareness. The trainers are (former) police officers who have great experience with police work. The HPM-training has three central goals. First, during the visit and the workshop, a link is made between human rights violation during the Holocaust and the present-day events and situations in which human rights are violated. Second, there is a strong focus on the universal mechanisms behind group violence. Central are not so much the historical events in themselves, but the processes that can lead ordinary citizens to commit atrocities. This approach automatically directs attention to issues such as peer pressure, polarization, and the spiral of violence and dehumanization. Because the police have the monopoly on the legitimate right to use force, special attention is paid to their role in the Holocaust. Third, the training focuses on the individuals' willingness to act and the possibility of saying 'no' to injustice even in the most extreme situations.

The HPM training tries to create awareness among the police officers to: (1) enable people to continue to use their existing leverage in challenging circumstances and not blindly execute commands, and (2) teach participants the skills that would enable them to recognize and analyze ethical dilemmas and make a well-reasoned choice. In sum, the HPM training attempts to move away from classic 'deontology' courses and teaches police officers how to deal with difficult situations in which ethical dilemmas arise. In the broader spectrum of peace education programs the training can be regarded as a type of remembrance education (Spruyt et al. 2014).

Data

The data collection started on February 2017 and lasted until the end of December 2017. During this time period, 83 sessions took place. Police officers taking part in the training were asked to participate and to complete the first questionnaire prior to the start of the training (i.e., the pre-test). With a few exceptions, everyone took part in the pre-test. At the end of the pre-test, participants were asked whether they were prepared to participate in the subsequent studies. The post-test survey was administered at the day after the training. Finally, the follow-up survey was administered 1 month after the initial visit.

Only participants who provided a valid email address on the pre-test could participate in the post-test study and the follow-up study. A total of 1255 participants were surveyed during the pre-test. About one-half (52.7% or 661) provided a working e-mail address and stated that they were willing to participate in the follow-up studies. About one-half (48.6% or 321) of these respondents who stated that they would be willing to participate in the subsequent studies and provided their email addresses actually responded to the email invitation and participated in the second survey (post-test). Our response rate—48.6%—is exactly the same response rate that Nix et al. (2017) reported as the average response rate for police surveys distributed using other means (e.g., e-mail, online). Finally, out of the respondents who expressed willingness to participated in the future studies and shared their email with the research team, about one-third (33.7% or 231) participated in the third and last survey (i.e., the follow up). After the initial e-mail invitation to participate in the post-test or follow-up, a reminder was sent after 1 week for those who did not started yet and those who started but hadn't completed the survey yet. Taking into account the fact that respondents could not be contacted in any other way than through the email address they provided to the research team, we consider this response rate to be acceptable and even exceeding the typical online survey response rate. Of the 207 remaining respondents, 65 were trainees, 105 police officers, and 37 respondents in management positions.

We investigated the extent to which the participants in the post-test group and the follow-up group were representative of the total group participating in the pre-test of the study. The non-response analysis showed that the selectivity in participation in the post-test is limited to a number of socio-demographic characteristics (i.e., age and language group) and the position that people have within the police (i.e., participation in the follow-up was lower among younger participants, French-speaking group, and among trainees). Weight coefficients were calculated for these differences. These ensure that the relative distribution for these characteristics in the data from the pre-test and the post-test is exactly the same as that of the group that followed the HPM training and participated in the pre-test. We found no indications of selectivity according to socio-political views and the specific working conditions.

Questionnaire

Police integrity studies rely on the hypothetical scenarios or vignettes. While police officers may not always behave in accordance with their attitudes and, hence, responses to the hypothetical scenarios may not be identical to the real-life reactions, some of the studies reported that the attitudes and opinions expressed when evaluating hypothetical scenarios may be strongly correlated with the actual behavior (e.g., Kim and Hunter 1993; Goudriaan and Nieuwbeerta 2007). One the factors increasing the greater fit between the responses to hypothetical scenarios and the actual behavior is the design of the scenarios in a way that provides realistic descriptions of the behavior that is also contextualized (e.g., Evans et al. 2015). Indeed, when designing the hypothetical scenarios for the first police corruption questionnaire, Klockars and colleagues did so in a way that the scenarios would be appropriate for the most frequent police assignment—patrol—and would be realistic in modern, industrial societies (e.g., Kutnjak Ivković 2015a, b, p. 12). In fact, "[s]ome scenarios were based on published studies that had employed a case scenario approach. Others drew on the experience of the authors" (Klockars et al. 2000, p. 4). The same approach was used for the design of the subsequent police integrity questionnaire (e.g., Kutnjak Ivković 2015a, b).

Our study contains three scenarios based on the police integrity questionnaire (Klockars et al. 2006). The first two scenarios are the slightly changed original versions of the scenarios, while the third scenario has been systematically changed from the original. In total, these were adapted in consultation with senior members of the Belgian police to fit better the Belgian context and to provide sufficient variation in the types of misconduct:

Case 1 "Physical violence": During an intervention in a bar fight, a young female colleague receives a black eye from one of the male fighters. The man is arrested, handcuffed, and while he is taken to a cell, a male member of your team punches him very hard in the region of the kidneys while saying "Hurts, doesn't it?"

Case 2 "Alcohol intoxication": At 2 A.M. a police officer, who is on duty, is driving his patrol car on a deserted road. He sees a vehicle that gat stuck in a ditch. He approaches the vehicle and realizes that the driver is not hurt but is obviously intoxicated. He also notices that the driver is a police officer. Instead of reporting this incident, he brings the driver to his home.

Case 3 "Ethnic prejudice": It is Saturday, 3 A.M. Together with a colleague, you are responsible for the intake at the police office. A man of foreign origin enters the office. He is accompanied by a number of friends. He is clearly emotional and outraged. He says that he and his friends wanted to go and drink something in a well-known pub. While his friends could all enter the pub, he was refused entrance. According to the security guard because he was "drunk." Your contact with the man shows that he does not show any outward signs of alcohol intoxication. The man asks what he can do about this. Your colleague replies that he should let it go and, if really necessary, report it tomorrow to the police office in his place of residence. Your colleague also indicates that there is a little chance that something will actually happen as a result of his complaint.

Following the description of misconduct in each scenario, the respondents were asked to answer seven questions developed by Klockars et al. (2006). These questions explore the respondents' familiarity with agency rules, their evaluations of misconduct seriousness, views about appropriate and expected discipline, as well as their expressed willingness to report misconduct.

Dependent Variables

Given our research objective, we focus on two questions measuring seriousness and willingness to report. The first question asked the respondents to assess misconduct seriousness ("How serious do you consider this behavior to be?"). Potential answers ranged from 1 "Not at all serious" to 5 "Very serious." The other question inquired about the respondents' willingness to report the misconduct ("Would you report a fellow police officer engaged in this behavior?"). Possible answers ranged from 1 "Definitely not" to 5 "Definitely yes."

Independent Variables

In this chapter we study whether people changed attitudes after having followed the HPM-training. We not only focus on the general change, but also look for differences among subgroups. Indeed, it seems plausible that some groups benefit more from remembrance education than others. To that end, a number of independent variables where used in the analysis.

First, we included gender (male, female), years of service with the police, and police function (trainees, police officers, police in management) in the analyses.

Second, we included a range of characteristics that reveal the more socio-psychological profile participants. *Ethnic prejudice* was measured by four items derived from an ethnocentrism scale developed by Billiet et al. (1990). The scale measures a general ethnocentric attitude in which migration and multiculturalism are considered undesirable. The items (e.g., "Foreigners are generally not to be trusted.") were rated on a 5-point Likert scale ranging from "Strongly disagree" to "Strongly agree" (Cronbach α = .75). Respondents' *contact with victims and perpetrators of criminality* was measured with five items (e.g., "How often do you come into contact with victims of serious crimes during your work?") based on a scale developed by Van Craen (2015). This concept was included as a robustness check for the training because it can be expected that participants with a great deal of experience with victims and perpetrators of crime might have become more accustomed to situations in which serious misconduct occurs and, as a result, might be less impressed by forms of misconduct and intergroup conflicts. Items were rated on a 5-point Likert scale ranging from "Each day" to "Never" (Cronbach α = .91). We also used an indicator that measured respondents' general belief in the *general effectiveness of peace education programs*, which we use as a proxy variable for openness to change. The item was measured dichotomously with 0 "No or doubts" and 1 "Yes".

Third, two indicators that referred to people's experiences during the training were included.

Perceived emotional impact of the training refers to the degree to which participants were emotionally touched by the training. Respondents were asked to what extent they experienced seven different emotions (e.g., anger, powerlessness, compassion) during the training. The answers ranged on a 5-point Likert scale from "Not at all" to "Often." *Perceived cognitive impact* refers to the extent to which the training cognitively affected participants; it was measured by four items. Items (e.g., "The training made me think about human rights") were rated on a 5-point Likert scale ranging from "Strongly disagree" to "Strongly agree." Both perceived emotional impact and perceived cognitive impact were measured in the post-test.

Finally, *perceptions of the police integrity of their colleagues and organization* were measured through three items from the Klockars and colleagues' police integrity scale (2006). In particular, these questions focused on the respondents' familiarity with the official rules ("Would this behavior be regarded as a violation of official policy in your force?"). We also included questions measuring the respondents' perceptions of peer culture by asking them to assess how their peers would evaluate misconduct seriousness ("How serious do most police officers in your force consider this behavior to be?") and how likely they would be to report misconduct ("Do you think most police officers in your force would report a fellow police officer who engaged in this behavior?").

Research Strategy and Analysis

The analysis consisted of three steps. Before assessing the impact of the training, we first used paired sample T-tests that revealed participants' initial judgement of the three types of misconduct in the pre-test (Table 1). As the three cases strongly differ in terms of the type of police misconduct, it was very likely that respondents would also perceive them as different in terms of seriousness. In the second step, the ANOVA analysis with repeated measures (within subject design) was used to investigate whether the training had an impact on the perceived seriousness

and reporting intent of the three types of misconduct over time (Table 2). In the third step, multivariate linear regression analysis was used to assess if the impact of the training differed between subgroups and through which mechanisms the training had an effect for perceived seriousness (Tables 3, 4, and 5) and willingness to report (Tables 6, 7, and 8). In this final step, we calculated a difference score between the pre-test and the post-test for each type of misconduct (e.g., perceived seriousness of case 1 before the training v. perceived seriousness of case 1 after the training). A positive difference score means that a desirable change has taken place after the HPM training. Only the difference between the pre-test and post-test was taken into account because our results show that the effects of the training remain stable between the post-test and the follow-up.

In each table the same 6 models were analyzed. First, the intake characteristics were entered in model 1 and 2. The second category of characteristics, focusing on the cognitive and emotional impact of the training, were entered in model 3. Model 3 provides insight into the extent to which the observed changes are the result of the HPM training and the mechanisms through which such effects are achieved. Models 4 through 6 add the perceived seriousness or reporting intent of the peers in the workforce and the organization.

Results

Pre-trial Assessments of Seriousness and Willingness to Report

Table 1 presents mean scores for perceived seriousness and willingness to report for the three cases of misconduct in the pre-test. Clear and significant differences emerged; the pattern was identical for both outcomes (i.e., seriousness evaluations, expressed willingness to report). On the one hand, the case about physical violence was considered the most serious and was most likely to be reported (Table 1). On the other hand, the case about ethnic prejudice was considered

Table 1 Seriousness and willingness to report by case scenario at the pre-test

Case outcome	Physical violence		Alcohol intoxication		Ethnic prejudice	
	Mean	S.E.	Mean	S.E.	Mean	S.E.
Own seriousness[1]	4.32$_a$	0.80	3.77$_b$	1.02	3.52$_c$	0.90
Own willingness to report[2]	3.31$_a$	1.02	3.18$_b$	1.17	2.85$_c$	1.09

Note: Means with different subscripts in the same row differ, $p < .05$, from each other
[1]Ranging from 1 (Not at all serious) to 5 (Very serious)
[2]Ranging from 1 (Definitely not) to 5 (Definitely yes)

Table 2 Seriousness and willingness to report by case scenario at three time points

	Physical violence		Alcohol intoxication		Ethnic prejudice	
	Mean	S.E.	Mean	S.E.	Mean	S.E.
How serious do you consider this behavior to be?[1]						
Pre-test (before the training)	4.30	0.07	3.79	0.10	3.49$_a$	0.07
Post-test (1 day after the training)	4.28	0.07	3.71	0.10	3.76$_b$	0.08
Follow-up (1 month after the training)	4.14	0.08	3.71	0.09	3.75$_b$	0.08
Eta-square	0.023		0.011		0.134***	
Would you report a fellow police officer engaged in this behavior?[2]						
Pre-test (before the training)	3.16$_a$	0.09	3.01$_a$	0.11	2.76$_a$	0.09
Post-test (1 day after the training)	3.35$_b$	0.10	3.09$_a$	0.10	3.03$_b$	0.10
Follow-up (1 month after the training)	3.44$_b$	0.09	3.32$_b$	0.09	3.34$_c$	0.09
Eta-square	0.082**		0.108**		0.226***	

Seriousness and reporting by case scenario at the pre-test
Note: Means with different subscripts in the same column differ, $p < .05$, from each other
[1]The scale ranged from 1 = "Not serious at all" to 5 = "Very serious"
[2]The scale ranged from 1 = "Definitely would not report" to 5 = "Definitely would report"
* $p < .05$, ** $p < .01$, *** $p < .001$

the least serious and least likely to be reported (Table 1). The evaluations of mean seriousness and willingness to report for the alcohol intoxication case are somewhere between the other two cases (Table 1). These differences in mean values among the three cases suggest that these cases represent a continuum of perceived seriousness of the misconduct.

At the same time, the average scores for each case are not very high and do not reach the seriousness/reporting end of the scale. This the good news because these results imply that the risk on the possible ceiling effects was limited and our instrument was capable of effectively measuring improvement over time, assuming, of course, that there is improvement over time. The only exception from this rule is for the respondents' seriousness evaluations in the case of physical violence.

In this case, because the mean is 4.32 out of 5 and close to the very serious side of the scale, the instrument cannot register a potentially large improvement over time, but only a moderate one.

The Effects of the HPM Training on Evaluations of Seriousness and Willingness to Report

Table 2 shows whether the perceived attitude toward the three cases of police misconduct changed after the HPM training. Single effects for each outcome were estimated after repeated measures ANOVA indicated a significant interaction between case type and time for perceived seriousness (Eta^2: 0.157, p: 0.001) and willingness to report (Eta^2: 0.089; p: 0.028).

Table 3 Regression model of changes in perceived seriousness for the scenario with physical violence

	Change in perceived seriousness: physical violence					
	Model 1	Model 2	Model 3	Model 4	Model 5	Model 6
Gender[a]	0.05	0.06	0.07	0.10	0.11	0.13+
Years of service	−0.21*	−0.21*	−0.21*	−0.18*	−0.21*	−0.19*
Police function[b]						
Trainee	−0.07	−0.05	−0.06	−0.05	−0.01	−0.02
Police in management	0.10	0.11	0.11	0.09	0.12	0.10
Training effective[c]	0.05	0.07	0.05	0.05	0.04	0.04
Confronted with victims and offenders	−0.00	0.00	0.02	−0.01	−0.03	−0.04
Ethnic prejudice		0.09	0.11	0.10	0.12+	0.11
Perceived emotional impact			0.04	0.02	0.05	0.04
Perceived cognitive impact			0.10	0.13+	0.08	0.11
Violation of official rules				−0.22**		−0.13+
Most police officers' perceived seriousness					−0.27***	−0.21**
N	210	209	209	208	208	207
Adjusted R^2	0.001	0.004	0.007	0.047	0.068	0.077

Cell entries are standardized beta coefficients
+ $p < .10$, * $p < .05$, ** $p < .01$, *** $p < .001$
[a]The reference category is "male"
[b]The reference category is "police officers"
[c]The reference category is "No or not sure"

The means reveal that there were hardly any shifts for the first two cases in the changes of the assessments of seriousness over time, but a clear and substantial change occurred for the case on ethnic prejudice (Eta[2]: 0.134, p: 0.000). Specifically, in the case of ethnic prejudice, compared to their views at pre-training, the respondents evaluated the scenario as more serious both immediately post-training and in the follow-up study. At the same time, there were no statistically significant differences between the assessment of seriousness in post-training and the follow-up, indicating that, once the effects of the HPM training have occurred, they remained stable over time. This implies that members of the police perceived the behavior in the ethnic prejudice case, which before the HPM training and compared to the other cases was considered to be the least serious, has started to be evaluated as more serious after the respondents took part in the HPM training. This is an important finding because the effect is present for the case that thematically corresponds closest to the objective of the HPM training.

One the other hand, we found that the respondents' willingness to report misconduct for all three cases has increased after the training and that the members of the police were more inclined to say that they would report the misbehavior of the colleague (Table 2). However, the effect on the case of ethnic prejudice was much stronger (Eta[2]: 0.226, p: 0.000) than in the case of physical violence (Eta[2]: 0.082, p: 0.002) or alcohol intoxication (Eta[2]: 0.108; p 0.001). Interestingly, for the alcohol intoxication and ethnic prejudice cases, a significant increase in the willingness to report occurred between the post-test and the follow-up. This suggests that the effect was not only sustainable, but even increased in intensity over time, particularly in the case of ethnic prejudice.

Multivariate Models of Changes in Seriousness

Tables 3 through 5 reveal a similar pattern for the change in perceived seriousness for the three cases of misconduct. Models 1 through 3 show that there

Table 4 Regression model of changes in perceived seriousness for the scenario with alcohol intoxication

	Change in perceived seriousness: alcohol intoxication					
	Model 1	Model 2	Model 3	Model 4	Model 5	Model 6
Gender[a]	−0.10	−0.08	−0.07	−0.10	−0.08	−0.08
Years of service	0.08	0.07	0.07	0.06	0.04	0.04
Police function[b]						
Trainee	0.01	0.03	0.02	0.03	0.05	0.05
Police in management	0.00	0.01	0.02	0.01	0.04	0.04
Training effective[c]	−0.21**	−0.19*	−0.22**	−0.21**	−0.22**	−0.22**
Confronted with victims and offenders	−0.07	−0.06	−0.04	−0.06	−0.09	−0.09
Ethnic prejudice		0.09	0.11	0.10	0.09	0.09
Perceived emotional impact		0.04	0.05	0.07	0.07	
Perceived cognitive impact			0.13+	0.15*	0.13+	0.14+
Violation of official rules				−0.18*		−0.06
Most police officers' perceived seriousness					−0.31***	−0.28***
N	203	202	202	200	200	200
Adjusted R²	0.024	0.024	0.034	0.059	0.121	0.119

Cell entries are standardized beta coefficients
+ p < .10, * p < .05, ** p < .01, *** p < .001
[a]The reference category is "male"
[b]The reference category is "police officers"
[c]The reference category is "No or not sure"

Table 5 Regression model of changes in perceived seriousness for the scenario with ethnic prejudice

	Change in perceived seriousness: ethnic prejudice					
	Model 1	Model 2	Model 3	Model 4	Model 5	Model 6
Gender[a]	−0.05	−0.03	−0.02	−0.02	−0.03	−0.03
Years of service	0.06	0.06	0.06	0.08	0.11	0.11
Police function[b]						
Trainee	0.01	0.03	0.03	0.05	0.09	0.09
Police in management	−0.04	−0.02	−0.02	−0.01	−0.01	−0.01
Training effective[c]	−0.03	0.01	−0.02	−0.00	−0.01	0.01
Confronted with victims and offenders	−0.07	−0.07	−0.05	−0.03	−0.05	−0.03
Ethnic prejudice		0.11	0.13+	0.10	0.13+	0.12
Perceived emotional impact			0.04	0.02	0.04	0.03
Perceived cognitive impact			0.12	0.17*	0.16*	0.18*
Violation of official rules				−0.20**		−0.10
Most police officers' perceived seriousness					−0.24**	−0.21*
N	197	196	196	194	195	194
Adjusted R²	−0.022	−0.016	−0.008	0.023	0.041	0.049

Cell entries are standardized beta coefficients
+ p < .10, * p < .05, ** p < .01, *** p < .001
[a]The reference category is "male"
[b]The reference category is "police officers"
[c]The reference category is "No or not sure"

Table 6 Regression model of changes in willingness to report for the scenario with physical violence

| | Change in reporting intent: physical violence | | | | | |
	Model 1	Model 2	Model 3	Model 4	Model 5	Model 6
Gender[a]	−0.08	−0.07	−0.07	−0.04	−0.05	−0.04
Years of service	−0.07	−0.08	−0.07	−0.06	−0.04	−0.03
Police function[b]						
Trainee	0.05	0.08	0.09	0.09	0.14	0.15
Police in management	0.06	0.07	0.08	0.06	0.09	0.08
Training effective[c]	−0.02	0.02	−0.01	−0.00	−0.02	−0.01
Confronted with victims and offenders	0.03	0.04	0.05	0.03	0.04	0.03
Ethnic prejudice		0.14+	0.16*	0.15*	0.18*	0.17*
Perceived emotional impact			0.00	−0.01	0.01	0.01
Perceived cognitive impact			0.12	0.14+	0.15*	0.16*
Violation of official rules				−0.15*		−0.09
Most police officers' reporting					−0.35***	−0.33***
N	206	205	205	204	205	204
Adjusted R²	−0.013	0.000	0.004	0.019	0.121	0.124

Cell entries are standardized beta coefficients
+ p < .10, * p < .05, ** p < .01, *** p < .001
[a]The reference category is "male"
[b]The reference category is "police officers"
[c]The reference category is "No or not sure"

was a little variation in sub-groups for the change in perceived seriousness between the pre-test and post-test. Most indicators are not significant for the three cases. Only for the alcohol intoxication case, years of service with the police was negatively related to perceived seriousness (Table 3).

Models 3 through 6 in Tables 3, 4, and 5 investigated the mechanisms through which a change in perceived seriousness is achieved. For both the alcohol intoxication (Table 4; Models 3–6) and ethnic prejudice case (Table 5; Models 3–6), the perceived cognitive impact—by which we mean having the feeling that one has really learned something—was positively related to change in perceived seriousness, while it was not significantly related to the change in seriousness for the physical violence case (Table 3). For perceived emotional impact—by which we mean having been emotionally touched by the training—no effects were found in any of the three cases. This indicates that the effect of training mainly follows a cognitive pathway rather than an emotional pathway.

For all three cases (Tables 3, 4, and 5; Models 4 and 5), we found that the extent that the misconduct was perceived to be a violation of official policy or the degree that fellow police officers would

consider this behavior serious, was negatively related to the changes in perceived seriousness. Interestingly, the effect of the perceived extent that the misconduct violates organizational policy was (completely) mediated by the perceived seriousness of the misconduct by fellow police officers. In other words, the influence of police culture (i.e., estimates of others' estimates of seriousness) seems to be stronger than the respondents' recognition of behavior as rule-violating. One explanation for this effect might be that members of the police that work in organizations where such forms of misconduct are perceived to be serious violations by fellow police officers already had high levels of ethical integrity. Indeed, most room for improvement is in organizations where such types of misconduct are less likely to be perceived as problematic by peers.

Multivariate Models of Changes in Willingness to Report

Tables 6 through 8 presents the results for the analyses on changes over time in willingness to report the misconduct. Similarities and differ-

Table 7 Regression model of changes in willingness to report for the scenario with alcohol intoxication

	Change in reporting intent: Alcohol intoxication					
	Model 1	Model 2	Model 3	Model 4	Model 5	Model 6
Gender[a]	0.03	0.05	0.06	0.06	0.05	0.05
Years of service	0.14	0.14	0.14	0.13	0.17+	0.16+
Police function[b]						
Trainee	0.07	0.08	0.07	0.08	0.12	0.12
Police in management	−0.03	−0.02	−0.02	−0.02	−0.01	−0.01
Training effective[c]	−0.15*	−0.13+	−0.17*	−0.16*	−0.17*	−0.17*
Confronted with victims and offenders	−0.08	−0.08	−0.05	−0.06	−0.06	−0.06
Ethnic prejudice		0.07	0.10	0.09	0.08	0.08
Perceived emotional impact			0.10	0.11	0.11	0.11
Perceived cognitive impact			0.11	0.12	0.11	0.12
Violation of official rules				−0.12+		−0.05
Most police officers' reporting					−0.22**	−0.20**
N	201	200	200	198	198	198
Adjusted R^2	0.007	0.008	0.024	0.033	0.065	0.063

Cell entries are standardized beta coefficients
+ p < .10, * p < .05, ** p < .01, *** p < .001
[a]The reference category is "male"
[b]The reference category is "police officers"
[c]The reference category is "No or not sure"

Table 8 Regression model of changes in willingness to report for the scenario with ethnic prejudice

	Change in reporting intent: ethnic prejudice					
	Model 1	Model 2	Model 3	Model 4	Model 5	Model 6
Gender[a]	−0.01	0.00	0.02	−0.01	0.00	−0.00
Years of service	0.07	0.06	0.07	0.08	0.10	0.10
Police function[b]						
Trainee	−0.04	−0.02	−0.02	0.01	0.03	0.03
Police in management	−0.04	−0.02	−0.02	−0.01	−0.02	−0.02
Training effective[c]	−0.06	−0.02	−0.05	−0.01	−0.01	−0.01
Confronted with victims and offenders	−0.02	−0.01	0.01	0.03	0.01	0.03
Ethnic prejudice		0.14+	0.17*	0.14+	0.18*	0.16*
Perceived emotional impact			0.07	0.05	0.06	0.06
Perceived cognitive impact			0.12	0.17*	0.15*	0.17*
Violation of official rules				−0.19*		−0.12
Most police officers' reporting					−0.22**	−0.18*
N	197	196	196	195	194	194
Adjusted R^2	−0.019	−0.006	0.007	0.034	0.049	0.055

Cell entries are standardized beta coefficients
+ p < .10, * p < .05, ** p < .01, *** p < .001
[a]The reference category is "male"
[b]The reference category is "police officers"
[c]The reference category is "No or not sure"

ences with perceived seriousness are visible. Models 1 through 3 show that there was little variation in sub-groups for the change in willingness to report the misconduct between the pretest results and the post-test results.

Our regression models indicate that ethnic prejudice was positively related to change in willingness to report the misconduct for the physical violence case (Table 6; Model 2) and the ethnic prejudice case (Table 8; Model 2). This means that members of the police who scored higher on ethnic prejudice at the pre-test were more likely to say that they would report misconduct in the post-test.

Models 3 through 6 investigated the mechanisms through which a change in perceived seriousness was achieved. Similar to the results for perceived seriousness, Models 3 through 6 (Table 6, 7, and 8) show that perceived cognitive impact, but not perceived emotional impact, was positively related to the change in willingness to report misconduct for the physical violence case (Table 6; Models 3–6) and the ethnic prejudice case (Table 8; Models 3–6), but not for the alcohol intoxication case (Table 7; Models 3–6).

Similarly to the changes we observed in estimates of misconduct seriousness, we found that the degree to which the misconduct was perceived to be a violation of official policy and the degree that the respondents assumed that fellow police officers would be willing to report this misconduct were both negatively related to the changes in willingness to report misconduct over time (Tables 6, 7, and 8; Models 4 and 5). The perceived extent that the misconduct violates organizational policy was completely mediated by the perceived willingness to report misconduct by peers (Tables 6, 7, and 8; Model 6). Thus, it seems that the perceived ethical integrity of peers is more important than the extent that this misconduct is perceived to be a violation of official policy.

Conclusion

In this chapter, we explored if and how a Holocaust remembrance training program designed as a police ethics training influences police integrity among 200 members of the Belgian police. Three cases on ethical misconduct (physical violence, alcohol intoxication, and ethnic prejudice) were presented to the members of the police before, right after (1 day), and 1 month after the training. Respondents were asked to rate how serious they considered the misconduct to be and how willing they were to report the misconduct.

The central objective of the Holocaust remembrance training is to teach its participants the causes and mechanisms behind collective violence. During the training it is emphasized that group violence often starts with relatively small discriminating events but can easily evolve through processes of dehumanization and polarization to collective widespread violence (i.e., spiral of violence). The HPM-training focuses on the role of the police during the Holocaust and makes a link to current events. Actual examples from the police workplace are used throughout the training. The ultimate goal is to provide members of the police tools and skills to deal with ethical dilemmas and group pressure. The bottom line of the training is the message that in any situation a member of the police always has room to say "no" to injustice and to take one's responsibility.

Our results show that the HPM-training had a clear and sustainable positive effect on police integrity. After the training, both immediately and after a month, members of the police considered the ethnic prejudice misconduct more serious than before the training. More importantly, after the training, members of the police were more inclined to state that they would react themselves by reporting a fellow police officer if he or she would partake in one of the three types of misconduct. These effects seemed to be sustainable as we did not only observe a significant and substantial improvement just immediately following the HPM training, but in the follow-up study done after about 1 month post-training.

Within the three types of cases (i.e., police corruption, use of excessive force, ethnic bias), the strongest effects were found for the case of ethnic bias. In other words, it seems that one of the core insights that lies at the heart of the HPM training—namely that relatively less serious forms of misconduct could easily slip into more serious forms—is clearly transmitted during the training. This was done not only in the form of cognitive awareness of the issue, but also in the form of individual willingness to act in such cases. Our results show that that the message that individuals have the power to say 'no' to injustice seems to have been successfully transferred through the HPM training.

Finally, it is clear that members of the police who reported more ethnic prejudice at the start of the training benefitted most from the training. A similar pattern was visible for police officers who worked with colleagues who would consider such behavior less problematic or in an organization where such behavior would be considered less a violation of the organizational policy. This implies that the greatest benefactors of the HPM training are those members of the police who, from a police integrity perspective, need such training the most.

The results of our study provide further evidence that methodology developed to measure police integrity could be successfully applied to assess any potential changes in the integrity level and capture a potential change in the respondents' individual integrity levels over time. In the context of police training, police integrity methodology should become a valuable tool for any police administrator or scholar who is interested in evaluating the degree to which trainees have mastered the ethical material presented to them and capturing any potential changes in their cognitive views. Indeed, our research shows that peace education in the form of a Holocaust remembrance training program adapted to the police has the potential to positively influence the ethical integrity of members of the police.

References

Antrobus, E., Thompson, I., & Ariel, B. (2019). Procedural justice training for police recruits: Results of a randomized controlled trial. *Journal of Experimental Criminology, 15*(1), 29–53.

Billiet, J., Carton, A., & Huys, R. (1990). Onbekend of onbemind? In *Een sociologisch onderzoek naar de houding van de Belgen tegenover migranten*. KU Leuven: Sociologisch onderzoeksinstituut.

Blue Courage. (2019). *Blue Courage consulting and training company*. Catalogue offerings. Retrieved March 6, 2019, from https://bluecourage.com/courses-offered/

Caldero, M. A. (2014). *Police ethics: The corruption of noble cause*. Abington: Routledge.

Conti, N., & Nolan, J. J., III. (2005). Policing the platonic cave: Ethics and efficacy in police training. *Policing and Society, 15*(2), 166–186.

Crank, J. P., & Caldero, M. A. (2004). *Police Ethics: The Corruption of Noble Cause*. Cincinnati, OH: Anderson Publishing Co.

European Union Agency for Law Enforcement Training (CEPOL). (2019). *Fundamental rights, police ethics training, step 1*. Retrieved March 6, 2019, from https://www.cepol.europa.eu/tags/police-ethics

Evans, S. C., Roberts, M. C., Keeley, J. W., Blossom, J. B., Amaro, C. M., Garcia, A. M., Odar Stough, C., Canter, K. S., Robles, R., & Reed, G. M. (2015). Vignette methodologies for studying clinicians' decision-making: Validity, utility, and application in ICD-11 field studies. *International Journal of Clinical and Health Psychology, 15*(2), 160–170.

Goudriaan, H., & Nieuwbeerta, P. (2007). Contextual determinants of juveniles' willingness to report crimes: A vignette experiment. *Journal of Experimental Criminology, 3*, 89–111.

Haberfeld, M. R. (2002). *Critical issues in police training*. Upper Saddle River, NJ: Prentice Hall.

Haberfeld, M. R. (2018). *Critical issues in police training* (3rd ed.). New York: Pearson Education Company.

Jonstone, C. (2017). *Radio Praha in English*. Retrieved Feb 22, 2019, from https://www.radio.cz/en/section/marketplace/why-the-czech-republic-scored-worse-in-corruption-index

Kazerne Dossin. (2019). *Training program: Holocaust, police and human rights*. Retrieved from https://www.kazernedossin.eu/EN/Onderwijs-vorming/Politie/Opleidingen/Opleiding-Holocaust,-politie-en-Mensenrechten

Kim, M. S., & Hunter, J. E. (1993). Relationships among attitudes, behavioral intentions, and behavior: A meta-analysis of past research, part 2. *Communication Research, 20*(3), 331–364.

Klitzman, R. (2015). *The ethics police? The struggle to make human research safe*. New York: Oxford University Press.

Klockars, C. B., & Kutnjak Ivković, S. (2004). Measuring police integrity. In M. J. Hickman, A. R. Piquero, & J. R. Greene (Eds.), *Police integrity and ethics*. Belmont, CA: Wadsworth Publishing.

Klockars, C. B., Kutnjak Ivković, S., Harver, W. E., and M. R. Haberfeld (2000). *The measurement of police integrity*. Research in brief. U.S. Department of Justice, Office of Justice Programs, National Institute of Justice. Government Printing Office: Washington, DC.

Klockars, C. B., Kutnjak Ivković, S., & Haberfeld, M. R. (Eds.). (2004). *The contours of police integrity*. Newbury Park, CA: Sage.

Klockars, C. B., Kutnjak Ivković, S., & Haberfeld, M. R. (2006). *Enhancing police integrity*. New York: Springer.

Kutnjak Ivković, S. (2009). The Croatian police, police integrity, and transition toward democratic policing. *Policing: An International Journal of Police Strategies and Management, 32*(3), 459–488.

Kutnjak Ivković, S. (2015a). Police integrity in Croatia. In S. Kutnjak Ivković & M. Haberfeld (Eds.), *Police integrity across the world*. New York: Springer.

Kutnjak Ivković, S. (2015b). Studying police integrity. In S. Kutnjak Ivković & M. Haberfeld (Eds.), *Police integrity across the world*. New York: Springer.

Kutnjak Ivković, S., & Haberfeld, M. R. (2019). Exploring empirical research on police integrity. In S. Kutnjak Ivković & M. Haberfeld (Eds.), *Exploring police integrity*. New York: Springer.

Kutnjak Ivković, S., & Klockars, C. B. (2004). Police integrity in Croatia. In C. B. Klockars, S. Kutnjak Ivković, & M. R. Haberfeld (Eds.), *The contours of police integrity* (pp. 56–74). Thousand Oaks, CA: Sage Publications.

Lobnikar, B., & Meško, G. (2015). Police integrity in Slovenia. In S. Kutnjak Ivković & M. Haberfeld (Eds.), *Police integrity across the world* (pp. 183–212). New York: Springer.

Maesschalck, J., & De Schrijver, A. (2015). The development of moral reasoning skills in police recruits. *Policing: An International Journal, 38*(1), 102–116.

Nix, J., Pickett, J. T., Baek, H., & Alpert, G. P. (2017). Police research officer surveys, and response rates. *Policing and Society, 29*, 530–550. https://doi.org/10.1080/10439463.2017.1394300.

Pagon, M., & Lobnikar, B. (2004). Police integrity in Slovenia. In C. B. Klockars, S. Kutnjak Ivković, & M. R. Haberfeld (Eds.), *The contours of police integrity* (pp. 212–231). Thousand Oaks, CA: Sage Publications.

Prenzler, T., & Ronken, C. (2016). Survey of innovations in development and maintenance of ethical standards by Australian Police Departments. In *Contemporary issues in law enforcement and policing* (pp. 89–106). Boca Raton, FL: CRC Press.

Roebuck, J. B., & Barker, T. (1974). A Typology of Police Corruption. *Social Problems, 21*(3), 423–437.

Skogan, W., & Frydl, K. (2004). *Fairness and Effectiveness in Policing: The Evidence* (Eds.). Washington, D.C.: The National Academies Press.

Skogan, W., Van Craen, M., & Hennessey, C. (2015). Training police for procedural justice. *Journal of Experimental Criminology, 11*(3), 319–334.

Spruyt, B., Elchardus, M., Roggemans, L., & Van Droogenbroeck, F. (2014). *Can peace be taught? Researching the effectiveness of peace education*. Brussels: Flemish Peace Institute. Retrieved from https://www.flemishpeaceinstitute.eu/sites/vlaams-vredesinstituut.eu/files/files/reports/can_peace_be_taught_revised.pdf.

Timm, H., & Christian, K. E. (1991). *Introduction to private security*. Pacific Grove, CA: Brooks/Cole Publishing.

Van Craen, M. (2015). *Vragenlijst voor het bevragen van politiemensen over interne en externe procedurele rechtvaardigheid*. Leuven. Unpublished document.

Index

© Springer Nature Switzerland AG 2019
S. Kutnjak Ivković, M. R. Haberfeld (eds.), *Exploring Police Integrity*,
https://doi.org/10.1007/978-3-030-29065-8

Printed by Printforce, the Netherlands